COLON

49 *p. 125*	50 *p. 125*	51 *p. 125*	52 *p. 125*	53	54 *p. 126*
Direct Quotation	Introducing a List	With Independent Clauses	Special Uses	Period	Question Mark

OTHER MARKS

55 *p. 127*	56 *p. 127*	57 *p. 128*	58 *p. 129*	59 *p. 129*	60 *p. 131*
Exclamation Point	Dash	Parentheses	Brackets	Quotation Marks	Direct Quotation

OTHER MARKS

61 *p. 133*	62 *p. 134*	63 *p. 134*	64 *p. 134*	65 *p. 134*	66 *p. 135*
Apostrophe in Possessives	Apostrophe in Omission of Letters	Apostrophe in Plurals	Hyphen in Word Division	Hyphen in Compounds	Ellipsis Mark

OTHER MARKS

67 *p. 135*	68 *p. 136*	69 *p. 138*	70 *p. 138*	71 *p. 139*	72 *p. 139*
Caret	Capitalization	Forms not Capitalized	Italics	Incorrect Abbreviations	Correct Abbreviations

WORD

73 *p. 140*	74 *p. 162*	75 *p. 165*	76 *p. 168*	77 *p. 168*	78 *p. 169*
Numbers	Spelling	Appropriate Preposition	Colloquialisms	Slang	Illiteracies

WORD

79 *p. 170*	80 *p. 172*	81 *p. 185*	82 *p. 186*	83 *p. 197*	84 *p. 202*
Wordiness	Concreteness	Mixed Figures	Triteness	Glossary of Usage	Topic Sentence

PARAGRAPH

85 *p. 205*	86 *p. 205*	87 *p. 207*	88 *p. 211*	89 *p. 217*	90 *p. 218*
Unity	Coherence	Emphasis	Development	Introductory Paragraphs	Concluding Paragraphs

OUTLINE — PRÉCIS

91 *p. 232*	92 *p. 234*	93 *p. 246*	
Division	Phrasing the Topic Outline	Using Own Wording	*Correction Chart*

UNIFIED
ENGLISH COMPOSITION

Unified
English Composition

APPLETON-CENTURY-CROFTS, INC., NEW YORK

Unified
English Composition

Gerald D. Sanders
Formerly, Michigan State Normal College

•

Hoover H. Jordan
Michigan State Normal College

•

Wallace H. Magoon
Ball State Teachers College

Third Edition

APPLETON-CENTURY-CROFTS, Inc., NEW YORK

PREFACE

THIS THIRD EDITION of *Unified English Composition* follows in main design the scheme of former editions. In many ways it benefits, we believe, by reflecting the views of teachers who have used earlier editions and who have shared with us their experiences and suggestions.

Our aim in all editions has been to provide a text that will save the time of instructors and will give to students in one volume all the materials they need in the freshman composition course. The wide use of previous editions leads us to assume that our general method is sound. At the same time, we think we have increased the effectiveness of the text by heeding the advice of many teachers on specific matters.

In addition to making changes in minor details throughout the text of the new edition, we have altered somewhat the order of chapters and have subjected some sections to rather thorough revision.

By moving the chapter, "The Précis," to the second part of the text, by putting the chapter on the Sentence before that on the Word, and by revising the chapter on Reading to make it conform more nearly to the needs of the majority of students as they enter college, we think we have achieved a better arrangement for instructors who like to follow a text as it is organized.

In response to suggestions from teachers whose opinions we value, we offer a more detailed treatment of sentence problems; we add new sections to the chapter on the Word; and we offer more copious illustrations of paragraph development, including examples of paragraphs developed by different methods from one topic sentence.

Though all sections in the latter half of the book are altered in details, the presentations of the précis and the research paper are revised most thoroughly. The précis section now has more complete instructions and more extensive illustrations. Changes concerning the research paper make clearer step by step the process of research from choosing the topic to submitting the completed manuscript, present a sample manuscript as a visual guide for the student, and consider matters of form in accordance with the practice outlined in "The MLA Style Sheet."

The reading selections in all editions of this textbook have purposely been of many different levels of difficulty and excellence. While most of the selections, both time-honored and current, are longer and more thoughtful than a student can be expected to write, yet, especially in the first sections of this edition, are numerous shorter articles on topics of a sort that students may themselves choose, so that these should serve not only as a stimulus to students in selecting and thinking about their own subjects but also as models for limiting subject matter, organizing it logically, and treating it in detail. At the end of almost every group of readings we offer suggestions for writing and at the end of the paragraph section a long list of suggestions.

A word about footnotes may be in order. We number our own footnotes consecutively throughout each section but retain the numbering of the author's own footnotes as in the original; this will explain such apparent discrepancies as that, for instance, on page 3. It should also be said perhaps that the footnote form used in giving credit to those who own the copyright on reading selections cannot be consistent throughout the book because of the requirement of various publishers that we follow their specified footnote form. For consistency, therefore, we have sometimes brought into harmony the footnote forms of an entire section of the textbook in a fashion that does not accord with our own recommendations in the section on footnoting.

We are grateful to the authors and publishers who have allowed us the use of material held in copyright and to all who have generously sent us suggestions for this revision. To our colleagues, especially Professors Elisabeth Carey, Notley Maddox, and O. I. Schreiber we are especially indebted for generous aid.

THE AUTHORS

CONTENTS

Chapter   *Page*

PREFACE   v

Orientation

I. A FOREWORD TO STUDENTS   1

Where Are We? Carl Becker (950) *   4
Studies That Build Men of Character, Archibald S. Foord (2000)   6
A Little Learning, Whitney Griswold (4200)   9

II. READING AND STUDYING   16

Employing Different Methods of Reading for Different Purposes, 17; Hindrances to Reading, 17; Studying Intelligently, 20; Acquiring Speed, 21

An Apology for Idlers, R. L. Stevenson (350)   22
How to Learn, Edward S. Robinson (2100)   23
From *The Hero as Man of Letters,* Thomas Carlyle (1600)   27
From *Of Kings' Treasuries,* John Ruskin (5600)   29
The Decline of Attention, Clifton Fadiman (4500)   38

III. FIRST CONSIDERATIONS   46

A. THE MANUSCRIPT   46
Form and Appearance, 46

B. PRELIMINARY PLANNING   48
Subject, 49; Audience, 50; Purpose, 51; Thesis, 51; The Outline; Making a Blueprint, 51; Tone, 52; Title, 53

C. WRITING AND EDITING   53
Proofreading and Revising, 54; Corrections, 54; Ethics Concerning Sources, 55

"The Witch Tree," Rose D. Meyer (400)   55
My Experience as a Book Agent, Wilbur L. Cross (750)   56
Do Animals Talk? Lillian Harriman (1400)   57

Parts of the Composition

I. GRAMMAR AND THE SENTENCE   61

A. PARTS OF SPEECH   61
Nouns, 62; Pronouns, 62; Verbs, 63; Adjectives, 68; Adverbs, 69; Conjunctions, 70; Prepositions, 70; Verbals, 71

B. THE SENTENCE   72
Parts of the Sentence, 72; Classes of Sentences According to Form, 76

Grammar, William Cobbett (750) *   78
Tu'imalila, Oldest Animal in the World, Mary Patterson (800)   79
An Electrical "Bath" in Yellowstone, William B. Sanborn (800)   81

* The figure in parentheses is a rough approximation of the number of words in the reading selection.

Chapter   *Page*

    Struck by Lightning, Henry H. Rusby (800)   83
    The Metamorphosis of Hell Week, Karl Detzer (900)   84

  C. ANALYZING THE SENTENCE   86
  Expository analysis, 86; Diagraming, 87; Simple Sentences for Analysis, 91

  D. APPLYING GRAMMATICAL PRINCIPLES   95
    1. Grammatical and Logical Completeness, 95
    2. Correctness and Correct Relationship of Sentence Elements, 97
    3. Position of Sentence Elements and Logical Sentence Patterns, 108

  E. WRITING EFFECTIVE SENTENCES   114

  F. PUNCTUATION   117
  The Comma, 118; The Semicolon, 123; The Colon, 125; The Period, 126; The Question Mark, 126; The Exclamation Point, 127; The Dash, 127; Parentheses, 128; Brackets, 129; Quotation Marks, 129; Punctuating Direct Quotation, 131; The Apostrophe, 133; The Hyphen, 134; The Ellipsis Mark, 135; The Caret, 135

  G. MECHANICS   136
  Capitals, 136; Italics, 138; Abbreviations, 139; Numbers, 140

    I Chose America, Percy Waxman (1600)   141
    The American Way of Life, Dorothy Thompson (1000)   143
    Credo, Thomas Wolfe (750)   145
    Where I Stand, Elia Kazan (850)   147
    How to Misunderstand the USA, Tibor Koeves (3000)   148

II. THE WORD   154

  A. THE DICTIONARY   154
  The Unabridged Dictionary, 154; The Abridged Dictionary, 154; The Thesaurus, 156

    Featherbeds and Parnassus, Carol Hovious (2500)   158

  B. SPELLING   162
  Rule for *ie* and *ei*, 162; Rules Governing Prefixes and Suffixes, 162; Rules Governing the Spelling of Plurals of Nouns, 162; Words Frequently Misspelled, 163

  C. WORDS FREQUENTLY CONFUSED   164

  D. THE APPROPRIATE PREPOSITION   165

  E. LEVELS OF USAGE   166
  The Common Level, 166; The Literary Level, 167; The Technical Level, 167; The Colloquial Level, 168; The Slang Level, 168; The Illiterate Level, 169

  F. THE RIGHT CHOICE OF WORDS   170
    1. Economy of Diction, 170
    2. Specific and Concrete Words, 172

    Co-operation versus Competition, John Ruskin (550)   174
    Basic English for Science, Tom Burns Haber (2600)   175
    I Can't Quite Hear You, Doctor, Joseph A. Brandt (3500)   178

    3. Imaginative Words, 184

    The Cliché Expert Takes the Stand, Frank Sullivan (500)   187
    Emotional Meanings, Robert H. Thouless (4400)   188
    On Word Magic, A. G. Gardiner (1400)   195

  G. GLOSSARY OF FAULTY USAGE   197

Chapter   *Page*

III. THE PARAGRAPH   202

A. DEFINITION   202
Length, 202; The Topic Sentence, 202; Transitional and Narrative Paragraphs, 204

B. UNITY, COHERENCE, AND EMPHASIS   205
Unity, 205; Coherence, 205; Emphasis, 207

    The Author's Account of Himself, Washington Irving (1000)   209

C. PARAGRAPH DEVELOPMENT   210
Detail, 211; Illustration, 212; Comparison, 212; Contrast, 212; Elimination, 213; Questions, 213; Combination, 213

D. INTRODUCTION AND CONCLUSION   216
The Introduction, 217; The Conclusion, 218

    College Football "Expendable," Robert M. Hutchins (750)   219
    My America, John Buchan (Lord Tweedsmuir) (4500)   221

Topics for Writing, 228

The Whole Composition

I. BASIC PRINCIPLES AND ORGANIZATION   231

A. THREE BASIC PRINCIPLES: UNITY, COHERENCE, EMPHASIS   231

B. THE OUTLINE   232
The Mechanical Form, 232; The Composition of the Outline, 232; The Topic Outline, 233; The Sentence Outline, 234

    The Conditions of Art, John Ruskin (1000)   238
    Skiing, Strand Mikkelsen (1400)   240
    Types of Industrial Organization, Willard L. Thorp (1800)   242

C. THE PRÉCIS   245

    Woodchuck Therapy, Robert Peel (1000)   247
    Nobel Prize Acceptance Speech, William Faulkner (500)   249
    Technology—Hope or Hobgoblin? Henry B. du Pont (1100)   250
    Humor and America, Max Eastman (4900)   252

II. THE FOUR FORMS OF WRITING   260

A. EXPOSITION   260
Definition, 260

    Donjon, Anon. (185)   264
    Bathtub, W. P. Gerhard (500)   264
    Radicalism and Conservatism, Arthur M. Schlesinger (900)   265
    A Gentleman, John Henry Newman (900)   267

The Process, 268

    How to Write a Book, Harold Nicolson (1600)   270
    How to Detect Propaganda, Clyde R. Miller *et al.* (2700)   273
    Be Your Own Weatherman, Carl Warden (1800)   **277**

Chapter

Page

Mechanisms and Organizations, 279

Under Mobile River, R. G. Skerrett (900)   281
Earthquakes, Rev. Joseph Lynch, S.J. (3100)   283
The Struggle for Existence, Henshaw Ward (3500)   288

Analysis, 293

The Business Type, James Truslow Adams (1500)   296
You Are One of These, Vergil D. Reed (1800)   299
Let's Join the Human Race, Stringfellow Barr (1150)   302

B. ARGUMENTATION   304
The Proposition, 304; The Issues, 304; The Methods of Reasoning, 305; Application of Reasoning to the Writing of Argument, 308; Final Precautions, 309

Work Your Way through College? Ralph Cooper Hutchison (1750)   312
Should Students Study? William Trufant Foster (3800)   315
World Government or World Destruction? Stephen King-Hall (1200)   321

C. DESCRIPTION   324
Accurate Observation, 324; Choice of Words, 325; Point of View, 327; Dominant Impression, 328; Choice of Details, 328

SENSE IMPRESSIONS, 329

On Observing Colors, John Ruskin (250)   329
Water, John Ruskin (400)   330
Christmas Tree, Herman Smith (180)   331
Water Hyacinths, Harnett T. Kane (350)   331
Rain in Mexico, Gertrude Diamant (450)   332
The Merry-Go-Round, Stephen Crane (270)   333
Sounds in Late Summer, Richard Jefferies (360)   333
Early Morning, Siegfried Sassoon (90)   334
Making Tortillas, Gertrude Diamant (250)   334
The Wind, R. C. Hutchinson (160)   335
Apples, John Burroughs (300)   335
Christmas Breakfast, Herman Smith (200)   336
Dinner at Cousin Lil's, Herman Smith (500)   336

PLACES, 337

Mexico City, Gertrude Diamant (1500)   337
Farmhouse Cellar, Herman Smith (350)   339
The Furnished Room, O. Henry (400)   340

PERSONS, 341

Captain Ahab, Herman Melville (400)   341
Eustacia Vye, Thomas Hardy (720)   341
Stina, Herman Smith (200)   343

CHANGING POINT OF VIEW, 343

A Road in England, R. C. Hutchinson (700)   343
A Steamboat Landing at a Small Town, Mark Twain (650)   344

Chapter   Page

D. NARRATION   347

The Initial Situation, 348; Action, 357; Conclusion, 354; Essential Qualities of Good Narration, 356; Types of Narration, 357

SIMPLE NARRATIVE, 358

Finding a Room, Gertrude Diamant (700)   359
Adventure of a Turtle, John Steinbeck (700)   360
Baker's Blue-Jay Yarn, Mark Twain (1900)   361
The Dinner Party, Mona Gardner (500)   364
The Evening Service, R. C. Hutchinson (2600)   366

THE SHORT STORY, 370

The Apparition, Guy de Maupassant (2400)   372
Foot in It, James Gould Cozzens (1200)   376
The Happiest Man on Earth, Albert Maltz (4000)   378
Brandy for Breakfast, Laurence W. Meynell (6200)   384
Laura, Saki (H. H. Munro) (1800)   393
You Could Look It Up, James Thurber (6000)   396
A New England Nun, Mary Wilkins Freeman (4800)   405
The Color of Mama Josefina's Life, Mary Main (3200)   412
The Law-Abiding, Marc Brandel (5300)   417
That Greek Dog, MacKinlay Kantor (4900)   426

III. BLENDING THE FOUR FORMS OF WRITING   434

A. THE RESEARCH PAPER   434
Choosing a Topic, 435; The Use of the Library, 435; Forms for Bibliography Cards, 441; Note-taking and the Use of Sources, 442; Evaluating Sources: Evidence, 444; The Outline, 446; Footnotes and Final Bibliography, 446; List of Common Abbreviations, 449

The Conspiracy of Aaron Burr, Lois Boeck   450
"I Have Not Yet Begun to Fight," Charles Lee Lewis (3200)   459

B. THE FEATURE ARTICLE   464
Finding Ideas for Feature Articles, 464; Making the Article Interesting, 465; The Feature Story Based on Library Research, 465; The Feature Story Based on the Interview, 466

Fifty Ideas for Newspaper Features   467
Solo, The Talk of the Town (800)   470
Sidewalk Fisherman, Meyer Berger (3400)   471
Enterprise and Old Iron, John Patric (2100)   477

C. THE BOOK REVIEW   480
How to Begin, 480; How to Criticize Exposition and Argument, 481; How to Criticize Narration, 481; How to Write the Review, 482

Review of
Sophocles   483
The Art of Scientific Investigation (175)   483
More About Words (280)   483
Dictionary of American History, Paul A. Palmer (1400)   484
Abraham Lincoln: The War Years, Charles A. Beard (1600)   485
You Can't Go Home Again, Louis B. Salomon (800)   487

Chapter   *Page*

    D. BIOGRAPHY   488
    The Character, 488

        The Office Bore, Mark Twain (600)   489
        The Country Gentlemen, T. B. Macaulay (1600)   490

    The Character Sketch, 493

        Heywood, Christopher Morley (800)   495
        Walt Whitman Old and Poor, Hamlin Garland (2300)   496

    The Biographical Sketch, 500

        Hu Shih: Sage of Modern China, Marquis W. Childs (3600)   501
        There Was a Young Englishman, Clarence Day (1400)   507

    The Autobiography, 509

        Digging a Well, John Muir (600)   512
        Why I Am a Naturalist, Alan Devoe (1500)   513

    E. THE LETTER   516
    The Friendly Letter, 516; Letters by William Cowper, 517; Sydney Smith, 517;
    Charles Lamb, 518; Thomas Moore, 518; The Formal Note, 519; The Business Let-
    ter, 520; The Claim Letter, 522; The Letter of Application, 522

    F. THE INFORMAL ESSAY   525
    Definition, 525; Procedure, 525

        My Fishpond, Stephen Leacock (1600)   528
        On the Floor of the Library, Simeon Strunsky (1300)   530
        A Little Moral Advice, Sydney Smith (800)   532

INDEX   535

WORKBOOK

    Jay Gould, Henry Adams, Exercise 48
    The Diffusion of Cultural Traits, Franz Boas, Exercise 48
    From *First Inaugural Address,* Thomas Jefferson, Exercise 49
    From *Of Education,* John Milton, Exercise 49
    From *Speech at the Cooper Institute,* Abraham Lincoln, Exercise 50
    Prospice, Robert Browning, Exercise 50
    The Last Word, Matthew Arnold, Exercise 51
    So Then, I Feel Not Deeply! Walter Savage Landor, Exercise 51

READING SELECTIONS

[By Subjects]

EDUCATIONAL MATTERS

Where Are We? Carl Becker, 4
Studies That Build Men of Character, A. S. Foord, 6
A Little Learning, Whitney Griswold, 9
How to Learn, E. S. Robinson, 23
The Metamorphosis of Hell Week, Karl Detzer, 84
College Football "Expendable," R. M. Hutchins, 219
Work Your Way through College? R. C. Hutchison, 312
Should Students Study? W. T. Foster, 315
Of Education, John Milton, WORKBOOK Ex. 49

THE AMERICAN WAY OE LIFE

I Chose America, Percy Waxman, 141
The American Way of Life, Dorothy Thompson, 143
Credo, Thomas Wolfe, 145
Where I Stand, Elia Kazan, 147
How to Misunderstand the USA, Tibor Koeves, 148
My America, John Buchan, 221
Humor and America, Max Eastman, 252
Enterprise and Old Iron, John Patric, 477

HISTORY, POLITICS, AND GOVERNMENT

Radicalism and Conservatism, A. M. Schlesinger, 265
Let's Join the Human Race, Stringfellow Barr, 302
World Government or World Destruction, Stephen King-Hall, 321
The Conspiracy of Aaron Burr, Lois Boeck, 450
"I Have Not Yet Begun to Fight," C. L. Lewis, 459
The Country Gentlemen, T. B. Macaulay, 490
From *First Inaugural Address*, Thomas Jefferson, WORKBOOK Ex. 49
From *Speech at the Cooper Institute*, Abraham Lincoln, WORKBOOK Ex. 50

BUSINESS AND ECONOMICS

Co-operation versus Competition, John Ruskin, 174
Types of Industrial Organization, W. L. Thorp, 242
Technology—Hope or Hobgoblin? H. B. du Pont, 250
The Business Type, J. T. Adams, 296
You Are One of These, V. D. Reed, 299

NATURAL HISTORY AND OTHER SCIENTIFIC MATTERS

"The Witch Tree," R. D. Meyer, 55
Do Animals Talk? Lillian Harriman, 57
Tu'imalila, Oldest Animal in the World, Mary Patterson, 79
An Electrical "Bath" in Yellowstone, W. B. Sanborn, 81
Struck by Lightning, H. H. Rusby, 83

Woodchuck Therapy, Robert Peel, 247
Be Your Own Weatherman, Carl Warden, 277
Under Mobile River, R. G. Skerrett, 281
Earthquakes, Rev. Joseph Lynch, S.J., 283
The Struggle for Existence, Henshaw Ward, 288
Digging a Well, John Muir, 512
Why I Am a Naturalist, Alan Devoe, 513

LANGUAGE AND WRITING

Grammar, William Cobbett, 78
Featherbeds and Parnassus, Carol Hovious, 158
Basic English for Science, T. B. Haber, 175
I Can't Quite Hear You, Doctor, J. A. Brandt, 178
The Cliché Expert Takes the Stand, Frank Sullivan, 187
Emotional Meanings, R. H. Thouless, 188
On Word Magic, A. G. Gardiner, 195
How to Write a Book, Harold Nicolson, 270
How to Detect Propaganda, C. R. Miller *et al.*, 273

LITERARY MATTERS, CRITICISM, AND AESTHETICS

From *The Hero as Man of Letters*, Thomas Carlyle, 27
From *Of Kings' Treasuries*, John Ruskin, 29
The Decline of Attention, Clifton Fadiman, 38
My Experience as a Book Agent, W. L. Cross, 56
The Conditions of Art, John Ruskin, 238
Nobel Prize Acceptance Speech, William Faulkner, 249
Humor and America, Max Eastman, 252
Book reviews, 483
Walt Whitman: Old and Poor, Hamlin Garland, 496
On the Floor of the Library, Simeon Strunsky, 530
So Then, I Feel Not Deeply! W. S. Landor, WORKBOOK EX. 51

BIOGRAPHY, PEOPLE, AND TYPES

My Experience as a Book Agent, W. L. Cross, 56
The Author's Account of Himself, Washington Irving, 209
A Gentleman, J. H. Newman, 267
The Business Type, J. T. Adams, 296
Captain Ahab, Herman Melville, 341
Eustacia Vye, Thomas Hardy, 341
Stina, Herman Smith, 343
Solo, The Talk of the Town, 470
Sidewalk Fisherman, Meyer Berger, 471
The Office Bore, Mark Twain, 489
The Country Gentlemen, T. B. Macaulay, 490
Heywood, Christopher Morley, 495
Walt Whitman: Old and Poor, Hamlin Garland, 496
Hu Shih: Sage of Modern China, M. W. Childs, 501
There Was a Young Englishman, Clarence Day, 507
Digging a Well, John Muir, 512
Why I Am a Naturalist, Alan Devoe, 513
My Fishpond, Stephen Leacock, 528
Jay Gould, Henry Adams, WORKBOOK EX. 48

DESCRIPTION: see Table of Contents

NARRATION: see Table of Contents

ESSAYS AND MISCELLANEOUS

An Apology for Idlers, R. L. Stevenson, 22
Skiing, Strand Mikkelsen, 240
Donjon, Anon., 264
Bathtub, W. P. Gerhard, 264
A Little Moral Advice, Sydney Smith, 532
The Diffusion of Cultural Traits, Franz Boas, WORKBOOK Ex. 48
Prospice, Robert Browning, WORKBOOK Ex. 50
The Last Word, Matthew Arnold, WORKBOOK Ex. 51
So Then, I Feel Not Deeply! W. S. Landor, WORKBOOK Ex. 51

Orientation

ʊʊʊʊʊ

I. A FOREWORD TO STUDENTS

BOTH EVIDENCE and experience prove that a student of average intelligence can master any subject in which he takes enough interest. That many students at the time they enter college are miserably prepared in the use of their own language indicates, then, that they have never become convinced of the value of knowing how to use language correctly and effectively in speaking and writing. If you are one of these and your attitude in the past has been one of repugnance or indifference towards the work of learning to write and speak well, you are asked to give thoughtful consideration to the following remarks.

Perhaps your reason for entering college was to prepare for a profession—that of engineering, dentistry, medicine, or some other —or to become a superior farmer or businessman, and you are impatient at having to spend time learning the skills and techniques of composition. It may therefore be important to you to learn that there is a direct relationship between ability to use English well and achievement in all your college work. This is not just the idea of some English professor. Many investigations, in various places and at different times, each conducted with scientific objectivity, prove its truth. We have space to report just a few of these, but all similar tests show like results.

(1) M. E. Gladfelter concluded after a study of the grades of freshmen at Temple University that a diagnostic English test, plus a psychological test, would reveal so clearly a student's ability to do college work that the high-school record need not be consulted, except to check upon desirable prerequisites.[1] (2) W. D. Templeman, after studying the record of 2,430 freshmen at the University of Illinois, reached a similar conclusion. His study verified a belief in the office of the Dean of Liberal Arts and Sciences at the University of Illinois "that, generally speaking, a student's grade in freshman rhetoric is a good index of his entire future academic ranking."[2] Among his findings were the following: of sixty-five engineering students who received E (the lowest grade) in rhetoric, all but three were below C in their general average. Likewise, of sixty-eight engineers who received A or B in rhetoric, all but nineteen were above B in all subjects. This relationship held in every college of the university—Engineering, Agriculture, Commerce, Physical Education, and Liberal Arts. (3) Johnson O'Connor conducted a survey which demonstrated that a close relationship exists between the size of a student's vocabulary and his success after graduation. In reporting on his survey, he stated: "An extensive knowledge of the exact meanings of English words accompanies outstanding success more often than any other single characteristic which the Human Engineering Laboratories have been able to isolate and

[1] "The Value of the Cooperative English Test in Prediction for Success in College," *School and Society*, XLIV (September 19, 1936), 384.
[2] "Vocabulary and Success in College," *School and Society*, LI (February 17, 1940), 2.

1

measure. . . . The balance of the evidence at the moment suggests that such a consciously, even laboriously, achieved vocabulary is an active asset." [1]

Now unless you have a closed mind, you will accept the weight of such evidence; and if you are intelligent and ambitious, you will determine to make the best use possible of the chance to learn the fundamental skills and techniques of communication, so that you will benefit in the ways these surveys indicated. You will be in a better position to do this, however, if you understand and accept two requisites: first, the responsibility of learning to write and speak well is yours alone; and second, the task entails hard, consistent, and intelligent effort.

You will, of course, have the help of a specialist—your instructor—who understands the principles and techniques of good communication. He can explain difficulties to you and advise you how to eliminate errors and better your style, but he cannot teach you to write well without your cooperation. If you are in earnest, you will strive diligently to follow his instructions. You will not wait for assignments before exploring sections of your text that treat of matters about which you are ignorant or on which you have become rusty. You will make it a rule to add something each day to your store of knowledge about how to write well.

You will be better fortified, moreover, if you keep in mind the fact that mastery of the skills and techniques of good writing and speaking will not come easily. Even the most expert and polished writers find composition difficult. The most fluent and smoothly flowing passages are often the ones over which a writer has labored longest. In his essay "Self-Cultivation in English," G. H. Palmer says, "I must write with pains that he may read with ease." If you find it necessary, therefore, to spend an undue amount of time on the course in order to perfect your skill in communication, you must not begrudge the time nor skimp your work. Just as the football player endures long, tedious hours of drill to win the plaudits of the crowd on Saturday afternoon, so you must spend long, trying hours in learning the principles set forth in your text, in studying the work of master writers, and in practicing the art of writing itself. This is the price you pay for being in arrears. But if you do learn the principles, if you make progress in applying them, your dividends will be great, both in the quality of all your college work and in your intellectual growth generally, for if you learn to express your ideas clearly, correctly, and logically, you will find this an aid in everything you do.

Nor will the advantage end with your college days. If you acquire the skill to write and speak well, you will find numerous ways to employ your ability after you leave college. You may need to explain your ideas or defend your opinions or actions to your business or professional colleagues or your community. You may have to talk at civic clubs, write reports of investigations you conduct, contribute material to your local newspaper; and always you will have to write letters—letters of application, business letters, and friendly letters. How well you do these tasks will in part determine your professional and social success. In this connection, Edward Menge makes a pertinent remark concerning one profession, that of engineering: "Every leader in engineering without exception places heavy emphasis upon the necessity of a thorough knowledge of English. J. A. W. Waddell, the famous civil engineer, justly says that an American engineer's greatest asset is his ability to write and speak correctly, elegantly, and vigorously." [2]

Writing is one of the best means, moreover, of achieving recognition in whatever profession you enter. Almost every business and profession has its publications, and if you are able to contribute to one of these, you can reach an audience far beyond your immediate circle and can bring to this audience your

---

[1] "Vocabulary and Success," *The Atlantic Monthly,* CLIII (February, 1934), 160-166.

[2] From Edward Menge, *Jobs for the College Graduate in Science* (New York, 1932), p. 72.

ideas and the results of your experiments and research. A teacher describes successful classroom techniques; a doctor analyzes his case histories; an engineer presents his methods of overcoming technical difficulties; a merchant describes successful advertising and merchandising programs. By doing this, each becomes better known and wins recognition for himself in a way that would not be possible if he lacked the ability to present his information to others.

But in an even more significant way than in economic success, social success depends on the ability to speak and write well. Ben Jonson wrote: "No glass renders a man's form and image so true as his speech." And it is true that a man's breeding and social grace are evident as soon as he speaks or writes. No one, of course, expects a person to write and speak correctly who has had no educational opportunities, but few will condone flagrant errors in the speech and writing of college students. Bad grammar, wrong idioms, faulty sentences, and like errors handicap a college graduate not only because they hinder precise transmission of thought from one mind to another, but because educated men and women do not make such errors. To do so makes one as suspect as a man who wears high yellow shoes or a woman who wears slacks to a formal ball.

But in a more profound sense than in any discussed so far is it important that you know how to use your language well. As the means of communication tend to make the world smaller, and as Americans are called on more and more to assume responsibilities in many parts of the earth, it is important that every educated citizen of the country become increasingly conscious of the value of language in general and of his own in particular, and that he take pride in it and in his knowledge of it. In this connection, consider the following pertinent statement by John Milton:

Whoever in a state knows how to form wisely the manners of men, and to rule them at home and in war with excellent institutes, him in the first place, above others, I should esteem worthy of all honor; but next to him the man who strives to establish in maxims and rules the method and habit of speaking and writing received from a good age of the nation, and, as it were, to fortify the same round with a kind of wall, any attempt to overleap which ought to be prevented by a law only short of that of Romulus. . . . The one, as I believe, supplies a noble courage and intrepid counsels against an enemy invading the territory; the other takes to himself the task of extirpating and defeating by means of a learned detective police of ears and a light cavalry of good authors, that barbarism which makes large inroads upon the minds of men, and is a destructive intestine enemy to genius. Nor is it to be considered of small consequence what language, pure or corrupt, a people has, or what is their customary degree of propriety in speaking it. . . . For, let the words of a country be in part unhandsome and offensive in themselves, in part debased by wear and wrongly uttered, and what do they declare but, by no light indication, that the inhabitants of that country are an indolent, idly-yawning race, with minds already long prepared for any amount of servility? On the other hand, we have never heard that any empire, any state, did not flourish moderately at least, as long as liking and care for its own language lasted.[1]

If, then, being able to communicate correctly and effectively will benefit you in so many ways, and if you are interested in your development and achievements, no urging should be needed to induce you to determine to master the rules and principles of correct communication. If as the result of past experiences you believe you lack the aptitude to communicate your ideas intelligibly to others, be assured that no special aptitude in language is requisite in order to learn to write and speak clearly and correctly. You will need intelligence, diligence, patience, and persistence; but these are needed for any sort of attainment. Just as through practice you can learn to play bridge or tennis with acceptable skill, though you may never become a Culbertson or a Budge, so by diligent application and conscientious practice you can learn to write in a workmanlike manner.

[1] From David Masson, *The Life of John Milton* (London, 1881), I, 790.

You will benefit most from this course by considering it for what it is—a foundation course in which to learn the best means of transmitting all the ideas you will ever have on any subject. To think of it as intended primarily for those who will make a profession of writing, and therefore not as your concern, is to mistake its whole purpose. The future creative writer will derive benefit from it, to be sure, for it contains the principles of his craft; but for him it is only the beginning of a long apprenticeship. For many others, it is the only course they will take that is devoted specifically to the best means of transmitting ideas. If these should treat it as "just another course" and fail to learn what it attempts to teach, they are very likely to remain handicapped in their thinking, talking, and writing; for if their medium of expression is poor, how can their ideas appear in a favorable light? But if they should accept the chance to learn to use their language effectively, and be willing to devote whatever time is required to bring this about, they will find both in college and afterwards ample rewards for their decision and efforts.

Where Are We?[1]

CARL BECKER

I WAS INTERESTED in the letter of Five Bewildered Freshmen, and in the discussion it gave rise to. The freshmen say they have been engaged in the intellectual life for more than two months and don't know what it's all about. This is bad, but who is to blame? Some say the students are to blame, and some say the professors. What is to be done about it? You suggest a foundation or an orientation course such as is given in other universities.

For my part, I don't blame anyone—not the freshmen, certainly. It's not especially the student's fault if he doesn't know what it's all about. If he did, he wouldn't need to come to college. That's why, I have always supposed, young people come to college—to get some notion, even if only a glimmering, of what it's about. They come to get "oriented." But why expect to be oriented in two months, or a year? The whole four-years college course is a course in orientation. It isn't a very satisfactory one, indeed. Four years isn't enough. Life itself is scarcely long enough to enable one to find out what it's all about.

Neither do I blame the professors—not particularly. Many people appear to think that professors possess some secret of knowledge and wisdom which would set the students right as to the meaning of things if they would only impart it. This, I do assure you, is an illusion. I could write you a letter on behalf of Five Bewildered Professors which would make the five bewildered freshmen appear cocksure by comparison. The professors are in the same boat. They don't know either what it's all about. They tried to find out when in college, and they have been trying ever since. Most of them, if they are wise, don't expect ever to find out, not really. But still they will, if they are wise, keep on trying. That is, indeed, just what the intellectual life is—a continuous adventure of the mind in which something is being discovered possessing whatever meaning the adventurer can find in it.

This effort to find out what it's all about is, in our time, more difficult than ever before. The reason is that the old foundations of assured faith and familiar custom are crumbling under our feet. For four hundred years the world of education and knowledge rested securely on two fundamentals which were

[1] This article appeared as a letter by Professor Becker in answer to one which had previously appeared in the columns of the newspaper. Reprinted by permission of the *Cornell Daily Sun*.

rarely questioned. These were *Christian philosophy* and *Classical learning*. For the better part of a century Christian faith has been going by the board, and Classical learning into the discard. To replace these we have as yet no foundations, no certainties. We live in a world dominated by machines, a world of incredibly rapid change, a world of naturalistic science and of physico-chemico-libido psychology. There are no longer any certainties either in life or in thought. Everywhere confusion. Everywhere questions. Where are we? Where did we come from? Where do we go from here? What is it all about? The freshmen are asking, and they may well ask. Everyone is asking. No one knows; and those who profess with most confidence to know are most likely to be mistaken. Professors could reorganize the College of Arts if they knew what a College of Arts should be. They could give students a "general education" if they knew what a general education was, or would be good for if one had it. Professors are not especially to blame because the world has lost all certainty about these things.

One of the sure signs that the intellectual world is bewildered is that everywhere, in colleges and out, people are asking for "Orientation" courses which will tell the freshmen straight off what it is all about. If we were oriented we shouldn't need such courses. This does not mean that I am opposed to an orientation course for freshmen. I would like an orientation course for freshmen. I would like one for seniors. I would like one for professors and trustees. I would like one for President Farrand and President Butler. Only, who is to give it? And what is it to consist of? I asked Professor Hayes, "What about your orientation course at Columbia?" He said, "It's a good thing for the instructors who give it." I asked a man whose son had taken the course, "What did he get out of it?" The reply

was, "He read three books in three unrelated fields of knowledge and got a kick out of one of them." Who knows the "background" or the "general field of knowledge"? If the course is given by many professors, the student will be taking several courses as one course instead of several courses as separate courses. If one man gives it what will it be? It will be as good as the man is. If we could get a really top-notch man to give a course, no matter what, and call it an orientation course, I should welcome it. H. G. Wells might give such a course, and it would be a good course. I doubt if it would orient any one or settle anything, but it would stir the students up and make them think. That would be its great merit. That is the chief merit of any course—that it unsettles students, makes them ask questions.

The Five Bewildered Freshmen have got more out of their course than they know. It has made them ask a question—What is it all about? That is a pertinent question. I have been asking it for thirty-five years, and I am still as bewildered as they are.

SUGGESTIONS FOR STUDY

1. State the attitude of the Five Bewildered Freshmen.
2. Why does not the author blame the freshmen?
3. Why does not the author blame the professors?
4. What makes certainty more difficult to find in our time?
5. What is the author's idea of the chief merit of any course?
6. Why then should the Five Bewildered Freshmen feel some consolation?
7. Write a composition suggested by this article. What do you expect to receive from your education? Have you experienced any bewilderment of this kind? What do you think of a course which primarily makes you ask questions rather than giving you specific answers? In what areas of study are some answers possible?

Studies That Build Men of Character[1]

ARCHIBALD S. FOORD

AT THE OUTSET let us look statistically at the academic opportunities before you. If you were to count the courses listed in the white pamphlet that directs you to your classrooms you would see that Yale offers approximately 930 terms of courses. It would take you a little more than 93 years to complete them all —a rather lengthy college career—for at the rate of 5 courses a year most of you will take only 40 terms of work to earn your degree. So your opportunities in this sense are practically boundless, far more than you can possibly take advantage of, and, considering the courses you are required to take for graduation, you face the problem of electing something less than 1/23 of what is available to you.

Well, perhaps that is not such an appalling task if you have a vocational purpose in mind. There are courses especially set up and prescribed for the budding doctor, chemist, engineer. If your aptitudes are equal to your intent you may solve your problem by choosing such a pre-professional course. And if so, well and good. Those courses are in the curriculum for a specific practical purpose. But there are also a great many courses in the curriculum—certainly the majority—which from a vocational point of view appear to be pretty useless. Unless you decide to teach them it is unlikely that the information they impart will ever directly help you to earn a nickel.

Of these a large proportion lies in the general field called the Humanities, traditionally the core of the Yale course of study. There is no official definition of the Humanities, but

we normally consider them to be the Classics —History (including the History of Art and Music), Philosophy, English and the modern foreign languages and literatures. You are required to take a certain number of these, but beyond the elementary level you have a wide range of choice. Thus your problem of choosing is made difficult both by the great numbers available and by the fact that these courses have no immediate practical application. How then do you take advantage of your superabundant opportunities in the field of the Humanities?

You do so first by understanding their purpose, which, if without economic value, is real enough. Their purpose is embodied in their name, bestowed upon them 600 years ago by an Italian scholar named Battista Guarino. Of all God's creatures, wrote Guarino, "To man only is given the desire to learn. Hence, what the Greeks called *paidia*, we call *studia humanitatis* . . . ," he continued, the study of "the pursuits, the activities proper to mankind." To Guarino, the Humanities, *studia humanitatis*, were fundamentally studies in the proper conduct of life. He urged the student to master language first, for without it you cannot begin to learn. Then turn to history, he went on, where you "will learn to understand the manners, laws, and institutions of different types of nations, the varying fortune of individuals and states, the sources of their success and failures." Side by side with history, he concluded, read poetry and fiction which exhibit "the realities of our own life under the form of imaginary persons and situations."

Now the concept of what studies are "proper to mankind" has expanded a good deal in the six centuries since Guarino. All

[1] This article was originally given as an address to the Class of 1955 at Yale University. From the *Yale Alumni Magazine* (December, 1951). Reprinted by permission of the *Yale Alumni Magazine*.

the social sciences, for example, have been developed; and the natural and physical sciences have made tremendous strides. But they have in no way supplanted the Humanities for what the old scholars called "learning and training in virtue," that is, for building men of character and integrity capable of leadership among their fellows. Indeed you will find that those who direct pre-professional studies urge their students to absorb all of the Humanities that they can, for professional competence without the breadth and depth of understanding to make it useful in the world of men is but a poor achievement. A wise old physician once observed, "It is much more important to know what sort of a patient has a disease, than what sort of a disease a patient has." The Humanities still constitute the "school of life."

But, you may well ask, how so? How am I trained for life by translating Vergil or memorizing the dates of Napoleon? In what way does mastering the subtleties of Spinoza or reading the works of Goethe and Shakespeare develop my character and integrity? The answer is not simple, but neither is it an academic mystery. You commence with a study of the facts, by sweating out rules of grammar, names, dates, and multifarious details. But these are not an end in themselves. The Humanists do not subscribe to the philosophy which Mr. Gradgrind imposed upon the Coketown school teacher when he said, "Facts alone are wanted in life. Plant nothing else, and root out everything else." Quite the reverse. The Humanist knows that you will forget most of your facts in a very short time. A knowledge of facts is merely an indispensable preliminary to two far more important accomplishments.

The first is the training of the mind and the increasing of its capacity to learn. It is in this sense that your teachers refer to a course as a discipline. For learning, it goes without saying, does not cease abruptly upon graduation. For the wise man it continues to the end of his life. If you have learned how to learn you possess an enormous advantage

over those who never submitted their minds to college disciplines. Your brain is alert, orderly, open to new ideas, quick to discern, and careful to discriminate. These qualities are not easily acquired. They come only from constant application, often sheer drudgery. There are no shortcuts. As old Hesiod observed, the gods have set much sweat between us and true manhood.

No course has a monopoly on effective discipline. For centuries Greek and Latin grammar were considered essential, and no one has yet invented better exercise for the growing intellect. The man who has mastered the order and precision of those tongues can tackle many a problem the ancients never thought of, and the qualities of mental discipline acquired will remain long after grammatical details have been forgotten. But the modern languages can serve the purpose too, and if philosophy sometimes begets dreamers, it has also nourished some of the clearest and most practical minds the world has ever known.

In a quite different sense history develops the same qualities. Here there is not to be found the logic and precision of grammar or philosophy, for in some ways history is a good bit of a muddle. The historian seeks truth in a rather jumbled past. When he examines an historical document, he cannot take it at face value. He must first determine the authenticity of the document, establish that it is what it purports to be. Then he must try to sift bias and prejudice from objective fact, compare his evidence with similar or conflicting evidence to determine the exactness of his information, and only then is he ready to give it an interpretation that is meaningful in the long stream of time. On every side his path is beset by snares, for the world is rich in forgeries, well meaning falsehoods, and unintentional errors. One mistake in the process can destroy all the value of the historian's labor. The mind trained to find historical truth is disciplined indeed. That explains why so many historians were made intelligence officers in the last war. They had little information of any practical value, but they had the mental qualities to learn quickly and handle dispassionately a large body of unfamiliar material.

This leads me to the other purpose of the Humanities, one that is broader and less easily explained. It used to be stated briefly as the acquisition of Culture, spelled with a capital C—but that word is ill-defined and much abused. Let me try to expound the meaning of Culture in two of its major aspects. The first is simply a pleasurable appreciation of man's literary and artistic heritage. A cultured man is one who can understand and enjoy for their own sakes the great achievements of the human race. This does not rule out the smaller pleasures of our own little world. They are part of our heritage too. The most cultured man I know is a baseball fan and thoroughly enjoys a good movie. He is no intellectual snob. But he is far removed from that sorry individual, to be numbered by the million, whose entire range of interests includes only his job, sports, and sex; whose mind withers in the dreary narrowness of his own arid life until his intellect dies or he becomes a psychiatric case. The most extreme example of this type is the top gambler called before the Kefauver Committee early this year. Though rich beyond the dreams of avarice, he privately confesses that he has no pleasures but the horse racing form, which occupies his attention for only a few minutes a day. There is many a man with a much better education who is as tightly imprisoned in his own intellectual vacuum. What we call Culture releases us from that mental bondage and sets us free to share the richest experiences of mankind. For those who know, the world can offer no greater thrill than a symphony by Beethoven or a painting by Da Vinci, and nothing stirs the emotions more deeply than a Shakespearean tragedy or a poem by Keats. Like the other sensations of the mind and heart, these cannot be put adequately into words, and since I cannot do so I ask you to accept the truth of what I say

upon the testimony of generations of cultured men.

But a good acquaintance with the Humanities gives you more than rich enjoyment— and here I come to the second aspect of the meaning of Culture—it gives you the philosophical insight, the deep serenity, and the broad understanding that are the hallmarks of the mature man, the man who is rightly attuned to the world in which he lives. On the one hand he finds moral and intellectual inspiration in our cultural heritage that makes him a creative and uplifting member of society. On the other, a knowledge of the past and its achievements steadies his course through the storms of existence. History does not repeat itself, but he who knows how men and nations have acted in times gone by cannot be stampeded into panic or lulled into false security by the gusty passions of the day. He sees his life in a perspective as clear as man can know. Such maturity, it is truly observed, is the gate of Paradise.

If you can accept what I have said, I believe that you have the clues to making the most of your opportunities in the Humanities. Keep constantly before you that their purposes are to train your mind, to enrich your pleasures, and to acquaint you with sources of inspiration and wisdom. Seek these things, and you shall find them.

To achieve these ends it probably is of little importance which of the Humanities you choose to take. "It must not be supposed," wrote a teacher 500 years ago, "that a liberal education requires acquaintance with them all . . . we do wisely," he went on, "to pursue that study which we find most suited to our intelligence and our tastes, though it is true that we cannot rightly understand one subject unless we can perceive its relation to the rest." That quotation contains my concluding advice. Don't worry about the humanistic courses you cannot take. Get the utmost in true value from the ones you do.

SUGGESTIONS FOR STUDY

1. What are the Humanities? How do these differ in purpose from the pre-professional courses?

2. In your own words, explain Guarino's statement of the purposes of the Humanities. Is the mastery of facts necessary to the humane studies? If so, in what sense?

3. What mental benefits accrue from the study of the humanities? What does the author mean by "culture"?

4. Consider this article very carefully to see what its ideas have to do with those in Professor Becker's "Where Are We?" Write a composition explaining one point of identity in these two articles. Be specific; refer frequently to what each author says, so that your generalizations will be made clear.

5. Define the following words from this article: vocational, integrity, academic, multifarious, discriminate, authenticity, dispassionately, heritage.

A Little Learning[1]

WHITNEY GRISWOLD

A little learning is a dangerous thing;
Drink deep, or taste not the Pierian spring:
There shallow draughts intoxicate the brain,
And drinking largely sobers us again.

I TAKE MY TITLE from these familiar lines of Alexander Pope's *Essay on Criticism.* The Pierian spring was the spring in North Thessaly from which the Muses drank and so refreshed the wisdom and skill in the arts and sciences with which they inspired the human race. It was the symbol of pure learning and revered as such in Greek mythology. It was the *fons et origo* of a culture that exalted truth, beauty, reason, and freedom, that became the foundation of Western civilization, and that still inspires the free nations in their effort to preserve that civilization.

We have done away with this mythology and with it, I sometimes think, all but done away with the culture that supported it (and was supported by it) as well. We have made a monkey out of Prometheus with our cyclotrons. We have left Mercury in the lurch with our jets. We have discarded the Muses and

their spring for teachers and books, and we are in the process of discarding the teachers and books for television and other mechanical marvels. We might better express Alexander Pope's sentiments as follows:—

A little learning is a difficult thing—
How *far* is it to the Pierian spring?
Let's have a quick one at the nearest bar,
Or better still, curb-service in the car.

Or we might render it:—

A little learning *is* a dangerous thing:
There may be poison in the Pierian spring!
They say it's Greek, but when we hear it gushin',
It sounds to us suspiciously like Russian!

Or, in short:—

IF A LITTLE LEARNING IS A DANGEROUS THING, A LOT OF LEARNING IS A MUCH MORE DANGEROUS THING.

This is a strange state of mind, is it not, for a people who more than three hundred years ago (1647) adopted the first general education act in modern times and founded nine colleges before achieving their independence. It is a strange state of mind for the descendants of Puritans who recognized ignorance as the chief weapon of "that old deluder, Satan," and the heirs of Thomas Jefferson who saw it as the chief instrument of dictators and

[1] This article was designed as an address to the students of Phillips Academy, Andover. From *The Atlantic,* CXC (November, 1952). Reprinted by permission of the author and of *The Atlantic Monthly.*

despots. It is a paradox in a nation that has led the world in bringing educational opportunities to its citizens and today sends more of them to school and college than any other free people has ever done in history.

Have I exaggerated our national attitude toward education? You can cite individual cases to prove that I have. This school is one. My university, I like to think, is another. But the attitude I describe is far too prevalent for those who have the welfare of American education at heart to be complacent about it, and even at Andover and Yale the attitude is not unknown. As a nation and a civilization we have wandered far from the Pierian spring, into an arid land where the waters of that spring are blended, bottled, and purveyed under a variety of persuasive labels but where, of the spring's pure essence, it is a long time between drinks. Here, intoxicated by blends and substitutes, we dispute the merits of the original without really tasting it, after the fashion of tipplers, confused yet sure of ourselves, to the detriment of our educational system and the equal detriment of our civilization and our country.

The pure essence that is so much wanting in our educational system is that which has for its purpose neither the filling of categories with quantitative knowledge nor the communication of vocational skills, but the awakening and development of the intellectual, moral, and aesthetic powers in man. This purpose is admirably stated in the recent report of a committee on general education, in the organization of which your headmaster was a prime mover. A liberal education, says this report, should help to "achieve the excellence of human nature," to instill in the individual such qualities as intellectual curiosity, a love of excellence, inner strength and integrity, and above all, the capacity for self-education. To achieve these results, the committee insists on three indispensable prerequisites: first, the recruiting and encouraging of imaginative, enthusiastic, creative teachers; second, making education a more personal affair through tutorials, seminars,

and small courses; third, more active participation and personal involvement on the part of the student in the educational process, in distinction to the passive absorption of materials.

With all due credit to those individual schools and colleges that are making progress toward these goals, and with high hopes that they may sustain their momentum, we must face the fact that the country as a whole has neither adopted the goals nor set aside enough of its resources even to keep within sight of them. Our committee gives top priority to the recruitment of "imaginative, enthusiastic and creative teachers" and calls for a much higher ratio of teachers of this caliber to students. Yet according to an editorial in the New York *Times* we graduated from college this year only 32,000 teachers of all calibers to meet a nation-wide demand for 160,000. This demand, by the way, is calculated not on the basis of small seminars that will make education an individual experience, but on the minimum ratio of teachers to overcrowded classrooms that will bring the students in off the fire escapes without increasing the local tax rate. As to the quality of this teaching, you may draw your own conclusions from the facts that of 600,000 elementary teachers in our public schools, 300,000 do not hold college degrees and, according to the National Education Association, 100,000 are so poorly prepared that their continued presence in the classroom is considered "dangerous to the mental and emotional health of America's youth."

There are reasons for these conditions, but there is no excuse. A principal reason is the low salaries paid to teachers, ranging on the average in our public schools from a high of $4500 in New York to a low of $1475 in Mississippi, for a national average of $3290. In 1950 the average annual earnings per full-time employee in American agriculture and industry was $3024. The comparable figure for public school teachers that year was $3097. There is this significant difference between the two figures. The first, the industrial, is an average of skilled and unskilled wages. The second, the educational, is an average of salaries paid to a skilled profession. The fact that the two figures are very nearly equal shows better than words not only the relative position of teaching in our national scale of values but also the teaching profession's relatively feeble powers of competition for the kind of recruits it needs. If we compare our average teacher's salary with the average salary of college graduates in other professions, we find 95 per cent of the latter earning $3000 or over, 79 per cent earning $5000 or over, and 59 per cent earning $7500 or over.

No one expects to get rich in teaching. We all take a vow of poverty when we enter the profession. But if a teacher is to fulfill the requirements set for him by our committee, he must be able to share liberally in the cultural opportunities of his fellow men—raise a family, read, travel, cultivate his intellectual and aesthetic tastes. Alas, he cannot afford these essentials. He has all he can do to pay the grocer.

I know one excellent schoolteacher who spends his summers running a hot-dog stand in an amusement park so that he can afford to stick by his profession the rest of the year. He should be reading Plato. Or better still Aristotle. Or writing a book.

The plain fact is that the teaching profession is cut off from the type of recruits it most urgently needs *at the source,* in our colleges, where hundreds of actual candidates and thousands of potential ones are lost every year to other professions. Money alone will not rectify these conditions. Every teacher must have a sense of mission. But until we pay our teachers a wage that enables them to fulfill that mission, our efforts to improve upon it with curricular reforms will be futile, and we shall continue to suffer an enormous waste of cultural and human resources.

We do not tolerate such a state of affairs in industry. Why do we tolerate it in educa-

tion? Our excuse is that we cannot afford to do better. How valid is this excuse? In 1950 the gross national product of the United States—that is, the total market value of all goods and services produced—was $282,000,000,000. Our educational expenditures that year, both public and private, were approximately $5,600,000 on primary and secondary education and $2,200,000 on higher education, a total of $7,800,000 or 2.7 per cent of our gross national product.

I will not compare this expenditure with our defense budget, as I do not wish to suggest that the latter should be reduced. But I will compare it with consumer expenditures on radio, television sets, and musical instruments (with the last finishing a very poor third) of $3,120,000,000 or 1.1 per cent of our gross product, and with expenditures on new and used cars, not counting trucks, of $19,447,000,000 or 6.9 per cent of our gross product. These figures and others showing the amounts we spend each year on pleasures and creature comforts quite apart from our necessities prove to my satisfaction, at least, that we could spend more on education: as much more as is needed to accomplish the goals we are discussing. Our excuse that we cannot afford to do so is a lame one. The truth is that we do not wish to do so. This is not because we are obdurate and hardhearted. It is because we are deluded—deluded by a little learning. That is all we are paying for and all we are getting for our money. It is a cultural, not an economic, phenomenon, though it does have an economic reckoning. For the sums we imagine we are saving on education are spent on juvenile delinquency and other social and economic diseases which education might have cured at half the cost.

Is there no compromise, no substitute for able teachers? Are there no curricular devices that will compensate for the lack of them? Here our delusions multiply, and vocationalism, unrelated gobbets of quantitative knowledge, and downright nature-faking crowd liberal learning to the wall. In our nation-wide secondary school curriculum, the milieu in which millions of individuals plan their lives each year, courses in office training, commercial occupation, effective living, band music, and radio broadcasting press heavily on the serried remnants of the liberal arts.

I do not assume that every student in our secondary schools can or should go to college, nor do I question the motive behind such "vocational" courses for those who do not. But I do question the results. For students who go on to college they represent not only a waste of time but a confusion of values that has made serious inroads into higher education. For those who do not go on, they are poor substitutes for vocational apprenticeship and the subjective experience of life itself. There is too great a tendency in the United States, even on the part of individuals who admit the value of a liberal education to students preparing for college and the professions, to discount its value to those for whom secondary school is the final educational experience. Too many of us are disposed to agree with Bentham's view that in the enjoyment of life "pushpin is as good as poetry," and, out of ignorance, laziness, or sometimes out of intellectual snobbery, and on the basis of highly inexact and often haphazard methods of selection, to relegate lives to pushpin that might have been redeemed by poetry.

I shall have more to say on this subject presently. Let me say here that I believe that for *all* students, those who go on to college and those who do not, the richer the experience of liberal education, limited only by the individual's capacity to assimilate it, the better for our culture and the better for our country; and that in relation to this type of education the type I am criticizing bulks far too large.

This is no condescending lament from the ivory tower. It is the plea of students who have been through the mill and who deserve better of their country than it is giving them. Let me cite one of them who might almost be said to have died in this cause. He is Bert Stiles, author of the recently published war book, *Serenade to the Big Bird* (Norton). Bert Stiles left college to enlist in the Army Air Force, flew as copilot on thirty-five bomber missions over France and Germany, won the Air Medal and Distinguished Flying Cross, and then, instead of taking up his leave and returning to the United States, requested transfer to fighters and was shot down in a P-51 over Germany in 1944, at the age of twenty-three.

Returning from a particularly savage mission over Munich one day—as it turned out, very near the end of his life—this young airman and his pilot rode their bicycles out into the English countryside, bought four pounds of strawberries, and while consuming them fell into a long educational colloquy in which our school and college committee will find strong support. I quote the part dealing with secondary education:—

"I was involved in an outfit called the Progressive Education Group, with forty picked members from the two feeding junior high schools, picked for character and brains and general affability. We stayed together all the way through high school. We were a hot outfit all right . . . two teachers and forty eager beavers on our way to the moon.

"The School Board signed away all its powers. We could take a shot at anything, any subject, any whim, for as long or as short as we desired. We could pick our courses and our teachers. We could go on field trips, and use the school bus. We could do anything we chose, for two hours of the school day. The first year it was three hours a day. Progressive English one hour a day, progressive social science one hour (the names didn't mean anything), and progressive science one hour.

"Progressive science turned out to be a spectacular flop and was discontinued. Each member of the class chose some scientific subject to investigate and report on to the others. It took a year to give all the reports.

"I chose sleeping bags, and the science of keeping warm in one, and made a gala report on this in April, and just sat there and slept the rest of the year. I think my report had something to do with their discontinuing the course. . . .

"I could remember most of the educational byways that class flung itself down . . . a speed-up course in psychology, a quick survey of adolescent sex problems. We started to produce a series of plays and never finished. . . .

"We wrote poems and short stories, and seriously delved into the art of letter writing. We spent one spring learning the stories of operas. We debated whether to spend a little time on history, and decided not.

"We spoke extemporaneously. We spoke out of turn. We ranted and raised hell and went out on field trips and took in the key movies, and had a few parties to develop social poise.

"When we made our reports at the end, I stated I hadn't gotten a whole hell of a lot out of it."

It is an easy step from these curricular delusions to the corruption of college athletics, which represents yet another symptom of shallow draughts from the Pierian spring. The whole sad, innocent and not so innocent confusion of values that produces such results as the West Point scandal and the basketball fixes; the million-dollar gate receipts; the open traffic in football scholarships and "additional compensations" averaging as high in some cases as three or four thousand dollars a year; the underground recruitment of football players by alumni and coaches of colleges that frown upon it in principle; the fantastic case histories of athletes majoring in physical education and receiving course credit for football, handball, elementary swimming, social dancing, rhythms, and fly fishing; the seamy double standard, spreading through college communities as from a tainted well . . . it is a tale of educational assets mortgaged to the entertainment industry, of educational opportunities squandered in the coliseum, of men content with a little learning and impatient with that if it gets in the way of a winning team.

Do you again suspect me of speaking from the ivory tower? I am uttering the thoughts of sports columnists as well as university presidents, of undergraduates as well as faculty members, of athletes as well as scholars, of athletes who are scholars and of scholars who are athletes. Two years of military service are crowding into the already overcrowded educational years of these young men, with perhaps an *Iliad* or an *Odyssey* lying beyond them, inclining their thoughts more and more to the unfinished business of Bert Stiles.

It is perfectly possible, I would say essential, to find room in these years for active participation in organized athletic sports. I am proud to represent a university in which no fewer than three thousand of its four thousand undergraduates participate in such sports, and I intend to do everything I can to increase rather than diminish this number. I believe this program should continue to include intercollegiate as well as intramural competition, and I hope we may be victorious at all times and events. But I also believe that the athletic cloth should be cut to the educational pattern: that intercollegiate competition should be conducted on a single-standard, amateur basis; that individual ethics should be substituted for the group ethics now governing that competition; and that according to these individual ethics it is no more justifiable for a college to recruit football or basketball players by special financial inducements or curricular concessions than it would be for me to inveigle your headmaster into a game of golf and then hire Sam Snead to disguise himself as me and go out and take the headmaster's watch and pocketbook away from him. To condone such practices in the name of education adds moral to intellectual confusion and puts one more delusion in the way of our proper educational goals.

Is learning safe? That is a question we often hear nowadays, and there are some

Americans who have concluded in the negative. Our schools and colleges are accused of subversive activities, textbooks are banned, teachers are suspected for what they do and say not merely as individual citizens but as members of their profession. If a little learning is dangerous, a lot of learning is much more dangerous. It will destroy our faith and make us traitors to our country.

I believe that the people who talk this way prove better than any evidence I have offered here that Alexander Pope was right. Books won't stay banned. They won't burn. Ideas won't go to jail. In the long run of history, the censor and the inquisitor have always lost. The only sure weapon against bad ideas is better ideas. The source of better ideas is wisdom. The surest path to wisdom is a liberal education.

The cold war is the great fact of our day. It is a war of ideas. What folly it is to suppose that the schoolboy who hears and sees discussions of these ideas on radio and television, in the newspapers and magazines on his living-room table, or in the books in his local bookstores and library, is being protected from them by not mentioning them in the classroom. The whole genius and strength of democracy is epitomized in the man who prefers the better because he understands the worse. He is the perfect embodiment of the liberal education for which this Academy stands. It is not in countries where this type of education has flourished that Communism has made progress, but in countries where great ignorant masses of peasants were denied even a little learning. Communism itself, with its philosophical pretensions and its double talk, its captive science and literature, is the full flower of a little learning. Is not the obvious defense against it those deeper draughts prescribed by Pope, prohibited in Russia, yet still permissible in the United States? Is it not contorted logic to believe that liberal education, which the Kremlin fears (and therefore prohibits), will be the death of Communism in Russia, will be the birth of it in the United States?

You will hear it said, finally, that there is too much learning, that when people get too well educated they won't want to work. Work at what? The learned professions? In these, work and education and satisfaction are synonymous. Work in industry? With their high wages and their forty-hour week, what will our factory workers do with their other 128 hours? Allowing 56 for sleep and 21 for meals, that still leaves 51 in which education might prove itself. What else will fill these hours? Television? Movies? Demagogues? A little learning? Often you will find that the man who argues too much education occupies the same cultural level as the man to whom he applies the argument. The minute he steps out of his office he steps into the same car, the same movie show, the same television program, the same sleepy evening; reads the same newspapers and magazines, drinks the same beer, smokes the same cigarettes, listens to the same radio broadcasts. Observing these two gentlemen in their use of leisure time, a man from another planet might conclude that their educational advantages had been identical. This is an infirm foundation, is it not, for the curtailment of these advantages to either. We all live in the same country, under the same government. We are all responsible for choosing this government and for understanding and judging its policies. We believe in equal opportunity. The proof of equal opportunity is mobility. The key to mobility is education. The idea that there can be too much education is all very well for a feudal system or a dictatorship, but it is a contradiction in terms in a democracy.

Gentlemen of Andover, your Academy was founded in the year 1778. This was a critical year in the history of our country. It is true that just the year before we had won the Battle of Saratoga and Benjamin Franklin had then signed certain treaties of commerce and alliance with France. But Washington was at Valley Forge and the British held New York and Philadelphia.

I will give you two propositions for the year 1778: a little learning was a dangerous thing, and so was being an American. It is to your everlasting credit that for over a century and three quarters, in the forefront of American education, your Academy has, with flawless logic, inspired teaching, and liberal learning, proved the first proposition and disproved the second. May you continue to do so, to the common benefit of American education and American democracy.

SUGGESTIONS FOR STUDY

1. What contrast is presented by the modern view on education and the older view?

2. What does the author feel is wanting most seriously in our educational system?

3. What life must a teacher live to be effective? What is necessary to recruit teachers? Is the cost too great for the country to bear?

4. What does the author believe will enrich all students and in turn our society?

5. What is wrong in college athletics? What can be done in remedy?

6. How can a liberal education best combat Communism?

7. What main idea is this essay asserting?

8. Define these words from the article: paradox, prevalent, rectify, obdurate, relegate, condone.

Orientation

II. READING AND STUDYING

IN THE EXCERPT from *Heroes and Hero-Worship* at the end of this chapter, Carlyle says that all "a university or final highest school can do for us is still but what the first school began doing—teach us to *read.*" The process of becoming a good reader is, in fact, a long and arduous one, requiring complex skills, severe mental discipline, and conscious effort and application. That few college freshmen have mastered it is evident from the inability of the majority to read with full understanding a simple poem, a page of ordinary English prose, or a chapter from a textbook in elementary science, to say nothing of subjects involving close reasoning and difficult terminology. Because students so handicapped will be frustrated at every turn in their efforts to acquire an education, their first task should be to improve as readers. This is especially true of students of writing, for there is a close correlation between ability to read well and write well. A poor reader nearly always is a poor writer; and a good reader, even when untrained in the techniques of composition, can usually express his thoughts well. For the composition student more than others, therefore, time spent in learning to be a proficient reader is time well invested.

To become a good reader requires intellectual curiosity; the ability to concentrate, to visualize, and to retain and organize for effective use ideas gained from reading; and attention to vocabulary. Without curiosity to explore what is to him undiscovered countries of the mind, to learn what others have found out about man and his environment and problems, no one is likely to make the effort necessary to become a good reader; but if his curiosity is deep enough, no frustrating circumstance, no handicap—poor eyesight or blindness, unfavorable surroundings, illness, poverty, grueling labor, nothing—can keep him from exploring the accumulated stores of knowledge preserved in books. Without the power to concentrate, to "tune out" worries and distracting noises and circumstances, a reader cannot report accurately what he has read in the sports page of a newspaper, let alone follow unfamiliar and closely reasoned ideas. Without the ability to visualize, he will receive from reading none of the vivid impressions that make what he reads come to life, take on extra dimensions as a picture does when viewed through a stereoscope, and linger in his mind and become a part of living experience. Without the ability to retain what he has read and to organize it in his mind for effective use, he will get from reading little more value than practice for the eyes. Finally, without knowing the precise meaning of words and constantly expanding his vocabulary, he will not improve as a reader. Words being symbols of ideas, it follows as a matter of course that until the symbols take on meaning, the ideas will remain obscure; and that the more words one knows and the more accurate their meanings to him, the more ideas he will have access to and the more precisely will he enter into an author's meaning. Obviously, no one can develop intellectual curiosity or acquire powers of concentration, visualization, retention, and orderliness of mind or become master of a large vocabulary in a moment. All this will come in time by discipline and effort. Meanwhile, a poor reader can make a start towards improvement by diagnosing his weaknesses and substituting good habits of study for poor ones.

EMPLOYING DIFFERENT METHODS OF READING FOR DIFFERENT PURPOSES

We read for many reasons—for isolated facts, for general information, for recreation, for exact knowledge. A good reader does not use a like method in all his reading, but skims, reads rapidly, or reads methodically and intensively as best suits the purpose for which he is reading. In his essay at the end of this chapter, Ruskin says "if you read this . . . you cannot read that" and makes the point that, in general, we should employ our time in reading good books of all time. If education is attaining to know the best that has been thought and said in the world, a student desiring the greatest good from his years in college cannot afford to spend much time on what is ephemeral. Yet, as he does not wish to be ignorant of contemporary problems and happenings, he must read newspapers, current magazines, and some of what Ruskin calls good books of the hour. To do this and yet have time for more important reading, he learns to skim—to get the sense of an article or chapter quickly by noting the thesis, observing the main outline, and looking for key words, topic sentences, transitions, and summaries. This method is especially useful for reading newspapers and news and picture magazines and for running down specific information or looking up isolated facts in books of reference. By attending to the headlines and leads, or first paragraphs, of news stories, passing by items of no moment, and noting a few important details in matters of some concern, a good reader in a few minutes can post himself on the day's news; and by focusing his attention on a key word or phrase and looking only for it in glancing through an article, he can check up on half a dozen facts while a plodding reader is finding one.

For reading that does not tax the faculties unduly but that he does not wish merely to skim—significant articles in periodicals, fiction, and popular works on such subjects as science, government, and the arts—a good reader employs a method that lets him cover much ground in the briefest time. He reads rapidly, rarely pausing to go back for something he has missed or to look up a word unless it is a key to an important passage, taking in the content of some paragraphs at a glance, perhaps skipping passages that have no important bearing on the topic.

For difficult assignments, tightly packed thought, and matter full of unfamiliar terms and ideas new to a reader, a different method is imperative. For such reading it is essential to follow every sentence with the closest attention and without omissions, to look up the meaning of all terms not clear from the context, to keep an alert eye for topic sentences, transitions, and connectives, to take careful heed of the organization, and to underline key statements, make marginal notes, or even outline or paraphrase the most difficult passages.

The purpose of reading being to get the precise meaning of something written, the wise reader will use whatever method lets him do this with the least expenditure of time and effort; but as he will not be satisfied with anything short of the exact meaning—whether of a news report of a college dance, Kant's *Critique of Pure Reason,* or Plato in the original Greek—he will use the method that insures this result. If he can get Kant's meaning by skimming, he will; if he must use a dictionary and paraphrase each paragraph to understand the report of the dance, he will do that—as he might if it were written in Magyar; but he will expend no more time and effort than he must with either.

HINDRANCES TO READING

A student who gets pleasure and meaning from what he reads may be as nervous as Samuel Johnson, have as poor eyesight as the historian Prescott, and have as poor facilities for reading as Franklin or Lincoln; yet he will not be deterred by these handicaps. It is different with a student who finds reading a bore and even easy assignments difficult. Until he masters the skills of reading and can read with ease, he needs to remove as many as he can of the obstacles that hinder him. These may be physiological (poor eyesight, incorrect posture, nervousness, vocalization, faulty eye movements), environmental (poor lighting, noise, interruptions), mental (daydreaming, worry, lack of purpose, improper phrasing, language difficulties), or a combination of all three. To remove these hindrances will not be easy, but the first step towards improvement is to find them and work intelligently to eliminate them.

Physiological Hindrances

Poor eyesight often causes strain of which a reader is unaware. If after reading a short time you find your eyes smarting or becoming tired, the words tending to blur, or a headache coming on, it would be wise to consult an oculist to see if you need reading glasses. *Poor posture* that causes muscle weariness or prevents correct breathing may also be a hindrance. When studying, sit erect at a desk or table and hold your book at the right distance and angle to see the print without strain. A book rest that you can adjust and that will leave your hands free for making notes may be useful. *Nervousness* is another hindrance. If you have a tendency to fidget as you read, try to develop control. Resist the temptation to put down one book and take up another, empty the ash tray, straighten up the desk or room, finger objects within reach, drum on the desk or chair, sway the head or body, or do any of the numerous things that betray nervousness. To overcome these tendencies will probably require conscious practice for set periods, but gradually you can extend the periods in which you sit still and concentrate on your work. A more serious hindrance to efficient reading is the habit of *vocalizing*—moving the lips in silent reading, making small movements of the tongue or throat muscles, silently sounding each word, or even making slight sounds in the throat. Reading aloud can be a fruitful practice, but vocalizing is the mark of an unskilled reader. If you have this habit, practice reading for brief periods without vocal-

izing, gradually extend the periods, and discipline yourself to stop the habit whenever you catch yourself reverting to it. As *faulty eye movements* are closely related to improper phrasing, they will be considered in more detail under mental hindrances. It will be sufficient here to point out that when we read, the eyes travel across the page from left to right in a series of movements. With each movement the retina receives an impression of a certain number of words, representing our eye span. An unskilled reader has a very short eye span, and therefore makes many movements to a line; moreover, he often glances back to look for something he missed. A chart of his eye movements would show the eye moving unevenly back and forth, up and down, instead of steadily along the line. Again, conscious practice in reading steadily along and on trying to take in as many words as possible at a glance will produce good results.

Environmental Hindrances

You need a *good light* when you read, both to protect the eyes and to make the print easy to follow. In reading by night, use a strong light, so located as not to shine in the eyes or make a glare on the page, preferably so that the beams fall on the page from across the left shoulder. *Noise, chatter,* and *interruptions* are major causes of inability to understand what you read. Obviously, anything that competes for attention is a hindrance to reading; yet some students deliberately turn on the radio or a record player before starting to study, maintaining they can study better under such circumstances. They, of course, are fooling themselves or, more likely, have no concept of what it means to study. The chatter of thoughtless roommates and acquaintances and interruptions that constantly divert attention from reading are more difficult to control. If a roommate is unreasonable and persistent in causing disturbance, the only redress may be to move or acquire another roommate, but usually you can settle matters amicably by stipulating for certain hours for study and being firm about adhering to the stipulation. After all, it is to the advantage of your roommate and neighbors to study too, and your firmness may aid them.

Mental Hindrances

More difficult to deal with than any of the matters considered so far are those that stem from mental habits and state of mind. To remove them requires severe mental discipline, but as they are obstacles to mental attainment, a student at all serious in his intentions will make the attempt.

You may have had the experience of "reading" a whole passage without having the faintest idea of what it was about because your mind was on other matters. More often, however, you have simply let the book drop and gazed into space while your mind drifted off in a reverie. Such inattentiveness comes from the habit of *daydreaming*. Nearly everyone does a certain amount of daydreaming. What you need to keep in mind is that the time for daydreams is not when you are engaged in study. If you are prone to this habit, be resolute in calling your mind sharply back to its task when you find it wandering. If you are weary mentally, an hour off for exercise will probably save you time in the end and aid you in applying yourself with fresh zest to your studies.

Worry is another inveterate foe of good study habits and reading comprehension. Some of us worry more than others, but all of us worry unnecessarily. If you find some problem nagging at your mind as you try to read, so that you can give only cursory attention to the ideas, you will be wise to take off a few minutes to consider whatever is causing the worry, or even take a brisk walk while you face the matter intelligently. If it is a problem you can do something about, make as intelligent a decision as you can on your procedure, and then dismiss the matter from your mind. If the problem is insoluble at the moment, the only wise course is to put it aside for time to resolve. This is easier said than

done, of course, but if you think a moment, you will realize that however acute the problem, worry will not resolve it.

A student without purpose in life, who has drifted into college and is drifting through without aim or plan, has a problem much too acute for consideration here. He needs wise counsel and the aid of the best guidance a college can provide. In a narrower sense, however, *lack of purpose* may apply to a student's reading. If he reads without design, simply because something is assigned or suggested to be read, he will read much less intelligently than if he has a clear idea of the purpose for which he is reading. A good procedure before starting to study any lesson or read any outside assignment is to take a moment to decide just what the lesson or outside reading is designed to accomplish, what its main purpose is in relation to the whole course, and then read the lesson or book with this purpose in mind. If the lesson consists of a set of rules, an intelligent student will decide whether the rules are an essential part of the knowledge he will be supposed to assimilate, and if they are, he will learn them. If in a history course he is asked to read a Victorian social novel, he will decide that the purpose of the assignment is to give him a "backstairs" view of the history of the time, and though he may enjoy the characterization and plot of the novel, he will look for the historical and social implications as he reads, and will emphasize these in his lesson report.

Another hindrance to efficient reading is *improper phrasing*. We communicate usually not by means of single words but groups of words, each a "breath group." We do not say, for instance, The . . . dog . . . has . . . not . . . been . . . fed, but Thedog . . . hasnotbeenfed, or Thedoghasn'tbeenfed. Because it is difficult to read words thus run together, we write or print them separately; but when we read, we take in at one sweep of the eye a combination of words that seem to belong together, as was explained under "faulty eye movements" on page 18. Since these combinations register separately on the mind, it follows that when a reader sees as one group a combination of words that were not meant by the writer to go together, his idea of what he is reading will be distorted. Very poor readers read one word at a time, without giving thought to how the words combine to form ideas. Only slightly better readers may read two or three words at each glance of the eye along the line, but without making sensible combinations. The good reader, on the other hand, sweeps his eye along the line, taking in at each glance, or fixation, large groups of words that combine readily to form ideas, or mental images. Good practice in correct phrasing is to take a passage and go over it till you are certain of the meaning, put bars between groups of words that obviously go together, and practice reading each group at one glance of the eye; then gradually increase the number of words you can take in at one glance. Constant practice of this procedure will increase your eye span and will help you read with more speed and more understanding.

A basic cause of inability to read is an inadequate vocabulary, but as this deficiency requires extended consideration, it is treated in a separate section in the chapter on "The Word."

STUDYING INTELLIGENTLY

Time Allotment

Students who have not learned to study properly often spend more time on their assignments with far poorer results than do those who know how to study intelligently, for it is not the length of time spent on a lesson that counts, but how the time is used. A student who knows the purpose of a given assignment and directs all his faculties to achieving this purpose can usually prepare his work well and still have time for recreation, social activities, or a job, if it is essential that he work.

A requisite for proficiency as a student is a schedule that takes into account time for study as well as for class attendance. If you are taking fifteen hours of class work a week, your schedule should provide for at least thirty hours of study. This does not mean that you will allot arbitrarily two hours of study to each assignment. The time required for an assignment is whatever it takes for thorough preparation. This may be less than an hour or many hours, but the average, depending on a student's ability, will be two to three hours. A sensible procedure, therefore, is to draw up a schedule in which you allot specific periods for study as well as for class attendance, and force yourself to adhere to this schedule, making only such adjustments as experience dictates.

You are unlikely to take the same degree of interest in every subject. If this is true, you may be tempted to study first, or when you are freshest and most alert, subjects that interest you most. A wiser procedure is to take up when you are least tired and inattentive those you find least interesting or most difficult.

In organizing your time, arrange your study periods, so far as possible, at hours when you will have the fewest distractions and the least noise to contend with and when you are least tired. If you have free periods during the day, when most students are away from the dormitory or when the library is least crowded, use these for studying your more difficult subjects. Remember, too, that the time for physical exercise is when you are mentally fagged, not when you are most awake. When the time comes to study, resist the temptation to attend to many trivial matters before you settle down, but begin at once, and keep to the task without interruption till it is done or the period over. The experience of a few months will prove to you how much more pleasant your life as a student will be if you follow some such system than if you study haphazardly or do everything else first and rush through your preparations at the last possible moment.

Methods of Study

A good first step is to become acquainted with your textbooks. When you acquire a textbook and before you begin to study individual assignments, take careful note of the title; see who the author is and if possible find out what his position is in his field; look at the copyright date (on the reverse side of the title page) to see if the text was written recently; go carefully over the table of contents, noting chapter headings or the headings of main and subdivisions, so as to get the organization clearly in mind; and read the preface. If the book has introductory and summary paragraphs for chapters or divisions, read these. In this way you will become informed of the purpose and limits of the text and of the author's objectives, and will have a clearer idea of the purpose of individual assignments.

When you begin to study a lesson, first take a few moments to glance over the whole assignment. In this survey, note what the assignment embraces, what relation it bears to the course as a whole, what is its specific objective, what are its main divisions and elements, and consider the best method to employ in studying it. If it involves rules and their application, you will need to drill—to go over them till you know them and how to apply them. If it is the study of a foreign language, you will need to memorize vocabulary, learn idioms, and drill on grammar. If it is general reading in literature, social science, or science, you may need to read it a number of times—perhaps the first time rapidly for main ideas; a second time more carefully for details, this time looking up all unfamiliar words and terms, underlining topic sentences, and making note of salient points; and, if necessary, a third time, passing over what is already clear and concentrating on difficult passages.

Finally, try to arrange a schedule that will allow you a brief period for review before each class. If this is impractical, take time for a rapid review of next day's lessons before you retire, or, better, get up early enough in the morning to review.

ACQUIRING SPEED

As the only purpose of reading is to glean the meaning of something written, comprehension is ultimately all that matters. Most authorities on reading hold, however, that comprehension and rate of reading are related and that a rapid reader tends to comprehend better than a slow one. Even if this were not true, the ability to read rapidly is desirable, for time to read is limited and things to read unlimited. Practice in acquiring a higher rate of speed is worth while, therefore, whatever one's rate may be.

One of the most useful methods of acquiring speed is that suggested in the section in this chapter on *improper phrasing,* for little gain is possible in the rate of reading without an increase in eye-span. After some practice in reading selections you have marked, you will find it more convenient to practice with selections in periodicals that have somewhat narrow columns. Also, in all your reading, try to take in at a glance all the words between punctuation marks. Constant practice of this procedure will aid you greatly in gaining speed.

Another method that will help you increase your speed is to read an article at your normal rate; determine what your normal rate is by dividing the number of words in the article by the number of minutes it took you to read it; then re-read the article as rapidly as possible; and again figure your rate. Gradually begin to apply the rate at which you read the second time to a first reading, being certain at the same time that you understand what you have read. The reading selections in this book will give you ready material for this practice, and to save you time in counting the words, the approximate number of words in each selection is given after the title in the table of contents.

A prime requisite for rapid reading is an adequate vocabulary. The more words you know in both their denotations and connotations, the fewer times you will have to stop to look up a meaning or to try to gather the meaning from the context; and the more rapidly will you take in ideas. In this connection, the chapter on "The Word," page 154, will aid you, and it will be well for you to study it carefully without waiting for it to be assigned. Furthermore, make a practice of keeping a list of words and definitions that recur in your reading, and give some time each week to reviewing this list. When one of them seems appropriate, use it in writing or speaking to help fix it in your memory. Increasing your vocabulary by whatever device will greatly increase your ability to read with both speed and understanding.

Reading a Sample Paragraph. One method of analyzing a reading selection is illustrated with the paragraph from Stevenson which follows.

(See *Workbook*, Exercises 48, 49, 50, 51.)

An Apology for Idlers

R. L. STEVENSON

JUST NOW, when everyone is bound, under pain of a decree in absence convicting him of *lèse*-respectability, to enter on some lucrative profession, and labor therein with something not far short of enthusiasm, a cry from the opposite party who are content when they have enough, and like to look on and enjoy in the meanwhile, savors a little of bravado and gasconade. And yet this should not be. Idleness, so-called, which does not consist in doing nothing, but in doing a great deal not recognized in the dogmatic formularies of the ruling class, has as good a right to state its position as industry itself. It is admitted that the presence of people who refuse to enter in the great handicap race for sixpenny pieces, is at once an insult and a disenchantment for those who do. A fine fellow (as we see so many) takes his determination, votes for the sixpences, and in the emphatic Americanism, "goes for" them. And while such a one is plowing distressfully up the road, it is not hard to understand his resentment, when he perceives cool persons in the meadows by the wayside, lying with a handkerchief over their ears and a glass at their elbow. Alexander is touched in a very delicate place by the disregard of Diogenes. Where was the glory of having taken Rome for these tumultuous barbarians who poured into the Senate house and found the Fathers sitting silent and unmoved by their success? It is a sore thing to have labored along and scaled the arduous hilltops, and when all is done, find humanity indifferent to your achievement. Hence physicists condemn the unphysical; financiers have only a superficial toleration for those who know little of stocks; literary persons despise the unlettered; and people of all pursuits combine to disparage those who have none.

A. Questions on literal meaning. Underline the correct elements.
  1. The ideas which are about to be stated may sound like (a) foolish and excessive talking, (b) excessive respectability, (c) sober wisdom.
  2. The idleness which is going to be discussed consists in (a) engaging in no activity, (b) engaging in activity which is not generally recognized as profitable, (c) engaging in bustling and money-grabbing.
  3. People who are energetically engaged in a particular activity are annoyed by people who disparage that activity because of (a) fear that the government will be overthrown, (b) fear that the stock market will be upset, (c) injury to their self-esteem.

B. Manner of expression.
  1. Choice of words: The language used in this passage is distinctly literary. The au-

thor has a large vocabulary, but his choice of words is not that of common speech or ordinary direct expression, indicating that he is consciously trying to produce unusual effects with his language. (Examples: *bravado and gasconade, dogmatic formularies, an insult and a disenchantment, takes his determination, plowing distressfully, tumultuous barbarians, arduous hilltops*.) The figures of speech (*decree in absence, great handicap race for six-penny pieces, scaled the arduous hilltops*) are ingenious and show imagination. The references to American slang, Alexander, and the sack of Rome indicate wide reading.

2. Sentence patterns: The characteristic sentence structure is long and rhythmical, but short sentences (such as "And yet this should not be.") spaced among the long ones prevent the style from seeming heavy. The sentences are artistically varied as to the positions of the various elements, flow smoothly, and give the effect of long experience in the use of literary English.

3. Structure of the paragraph: The paragraph proceeds logically from a statement of the leading idea to a restatement of it and then to a set of illustrations. The paragraph is well integrated. The last sentence, with its balanced series of independent clauses, the last of which returns to a statement of the leading idea, produces an effect of good craftsmanship and finality.

C. The speaker: Robert Louis Stevenson, a professional English author of the latter half of the nineteenth century, was particularly successful with romantic stories of action and adventure and with informal essays of a lei-

surely type. A chronic invalid, he spent some time in the United States and lived his last years on an island in the South Seas in pursuit of simple living and colorful romance.

D. The audience: Judged on the basis of vocabulary, sentence structure, and allusions, the audience for which Stevenson was writing was composed of educated, well-read people with time and a taste for considering ideas for their own sake.

E. The purpose: To explain and defend an attitude towards life which does not set the ordinary high premium on a busy pursuit of money.

F. The place: A British magazine devoted to literary and political writing.

G. The time: The year 1877, a time when industrial expansion, in both the United States and England, was reaching a high point in its history.

Denotation: In spite of its unpopularity at the present time, owing largely to the tendency of human beings to be annoyed by modes of living different from their own, the point of view of the person who does not wish to join in the busy pursuit of money deserves to be stated.

Connotations: I, an artist in words, find this era of industrialism in which I live uncongenial to my tastes. As an artist, a connoisseur of things that cannot be valued in money, I resent being looked down upon by those who consider money and the activities which procure it of highest value. I like to think that those whose lives are consumed in lucrative industry are not as bad as they seem, but that they have made an unwise choice, and, having made the choice, find it necessary to disparage people like me in order to protect their own self-esteem.

How to Learn[1]

EDWARD S. ROBINSON

THE OLD SAW says that *Practice makes perfect*. And certainly perfection is unattainable in any of the complex forms of human activ-

[1] From Edward S. Robinson, *Man as Psychology Sees Him* (New York, 1932). Reprinted by permission of The Macmillan Company.

ity without practice. Mere practice, however, is not enough. There are circumstances when much practice will produce either very little learning or none at all.

A man may pass along a street day after day for years without learning the order of the houses or all the details of their color and shape. Many things along this route he does learn, yet many others he does not learn, even though he is often conscious of them. Of course, if he were told that he had to pass an examination on these familiar scenes, his attitude in passing them would undergo a decisive change. He would now look upon the places that he passed in the attitude of actively intending to remember them. The distinction is between what psychologists call *incidental learning* on the one hand, and *intentional learning* on the other.

The difference in effectiveness of these two types of learning has been brought out by many experiments. Learning is frequently studied by means of an instrument known as the stylus-maze—a labyrinth cut as a groove in a metal sheet. The subject, who is blindfolded, pushes the stylus through the groove until he is able to find the shortest route, the route not involving culs-de-sac. Dr. Louis W. Gellerman recently put two groups of subjects through such a task. The members of one group were told that they were to learn the pattern. Those in the other group were instructed to "run" the maze, but they were not told to learn its pattern. Those who had the conscious intent to learn did learn in about one-fifth the practice required by those without this intent. Some of the latter never did learn the maze. A number of experiments have brought out the same facts for memorization. William McDougall and May Smith, his collaborator, once found that the reading, with no intent to learn, of a list of meaningless syllables would produce learning only after eleven times as many trials as would be required if the intent to learn were consciously present.

The presence of the intent to learn is, then, a prime requisite for effective learning. In much of our reading, typewriting, tennis playing, we are careless in this regard. We put too much faith in sheer repetition and fail to keep in mind the fact that we are trying to improve our knowledge or skill. Any kind of motivation that keeps us conscious that we are seeking to increase our efficiency is likely to be helpful. Competition, which encourages us to compare our own performance with that of others, is an especially good device for establishing and maintaining a strong intention to learn.

Another important supplement to sheer practice is an understanding of the task before us. Students frequently underscore what they consider important in the text. But too often they underscore almost every line. This indicates that they have not made clear to themselves the exact nature of the task. They hope that they will learn enough, but they do not think over the nature of the lesson. If they did they would not give equal importance to so many items. They would see the relations of parts to whole; they would see a logical structure. Suppose that one is trying to learn about Russia, the gold standard, or the Republican party. He reads books in order to acquire information. But he is likely to learn little unless he thinks as he reads—unless he constantly raises in his own mind the question as to what is important and therefore worthy of special attention and what is unimportant and a proper subject for neglect. Rarely, indeed, does one have reason to learn all that is in a book. But unless one decides on rational grounds what he wants to learn, he will acquire only a few scattered fragments of information which, because of their lack of logical coherence, will soon be forgotten.

There are various ways in which an act of skill or a body of knowledge can be understood, and not all of these are equally useful in aiding the learning process. We have pointed out that the golfer may become concerned with too many features of his play, so that his very understanding constitutes a distraction. Similarly in the acquisition of information, it is possible to understand what one is trying to learn, but at the same time to lay out for oneself a wholly impracticable task. The difficulty is not a lack of understanding of the subject to be mastered, but a lack of *selective* understanding based upon a realistic judgment of the time available and of one's capacity for the task. For adults who wish to go on acquiring useful and interesting knowledge, the importance of the selection in connection with learning can hardly be overestimated. Many a man who has decided to inform himself in regard to the banking system, tariff legislation, or modern painting has soon given up in discouragement; his progress has been impeded by a lack of any clear conception of what he wants to learn.

True, there are difficulties in the way of selecting the critical points in relatively unfamiliar materials. How can one know what parts of a book may safely be neglected until after one has mastered the text as a whole? Unless one is concerned with exceedingly close-knit and technical material, where a thorough understanding of each point is necessary before its successor can be met, the best plan is to begin by reading the entire book as rapidly as is comfortable. This will give one a reasonably accurate idea of the general framework, which in most cases is fairly simple. Then one can go back to the text and pick out and emphasize to oneself the essential ideas. An initial perspective can often be gained by reading the first and last chapters and then proceeding to the middle ones.

Especially in the case of informational learning, a principal cause of inefficiency lies in the fact that the first impression is not adequately supplemented. In one of the most important scientific studies of memory Hermann Ebbinghaus, in 1887, showed that forgetting proceeds very rapidly for material that has been just barely learned. He found that 42% of a list of meaningless syllables were forgotten within twenty minutes. Two days after learning, 72% had been forgotten. After that, forgetting proceeded very slowly, but of course most of the possible loss had occurred. Forgetting of meaningful facts does not take place so rapidly as that of meaningless materials, but the general nature of the process is much the same. Immediately following reading there is typically a swift disintegration of

a considerable part of what has been learned. The application of this principle is simple. If one hears a simple fact like a name or a complex set of facts like a play, the time to reenforce the first impression and to cut off the normal process of rapid disintegration is as soon as possible after impression. A number of years ago Harold E. Jones, then at Columbia University, conducted a pretty demonstration of the importance of checking the progress of forgetting. He found that eight weeks after a lecture a college class remembered only 24% of the material that had been presented. But some of the students had been forced to use their knowledge by taking a test right after the lecture. Eight weeks later these students remembered approximately twice as much as did those who had not reënforced their first impression.

There are two important methods of reënforcement. In the case of material that has been read, we may simply turn back to the printed pages and read them over again. Or we may attempt, by our own efforts, to recall what we have read. In most instances the latter is by far the more effective procedure. It may be well to check the correctness of one's recall by referring to the printed page, but this should be done only after the effort to recall has been made. One reason for the difference between these two methods of reënforcement is to be found in the fact that the second involves the kind of use that one will ultimately want to make of one's knowledge. And the sooner the knowledge is put to such active use, the better adapted it will be to that purpose. Another important feature of reënforcement through active recall is that one is forced to put his whole attention upon the facts involved. If one simply reads and re-reads, his rehearsals are likely to become half-hearted.

There is some evidence that skills like golfing and typewriting, which involve adjustments among muscular movements, are not so readily forgotten as is newly acquired information. It is nevertheless important that each lesson be followed by a reënforcing practice and that the practice be of the best kind. As a result of a number of laboratory studies at the University of Chicago, Professor Harvey Carr and his students have shown that, just as in the case of intellectual acquisitions, the person acquiring a motor skill must be put upon his own. It is possible to learn a maze pattern, if through the blocking of the blind alleys, one is forced to go through the correct pathway again and again. This is a good deal like learning a lesson by going over it time after time while looking at the printed page. But this is not an efficient learning method. One will learn more quickly if he is forced to go through the maze while the blind alleys are open. If the performance of a certain task in actual practice involves the temptation to make certain errors, then it is desirable during at least part of the practice to expose the person to some of the errors. In complex skills learning consists quite as much in weakening the wrong acts as it does in strengthening the right ones.

There are applications of this principle in the realm of character building. A schoolmaster was known far and wide for his dominating personality and for his almost complete control over the boys in his school. Yet this sequel is also told. These boys were especially prone to get into trouble of one kind or another after their entrance into university life, where they were thrown upon their own resources. They might have been better prepared to control themselves if, during school days, they had had a little better acquaintance with their own propensities for mischief.

There are certain formal aspects of practice or rehearsal that have to be taken into account in arriving at the conditions of most efficient learning. How long is one to practice at one time, and how frequently is one to repeat the practice sessions? In the early days of experimental psychology there was hope of discovering some single simple formula regarding the optimal distribution of practice. But as this problem has been worked over, it appears that the best distribution of practice

varies for the act or material being learned. Unless we are dealing with a very complicated act or a very large body of material, it is better to have the rehearsal period long enough to enable the learner to go through the task as a whole. If, for example, one is trying to learn a speech which is to take a half hour for delivery, it would surely be better not to curtail the single learning period to less than a half hour. The same principle would probably hold for considerably longer units of material. In other words, if the task to be learned has any real unity, it is best to preserve that unity by going through the task as a whole rather than through part of it at one session and another part at another session. There are, of course, limits to this rule. One cannot get all of American history or all of typewriting into a single study period. In such cases, however, it is always possible to find smaller subordinate unities within the larger subject matter. It is probably never justifiable to determine the length of the practice period simply in terms of time. The time element should always be brought into relation to the question of natural divisions within the task. Early investigators, studying the acquisition of fairly simple habits, found that very short practice periods were usually advantageous and their findings were undoubtedly sound for the tasks studied, but when we consider the complexity of a large part of our learning in practical life, we can see that one must reject the simple rule that practice should be interrupted as frequently as possible.

As to the optimal interval between rehearsals, this depends upon the rate at which the material being learned is forgotten. It is desirable, as we have seen, to reënforce the early impressions fairly promptly, because otherwise their influence will be rapidly lost. Later in the learning the intervals may be increased without harm and sometimes with actual advantage. In the main, muscular habits like golfing or typing do well with considerable periods between rehearsals, while ideational habits such as poems or language lessons require earlier repetitions for the best results.

SUGGESTIONS FOR STUDY

1. Distinguish incidental learning from intentional learning.

2. How much more effective is intentional learning than incidental learning?

3. What is wrong with trying to memorize everything in a given assignment? After reading this article, select from it those main principles which should be learned.

4. State two important methods of reënforcing initial impressions. Which method is the more valuable?

5. Are skills which involve muscular movement likely to be retained longer than those which involve the acquisition of information?

6. Is it better in learning to follow just the right pattern each time or to strike out on your own and expose yourself to possible errors?

7. Are short periods of practice usually advantageous? What limitations are imposed upon this rule?

8. Formulate a rule for determining the time intervals to elapse between repetitions of a skill to be learned.

9. Write down as succinctly as possible the three major principles of learning formulated here. Then under each principle add the significant minor suggestions that will assist you in learning.

10. Define the following words from this article: stylus, cul-de-sac, impracticable, disintegration, prone, optimal, collaborator.

from
The Hero as Man of Letters

THOMAS CARLYLE

OUR PIOUS FATHERS, feeling well what importance lay in the speaking of man to men, founded churches, made endowments, regulations; everywhere in the civilized world there is a pulpit, environed with all manner of complex dignified appurtenances and furtherances, that therefrom a man with the tongue may, to best advantage, address his fellow men. They felt that this was the most important thing; that without this there was no good thing. It is a right pious work, that of theirs; beautiful to behold! But now with the art of writing, with the art of printing, a total change has come over that business. The writer of a book, is not he a preacher preaching not to this parish or that, on this day or that, but to all men in all times and places? Surely it is of the last importance that *he* do his work right, whoever do it wrong—that the *eye* report not falsely, for then all the other members are astray! Well; how he may do his work, whether he do it right or wrong, or do

it at all, is a point which no man in the world has taken the pains to think of. To a certain shopkeeper, trying to get some money for his books, if lucky, he is of some importance; to no other man of any. Whence he came, whither he is bound, by what ways he arrived, by what he might be furthered on his course, no one asks. He is an accident in society. He wanders like a wild Ishmaelite, in a world of which he is as the spiritual light, either the guidance or the misguidance!

Certainly the art of writing is the most miraculous of all things man has devised. Odin's *Runes* were the first form of the work of a hero; *books*, written words, are still miraculous *runes*, the latest form! In books lies the *soul* of the whole past time; the articulate audible voice of the past, when the body and material substance of it has altogether vanished like a dream. Mighty fleets and armies, harbors and arsenals, vast cities, high-domed, many-engined—they are precious, great; but what do they become? Agamemnon, the many Agamemnons, Pericleses, and their Greece—all is gone now to some ruined fragments, dumb mournful wrecks and blocks; but the books of Greece! There Greece, to every thinker, still very literally lives; can be called up again into life. No magic *rune* is stranger than a book. All that mankind has done, thought, gained, or been—it is lying as in magic preservation in the pages of books. They are the chosen possession of men.

Do not books still accomplish *miracles*, as *runes* were fabled to do? They persuade men. Not the wretchedest circulating-library novel, which foolish girls thumb and con in remote villages, but will help to regulate the actual practical weddings and households of those foolish girls. So "Celia" felt, so "Clifford" acted: the foolish theorem of life, stamped into those young brains, comes out as a solid practice one day. Consider whether any *rune* in the wildest imagination of mythologist ever did such wonders as, on the actual firm earth, some books have done! What built St. Paul's Cathedral? Look at the heart of the matter, it was that divine Hebrew BOOK—the word partly of the man Moses, an outlaw tending his Midianitish herds, four thousand years ago, in the wilderness of Sinai! It is the strangest of things, yet nothing is truer. With the art of writing, of which printing is a simple, an inevitable and comparatively insignificant corollary, the true reign of miracles for mankind commenced. It related, with a wondrous new contiguity and perpetual closeness, the past and distant with the present in time and place; all times and all places with this our actual here and now. All things were altered for men, all modes of important work of men: teaching, preaching, governing, and all else.

To look at teaching, for instance. Universities are a notable, respectable product of the modern ages. Their existence too is modified, to the very basis of it, by the existence of books. Universities arose while there were yet no books procurable; while a man, for a single book, had to give an estate of land. That, in those circumstances, when a man had some knowledge to communicate, he should do it by gathering the learners round him, face to face, was a necessity for him. If you wanted to know what Abelard knew, you must go and listen to Abelard. Thousands, as many as thirty thousand, went to hear Abelard and that metaphysical theology of his. And now for any other teacher who had also something of his own to teach, there was a great convenience opened: so many thousands eager to learn were already assembled yonder; of all places the best place for him was that. For any third teacher it was better still; and grew ever the better, the more teachers there came. It only needed now that the king took notice of this new phenomenon; combined or agglomerated the various schools into one school; gave it edifices, privileges, encouragements, and named it *Universitas*, or School of all Sciences: the University of Paris, in its essential characters, was there. The model of all subsequent universities, which down even to these days, for six centuries now, have gone on to found themselves. Such, I conceive, was the origin of universities.

It is clear, however, that with this simple circumstance, facility of getting books, the whole conditions of the business from top to bottom were changed. Once invent printing, you metamorphosed all universities, or superseded them! The teacher needed not now to gather men personally round him, that he might *speak* to them what he knew: print it in a book, and all learners far and wide, for a trifle, had it each at his own fireside, much more effectually to learn it!—Doubtless there is still peculiar virtue in speech; even writers of books may still, in some circumstances, find it convenient to speak also—witness our present meeting here! There is, one would say, and must ever remain while man has a tongue, a distinct province for speech as well as for writing and printing. In regard to all things this must remain; to universities among others. But the limits of the two have nowhere yet been pointed out, ascertained, much less put in practice; the university which would completely take in that great new fact, of the existence of printed books, and stand on a clear footing for the nineteenth century as the Paris one did for the thirteenth, has not yet come into existence. If we think of it, all that a university or final highest school can do for us, is still but what the first school began doing—teach us to *read*. We learn to *read*, in various languages, in various sciences; we learn the alphabet and letters of all manner of books. But the place where we are to get knowledge, even theoretic knowledge, is the books themselves! It depends on what we read, after all manner of professors have done their best for us. The true university of these days is a collection of books. . . .

On all sides, are we not driven to the conclusion that, of the things which man can do or make here below, by far the most momentous, wonderful, and worthy are the things we call books! Those poor bits of rag paper with black ink on them—from the daily newspaper to the sacred Hebrew BOOK, what have they not done, what are they not doing! For . . . whatever be the outward form of the thing (bits of paper, as we say, and black ink), is it not verily, at bottom, the highest act of man's faculty that produces a book? It is the *thought* of man; the true thaumaturgic

virtue; by which man works all things whatsoever. All that he does and brings to pass, is the vesture of a thought. This London City, with all its houses, palaces, steam engines, cathedrals, and huge immeasurable traffic and tumult, what is it but a thought, but millions of thoughts made into one—a huge immeasurable spirit of a THOUGHT, embodied in brick, in iron, smoke, dust, palaces, parliaments, hackney coaches, Katherine docks, and the rest of it! Not a brick was made but some man had to *think* of the making of that brick. The thing we called "bits of paper with traces of black ink," is the *purest* embodiment a thought of man can have. No wonder it is, in all ways, the activest and noblest.

SUGGESTIONS FOR STUDY

1. What change have books and reading made between our time and that before books existed?

2. In what sense are books greater than fleets, armies, cities?

3. List the specific "miracles" which Carlyle attributes to books.

4. Explain how universities came into being, according to Carlyle.

5. What is the main use of schools?

6. Define these words from the article: appurtenances, corollary, contiguity, procurable, metaphysical, theology, agglomerated, edifices, metamorphosed, superseded, thaumaturgic.

from
Of Kings' Treasuries

JOHN RUSKIN

MY FIRST DUTY this evening is to ask your pardon for the ambiguity of title under which the subject of this lecture has been announced: for indeed I am not going to talk of kings, known as regnant, nor of treasuries, understood to contain wealth; but of quite another order of royalty, and another material of riches, than those usually acknowledged. I

had even intended to ask your attention for a little while on trust, and (as sometimes one contrives, in taking a friend to see a favorite piece of scenery) to hide what I wanted most to show, with such imperfect cunning as I might, until we unexpectedly reached the best point of view by winding paths. But— and as also I have heard it said, by men practiced in public address, that hearers are never so much fatigued as by the endeavor to follow a speaker who gives them no clue to his purpose—I will take the slight mask off at once, and tell you plainly that I want to speak to you about the treasures hidden in books; and about the way we find them, and the way we lose them. . . .

Granting that we had both the will and the sense to choose our friends well, how few of us have the power! or, at least, how limited, for most, is the sphere of choice! Nearly all our associations are determined by chance, or necessity; and restricted within a narrow circle. We cannot know whom we would; and those whom we know, we cannot have at our side when we most need them. All the higher circles of human intelligence are, to those beneath, only momentarily and partially open. We may, by good fortune, obtain a glimpse of a great poet, and hear the sound of his voice; or put a question to a man of science, and be answered good-humoredly. We may intrude ten minutes' talk on a cabinet minister, answered probably with words worse than silence, being deceptive; or snatch, once or twice in our lives, the privilege of throwing a bouquet in the path of a princess, or arresting the kind glance of a queen. And yet these momentary chances we covet; and spend our years, and passions, and powers in pursuit of little more than these; while, meantime, there is a society, continually open to us, of people who will talk to us as long as we like, whatever our rank or occupation—talk to us in the best words they can choose, and of the things nearest their hearts. And this society, because it is so numerous and so gentle, and can be kept waiting round us all day long—kings and statesmen lingering patiently, not to grant audience, but to gain it!—in those plainly furnished and narrow anterooms, our bookcase shelves—we make no account of that company—perhaps never listen to a word they would say, all day long!

You may tell me, perhaps, or think within yourselves, that the apathy with which we

regard this company of the noble, who are praying us to listen to them; and the passion with which we pursue the company, probably of the ignoble, who despise us, or who have nothing to teach us, are grounded in this—that we can see the faces of the living men, and it is themselves, and not their sayings, with which we desire to become familiar. But it is not so. Suppose you never were to see their faces—suppose you could be put behind a screen in the statesman's cabinet, or the prince's chamber, would you not be glad to listen to their words, though you were forbidden to advance beyond the screen? And when the screen is only a little less, folded in two instead of four, and you can be hidden behind the cover of the two boards that bind a book, and listen all day long, not to the casual talk, but to the studied, determined, chosen addresses of the wisest of men—this station of audience, and honorable privy council, you despise!

But perhaps you will say that it is because the living people talk of things that are passing, and are of immediate interest to you, that you desire to hear them. Nay, that cannot be so, for the living people will themselves tell you about passing matters, much better in their writings than in their careless talk. But I admit that this motive does influence you, so far as you prefer those rapid and ephemeral writings to slow and enduring writings—books, properly so called. For all books are divisible into two classes: the books of the hour, and the books of all time. Mark this distinction—it is not one of quality only. It is not merely the bad book that does not last, and the good one that does. It is a distinction of species. There are good books for the hour, and good ones for all time; bad books for the hour, and bad ones for all time. I must define the two kinds before I go farther.

The good book of the hour, then—I do not speak of the bad ones—is simply the useful or pleasant talk of some person whom you cannot otherwise converse with, printed for you. Very useful often, telling you what you need to know; very pleasant often, as a sensible friend's present talk would be. These bright accounts of travels; good-humored and witty discussions of questions; lively or pathetic storytelling in the form of novel; firm fact-telling by the real agents concerned in the events of passing history—all these books of the hour, multiplying among us as education becomes more general, are a peculiar possession of the present age: we ought to be entirely thankful for them, and entirely ashamed of ourselves if we make no good use of them. But we make the worst possible use if we allow them to usurp the place of true books: for, strictly speaking, they are not books at all, but merely letters or newspapers in good print. Our friend's letter may be delightful, or necessary, today: whether worth keeping or not, is to be considered. The newspaper may be entirely proper at breakfast time, but assuredly it is not reading for all day. So, though bound up in a volume, the long letter which gives you so pleasant an account of the inns and roads and weather last year at such a place, or which tells you that amusing story, or gives you the real circumstances of such and such events, however valuable for occasional reference, may not be, in the real sense of the word, a "book" at all, nor in the real sense, to be "read." A book is essentially not a talked thing, but a written thing; and written not with a view of mere communication, but of permanence. The book of talk is printed only because its author cannot speak to thousands of people at once; if he could, he would—the volume is mere *multiplication* of his voice. You cannot talk to your friend in India; if you could, you would; you write instead: that is mere *conveyance* of voice. But a book is written, not to multiply the voice merely, not to carry it merely, but to perpetuate it. The author has something to say which he perceives to be true and useful, or helpfully beautiful. So far as he knows, no one has yet said it; so far as he knows, no one else can say it. He is bound to say it, clearly and melodiously if he may; clearly, at all events. In the sum of his life he

finds this to be the thing, or group of things, manifest to him—this, the piece of true knowledge, or sight, which his share of sunshine and earth has permitted him to seize. He would fain set it down forever; engrave it on rock, if he could; saying, "This is the best of me; for the rest, I ate, and drank, and slept, loved and hated, like another; my life was as the vapor, and is not; but this I saw and knew: this if anything of mine, is worth your memory." That is his "writing"; it is, in his small human way, and with whatever degree of true inspiration is in him, his inscription, or scripture. That is a "Book."

Perhaps you think no books were ever so written?

But, again, I ask you, do you at all believe in honesty, or at all in kindness? or do you think there is never any honesty or benevolence in wise people? None of us, I hope, are so unhappy as to think that. Well, whatever bit of a wise man's work is honestly and benevolently done, that bit is his book, or his piece of art. It is mixed always with evil fragments—ill done, redundant, affected work. But if you read rightly, you will easily discover the true bits, and those *are* the book.

Now, books of this kind have been written in all ages by their greatest men—by great readers, great statesmen, and great thinkers. These are all at your choice; and life is short. You have heard as much before; yet, have you measured and mapped out this short life and its possibilities? Do you know, if you read this, that you cannot read that—that what you lose today you cannot gain tomorrow? Will you go and gossip with your housemaid, or your stableboy, when you may talk with queens and kings; or flatter yourselves that it is with any worthy consciousness of your own claims to respect that you jostle with the hungry and common crowd for *entrée* here, and audience there, when all the while this eternal court is open to you, with its society, wide as the world, multitudinous as its days, the chosen and the mighty of every place and time? Into that you may enter always; in that you may take fellowship and rank according to your wish; from that, once entered into it, you can never be an outcast but by your own fault; by your aristocracy of companionship there, your own inherent aristocracy will be assuredly tested, and the motives with which you strive to take high place in the society of the living, measured, as to all the truth and sincerity that are in them, by the place you desire to take in this company of the Dead.

"The place you desire," and the place *you fit yourself for*, I must also say; because, observe, this court of the past differs from all living aristocracy in this—it is open to labor and to merit, but to nothing else. No wealth will bribe, no name overawe, no artifice deceive, the guardian of those Elysian gates. In the deep sense, no vile or vulgar person ever enters there. At the portières of that silent Faubourg St. Germain,[1] there is but brief question: "Do you deserve to enter? Pass. Do you ask to be the companion of nobles? Make yourself noble, and you shall be. Do you long for the conversation of the wise? Learn to understand it, and you shall hear it. But on other terms?—no. If you will not rise to us, we cannot stoop to you. The living lord may assume courtesy, the living philosopher explain his thought to you with considerate pain; but here we neither feign nor interpret; you must rise to the level of our thoughts if you would be gladdened by them, and share our feelings if you would recognize our presence."

This, then, is what you have to do, and I admit that it is much. You must, in a word, love these people, if you are to be among them. No ambition is of any use. They scorn your ambition. You must love them, and show your love in these two following ways.

I. First, by a true desire to be taught by them, and to enter into their thoughts. To enter into theirs, observe; not to find your own expressed by them. If the person who wrote the book is not wiser than you, you need not read it; if he be, he will think differently from you in many respects.

[1] A quarter in Paris where the nobility lived.

Very ready we are to say of a book, "How good this is—that's exactly what I think!" But the right feeling is, "How strange that is! I never thought of that before, and yet I see it is true; or if I do not now, I hope I shall, some day." But whether thus submissively or not, at least be sure that you go to the author to get at *his* meaning, not to find yours. Judge it afterwards if you think yourself qualified to do so; but ascertain it first. And be sure also, if the author is worth anything, that you will not get at his meaning all at once—nay, that at his whole meaning you will not for a long time arrive in any wise. Not that he does not say what he means, and in strong words too; but he cannot say it all; and what is more strange, *will* not, but in a hidden way and in parable, in order that he may be sure you want it. I cannot quite see the reason of this, nor analyze that cruel reticence in the breasts of wise men which makes them always hide their deeper thought. They do not give it you by way of help, but of reward; and will make themselves sure that you deserve it before they allow you to reach it. But it is the same with the physical type of wisdom, gold. There seems, to you and me, no reason why the electric forces of the earth should not carry whatever there is of gold within it at once to the mountaintops, so that kings and people might know that all the gold they could get was there; and without any trouble of digging, or anxiety, or chance, or waste of time, cut it away, and coin as much as they needed. But Nature does not manage it so. She puts it in little fissures in the earth, nobody knows where; you may dig long and find none; you must dig painfully to find any.

And it is just the same with men's best wisdom. When you come to a good book, you must ask yourself, "Am I inclined to work as an Australian miner would? Are my pickaxes and shovels in good order, and am I in good trim myself, my sleeves well up to the elbow, and my breath good, and my temper?" And, keeping the figure a little longer, even at cost of tiresomeness, for it is a thoroughly useful one, the metal you are in search of being the author's mind or meaning, his words are as the rock which you have to crush and smelt in order to get at it. And your pickaxes are your own care, wit, and learning; your smelting furnace is your own thoughtful soul. Do not hope to get at any good author's meaning without those tools and that fire; often you will need sharpest, finest chiseling, and patientest fusing, before you can gather one grain of the metal.

And, therefore, first of all, I tell you earnestly and authoritatively (I *know* I am right in this), you must get into the habit of looking intensely at words, and assuring yourself of their meaning, syllable by syllable —nay, letter by letter. For though it is only by reason of the opposition of letters in the function of signs, to sounds in the function of signs, that the study of books is called "literature," and that a man versed in it is called, by the consent of nations, a man of letters instead of a man of books, or of words, you may yet connect with that accidental nomenclature this real fact—that you might read all the books in the British Museum (if you could live long enough), and remain an utterly "illiterate," uneducated person; but that if you read ten pages of a good book, letter by letter—that is to say, with real accuracy—you are forevermore in some measure an educated person. The entire difference between education and noneducation (as regards the merely intellectual part of it) consists in this accuracy. A well-educated gentleman may not know many languages—may not be able to speak any but his own—may have read very few books. But whatever language he knows, he knows precisely; whatever word he pronounces, he pronounces rightly; above all, he is learned in the *peerage* of words; knows the words of true descent and ancient blood, at a glance, from words of modern canaille; remembers all their ancestry, their intermarriages, distant relationships, and the extent to which they were admitted, and offices they held, among the national noblesse of words at any time,

and in any country. But an uneducated person may know, by memory, many languages, and talk them all, and yet truly know not a word of any—not a word even of his own. An ordinarily clever and sensible seaman will be able to make his way ashore at most ports; yet he has only to speak a sentence of any language to be known for an illiterate person; so also the accent, or turn of expression of a single sentence, will at once mark a scholar. And this is so strongly felt, so conclusively admitted, by educated persons, that a false accent or a mistaken syllable is enough, in the parliament of any civilized nation, to assign to a man a certain degree of inferior standing forever.

And this is right; but it is a pity that the accuracy insisted on is not greater, and required to a serious purpose. It is right that a false Latin quantity should excite a smile in the House of Commons; but it is wrong that a false English *meaning* should *not* excite a frown there. Let the accent of words be watched, and closely; let their meaning be watched more closely still, and fewer will do the work. A few words, well chosen and distinguished, will do work that a thousand cannot, when every one is acting, equivocally, in the function of another. Yes; and words, if they are not watched, will do deadly work sometimes. There are masked words droning and skulking about us in Europe just now— (there never were so many, owing to the spread of a shallow, blotching, blundering, infectious "information," or rather deformation, everywhere, and to the teaching of catechisms and phrases at schools instead of human meanings)—there are masked words abroad, I say, which nobody understands, but which everybody uses, and most people will also fight for, live for, or even die for, fancying they mean this or that, or the other, of things dear to them: for such words wear chameleon cloaks—"ground-lion" cloaks, of the color of the ground of any man's fancy: on that ground they lie in wait, and rend him with a spring from it. There never were creatures of prey so mischievous, never diplomatists so cunning, never poisoners so deadly, as these masked words; they are the unjust stewards of all men's ideas: whatever fancy or favorite instinct a man most cherishes, he gives it to his favorite masked word to take care of for him; the word at last comes to have an infinite power over him—you cannot get at him but by its ministry. . . .

And now, merely for example's sake, I will, with your permission, read a few lines of a true book with you carefully; and see what will come out of them. I will take a book perfectly known to you all. No English words are more familiar to us, yet few perhaps have been read with less sincerity. I will take these few following lines of "Lycidas."

Last came, and last did go,
The Pilot of the Galilean lake.
Two massy keys he bore of metals twain
(The golden opes, the iron shuts amain).
He shook his mitred locks, and stern bespake:—
"How well could I have spared for thee, young
    swain,
Enow of such as, for their bellies' sake,
Creep, and intrude, and climb into the fold!
Of other care they little reckoning make
Than how to scramble at the shearers' feast,
And shove away the worthy bidden guest.
Blind mouths! that scarce themselves know how
    to hold
A sheep-hook, or have learned aught else the
    least
That to the faithful Herdman's art belongs!
What recks it them? What need they? They are
    sped,
And when they list, their lean and flashy songs
Grate on their scrannel pipes of wretched straw;
The hungry sheep look up, and are not fed,
But swoln with wind and the rank mist they
    draw,
Rot inwardly, and foul contagion spread;
Besides what the grim Wolf with privy paw
Daily devours apace, and nothing said."

Let us think over this passage, and examine its words.

First, is it not singular to find Milton assigning to St. Peter, not only his full episcopal function, but the very types of it which Protestants usually refuse most passionately? His "mitred" locks! Milton was no bishop-lover; how comes St. Peter to be "mitred"?

"Two massy keys he bore." Is this, then, the power of the keys claimed by the Bishops of Rome, and is it acknowledged here by Milton only in a poetical license, for the sake of its picturesqueness, that he may get the gleam of the golden keys to help his effect?

Do not think it. Great men do not play stage tricks with the doctrines of life and death: only little men do that. Milton means what he says; and means it with his might too —is going to put the whole strength of his spirit presently into the saying of it. For though not a lover of false bishops, he *was* a lover of true ones; and the lake pilot is here, in his thoughts, the type and head of true episcopal power. For Milton reads that text, "I will give unto thee the keys of the kingdom of Heaven," quite honestly. Puritan though he be, he would not blot it out of the book because there have been bad bishops; nay, in order to understand *him*, we must understand that verse first; it will not do to eye it askance, or whisper it under our breath, as if it were a weapon of an adverse sect. It is a solemn, universal assertion, deeply to be kept in mind by all sects. But perhaps we shall be better able to reason on it if we go on a little farther, and come back to it. For clearly this marked insistence on the power of the true episcopate is to make us feel more weightily what is to be charged against the false claimants of . . . power and rank in the body of the clergy: they who, "for their bellies' sake, creep, and intrude, and climb into the fold."

Never think Milton uses those three words to fill up his verse, as a loose writer would. He needs all the three—specially those three, and no more than those—"creep," and "intrude," and "climb"; no other words would or could serve the turn, and no more could be added. For they exhaustively comprehend the three classes, correspondent to the three characters, of men who dishonestly seek ecclesiastical power. First, those who "creep" into the fold; who do not care for office, nor name, but for secret influence, and do all things occultly and cunningly, consenting to any servility of office or conduct, so only that they may intimately discern, and unawares direct, the minds of men. Then those who "intrude" (thrust, that is) themselves into the fold, who by natural insolence of heart, and stout eloquence of tongue, and fearlessly persever-ant self-assertion, obtain hearing and author-ity with the common crowd. Lastly, those who "climb," who, by labor and learning, both stout and sound, but selfishly exerted in the cause of their own ambition, gain high dignities and authorities, and became "lords over the heritage," though not "ensamples to the flock."

Now go on:

Of other care they little reckoning make,
Than how to scramble at the shearers' feast.
Blind mouths—

I pause again, for this is a strange expres-sion: a broken metaphor, one might think, careless and unscholarly.

Not so; its very audacity and pithiness are intended to make us look close at the phrase and remember it. Those two monosyllables express the precisely accurate contraries of right character, in the two great offices of the Church—those of bishop and pastor.

A "bishop" means "a person who sees."

A "pastor" means "a person who feeds."

The most unbishoply character a man can have is therefore to be Blind.

The most unpastoral is, instead of feeding, to want to be fed—to be a Mouth.

Take the two reverses together, and you have "blind mouths." We may advisably fol-low out this idea a little. Nearly all the evils in the Church have arisen from bishops de-siring *power* more than *light*. They want authority, not outlook. Whereas their real office is not to rule; though it may be vigor-ously to exhort and rebuke; it is the king's office to rule; the bishop's office is to *oversee* the flock; to number it, sheep by sheep; to be ready always to give full account of it. Now, it is clear he cannot give account of the souls, if he has not so much as numbered the bodies of his flock. The first thing, therefore, that a

bishop has to do is at least to put himself in a position in which, at any moment, he can obtain the history, from childhood, of every living soul in his diocese, and of its present state. Down in that back street, Bill and Nancy, knocking each other's teeth out! Does the bishop know all about it? Has he his eye upon them? Has he *had* his eye upon them? Can he circumstantially explain to us how Bill got into the habit of beating Nancy about the head? If he cannot, he is no bishop, though he had a mitre as high as Salisbury steeple; he is no bishop—he has sought to be at the helm instead of the masthead; he has no sight of things. "Nay," you say, "it is not his duty to look after Bill in the back street." What! the fat sheep that have full fleeces—you think it is only those he should look after, while (go back to your Milton) "the hungry sheep look up, and are not fed, besides what the grim Wolf, with privy paw" (bishops knowing nothing about it), "daily devours apace, and nothing said"?

"But that's not our idea of a bishop." Per-haps not; but it was St. Paul's; and it was Mil-ton's. They may be right, or we may be; but we must not think we are reading either one or the other by putting our meaning into their words.

I go on.

But swoln with wind and the rank mist they
draw.

This is to meet the vulgar answer that "if the poor are not looked after in their bodies, they are in their souls; they have spiritual food."

And Milton says, "They have no such thing as spiritual food; they are only swollen with wind." At first you may think that is a coarse type, and an obscure one. But again, it is a quite literally accurate one. Take up your Latin and Greek dictionaries, and find out the meaning of "Spirit." It is only a contrac-tion of the Latin word "breath," and an in-distinct translation of the Greek word for "wind." The same word is used in writing, "The wind bloweth where it listeth"; and in writing, "So is every one that is born of the

Spirit"; born of the *breath,* that is; for it means the breath of God, in soul and body. We have the true sense of it in our words "inspiration" and "expire." Now, there are two kinds of breath with which the flock may be filled: God's breath and man's. The breath of God is health, and life, and peace to them, as the air of heaven is to the flocks on the hills; but man's breath—the word which *he* calls spiritual—is disease and contagion to them, as the fog of the fen. They rot inwardly with it; they are puffed up by it, as a dead body by the vapors of its own decomposition. This is literally true of all false religious teaching; the first, and last, and fatalest sign of it is that "puffing up." Your converted children, who teach their parents; your converted convicts, who teach honest men; your converted dunces. who, having lived in cretinous stupefaction half their lives, suddenly awaking to the fact of there being a God, fancy themselves therefore his peculiar people and messengers; your sectarians of every species, small and great, Catholic or Protestant, of high church or low, in so far as they think themselves exclusively in the right and others wrong; and pre-eminently, in every sect, those who hold that men can be saved by thinking rightly instead of doing rightly, by word instead of act, and wish instead of work —these are the true fog children—clouds, these, without water; bodies, these, of putrescent vapor and skin, without blood or flesh: blown bagpipes for the fiends to pipe with— corrupt, and corrupting—"Swoln with wind and the rank mist they draw."

Lastly, let us return to the lines respecting the power of the keys, for now we can understand them. Note the difference between Milton and Dante in their interpretation of this power; for once, the latter is weaker in thought; he supposes *both* the keys to be of the gate of heaven; one is of gold, the other of silver: they are given by St. Peter to the sentinel angel; and it is not easy to determine the meaning either of the substances of the three steps of the gate, or of the two keys. But Milton makes one, of gold, the key of

heaven; the other, of iron, the key of the prison in which the wicked teachers are to be bound who "have taken away the key of knowledge, yet entered not in themselves."

We have seen that the duties of bishop and pastor are to see, and feed; and of all who do so it is said, "He that watereth, shall be watered also himself." But the reverse is truth also. He that watereth not, shall be *withered* himself; and he that seeth not, shall himself be shut out of sight—shut into the perpetual prisonhouse. And that prison opens here, as well as hereafter; he who is to be bound in heaven must first be bound on earth. That command to the strong angels, of which the rock-apostle is the image, "Take him, and bind him hand and foot, and cast him out," issues, in its measure, against the teacher, for every help withheld, and for every truth refused, and for every falsehood enforced; so that he is more strictly fettered the more he fetters, and farther outcast, as he more and more misleads, till at last the bars of the iron cage close upon him, and as "the golden opes, the iron shuts amain."

We have got something out of the lines, I think, and much more is yet to be found in them; but we have done enough by way of example of the kind of word-by-word examination of your author which is rightly called "reading"; watching every accent and expression, and putting ourselves always in the author's place, annihilating our own personality, and seeking to enter into his, so as to be able assuredly to say, "Thus Milton thought," not "Thus *I* thought, in misreading Milton." And by this process you will gradually come to attach less weight to your own "Thus I thought" at other times. You will begin to perceive that what *you* thought was a matter of no serious importance; that your thoughts on any subject are not perhaps the clearest and wisest that could be arrived at thereupon: in fact, that unless you are a very singular person, you cannot be said to have any "thoughts" at all; that you have no materials for them, in any serious matters—no right to "think," but only to try to learn more of the facts. Nay, most probably all your life (unless, as I said, you are a singular person) you will have no legitimate right to an "opinion" on any business, except that instantly under your hand. What must of necessity be done, you can always find out, beyond question, how to do. Have you a house to keep in order, a commodity to sell, a field to plough, a ditch to cleanse? There need be no two opinions about these proceedings; it is at your peril if you have not much more than an "opinion" on the way to manage such matters. And also, outside of your own business, there are one or two subjects on which you are bound to have but one opinion. That roguery and lying are objectionable, and are instantly to be flogged out of the way whenever discovered; that covetousness and love of quarreling are dangerous dispositions even in children, and deadly dispositions in men and nations; that in the end, the God of heaven and earth loves active, modest, and kind people, and hates idle, proud, greedy, and cruel ones;—on these general facts you are bound to have but one, and that a very strong opinion. For the rest, respecting religions, governments, sciences, arts, you will find that, on the whole, you can know NOTHING—judge nothing; that the best you can do, even though you may be a well-educated person, is to be silent, and strive to be wiser every day, and to understand a little more of the thoughts of others, which so soon as you try to do honestly, you will discover that the thoughts even of the wisest are very little more than pertinent questions. To put the difficulty into a clear shape, and exhibit to you the grounds for *indecision*, that is all they can generally do for you!—and well for them and for us, if indeed they are able "to mix the music with our thoughts, and sadden us with heavenly doubts." This writer, from whom I have been reading to you, is not among the first or wisest: he sees shrewdly as far as he sees, and therefore it is easy to find out his full meaning; but with the greater men,

you cannot fathom their meaning; they do not even wholly measure it themselves, it is so wide. Suppose I had asked you, for instance, to seek for Shakespeare's opinion, instead of Milton's, on this matter of Church authority?—or for Dante's? Have any of you, at this instant, the least idea what either thought about it? Have you ever balanced the scene with the bishops in Richard III against the character of Cranmer? the description of St. Francis and St. Dominic against that of him who made Virgil wonder to gaze upon him—"*disteso, tanto vilmente, nell' eterno esilio*";[1] or of him whom Dante stood beside, "*come 'l frate che confessa lo perfido assassin*"? Shakespeare and Alighieri knew men better than most of us, I presume! They were both in the midst of the main struggle between the temporal and spiritual powers. They had an opinion, we may guess. But where is it? Bring it into court! Put Shakespeare's or Dante's creed into articles, and send *it* up for trial by the Ecclesiastical Courts!

You will not be able, I tell you again, for many and many a day, to come at the real purposes and teaching of these great men; but a very little honest study of them will enable you to perceive that what you took for your own "judgment" was mere chance prejudice, and drifted, helpless, entangled weed of castaway thought; nay, you will see that most men's minds are indeed little better than rough heath wilderness, neglected and stubborn, partly barren, partly overgrown with pestilent brakes, and venomous, windsown herbage of evil surmise; that the first thing you have to do for them, and yourself, is eagerly and scornfully to set fire to *this*; burn all the jungle into wholesome ash heaps, and then plough and sow. All the true literary work before you, for life, must

[1] Longfellow translates this and the quotation in the next line as follows:

"O'er him who was extended on the cross
So vilely in eternal banishment."

"I stood even as the friar who is confessing
The false assassin."

begin with obedience to that order, "Break up your fallow ground, and *sow not among thorns.*" [2]

[2] Having made his first point—that a reader must enter into the thoughts of an author—Ruskin continues in the part of the essay here omitted to expound his second point—that a reader must enter into the author's heart.

SUGGESTIONS FOR STUDY

1. Into what main classes can books be divided?

2. Would you rather listen to the "studied, determined, chosen addresses of the wisest of men" or to their "casual talk"? Why?

3. Are the books written for all time to be read by anybody and everybody? What bearing might Ruskin's answer to this question have on educational practices?

4. What, according to Ruskin, is the proper spirit in which to approach a great book? Does this spirit exclude critical reading?

5. In what respects is Ruskin's interpretation of the lines from "Lycidas" likely to be different from that of the ordinary reader? What causes this difference?

6. What are "masked words"?

7. Explain the meaning of redundant, entrée, inherent, circumstantially, cretinous, Elysian, equivocally, catechism, chameleon, episcopate, ecclesiastical, servility, sectarians.

The Decline of Attention[1]

CLIFTON FADIMAN

ALMOST fifty years ago Henry James, a novelist desperately in search of an audience, isolated, in the course of a letter of December 11, 1902, to William Dean Howells, one reason for commercial failure. He wrote (*italics his*): "The *faculty of attention* has utterly vanished from the general anglo-saxon mind, extinguished at its source by the big, blatant Bayadère of Journalism, of the newspaper and the *picture* (above all) magazine; who keeps screaming, 'Look at *me*, I am the thing, and I only, the thing that will keep you in relation with me *all the time* without your having to attend *one minute* of the time.' . . . Illustrations, loud simplifications and *grossissements*, . . . the prose that is careful to be in the tone of, and with the distinction of a newspaper or bill-poster advertisement—these, and these only, meseems, 'stand a chance'."

The first thing that strikes one about this pronouncement is its extraordinary accuracy if considered as prophecy. All the evils of which poor James complained would seem

[1] From the *Saturday Review of Literature*, XXXII (August 6, 1949). Reprinted by permission of the author and of the *Saturday Review of Literature*.

to have intensified since his day. Yet James did not think of himself as prophetic; apparently the decline of attention in the reading public was already, in 1902, a salient phenomenon.

Let us move back another hundred years. We find Wordsworth writing, in the preface to the 1802 edition of the "Lyrical Ballads": "For a multitude of causes unknown to former times are now acting with a combined force to blunt the discriminating powers of the mind, and, unfitting it for all voluntary exertion, to reduce it to a state of almost savage torpor. The most effective of these causes are the great national events which are daily taking place, and the increasing accumulation of men in cities, where the uniformity of their occupations produces a craving for extraordinary incident which the rapid communication of intelligence hourly gratifies."

It is interesting to note, first, that the decline of attention had been clearly spotted as far back as 1802; and, second, that some of its causes—nationalism and industrialism—were more philosophically identified in that early era than in James's time. What

James took to be the sources of the decline of attention—the blatancies of journalism and particularly of pictorial journalism—are really secondary effects or symptoms. At most they lend a helping hand; they are aids to inattention.

Let us be clear as to what we mean by attention. The faculty of attention itself cannot disappear. But it may be paralyzed by various pressures: the pressure of the German torture chamber, of the Kremlin propaganda mill, of the sensational journalism of James's complaint. It may also be displaced as to its objects; that is, attention may be unwilling or unable to fasten on the matters James cared for—the world of art and thought—and quite willing and able to fasten on a quite different set of objects: the mechanisms of industrial production, of a baseball game, of war.

It seems fairly clear that in our time the attrition of one kind of attention—the ability to read prose and poetry of meaning and substance—is becoming more and more widespread; and that the faculty of attention in general is undergoing a wholesale displacement away from ideas and abstractions toward things and techniques. The movement toward displacement is the result of calculated policy in such police states as the Soviet Union. It is a natural phenomenon, by no means universal, in free countries such as our own. The final consequence of both the paralysis and the displacement may be glimpsed in the pages of those Utopias which began with "Erewhon," continue with "Brave New World," and culminate in a crescendo of horror in George Orwell's "Nineteen Eighty-four."

I use the word horror, but I use it improperly because subjectively. When reflecting on these Utopias, it is important to remember that they were conceived by literary men, that is, by men belonging to the class most gravely menaced by the paralysis and displacement of attention. Such men—Wordsworth, James—are naturally the first to notice the phenomenon from which they

have most to fear. But there is a larger class —technicians, generals, Mr. Burnham's admired "managers," certain kinds of journalists, certain kinds of government and labor bureaucrats—which has much to gain from the same phenomenon; and there is a very large class indeed which simply feels more comfortable in a society that does not demand from it any considerable systematic effort of the mind.

Here is Cyril Connolly in a recent number of *Horizon*:

The great artists of the past, despite the love lavished on them by scholars and esthetes, are becoming more and more remote and unfamiliar. They are not replaced by others because we are moving into a word of non-art. One has only to compare the world of the long sea voyage: sunsets—leisure—complete works of so-and-so—with the still mildly esthetic world of the train and then with the completely incurious existence of the air-passenger with his few reassuring leaflets issued by the company, his meals wrapped up in cellophane in a cardboard box, his copy of *Time* in case the sleeping pill doesn't work. This unseeing, unreading traveler is a symbol of the new public. Poetry for this civilization may well cease to exist, for no one except a few professors will possess the necessary ear to follow its subtleties. Reading aloud is almost extinct and the poet who wrestles with his subtle tone-effects secures his victories for himself alone. The hopeless are the irresponsible, the irresponsible are the lazy: we must accustom ourselves to a reading public which is both too slothful and too restless to read until a sense of values is restored to it.

But what meaning would this tirade hold for a publisher of comic books or a seller of big-magazine advertising space: men who are quite as good citizens as is Mr. Connolly and possess souls quite as immortal as his? To them all the things of which Mr. Connolly complains seem good, not bad; inability to read poetry is for them a sign of decency and inner happiness. No cheap irony is here intended; I wish merely to suggest that the decline in the ability to read is distressing only from a certain traditional —indeed, one might say reactionary—point of view. In larger perspective it may seem merely an inevitable change in man's mental outlook as he moves into a new phase of culture—or anticulture. The poet will view this change differently from the anthropologist, who will view it differently from the grand masters of pictorial journalism, who will view it differently from the straphanging reader of a tabloid newspaper.

Let us try, then, to consider the decline of attention, not as lobbyists for the mind, but as objectively as possible.

The first thing to make clear is that excellent books are being consistently produced and eagerly read. The question to ask, however, is this: do such books, read by a minority, make a connection with the *center* of our culture in the same sense that the latest issue of a picture-magazine or the latest product from Hollywood *does* make such a connection? Our anthropologist would be forced to answer in the negative. I think he would have to admit that the success of such a book as Toynbee's "A Study of History," is an eccentric rather than a normal phenomenon.

I believe, furthermore, examination would reveal that such books are the consolation of the few (still fairly numerous—possibly a million in all) whose faculty of attention has been neither paralyzed nor displaced, but who fearfully sense such paralysis and displacement all about them. Quite literally such books give aid and comfort to the enemy—that is, the enemy of "progress," of the probable future. The cults of Faulkner, James, Eliot, Kafka; the excitement over the often admirable "new criticism"; the multiplication of little magazines with littler and littler circulations; the flowering of "difficult" poetry; the modest successes of such an uncompromising publishing house as New Directions, or such a vanguard magazine as *Partisan Review*; the limited but definite triumphs of the Great Books movement; the attention given to such educational "experiments" as St. John's College and such traditional pronouncements as

those by educators like Hutchins and Conant —all these apparently disparate phenomena are really symptoms, not of the numerical growth of those who cultivate the faculty of attention, but rather of the growth of the intensity of their need for some mental pabulum other than that supplied by the central culture-purveyors of our time.

We may put it another way. From the time of the Greeks and early Hebrews up to the triumph of the nationalist spirit, and the industrial revolution, the "highbrow"— Moses, Socrates, Thomas Aquinas, Voltaire —was instinctively regarded, however vaguely, as a leader of the human race. He fought, even if unsuccessfully, a vanguard action. Today the "highbrow"— Schweitzer, Hutchins, Einstein, Freud, Sir Richard Livingstone—is instinctively regarded, even when accorded a certain mechanical respect, as contrary to the trend of the times. He is attacked regularly, not by obscurantists, which is to be expected, but in the columns of the most thoughtful and responsible newspapers and periodicals. He fights a rear-guard action.

If we limit our attention to literature alone, the fact that this action is rear-guard manifests itself in dozens of ways. For instance, in a nation of 140,000,000, we have only two serious monthly magazines of general appeal—*Harper's* and *The Atlantic Monthly*. As we should expect (for they satisfy the intense thirst of a cultural outgroup) their circulation is faithful, but it is also limited, and does not keep pace either with the growth of the general population, or with that of the specifically "literate." These and a few other serious magazines— including your own *Saturday Review*—make valiant efforts to print material that demands a real effort of the attention.

But it is needless to point out that the magazines that really talk to the heart of our country are not these, but the others— the digests, the pulps, the picture magazines, the weekly news catalogues, the smooth-paper monthly mammoths. These vary widely in literary finish and "sophistication" —but they have in common this: they make no rigorous demand on the faculty of attention.

Some of the obvious characteristics of this journalism are: brevity, superficiality, simplification, the emphasis on timeliness (with its corollary, the conscious neglect or unconscious ignorance of the past), planned non-literary English, the avoidance of abstract ideas, the compartmentalization of life (this compartmentalization, as in the news magazine, is the verbal analogue of mass production's division of labor), the emphasis on "personalities" as well as the avoidance of *personality*, the exploitation of the "column" as against the discursive essay, the preference of the wisecrack to wit, the featuring of headlines (here, as elsewhere, modern journalism reveals its kinship, quite proper and natural, with advertising), the often remarkable ingenuity displayed in "packaging," an almost religious veneration for the "fact" (to be "well informed" is our substitute for the capacity to reflect), the rapid alternation of appeals (known as "balance," or something for everybody), and the careful exploitation of certain not highly cerebral interests, mainly in the areas of vicarious sex, criminality, violence, "inspiration," gadget-worship, and the idolization of contemporary gods, such as cinema stars, sports heroes, and clean-faced high-school girl graduates.

In general, a successful, technically admirable attempt is made to *attract* the attention without actually *engaging* it; to entertain rather than challenge; or, to use the editors' quite legitimate phrase, to be "readable"—that is, to present material which can be read easily and forgotten quickly.

(The reader is reminded that the above description is not intended to be pejorative or scornful. No reflection is here cast on the editors or publishers of these magazines. The appeal to inattention is as natural a development of our culture as is the mass-produced washing machine. There is nothing Machiavellian—with a few exceptions—about those who manipulate this appeal. To be indignant at them is equivalent to not loving our fate, and Spengler has told us how stupid and illogical *that* is.)

Pater thought the goal of all the arts was to approach the condition of music. It would seem that today the goal of the word is to approach the condition of the picture. The great triumphs of modern journalism have been accomplished not with the typewriter but with the camera; the lens is mightier than the sword. This is natural enough: the photograph (I am not referring here, of course, to the occasional production of a great camera-artist, such as a Steichen or a Gjon Mili) makes less demand on the attention than even the simplest sentence. It attracts at once; it induces an immediate stimulus, and it is forgotten directly. It is the ideal medium of communication without real connection, so ideal as to make it inevitable that the two great communications inventions of our time—the radio and the movie—should somehow copulate and engender television.

It was advertising that did most of the pioneering for modern journalism, that discovered the value of the pictorial and the visible. Advertising led the assault on the solid page of prose, led it so successfully that nowadays even the editors of serious magazines worry about "breaking up" the page, introducing "white space," and similar problems. Visibility is the thing: the comic strip represents its outstanding triumph, and sky-writing its enthronement in heaven. (It is a curious fact that, when it is really and genuinely desired that the reader should *think*, a throwback is made to the old-fashioned "solid page." This is true whatever the content of the message—be it an advertisement for world government or one of the highly interesting arguments advanced by McGraw-Hill.)

The victory of the visible is closely associated with another victory—that of the clock. The long piece, the discursive essay, the attempt at a complete view of anything—these find publication only with difficulty. When *The New Yorker* devoted an entire issue to John Hersey's "Hiroshima," admiration for the narrative's qualities was far less intense than astonishment (shock is really the word) at the mere fact that so long a piece of prose should be presented to the magazine reader for a single reading. The shortened paragraph, the carefully measured column, the "punchy" sentence are, of course, minor by-products of our clock-worship which began, as Mumford has brilliantly demonstrated, in the late Middle Ages with the advent of the commercial spirit, and underwent a vast development with the triumph of industry and technique. We modern readers want to "understand" a piece of prose as quickly as, let us say, we can understand the dashboard of our new cars. In both cases we wish to increase the sense of our own "efficiency" by subordinating ourselves to the errorless perfection of a machine.

Hence the digest; hence the remarkable *Quick* (unaccountably so spelled instead of *Kwik*), which is a news digest of news digests. I find *Quick,* by the way, wholly admirable; it persuades me absolutely that there is no need to read a newspaper. (Yet, of course, the newspaper must be produced so that it may in turn produce *Quick.*) This super-digest not only makes little demand on one's mental attention; it makes little demand on one's physical or muscular attention. It fatigues neither the brain nor the eye. My only objection to it is that it seems to prove the needlessness of reading the news at all. One can easily imagine a digest of *Quick* (*Quicker*) and finally one of *Quicker* (*Quickest*). From *Quickest* to the non-reading of the news seems a logical next step, and one which we should contemplate with horror. We already know the possible consequences of such a habit: Thoreau's "Walden."

As already pointed out, we must beware of assuming that the prime *causes* of the decline of attention are to be found in such symptoms as *Quick,* advertising, the radio, television, the gossip column, the picture magazine, the soap opera, the mass-newspaper, the comic book, the pulps, the mammary-glandular "historical" works of fiction, the inspirational best seller, the cinema, the juke-box, the monosyllabic novel. They aid in the relaxation of attention, but they do not cause it. They are merely carriers of the germ.

Similarly, it is both ungenerous and superficial to blame our educational system. That, too, is a carrier, not a cause. It is true, as educators such as Bernard Iddings Bell have pointed out, that on the whole our primary schools no longer really teach the child certain basic skills (how to read, write, speak, listen, and figure) the non-possession of which works against the development of attention. It is true, as Bell says, that many of our primary schools, through the system of mass-promotion ("Everybody has won," said the Dodo, "and all must have prizes") place a premium on mental laziness. It is true also that many of our high schools proceed on the make-the-work-interesting-to-the-student theory—which hardly conduces to the development of the intellect. Finally, it is true that the college, therefore, is forced to neglect its true function—which is to produce mentally mature leaders—in favor of performing, belatedly and therefore inefficiently, the elementary educational duties that are properly the province of the primary and secondary schools.

The school is an instrument of our society; it cannot be that and at the same time an agent of intellectual revolution. It cannot teach the virtues of attentiveness if the society of which it is a part indoctrinates the child hourly with the virtues of inattentiveness, or, rather, with the virtues of attentiveness to things, techniques, machines, spectator sports, and mass amusement, as against the virtues of attentiveness to knowledge, wisdom, and the works of the creative imagination.

The school—there are, of course, notable exceptions—has in general become a kind of asylum or refuge rather than an educational institution. In his noble jeremiad "Crisis in Education," Dr. Bell quotes a high-school principal as saying: "My real business is to keep adolescent boys and girls, regardless of educational aptitude and desire or the lack of them, from running the streets, getting into trouble, and becoming an intolerable nuisance in the community. The easiest way to keep them willing to submit to the school's control and so, incidentally, to hold my job, is to provide for them a vast amount of amusement and a minimum of work to do."

This seems a fair statement. All it means is that if our culture desires to produce, not rational men, but producers and consumers, the school becomes a useful place in which to quarter and divert the youthful citizen until he is old enough to produce and consume. The point is well put, entirely without irony, by Professors Russell and Judd, of the University of Chicago, in "The American Educational System": "Most young people today are not able to enter industry or other types of gainful employment before age eighteen; in many cases not before age twenty. The best method of occupying the time of such young people is an important problem, and the solution of this problem by requiring an extended educational period, regardless of the immediate value of the education as such, may be socially wise." Dr. Bell further quotes them as saying that American education may have to depart from the usual academic and vocational disciplines if it is to be "made of sufficient interest to appeal to most young people in this country."

It is clear that this conception of the school is not at all eccentric or cynical. It is realistic. It simply tunes in on the wave-band of our society in general. However, it is also clear that it will hardly be apt to produce men and women capable of paying attention to a reasonably complex story or exposition, much less capable of reacting to the highest types of literature, such as poetry, tragic drama, philosophy, or religious reflection.

The phrase quoted above, "of sufficient interest to appeal," is the crux of the matter. The future citizen is made the criterion; you must "appeal" to him, or be lost. Thus the reading public becomes a "consuming public" that must be *sold* words and thoughts. In consequence the writer tends more and more to obey the doctrine of cultural Jacobinism—to wit, that he is equal to his audience, but not superior to it. He must "please," and the quickest way of pleasing involves simplification, overemphasis, and all the other ingenious techniques of modern communication.

Naturally, a great many writers, members of the outgroup, reject this theory. They believe that if they do not know and feel more than their audience, there is no particular point in being a writer. They write, therefore, in accordance with outmoded standards—and to date have succeeded, as a general thing, in finding an audience of people more or less like themselves, relics, holdovers. This audience, particularly in free countries like our own, is still quite numerous. It supports many excellent publishers, several book clubs, a multitude of good bookstores. It welcomes eagerly such novelists as Graham Greene, Miss Compton-Burnett, Elizabeth Bowen—writers who are not ashamed, nay, are proud, to make stiff demands on the attention of the reader. But, whatever it may contribute to our culture, it does not appear to be solidly in the mainstream.

That mainstream is composed largely of men and women whose faculty of attention is in process either of decay or displacement. In decay it is incapable of grasping reasonably complex works of literature or speculation. In displacement it is highly capable of grasping the often formidable intricacies of business, machinery, technique, sports, and war. (War and sports seem to be particularly favored as the areas in which our faculty of attention deploys itself most efficiently; war—when not fought for a principle—and sports merge the maximum of movement with the minimum of meaning.)

For the fundamental causes of the decline of attention, we shall have to go back to our quotation from Wordsworth. They lie deep in the history of the last 300 years and are almost surely connected with the rise of aggressive nationalism and the victory of the industrial revolution. At some point in the not very remote past a profound shift in our thinking took place. An interest in altering and vanquishing the environment by means of mechanical techniques plus an interest in material accumulation began to oust our traditional interest in discovering the nature of man and expounding his relation to God. Nationalism set itself up against universal thought, substituting for it local and temporal dogma. Industrialism erected definite, easily understandable standards of values, quite at variance with the ethical, religious, and esthetic standards that had, at least in theory, prevailed before its time. These standards "paid out"—that is, the man who lived by them found himself becoming "successful" or "adjusted."

It seemed more useful to fix the attention on a new system of double-entry bookkeeping or the mechanism of the internal-combustion engine than on "Hamlet." It *was* more useful: it was also more enjoyable.

If the man who likes "Hamlet" finds himself a member of an outgroup, even a tolerated outgroup, sooner or later he may wonder whether it's worthwhile to like "Hamlet." If there are no, or few, social rewards accruing from the exercise of the faculty of attention, he may tend increasingly to permit its attrition. If the rational man is made more and more to look like a fool (and, in our time, let us confess it, he *does* look like a fool, even though he is not one) he may cease to prize his rationality. Very few like to be reactionary, setting themselves against the current of their time. Most of us want to

be part of contemporary history, and if contemporary history does not demand of us any rigorous ordering of the faculty of attention, we will either allow it to decline or we will fix it upon those objects or processes in which the majority of our fellow-citizens seem to be genuinely interested.

The humanist will cry out against all this; but he forgets that humanism itself is no more than 3000 years old, a short parenthesis in history. At one time the mental habits of the caveman prevailed over the earth. There seems no absolute reason why the mental habits of George Orwell's robot man of 1984 should not come to prevail during the next few hundred years. Those reactionaries who believe that man is unchangeably a rational soul will have faith that Orwell's world, too, will pass; and that man is bound to return to the pursuit of those goods Socrates and Jesus pointed out to him. But it is doubtful that this return will on a large scale come to pass in our own time. For the moment the humanist would seem constrained to bide his time and conserve the faculty of attention as the church conserved the riches of the classical tradition during what is unfairly called the Dark Ages.

There is a hope—not a great one—that he may enjoy a victory even in his own time. For, underneath all the triumph of the machine and aggressive nationalism and the closed police state, there seethes a vague unease which has nothing to do with class or race or nation. It does not understand itself, this unease; and so far, because it does not understand itself, it has been easily neutralized or harmlessly canalized. It may not come to the surface. But it may. If it does, it will find some of its leaders among those whose faculty of attention has not atrophied, among those who are now being made to feel a bit alien, a bit suspect—among philosophers, educators, scientists, humanists in general. Mind-man has not fought his last battle; nor has Thing-man quite won his first.

SUGGESTIONS FOR STUDY

1. In what did James and Wordsworth agree?

2. How does the author define *attention* for the use of the term in this article? What kind of attention does he believe to be declining?

3. Why does Cyril Connolly believe poetry "may well cease to exist" for this civilization?

4. Is the current publication of excellent books a sign of a literate culture with us?

5. What change of attitude in regard to the "highbrow" has taken place in modern times?

6. What magazines "talk to the heart of our country"?

7. Enumerate several characteristics of modern journalism which the author deplores. Does such journalism engage attention?

8. What effect does the picture have on attention?

9. What change has come to school systems so that they do not encourage attention?

10. Where does the author believe the fundamental causes of the decline of attention lie?

11. Is the author completely pessimistic about the future?

12. Define these words used in the article: salient, torpor, blatancy, attrition, eccentric, pabulum, obscurantist, pejorative, discursive.

Orientation

ﻬﻬﻬﻬﻬ

III. FIRST CONSIDERATIONS

A. The Manuscript

EW WHO STUDY freshman composition will ever be professional writers; hence such a course does not aim primarily at training students to become creative artists, but to use their language effectively in the ordinary affairs of life. Yet in many fundamentals, the standards are the same for the college student writing a letter home and the great novelist composing a masterpiece of fiction. The rules and practices commonly employed in all forms of writing are not the results of some individual's idiosyncrasies, but have been accepted for reasons of logic, convenience, common sense, or good taste. And a student who learns and adheres to them in his writing may have the satisfaction of knowing that he is using methods which are correct for all his written work, whether it be a class report, a term paper, a master's thesis, an address, a novel, or a poem.

FORM AND APPEARANCE

The basic rules for the form and appearance of manuscripts depend on good taste and courtesy rather than on grammatical or rhetorical principles. If a person has good taste and courtesy, for instance, he will not expect someone to read a manuscript that is slovenly in appearance and partly illegible. Almost no one, of course, prepares a first draft which is perfect in these respects; hence when the ideas are stated as well as a writer is capable of stating them, and all corrections have been made, it is essential to make a fair copy of the manuscript before submitting it to a reader. The following directions, if learned and followed, will insure a manuscript's being neat in appearance and conforming to the best practices of professional writers.

1. **PAPER.** Use standard-size (8½ x 11 inches), white unruled typewriting paper, unless your instructor requires another kind.

2. **INK.** Use black or blue-black ink; or, if a typewriter is employed, use a black ribbon.

1a. 3. **TITLE.** About two inches from the top of the page, center the title, leaving equal space between it and each margin.

If it is more than a line in length, fill up the first line and center the second. Leave about an inch between the title and first line of the composition. Capitalize the first word of the title and all the other words except articles, conjunctions, and prepositions. Do not underline or use quotation marks unless these marks are required according to rules for italics and quotation marks (see pp. 138, 129 ff). Do not use a period after a title, but use a question mark if the title is a question, and an exclamation point if it is exclamatory.

In typescript capitalize all letters in the title. All other directions are the same as in the preceding paragraph.

1b. 4. **INDENTION.** Indent the first line of each paragraph about an inch.

1c. 5. **MARGINS.** Margins should be wide and even.

The left margin should be about 1½ inches wide, to allow plenty of room for the instructor's comments and marks. The right margin should be about an inch wide. When possible, avoid dividing words at the end of lines, but if it is necessary to divide a long word to insure a good-looking margin, use the hyphen in accordance with the required rules (see page 134). Never divide a short word. Never leave a wide space at the end of a line, except at the end of a paragraph, and never crowd letters together towards the right margin.

Leave margins of about an inch at the top and bottom of the page.

1d. **Always write to the end of a line at the bottom of a page unless it is at the end of a paragraph.**

6. ERASURES AND CORRECTIONS. If there are several erasures or additions on a page of manuscript, the page should be recopied; but it is not necessary to recopy a page for an occasional change after the final draft is written. For an addition, use the caret, and write the omitted word in the space above, thus:

spent
Six of us the night at the camp.
∧

To erase a passage, run two or three straight lines through the words to be omitted. The method of denoting a passage to be omitted by enclosing it in parentheses is incorrect. Parentheses have a very definite function which has nothing to do with marking an omitted passage.

7. PAGING AND ENDORSING. Write on one side of the page only. Check each manuscript carefully to see that the pages are not jumbled. Then, beginning with the second page, number each page in the upper righthand corner—using arabic numerals— and after the page number, write your last name or the title of your paper, as your instructor prefers, so that if the manuscript becomes disarranged, the instructor can reassemble it without undue trouble.

The two commonly accepted methods of folding and endorsing college compositions are sketched on page 48.

NOTE: Method *b* should never be used elsewhere than in college classes. When submitting a manuscript for publication, do not fold the manuscript at all if it has many pages. If it consists of a few pages only, fold as noted in method *a,* or fold twice in the manner of a business letter. If the manuscript is one submitted for publication, the endorsement should be made according to method *a* except that the address is used instead of the number of the course, the date, and the other details required in college courses.

8. LEGIBILITY. In preparing manuscripts, use a typewriter if one is available. If no typewriter is available, however, you are obligated to see that your manuscript is legible.

(a) Do not crowd lines close together so that the letters of one line overrun those of another. On the other hand, do not leave a noticeable space between lines.

(b) Leave space enough between words so that a reader can distinguish one word from another without hesitation. Leave a slightly greater space between sentences. Do not leave a gap between letters of the same word.

(c) Avoid idiosyncrasies of handwriting, such as making certain letters with curlicues or large flourishes, writing certain words—as *and*—slantwise across the line, making a circle instead of a dot over *i*'s and for periods. Cultivate a simple, clear style of handwriting.

(d) Take pains in forming your letters. Especially, write *m*'s and *n*'s and *u*'s and *v*'s, *a*'s and *o*'s, and *e*'s and *i*'s so that they are distinguishable.

9. INSTRUCTIONS FOR TYPING. When using a typewriter, double-space the lines, except for footnotes and for quotations of several lines, which are single-spaced.

Underline—to designate italics—by using the interlinear mark, which on standard keyboards is on the key with the figure 6.

Use a single hyphen mark for the hyphen and two of these for the dash, with no space

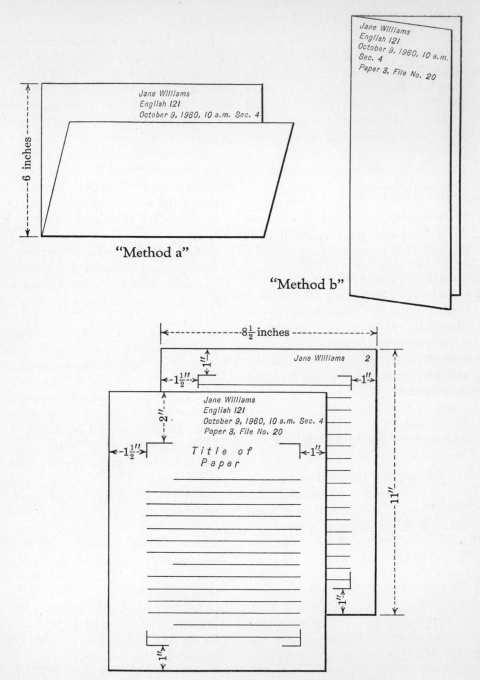

Jane Williams
English 121
October 9, 1960, 10 a.m. Sec. 4

"Method a"

Jane Williams
English 121
October 9, 1960, 10 a.m.
Sec. 4
Paper 3, File No. 20

"Method b"

8½ inches

1″

1½″

Jane Williams   2

1″

2″

Jane Williams
English 121
October 9, 1960, 10 a.m. Sec. 4
Paper 3, File No. 20

1½″

Title of
Paper

1″

11″

1″

1″

METHOD "A" OF PAGING AND ENDORSING.

before or after the mark, whether it designates a hyphen or a dash.

Leave one space between words and after commas, semicolons, colons, parentheses, question marks, and the like within a sentence, but two spaces between sentences, regardless of what mark closes the sentence.

B. Preliminary Planning

A student who wishes to write interesting and successful papers instead of the dreary, formless ones that are too common a feature of the freshman composition course must do a certain amount of planning before he even starts to write. The minimum initial planning for a reasonably satisfactory result consists of choosing a subject you know something about or have some interest in, narrowing the scope of your paper to one or two topics that can be treated adequately in a short article, writing to a specific audience, and having in mind a specific purpose as you write.

SUBJECT

Do not make a big problem of choosing a subject on which to write. No one expects you to have world-shaking ideas or to report sensational experiences. Settle on something about which you have information already at hand or about which you have ideas of your own. You should spend the bulk of your time in organizing your ideas and trying to present them correctly, not in worrying about a subject on which to write.

Your instructor may allow you to choose all your subjects, he may assign all subjects, or he may vary the procedure by assigning some and allowing you to choose some. But even when he assigns the subjects, he will usually allow a choice among several, or permit you to adapt the subject to your own knowledge and experience. The assignment, for instance, might be to explain how you secured spending money when attending high school. In this assignment, there is leeway enough to allow any student to write on the subject. One with a definite experience in finding and working at a job whereby he secured his spending money might perhaps have less trouble getting started than one who never had a job; yet even a girl who never earned a penny by working might write a very interesting paper on how she wheedled an allowance from an unwilling parent; and another who managed to go through high school without having any spending money might write a whimsical

and interesting explanation of how such a feat was accomplished. It is good practice, incidentally, to write from assigned subjects, since one often is required to make reports, to give talks, and to write articles on specified topics.

When a writer has to choose a subject himself, he should select one he knows something about or is sufficiently interested in to investigate. A person, for instance, who was born and bred in a city, who never visited a farm, and whose interest in pigs is confined to the crispness of his breakfast bacon, would hardly be the one to write on "The Best Method of Feeding a Pig Which Is Being Prepared for Exhibit at a Fair"; and an article on "Recreational Facilities in Blank City" would probably have little value, and be a difficult chore besides, if it were undertaken by one born and brought up on a farm and with no interest in or knowledge of life in a city.

2. Once you have selected a general subject, the next step is to narrow it so that in a short paper you can treat adequately and fully the point you are making. Unless one has the skill of a Francis Bacon, it is difficult to say anything interesting in a brief article on such broad topics as "Truth," "Nature," "Patriotism," "Football," "College Athletics," and the like. One of the most common faults of inexperienced writers is that they say so little on such broad and general topics as those noted. "Recreational Facilities in Chicago," for instance, is much too broad a subject to be treated adequately in five hundred words.

The following examples will indicate how broad topics may be narrowed to make them suitable for brief compositions.

BROAD TOPIC	TOPIC NARROWED FOR LONG ARTICLE	TOPIC FURTHER NARROWED FOR A SHORT PAPER
Collegiate sports	First steps in archery	How to hold a bow How to string a bow

BROAD TOPIC	TOPIC NARROWED FOR LONG ARTICLE	TOPIC FURTHER NARROWED FOR A SHORT PAPER
Advertising	Advantages of television as a medium in advertising	Arthur Godfrey's method of advertising— Different appeal to smokers by cigarette manufacturers in current magazines
Architecture	The design and construction of a Georgian house	How to recognize a Doric column What is a frieze
Cookery	Dinner for a gourmet	How to cook a mountain trout The best menu for a class banquet
Sailing	Learning to sail a boat	How to sail against the wind
Camping	What one must know and do to have a successful camping trip	Building an outdoor fire with damp materials Putting up a tent
Swimming	The correct method of learning to swim	How to float How to do the breast stroke
Photography	Effective use of shadows in outdoor photography	How to get a good snapshot of a child Photographing a lake at sunset
Motoring	Being a safe driver	How to enter a curve Returning to the pavement after running off on the shoulder
Poetry	The main classes of poetry	An explanation of Housman's "Loveliest of Trees"

AUDIENCE

Whenever you write, whatever you write, always write for a specific audience. Billboards in wartime used to display pictures of a stern Uncle Sam pointing a finger and looking directly at passers-by to whom he was saying, "The army wants you"; and in Coleridge's poem, the ancient mariner held the wedding guest with his glittering eye till he had told him the story of the slain albatross. You must use a defter approach, but your appeal to the attention of your audience must be as dramatic, if more subtle; and how can you hope to attract attention when you have no idea whom you are addressing? A student may argue, of course, that as he does not intend to become a professional writer, he does not need to develop the ability to hold a reader's interest. Yet if he should never write anything except letters, he will write more attractive and interesting letters if he makes a conscious effort to please, to inform, or to convince his correspondent; and if he should ever write anything for publication, he must be aware of the audience he wishes to reach so that he can use the best means of catching and holding its interest. A writer on college football, for instance, would prepare very different articles for the sports page of a college newspaper and for a magazine devoted to college administrative problems. An expert would write different articles on stamp collecting for the boys' page of a Sunday newspaper supplement and for a philately journal. Professional writers who hope to sell stories or articles to a specific magazine make a practice of reading the magazine for a considerable period in order to learn the level and interests of its audience. You need not plan to be a professional writer to benefit from the practices of professionals. For any piece of writing, then, decide on the audience you wish to reach and inform your instructor of your decision so that he can judge whether you have been successful in your appeal to this audience.

PURPOSE

To be a successful writer, you should be acutely aware of your *general purpose* and *specific purpose* in each composition you undertake. Your general purpose will be to inform, to persuade, or to entertain your readers. Knowing which of these you are trying to do will help you escape such common faults of inexperienced writers as starting to explain how to build a camp (to inform) and rambling off into the relation of an exciting adventure on a camping trip (to entertain), or as setting out to explain the T-formation in football (to inform) and becoming sidetracked into an argument that the team needs a new coach who will produce more versatile players (to persuade). As you develop skill as a writer, you may of course have more than one general purpose in a given article; yet one purpose should be uppermost, and until you acquire great skill, you should probably have only one general purpose in mind.

In addition to the general purpose, you should have a specific purpose for each composition. Suppose your general topic is camping and that you have narrowed it for a short article to an explanation of how to build a successful camp. You might state your specific purpose in this way: to inform a group of city boys of junior-high-school age, who are without experience as campers, of what supplies and equipment to take on a camping trip, how to select a site, and just how to build the camp. Or suppose in a letter home your specific purpose is to coax an extra allowance from a reluctant parent. You will stress unexpected calls on your purse and increased items of expense and will carefully avoid mention of any extravagancies on your part. You might state your specific purpose as follows: to persuade my father that

though I have been frugal, I cannot meet my necessary expenses, buy books and supplies, and have anything left for necessary items of clothing and for participation in any of the social affairs of the college. You will note in these examples that the statement of specific purpose begins with an infinitive ("to inform," "to persuade") and includes the main points of your article, stated as exactly and precisely as possible.

THESIS

Every well-organized paper is the development of a thesis—a brief statement of the central idea of the whole composition. The thesis is the specific purpose stated in a declarative sentence. The subject of the thesis sentence is normally the same as the topic, and the predicate is what you intend to bring out about the topic. For example, suppose you are writing a paper to persuade the city council or park commission of your city to establish a proposed playground in a particular spot. Your thesis sentence might read, "The location of the playground provided for by the recent act of the City Council should be on the North Side on the vacant lot at Lake and Huron Streets."

Up to this point in your planning, the steps you have taken may be illustrated by the following summary:

TOPIC: city playgrounds
NARROWED TOPIC: the location of a playground for Haysville
AUDIENCE: the Haysville Park Commission
PURPOSE:
   General: to persuade
   Specific: to induce the Park Commission to locate the playground provided for by the recent act of the Council on the vacant lot at Lake and Huron Streets on the North Side
THESIS SENTENCE: The location of the proposed playground for Haysville should be on the North Side on the vacant lot at Lake and Huron Streets.

THE OUTLINE: MAKING A BLUEPRINT

The problem of any writer is to begin at the right place, to proceed without detours on the main track to his destination, and, having covered all the ground, to end at the right place. The best way to meet this problem is to begin by making an outline. For long, complex articles, lengthy, detailed outlines may be necessary, and to make these involves careful study (see pages 232-235); but for short papers of the sort usually required during the first months of a freshman composition course, simple outlines that can be prepared in a few minutes are sufficient. Taking the time to make such an outline will save wasted effort and will insure the article's being orderly and consistent instead of an ill-organized jumble of ideas put together without evidence of any relationship between them and with minor elements given equal prominence with major ones.

Making an outline is essentially a problem in order and division. A good outline indicates main divisions and subdivisions and the order of arrangement. It therefore insures a writer's emphasizing the most important ideas and placing subordinate ideas in the proper relationship to the main ones, and it insures coherence in the arrangement of the various ideas, so that the thought proceeds in an orderly and logical way throughout the composition. It is customary in outlines to use roman numerals for the main divisions (I, II, III), capital letters for the main subdivisions (A, B, C), arabic numerals for minor subdivisions (1, 2, 3), and lower-case letters for still smaller subdivisions. For short papers it is usually sufficient to note main divisions and main subdivisions, with perhaps an occasional minor subdivision.

The following outline for an article in a children's magazine on how to plan and conduct a picnic is an example of simple outlining.

ORGANIZING AND CONDUCTING A SUCCESSFUL PICNIC

I. *Size and personnel of the group*
  A. Best number for a successful picnic
  B. Best age groups for compatibility and similarity of interests
  C. Relative number of boys and girls
II. *Food and drinks.*
  A. Kind and amount of food
    1. Food to be prepared at home
    2. Food to be prepared at picnic grounds
  B. Kind and amount of drinks
    1. Cokes, pop, lemonade
    2. Coffee for chaperone
III. *Site for picnic*
  A. Main features
    1. Privacy
    2. Room for games and activities
  B. Other features
    1. Place for cooking and building camp fire
    2. Place near by for swimming
IV. *Entertainment*
  A. Outdoor games
  B. Singing around the camp fire
    1. A capable leader
    2. Familiar songs
V. *Necessary chores*
  A. Cleaning up
  B. Putting out the camp fire

This outline—or any other—may of course be condensed or extended considerably. Its main use for an inexperienced writer is that it permits him to spot omissions or unnecessary inclusions and to see that the parts are properly related and set down in an orderly way. If you form the habit of making an outline before starting to write, you will soon find the procedure so useful that the slight drudgery involved will not be irksome.

TONE

The tone in which you write your composition is something to decide upon before you begin. It may be serious, whimsical, gay, sober, satirical, pathetic, grave, solemn, earnest, sprightly, merry, or any of a hundred shadings, depending on the subject, on the audience to which you wish to appeal, and on your own abilities. Obviously it would be in poor taste to use a mirthful tone when writing to someone lately bereaved or to use a satirical tone about marriage when congratulating someone just married. It would be an error for a heavy, plodding person to attempt a playful tone in his writing, or, except in burlesque, for the campus clown to assume a mood of pathos. The choice of tone should be made consciously and should be appropriate to the topic, audience, and purpose of the writer.

TITLE

Choosing an interesting or expressive title is an important, if minor, item in the production of a successful manuscript. It should therefore not be done haphazardly or carelessly. Its chief purpose should be to give the reader an accurate idea of what the composition is about or to attract his notice and make him want to read it. First, it should not be too broad or too general. The title "Crows," for example, is too general to interest most readers and too broad for a paper of five hundred words. A writer who has made a study of crows or has owned a pet crow, however, might select as an effective title "The Value of the Crow to Farmers" or "How to Keep a Pet Crow and Stay Sane." These examples suggest a second point: not only should the title suggest the scope of the paper, but it should indicate the tone, for readers would expect to find in an article with the first title a serious treatment of the subject and in one with the second title a humorous and entertaining treatment. Make a practice of observing the titles of magazine articles, and try to determine the reason for the choice of each. In your own titles, tend to select ones that are simple, natural, and reasonably short, that suggest the tone of your composition, and that will attract the notice of a reader or inform him of the nature of the composition.

C. *Writing and Editing*

If you take to heart the foregoing suggestions about preliminary planning and try to profit from them, the actual writing of a composition should not be difficult, for you will have settled the matter of the content and scope of your paper before you begin to write and will have determined the order and roughly the amount of space of the various divisions. A few additional suggestions may help you until you learn through prac-

tice more precise rules of procedure. First, avoid general introductions or opening paragraphs that have no direct bearing on your topic. You need a good beginning, of course —one that will catch the attention of a reader and start him off in a good mood to read your composition; but this beginning should be relevant to the thesis, should never be an apology of any sort, should never include a reference to your problem as a writer approaching his topic, and should lead your reader directly into the subject you propose to treat.

Suppose, for example, that your topic is an explanation of the activities of registration day and that your audience is a group of high-school friends who are not attending college. Instead of beginning with a paragraph on your feeling of sadness at being separated from your friends, a general statement about your excitement or happiness or bewilderment at being at last on the campus of Old Siwash, or an apology for having to write on such a dull topic or for your inability to write something worth reading at all, begin without preamble in some such manner as follows: "Hundreds of freshmen —all a little green, all a little bewildered, though the more sophisticated ones were trying to appear nonchalant and knowing— were massed in front of the gymnasium where we were to register. In the press, we stepped on one another or elbowed our way through the crowd to someone we knew. After waiting for what seemed hours, we saw the doors swing open and piled through— lambs going to the slaughter!"

Once you have achieved a good opening, proceed from point to point as laid out in your outline, making certain that you support each point by as many specific and interesting details as you can bring together. In moving on from one point to the next, see that you carry your readers along with you by calling their attention to each new step by the proper signs. These signs are transitional words, phrases, or sentences. After the opening paragraph on registration, for instance, you might begin the next paragraph in this way: "Inside the gymnasium, we looked in bewilderment at the many signs directing us where to go and at the dozens of professors waiting to advise us." Here "Inside the gymnasium" keeps your readers aware of your progress and warns them that the scene has changed. Succeeding paragraphs might begin with some such transitional elements as these: "Having at last found out where to go first . . ."; "Now that we had filled out our cards . . ."; "At last, having reached an understanding with our advisers over our program, we were free to leave the gymnasium."

Finally, when you have developed the points of your outline, end your paper quickly and without any elaborate closing remarks. In a short paper you need not summarize what you have written, but the final sentence should give your readers a sense of coming to the end of the article. A very few words, however, will do this. The article on your experiences on registration day, for example, might close somewhat as follows: "As we emerged from the administrative offices with our numerous cards signed, most of our money extracted from us, and the past few hours a maze in our minds, we flopped down on the grass in the quadrangle with a sigh of contentment. We were full-fledged students at Old Siwash"; or it might be more simple yet: "So we came to the end—or was it the beginning?"

PROOFREADING AND REVISING

A writer's job is hardly more than half done when he has arranged his ideas in an orderly manner and written the first draft of his paper. The remaining part of the job consists in going over the manuscript for various sorts of errors and making corrections. Professional writers often polish their work for months before they allow it to go to a printer. Some of the greatest poets—Shelley and Tennyson, for instance—apparently expended more time revising some of their writings than in the original composi-

tion. An inexperienced writer will not find all his errors, of course. In fact, as you are able to detect errors, your first advance as a writer will be apparent. A few things, however, you can check from the beginning. One of these is spelling. Unless you are a good speller, you will not always know which words you misspell. Form the habit, therefore, of checking in a dictionary all the words that you have the least suspicion you may have misspelled and many that you may think correct. The little time this will take will repay you richly for the trouble. Another matter you can check is complete, correct sentences. You doubtless know that a sentence contains a subject and a predicate and makes logical and grammatical sense, but in the hurry of writing, you may not invariably write correct sentences. Again you will raise the quality of your composition by checking for incomplete or run-on sentences (see rules 3 and 46a). Check too to see if you have shifted tense, mood, or voice unnecessarily, if the verbs agree with the subject in number and person, if pronouns agree with their antecedents, if you have used the proper transitional elements, especially between paragraphs, and if in an effort to sound literary you sound entirely unlike your normal way of talking. Until you become expert at revising it will be best to read the manuscript a number of times, checking for different errors at each reading.

When you have done your best to eliminate errors, make a final copy that is as neat and correct as you can make it, correct minor errors that may have crept in during copying, and have the composition ready to hand in at the beginning of class on the day it is due.

CORRECTIONS

After the instructor has read your composition, he will return it with notations of errors and suggestions for revision or rewriting. As instructors differ widely in their requirements for revision, it will be best to copy in your notebook the method your instructor wishes you to follow in making revisions.

ETHICS CONCERNING SOURCES

A final matter that every student should have in mind is that whatever any writer offers as his composition should really be his. Using the product of someone else's mind as one's own is as much theft as taking his purse. The young writer, moreover, should do his own work, not only because it is unethical for him not to do so, but because the only way he can learn to write with

decency and competency is to work matters out for himself. Later in the course you will receive instruction in the use of literary sources (see pp. 434 ff). For the time being make it a matter of personal honor never to use ideas that have appeared anywhere in print or the work of another student without using quotation marks and stating the source of what you quote. Quotation marks were invented to allow a writer to quote matter not his own without laying himself open to the charge of plagiarism.

"The Witch Tree"[1]

ROSE D. MEYER

ONE OF MINNESOTA'S oldest landmarks is a wind-twisted cedar known as "The Witch Tree." For more than 300 years it has braved the elements that storm the north end of Hat Point on the scenic Lake Superior North Shore. Long ago, early traders and Indians glided by this point of rocks in their swift canoes on the way to Grand Portage, four miles distant, western headquarters of the Northwest Company organized in 1778, absorbed into the Hudson Bay Company in 1821, and recently set aside as Grand Portage National Historical Site. Its huge stockade in the yard, where thousands of canoes once were placed, now has been restored, and buildings erected by the Minnesota Historical Society on the site of the original ones follow the early pattern.

The trail leading to the ancient Witch Tree, four miles from Grand Portage, winds through dense forest that sweeps down over high granite cliffs to the water's edge. To get to the tree, one follows a ghostlike trail. Gulls wheel and cry overhead, and the crystal-clear water of Lake Superior laps

the craggy shoreline, just as it did when this strangely gnarled cedar was a sapling on the rock that juts out into the Lake toward which it now leans. The upper branches are bare and bleached. The lower ones bear sparse evergreen foliage bearded with graying hairy moss. And the distorted roots give the appearance of weird old serpents intertwining the natural granite pedestal.

In the old days Indians made round-about portages to avoid passing this awesome tree. They believed it harbored an evil spirit in the form of a dark brown eagle-like bird with huge wide-spread wings and vicious beak and claws. Only in large groups would they venture to approach it, and then with drumming of tomtoms, and songs and gifts of tobacco, which they deposited in an opening in the base to propitiate the evil spirit.

However, it is said, the coming of the white man with his guns scared the evil bird and it fled. Nevertheless, for many years the tobacco offerings were continued, just to make sure of good faith and good luck on hunting and trapping expeditions in the environs.

Chippewas, still living in Grand Portage.

[1]From *Nature Magazine*, XLIV (December, 1951). Reprinted by permission of *Nature Magazine*.

tell the legend of The Witch Tree, and about their grandfathers, who were among those who deposited tobacco by the ancient tree.

SUGGESTIONS FOR STUDY

1. What sort of details are in paragraph one? What do these tell you about the reader's knowledge, in the author's estimation? Examine the whole article in terms of what the author expects the reader to know. Would an author include all this information in writing for all groups of readers? Explain.

2. What is the general purpose of this article? Is it primarily to argue some idea, arouse emotions, or give information about a tree? If the author shifted the general purpose, how would it alter the character of the article?

3. State the subject, general and specific purposes, and thesis of the article. Remember that the thesis must be one complete sentence that makes a statement about the subject of the article.

4. Write a composition about some point of interest in your locality. Be sure to write it in terms of a specific reader, purposes, and thesis.

My Experience as a Book Agent[1]

WILBUR L. CROSS

I TOOK, as the scene of my first and last experience as a book agent, West Greenwich, for the most part a farming district, where before the summer was over I was threatened with being tarred and feathered if I did not get out of my own free will.

My very first sale was made in a farmhouse kitchen, where I explained to the farmer and his wife that I had called upon them first of all because I had been told they were readers of good books. Thereupon I pulled out a prospectus which hung concealed under my coat and began to set forth the marvelous things of the ancient world. While I was telling the story of the eruption of Mt. Vesuvius and the destruction of Pompeii, I noticed that the farmer kept shaking his head as if from some nervous affliction. But I soon discovered that there was nothing the matter with his neck, for when his wife took pencil in hand to put her name down for a copy of the book, he jumped up and shouted that everything I had said was a lie, you couldn't get ashes enough to bury a city, and he wouldn't have the book in the house. His wife reduced him to silence by saying that she was buying the book for herself, not

for him, that she had money of her own to pay for it, that the house and the land were hers, anyway.

As soon as the quarrel seemed to be over, I shook hands with the wife, tried to shake hands with the husband, and so departed, happy over a sale on my first trial. In my innocence I was only amused by the scene, not anticipating that tinder had been lighted in that kitchen which would set the town on fire against me. For three weeks thereafter I tramped over the hills of West Greenwich, miles upon miles, with one excursion into Voluntown across the border in Connecticut. By that time I had decided to quit business. To make easy a release from my agreement with the publishers, a young local physician, with whom I passed a pleasant hour, kindly certified that on examination he found me greatly debilitated, physically and mentally, partly owing to long tramps under a hot sun, and that I should be unable to go back to college unless I gave up the job and took a long rest in the shade.

I still had to return to deliver some sixty copies of the book to subscribers. It had been arranged that one of them, an intelligent and substantial farmer named Benjamin T. Gorton, was to drive me through his part of the town to leave the books with subscribers

[1] From Wilbur L. Cross, *Connecticut Yankee* (New Haven, 1943). Reprinted by permission of the Yale University Press.

and collect my money. When I arrived at his house with the books one evening three weeks later, he turned a cold shoulder on me, even refusing at first to take me in and urging me to get out of town as quickly as I could. I asked him what it was all about. "Well," he said, in substance, "two years ago a man came over here from Providence and sold the farmers in the town a receipt for a substitute for paint. Some of them who tried it out found that it cost more than lead paint and that one good rain washed it all off their houses. If that man should ever show himself here again, he would get tar and feathers and a rail. My man [the manager of his farm] who goes over to the store most every day, says that they are all ready for you because you're a worse liar than the man who sold them the receipt for a worthless paint." I certainly was a bit skeered.

I had some difficulty in persuading Mr. Gorton to let me stay over night, but at last when his wife intervened in my behalf, he consented. The next morning I had a talk with his man, who brought in the ringleader of the opposition before the day was over. The ringleader, to whom I had sold no book, came with fire in his eyes. I greeted him cordially and showed him the book. We went over it together. I assured him that it contained no lies. He got interested as I turned page after page and read here and there. Finally I gave him a damaged copy. We clasped hands and he went away with the book under an arm. Within a day or two I had similar talks with others in the posse.

The result was that the next week I delivered all the books, with the aid of Mr. Gorton and his horse and buggy.

In order to bring my nerves back to normalcy I stayed on for another week, and listened to my host's racy stories of the countryside, which ran back to training days when he was an officer in the militia. Nor should I forget Mrs. Gorton who knew how to manage her house as well as her husband. We began the day with a nourishing breakfast, starting with three fingers of hard cider for Mr. Gorton and myself with a teaspoonful of saleratus added to make it foam; then delicious johnnycakes with maple syrup—I forget the rest.

SUGGESTIONS FOR STUDY

1. How did the author make his first sale? Why was he in trouble when he returned to deliver his copies? How did he escape from his difficulty?

2. Consider the article in terms of its reader. What point of interest does the author try to arouse in paragraph one? Does he anticipate that the reader knows anything of his personal circumstances? Is the vocabulary so difficult that many readers would be unable to understand the selection?

3. What is the author's general purpose—is he trying to entertain by getting the reader to laugh with him about his experiences, is he trying to argue with us about book selling, or is he simply giving us information?

4. State the subject, purposes, and thesis of this article.

5. Write a composition detailing some similar experience of your own; specify the reader, purposes, and thesis.

Do Animals Talk?[1]

LILLIAN HARRIMAN

SOMEWHERE, recently, I heard a story that ran like this:

[1] From the *National Humane Review* (March, 1952). Reprinted by permission of the *National Humane Review*.

A man walked into his club one evening and was surprised to see a dog playing poker with three of the club members. He exclaimed admiringly at the dog's ability.

"Aw, the dog's not so smart," said one of

the other poker players. "When he gets a good hand, he always wags his tail."

It is in much the psychological spirit of this answer that human beings, including learned psychologists, too often attempt to investigate manifestations of animal intelligence such as their means of communication. There is a vast literature, from scientific and non-scientific sources, on the subject of animal language. The quotable experts range from Professor Heavybrow, who used all the laboratory equipment in Vienna to prove that a hamster can't learn to repeat "Simple Simon picked a peck of pickled peppers," to the old lady in Dubuque who absolutely knows that her cat can talk because she carries on long conversations with it.

The learned literature adds up to a total of just about nothing, and for one good reason: the trouble is that almost all investigators start out by assuming that if animals talk, the talk must somehow be intelligible to humans. They reason like the poker player —it is not enough that a dog should play poker; to prove intelligence, he must also (because human beings do so) refrain from wagging his tail when he gets four aces. An animal isn't talking, this kind of argument runs, unless *we* can understand the language used.

To persons who can rid themselves of this self-centered point of view, there seems to be a lot of evidence that animals—all animals—talk. They tell each other of danger, of love, of food, of fear, of pain. They organize vast societies as complex as any in human experience. They work out almost instant cooperation of family groups and communities in emergencies. They play and they war. And, at times, they perform feats of communication that even radio and television will not equal for man.

"Ah," says Professor Heavybrow triumphantly, at about this point in the discussion, "but you said that animals *talk*. It is granted that a bluejay warns his avian col-

leagues of danger with a shrill outcry, and that a beaver does the same thing with a whack of his tail on water. That, however, is not *talk*."

It *is* talk, though, and so is the twinkle of a female glow worm, and so is the awkward gesticulation of a male fiddler crab when he stands before his lady-love, and so is the purr of a cat and the bark of a dog. It is talk in *precisely* the sense in which we use the word when we say men talk.

After all, what is "talk." It is a means of communication. It is perfectly obvious, from every-day experience of virtually everybody, that many animals communicate by sound. It is not germane to the argument whether the ideas communicated are as complex as Professor Heavybrow's ideas. When the professor tells his wife that "I love you," he is talking, even though the idea expressed is primitive and purely sensory. When a ruffed grouse drums for his hen, he too is talking.

The fact that man "talks" by making noises with his tongue, palate, lips, vocal chords, and nose, while the grouse uses its wings and the beaver sometimes its tail, is irrelevant to the question. Man would still be "talking" if he had decided, in the course of his evolution, to communicate by patting his hands together in Morse code instead of by waggling his tongue and chin. The same conclusion must be granted to the animals.

But the most interesting part of the evidence that animals talk is not in the irrefutable proofs that they communicate by sound. (Incidentally, there is pretty good evidence that all animals make some kind of sound, although many of them are below or above the range perceptible to the human ear.) Fascinating far beyond the proof of meaning in a pussycat's meaningful purr are the occasional tantalizing indications that animals can and do talk *without* sound.

Consider the case of two cats once described by Alan Devoe, the famous nature writer. Their names were Sim and Sam. Sim (or perhaps it was Sam), Devoe says, liked to go hunting in the nearby meadow, while Sam (or Sim) preferred lolling on a chair in the house. But he many times observed, Devoe reports, that the house cat rose abruptly from a sound sleep, lifted his ears, twitched his tail, trotted to a door and requested exit, and then headed in a direct bee-line across the meadow. Invariably on such occasions, says Devoe, the house cat went directly to the hunting cat and, invariably, investigation showed that the hunter had just caught a field mouse or some other prey.

Did the two cats communicate? Did they "talk"?

Dr. J. B. Rhine, professor of psychology at Duke University, says categorically that some animals have been found capable of telegraphic communication under rigidly controlled experimental conditions. Dr. Rhine and his wife, Dr. Louisa E. Rhine, have been investigating extra-sensory perception in animals for many years.

Dr. Rhine tells of a horse, named *Lady*, a four-year-old filly owned by Mrs. C. D. Fonda, near Richmond, Va. *Lady* had a trick of answering questions by spelling out answers with printed blocks nuzzled into complete words. Dr. Rhine, of course, suspected chicanery or involuntary and subconscious signals from Mrs. Fonda to the horse. But when he and his wife ran the tests for six full days, he became convinced that *Lady* was receiving telepathic communication from Mrs. Fonda. To test the theory, he placed Mrs. Fonda in one room, *Lady* in another. The horse still spelled out correct answers to questions asked of Mrs. Fonda. Then Dr. Rhine tried it himself and found that the horse could receive messages from him as well as from its mistress.

Was Dr. Rhine "talking" to the filly?

Or consider the case of Pikki, a fox terrier, which was studied for many months by the famous Russian neurophysiologist, Dr. W. Bechterev, in St. Petersburg just before World War I.

Pikki, Dr. Bechterev discovered, would carry out any kind of simple instruction formulated in the mind of his master. With master and dog placed in rooms a mile apart, Dr. Bechterev would request the man to "tell" Pikki to jump on a table, or pick up a bone left in a corner, or to bark, or to lie down. The man would merely concentrate on a mental image of what he desired the dog to do. There was no possible way that he could signal the dog, by sound or sight.

Invariably, Dr. Bechterev reported, through hundreds of tests, the dog did as instructed.

Was there talk between the man and dog?

Scientists such as Dr. Rhine and Dr. Bechterev, not to mention reputable and experienced observers such as Alan Devoe, have compiled records of many hundreds of similar cases of telepathic communication between men and animals and between animal and animal. There is a constant attempt to discredit such observations by attributing the phenomena to "instinct" or some other indefinable attribute of animals. But this attempt is unscientific because it attempts to deny the only hypothesis which will explain all the observed phenomena by advancing a theory which explains nothing.

There is a vast amount of solid, scientific evidence that animals talk; that they talk in precisely the sense that humans talk. There is no evidence that they *don't* talk.

The answer to the question in the title of this article is, therefore:

Animals talk!

SUGGESTIONS FOR STUDY

1. Why do a great number of people assume that animals cannot talk? What sort of communication do animals customarily hold with each other? How does the author define the verb "talk"? Do animals always talk in our sound range? Explain.

2. The author begins the article with an amusing anecdote. What does this beginning indicate about the reader; is his interest in the subject high or low, in the author's estimation, before he begins to read? Does this anecdote

give evidence to the reader that the article is for scientific specialists in the subject or for amateurs? Is this same conclusion borne out by any wording in the paragraph beginning "It is in much the psychological spirit"?

3. What is the general purpose of the article?

How soon in the article is this purpose clearly established?

4. State the subject, purposes, and thesis of the article.

5. Use the material in this article to construct a composition which will have a different general purpose from this one.

Parts of the Composition

꙳꙳꙳꙳꙳꙳

I. GRAMMAR AND THE SENTENCE

GRAMMAR is the branch of study that deals with the classes of words, their inflections, and their relations and functions in sentences. For most college students, the chief reason for studying grammar is that a knowledge of its principles is an aid to correct and effective writing and speaking. As a map helps a driver through the maze of twists and turns, intersections, and branching roads to his destination in a large city, so grammar helps a writer through the labyrinths of language to clear and correct expression.

As in other fields of learning, authorities differ over many minute points in grammar, even some of the terms being different in different textbooks, but these differences need not concern you. In this chapter, the terms in more common use are employed, and only such matters are considered as are likely to aid you in your writing.

A. Parts of Speech

For convenience in referring to the functions of words in sentences, most authorities on the English language recognize eight classes, called *parts of speech:*

1. **Nouns**—words that function as the name of something, as a person, place, thing, or quality. (*Green* is my favorite *color. Lay* is a transitive *verb.*)

2. **Pronouns**—words used as substitutes for nouns. (Tom laid *his* book on *yours. This* is *mine, that yours. Who* went with *you?*)

3. **Verbs**—words used to express action, condition, or being. (He *caught* the ball and *threw* it to first. The crowd *remained* silent. The treaty *exists.*)

4. **Adjectives**—words used to modify (describe, limit) nouns, pronouns, or other substantives. (*The dark brown* suit is *an old* one. He is *taller* than I.)

5. **Adverbs**—words used to modify or limit verbs, adjectives, or other adverbs. (He will come *soon.* He ran *doggedly.* He is *very* tall. He talked *more freely* today.)

6. **Conjunctions**—words used to connect words, phrases, and clauses. (Tim *and* I wondered whether to go *or* stay, *but* we have decided to stay *because* the fishing is too good to leave.)

7. **Prepositions** — words, generally with some meaning of position, time, or other abstract relation, placed before nouns or other substantives to indicate their relation to other words or their function in the sentence. (He went *to* town *in* the morning and returned *in* the afternoon *with* supplies *for* a week.)

8. **Interjections**—exclamatory words introduced into a sentence for emphasis or to indicate feeling. (*Oh,* you can't believe that. He was, *alas,* my friend.)

In determining the part of speech of any word in a sentence, you must know the function of the word in the sentence, for no word by its nature belongs to any specific class. Consider the following sentences, for example: Lois *Green,* the girl in the *green* outfit, in her approach to the *green* appeared rather *green* as a golfer. Howard *Fast* worked *fast* in making the *fast* horse *fast* to the post. If

61

you learn the few ways in which words function in a sentence and the terms used for these functions, grammar should be a minor problem for you. You will soon note certain similarities among various groups. For instance, nouns, pronouns, and other noun equivalents—to be explained later—form a closely related group for which the general term *substantive* is used. Adjectives and adverbs form another closely related group, the modifiers. Conjunctions and prepositions are both connectives. The point is that by looking at the way a word functions in the sentence, you reduce greatly what you need to learn in order to have a working knowledge of grammar.

NOUNS

Proper and Common Nouns. Nouns are classified as proper or common. Proper nouns, always capitalized, name a particular person, place, or thing (*Central Park, John Milton, Detroit*). Common nouns name any member of a group (*park, man, city, book*).

Common nouns are of three kinds: *concrete,* the names of objects perceived by the senses (*book, stone, wool*); *abstract,* the names of objects not perceived by the senses (*loyalty, wisdom, patriotism*); *collective,* the names applied to entire groups considered as single units (*family, army, class*).

Number. Nouns are *singular* or *plural,* singular referring to one, plural to more than one. (For rules on forming plurals of nouns, see page 162.)

Gender. In modern English, gender indicates the sex of the being or thing named. The genders are *masculine* (*brother, boy, gander, Patrick*); *feminine* (*sister, girl, goose, Patricia*); *neuter* (*stone, city, table, tree*); and *common* (when reference is to something either masculine or feminine: *parent, cousin, child, chicken*).

Masculine and feminine nouns are distinguished as follows:

1. By using different words: *buck—doe, rooster—hen, king—queen.*

2. By adding a feminine suffix to the masculine form, usually *-ess* or *-ix*: *actor—actress, host—hostess, aviator—aviatrix.*

3. By adding a masculine suffix to the feminine form: *widow—widower.*

4. By placing a word indicating the sex before or after another word to make a compound noun: *manservant—maidservant, foreman—forewoman, landlord—landlady.*

5. By changing the *-us* to *-a* in Latin words: *alumnus—alumna.*

Case. English nouns have three cases: *nominative, possessive,* and *objective.* Of these the nominative and objective forms are always alike, and as these are the forms given in dictionaries, they will cause a writer no trouble. The possessive case is indicated by an apostrophe or apostrophe and *s* (for rules relating to the formation of the possessive case, see page 133): *boy's* arm, *man's* hand, *Jones's* watch, the *Joneses'* house, *students'* notes, *children's* toys.

(See *Workbook,* Exercises 14 and 15.)

PRONOUNS

A pronoun is the most common substitute for a noun. If the English language lacked pronouns, we should have to use such awkward expressions as "Guy laid Guy's book on Guy's desk and picked up Guy's racket." To avoid this awkwardness, we substitute a pronoun for the noun after the first reference. The noun to which the pronoun refers or for which it is substituting is called its **antecedent.** English pronouns are usually divided into eight classes.

Personal Pronouns. Personal pronouns are inflected for gender, number, case, and person. The *first person* is used when the pronoun refers to the speaker, the *second person* when it refers to the person addressed, and the *third person* when it refers to someone being spoken of. (See facing page.)

Relative Pronouns. Relative pronouns—*who, which, what, that*—connect adjective

Personal Pronouns

NUMBER	CASE	1ST PERSON	2ND PERSON	3RD PERSON		
				masc.	*fem.*	*neut.*
	Nominative	I	you	he	she	it
SINGULAR	*Possessive*	my, mine	your, yours	his	her, hers	its
	Objective	me	you	him	her	it
	Nominative	we	you	they		
PLURAL	*Possessive*	our, ours	your, yours	their, theirs	same for all genders	
	Objective	us	you	them		

clauses to their antecedents (see page 76 for adjective clauses). They are not inflected for gender or number, and only *who* is inflected for case: nominative—*who*, possessive—*whose*, objective—*whom*.

Interrogative Pronouns. Interrogative pronouns—*who, which, what*—are used in asking questions: *Who* went? *Which* is yours? Of these, only *who* is inflected, its forms being the same as the relative *who*.

Demonstrative Pronouns. The demonstrative pronouns—*this, that, these, those*—are used to point out or identify: *This* is my book, *that* yours.

Indefinite Pronouns. Indefinite pronouns —*another, anybody, anyone, each, either, everyone, little, none, someone, such; all, both, few, many, several, some,* and similar words—are used in impersonal generalizations and when the antecedent is unknown: *Everyone* likes Jane. *Some* brought their books. *Little* is known of him.

What and the compounds *whoever, whichever,* and *whatever* are placed in this class when they introduce noun clauses (see page 76) and the antecedent is not present: I know *what* you want. Send *whomever* you wish.

Reciprocal Pronouns. The reciprocal pronouns are *each other* (when two are involved) and *one another* (when more than two are involved): Joan and Jean help *each other*. The people on this street always help *one another*.

Reflexive Pronouns. Reflexive pronouns refer to the subject of the sentence and are formed by adding *self* or *selves* to personal pronouns: *myself, yourself, oneself, ourselves.* He cut *himself* while shaving. We bought *ourselves* a boat.

Intensive Pronouns. Intensive pronouns are formed in the same way as reflexive pronouns. Their function is to emphasize a noun or pronoun: John *himself* will be here. We could do it *ourselves.*

(See *Workbook*, Exercise 16.)

VERBS

Verbs force a group of words to make a statement, give a command, express an emotion, or ask a question. If the action expressed is performed by the subject and is directed upon some object, the verb is classified as *transitive:* He *hit* the ball. If the action or state expressed is limited to the subject, or agent, the verb is classified as *intransitive:* He *runs* fast. A special class of intransitive verbs (*be, become, seem, appear,* and often such sensory verbs as *taste, feel,* and *look*) are called *linking* verbs because they serve merely to join the subject with a word that completes its meaning: He *is* tall. She *appears* happy.

Regular and Irregular Verbs. Verbs are classified in another way as *regular* or *irregular,* depending on the way in which they form the *principal parts.* The principal parts of English verbs are the *present infinitive* (*be*), *past tense* (*was*), and *past participle* (*been*).

Regular verbs, comprising all except a few hundred of all English verbs, form the past tense and past participle by adding *-ed, -d,* or *-t* to the present infinitive (*stop, stopped,*

stopped). They are descended from a class of Old English verbs called *weak verbs* and are sometimes called weak verbs in modern English.

Irregular verbs form the past tense by internal vowel change, and the past participle by internal vowel change, the addition of *-en*, or both (*begin, began, begun; rise, rose, risen*). These are descended from a class of Old English verbs called strong verbs and are therefore sometimes called strong verbs in modern English. This class was once far larger than it is now, but many verbs that were once irregular have become regular; the tendency of English verbs is to shift from irregular to regular. This tendency may be seen in some verbs now in the process of shifting and hence having both forms: *strive, strove* or *strived, striven* or *strived*.

Because the tenses of English verbs are formed from the principal parts, you should learn the principal parts of all irregular verbs and of a few weak verbs that often give trouble. As there are only two or three hundred irregular verbs altogether, the task of committing them all to memory is not a difficult one. Below is a list of some fifty of the most bothersome ones. These, at least, should be learned.

Conjugation of Verbs. Conjugation is the special term used for the inflection of the verb. English verbs are inflected to show

INFINITIVE	PAST TENSE	PAST PARTICIPLE	INFINITIVE	PAST TENSE	PAST PARTICIPLE
arise	arose	arisen	rend	rent	rent
begin	began	begun	ring	rang	rung
bid	bade	bidden	rise	rose	risen
bind	bound	bound	run	ran	run
bite	bit	bitten	see	saw	seen
blow	blew	blown	seek	sought	sought
break	broke	broken	send	sent	sent
bring	brought	brought	set	set	set
build	built	built	shake	shook	shaken
burst	burst	burst	shed	shed	shed
choose	chose	chosen	shine	shone	shone (intransitive)
cling	clung	clung			
come	came	come	shoot	shot	shot
dive	dived	dived	shrink	shrank	shrunk
do	did	done	sing	sang	sung
draw	drew	drawn	sink	sank	sunk
drink	drank	drunk	sit	sat	sat
drive	drove	driven	slay	slew	slain
eat	ate	eaten	sling	slung	slung
fall	fell	fallen	slink	slunk	slunk
feed	fed	fed	speak	spoke	spoken
fling	flung	flung	spring	sprang	sprung
fly	flew	flown	steal	stole	stolen
forsake	forsook	forsaken	sting	stung	stung
freeze	froze	frozen	swear	swore	sworn
give	gave	given	swell	swelled	swollen (swelled)
grind	ground	ground			
grow	grew	grown	swim	swam	swum
know	knew	known	take	took	taken
lay	laid	laid	tear	tore	torn
lead	led	led	think	thought	thought
lend	lent	lent	throw	threw	thrown
lie	lay	lain	write	**wrote**	**written**
meet	met	met			

person, number, mood, voice, and tense.

TENSE. Tense is the inflection of the verb to express distinctions of time, there being six tenses—present, past, future, present perfect, past perfect, and future perfect.

The *present tense* ordinarily expresses an action or condition taking place in present time (He *hears* her call. I *see* the airship.); but it may also state a universal truth (In a vacuum, light and heavy bodies *fall* at the same speed.), refer to a future action (He *leaves* for Europe next month.), or refer to a past action for dramatic effect (Lincoln *surveys* the vast crowd and without preamble *begins,* "Fourscore and seven years.").

The *past tense* refers to simple past time (John *entered* three events. She *went* home.). As the verb alone indicates an indefinite time in the past, additional information must be added to make the time definite. (She went home *last night.*)

The *future tense* expresses an action or condition presumed to take place in the future. To form the future tense, we have to use the *auxiliary* (helping) verbs *shall* and *will.* (He *will leave* Monday. I *shall stay* here till autumn.)

The *present perfect tense* expresses an action or condition completed at the present time. To form this tense requires the use of the auxiliary *have* or *has.* (He *has eaten* his lunch.)

The *past perfect tense* expresses an action or condition complete at some past time. To form this tense requires the use of the auxiliary *had.* (He *had locked* the door when I arrived.)

The *future perfect tense* expresses an action or condition that will be completed at some future time. (The birds *will have eaten* all the cherries before you arrive. By five o'clock the game *will have been* over an hour.)

In addition to the simple tense forms just explained, two other forms are in common use—the *progressive* and the *emphatic.* The progressive-tense form indicates that an action is continuing over a period of time (I *am commuting* this year. I *was commuting* all last year. I *shall be commuting* till autumn. *I have been commuting* for a month. *I had been commuting* till this week. *I shall have been commuting* for a year in June.). The emphatic form—made by using *do* or *did* with the perfect infinitive—is employed when special emphasis is required and in questions and negative statements that require no special emphasis. (I *do study.* I *did study* this lesson. *Did* you *study?* I *did* not *study* that section.)

MOOD. Mood is the inflection of the verb to express the manner in which the action or condition is thought of—whether as a fact, a command, a wish. English verbs have three moods—indicative, imperative, and subjunctive.

The *indicative mood*—by far the most common of the three—expresses a simple statement of fact or asks for direct information. (The train *was* late. I *shall go* tomorrow. *Are* you *going?*)

The *imperative mood* expresses a command or request. (*Fill* out all the forms. *Come* for a walk with me.)

The *subjunctive mood* expresses doubt or uncertainty, a condition unreal or contrary to fact, a concession, or an improbability. It is used in prayers, exclamations, parliamentary proceedings, after such verbs as *desire, order, beg,* and *entreat,* and in negative clauses of purpose.

UNCERTAINTY: If the rain *should hold* up, we *might go.*

CONDITION CONTRARY TO FACT: I wish vacation *were* here.

CONCESSION: *Be* it as you wish.

IMPROBABILITY: If war *were* outlawed, we *might claim to be civilized.*

PRAYER: Heaven *help* us!

PARLIAMENTARY PARLANCE: I move the remark *be stricken* from the record.

AFTER VERBS OF COMMAND: I desire that they *be told.*

NEGATIVE CLAUSES OF PURPOSE: He entered quietly lest he *wake* the baby.

Voice. Voice is the distinction of form in the verb to show the relation of the subject of the verb to the action that the verb expresses. English verbs have two voices—active and passive.

The *active voice* represents the subject as the doer of the action. (The storm *destroyed* many trees.)

The *passive voice* represents the subject as the receiver of the action. (Many trees *were destroyed* by the storm.) The passive voice is formed by using some part of the verb *be* with the past participle of the principal verb. Because in the passive voice the subject receives the action, only transitive verbs—in which the action must pass over from an agent to a receiver of the action—have a passive voice.

Number. Verbs are inflected to indicate reference to one or more than one. English verbs have two numbers—singular and plural. *Singular number* refers to one person, thing, or quality, *plural number* to more than one. The form of the verb is the same for both numbers except in the third person present indicative of all verbs and in the present and past indicative of the verb *be*.

Person. Verbs are inflected to indicate the person or thing speaking, spoken to, or spoken of. In English there are three persons—the *first person* (the one speaking: I *am* at home), the *second person* (the one spoken to: You *are* at home), and the *third person* (the one spoken of: He *is* at home). In usage, the verb agrees with its subject in number and person. The form of the verb is the same for all persons except in the third person singular present tense of the indicative mood

of all verbs and in the first and third person singular of the present and past tenses of the indicative mood of *be*.

Examples of Conjugation. A complete conjugation consists of all the persons, numbers, tenses, and moods, both active and passive voice; but to clarify some point, it may be necessary to conjugate only one part of the verb, as for instance the present tense, active voice, indicative mood of *sing:* I sing, you sing, he sings; we sing, you sing, they sing.

The synopsis of a verb is a condensed statement of the specific forms asked for. For example, a synopsis of the third person singular, indicative mood, active voice of the verb *see* would be given in this way: *present* —he sees, *past*—he saw, *future*—he will see, *present perfect*—he has seen, *past perfect*— he had seen, *future perfect*—he will have seen. A synopsis of the verb *find* in the third person plural, subjunctive mood, passive voice would be: *present*—they be found, *past*—they were found, *present perfect*— they have been found, *past perfect*—they had been found.

The following examples show the conjugation of a regular and an irregular verb in all tenses of the indicative mood and the complete conjugation of the verb *to be*.

Besides these primary moods of the verb are many other modal forms, which furnish additional shades of meaning. That is, in English one may say not only *I plan*, but such other variants as *I am planning, I do plan, I may plan, I can plan, I must plan,* and *I ought to plan*, all forms of the verb "to plan."

(See *Workbook*, Exercises 17, 18, and 19.)

REGULAR VERB: **to look**		IRREGULAR VERB: **to sit**	
PRESENT TENSE			
SINGULAR	PLURAL	SINGULAR	PLURAL
1. I look	1. we look	1. I sit	1. we sit
2. you look	2. you look	2. you sit	2. you sit
3. he looks	3. they look	3. he sits	3. they sit

Method of forming: Use first principal part unchanged for all forms except third person singular, which adds an *s*.

PAST TENSE

looked   (the same for all persons and numbers)
sat   (the same for all persons and numbers)

Method of forming: Second principal part unchanged throughout.

FUTURE TENSE

1. shall look	1. shall look	1. shall sit	1. shall sit
2. will look	2. will look	2. will sit	2. will sit
3. will look	3. will look	3. will sit	3. will sit

Method of forming: Add *shall* or *will* before the first principal part. NOTE: The formal usage is retained here, but in normal usage for the simple future without special emphasis *will* is common for all persons, especially in speech. Meticulous speakers and writers, however, preserve the distinction as noted, and in formal writing students will do well to follow their example.

PRESENT PERFECT TENSE

1. have looked	1. have looked	1. have sat	1. have sat
2. have looked	2. have looked	2. have sat	2. have sat
3. *has* looked	3. have looked	3. *has* sat	3. have sat

Method of forming: Add third principal part (past participle) to present tense of the verb *have*.

PAST PERFECT TENSE

had looked   (the same for all persons and numbers)
had sat   (the same for all persons and numbers)

Method of forming: Add third principal part (past participle) to past tense of the verb *have*.

FUTURE PERFECT TENSE

1. shall have looked	1. shall have looked	1. shall have sat	1. shall have sat
2. will have looked	2. will have looked	2. will have sat	2. will have sat
3. will have looked	3. will have looked	3. will have sat	3. will have sat

Method of forming: Add *shall have* or *will have* before third principal part (past participle). For *shall* or *will* see the note under *future tense* above.

to be

PRESENT INFINITIVE	PAST	PAST PARTICIPLE
be	was	been

INDICATIVE MOOD

PRESENT TENSE		PRESENT PERFECT TENSE	
I am	We are	I have been	We have been
You are	You are	You have been	You have been
He is	They are	He has been	They have been

PAST TENSE		PAST PERFECT TENSE	
I was	We were	I had been	We had been
You were	You were	You had been	You had been
He was	They were	He had been	They had been

FUTURE TENSE		FUTURE PERFECT TENSE	
I shall be	We shall be	I shall have been	We shall have been
You will be	You will be	You will have been	You will have been
He will be	They will be	He will have been	They will have been

SUBJUNCTIVE MOOD

PRESENT TENSE		PRESENT PERFECT TENSE	
I be	We be	I have been	We have been
You be	You be	You have been	You have been
He be	They be	He have been	They have been

PAST TENSE		PAST PERFECT TENSE	
I were	We were	I had been	We had been
You were	You were	You had been	You had been
He were	They were	He had been	They had been

IMPERATIVE MOOD

SINGULAR	PLURAL
Be	Be

VERBALS

PARTICIPLES	GERUNDS	INFINITIVES
Present: Being	Present: Being	Present: To be
Past: Been	Perfect: Having been	Perfect: To have been
Perfect: Having been		

ADJECTIVES

An adjective is a word that modifies (describes, limits, points out) a substantive (a noun or noun substitute). Its function is to answer the question *which? what kind? how many?* as applied to the substantive. Adjectives are inflected only to show *comparison,* of which there are three degrees: *positive* (the simple form, involving no actual comparison), *comparative* (a comparison involving *two* objects or persons), and *superlative* (a comparison involving more than two). Comparison is indicated in three different ways: (1) by adding *-er* or *-est* to the positive, (2) by using *more* or *most* with the positive, and (3) by using different words for each degree:

The general rule is to form the comparative and superlative degrees of words of one syllable by adding *-er* and *-est* and of words of two or more syllables by adding *more* and *most* or *less* and *least,* but the rule is not absolute. The tendency in American usage is to employ *more-most* and *less-least* even with one-syllable words, whereas in English usage the *er-est* forms are often used with words of several syllables (*delightfuler, delightfulest*). A few adjectives by their nature cannot logically be compared—e.g., *chaste, dead, round, square,* and *unique.* The quality of death is absolute; so is the quality

POSITIVE	COMPARATIVE	SUPERLATIVE
tall	tall*er*	tall*est*
sweet	sweet*er*	sweet*est*
bitter	*more* bitter	*most* bitter
colorful	*more* colorful	*most* colorful
bad	worse	worst
good	better	best
little	less (lesser)	least
many (much)	more	most

of roundness, squareness, and uniqueness. Others that cannot be compared are the cardinals (one, two, three, etc.) and the ordinals (first, second, third).

Adjectives, like nouns, may be classed as common or proper. *Proper adjectives* are those derived from proper nouns (a *Canadian* flag, an *Indian* arrow, an *English* or a *Spanish* class), and like proper nouns they are always capitalized. *Common* adjectives are all those that are not proper (a *red* hat, an *old* man).

The definite and indefinite articles are adjectives that, as their names imply, indicate a definite person, place, or object (*the* man, *the* park, *the* oak) or an indefinite one (*a* man, *an* owl). In usage, *a* is employed before a consonant sound and *an* before a vowel sound (*a* cat; *a* or *an* historical occasion, depending on whether the *h* is sounded; *an* hour; *an* eel).

The usual position of adjectives is before the noun (the *red* rose) or after a linking verb (the rose is *red*), but pairs of adjectives

ADVERBS

An adverb is a word that modifies a verb, adjective, or other adverb. Its function is to answer the question *how? when? where?* or *how much?* concerning the word it modifies. In answering the question *how?* it expresses *manner* (He walks *rapidly*. Examine the evidence *carefully*.); in answering the question *when?* it expresses *time* (He went *yesterday*. Come *soon*.); in answering the question *where?* it expresses *place* (I found the pen *there*. Come *home*.); and in answering the question *how much?* it expresses *degree* (He was *very* serious. The tire was *almost* flat.).

Adverbs are like adjectives in being inflected only to show degree, and also like adjectives, they have the three degrees *positive, comparative,* and *superlative.* They form the comparative and superlative degrees in the same manner as adjectives, although the forms *more-most* and *less-least* are even more frequently employed with adverbs than with adjectives. A few have irregular comparisons:

POSITIVE	COMPARATIVE	SUPERLATIVE
badly (ill)	worse	worst
far	farther (further)	farthest (furthest)
little	less	least
many, much	more	most
well	better	best

and those that are grouped with modifiers of their own frequently come after the noun (the child, *pink* and *chubby*).

Since linking verbs—*be, become, seem,* and *appear,* and very often the sensory verbs *feel, look, smell, sound,* and *taste*—serve merely to connect the subject and the modifier that comes after the verb, the modifier after a linking verb is always an adjective. (He is *tall*. He seems *hungry*. He appears *cheerful*. He feels *bad* about losing the game.) Note, however, that when the predicate is not a linking verb, the modifier is an adverb (see the next section).

(See *Workbook,* Exercise 20.)

Again like adjectives, some adverbs by their nature cannot be logically compared—for example, *entirely, fatally,* and *quite.*

The majority of adverbs end in *-ly,* but this ending must not be taken as an infallible sign of an adverb, for many adjectives end in *-ly* (the *manly* youth, the *surly* man), and nouns often function as adverbs (She hurried *home*. The class meets *Monday*.). The way the word functions in the sentence determines its part of speech. Whatever part of speech a word may appear to be, it is an adverb when it qualifies or limits a verb, adjective, or adverb.

In the section on the adjective, it was said

that the modifier after a *linking* verb is an adjective, but such verbs as *appear* and the sensory verbs are not always linking verbs. When the modifier after such verbs refers to the verb rather than to the subject, it is of course an adverb. (He appears *cheerfully* each day for his handout. He felt the sharp edge *gingerly*. He tasted the new dish *cautiously*.)

(See *Workbook*, Exercise 21.)

CONJUNCTIONS

A conjunction is a connective whose function is to join words and groups of words (phrases and clauses). There are two classes of conjunctions: co-ordinating and subordinating.

A *co-ordinating conjunction* joins words and groups of words of equal rank. Conjunctions belonging to this class are *and, but, for, or,* and *nor,* and certain pairs, called *correlative conjunctions*, that always go together: *both—and, either—or, neither—nor,* and *not only—but also.* In contemporary usage, some writers treat the conjunctive adverbs *so* and *yet* as co-ordinating conjunctions, but careful stylists avoid the practice. These conjunctions have precise meanings and should be used with care. *And* and *not only—but also* indicate addition; *but* indicates contrast; *for* indicates reason or motive; *or, nor, either, neither, either—or,* and *neither—nor* indicate alternation or choice.

Jack *and* Jill went up the hill.
The entertainers sing *and* dance.
The shrub is sturdy *and* hardy.
We asked them *both* to sing *and* to dance.
He is small *but* powerful.
She is going to Florida, *for* her family is now living there.
Either come *or* telephone me.
Neither rain *nor* hail stays these couriers.

A *subordinating conjunction* joins words and groups of words of unequal rank. Belonging to this group are the simple subordinating conjunctions *after, although, because, before, if, since, that, though, unless,* *when, whereas, wherever, while,* and the compounds *as if, even though, inasmuch as, in order that, in spite of the fact that, no matter what, notwithstanding that, so that,* and many others.

I have seen him only once *since* he left.
She will not go *unless* you go also.
Fishing is best *when* the lake is calm.
In order that he may go, I shall stay here.
I shall not go *even though* they pay my expenses.

Relative pronouns also function as subordinating conjunctions, and a special class of adverbs indicate exact shades of relationship between co-ordinate clauses and sentences. These latter are usually called *conjunctive adverbs.* Examples of words often employed to mark transitions are *accordingly, consequently, furthermore, hence, however, indeed, likewise, meanwhile, moreover, namely, nevertheless, similarly, still, therefore, thus, yet,* and the compound forms (transitional phrases): *as a result, for example, for instance, for this reason, in addition, in fact, in other words, of course, on the contrary, on the other hand,* and *that is.*

Choice of the right connective is highly important for the writer who wishes his meaning to be unmistakably clear (see page 106).

(See *Workbook*, Exercise 22.)

PREPOSITIONS

A preposition is a word that joins a substantive (noun, pronoun, or other noun substitute) to another word and shows the relationship of the words so joined. A preposition usually carries a meaning of direction, position, time, or some other abstract relation (*to* the house, *on* the table, *at* five o'clock). As the definition indicates, a preposition always appears in company with a substantive, which is called the *object of the preposition.* The preposition and its object make a *prepositional phrase.* Because the term *preposition* is derived from a Latin word that meant "to place before," some purists maintain that the only position for a preposition is before the substantive. Nine times out of ten, prepositions do come before their objects, but occasionally they come after: That is what we are asking *for.*

According to form, prepositions are simple (*at, by, for, of, through, to, up*) or compound (*according to, as to, because of, in regard to, in spite of, instead of, on account of, out of*).

He likes to walk *in* the rain.

They opened the door *with* a borrowed key.

The game ended *because of* darkness.

We went *in spite of* the weather.

(See *Workbook*, Exercise 22.)

VERBALS

Three classes of words that are not recognized as parts of speech, yet are highly important to students of composition, are *gerunds, participles,* and *infinitives.* These forms are derived from verbs—hence the general term *verbal* for all of them—but function as other parts of speech.

Gerunds. A *gerund* is a word that is derived from a verb and *functions as a noun;* consequently it has certain characteristics of both verbs and nouns. Like the verb it expresses tense and voice, takes adverbial modifiers and objects, and expresses action or state of being; and like the noun it may be modified by adjectives. It is formed by adding -*ing* to the first principal part of the verb.

Swimming is good exercise.

Joan likes *playing* the piano.

Show your interest by *voting.*

Although the majority of gerunds are in the present tense, active voice, the gerund may be found in any of four forms:

	ACTIVE VOICE	PASSIVE VOICE
PRESENT	liking	being liked
PERFECT	having liked	having been liked

Note that in the compound forms, the -*ing* is added to the first word of the auxiliary.

The logical subject of the gerund is a possessive modifier: I like *Kate's* singing.

Participles. A participle is a word that is derived from a verb and *functions as an adjective.* It has certain characteristics of both verbs and adjectives: like the verb, it may be transitive or intransitive, it may show tense and voice, and it may take objects; and like the adjective, it modifies a substantive.

English verbs have three participles: present, past, and present perfect. The present participle is formed by adding -*ing* to the first principal part of the verb; the past participle is the third principal part of the verb.

The *racing* car just missed us.

Leaning over, he grabbed the line.

Bent twigs become crooked trees.

Please submit a *written* report.

The following table illustrates the tense and voice forms of participles:

	ACTIVE VOICE	PASSIVE VOICE
PRESENT	liking	being liked
PAST	(none)	liked
PERFECT	having liked	having been liked

The present tense of the participle generally indicates the same time as that of the principal verb, and the past and perfect participles a time prior to that of the main verb: *Reading* the letter, he walked slowly to his room. *Having written* the letter, he mailed it.

Infinitives. An *infinitive* is a word that is derived from a verb and *functions as a noun, an adjective,* or *an adverb.* It is the first principal part of the verb and is usually introduced by *to* (called the sign of the infinitive), although the *to* is frequently omitted. Being derived from a verb, it expresses tense and voice, may have a subject, may take an object or complement, and may be modified by an adverb. The tense and voice forms of the infinitive are as follows:

	ACTIVE VOICE	PASSIVE VOICE
PRESENT	to like (progressive: to be liking)	to be liked
PERFECT	to have liked (progressive: to have been liking)	to have been liked

The following examples indicate ways in which the infinitive functions:

AS A NOUN: *To know* him is *to love* him.
                    I like *to swim.*
AS AN ADJECTIVE: He has a lesson *to study.*
AS AN ADVERB: He stopped *to ask* the way.
                    To find peace, he went to the woods.
                    He is too old *to live* alone.

(See *Workbook,* Exercises 23 and 24.)

B. The Sentence

Nothing in the study of composition will reward you more than acquiring a thorough understanding of the sentence. You need to know the kinds of sentences and the names and relationship of various parts of a sentence to profit from class discussions and from comments about your own writing, and you need to analyze sentences and to know what rules apply, in order to write sentences that conform to the standards of acceptable usage.

In normal practice, *a sentence is a group of words, containing a subject and a predicate, that expresses an idea all the parts of which have a logical relationship and together form a grammatically complete unit.* It always begins with a capital letter and ends with a period, a question mark, or an exclamation point.[1] Once you have mastered the principles that apply in general usage, you may be allowed certain liberties in writing sentences, but until then, you will do well to follow normal patterns.

PARTS OF THE SENTENCE

Subject and Predicate. With a few exceptions (see page 78), every sentence has a subject and a predicate. The *subject* is the person, place, thing, or quality with which the sentence is primarily concerned—that about which a statement or assertion is made, a question is asked, an emotion is expressed, or to which a request or command is addressed. The *predicate* expresses the action or the state of being of the subject; or, to put the matter as simply as possible, it is what is said of the subject.

SUBJECT	PREDICATE
Roy	walks.
The park	is open.
The tree	is old.
Superstition	is not dead.
He	lives in Ohio.

The subject of a sentence is always a substantive—a noun or noun substitute (pronoun: *He* is here; gerund: *Whistling* may be an art; infinitive: *To draw* well requires practice.). It may be a single word, a phrase, or a clause. The *predicate* is always a verb—never any other part of speech or a verbal.

COMPOUND SUBJECT AND PREDICATE. Both the subject and the predicate may consist of one word or of two or more words. A subject comprising two or more words or groups of words of equivalent value is called a *compound subject* (*Jean* and *Sue* play. *To play* tennis or *to study* is my problem.). A predicate comprising two or more verbs of equivalent value is called a *compound predicate* (Sue *plays* and *sings.* He *will come* tomorrow or *will write.*).

SIMPLE AND COMPLETE SUBJECT AND PREDICATE. Except for absolute constructions (see page 75), every part of the sentence is related either to the subject or to the predicate. The specific person, place, thing, or quality spoken of is the *simple subject.* The single word or combination of words that expresses the action or state of being of the subject is the *simple predicate.* The simple subject and all the sentence elements that relate to it are the *complete subject,* and the simple predicate and all the elements that relate to it are the *complete predicate.* Nor-

---

[1] Classed according to meaning, sentences are *declarative* if they state a fact or make an assertion (*Beethoven wrote nine symphonies. No one will fly to Mars.*); *imperative* if they express a command or request (*Leave by the main gate. Lend me a pen.*); *interrogative* if they ask a question (*Who will go with me?*); and *exclamatory* if they express an emotion (*How good it is to see you!*). Note that declarative and imperative sentences end with a period, an interrogative sentence with a question mark, and an exclamatory sentence with an exclamation point.

mally, the terms *subject* and *predicate* refer to the simple subject and simple predicate, and will be so used hereafter in this chapter. In the examples that follow, a slanting line separates the complete subject and complete predicate, and italics designate the simple subject and simple predicate.

Men / walk.

The old *men / walk* slowly in the sun.

Two old *men,* watery-eyed and scraggly-bearded / *walk* slowly and painfully along the parched path in the blistering August sun.

He / will not *have heard* from home yet.

The *boys* and *girls / have gone* on a picnic.

Swimming / is good exercise.

Jane, Jean, and *Joan / room, study,* and *attend* class together.

IDENTIFYING THE SUBJECT. Students rarely have trouble identifying the predicate of a sentence, but they do sometimes have trouble identifying the subject. The problem usually arises in inverted sentences (those in which the predicate precedes the subject) and in long, complicated sentences. When you cannot readily name the subject, a good method is to identify the predicate and then place *who* or *what* before it, thus making a question. The word that best answers the question will be the subject. As examples, consider the following sentences:

1. Down came the rain.
2. With a blinding flash of lightning and a terrific clap of thunder, down in a pouring deluge, almost without warning, came the beating rain, sending the hardiest fishermen scurrying to cover.
3. A list of eligible players was posted.
4. There on the bulletin board, as casually as a notice calling an extra practice session, was posted the list of players eligible to go on the trip for the great game of the year.
5. There were seats in the bus for thirty men.

Having identified the predicate of *1* and *2* as *came* and of *3* and *4* as *was posted,* ask, Who or what came? Who or what was posted? Then test each term for a sensible answer. As *rain came* makes sense and *down came* does not, you decide that *rain* is the subject. In *3* and *4* you note that *post* is used in the sense of "to affix to a wall" rather than of "to inform," and you decide that as a list may be affixed to a wall but players may not, *list* is the subject. In *5* a hasty glance might lead you to think *there* the subject, but again the question, What were in the bus? will give you the right answer—*seats.*[1]

Besides a subject and predicate, a sentence may have modifiers, connectives, and complements. A *modifier* is any word or group of words that describes, qualifies, or limits any sentence element, such as the subject, the predicate, or a complement. (See the sections on adjectives and adverbs in the chapter on grammar, and the sections on phrases and clauses in this chapter.) A *connective* is a word whose function is to join words and larger elements of a sentence or to show the relationship between sentence elements, sentences, and paragraphs. (See the sections on conjunctions and prepositions in the chapter on grammar.) A *complement* is a word or group of words that helps a verb make an assertion; that is, it is an addition to the verb necessary to complete the predicate. Most intransitive verbs make complete assertions and are therefore called *verbs of complete predication* (The parrot *talks.* He *drives,* but I *walk.*). Transitive verbs in the active voice and the class of intransitives called linking verbs require the help of complements to complete their meaning and are therefore called *verbs of incomplete predication* (He COLLECTS *stamps.* She IS *secretary.*). Complements most frequently employed are called *subjective complements* and *direct objects.* These and various minor sentence elements are explained in the following sections.

The Subjective Complement. A *subjective complement* is a substantive or an adjective

---

[1] In sentences beginning *there is, there are, there once lived, there* is an expletive, and the subject is said to be *delayed. It* is also an expletive in such sentences as *It is true that he was absent.*

that comes after a linking verb and describes, limits, or identifies the subject. The linking verb joins the subject and complement and serves to express the relationship between them. The most common linking verb is *be*, but a few others—such as *become, seem,* and *appear*—ordinarily serve as linking verbs, and still others—such as *taste, feel, look,* and *grow*—often function as linking verbs. The following examples illustrate ways in which various forms of the substantive and the adjective function as subjective complements:

NOUN: The speaker is a *doctor*. The principal crop was *wheat*.

PRONOUN: The first to arrive were *they*. The one who reported it was *I*.

GERUND: His hobby is *sailing*, but mine is *canoeing*.

INFINITIVE: To see is *to believe*. My plan is *to leave* tomorrow.

ADJECTIVE: He seems *cheerful*. He has grown *tall*.

PARTICIPLE: The weather seems *threatening*. He appears *thriving*.

Notice in each of these examples that the complement tells something important about the subject: *wheat* crop, *threatening* weather.

Because verbals are derived from verbs, they may be intransitive and therefore also take a subjective complement:

GERUND: Being *president* is a great responsibility.

PARTICIPLE: Marilyn, being *tired*, has gone to bed.

INFINITIVE: To be *ready* at all times is our motto.

The Direct Object. A *direct object* is the person or thing that receives an action of the subject as expressed by the verb. Transitive verbs in the active voice require a direct object to complete their meaning. The difference between a subjective complement and a direct object is that the subjective complement is identical with the subject or describes or limits it, whereas the direct object is the recipient of an action performed by the subject. Any substantive may be a direct object.

NOUN: The ruling caused many *strikes*. Sue baked a *cake*.

PRONOUN: I saw *him* after the game. Invite *whomever* you like.

GERUND: John enjoys *swimming*. He admits *speeding*.

INFINITIVE: She began *to plan* for the party. He tried *to carve* the fowl.

Except for the past participle, verbals derived from transitive verbs may also take a direct object:

GERUND: Sending a *letter* will not solve the problem.

PARTICIPLE: Denouncing their *policy*, he made a bitter speech.

INFINITIVE: To make a *hit* is not easy in this game.

The Indirect Object. An indirect object is the person or thing *to whom* an action is directed or *for whom* it is performed. It is usually required after such verbs as *ask, bring, cook, give, lend, make, read, sing, teach,* and *write* to complete the meaning of the verb. It may be identified by the *absence of a preposition*, for if the preposition is present, the word becomes the object of the preposition instead of the indirect object of the verb. Examples are the italicized words in the following sentences:

Ask *me* the answer. He will bring *us* a report. Sue baked the *boys* a cake. I gave *Jean* my book. He lent *us* his car. Sing *me* a song.

The Objective Complement. An *objective complement* is a noun or an adjective that completes the predicate by telling something about the direct object. It is used with such verbs as *appoint, call, choose, elect, make, name,* and *nominate*. As it complements the direct object, it is present only when there is a direct object, and *it always follows the direct object*. A test for identifying the objective complement is to insert the infinitive *to be* between it and the direct object. If the statement then makes sense, the noun or adjective following the direct object is an objective complement.

NOUN: We elected him *secretary.* Columbus thought the new land *India.*

ADJECTIVE: I like my coffee *black.* They call the result *excellent.*

The Objective Infinitive. The *objective infinitive* is a term given to a special form of the direct object. It consists of a noun or pronoun *in the objective case* followed by an infinitive, of which the noun or pronoun is the subject. The sign of the infinitive *to* may be either stated or implied.

> Her father wanted *her to have* an education. Our friends advised *us to accept* the offer. We saw *Tom win* the low hurdles. I heard the *car roar* past.

Appositives. An *appositive* is a substantive attached to another substantive and denoting the same person or thing. It always comes after the substantive to which it is attached and is said to be *in apposition* with this substantive.

> This is my brother *Tom.* Mr. Allen, a *doctor,* is at his summer cottage, *Green Gables,* where he is enjoying his favorite pastime, *fishing.*

Nominative of Address. A *nominative of address* is a noun or pronoun used in addressing a person or thing.

> Where were you today, *George?* Go, *lovely rose,* with my message.

Nominative Absolute. A *nominative absolute* consists of a substantive in the nominative case and a participle expressing cause, circumstance, or time of an action. Although independent of the rest of the sentence, it is in effect an adverbial modifier.

> *The storm being over,* we left the shelter. *Swimming having left us tired,* we lay on the beach.

Absolute Infinitive Phrase. An *absolute infinitive phrase* consists of an infinitive and its complement or modifiers.

> *To tell the truth,* I have no excuse.

(See *Workbook,* Exercises 25 and 26.)

Phrases. Phrases are extremely important word-groups used as sentence elements. A *phrase is a group of two or more words, lacking a subject and predicate, that functions as a single word.* To identify a phrase readily, keep in mind four things: (1) it is a group of two or more words, never one word; (2) the words must be closely related to form a sense unit, not just any two or more words that come together; (3) it does not have a subject and predicate; that is, the group lacks predication; and (4) the word-group functions as a single word in the sentence. Named according to their formation, the most important phrases are *prepositional, participial, gerund,* and *infinitive.*

A PREPOSITIONAL PHRASE consists of a preposition and a substantive (its object) and any modifiers present. It functions as an adjective, an adverb, or a noun.

ADJECTIVE: The dog *with the brown spots* is mine. (modifies subject)

> My cousin is the girl *in the red jacket.* (modifies subjective complement)

> I asked the man *from the garage* to help us. (modifies direct object)

ADVERB: We studied *in the afternoon.* (modifies verb—tells when)

> Put your coat *on the hanger.* (modifies verb—tells where)

> He is youthful *in appearance.* (modifies adjective)

NOUN: *In the morning* is when I practice. (subject of *is*)

A PARTICIPIAL PHRASE consists of a participle and its modifiers and complements. It always functions as an adjective and must therefore modify a specific substantive present in the sentence.

> *Running swiftly,* he grabbed the child. (modifies subject)

> *Being now a citizen,* you should vote. (modifies subject)

> That is John *holding the child.* (modifies subjective complement)

> They applauded the man *playing left end.* (modifies direct object)

A GERUND PHRASE consists of a gerund and its qualifiers and objects. It always functions as a noun.

Getting up in the morning was his big problem. (subject)

She enjoys *doing the shopping.* (direct object)

Whoever heard of *going to bed at this hour?* (object of preposition)

AN INFINITIVE PHRASE consists of an infinitive and its qualifiers and objects. It functions as an adjective, an adverb, or a noun.

ADJECTIVE: The forms *to fill out* have come. (modifies subject)

He made an effort *to reach the stranded boy.* (modifies direct object)

ADVERB: He went *to check on the time.* (modifies verb—tells purpose)

Joan was willing *to serve as leader.* (modifies adjective)

NOUN: *To go at once* was our decision. (subject)

Keith offered *to provide transportation.* (direct object)

A VERB PHRASE consists of a verb and its auxiliaries. It is always a predicate.

He *will* already *have been gone* an hour.

(See *Workbook,* Exercise 27.)

Clauses. *A clause is a group of words, containing a subject and predicate, that forms part of a sentence.* To identify a clause, therefore, note whether the group of words has a subject and a predicate and whether it is a part of the sentence. According to its function in the sentence, a clause is classified as. *independent* (also called *main* or *principal*) or *dependent* (also called *subordinate*).

AN INDEPENDENT CLAUSE has two distinguishing features: in content it deals with whatever is the principal concern of the sentence (that is, it carries the main predication), and in structure it has grammatical completeness (is capable, if detached from the other elements of the sentence, of standing alone as a sentence).

The house will not fall, because it is built upon a rock.

When the rain is over, *we can finish the game.*

A DEPENDENT CLAUSE as a general rule ex-presses some part of an idea that has less importance than that expressed in the independent clause; and in structure it does not make complete grammatical sense, either because the arrangement of the words leaves the idea incomplete or because it includes a subordinating connective that indicates its dependence on another clause. (Occasionally, however, the connective is understood: He said [*that*] he would go; or the words in the dependent clause are so arranged as to make a connective unnecessary: *Had it happened that way,* I should have known.)

Like phrases, dependent clauses function in the sentence as single words; and according to their function they are called *noun clauses, adjective clauses,* and *adverbial clauses.*

NOUN CLAUSE: *What happened* was something we could not foresee. (subject)

He said *the report was true.* (direct object)

He is *what one may call a gourmet.* (subjective complement)

ADJECTIVE CLAUSE: The man *who just spoke* is the coach. (modifies subject)

He bought the calf *that won first prize.* (modifies direct object)

John is the lad *who won the game.* (modifies subjective complement)

ADVERBIAL CLAUSE: He walked *as if he were in a hurry.* (modifies predicate—tells manner)

Should he go, I shall report it. (modifies predicate)

He ran as rapidly *as he could.* (modifies adverb)

CLASSES OF SENTENCES ACCORDING TO FORM

According to their formation or structure, sentences are classified as *simple, complex, compound,* and *compound-complex.* The basis on which this classification is made is the number and kind of clauses in a sentence. If you can identify a clause and can differentiate between independent and dependent clauses, you should have no problem over this classification.

The Simple Sentence. A *simple* sentence consists of *one independent clause.* It may contain any number of phrases and other modifiers, so long as the modifiers are not clauses. Either the subject or the predicate may be compound, but it must not contain more than one clause, nor may it be introduced by a subordinating connective. The length of a sentence has nothing to do with its classification: a simple sentence may extend to many lines, and a complex or compound sentence may have as few as three or four words. The following are all examples of simple sentences:

Go.

Birds fly.

Where is Sylvia?

What a beautiful sunset that is!

Being tired of studying, he has gone for a walk.

The dog and the boys and girls romp and play together.

Having a nose for news and being fond both of people and gossip, Aunt Priscilla, my mother's youngest sister—the only one of my mother's family staying with us for any length of time in my childhood—used to circulate around the village gathering all the bits of information from all the gossipy matrons, spinsters, and even bachelors in the place, and afterwards making it all into a beautifully fashioned fabric for the entertainment and delight of our whole family, even including father.

The Complex Sentence. A *complex* sentence contains *a single independent clause and at least one dependent clause.* It may have any number of dependent clauses (it must have one); but if it has more than one independent clause, it is not classified as a complex sentence. The dependent clause may function as a noun (as subject, subjective complement, direct object, object of a preposition) or as an adjective or adverb.

NOUN: *That he writes well* is to his credit. (subject)

The report is *that he will be here.* (subjective complement)

I know *who he is.* (direct object)

I shall give it to *whoever needs it.* (object of preposition)

The fact *that the world is round* was proved by Columbus. (appositive)

ADJECTIVE: Anyone *who is discriminating* will like the play. (modifies subject)

This is the place *where I found the watch.* (modifies subjective complement)

I found the bicycle, *which is a Sterling.* (modifies direct object)

ADVERB: I left *before my family returned.* (modifies verb—tells time)

Because he was too tall, he was rejected. (modifies verb—tells cause)

The Compound Sentence. A *compound* sentence contains two or more independent *clauses.* It contains no dependent clause. The independent clauses should be closely related in thought. In writing compound sentences, be careful to use the right connective and punctuation (see the sections on conjunctions, page 70; on connectives, page 106; and on the use of commas, page 118, and semicolons, page 124).

The signal was flashed, *and* the plane moved toward the runway.

The order was sent, *but* it was lost in transit.

Both sides must agree to the terms, *or* the war will continue.

Platinum is a catalyst; *that is,* it promotes a reaction without itself being affected.

We wrote last week; *therefore* we should hear soon.

The Congress is working on a revision of the law; meanwhile the old act is being enforced.

The Compound-Complex Sentence. A *compound-complex* sentence contains *two or more independent clauses and one or more dependent clauses.*

He is a native of Holland, where he lived till he was sixteen, but for the last twenty years he has lived in the United States.

Although a strike was called, labor took a conciliatory policy, and the government did not have to intervene.

Irregular Sentences. Although as was said at the beginning of this chapter, a sentence normally contains both a subject and a predicate, there are some permissible exceptions to this rule. Exclamatory words and phrases are of course permissible. In questions and answers, a phrase may be used when the meaning is obvious. A phrase may also be used to mark main transitions, especially in lengthy articles where the subdivisions are themselves long. Again, in writing conversation, phrases are often used to give the conversation an effect of reality. In modern fiction and poetry, an author may at times treat a series of phrases and elliptical sentences as if they were normal sentences. This device is rarely employed except in descriptions and in summaries of the thoughts running through the mind of some character, its purpose being to create an impression rather than to give a detailed picture or explanation.

Although you may have occasion, especially in writing conversation, to use elliptical sentences or to treat single words or phrases as sentences, as a rule you should avoid irregular sentences. When you are a master of the techniques of writing, you will then be able to decide when you may safely diverge from the patterns in which sentences are normally cast.

(See *Workbook*, Exercise 28.)

Grammar[1]

WILLIAM COBBETT

WITHOUT UNDERSTANDING [the grammar of your own language] you can never hope to become fit for anything beyond [menial labor]. It is true that we do (God knows!) but too often see men have great wealth, high titles, and boundless power heaped upon them, who can hardly write ten lines together correctly; but, remember, it is not *merit* that has been the cause of their advancement; the cause has been, in almost every such case, the subserviency of the party to the will of some government, and the baseness of some nation who have quietly submitted to be governed by brazen fools. Do not you imagine that you will have luck of this sort; do not you hope to be rewarded and honored for that ignorance which shall prove a scourge to your country, and which will earn you the curses of the children yet unborn. Rely you upon your merit, and upon nothing else. Without a knowledge of grammar, it is impossible for you to write correctly, and it is by mere accident if you speak correctly; and pray

[1] From William Cobbett, *Advice to Young Men.*

bear in mind that all well-informed persons judge of a man's mind (until they have other means of judging) by his writing or speaking. The labor necessary to acquire this knowledge is, indeed, not trifling: grammar is not, like arithmetic, a science consisting of several distinct departments, some of which may be dispensed with; it is a whole, and the whole must be learned, or no part is learned. The subject is abstruse; it demands much reflection and much patience; but when once the task is performed, it is performed *for life,* and in every day of that life it will be found to be, in a greater or less degree, a source of pleasure or of profit or of both together. And what is the labor? It consists of no bodily exertion; it exposes the student to no cold, no hunger, no sufferings of any sort. The study need subtract from the hours of no business, nor, indeed, from the hours of necessary exercise; the hours usually spent on the tea and coffee slops and in the mere gossip which accompany them, those wasted hours of only *one year,* employed in the study of English grammar, would make you a correct speaker and writer for the rest of your life. You want no school, no room to study in, no expenses, and no troublesome circumstances of any sort. I learned grammar when I was a private soldier on the pay of sixpence a day. The edge of my berth, or that of the guard bed, was my seat to study in; my knapsack was my writing table; and the task did not demand anything like a year of my life. I had no money to purchase candle or oil; in winter time it was rarely that I could get any evening light but that of *the fire,* and only my *turn* even of that. And if I, under such circumstances, and without parent or friend to advise or encourage me, accomplished this undertaking, what excuse can there be for *any youth,* however poor, however pressed with business, or however circumstanced as to room or other conveniences? To buy a pen or a sheet of paper I was compelled to forego some portion of food, though in a state of half starvation; I had no moment of time that I could call my own; and I had to read and to write amidst the talking, laughing, singing, whistling, and brawling of at least half a score of the most thoughtless of men, and that, too, in the hours of their freedom from all control. Think not lightly of the *farthing* that I had to give, now and then, for ink, pen, or paper! That farthing was, alas! a *great sum* to me! I was as tall as I am now; I had great health and great exercise. The whole of the money,

not expended for us at market, was *twopence a week* for each man. I remember, and well I may! that upon one occasion I, after all absolutely necessary expenses, had on a Friday made shift to have a halfpenny in reserve, which I had destined for the purchase of a red herring in the morning; but, when I pulled my clothes off at night, so hungry then as to be hardly able to endure life, I found that I had *lost my halfpenny!* I buried my head under the miserable sheet and rug, and cried like a child! And again I say, if I, under circumstances like these, could encounter and overcome this task, is there, can there be, in the whole world a youth to find an excuse for the nonperformance? What youth, who shall read this, will not be ashamed to say that he is not able to find time and opportunity for this most essential of all the branches of book learning?

SUGGESTIONS FOR STUDY

1. Why does Cobbett believe a knowledge of grammar is necessary?
2. Although the study of grammar requires labor, why is not the learning of it arduous?
3. What equipment is needed to learn grammar? What surroundings?
4. From a rhetorical point of view, why does Cobbett include the personal illustration that occupies the last half of the article?
5. Define the following words from the selection: subserviency, brazen, dispensed, abstruse, forego, farthing.

Tu'imalila, Oldest Animal in the World[1]

MARY PATTERSON

IF LIFE be a blessing, then Tu'imalila—the King of Malila—probably is the most blessed of all the creatures of earth. For Tu'imalila is, according to carefully investigated records, the oldest living animal of the

[1] From the *National Humane Review* (April, 1952). Reprinted by permission of the *National Humane Review.*

world. There may be older creatures in the dark depths of some ocean or jungle but none so old for which there is a reliable record.

Tu'imalila is a giant tortoise, resident in the grounds of the palace of the Queen of Tonga—the Friendly Islands—in the Western Pacific. Palace records show that Tu'imalila was brought to Tonga by Captain James Cook in 1777. That was 175 years ago. Captain Cook presented Tu'imalila to the Tonga king. No one knows exactly how old the giant tortoise then was, of course, but circumstantial evidence indicates that he was at least 100 years old.

It is overwhelmingly probable, therefore, that Tu'imalila is at least 250 years old!

Today Tu'imalila weighs approximately 450 pounds. He is blind in one eye, the result of having been run over by a dray some 50 years ago. He has survived two great bush fires that scarred his shell. He is a lonely old man, without companionship of his species. But the King shows no loss of interest in life. His horny beak snaps as avidly as ever at beetles and grubs, and he carries his 450 pounds around the palace grounds with unflagging vigor.

Tu'imalila came by his name and title honestly. The word Tu'i means King. The compound of the Tu'i Tonga at the time that Captain Cook visited the island was called Malila. Because the giant tortoise was a valued and even awesome gift, the Tu'i Tonga organized a ceremony which made the tortoise an official Chieftain of Tonga and conferred on him the title of Tu'imalila —King of the Malila.

From that ancient day until now, Tu'imalila has had an apartment in the palace. On ceremonial occasions he is placed among the other Chiefs and is served his cup of *kava*.

When Robert Gibbings, British artist and author, visited the Friendly Islands about two years ago, he obtained permission to paint Tu'imalila's portrait.

"When he came to me to sit for his portrait," Gibbings said, "he traveled in a royal car. I had expected that so venerable a subject would be an ideal model, but it was with difficulty that I persuaded him to keep still and not wander off to inspect the garden."

The Giant Tortoises, Tu'imalila's clan, are terrestrial tortoises that once were extremely numerous on several groups of South and West Pacific islands. Several specimens have been found that weighed more than 600 pounds, with a shell length of more than four feet.

Unfortunately for the great beasts, sailors of Captain Cook's day discovered early that tortoises could live for many months without food or water and that they were delicious food. For a century afterward sailing ships regularly put into the Galapagos, Mascarene or Seychelles-Aldabra Islands and stocked up with Giant Tortoises. The animals were either dumped unceremoniously into the hold or were turned on their backs and tied on deck, to broil in the equatorial sun until wanted by the cook.

Chiefly because of this wanton use of the animals, the Giant Tortoises today are rare and are found chiefly in the Galapagos.

The exact age of Tu'imalila and other Giant Tortoises that have been long kept in captivity has been the subject of much scientific research and speculation. Another tortoise, known to zoologists as "Marion's tortoise," was accidentally killed in 1918 after having lived in the artillery barracks at Port Louis, on Mauritus, since 1766. Another giant tortoise, the survivor of a pair, lives at Plantation House, the residence of the Governor of St. Helena. The age of this animal is uncertain, but J. C. Mellis, historian, wrote in 1875 that tradition indicated that "two of these very large tortoises have lived at Plantation for a century or more." That would indicate that Jonathan, the survivor, is at least 175 years old.

The circumstantial evidence most compellingly pointing to the conclusion that Tu'imalila was at least 100 years old when Captain Cook presented him to the Tu'i Tonga is in the very fact that Cook chose him as a royal gift. In all probability Tu'imalila was one of several of the great reptiles stored on Captain Cook's ship, waiting to be eaten. Cook's crew would, naturally, have chosen only full-grown tortoises for this purpose. And Cook, naturally, would have selected the largest to please the King of Tonga.

Giant Tortoises continue growing for well over 100 years, and it is reasonable to suppose, therefore, that Tu'imalila had reached this stage of adulthood when he arrived in Tonga.

It is certain, at any rate, that Tu'imalila has lived happily in the Tonga palace grounds while billions of men, of a half-dozen generations, have lived, struggled, and died. Tu'imalila might be pardoned if occasionally he feels a slight contempt for the race that waits on him.

SUGGESTIONS FOR STUDY

1. What are the size and age which Giant Tortoises may attain? For how long do they continue to grow?
2. What accounts for their rarity?
3. Why has Tu'imalila been especially honored?
4. Study carefully how the reader's interest has been sustained by specific details rather than generalizations. Observe also how the narrative bits about Tu'imalila—his introduction to the island and his sitting for a portrait—increase interest. Such bits do much to enliven non-narrative writing. What is the general purpose of this article?

An Electrical "Bath" in Yellowstone[1]

WILLIAM B. SANBORN

IN EARLY SEPTEMBER of 1949 I had occasion to drive from Madison Junction to Mammoth Hot Springs in the Yellowstone Park, and dusk was gathering when I drove onto the stretch of straight highway that parallels Swan Lake. A violent electrical storm was centered over Electric Peak, extending several miles eastward into the Beartooth Range. Heavy bolts of lightning frequently stabbed downward, and the clouds themselves seemed to be constantly flickering with an orange light. The display was so spectacular that I pulled off the road near the north end of Swan Lake and stepped out of the car to watch it.

It was then that I noticed a bluish light coming from over the low ridge to the west of Swan Lake. My first thought was of a fire, perhaps caused by lightning. I watched the ridge for a moment and was amazed to see what can best be described as a hazy patch of blue light coming over the ridge and moving down the hill slope toward the flats

around the lake. It was then that I observed a very low lead-gray cloud moving swiftly above the patch of light. The patch moved through the marshy north end of Swan Lake and caused several waterfowl to rise in hurried flight.

The patch of light moved off the lake and onto the flats at a steady rate and proceeded directly toward my viewpoint. When the patch was but a few yards away, I noticed a sudden calm in the air and a marked change in temperature, as well as what I believe was the odor of ozone. It was then that I realized that the display before me was some manner of static electricity, comparable perhaps to St. Elmo's fire and directly controlled by the low cloud moving above.

The patch, which actually was a static field, enveloped my immediate area. To describe the weird feeling caused by viewing the progress of this phenomenon is difficult. It kept low to the ground, actually "flowing around" everything that it came in contact with, coating it with a strange pulsating light. Each twig on the sagebrush was surrounded by a halo of light about two inches in diameter. It covered the automobile and

[1] From *Natural History*, LIX (June, 1950). Reprinted by permission of the author and *Natural History* and the American Museum of Natural History.

my person but did not cover my skin. There was a marked tingling sensation in my scalp, and brushing my hair with the hand caused a snapping of tiny sparks.

The most unusual aspect of the disturbance occurred when I threw a rock along the ground in much the way one skips a stone over a pond or lake. Every time the rock hit the ground or a piece of brush it gave the appearance of "splashing." The light would momentarily disappear from the contact spot but immediately build up again. I noted that the static could be brushed off the car surface, and it also would establish the light again in a matter of seconds. I obtained no shock from touching any object on the ground or the outside of the car.

My estimate of the speed of the disturbance was about three or four feet a second, or faster. The field seemed to be about 50 yards wide and perhaps some 250 yards in length, roughly comparable to the low cloud above.

I watched the display move quickly up the valley toward Electric Peak until it faded from view and darkness closed in. (It might be mentioned that Electric Peak derives its name from the electric storms that frequent its heights and the surrounding region. It is the highest peak in the northern part of the park.) Upon getting into the car and closing the door, I touched the horn ring and was rewarded with a most substantial shock, the effect of which caused numbness in my arm for several hours. Probably the car had become charged negatively, since it was insulated from grounding by the tires. I must have carried a positive charge from my contact with the ground and the disturbance.

When the experience was described to Ross Gunn, Director of Physical Research at the United States Weather Bureau, he commented that phenomena of this sort are reasonably common in mountainous regions during periods of thunderstorm activity. "Usually the described effects," he commented, "are short-lived and precede a lightning discharge. The glow results from ionization induced by a highly electrified cloud overhead. The electric field necessary to produce an observable glow usually exceeds 2000 volts per centimeter. It is entirely adequate to make one's hair stand on end. In the described case, the overhead cloud was doubtless millions of volts above the potential of the ground. It is a very interesting instance of this sort of occurrence because of its great length and apparent stability."

I don't know whether I would have been able to observe events as carefully as I did if I had known that it was "millions of volts," but in any case I shall certainly remember the experience for a long time as one of the most outstanding displays in nature that I have ever observed.

SUGGESTIONS FOR STUDY

1. Observe what details of setting the author establishes. What do these details indicate about the author's understanding of the knowledge possessed by the reader?

2. Mention two or three details observed by the author while the electrical "bath" surrounded him. Such details make vivid writing.

3. How fully described is the physics of the electrical phenomenon? What does the author assume then about his reader?

4. Study the organization. Observe how a clear presentation is effected by relating the events chronologically up to the final explanations.

Struck by Lightning[1]

HENRY H. RUSBY

FROM LA PAZ I dispatched my luggage to Valparaiso by freight, hastening, myself, to Arica to catch a steamer. On this first part of my journey, I was accompanied by two friends, Abraham Gainsborg and a Mr. Quinn, former manager of the Homestake Mine, and with them I endured the parallel of my experience with lightning stroke in New Mexico, four years previously.

We were climbing to the summit of a spur, through a hail and snow storm, and dismounted to don our rubber clothing. Gainsborg, about fifty yards ahead and perhaps fifty feet higher, had remounted and was waiting for us. Quinn, midway between us, was just placing his foot in the stirrup. I had my foot on a pile of stones, and was buckling on my spur when I experienced two blinding flashes of lightning and two deafening crashes of thunder. The two were in such quick succession as to be scarcely distinguishable.

I felt the prickling of a thousand needles all over my body, and wondered whether my gun had exploded. I did not note the lapse of any time before I found myself scrambling up from the ground on my hands and knees. No animals were in sight upon the road, but against the hillside, perhaps an eighth of a mile away, stood Quinn's mule and mine. Evidently I had lain unconscious for some time, for they must have stampeded to that point, from which they were watching us in great excitement, ears pricked forward, and eyes glued upon the road where we were.

I looked up and saw Gainsborg's mule flat upon his belly, his front legs stretched out

and his head lying between them. Gainsborg lay to one side, apparently dead, coagulated blood upon the ground beside him. Quinn lay on his back among the stones.

I ran to release Gainsborg, and as I came up his mule began to quiver, then to struggle, and, before I could act, was on his feet, quite crazy, and prancing wildly. Gainsborg hung from the stirrup, his head striking the roadway as the mule jumped about. I had hold of the bridle, but could not let go without exposing Gainsborg to immediate death, although unless he was quickly released the same result must ensue more slowly.

I drew my pistol to shoot the mule, just as Quinn came running up. He released Gainsborg from his dangerous position, and demanded who had struck him, declaring someone had hit him on the back of the head with a club! Now Gainsborg moaned, and we knew that he was alive. He vomited blood, which probably saved his life. We applied restoratives and soon had him bound upon his mule. Quinn led the animal, while I rode ahead six miles to the Indian *tambo* of Chulan Callani, to prepare a place for him.

Here fire was refused me on the ground that fuel was scarce, and I was obliged to threaten the Indians with my revolver. I had great difficulty in restoring circulation to Gainsborg's feet. He declared that they were freezing, and the hottest water bottles made no apparent difference. Eventually, we succeeded. He remained totally blind until about three in the morning, when he announced that he could see the light of the candle. He was able to resume his journey late on the following day.

It developed that neither he nor Quinn had had any knowledge of thunder or lightning, and I must assume that since I saw

[1] From Henry H. Rusby, *Jungle Memories* (New York, 1933), published by Whittlesey House. Reprinted by permission of the McGraw-Hill Book Company.

and heard two flashes and claps, I must have been struck by a third discharge.

I have found the succession of events in this experience of the greatest interest in enabling me to understand the nature of such an electric shock. It seems to indicate that the discharge of electricity from such a hillside is not uniform, in either time or intensity. I distinctly heard two discharges which, although almost instantaneous, were evidently in succession. Their effect on me was almost blinding, by the intensity of the flash, and at the same time produced a strong prickling sensation, but without any mechanical shock that I could distinguish. I think there may have been such a shock, but it was unnoticed, because of the effects on sight and hearing and on the surface of the skin. Before proceeding to put on my spurs, I had stood my gun in a leaning position, and my instant thought when I heard the discharge and felt the prickling sensation, was that my gun had exploded. Even this flash of thought regarding my own gun was preceded by one that I had been shot at by someone else. The lapse of time during which these ideas presented themselves must have been incalculably short, indicating the superior rapidity of thought over electricity,

since the shock which prostrated me had not yet occurred. Undoubtedly, the third discharge must have been unheard and unseen by me just as Gainsborg and Quinn did not see or hear those which had prostrated them. Finally, I refer to the total absence of any sense of the passage of time while I lay prostrated. When one wakes from a sleep, he is conscious of time having elapsed during that sleep, no matter how sound, but in this case there was no such consciousness whatever. My first glance about, as I rose from the ground, appeared to be a continuation of my seeing and hearing the first lightning flash. It required the evidence of the staring mules on a distant hillside to convince me that there had been a lapse of time.

SUGGESTIONS FOR STUDY

1. Trace the effect of the lightning bolt on the author and on Gainsborg.
2. Does the author believe that he heard or saw the flash which prostrated him? What does he conjecture about the speed of thought?
3. What phenomenon concerning the passing of time did he experience?
4. Observe how the organization is clearly set forth by the chronological series of events leading up to the final analysis of the experience.

The Metamorphosis of Hell Week[1]

KARL DETZER

TWENTY-SIX Lynchburg College students were suspended several years ago when a freshman lost an eye as the result of hazing. Two youngsters at the University of California were hospitalized for severe nitrate burns resulting from an initiation.

A fraternity pledge died of burns caused by an initiation stunt at St. Louis University. Dickinson College abolished hazing when

[1] From the *Reader's Digest* (September, 1951), condensed from *Guideposts* (September, 1951). Reprinted by permission of the *Reader's Digest*.

a boy died of blood poisoning after being hurt in a fraternity ruckus.

In 1949 at Brown University, Pledge Week ended in a free-for-all with one sophomore dead and another in the hospital. At the University of Alberta, one youth, dragged along corridors, beaten, held under cold showers, became hopelessly insane. Another student died last March at Alabama's Northwest State College following fraternity initiation.

A lanky Hoosier athlete named Bob Lollar was striding across the campus of Indiana

University one February morning in 1949 when he came upon a sight which set him thinking. Half-a-dozen young pledges to Greek-letter fraternities were undergoing "Hell Week." Wearing freak haircuts and silly clothes, they were moving stone piles that had only to be moved back, or rushing back and forth with empty wheelbarrows. They were doing these absurd things merely to prove themselves worthy of wearing certain fraternity pins.

Lollar, "pledge trainer" for his own fraternity, Alpha Tau Omega, was expected in the next few days to dream up similar silly antics for twenty youngsters. The more he thought about it the worse it seemed. The next day he walked into the office of a smart young assistant dean named Gary Schwartz.

"Look here, Gary," Lollar began earnestly, "the fraternities are wasting manpower and brains. Isn't there something constructive for these kids to do, some job on the campus that needs to be done? Why can't Hell Week be Help Week?"

As the campus was getting along nicely without the help of fraternity pledges, Schwartz grabbed the idea for the city of Bloomington. He called a minister friend. Indeed, there was a job to be done! A drab old community-service building operated by half-a-dozen churches needed painting.

Lollar's twenty pledges were enthusiastic. They bought, begged, and borrowed paint brushes, wangled gallons of paint from local merchants. At eight o'clock one morning Alpha Tau Omega began its initiation with Lollar acting as foreman. The youngsters scrambled up ladders, scraped off old paint, sanded the siding, slapped on a first coat; the next Saturday finished the job.

Other fraternity chapters soon joined the movement, with Dean Schwartz as adviser. Public officials, health and welfare groups, the Chamber of Commerce, and churches submitted lists of needs to the Interfraternity Council.

The Salvation Army reported a family, bogged down by illness, that lived in a house with a leaky roof. Lollar and his pledges soon were prying roofing and nails out of building-materials dealers. At the end of a hard Saturday's work the family had a new roof. Not only the pledges were on the job; older members of the fraternity joined them, knew the satisfaction of giving an appreciated helping hand.

On a cold winter morning Lollar and his crew tramped out into the country to a house reported by the county welfare department. In it lived a widow with five small children. A relief truck had dumped a big load of stove wood beside the highway, an uphill mile from the widow's door. The young huskies of Alpha Tau Omega settled that problem fast. By noon, an armload at a time, they carried the wood and stacked it neatly outside the woman's door.

Townspeople in Bloomington began to take notice. Maybe there was some sense in these wild fraternity kids, after all.

Within a year, more than twenty of the thirty-one fraternities on the Hoosier campus were engaged in their own good works. Help Week is now universal at Indiana, and other midwest colleges have adopted it. Purdue, old-time football rival of Indiana, was first to follow its good example; then came Butler, Bowling Green, and DePauw. The idea has spread to Cornell University and to schools in the South and Far West. Everywhere Help Week was tried, the steadily growing opposition to college fraternities subsided.

At Indiana now, whole fraternity chapters, not just the pledges, go out together on helpful community jobs. Sigma Chi discovered that the children of married students who occupy a big trailer court had no suitable place to play. Pledges and their elder brethren smoothed off a vacant space in the center of the trailer village, rolled and seeded it. Lumber and hardware dealers in the city donated supplies. The boys built swings and teeter-totters. The new playground is used by children from the whole neighborhood.

Fraternity boys painted the city bandshell, a long, hard job. They cut grass in the parks. Last fall leaves from Bloomington's thousands of shade trees filled the streets, making a fire hazard. City crews could not get rid of them fast enough. So a gang of husky young men from the fraternity houses helped out with brooms, rakes, and shovels. One group took as its project the rehabilitation of a Boy Scout camp near Bloomington.

On this same Indiana campus several years ago nine pledges went to jail for breaking into a grocery while on a scavenger hunt which was part of their initiation.

Bloomington's Mayor Tom Lemon says, "Police don't have any more trouble with these kids, and the townspeople have a new feeling toward the campus. We're working together and getting on fine."

Hell Weeks are on the wane all over America. The Indiana faculty, after watching the new spirit at work for more than two years, is convinced that the Greek-letter societies have come of age. They say the GI students, who brought serious purpose to school, probably are greatly responsible for the new attitude.

Bob Lollar, who started it all at Indiana, was a veteran. To men who had been through real Hell, "Hell Week" seemed mighty silly.

SUGGESTIONS FOR STUDY

1. What sort of grievances have led to concern over Hell Week activities?
2. What change in community attitude was effected at Indiana University by Help Week activities?
3. How have colleges generally reacted to Help Week?
4. In what ways have the pledges profited by the change of activity?
5. State the general purpose. Then notice how the general purpose was effected through a series of very specific incidents illustrating the activities of the pledges. Get into the habit of using such illustrations in your writing.

Suggestions for Writing

The four preceding articles suggest numerous topics. Have you seen or read of unusual animals or botanical specimens which you can describe as Tu'imalila is described? Have you or any of your friends had personal experiences comparable to those of William Sanborn and Henry Rusby? These could involve all sorts of experiences, such as those with lightning, snow, ice, fogs, sleet, rain, and so on. The article on Hell Week presents the sort of activity which is found on almost all campuses. What are your fraternities doing about Help Week? What is the community attitude toward fraternities or toward your college generally? Are students engaged in any activities similar to those related in the article? Are there student problems on your campus which need solution?

C. Analyzing the Sentence

An understanding of the various parts of a sentence, as explained in the preceding sections of this chapter, should make it possible for you to analyze any sentence; and the ability to analyze sentences should in turn help you to write more effective sentences.

There are two methods of analyzing sentences, by exposition and by diagraming. Which method is better is a matter of individual preference. You may prefer diagraming because it is a graphic method, insuring that no part of the sentence will be overlooked and allowing you to demonstrate the relationship of the various elements.

EXPOSITORY ANALYSIS

An expository analysis consists of an explanation of the function of every word in a sentence and of the relationship of every element to other sentence elements. As an example of the process, consider the following sentence: *Ralph served the ball over the net with blinding speed and completely bewildered his nervous opponent.* The analysis runs as follows: The subject of the sentence is *Ralph.* The predicate is compound, consisting of the verbs *served* and *bewildered. Ball* is the direct object of *served, opponent* the direct object of *bewildered.* The verb *served* is modified by two adverbial prepositional phrases—*with blinding speed,* which tells how the ball was served, and *over the net,* which tells where it was served. *Blinding* is a participle modifying *speed; completely* is an adverb modifying *bewildered*. The two adjectives (articles) *the* modify the nouns *ball* and *net;* and the two adjectives *his* and *nervous* modify the noun *opponent*. *And* is a conjunction linking the two parts of the compound predicate.

DIAGRAMING

Diagraming is a method of sentence analysis that makes use of certain graphic devices to show the relationship of sentence elements. Learning the specific devices requires a bit of study, but once you know them, you can analyze a sentence more quickly by a diagram than by expository analysis. Another advantage is that a diagram can be followed better by others. The following system of devices used in diagraming is now widely used, but it is not the only one, and may be subject to modification by your instructor.

SUBJECT AND PREDICATE. Place the subject and the predicate on a horizontal line, and separate them by a vertical line that *extends below* the horizontal line.

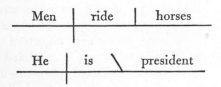

DIRECT OBJECT AND SUBJECTIVE COMPLEMENT. Place the direct object or the subjective complement on the horizontal line just to the right of the predicate. To show that the complement is a direct object, separate it from the predicate by a vertical line that extends *only to* the horizontal line. To show that the complement is a subjective complement, separate it from the predicate by a slanting line, the top of which leans towards the subject.

| Men | ride | horses |

| He | is \ president |

ADJECTIVES AND ADVERBS. Place adjectival and adverbial modifiers on a slanting line below the word they modify.

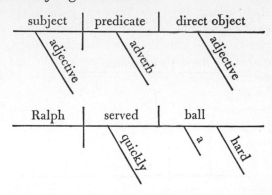

PREPOSITIONAL PHRASE. Place a prepositional phrase on a combined slanting and horizontal line *below* the word it modifies.

Ralph served the ball <u>over</u> <u>the net with great speed</u>.

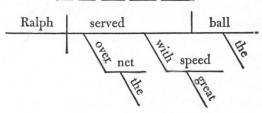

VERBALS. Place a participle *below* the word it modifies, using a line similar to that used for the prepositional phrase. Place a gerund on *a jagged line set on a stilt:* When an infinitive functions as an adjective or adverb, place it *below* the word it modifies on a line similar to that used for the prepositional phrase; and when it functions as a noun, place it on a similar line set *on a stilt.*

CONJUNCTIONS AND COMPOUND ELEMENTS. If the subject, predicate, or other element is compound, place it on a brace, one element of the compound on each part, and place the conjunction on a dotted line running between the elements which the conjunction joins: ———⟨ ┊ . The following examples illustrate the methods of diagraming verbals and compound elements.

Trying to buy costumes discouraged me.

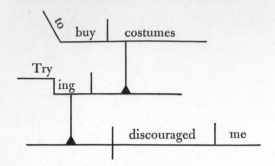

Traveling is an expensive hobby.

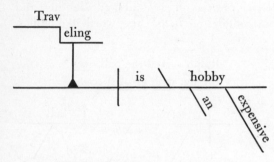

Tiring suddenly, he ceased running and sprawled on the grass.

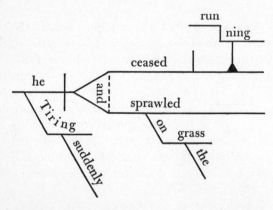

Running very swiftly, he slipped on the ice.

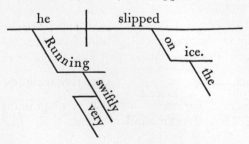

To buy costumes is difficult and taxes one's ingenuity.

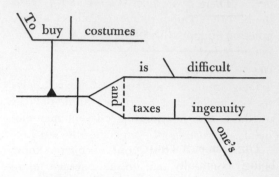

This morning Tom and Bob accompanied us to buy eggs.

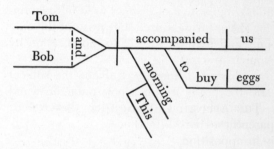

The following examples illustrate methods of diagraming imperative and interrogative sentences and those containing an expletive.

Bring the basket to me.

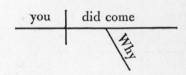

Why did you come?

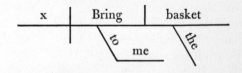

What do you want?

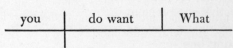

There are ten men in the room.

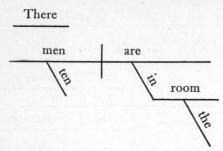

THE INDIRECT OBJECT. The indirect object being essentially an implied prepositional phrase, it is diagramed like the prepositional phrase, but with an *x* on the slanting line.

They gave him a costly gift.

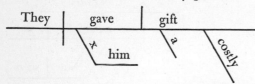

THE APPOSITIVE. Place the appositive in parentheses beside the word with which it is in apposition.

My brother Dick visited us.

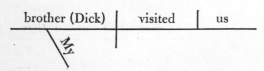

THE NOMINATIVE OF ADDRESS. Having no grammatical connection with the rest of the sentence, the nominative of address is set off by itself on a separate line.

Have you heard the news, John?

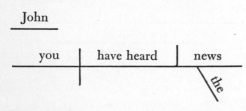

THE OBJECTIVE COMPLEMENT. Place the objective complement just to the right of the direct object and separated from it by a slanting line.

The voters elected him governor.

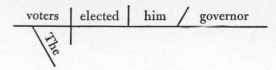

THE NOMINATIVE ABSOLUTE. As the nominative absolute has no grammatical relationship with the rest of the sentence, place the noun form on a separate line with the participle modifying it.

The car having gone, we walked to town.

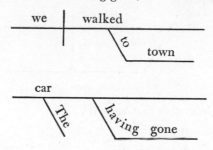

THE OBJECTIVE INFINITIVE. Place the entire objective infinitive construction on a stilt with a vertical line between the direct object and the infinitive.

He asked me to play the piano.

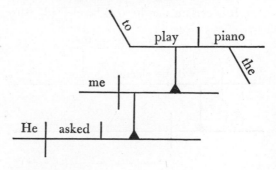

THE COMPLEX SENTENCE.
Noun clause. Place the noun clause on a separate line raised on a stilt above the point in the independent clause where it functions. Place the subordinating conjunction above the noun clause.

That he speaks well is obvious.

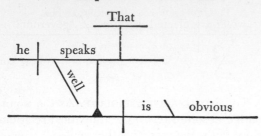

The man whom I know is very tall.

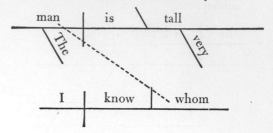

The Major converses with whoever is present.

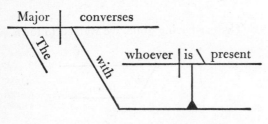

The house where he was born is a museum.

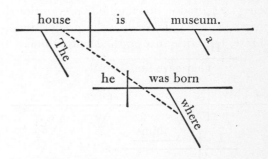

John says that he will come.

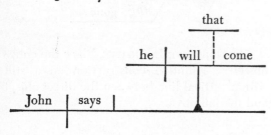

She bought a dress that fits her.

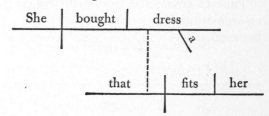

It is certain that he will be elected.

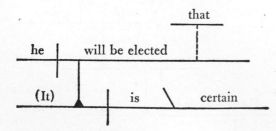

The car in which we rode is a coupe.

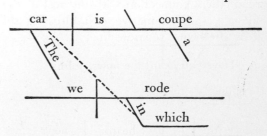

Adjective clause. Place the adjective clause on a separate line from the independent clause, and link the adjective clause to the independent clause by a dotted line from the relative pronoun to the word the clause modifies.

Adverbial clause. Place the adverbial clause on a separate line below the independent clause, with a subordinating conjunction on a dotted line from the dependent clause to the word modified in the independent clause.

Because he will not wait, he will lose his money.

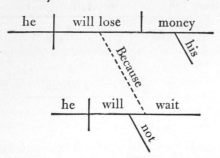

He ran more swiftly than I did.

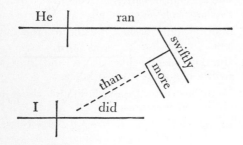

THE COMPOUND SENTENCE. Place the co-ordinating conjunction on a dotted line between the two independent clauses.

The vase was dropped, but no damage was done.

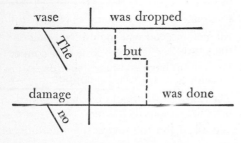

Buy this radio, or I shall sell it to Joe.

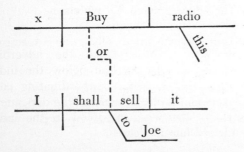

SIMPLE SENTENCES FOR ANALYSIS

1. The box contained twenty matches.
2. Send the remittance to our office.
3. Thayer is the treasurer.
4. A discount will be granted under those conditions.
5. The mayor, planning a safety campaign, sought the aid of the public.
6. The campaign began last month and proved a huge success.
7. Reducing fatalities was the aim of the campaign.
8. During the month fifty lives were spared by the careful motorists.
9. A new highway was built to relieve traffic congestion.
10. The highway had four lanes and no intersections.
11. The engineers promoted safety by banking the corners scientifically.
12. To prevent excessive speeds, the police enforced a speed limit.
13. Guessing the next move, my opponent maneuvered his men on the board to avoid a trap.
14. Soon I made an error of judgment and lost the game.
15. Pushing into the wilderness, we soon lost sight of civilization.
16. For six days we did not come to a single human habitation.
17. On the seventh day a trapper appeared and courteously shared his food with us in his rude shack.
18. His fare was venison, cooked well.
19. To keep our directions more easily, we followed the river for fifty miles.
20. Hungry and cold, we emerged from the forest near the Canadian border.
21. These botanists, loving flowers well, studied them assiduously.
22. In the low valleys I found many new species hidden from the casual eye.
23. These specimens they took home.
24. Other botanists have known flowers well but have not loved their beauty.
25. Planting seeds by mid-summer will yield abundant harvest.
26. By picking flowers each day, you increase the production of each plant.

27. To frighten us, the pirates hoisted a black flag.

28. We replied by sending a volley across their bow.

29. The fight soon began and lasted into the night.

30. Battling with fury, we drove them to their ship and escaped with no loss.

31. The little child ran along the road begging money from us.

32. We could not resist the childish appeal.

33. Soon we passed an ancient temple built by the Romans.

34. Deeply impressed, we admired its remarkable state of preservation.

35. Its statuary was beautiful and hardly touched by time.

36. Initials of many tourists were written around the base of each column.

37. Former emperors had occasionally taken marble slabs from the walls to ornament their own temples.

38. Despite these desecrations the temple kept its original grace and dignity.

39. Here was the huge ruin of a mighty stadium.

40. The Coliseum is still an inspiring sight for the tourists.

41. The committee awarded me a bronze medal.

42. Jones, chairman of the committee, congratulated every contestant.

43. The ceremony having ended, the audience went home quickly.

44. Bill, why did you go to the convention?

45. The board asked me to go and paid my expenses.

46. Then the committee on nominations elected me secretary of the association.

47. They also wanted me to be treasurer but did not insist.

48. The committee knowing my desires, my name was not mentioned again.

49. The railroad reserved me a lower berth.

50. Making the reservation fortunately was not difficult.

51. The ticket agent, a friend of mine, got me the reservation without delay.

52. I wish to go by plane on the next trip.

53. Saving a few hours in that way, I can transact more business.

54. The ten breeds being timed, the greyhound proved to be the fastest dog.

55. Running for short distances, the greyhound can defeat the race horse.

56. Over long distances the horse, being larger and stronger, has superior speed and stamina.

57. Many people believe the jackrabbit to be the fastest animal.

58. In a straight course the greyhound can overtake the jackrabbit swiftly.

59. The cheetah, a jungle animal trained to hunt, can probably exceed the swiftest greyhound in speed.

60. The cheetah, a native of Asia and Africa, is a member of the cat family.

61. Built for quick dashes, it can catch the antelope.

62. Hunting silently like a cat and running swiftly like a dog, it is a killer.

63. To the instructor I spoke hesitantly about my ideals and dreams.

64. In old age, shorn of strength, the veteran athlete did not lose courage.

65. From the workers in the fields sounds of merriment could be heard.

66. Keats, a youthful genius, was a target for hostile criticism.

67. My father bought me a beautiful red dress.

68. Slender and graceful, he appeared a prince in disguise.

69. Clear and true were the notes of the carillon.

70. All men of good will should lend their aid to the cause.

71. Wishing to have company, she forced me to go with her.

72. The notes of the bugle having sounded, the first rank began its charge.

73. We asked Jim to provide the entertainment.

74. The manuscript, carelessly written, was returned to its author.

75. The editor granted me more time to complete the manuscript.

76. The salesman tried selling an expensive product.

77. Making no sales, he soon became weary.

78. Taking him from his former position, they made him a district manager.

79. The promotion gave him a larger salary and pleased him immensely.

80. The rumor spreading this morning is a libel on our candidate.

SIMPLE, COMPLEX, AND COMPOUND SENTENCES FOR ANALYSIS

1. Explain our reasons to whoever asks.
2. Where have you put the book that was on the table?
3. Anyone who reads the newspapers can follow current events.
4. All who enter these doors must expect labor and hardship.
5. Few who take these tests can pass them.
6. The territory in which we landed was inhabited by cannibals.
7. The sonnets of Wordsworth which are found in this book are beautiful.
8. The airplane from which we leaped crashed in the swamp.
9. If she had realized her mistake, she could have rectified it.
10. The tyranny that has enslaved our people must be ended.
11. Bill decided to leave school, but Tom preferred to continue his studies.
12. Having graded the papers, the professor strode from the classroom.
13. Because he studied diligently, he was not dreading the examination.
14. When I whistled to the dog, he stopped and looked back.
15. By entering his name late, he avoided paying his fees.
16. He waited until the fire had been extinguished.
17. Although he is my friend, I am suspicious of his motives.
18. During the night we labored assiduously to complete the job.
19. Shylock asserted that Antonio owed him a pound of flesh.
20. I have never seen anyone who could equal John's record.
21. Send me the latest news that reaches you from Brazil.
22. If he knew the truth, he would stop the game immediately.
23. It is clear that you have not followed the course of events.
24. Guy refused to play tennis, but his friend Al was captain of the team.
25. Lacrosse has been played by the Indians for many years.
26. We might have known that you would object.
27. The Finger Lakes, which lie in the beautiful valleys of central New York, attract many tourists each year.
28. The man who should have sent me the car is holding a conference.
29. We enjoy a long walk while the dew is on the grass.
30. One of my friends once left a dollar in a library book.
31. If you exercise frequently, you probably have good health.
32. Because the sentence was answered incorrectly, the answer was heavily underscored in red ink.
33. In spite of his father's influence, he did not retain his position.
34. My roommate said that he wanted to borrow my tuxedo.
35. I am a midget, but my brothers are very tall.
36. He waited until the walks had been cleared.
37. Defiantly he waved the club over his head, but his friend merely laughed.
38. Walking home through the drifting snow was very enjoyable.
39. When he called last night, I told him that I had decided to go home.
40. With great care he packed his parachute.
41. One pastime of the idle is collecting shells.
42. I see no reason for believing this doctrine.
43. The rumor is that a break in market prices is imminent.
44. The broker that whispered the rumor to me has commanded great respect in the past.
45. The regulation that all sales must be cash may avert a sharp decline.
46. Stripping top soil from millions of acres was the result of ignorance.
47. To catch trout, drop your line in a running stream.
48. All summer we have been looking for a house to rent.
49. The printer should have been enraged by the manuscript, which was covered with blots and emendations.

50. The minstrel boy slung the harp over his shoulder and went to the wars.

51. Feeling tired, Jack dropped the oars and drifted with the current.

52. After trying in vain to attract our attention, the little dog trotted away.

53. After Joe was elected to office, his manner became insufferable.

54. The rumor that we pay our athletes is utterly false.

55. Every athlete who plays on our teams is primarily a scholar.

56. We do not even provide jobs for those who play football for us.

57. We believe that students should come to college to study.

58. Football should be played for the sport it gives to the players.

59. Rattling along the road in his ancient car, Tom was enjoying himself.

60. Borne up by the waves, the cask approached the shore.

61. Being frightened by a large dog, the tramp raced for the nearest tree.

62. Whoever buys a dog should give it excellent care.

63. If a dog receives attention, it will probably be happy and healthy.

64. Our landlord would not rent an apartment to anyone who had a baby.

65. A shortage of supplies has hampered our work this year, but that shortage may soon be a thing of the past.

66. Bring your textbook to class when you come tomorrow.

67. The plane in which we traveled was built by Lockheed.

68. This new plane will fly faster than previous planes of any make.

69. It is possible that both our candidates will be elected.

70. Discuss this matter with the friends whom you trust.

71. When you write, mention the name of the pilot with whom we rode.

72. On request he resigned, but he refused to stop fighting for his ideals.

73. That he fought well cannot be disputed, even though he lost.

74. The sergeant under whom we drilled was a severe taskmaster.

75. He could talk faster than I can, but I did not always listen.

76. Though he was satisfied with our work, he kept drilling us every day.

77. One day he asked me to drill the squad.

78. Because I had never given commands, I refused.

79. He then made me platoon leader and forced me to take command.

80. The loyal fans gave him a new car in appreciation of his services.

81. Bowed with grief, he slowly left the room.

82. Soon gaining control of himself, he returned with a jaunty air.

83. The conditions under which we conducted the experiment were not ideal.

84. Proving our contention was not easy.

85. Scientists who had not studied our evidence were highly skeptical.

86. Despite all the criticism our theory has lasted extremely well.

87. We hope that soon it will be a scientific law.

88. Gaily whistling as he walked, the postman neared the house.

89. The novel which we read contains a stimulating theme.

90. The narrative is told very well, but the characterization is very weak.

91. After reading a book, a student should make a précis of its contents.

92. It is good practice to write a paragraph every day.

93. To write fluently, one must write frequently.

94. Even though you do not have genius, you still may learn to write clearly.

95. By taking us through a dense wood, the guide confused us.

96. We could not find our way at night.

97. The tolerance that comes from experience will deepen your character.

98. The conclusion you have reached does not do credit to your mind.

99. By walking every day, I maintain good health.

100. The diagrams which you have been making illustrate your ability to analyze a sentence and also demonstrate that you will

understand the basic structure of any sentence which you write.

D. *Applying Grammatical Principles*

Many studies of the writing of college freshmen indicate that certain errors tend to recur over and over in the work of those who lack proficiency as writers. This section deals with these errors. Some have to do with the relationship of sentence elements, others with improper usages that leave the thought incoherent. A careful study of the following section should help you recognize and avoid these errors in your own writing.

1. GRAMMATICAL AND LOGICAL COMPLETENESS

In constructing sentences, aim first at completeness. Although any one sentence will convey only a small part of the thought of the whole composition, this segment should be both grammatically and logically complete. A sentence should not leave a reader asking questions about it. The word-groups *Roy being my brother*, *If Roy goes*, and *Since Roy left for college* all raise questions: What about Roy's being your brother? If Roy goes, what? If you know the preceding sections of this chapter, you will see what

is wrong. The first example contains a participle instead of a verb—and only verbs make statements about a subject. Although each of the other examples contains a noun and a verb, it also includes a subordinating connective, indicating the dependence of the group of words on something else—and a sentence must be complete in itself. The following rule, therefore, is very important.

3. Do not treat a fragment as a sentence.

Violation of this rule is called the *period fault*, for it involves cutting off by a period a fragment—such as a phrase or other modifier, an appositive, part of a compound predicate, or a dependent clause—that should be attached to the independent clause. Usually the error can be remedied by employing the proper punctuation—often by using a comma instead of a period, sometimes by omitting the punctuation altogether. At any rate, an analysis of the fragment will show that the word-group is not a sentence and that a period is incorrect. If the fragment is of sufficient importance, it may be made into a sentence by changing the verbal to a finite verb or by omitting the subordinating connective. The following examples illustrate the period fault and methods of correcting it.

PERIOD FAULT	EXPLANATION	AS CORRECTED
In an old dilapidated outfit and battered hat. He sat on the wharf and gazed at the water.	The prepositional phrase modifies the subject *he;* it belongs logically with the main clause.	In an old dilapidated outfit and battered hat, he sat. . . .
Being of hardy stock and of simple habits. He lived to a ripe old age.	The participial phrase modifies the subject of the main clause; it should be attached to the main clause.	Being of hardy stock and of simple habits, he lived. . . .
I saw him an hour ago. *Standing by the road and trying to thumb a ride.*	The participial phrase modifies the direct object *him* and should be attached to the main clause.	I saw him an hour ago standing by the road. . . . *or* I saw him an hour ago. He was standing. . . .
He threw the ball to first. *And then rushed towards third to back up the third baseman.*	The italicized element is part of a compound predicate, not a clause.	He threw the ball to first and then rushed. . . .

I feared he would not come. *Because he had a dozen excuses when I asked him.*

The italicized clause is dependent; it modifies the verb of the main clause.

I feared he would not come because he. . . .

Although it may seem silly. I dislike walking under a ladder.

The italicized clause modifies the verb *dislike;* it should be attached to the main clause.

Although it may seem silly, I dislike. . . .

I gave the book to Uncle Jack. *My father's youngest brother.*

The italicized element is in apposition with *Jack.*

I gave the book to Uncle Jack, my father's. . . .

An incomplete sentence sometimes may result from the omission of a single word. This indicates how closely you need to check your sentences to see that they are correct and logical. As a writer, you must remove every obstacle to a reader's understanding of your precise meaning. One way to do this is to take enough care with each sentence to see that every term necessary for clarity is included. Note especially the rules that follow.

4. **Do not omit a word needed to complete a comparison.**

4a. Do not omit *than* or *as* in double comparisons.

Incomplete: This melon is as sweet, if not sweeter, than the other.
[The omission of *as* after *sweet* makes the sentence read, "This melon is as sweet than the other." Say, ". . . as sweet *as,* if not sweeter *than.* . . ." Better still is ". . . as sweet as the other, if not sweeter," for if you complete the first part of the comparison, usage allows an ellipsis in the second part.]

4b. Do not omit *other* after *than* or *as* in a comparison of one of a group with all the others in the group.

Incomplete: Nancy is more studious than any girl in her class.
[Nancy is a member of the class. It is illogical to say she is more studious than herself. Say, ". . . more studious than any *other* girl. . . ."]

4c. Do not omit part of a comparison.

Incomplete: I like to play tennis with Earl better than Dwight.
[Say, ". . . better than *with* Dwight" or "better than Dwight does."]

Incomplete: This lake is prettier.
[Prettier than what? Add the term that completes the comparison.]

4d. **Do not omit a term when doing so leads to a comparison of unlike things.**

Incomplete: The wages of a mason are higher than a carpenter.
[Omission of *wages of* or *those of* after *than* forces a comparison between wages and carpenter. Only like elements may be compared.]

5. **Do not omit a term that is needed to make the thought clear and logical.**

5a. **Do not omit part of a verb phrase in a compound involving different times.**

Incomplete: He said only what others have and are saying.
[Omission of *said* after *have* makes the sentence read, ". . . what others have saying."]

5b. **Do not omit the second verb when different numbers are referred to.**

Incomplete: He is in his room and his roommates in the library.
[By trying to make one verb do the work of two, the writer makes his sentence say, ". . . his roommates *is* in the library." Since one subject is singular and one plural, two verbs are necessary.]

5c. **Do not omit a verb necessary in a series to give logical meaning.**

Incomplete: She is eighteen, brown eyes, and a pretty nose.
[As the sentence has only one verb, all three elements are subjective complements; the sentence says, "She is brown eyes; she *is* a pretty nose." Say, "She *is* eighteen and *has* brown eyes. . . ."]

5d. Do not omit one preposition when in two prepositional phrases idiomatic usage requires different ones.

Incomplete: He was both familiar and afraid of the lake.
[The idiom is *familiar with*. Because one preposition tries to do the work of two, the sentence reads, "He was familiar *of* the lake."]

5e. Do not omit a necessary preposition in references to time and other constructions.

Incomplete: Autumn I used to go nutting.
Incomplete: When I was eighteen I graduated high school.
[Say, "*In* autumn" and "graduated *from*."]

5f. Do not omit the connective *that* in constructions where the omission will mislead a reader.

Incomplete: We saw the crews, appearing around the bend, were racing neck and neck.
[The omission of *that* after *saw* leads a reader to assume that *crews*, rather than the whole clause, is the object; then when he comes to *were racing* he has to revise his idea. To prevent this momentary confusion, say, "We saw *that* the crews. . . ."]

5g. Do not omit the subject and predicate in a dependent clause when the subject is not the same as in the main clause.

Incomplete: While hurrying down town the noon whistle blew.
[This error is called a *dangling elliptical clause*. As it stands, the sentence says the whistle blew while *it* was hurrying down town. Say, "While I was. . . ."]

5h. Do not omit the subject of the main clause following a dependent clause.

Incomplete: When he was thirteen went to sea as an apprentice.
[As the sentence stands, the subject of the verb is the clause *When he was thirteen,* but this does not make sense. Say, ". . . *he* went to sea. . . ."]

(See *Workbook,* Exercise 29.)

2. CORRECTNESS AND CORRECT RELATIONSHIP OF SENTENCE ELEMENTS

To be effective, sentences must have unity and coherence. This means that all the parts must be expressed according to correct current usage and that they must show the proper grammatical and logical relationship. Subject and predicate must agree, pronouns must agree with their antecedents, modifiers must be grammatically and logically related to the words they modify, connectives must show the precise relationship of the elements they join, and clauses must be logically related in thought. The difference between a writer who throws together sentence elements without regard to their congruity and one who builds good sentences is much the same as the difference between a carpenter who can do a rough job of nailing together pieces of lumber and an expert cabinetmaker or between a cook who throws together a few ingredients and makes a dish that is barely edible and one who can prepare a dish to please a gourmet.

Verbs

A verb is the heart of a sentence. It gives a sentence life, changes a group of words from a mere impression into an idea, and helps all the other parts of the sentence perform their functions properly. Using the correct form of the verb is essential, therefore, for sentence effectiveness. Most errors involving verbs come from a writer's failing to distinguish between transitives and intransitives in a few somewhat similar pairs of verbs or from his using the wrong principal part, the wrong number, or the wrong tense.

6. Use the correct form of the verb.

College students rarely use such expressions as "I *see* him go down the street" for a past action, or "I *seen* him coming," He *throwed* me the ball," "I *taken* my brother along," and "I *brung* my raincoat today"; but they frequently do use the wrong principal part of some verbs. As the verbs **that** cause most trouble are few, a good procedure is to memorize the whole list (see page 64) and practice using the correct forms until correct usage becomes a habit. Note especially the difference between the past tense and the past participle, and use only the past participle after an auxiliary verb (such as *be* and *have*).

> The game *has begun* (not *has began*).
>
> The dog *has bitten* three people (not *has bit*).
>
> I *have been chosen* leader of the troop (not *have been chose*).
>
> The bird *has flown* out of the cage (not *has flew*).
>
> Everyone *has gone* to the game (not *has went*).
>
> My hat *is worn* out (not *is wore*).

Especially troublesome to many students are the somewhat similar pairs *lie—lay, rise—raise,* and *sit—sat.* Confusing these verbs results from failure to distinguish between transitive and intransitive verbs. The first verb in each pair is intransitive,[1] the second transitive; that is, *lie, rise,* and *sit* do not take an object, whereas *lay, raise,* and *set* do (except that *set* in one or two idiomatic usages is intransitive: *the sun sets; a dye sets*). The best way to learn to use these verbs correctly is to practice using them in sentences till it becomes a habit to use them correctly.

(See *Workbook*, Exercise 29.)

7. A verb agrees with its subject in number and person.

Agreement in person offers almost no problem in English sentences. In the matter of agreement in number, however, occasions for errors are numerous. First, there is the problem of identifying the subject and making the verb agree with it rather than with some other element in the sentence. Then there are problems involving the proper form of the verb with compound subjects, collective nouns, indefinite and relative pronouns,

[1] It may help you to remember this if you associate the *i*-verbs—*lie, rise, sit*—with the initial *i* in *intransitive.*

and in a number of special usages. Attention to the following rules will prevent virtually all errors you are likely to make in the agreement of subject and predicate.

7a. An intervening modifier does not affect the agreement of verb and subject.

Be especially careful to choose the correct form of the verb when the subject is followed by a parenthetical phrase or clause introduced by such terms as *together with, accompanied by, as well as,* and *with* or by a prepositional phrase beginning with *of.* See that the verb agrees with the subject and not with some substantive in the modifying element.

> Each *member* of the three classes *was* to report.
>
> *Eileen,* together with her uncle and two brothers, *is coming.*
>
> The *general,* accompanied by several aides, *has arrived.*
>
> An innocent *man* as well as those who were guilty *was punished.*
>
> *John* with others of the squad *is* out for practice.
>
> *This* no less than other laws *needs* to be tested.

7b. In sentences beginning with the expletive *there,* the verb agrees with the subject, but in those beginning with the expletive *it,* the verb is singular.

> There *are* many *birds* in this wood. There *is* a *cardinal* nesting here.
>
> It *is* the children making all the noise.

7c. A verb agrees with the subject, not with the subjective complement.

Errors under this rule are likely to occur when a parenthetical element comes between the subject and verb and the complement is in a different number from the subject.

> The *cause* of the scarcity *is* the many strikes that prevent shipments.
>
> The *reason* for his poor showing *is* too many activities and too heavy a load.

7d. A plural verb is used with a compound subject joined by *and*.

Errors under this rule usually occur in questions or other constructions when the predicate comes before the subject. Of the following examples, the first two are regular; the others illustrate sentences in which errors are most likely to occur.

Blossoms and fruit *appear* together on orange trees.

Courage, intelligence, and obedience *are* traits of these dogs.

Are chemistry and physics both required on this curriculum?

How *have* the depression and the upheaval of war affected education?

In this sale *are* included a Buick sedan, a Dodge truck, and a Ford roadster.

7dx. Exceptions to rule *7d* are the following: A singular verb is used (1) when the subject consists of a series, each of which refers to the same person or thing and (2) when each part of a compound subject is considered individually, especially if a singular adjective accompanies the noun.

A soldier, a statesman, and a great American *is* dead. [One person]

The flag-waver, the professional patriot, the "hundred-percent" American *is* not always the best citizen. [All terms refer to one person.]

My friend and colleague *is* about to address you. [One person]

The secretary and treasurer *is* not here. [One person; if different persons hold the two offices, *repeat the article* and use a plural verb.]

Every freshman and sophomore *is* required to take the test.

7e. With compound subjects joined by *or, nor, but,* or the correlatives *neither—nor, either—or,* and *not only —but also,* the verb agrees with the nearest word in the subject.

John or I *am scheduled* for that event. [This is correct, but because of the awkward sound, most writers prefer to recast the sentence:

Either John is scheduled for that event or I am.]

Joan, you or Sally *is* to go. [Or, Sally or you *are* to go.]

Not Wells but his lawyers *are* to blame.

Neither Homer nor Dante *is* much *read* by college students.

Neither Homer nor the Greek dramatists *are* much *read* by college students.

Daffodils and tulips or a weigela *is* best for that corner.

7f. With the indefinite pronouns *all, any, none,* and *such,* use a singular verb if the group is considered as a unit, and a plural verb if the members of the group are considered individually.

All *are* to take cameras. All *is* as we left it.

None *is* free from some prejudice. None *are* yet ready to start.

7g. With collective nouns, use a singular verb if the group is thought of as a unit and a plural verb if the members of the group are thought of individually.

The family *is* living in Vermont. The family *are* scattered for the summer.

The class *is* agreed on one point. The class *are* of several opinions.

Because of the awkward sound of a plural verb with a collective noun, many writers prefer such constructions as "Members of the class are scattered" and "Members of the class are of several opinions."

7h. A verb in a dependent clause that is introduced by a relative pronoun— *who, which, that*—agrees with the antecedent of the pronoun.

In applying this rule, first identify the dependent clause and then the antecedent of the relative pronoun.

He is the one *man* in his group who *acts* on his principles.

He is one of those *men* who *act* on their principles.

The following special usages regarding agreement between noun and verb are exceptions to the rule that the two must agree.

7i. **A literary title, whether singular or plural in form, takes a singular verb.**

"The Killers" *was written* by Ernest Hemingway.

Romeo and Juliet is about a family feud and young love.

Henry James's *The Ambassadors is* a novel of character.

7j. **Sums of money and measurements considered as a unit take a singular verb.**

Twenty dollars *is* my highest bid. [But, The dollars *were* stacked in a pile.]

A thousand miles *is* a long trip. [But, The miles *seem* endless.]

Six times nine *is* fifty-four. [The plural form is also correct.]

Seven ninths *is* the correct answer.

7k. **Certain nouns that are plural in form but singular in meaning take a singular verb.**

Such nouns as *billiards, measles, molasses, mumps,* and *news,* although plural in form, take a singular verb. Also nouns ending in *-ics* when they denote a science or art or its subject matter take a singular verb, although when they denote activities or practices, they take a plural verb.

Measles *is* considered a disease of childhood.

Economics *is* required on this curriculum.

The economics of those advocating this policy *need* revision.

Mathematics *is* one of my subjects; physics *is* another.

(See *Workbook,* Exercise 29, **C.**)

8. **Use the correct tense in expressing time.**

Most errors in tense result from employing the wrong tense in a sequence and from failing to observe certain conventional usages. For the normal functions of tenses, see page

65. The following rules cover most problems involving tense.

8a. **Use the present tense to state something that is true at all times.**

In connection with this rule, note that in indirect discourse, a permanent truth stated in a subordinate clause should be in the present tense.

Clyde argued that Texas *is* larger than Alaska, but upon checking up, he found that Alaska *has* more than twice the area of Texas.

8b. **Distinguish between the past tense and the present perfect tense.**

Use the past tense if the action expressed by the verb was completed at some past time, but if the action was performed in the past and continues into the present time, use the present perfect tense.

Incorrect: His novels deal with how people *have lived* in frontier days. [Since frontier days were in the past, the present perfect is not correct. Omit *have.*]

Incorrect: To this day war *was* the method of settling international disputes. [As war is still the method, use the present perfect "war *has been* the method."]

8c. **Observe the proper sequence of tenses in main and subordinate constructions.**

With the exception already noted of permanent truths, the verb of the main clause governs the tense of the whole sentence. The tense of a phrase or dependent clause must show unmistakably whether the action it expresses takes place before, at the time of, or after that expressed by the verb of the independent clause. It is especially important to watch the sequence of tenses in indirect discourse.

Mark said that he *had studied* his lesson. [Action expressed in dependent clause was prior to that of main clause. Direct discourse: *I studied.*]

Mark said that he *was studying.* [Action in dependent clause is concurrent with that of main clause. Direct discourse: *I am studying.*]

Mark said that he would study his lesson. [Action in dependent clause subsequent to that of main clause. Direct discourse: *I shall study.*]

Before I met him I *had heard* that he *is* a good athlete. [Action expressed in dependent adverbial clause is subsequent to that of main clause; action in dependent noun clause is in present tense because still true.]

8d. Observe proper tense sequence with participles and infinitives.

The verbals do not follow the rule stated in the preceding paragraph. Regardless of the tense of the verb, a *present participle* is used to indicate action taking place *at the same time* as that of the verb; a *present infinitive*, action taking place *at the time of or after* that expressed by the verb; and a *perfect participle* or *perfect infinitive*, action taking place *before* that expressed by the verb. The chief errors under this rule are (1) using a present participle instead of a perfect participle when the action expressed by the participle is prior to that of the verb (*Hearing* [instead of *having heard*] the news, I left for home) and (2) using a perfect infinitive with the past tense of the verb (I hoped *to have written* [instead of *to write*] you earlier).

Pronouns

Students are especially prone to make mistakes in the use of pronouns; yet most errors involving pronouns can be avoided if you will take pains to see that each pronoun you use points unmistakably to the word for which it is substituting (called its *antecedent*) and is in agreement with it.

9. Except for indefinite pronouns, a pronoun must have a definite, specific antecedent.

In using pronouns, make your aim not merely to be clear, but to be so clear that a reader cannot possibly misunderstand your meaning. Such an aim requires that the reader should never be puzzled over the exact word for which the pronoun is substituting. If this word is omitted altogether or

may be one of several words, or if instead of a pronoun's substituting for one word, it tries to substitute for a general idea as expressed in a whole clause, in all probability a reader will have difficulty understanding your meaning.

9a. A pronoun should not refer to a vague or implied antecedent.

Do not use a pronoun unless you can point to a specific substantive and say, "This is the word for which the pronoun is substituting." The following examples illustrate violations of the rule.

ANTECEDENT

IMPLIED: As I have always liked physics, I have decided to become *one*. [No antecedent for *one* being present, a substantive (*a physicist*) must be used instead of the pronoun.]

IMPLIED: Drama flourished in inn yards. People going there enjoyed *them*. [To what does *them* refer? Perhaps to *inn yards*, but the writer apparently is dealing with drama, and *drama* in the sense here used and *dramas* are not the same. Say, ". . . enjoyed plays."]

VAGUE: *They* often have accidents at this crossing. [Who? Say, "Motorists. . . ."]

VAGUE: *It* says on the bulletin board that the meeting is canceled. [Say, "A notice . . . says. . . ."]

9b. A pronoun should refer unmistakably to *one* antecedent.

If a sentence contains two words, either of which might be the antecedent, repeat the noun or recast the sentence.

She took the dresses from the hangers and laid *them* on the bed. [*Them* may refer to *dresses* or *hangers*. Instead of *them*, repeat the noun meant.]

He told John *he* would make an A in the course. [A reader cannot know whether the speaker or John is meant. Say, "He told John of his intention. . . ." or, "He told John, 'You will make. . . .'" or, "He told John the latter. . . ."]

In an attempt to remedy the defect in a sentence like the last example, a student sometimes resorts to the device of putting the noun in parentheses after the pronoun, but this only calls attention to the fact that he knows the reference is vague, yet is too lazy or indifferent to revise the sentence.

9c. A pronoun should not refer to a remote antecedent.

The dock lay in ruins. The boards were warped, and many were gone. Two ancient boats, their keels rusting away, lay abandoned. *It* showed years of disuse. [Although no singular noun lies between the pronoun and its antecedent, the two are so far apart that the noun should be repeated or the sentences revised. An exception is a whole paragraph in which each sentence begins with a pronoun referring to the subject of the first sentence.]

9d. A relative pronoun should not be separated from its antecedent by a word that might be mistaken for the antecedent.

His wife was operated on for appendicitis at the Good Samaritan Hospital, *which* suddenly attacked her Sunday. [What attacked her—the hospital?]

The price of the tickets will be $1, *which* may be obtained at the door. [Are dollars given away at the door?]

She asked me to find an electrician for her brother *who* knew how to repair a television set. [Omit *for* and transfer *her brother* to after *find.*]

9e. The pronouns *this, that,* and *which* should not refer to a whole idea expressed in a preceding clause.

Even good writers sometimes violate this rule, but because of the many occasions on which the reference is obscure, the rule is a good one to observe. It is especially important to follow the rule when the preceding clause contains a noun that might be mistaken for the antecedent.

After tramping the hills all day without lunch, we ate a big dinner, *which* was not to be wondered at. [Apparently the dinner is not to be wondered at, though the writer doubtless intends the pronoun to refer to the whole idea expressed in the main clause. The simplest

revision is to substitute *and no wonder* for the final clause.]

The stream, a month ago only a trickle, now filled its banks, carrying with it cacti and an occasional animal. *This* surprised us. [Is the antecedent *stream, animal,* or the whole idea expressed in the first sentence? Say, "The change surprised us," or better, "We were surprised to see the stream . . . now filling. . . ."]

9f. A pronoun should not refer to an antecedent occupying a subordinate position in a construction.

In Mrs. Gaskell's *Mary Barton* she deals with social conditions in Manchester. [Say, "In *Mary Barton,* Mrs. Gaskell deals. . . ."]

As I grabbed for the dog's collar, *it* ran down the street. [Say, "As I grabbed for its collar, the dog ran. . . ."]

9g. When two or more pronouns in a construction refer to different antecedents, avoid using the same pronoun.

This book deals with the elements of chess. *It* says *it* is not difficult to learn *it.* [The reference of the various *it's* is vague. Say, "This book, which deals . . . , says the game is not difficult to learn."]

10. Use a pronoun instead of such indefinite terms as *said* and *name.*

I bought the books you recommended and read *same.* [Say, ". . . read *them.*"]

The effect of *said* ruling is to work a hardship on commuters. [If the antecedent is clear, say, "*this* ruling"; if it is not, say, "The effect of the ruling that students may not have cars is. . . ." Such terms as *said* and *same* as here used are correct only in legal and technical papers.]

11. A pronoun agrees with its antecedent in person, gender, and number.

PERSON. Because nouns normally are considered to be in the third person, a pronoun substituting for a noun ordinarily is in the third person. This is true also when the antecedent is an indefinite pronoun used in an impersonal sense, except that in a strictly formal style, some writers prefer to repeat *one* throughout a construction instead of using the personal pronoun. The chief matter to keep in mind regarding agreement of person is to avoid shifts from one person to another without an excellent reason, and if a shift is essential, to see that the reader is warned by a proper transitional element. The following examples are correct.

John lent me *his* pen. Sue has *her* book. The dog lost *its* collar.

Look at that tree. *It* is loaded with fruit.

Everyone has *his* chores at the camp.

One took *his* (or *one's*) duties seriously in those days.

GENDER. If the sex of the antecedent is known, pronouns that are inflected for gender should be in the same gender as the antecedent. In English usage, when an antecedent may refer to either sex or both sexes, or if the sex is not known, the masculine pronoun is used. Unless special emphasis is required, do not say *"him or her"*: *him* is used conventionally for either sex when the antecedent is an impersonal singular pronoun or a noun of common gender. In employing relative pronouns, use *who* when referring to a masculine or feminine antecedent and *which* when referring to a neuter antecedent. *That* may be used with any gender.

Every American must now face *his* responsibilities.

Each of you will bring *his* manual to the laboratory next day.

A servant is worthy of *his* hire.

At slumber parties, each girl wears *her* prettiest pajamas.

The *man who* located the ore is a geologist.

There is the *woman who* bought the painting.

Martin returned the *book, which* I now hope to read.

Martin returned the *book that* I had lent him.

This is the *dog that* chased the cat.

NUMBER. Only a few matters need special emphasis concerning agreement in number.

11a. A pronoun referring to two or more antecedents connected by *and* is plural.

Lois and Norma left *their* tennis rackets in my room.

John and I brought *our* bathing suits.

The *freshmen and sophomores* have the pool to *themselves* today.

11b. A pronoun referring to two or more antecedents connected by *or, nor, either—or, neither—nor,* or *not— but* is singular.

George or Ralph left *his* hat in my room.

Not Mr. Jackson but Mr. Phillips sent *his* car for us.

Neither the *president nor* the *secretary* made *his* report.

11c. A pronoun referring to a singular general noun or to a singular indefinite pronoun is singular.

No one likes *his* motives questioned.

Everyone will bring *his* camera on the trip.

Every student there should express *his* opinion.

Each of the carpenters had *his* own tools with *him.*

Neither of the players won *his* event.

A person shows *his* manners by *his* actions at a game.

11d. A pronoun referring to a collective noun is singular or plural according to whether the group is thought of as a unit or as individuals.

The *orchestra* will gives *its* first concert Tuesday evening.

The *orchestra* filed in slowly and took *their* seats.

12. The case of a pronoun is determined by the way the pronoun functions in its clause.

The case of a pronoun is not determined by the case of the antecedent, but by the function of the pronoun in its own construction. If a pronoun acts as a subject or subjective complement or is in apposition with the subject or subjective complement, it is in the *nominative* case. If it is a direct object, the object of a preposition, in apposition with an object, or is the subject of an infinitive, it is in the *objective* case. If it modifies a noun or pronoun or modifies and precedes a gerund, it is in the *possessive* case.

12a. The case of a relative pronoun is determined by the function of the pronoun in its own clause, not by the case of its antecedent.

To determine the case of the relative pronoun, isolate the clause that the pronoun introduces, and then analyze the clause to see what function the pronoun performs in the clause.

I must see *who* is going. [Although the dependent clause is the direct object of the sentence, *who,* as the subject of the dependent clause, is in the nominative case.]

Tell *whoever* is there to come. [The explanation is the same as in the preceding example.]

We talked with the officer *who* reported the accident. [Although *officer,* the antecedent of *who,* is in the objective case because it is the object of a preposition, *who,* as the subject of the dependent clause, is in the nominative case.]

Give the message to *whomever* the chairman appointed secretary. [*Whomever* is in the objective case because it is the direct object of *appointed.*]

Give the message to *whoever* is secretary. [*Whoever* as the subject of the dependent clause is in the nominative case.]

Whom are you waiting for? [*Whom* is the object of the preposition *for,* and is therefore in the objective case.]

Who do you think will be elected? [*Who* is in the nominative case because it is the subject of the independent clause, "Who will be elected?"]

12b. In comparisons employing *than* or *as,* the case of the pronoun following the connective is determined by the function of the pronoun in the elliptical clause.

Stanley is older than *she* [is].
The dog likes her better than [it likes] *me.*

You go to town as often as *we* [go].
The children mind us as well as [they mind] *them.*

In such sentences, *than* and *as* are connectives that join an independent and a dependent elliptical clause. Completing the elliptical clause makes it easy to determine the correct case form.

12c. In appositional constructions, a pronoun takes the case of the word with which it is in apposition.

The secretaries—*you* and *I*—will frame the proposal. [Nominative case—in apposition with the subject.]

They are a happy couple, *he* and *she.* [Nominative case—in apposition with the subjective complement.]

Father took the girls—Doris, Edith, and *me*—to camp. [Objective case—in apposition with the direct object.]

Let's *you* and *me* go to the game. [The subject is *you* understood. *Let's* is a contraction for *let us, us* being in the objective case because it is the direct object. Since *you* and *me* are in apposition with the direct object, they too are in the objective case.]

12d. When two pronouns are joined by *and, or,* or *nor* to form a compound, both pronouns are in the same case.

The main problem in connection with this rule has to do with the personal pronoun, especially with the first person. Because as a child you were drilled to say "Dora and I" or "Philip and I," your pen betrays you into writing, "Uncle Mark took Dora and I to dinner." No one ever writes, "Uncle Mark took I to dinner"; it is only when Dora or Philip are along that the grammatical car runs off the road. Be especially careful with compounds after the prepositions *between* and *but.* Again the impulse to use *I* instead of *me* may lead you to write "Between you and I" or "No one is here but Tim and I," whereas the rule that the object of a preposition is in the objective case requires "Between you and me" and "No one is here but Tim and me."

12e. A pronoun functioning as the subject or subjective complement of an objective infinitive is in the objective case.

The captain ordered *them* to attack. (Subject of infinitive)

They asked Sue and *her* to be tellers. (Subject of infinitive)

He always tried to be *himself*. (Subjective complement of infinitive)

Evelyn took Peter to be *me*. (Subjective complement of infinitive)

This is an exception to the rule that subjects and subjective complements are in the nominative case. You will not err in writing such sentences as the first example; but in compounds, such as the second example, you need to keep the rule in mind.

13. Do not use an intensive pronoun in constructions calling for a personal pronoun.

He called for Henry and *me* (*not* "Henry and *myself*").

14. A pronoun is in the possessive case when it modifies a noun or pronoun or when it modifies and precedes a gerund.

His sweater is torn.

I like *his* pitching.

Ann likes tennis. She watched *Joan's* and *my* playing today.

The policeman did not like *their* driving.

Be certain that the word introduced by the pronoun is a gerund, for if it is a participle, the pronoun is in the objective case. In the third example above, for instance, it was the playing that Ann watched. If her interest had been in the players, the sentence would read, "Ann likes us. She watched Joan and me playing tennis today."

14a. The possessive case of personal, relative, and interrogatory pro-

nouns never requires an apostrophe —yours, his, hers, ours, theirs, whose, its.

If you write "It's a warm day," the sentence means "It is a warm day"; the possessive pronoun *its* is properly used in the sentence "The dog lost *its* bone." Similarly, "Who's there?" means "Who is there?" but the sentence "Whose hat is this?" contains a true possessive form.

(See *Workbook*, Exercises 30, 31, and 32.)

Modifiers

Modifiers are either adjectival (when they modify a substantive) or adverbial (when they modify a verb, an adjective, or an adverb). Errors in the use of modifiers result usually from failure to distinguish between adjectives and adverbs or to employ the correct form in comparisons.

15. Distinguish between adjectives and adverbs and use the part of speech proper to the literary level.

People whose speech is on a substandard level of usage (see p. 169) constantly confuse adjectives and adverbs in such sentences as "He worked *good* today" and "She is *some* better." Even college students often confuse *real* and *really*, *sure* and *surely*, and *most* and *almost*. As the list of words that cause most trouble is short, a good procedure would be to copy the list and use the words in sentences until correct usage becomes habitual.

ADJECTIVES	ADVERBS
good	well
most	almost
real	really
some	some, somewhat
sure	surely

Errors occur also through the use of an adverb instead of an adjective after a linking verb (see p. 69). To avoid making this error, remember that if the modifier limits or describes the subject, it should be an adjective, and if it qualifies the verb, it should be an adverb.

16. Use the proper degree in comparisons.

Do not compare a word that by its nature cannot be compared (see p. 68 f), and do not form a comparison from the comparative degree (as *worser, worsest,* from *worse,* the comparative degree of *bad*).

Because the distinction between the comparative and superlative is beginning to break down in comparisons of two objects, many reputable grammarians now countenance the use of the superlative in such sentences as "Of the two hats, I like the blue one *best*"; but in formal style it is desirable to preserve the distinction between the use of the comparative when comparing two objects and of the superlative when comparing more than two.

She is the *taller* of the two. She is the *tallest* of the group.

My raincoat is *older* than yours. My raincoat is the *oldest* of those here.

17. Use the correct form of the adjective.

17a. A noun functioning as an adjective is ordinarily singular (*freshman* class, *student* affairs, *senior* sports), although when the sense requires it, a plural form is used (*men* students).

17b. When a noun has a corresponding adjective (*agriculture—agricultural, industry—industrial*), the adjective and not the noun must be used to modify a substantive.

The *agricultural* experiments have been promising.

The *industrial* output is up this quarter.

17c. A demonstrative pronoun functioning as an adjective agrees in number with the word it modifies (*this* kind, *these* kinds; *that* group, *those* groups).

17d. A personal pronoun functioning as an adjective agrees with its antecedent, not with the substantive it modifies.

Tom invited *his* friend to the game.
Tom invited *his* friends to the game.
They invited *their* friend to the game.

ADVERBS IN DOUBLE NEGATIVE CONSTRUCTIONS. Because the adverbs *hardly* and *scarcely* have a negative meaning, it is incorrect to use them with *not*. Say, "I can hardly hear him" or "I cannot hear him," not, "I cannot (or can't) hardly hear him."

USAGE OF ADVERBS HAVING TWO FORMS. Many adverbs have two forms (*loud—loudly, quick—quickly, slow—slowly*). In the United States, it is customary in ordinary speech to use the form without the *-ly*, but in formal style, those ending in *-ly* are still preferred.

(See *Workbook*, Exercise 33.)

Connectives

Conjunctions and other connectives are minor yet highly important parts of a sentence, for they not only join sentence elements and sentences but show the relationship between them. A writer who cares whether his thought is clear must therefore exercise judicious care in choosing the proper connective to convey his exact meaning.

18. Use the proper connective to show the precise relationship between sentence elements.

The most common fault in the use of connectives is employing one that does not suggest the relationship the writer intended. Sentence elements are co-ordinate or subordinate. Obviously to use a subordinating connective when the elements are co-ordinate or a co-ordinating connective when one element is subordinate to another makes for incoherent thought. There are, moreover, many possible relationships among both co-ordinate and subordinate elements; and use of the wrong connective prevents a reader from perceiving the relationship the author has in mind. The following examples illustrate the proper use of connectives.

Co-ordinating Connectives

ADDITION:	He is hot *and* tired.
	The wind is sharp *and* piercing, *and* leaden clouds hide the sun.
	He is *not only* hot *and* tired *but also* hungry *and* thirsty.
	The wind is sharp *and* piercing; *moreover* it looks like snow.
ALTERNA-TION:	It is going to rain *or* snow.
	Either he was famished *or* the dinner was especially good.
	Neither Edith *nor* her sister is able to be here.
CONTRAST:	The sun is shining, *but* the wind is cold.
	She is wearing a dress that is pretty *but* old-fashioned.
	The sun is shining; *however*, the wind is cold.
REASON:	He will not get to the coast, *for* his car is falling apart.

Subordinating Connectives

CAUSE:	He is here *because* we invited him.
	Since he is invited, we must make him welcome.
	As we must leave now, we shall not see him.
COMPARI-SON:	He sings better *than* he plays.
	He runs *as* fast *as* any member of the team.
CONCES-SION:	*Although* we had a heavy line, we were defeated.
CONDI-TION:	*If* he had more patience, he would play better chess.
	Unless I am mistaken, your diagnosis is right.
	Provided we support him, he will win.
CONTRAST:	*Whereas* Jean prefers physics, I prefer French.
DEGREE:	*As much as* I admire him, I cannot vote for him.
	Go with us *as far as* Sue goes.
MANNER:	He left *as though* he hated to go.
	He acted *as if* he believed our story.

PLACE:	I hid the candy *where* you cannot find it.
	Who knows *whither* the clouds have sped?
PURPOSE:	He left *so that* I could get my studying done.
	He drove by *in order that* we could go home with him.
RESULT:	We were *so* tired *that* we went no further.
TIME:	He will come *when* he can have the car.
	Come to my room *as soon as* your class is over.

18a. Use a connective that shows the proper relationship between coordinate elements.

A co-ordinating connective joins like elements—two or more related nouns, two or more verbs, modifiers, clauses. It should also indicate the precise relationship between the elements it joins. What you mean will usually determine your choice of connective, but by their very nature, some elements will require a specific connective. To say, "He is tired *but* thirsty" is illogical. The most common error in choosing a connective is the use of *and* to join clauses that suggest contrast, alternation, or reason, as in the following examples.

I went to the game, *and* I did not enjoy it because of the poor fielding. [The sense of the second clause indicates that *but* is the proper connective.]

He came yesterday, *and* he had to be here last night for the game. [Since the second clause seems to state a reason for the action expressed in the first clause, the proper conjunction is *for*.]

This novel is about colonial days, *and* I like it very much. [As the second clause apparently is meant to state a result or consequence, the proper connective should be *therefore*.]

Another common error is using a subordinating connective to join clauses that have a co-ordinate relationship, as in sentences like the following: "In the second half our team encountered the stiffest opposition, *although* our rivals were playing inspired ball." *Although* denotes concession, but the second clause is not concessive. Rather, it states a reason; hence the connective should be *for*.

18b. Use the proper connective to show the relationship of subordinate elements.

The commonest errors in denoting the relationship between unequal elements are employing the co-ordinating conjunction *and* and employing subordinating connectives that do not show the relationship meant, as the following examples illustrate.

A storm was coming up, *and* we started for the shore. [The action in the second clause is not an addition to that expressed in the first clause, but a result. Say, "As a storm . . . , we started. . . ."]

Nancy was pleased *when* she won the scholarship. [The relationship between the clauses is not one of time but of cause; the connective should be *because*.]

While Aunt Kate is well, she cannot stand crowds and noise. [Say, "*Although* Aunt Kate. . . ."]

Another sort of error results from trying to make a preposition do the work of a subordinating conjunction, as in the following examples.

Use the oars *like* I showed you. [Instead of *as* or *in the manner that*]

I cannot go *except* you bring me home. [Instead of *unless*]

18c. Use the proper connective to mark transitions between sentences.

Connectives usually employed to denote transitions are conjunctive adverbs (see page 70). The following examples illustrate the wrong choice of such terms.

We plodded along all night. In the morning, *however,* we were very tired. [The condition expressed in the second sentence is obviously a result of the action expressed in the first sentence; hence the connective should be *therefore*.]

The sophomores were eager for the class games to begin. *On the other hand,* the freshmen were also eager. [The connective used indicates contrast, but as both freshmen and sophomores were eager, the connective should be *moreover* or *besides* to show addition. Here, since the state of each group is the same, it would be better to write, "Both the sophomores and freshmen were eager. . . ."]

The wind was biting, and the dry snow, driven by the wind, cut our faces. The sun, *moreover,* was shining brightly. [As the second sentence suggests contrast, the transitional word should be *however*.]

Prepositions

Errors in the use of prepositions are confined normally to employing the wrong preposition in idiomatic expressions and to adding a superfluous preposition in such constructions as, "Where is he *at?*" and "Where is he going *to?*" An idiom is a usage that has no specific grammatical basis, but is an accepted way of saying something. The only way of being certain to use the correct idiom is to observe the practice of good writers and speakers. For examples of correct use of prepositions, see pages 165 ff. (See *Workbook,* Exercise 33.)

3. POSITION OF SENTENCE ELEMENTS AND LOGICAL SENTENCE PATTERNS

To write sentences that are clear and effective, you must take pains to see that closely related sentence elements—such as a pronoun and its antecedent—are in agreement, that they are so placed in the sentence that their relationship to other elements is unmistakably clear, and that they show by their arrangement and pattern a logical relationship of ideas.

19. Place modifiers so that they do not modify the wrong element.

ADJECTIVES. In the placement of single adjectives, errors are likely to occur only in constructions in which several adjectives modify a substantive and one of the adjectives is a noun functioning as an adjective (called a *nounal adjective*). The error here results from placing a regular adjective before the nounal adjective, so that the former seems to modify the nounal adjective rather than the substantive.

ADJECTIVE

MISPLACED: I found a *red* woman's pocketbook today. [Say, "woman's red pocketbook."]

MISPLACED: Attend our sale of *defective* men's umbrellas. [Say, "men's defective umbrellas."]

MISPLACED: He was wearing a *dilapidated* child's hat at the picnic. [Say, "child's dilapidated hat."]

ADVERBS. An adverb normally comes after a verb it modifies and precedes an adjective or adverb. The position of the adverb may effect materially the meaning of a sentence. Watch especially the position of the following adverbs, for if they are placed improperly, they may give an altogether different meaning to your sentence from what you intended: *almost, even, ever, hardly, merely, never, not,* and *scarcely.* Note, for instance, how the meaning changes in the following sentences with the different positions of the adverbs.

Only I went to the picnic. [No one else went.]

I went *only* to the picnic. [I went nowhere else.]

I went to the *only* picnic. [There was just one picnic.]

All students are *not* careless. [No student is careless.]

Not all students are careless. [Some are careful.]

PHRASES AND CLAUSES. Misplacement of an adjectival or adverbial phrase or clause is almost certain to result in an obscure or illogical sentence. The normal position of such modifiers is next to the word they modify. If you can produce a better sentence by separating the elements, that is your privilege, but it is also your obligation to see that they are near enough to each other to make their relationship unmistakable to a reader. Guard especially against allowing a term that the phrase or clause might logically modify to

intervene between it and the word to which it refers. In the following examples, the misplaced modifiers are italicized, and carets indicate their proper position in the sentences.

He came ∧ just as we thought we had finished *with a dozen more jobs.*

∧ We visited the house where Emerson lived *last summer.*

I number among my friends ∧ an actress who retired to raise four children, *two schoolteachers, and the proprietor of a grocery store.*

The conference ∧ will be held in Detroit, *which will consider problems of industrial areas.*

His novel ∧ is about forest fires *which I like best.*

19a. Do not write a sentence that contains a squinting modifier.

A modifier placed between two elements either of which it may modify is called a *squinting modifier* because it seems to look two ways at once. The error is serious in that a reader cannot know to which element the modifier refers, although there may be a wide difference in meaning according to the way the sentence is interpreted. The squinting modifiers are italicized in the following examples.

He asked me *when the match was over* to go to his room. [Place the italicized clause at the beginning or the end of the sentence according to the meaning intended.]

He wrote that if he could not collect *within a week* he would turn the matter over to a lawyer. [A comma after either *collect* or *week* will clarify the meaning, but if the writer meant that he would turn the matter over to a lawyer within a week, a better revision is to place the phrase at the end of the sentence.]

(See *Workbook,* Exercise 34.)

19b. Do not write a sentence that contains a dangling modifier.

A modifier that does not bear a direct relationship to some word present in the sentence is called a *dangling modifier.* The term is also applied to a modifier that from its position seems to refer to a word it cannot logically modify. Modifiers to watch under this rule are participial phrases, adjectival and adverbial infinitive phrases, and prepositional gerund phrases. Elliptical phrases and clauses also lend themselves to the error. Be especially watchful when writing sentences in which a verbal phrase precedes the main clause, for if the agent of the action or state expressed in the phrase is not the same as the subject of the main clause, the phrase will dangle. To test for a dangling modifier, read the subject of the main clause and then the modifying phrase. If the two are not logically related, remedy the error either by turning the phrase into a dependent clause or by revising the main clause so as to make its subject the same as the agent of the action or state expressed in the phrase.

Dangling Modifiers

PARTICIPIAL PHRASE: *Carrying our bags*, the campus came into view. ["We," not the campus, carried the bags. Say, ". . . , we came in sight of the campus."]

Walking fast from the inn, the lake was soon reached. [A reader has no way of guessing the agent of the action expressed in the phrase. Certainly the lake did not walk. Say, ". . . , we (he, John, Joan) soon reached the lake."]

He stopped to telephone, *causing him to miss the bus*. [This is a dangling participial phrase of result. What or who caused him to miss the bus? Recast the sentence: "Stopping to telephone caused him. . . ."]

INFINITIVE PHRASE: *To receive compensation*, the accident must occur while the insured is in the plant. [Here one can guess the writer's meaning, but such short cuts produce at least a sloppy style. Say, ". . . , the one insured must sustain the accident while he is. . . ."]

To register late, a fee of $10 must be paid. [Again this is understandable, but why force a reader to supply the missing term? Say, ". . . , a student must pay. . . ." or better, "Late registration requires a fee of $10."]

GERUND PHRASE: *By winning the finals at Newport*, the cup came to America. [A reader cannot tell who or what is the agent of the action expressed in the phrase. Certainly it was not the cup. Say, ". . . , the American team brought the cup home" or "Smathers brought the cup to America."]

After scanning the skies, the game was postponed. [Who scanned the skies? Say, ". . . , the umpire postponed the game."]

PREPOSITIONAL PHRASE: *At the age of four* both his parents died. [Although the idea is absurd, a reader has to interpret this as meaning that the parents died when they were four. Say, ". . . , he became an orphan" or "When *he was* four, both his parents died."]

ELLIPTICAL CLAUSE: *After college*, the army claimed him. [Did the army attend college? Say, "After he finished college, ..." or "After college, he entered the army."]

When a girl, the lake was her chief joy. [Say, "When she was a girl. . . ."]

Do not eat pork *unless well cooked*. [Who or what must be well cooked? A reader can guess, of course; but why not say, ". . . unless it is well cooked"?]

Some participial phrases are used so frequently in a general sense that they are not considered dangling modifiers, although the word to which they refer is omitted from the sentence. The following examples illustrate commonly accepted usage:

Speaking of sports, our teams have done well this year.

Glancing at politics, several observations may be made.

Assuming your postulates, the outcome is certain.

(See *Workbook,* Exercise 38B.)

20. Avoid excessive co-ordination.

The practice of placing all ideas, major and minor alike, in co-ordinate clauses simply by adding one to another is a heritage from grammar-school days. To achieve a mature style, you must use care in the choice of connectives and must show by the structure of your sentences the proper relationship between the ideas. In the sentence, "I bought a house, and it was painted gray," the color of the house is given as much prominence as the purchase. Since ordinarily the purchase of a house is important, this idea should be in the independent clause, and the less important idea should be in a dependent clause or phrase, "I bought a house, which was painted gray." If an article were dealing with the color gray, the sentence might read, "I bought a gray house." The following is an example of excessive co-ordination carried to the extreme:

> We lived on a lake, and I learned to swim before I was six, and we used to have a rowboat, and I was accustomed to get in it and row all about the inlet, but one day when I was about nine I was in the boat, and a sudden squall came up, and the boat turned over, and I would certainly have drowned, but I was a good swimmer and was able to swim to shore.

In this passage, although the punctuation is correct and the ideas are arranged in logical sequence so that a reader can follow the thought easily enough, the monotony of the style, resulting from excessive co-ordination, repels a reader, and no indication is given of the relative importance of the various ideas.

21. Avoid a sequence of overlapping dependent clauses.

Akin to the fault of excessive co-ordination is that of excessive subordination—joining a succession of dependent clauses by *that, which,* or *who,* as in the following example:

> In the two-mile race, I watched Benson so closely that I failed to notice that two other runners who had not been written up were staying so close to me that they could pass me the moment that I began to weaken.

Here again, though the thought is clear, the repetitious style becomes monotonous.

22. Avoid "upside-down" subordination.

The term *upside-down subordination* is applied to a sentence in which a relatively unimportant part of the idea is expressed in the main clause, and the principal idea is relegated to a phrase or dependent clause. The following examples illustrate this error:

> Jane glanced at the clock, it being 8:20. [The time, not the act of looking at the clock, is important. Say, "Glancing at the clock, Jane saw that it was 8:20."]
>
> He exerted a burst of speed, forging ahead in the last few yards to win. [Winning the race is important, the burst of speed incidental. Say, "Exerting a burst of speed, he forged ahead. . . ."]
>
> Congress passed the bill, which caused widespread anxiety in the country. [Two errors mar this sentence: (1) The antecedent of *which* is obscure, and (2) the anxiety of the country is the important idea. Say, "The bill which the Congress passed caused. . . ."]

23. Avoid mixed constructions.

Once you have begun a sentence, keep to the pattern you have selected instead of making an illogical shift to some other pattern. Of the examples of mixed constructions given below, the first two are the obvious result of carelessness; but students who normally write well sometimes make errors of the sort exemplified in the last three sentences. The "something-is-when" and "reason-is-because" errors result from using an adverbial clause as a subjective complement in constructions that require a noun clause.

> We came on a hovel which by gathering fir boughs to lie on *we could sleep comfortably.* [Apparently the insertion of the long phrase deflected the writer from what he started to say. As it stands the sentence reads, "We came on a hovel which we could sleep comfortably."

Change the italicized clause to read, "we made into comfortable sleeping quarters."]

We surveyed that tract, an area, as we found on compiling our figures, *was five thousand acres*. [Forgetting that he began with an appositive, the writer shifts to a clause (*an area was five thousand acres*) that has no logical relationship to the main clause. Changing *was* to *of* or *that comprised* will remedy the fault.)

Success in football is *when a player receives his letter*. [A subjective complement must be a substantive or an adjective, not an adverb. Say, "Success . . . is apparent when. . . ."]

The reason I was late was *because I had a flat tire*. [The error is the same as in the preceding sentence. Change *because* to *that* or recast the sentence.]

I had to go home was the reason I was absent. [An independent clause is made the subject of the verb. Recast the sentence: "I was absent because I had to go home."]

24. Use parallel structure for sentence elements that have similar grammatical functions or that express co-ordinate ideas.

Shifts in the structure of parallel elements are always confusing to a reader. Parts of the sentence that should be expressed similarly are main clauses, dependent clauses, phrases, and single words that perform similar functions. Keep this rule in mind especially in writing a compound construction or a series. The following examples illustrate faulty parallel structure.

For exercise I swim, box, and *a game of tennis is always welcome*. [The first two items in the series are verbs, the third an independent clause. Change the clause to a verb and object: *and play tennis*.]

He is a writer, a painter, and *plays a musical instrument well*. [The first two items in the series are nouns, the third a verb and object. Make the last element a noun also: *and a musician*.]

He went slowly and *with reluctance* to the bench. [Make the modifiers parallel by changing the prepositional phrase to an adverb: *reluctantly*.]

It is my favorite sport and *which I never tire of watching*. [Here the writer attempts to make an independent and a dependent clause co-ordinate. The omission of *and* will improve the sentence, but a better revision is to change *and which* to *one*, thus making the second element an appositive.]

25. Place correlative conjunctions before similar or parallel elements.

In using correlative conjunctions (*both—and, either—or, neither—nor, not only—but also*), place each before a similar element: if one precedes an infinitive, make the other precede an infinitive; if one precedes a verb, make the other precede a verb, and so on.

CORRELATIVES WRONGLY PLACED: He *neither* feared man *nor* beast. [Say, "He feared neither man nor beast."]

This decision should *not only* be considered by students *but also* by citizens of the town. [Place the first correlative before *by students*, which is parallel with *by citizens*.]

(See *Workbook*, Exercise 35.)

26. Do not insert a lengthy element between parts of a construction that have a close relationship. As a rule, avoid any split construction that does not make for clarity, ease, and effectiveness in the sentence.

Do not split co-ordinate elements, a verb phrase, a comparison, or an infinitive to insert any term unless you can show that the result makes for sentence effectiveness; and never split one of these constructions to insert a long phrase, a long clause, or a series of elements. Make it a rule also to avoid inserting a lengthy element between the subject and predicate or between the verb and its complement. With a little care you can arrange all the parts of a sentence properly without resorting to awkward split constructions.

AWKWARD SPLIT CONSTRUCTIONS

CO-ORDINATE ELEMENTS: *As it was a rainy day*, the match was postponed, *as the courts were wet*. [Say, "As it was a rainy day and the courts were wet, ..." or recast the sentence.]

A VERB PHRASE:

He is, *or so his sister told me,* going. [Say, "He is going, or so. . . ." or better still, "His sister told me he is going."]

The ship was, *so far as the eye could perceive,* hardly moving. [Place the italicized clause at the beginning of the sentence.]

A COMPARISON:

October was colder, *although you may not believe this because of the few cloudy days,* than it was last year. [Place the italicized clause at the beginning or end of the sentence.]

AN INFINITIVE:

Football players find it hard to, *day after day, week after week, for three months,* go out for practice. [Place the italicized elements at the end of the sentence.]

It is hard to, *while you wait for your girl to get ready,* be relaxed and at ease. [Place the italicized clause at the beginning or end of the sentence.]

The insertion of an adverb or even a short adverbial phrase between an auxiliary and the main verb is conventional practice in English: The ship was *hardly* moving. It is also normal English usage to split an infinitive in such constructions as the following: We hope to *more than* double our output this month. The insertion of an adverb before the participle in the passive and perfect infinitive constructions is not considered a split infinitive: to have *recently* conferred; to be *quite* decided.

27. Do not make a needless shift in subject, type of discourse, voice, mood, or tense.

One of the most obvious signs of immaturity in a writer is needless shifting from one subject to another, from the active to the passive voice, from one mood to another, and the like. Remember that any unnecessary shift in your point of view will tend to break up the logical pattern of your sentences and will lead to incoherence and disunity. Once you have established a pattern for a sentence or for the whole composition, keep to that pattern.

27a. Avoid a shift of subject between clauses when the agent for both is the same.

In compound and complex sentences if the agent performing the action is the same in both clauses, do not be afraid to repeat the subject. If the subject is a personal pronoun and the subject of both clauses is the same, use the same person for both. The following examples illustrate unnecessary shifts in the subject:

We climbed the mountain, and the *city* lay stretched out below us. [Say, ". . . and saw the city. . . ."]

As *you* come to a break in the hedge, a *glimpse* of the river greets you. [Say, ". . . , you catch a glimpse of the river."]

We children had our chores to do, and *you* had better do them. [Say, ". . . , and we were held strictly accountable for doing them."]

27b. Avoid a shift in the form of discourse in a sentence.

If you begin the report of a conversation by using indirect discourse, do not change to direct discourse without a clear warning to your reader. Note, for instance, the awkwardness of the following sentence:

My roommate has spent the week discussing whether the band will be a good one and what dress shall I wear? [Say, ". . . and what dress she will wear" or ". . . discussing such matters as 'Will the band be a good one?' and 'What dress shall I wear?' "]

27c. Avoid an unnecessary shift in voice.

Unless there is an imperative need to shift, keep the same voice in consecutive clauses within a sentence. Guard especially against shifting from the active to the passive voice in the second clause of a compound sentence.

We went to Portage Lake for our picnic, and a good time was had by all. [Say, ". . . , and we all had a good time," or better still, "We all had a good time on our picnic at Portage Lake."]

We stayed on deck all day, and the sea was

scanned for flying fish. [Say, ". . . and scanned the sea. . . ."]

27d. Avoid an unnecessary shift in mood.

Before you begin to write, give some thought to the mood you will use in your composition, and having decided, keep to that mood, whether it is the indicative, the imperative, or the subjunctive. Be especially careful to keep the same mood in passages containing instructions on how to do something. In the following brief passage, for instance, note how the writer shifts from the imperative mood in the first sentence to the indicative in the second and third sentences, back to the imperative in the fourth sentence, and then to the subjunctive in the fifth.

> Take a knife and cut the limb off square without damaging the bark. I use a sharp knife for this. Next I cut the bark all round about two inches from the end of the limb. Next beat the bark with the back of the knife. You should not beat too hard lest you break the bark. [Say, "Using a sharp knife, cut the limb off square. . . . Next, cut the bark . . . and beat the bark gently with the back of the knife so as not to break the bark." You might, of course, use the indicative mood throughout. The point is: Having decided on one mood, do not shift to another.]

27e. Avoid an unnecessary or illogical shift in tense.

The same caution as was given concerning mood is necessary concerning tense: once you are committed to using the past or the present tense, keep to that tense. Note how confusing is the following report because the writer shifts so often from one tense to another.

> We took our seats while the guides explain the origin and history of the caverns. The lights were then turned off, and we are in total darkness. We hear someone singing "Rock of Ages." Next, the lights came on gradually. A guide tells us to follow him. After a considerable distance, we came to what looked like a large room.

(See *Workbook,* Exercise 36.)

E. Writing Effective Sentences

A person learning to play golf or tennis, to swim, bake, sew, carpenter, paint, play a musical instrument, or to do anything that requires practice in order to gain proficiency, first learns the rudiments and then works patiently and persistently to acquire ease and expertness. The process is the same for you in learning to write. You work first for correctness and clarity; then as you become competent in those matters, you begin to work for sentence effectiveness. To that end you will need to study the methods and analyze the style of good writers and to expend much critical labor in combining, deleting, sifting, rephrasing, and trying this or that position and construction; but meanwhile you can increase the effectiveness of your sentences by learning to apply some of the elementary principles considered in this section.

28. Make your sentences emphatic.

Every writer recognizes the need to make his sentences emphatic. Perhaps in the past you have resorted to the use of exclamation points, underlining, and other artificial means to emphasize what you considered important. Now you are ready to discard these devices of immaturity and to gain emphasis by the arrangement of sentence elements.

28a. Gain emphasis by the use of periodic sentences.

Sentences are classed as *loose* and *periodic* on the basis of the arrangement of sentence elements. A *loose sentence* is one in which the important ideas come near the beginning and less important ones—those that merely add details—at the end. A *periodic sentence* is one in which the modifying phrases, dependent clauses, and other minor elements come first, and the main idea is stated at the end. Because the normal pattern of English sentences is subject → verb → complement, any inversion of this order will serve to emphasize the element not in its normal position. The following examples illustrate the difference between loose and periodic sentences.

LOOSE: He leaped the chasm, though he had to exert great effort.

PERIODIC: With a tremendous effort he leaped the chasm.

LOOSE: He avoided attention by inching towards the door and keeping behind those entering.

PERIODIC: By keeping behind those entering . . . , he avoided attention.

28b. Gain emphasis by placing important ideas at the beginning or end of the sentence.

The most emphatic positions in a sentence are at the beginning and the end, especially the latter. To gain emphasis, therefore, reserve these positions for important ideas, and tuck connectives, absolute constructions, and minor modifiers within the sentence, as is done in the following examples.

His place, *he said,* was with his troops.

His advice, *to be sure,* was not of the best.

The way to handle this problem, *in my estimation,* is to submit it to a vote.

The tree, *standing in splendid isolation,* is a familiar landmark.

28c. Gain emphasis by climax.

In a series, place the items in the order of ascending importance—the least important first, the next important next, and so on.

WEAK: The boys at this camp are taught to cook simple dishes, to get along socially with other boys, to swim, to make campfires, and to tie various knots.

EMPHATIC: At this camp the boys are taught to tie various knots, to make campfires, to cook simple dishes, to swim, and to get along socially with other boys.

WEAK: The book is boring, long, and poorly bound.

EMPHATIC: The book is poorly bound, long, and boring.

28d. Gain emphasis by repetition.

Because as a child you were warned against monotonous repetitions in your writing, you may consider it bad form to repeat any word or construction in a sentence. Certain kinds of repetition do make for monotony, but the right sort of repetition is one of the most effective ways to gain emphasis. Such statements as Lincoln's "of the people, by the people, for the people" and Lowell's words about Garfield, "The soil out of which such men as he are made is good to be born on, good to live on, good to die for and to be buried in" gain in emphasis by the repetitions. For an excellent example of effective repetition, study the whole of Lincoln's Gettysburg Address or consider the following passage from St. Paul's letter to the Corinthians:

Though I speak with the tongues of men and of angels, and have not charity, I am become as sounding brass, or a tinkling cymbal. And though I have the gift of prophecy, and understand all mysteries, and all knowledge; and though I have all faith, so that I could remove mountains, and have not charity, I am nothing. And though I bestow all my goods to feed the poor, and though I give my body to be burned, and have not charity, it profiteth me nothing. Charity suffereth long, and is kind; charity envieth not; charity vaunteth not itself, is not puffed up, . . . thinketh no evil; rejoiceth not in iniquity, but rejoiceth in the truth; beareth all things, believeth all things, hopeth all things, endureth all things. Charity never faileth: but whether there be prophecies, they shall fail; whether there be tongues, they shall cease; whether there be knowledge, it shall vanish away. . . . When I was a child, I spake as a child, I understood as a child, I thought as a child; but when I became a man, I put away childish things. For now we see through a glass, darkly; but then face to face: now I know in part; but then shall I know even as also I am known. And now abideth faith, hope, charity, these three; but the greatest of these is charity.

This passage from St. Paul's letter illustrates two kinds of repetition: the use of the same word over and over and the use of the same structure throughout a sentence or even a whole passage—both effective ways of gaining emphasis when they are skilfully employed.

The best example of the repetition of sentence structure is the *balanced sentence*—one containing two parts, similar in structure and of about equal length, in which two ideas are compared or contrasted. The balanced sentence—once popular but not much used today—if constructed with care is an effective way of gaining emphasis.

> The mirth of Swift is the mirth of Mephistopheles; the mirth of Voltaire is the mirth of Puck.—Macaulay.

> Othello and Desdemona were different in almost every way. He was black; she was white. He was old; she was young. He knew only war and what pertained to war; she knew only such feminine matters as sewing and music.

(See *Workbook,* Exercise 37.)

29. Make your sentences concise.

After you have finished the first draft of your manuscript, weed out from your sentences padding, irrelevant items, and elements you included for their ornamental effect only or because you like the sound of the words. Conciseness is always effective, though to be concise you need not omit all rhetorical devices or write as if you were composing a telegram. In her narrative, "The Perfect Tribute," Mary Chapman Andrews says of Lincoln's writing the Gettysburg Address, that "he cut here and there an adjective, here and there a phrase, baring the heart of his thought, leaving no ribbon . . . of rhetoric." Make as your goal, sentences in which nothing pertinent is omitted and nothing irrelevant is included, in which you "bare the heart of your thought." In the following examples, elements that should be deleted are italicized.

> The prim little lady, *one of whose ancestors is said to have sailed with Captain Kidd,* motioned to the maid, *a gaunt, dour woman whose parents homesteaded in the Dakotas,* and told her to bring in the tea. [The italicized elements are certainly more interesting than

what is left, but in this sentence they have no possible relationship to the main idea.]

> GRAPES OF WRATH deals with tenant farmers who drift away from their farms in Oklahoma, *which is one of our leading oil-producing states.*

> We had a pleasant vacation last summer at White Lake, *near which is some excellent farming country.*

> I like my chemistry professor. He is always pleasant, and his lectures are clear. *Two of his children had mumps this winter.*

(See *Workbook,* Exercise 38.)

30. Avoid monotony by varying your sentence patterns.

A monotonous style is never effective; yet there are students who will employ the same sentence pattern throughout a whole passage or even an entire composition. A little study will suggest to you many ways of gaining sentence variety. An obvious way is to mix simple, complex, and compound sentences; another is to insert an occasional periodic sentence among loose ones. In adjective constructions, you may use a single adjective, a prepositional phrase, a participial phrase, or a clause (the *spired* church, the church *with the spire,* the church *having a spire,* the church *which has a spire*), and in adverbial constructions, you may use a single adverb, a prepositional phrase, or a clause (He dashed *quickly* into the wood; *With a burst of speed,* he dashed into the wood; He dashed into the wood *as fast as he could run*). You can vary the pattern of sentence beginnings, or use an appositive now and then instead of a dependent clause, or occasionally place an adjective or participle after the word it modifies instead of before. You may find it valuable to analyze a passage from the work of several authors and see what variations each uses for beginning sentences. For instance, in the first paragraph of the selection from Hardy's *Return of the Native* on page 341 of this text, the sentences in order begin as follows: with the subject, with an adverbial phrase, with a pronoun referring to the subject, with the verb of a dependent clause, and with an expletive. Again you may find it valuable to analyze frequently the entire sentence patterns of passages from several good writers to see what variations they employ in their sentences. Such a study will suggest to you many ways in which you can vary your own sentences in order to avoid monotony and maintain the interest of your readers.

31. Work consciously to achieve a pleasing style.

A beautiful style is certain to be an effective style. In our day simplicity is considered one element of beauty; hence modern authors avoid ornateness, high-flown rhetoric, overelaborate and highly figurative language. Another element of beauty is restraint. A heightened sentimentality or gushiness in writing or speaking is never pleasing. A third element of beauty is euphony— pleasing sounds. In every language certain sounds are considered pleasant, others unpleasant. In English, combinations of hard consonants and too many sibilants—s-sounds —are unpleasant; hence Tennyson, whose poetry is noted for its pleasing sounds, used to revise his verse to eliminate sibilants— "I must remove my geese," he would say.

In the process of composition the time to work for sentence effectiveness is during revision. With an outline of what you wish to say before you, write the first draft with your attention focused on the thought. Then with the ideas set down, direct all your critical faculties to the business of making what you have said effective and pleasing. If you find that your sentences are long and involved, see whether you have combined ideas that are not logically related. Here cut down a dependent clause to a prepositional, a verbal, or an appositional phrase, and a phrase to a single word; there strike out a modifying element that seems unnecessary; and in still another place, turn a dependent clause into a simple sentence. On the other hand, if the sentences are too short and choppy, consider

how you may combine some of them to form complex and compound sentences. You may also achieve variety within the sentences by beginning one with a modifying element— an adverbial phrase or clause or an adjectival modifier—and another with the subject; by employing inversion; and by alternating loose and periodic sentences. Make your aim to write so interestingly that once someone begins to read your manuscript, he will want to continue. To that end, use every resource a writer can employ—correctness, clearness, emphasis, conciseness, and variety. Then having made what you consider your final draft, read the manuscript aloud, paying attention to the sounds to see if the sentences read smoothly and easily and if the ideas seem to be expressed logically and clearly. In these ways you will be taking the first steps towards a pleasing and an effective style.

(See *Workbook,* Exercises 39, 40, 41, 42, and 43.)

F. Punctuation

A speaker relies on the tone in which he speaks, the stress he places on certain words, and pauses to convey his exact meaning. A writer has to substitute for these aids some device familiar enough to a reader to suggest where pauses are intended and where stress is needed, and the substitute on which he must chiefly rely is punctuation. Obviously, then, he must not use some private system of punctuation that he alone knows, but a system as familiar to his reader as to himself. Although usage in matters of punctuation is not uniform wherever English is written, and varies somewhat in different periods, the rules stated in the following sections are employed at the present time by virtually all writers who are careful in matters of style, and are enforced by publishers of books, learned publications, and magazines of literary quality. Some differences of usage will be found in newspapers and in magazines that affect a journalistic style, but these are minor and will be noted where the difference is sufficient to matter. The general tendency in modern practice is to employ less punctuation than in former times, but to be more consistent in the use of such rules as are the accepted practice.

THE COMMA

According to a number of studies, three fourths of all punctuation errors in the writing of college students are in the use of the comma. If using the comma correctly will reduce your errors in punctuation by three fourths, it seems obvious that it will repay you to give close attention to mastering these rules.

32. Use a comma to separate independent clauses that are linked by a co-ordinating conjunction—*and, but, for, or, neither, nor.*

It was a lazy October day, *and* in the still air not a leaf was stirring.

This is completely different from the original version, *nor* has it anything to do with the *Clair de lune.*

He sat in the shade all afternoon, *for* the day was too hot to work.

Let not your heart be troubled, *neither* let it be afraid.

In journalistic writing the comma is usually omitted between independent clauses, especially if they are short and have no internal punctuation, but in all formal writing it is regularly retained.

33. Use a comma to separate each item when three or more co-ordinate elements—words, phrases, or clauses—form a series without linking words between all of them.

Wooded hills, fields, roads, and lakes lay below us.

For breakfast we had *orange juice, poached egg on toast, and coffee.*

We have not decided whether to go *by car, by train, or by plane.*

He was one *who was aggressive without being offensive, who was calm without being phleg-*

matic, *who was friendly without being obsequious.*

In journalistic writing the comma is omitted between the last two items in a series, but as the omission often leads to ambiguity (*The flags were red, blue, yellow and white*—were there three flags or four?), the retention of the comma before the *and* is insisted on in all formal writing, except in connection with the name of a company (*Smith, Barney and Company* is correct). Note, however, (1) that if a co-ordinating conjunction is used between all elements in a series, the comma is omitted unless it is desired to emphasize each element (*Caesar came and saw and conquered; He was not gone, nor going, nor about to go*); and (2) that a comma does not separate *two* words or phrases joined by a co-ordinating conjunction (poor *but* honest, tall *and* straight).

34. Use a comma to separate consecutive adjectives that modify the same noun when the adjectives have a co-ordinate relationship.

Note that the adjectives must be co-ordinate—must have about the same degree of relationship to the substantive—for this rule to apply. If the final adjective is so closely related to the noun as to make virtually a hyphenated word, the adjectives are not separated by commas. A test for using the comma is to supply *and* between the adjectives: if the construction makes good sense with the *and*, include the comma. In the following examples, for instance, one might say "The gaudy *and* showy binding," but not "old *and* straw hat."

Note also that the final adjective is not separated from the noun by a comma.

The *gaudy, showy* binding detracted from the appearance of the book.

His *sharp, bright, bitter* epigrams appealed to his readers.

He wore a *tattered old straw* hat.

He was a *prominent public* official.

35. Use commas to set off nonrestrictive clauses and phrases.

A nonrestrictive clause or phrase is one that does not identify or limit the element it modifies, but merely gives added information about it. It could be omitted from a sentence without altering the meaning. Whether an element is restrictive or nonrestrictive is a matter not of grammar but of logic. If the word that is modified is something a reader identifies readily, as *Conrad Aiken, Grand Canyon, Boston, only brother,* the modifying phrase or clause is always nonrestrictive; but if the word modified is a common noun and is not already limited by some such word as *only,* a reader cannot know without other information whether the phrase or clause is restrictive or nonrestrictive; hence the punctuation must supply the information. For instance, in the sentence, "My blue tie, *which John is wearing,* was a birthday present," the commas tell us that the author has but one blue tie, and the clause merely adds the information that John is now wearing it. If he had more than one blue tie, no commas should be used, as the clause would then be needed to point out which tie was the birthday present.

In setting off a nonrestrictive element, be careful to use *two* commas, one at the beginning and one at the end, when it is inserted within the sentence.

> Conrad Aiken, *who is an American poet and short-story writer,* lived for many years in England. [The dependent clause is not needed to identify Conrad Aiken; it merely adds some information about him and is therefore set off by commas.]
>
> My only brother, *who served in the Korean campaign,* is an engineer. [If the speaker had more than one brother, the italicized clause would have to be restrictive to tell which one is the engineer; but as the engineer is an *only* brother, the clause merely adds a bit more information.]
>
> I must have a talk with Roger, *as we have a number of matters to discuss.* [The statement of the main clause is in no way affected by the adverbial dependent clause; hence the latter is nonrestrictive.]

> My brother John, *now living in Wheeling,* is going to be married. [As the name *John* identifies which brother is to be married, the phrase about where he is living is merely additional information.]
>
> The Grand Canyon, *in northern Arizona,* is one of nature's marvels. [It is not necessary to identify anything so well known as the Grand Canyon; its location is therefore only added information.]
>
> The mall needs a few more evergreens, *such as fir and spruce.* [The italicized phrase in no way limits *evergreens;* it merely offers examples of what sort of evergreens are meant.]

Note that if the clause is restrictive it is not set off by commas.

> The mason *who laid the stones* is a Swede.
>
> The book *that you borrowed* has to be returned to the library.

36. Use commas to set off an appositive element.

An appositive—a word that stands next to another and is its equivalent—is set off by two commas. (If it comes at the end of a sentence, it is of course separated by a single comma from the word with which it is in apposition.) Exceptions to the rule are (1) historical characters to whose names the descriptive phrase has become attached as part of the name, as *Charles the Bold, Peter the Great,* and (2) appositives that are used in a restrictive sense, as *my brother Joseph, the poet Frost, the term* Il Faut.

> My father, *Robert Browning Jones,* was named for the poet.
>
> The Grand Canyon, *one of nature's marvels,* is in northern Arizona.
>
> This letter is to my best friend, *Edwin French.*

37. Use commas to set off parenthetic elements.

Remember that a parenthetic element interrupts the main thought and that *two* commas are required—one before and one after the parenthetic element—unless the parenthetic construction comes at the beginning or end of the sentence.

37a. Use commas to set off additional elements in addresses, geographical locations, and dates.

When an address, a reference to a location, or a date contains more than one item, the various parts are separated by commas; but a comma is *not* placed between a preposition and the first element of the address or date. In journalistic style there is a tendency to omit the comma after the final item in the series, but this usage is not followed in formal writing. The following sentences are punctuated in accordance with formal usage:

Stephen Foster was born in Pittsburgh, *Pennsylvania,* in 1826.

She lives at 222 West Congress Street, *Tucson, Arizona,* but she is now in San Diego, *California.*

St. Louis, *Missouri,* and Memphis, *Tennessee,* are towns on the Mississippi River.

Stephen Foster was born on July 4, *1826,* in Pittsburgh.

Stephen Foster was born in July, *1826.*

At 11 a.m., *November 11, 1918,* the First World War officially ended.

Note, however, that a comma does not separate a single item from the rest of the sentence. The following are correct:

Stephen Foster was born in Pittsburgh in 1826.

She is staying at a hotel in Los Angeles.

37b. Use commas to set off an additional item in a reference.

A single item, however, is not separated from the rest of the sentence by a comma. The following sentences are punctuated correctly:

In *Hamlet,* II, ii, 255, you will find the reference you ask about.

In *Paradise Lost,* III, 30-40, Milton refers to his blindness.

You will find that quotation in *Hamlet.*

37c. Use commas to set off a noun used in direct address.

Is it true, *John,* that you have been to New Orleans?

Tell me, *Sue,* what you and Jane talked about.

37d. Use commas to set off introductory and directive elements and those modifying the whole sentence.

Well, I should not believe that if I were you.

Yes, I told him I would go.

No, there is no evidence to support such an assumption.

Surely, I shall try to oblige you.

There is a tendency to omit the comma with such words as *too, indeed, at least,* and *perhaps* when they have a close relationship to the whole sentence.

We had to procure supplies. Then *too* there was the problem of transportation.

Indeed I know the whole story.

At least wait till I get my raincoat.

37e. Use commas to set off transitional words and phrases.

You must, *however,* follow the advice of others in this matter.

It is true, *nevertheless,* that this regulation cannot be enforced.

I hold, *in the second place,* that the plan will not work.

The restrictive clause, *on the other hand,* limits the main clause.

If there is no danger of misreading, a conjunctive adverb introducing the second clause in a compound sentence need not be set off by a comma.

They are our guests; *therefore* we must pardon their actions.

He did not come yesterday; *consequently* I expect him today.

37f. A comma instead of an exclamation point is normally used to set off a mild interjection.

Alas, I had to give up the idea.

Ah, that is something I must not tell.

I knew him, *oh,* ages ago.

37g. Use commas to set off absolute phrases and clauses.

That being true, nothing remains to be said.

We had to hurry, *John wishing to start at once.*

There is nothing to do, *it seems to me,* but to obey the instructions.

37h. Use commas to set off a title after a proper name; but if the title precedes the name, it is not separated from the name by a comma.

Stith Gordon, *professor of history,* and Samuel James, *president of the college,* were on the program.

Defeated were Joram, *senator from Ohio,* and Stile, *representative from Iowa.*

Professor Stith Gordon and *President* Samuel James were on the program.

Senator Joram, of Ohio, and *Representative Stile,* of Iowa, were defeated.

37i. A comma does not separate a directive element in indirect discourse.

She said that she would stay.

For the use of the comma in direct discourse, see pages 131-132.

37j. Use commas to set off a nonrestrictive adjectival modifier that comes *after* the substantive.

The house, *unpainted and ramshackled,* had seen its best days.

The tower, *standing on a high hill,* was a sort of landmark.

Macbeth, which Shakespeare probably wrote for the court, deals with Scottish history.

38. Use a comma to separate an introductory participial, infinitive, or prepositional gerund phrase from the clause that follows.

Driving as rapidly as possible through heavy traffic, he arrived just in time.

Leaning against the post office, old Mack surveyed all passers-by.

To reach that goal, you have to be good in mathematics.

After winning the election, Brown was jubilant.

A short prepositional phrase preceding the subject is not usually set off by a comma

because as a rule it has a restrictive quality, but if it is long it may be set off.

Behind the farthest mountains of the range, dark clouds were just visible.

After a long day's ramble over steep hills, I was ready for bed.

In the meantime there was nothing to do.

After dusk the fireflies light up the glade.

In autumn we used to go nutting.

39. Use a comma to set off a long introductory adverbial clause.

When the adverbial clause is not introductory, the rules for restrictive and nonrestrictive clauses apply as with any other dependent clause.

As I was on my way to work this morning, I met a friend whom I had not seen for many years.

As soon as we received the storm warnings, we started for the harbor.

While we were on our way to class this morning, we made plans for the week end.

40. A comma is used to separate elements that are sharply contrasted.

She told us to walk, *not run.*

The word to use is effect, *not affect.*

41. Use a comma to separate an elliptical question added to a direct statement.

He was due this afternoon, *wasn't he?*

You will go with us, *will you not?*

42. Use a comma to separate elements that might be misread if the comma were omitted.

It is usually better, however, to recast such sentences than to rely on the comma to make the sentence clear.

Inside, the cat was yowling and the dog barking.

As we ate, the dog came running up the beach.

Abruptly the car stopped, throwing her forward.

While we were watching, the coach, a stockily built man, came over to us.

As we approached, the gate was on our left.

No ambiguity would result if one were to write "As I approached he held out his hand," since we do not say *As I approached he;* but if the sentence were "As I approached John held out his hand," the reader would not realize until he had reached *held* that *John* is the subject of *held* rather than the object of *approached.* A moment's confusion would therefore have resulted; and to save the reader even momentary confusion, the comma is inserted.

43. Use a comma after a parenthesis if one is normally required at the point where the parenthesis is inserted.

He returned my book (Conrad's *Lord Jim*), which he said he had enjoyed.

44. Use a comma after the salutation in an informal letter and after the complimentary close in a formal or informal letter.

After the salutation in an informal letter (*Dear John, Dearest Sue, Dear Mother*), the comma is conventionally used; but after a salutation in a formal letter (*Dear Sirs, Dear Mr. White*), a colon is used. After the complimentary close, whether in a formal or informal letter, a comma is used (*Yours truly, Sincerely yours, Yours ever, Yours with love*).

45. Do not use a comma unless there is a rule for its use.

45a. Do not use a comma (but a semicolon) to separate independent clauses that are not joined by a co-ordinating conjunction.

Independent clauses that are joined by a conjunctive adverb (*therefore, however, nevertheless,* and the like) or that have no connective should be separated by a semicolon (see page 124) or should be written as separate sentences. To separate them by a comma is to commit an error called the *comma splice* or *comma fault.* This error is usually considered worse than other errors in the use of the comma because of the im-

plication that a student who commits it does not understand the basic principles relating to compound sentences. The following sentences are punctuated correctly. If a comma were used instead of a semicolon or period, the result would be a comma-splice error.

I heard him out; however, I did not heed him.

He was thoroughly wet; moreover he was chilled to the bone.

We shall listen to all the arguments; then we shall decide.

The north bank was wooded; the south bank was grassy.

The cat was away. The mice were playing.

45b. Do not use a comma to set off restrictive elements.

This rule has been considered briefly in connection with that relating to nonrestrictive clauses (see page 119). A restrictive phrase or clause is one needed to identify or one that limits the word it modifies. If it is omitted, the sentence does not make logical sense or means something different from what the writer intended. To test whether the phrase or clause is restrictive, read the rest of the sentence. If the word that the omitted element modifies is not properly identified, the modifier is restrictive and should not be set off by commas.

A bird is nesting in the oak tree *that is just outside my bedroom.* [*Oak tree* is a common noun. Doubtless many oak trees are in the neighborhood. The dependent clause is necessary to point out which one the bird is nesting in; hence it is restrictive and is not separated from the word it modifies by a comma.]

The statement *that democracy has failed* remains to be proved. [Many statements remain to be proved. The writer refers to one only— *that democracy has failed;* hence the clause is restrictive.]

The bird *nesting over my east window* is a robin. [If the writer were to omit the italicized phrase, we could not identify the bird he means; hence the phrase is restrictive.]

He picked up the book *lying on the desk.* [The italicized phrase identifies the book he picked up.]

45c. Do not use a comma to separate sentence elements that have a close grammatical relationship.

Unless a parenthetical element is inserted at the spot, be especially careful not to employ punctuation between the following: (1) subject and verb, (2) verb and object, (3) adjective and noun, (4) preposition and object, (5) conjunction and the clause it introduces, (6) relative pronoun and the clause it introduces, (7) intensive pronoun and its antecedent, (8) two co-ordinate words or phrases joined by *and* or *or*, (9) correlatives, and (10) parts of a comparison. In the following examples the incorrectly inserted commas are inclosed in brackets.

INCORRECT USE OF COMMA
BETWEEN

1. SUBJECT AND VERB: The poem about the man with the hoe[,] was written by Edwin Markham.

The vacation to which she had looked forward all year[,] proved to be a disappointment.

2. VERB AND OBJECT: He told her[,] that he would come Thursday.

She said[,] that she would meet him at 3 o'clock.

This device will do[,] what the manufacturer promises.

3. ADJECTIVE AND NOUN: She walked down the grassy, winding[,] path.

White, fleecy[,] clouds were in the sky.

4. PREPOSITION AND OBJECT: John has worked in turn at[,] a furniture factory, an oil station, and an automobile plant.

His experience with[,] boys at camp, boy scouts, and a boating club[,] helped him obtain the job.

NOTE. The first and last elements in a series are not separated from preceding or succeeding elements of a sentence unless the series as a whole is nonrestrictive: Pies, cakes, and pastries[,] were excluded from the menu.

5. CONJUNCTION AND CLAUSE: He intended to go yesterday, but[,] he could not leave until today.

The speech was long and uninteresting, and[,] the audience was restless and noisy.

NOTE. The comma comes *before* the conjunction which joins co-ordinate clauses, not after.

6. PRONOUN AND CLAUSE: They were visited last week by their uncle after whom[,] their oldest son is named.

They were given a Siamese kitten which[,] they did not want.

7. INTENSIVE AND ANTECEDENT: He would give the message only to the manager[,] himself.

She was wearing a dress she[,] herself[,] had made.

8. TWO CO-ORDINATE ELEMENTS: Every game was played in the rain[,] or in the snow.

The morning for work[,] and the afternoon for play[,] was his motto.

9. CORRELATIVES: He was *as* tall[,] *as* his brother.

He was *both* willing to aid us[,] *and* ready to do so.

Neither the manager of the firm[,] *nor* the secretary was in.

The applicant must be *either* a junior[,] *or* a senior.

10. PARTS OF A COMPARISON: He is taller[,] than his sister.

This is farther[,] than I intended to go.

(See *Workbook*, Exercise 44.)

THE SEMICOLON

The semicolon has a function in punctuation about midway between that of the comma and the period. At times it substitutes for the comma, at other times for the period. But when it replaces a comma or period, there must be a logical basis for the substitution; it must not be used indiscriminately, according to the mere whim of a writer. The few rules discussed below should give you an intelligent conception of the uses of the semicolon.

46. Use a semicolon to separate the co-ordinate clauses of a compound sentence when they are not linked by a co-ordinating conjunction.

Sometimes the relationship between the clauses of a compound sentence is so apparent that a linking word is not required to show the relationship. When this is true, the clauses are separated by a semicolon:

Control your emotions; consider the facts calmly.

He did not join the air corps; he joined the artillery.

If you use a conjunctive adverb between independent clauses without an accompanying co-ordinating conjunction, place the semicolon before the conjunctive adverb. The most common conjunctive adverbs are *therefore, nevertheless, however, moreover, besides, so, consequently, accordingly, thus,* and *furthermore.*

We used a new method of cultivation; therefore the yield was greater.

I warned him that the bridge was out; nevertheless he went ahead.

The team suffered from lack of practice; moreover several players were ill.

Modern practice is to omit the comma after the conjunctive adverb except when it is necessary to avoid misreading. In such a sentence as "I plan to go this week; however, the transportation must be considered," a reader might suppose *however* to be a simple adverb and expect it to modify some word in the second clause till he had read to the end of the clause. To save him from this error, the comma is used after *however.* There would be no danger of such misreading in the three examples given above; therefore the comma is omitted after the conjunctive adverb.

46a. Avoid the run-together sentence.

This kind of sentence results from running together independent clauses without co-ordinating conjunction, period, or semicolon between them. Separate the clauses by a semicolon when the clauses are closely related; place a period between them when they are not component elements of one complete thought.

He looked strong; I felt weak.

He had all the symptoms of a cold. The next day he went swimming.

47. When the internal punctuation of the sentence is complicated, for the sake of clarity use the semicolon to separate elements ordinarily separated by the comma.

1. In a compound-complex sentence when some of the dependent clauses are nonrestrictive, a semicolon marks the main divisions, even when the linking words are co-ordinating conjunctions. Since the nonrestrictive modifiers are separated by commas, the semicolon is needed to mark the main divisions.

On our trip we went to the Grand Canyon by Route 66, which skirts the Ozarks, bisects the oil fields of Oklahoma, and cuts through northwestern Texas; and from the Grand Canyon we turned south, going to Phoenix and Tucson, Arizona, and on to Nogales, Mexico; but there we turned back towards home.

2. In complex sentences containing several dependent clauses which have internal punctuation, the semicolon is generally used to mark the main divisions.

I hold that democracy, in spite of its inefficiencies, the slowness with which it achieves results, and the danger of demagoguery inherent in it, is the best form of government; that the modicum of freedom we possess, though it has been bought with suffering and misery and torture and death, is worth what it cost; and that this form of government is worth living for, fighting for, and if need be dying for.

Note that the semicolon must not be used to separate the dependent clause nearest the main clause from the latter: for example, *I hold; that democracy . . .* It separates only co-ordinate elements, not those of different value, such as main and dependent clauses.

3. In simple sentences containing a complicated series, or elements having internal punctuation, the semicolon is generally used to separate the main divisions.

> We must get butter, bread, coffee, and eggs at the grocery store; bacon, sausage, and lamb chops at the meat market; soap and toothpaste at the drug store; and some waxed paper at the dime store.

48. Do not use the semicolon (1) to set off dependent sentence elements, such as nonrestrictive clauses, verbal or prepositional phrases, or other elements not co-ordinate, (2) to follow the salutation in a letter, (3) to precede a direct quotation.

After the salutation in a letter, use the comma if the letter is informal, the colon if it is formal; before a direct quotation, use a comma if the quoted passage is short or if the style is informal, a colon if the passage is long. If there is a rule for using the semicolon, use it; if there is none, do not use it.

(See *Workbook,* Exercise 45.)

THE COLON

The colon is a mark of introduction or anticipation, and in general it denotes formality. In very long and complicated sentences wherein the elements separated by semicolons are not the chief divisions, it is sometimes used to mark the main divisions; but students in the apprentice stage of writing should probably avoid writing sentences of this sort. For ordinary composition, it will suffice to know the following rules.

49. Use the colon to introduce a long or formal direct quotation.

> An entry in his diary is his best epitaph: "Well, I have had a happy life. I do not know that anybody whom I have seen close has had a happier."

> In his essay "The Function of Criticism," Matthew Arnold says: "It is of the last importance that English criticism should clearly discern what rule for its course . . . it ought to take.

The rule may be summed up in one word— *disinterestedness.*"

50. Use the colon to introduce a number of examples or a list of any sort.

> He has played a number of minor Shakespearean roles: Bardolph, the disreputable associate of Prince Hal; Shallow, the country justice; Dogberry, the ignorant law officer; and Sir Andrew Aguecheek, the drunken companion of Sir Toby Belch.

> The team met eight opponents in seven weeks: Northern, Central, Southeastern, Western, Tech, St. Joseph's, Northeastern, and Bascombe.

51. Use the colon between independent clauses when the second amplifies the first, or when the second gives a concrete illustration of a general statement in the first.

> In time, however, one of his favorite contentions was justified: in the long run, the majority of those who apply themselves to a matter will arrive at the right opinion, no matter how vociferous and professedly expert the opposition.

> Bridges in one of his sonnets says that the very names of things beloved are dear to us: the name of the one to whom he addressed the poem seemed to him the loveliest of all names.

52. The colon by common acceptance is used in the following specific instances:

1. After the salutation in a formal or business letter—

Dear Sir: Dear Professor Garrison:
Dear Mr. Jones: Dear Madam:

2. Between the hour and minute when time is expressed in figures—12:15 o'clock; 2:30 p.m.

3. Between chapter and verse in Bible references—*Genesis* 9:10.

4. Between the place of publication and the name of the publisher in bibliographical references—New York: Appleton-Century-Crofts.

NOTE. Do not capitalize the first word after a colon unless it is the beginning of a quotation or the beginning of an independent sentence.

Do not use the colon to introduce an indirect statement, nor to introduce an informal list (*Bring with you slacks, a warm sweater, and walking shoes.*).

(See *Workbook*, Exercise 45.)

THE PERIOD

Every college student knows, of course, that a period is used at the end of a declarative or imperative sentence, and at the end of certain legitimate fragmentary sentences (see page 78). What every college student does not *do*, however, is to observe this rule always in his writing. As was discussed in an earlier section, the period is often employed illegitimately to cut off phrases and dependent clauses. Such use is called the *period fault;* and it is considered a major error in writing, because it indicates that those who commit it lack a knowledge of the most rudimentary principle of composition—what a sentence is.

53. The period has but two uses: to mark the end of a declarative or imperative sentence and to mark an abbreviation.

Concerning the first use enough has been said, except to add the caution to be certain that it is a *sentence* (or a *legitimate* fragmentary sentence) at the end of which you place a period. Concerning the second usage, little more need be said. Some of the abbreviations most frequently used are *viz., e.g., Mr., Mrs., Dr., Ph.D., LL.D., A.B., M.A., A.M., P.M., B.C., p.* or *pp., etc.* The following usages should be kept in mind:

1. When a period is used after an abbreviation, it is followed, except at the end of a sentence, by whatever mark of punctuation would normally be used there.

Washington, D.C., is the capital.

Breakfast is served at 8 a.m.; lunch is served at 12:30 p.m.; dinner is served at 6:30 p.m.

2. When the abbreviation comes at the end of a sentence, one period serves two pur-

poses—to mark the abbreviation and to end the sentence.

3. Formerly a period was used after Roman numerals, but this is no longer done. One now writes "Henry VII was the first Tudor King."

4. Do not use a period after your own title of an essay, poem, or story.

5. Do not use a period after contractions in which the omission occurs within the word and is marked by an apostrophe, as in *hasn't, doesn't, weren't.*

THE QUESTION MARK

54. The question mark is used after every direct question.

What are you doing?

When can you come to see me?

It is not used after indirect questions.

He asked what you are doing.

I am writing to ask when you can come to see me.

1. In a series, a question mark may follow each question if special emphasis is desired. When used thus, it takes the place of a comma, and each element begins with a small letter (*Where is my text? my pen? my notebook?*). If it is not desired to emphasize each question in the series, use a comma except at the end of the sentence.

2. The question mark, in parentheses, indicates doubt concerning the authenticity of some fact (*Nathaniel Bacon was born in 1642 (?). Among Shakespeare's friends were Marlowe (?), Jonson, and Drayton.*). It should not be used to call attention to the fact that one is making a joke or is being ironical. (*Ben is the most studious (?) member of the family.*). Such usage shows poor taste, since it implies that the reader is not intelligent enough to see that one is joking or being ironical. If the reader is not well enough acquainted with the matter under discussion to catch the writer's intention, the sentence should be changed; if he is ac-

quainted with it, the question mark is unnecessary.

THE EXCLAMATION POINT

55. Use the exclamation point at the end of an exclamatory sentence and after words that express strong emotion or feeling.

What a world for men of good will to live in!
Look out! You'll fall!
What! I don't believe it.

Avoid using the exclamation point to label irony or humor. Such usage is in bad taste. In fact, the excessive use of the exclamation point anywhere is considered in poor taste. The constant resort to exclamation points indicates inability to gain effects by normal means, and hints that the writer is shallow or flighty and his statements probably untrustworthy.

THE DASH

56a. Use the dash when a sentence is abruptly broken off and something entirely different added.

The game will be—by the way, are you going to the game?
It says in this story—but I can't tell you all that now.

56b. Use the dash in writing conversation to show that a speech is not finished.

When this is done, no period follows the dash, though a question mark or exclamation point is used if it would be required in the completed sentence.

"The result will be——"
"I don't care what the result will be."
"But let me tell you what——"
"No, my mind is made up."
"Isn't that a stubborn——?"
"Not stubborn—firm."

56c. Use the dash to show hesitation or confusion on the part of a speaker.

This use is generally restricted to reporting conversation.

Where is the—er—the—tidying up you promised to do?
"I say I—would you—I'm sorry, but I left my money in my other coat pocket—will you buy the tickets?" he stammered.

56d. Use the dash to indicate the omission of words or letters.

Little acorns—great oaks, you know.
Have you read Poe's poem entitled "To F——s S. O——d"?

56e. Use the dash before a statement that summarizes a preceding series when the summary is an emphatic repetition of the preceding statement or when it is introduced by *namely, e.g.,* and the like.

The professional patriot, the constant flag-waver, the agitator who would pass laws to compel men to go through forms of appearing patriotic—all these are abhorred by those whose sense of patriotism lies too deep for words and trivial outward forms.

All his books are written in a learned language—in a language which nobody hears from his mother or his nurse.—MACAULAY.

Every rule in composition suggests three acts on your part—namely, learn it, use it, check your writing to see if you have observed its use correctly.

Some pairs of words are bothersome to students—*e.g.,* affect and effect, loose and lose, sit and set.

56f. Use the dash to designate an ironical contrast.

My opponent loudly affirms that he is for labor—and hobnobs with lobbyists for large corporations; he says he is against alcohol—and keeps a bar in his house; he claims he is a friend of education—and votes to cut school appropriations.

56g. The most common use of the dash is to set off (a) appositives that are emphatic or have internal punctuation and (b) other modifying expressions that have internal punctuation or have a very loose connection with the sentence in which they stand.

In this usage there are always two dashes—one at the beginning of the modifying expression and one at the end—unless the second dash coincides with a period or semicolon, when it is absorbed by the period or semicolon. The following examples, from Macaulay's essays, show these uses:

Compared with the labor of reading through these volumes, all other labor—the labor of thieves on the treadmill, of children in factories, of Negroes in sugar plantations—is an agreeable occupation.

They have in consequence been thrown in the shade by writers who . . . understood far better the art of producing effect—by Livy and Quintus Curtius.

In an evil day, though with great pomp and solemnity—we quote the language of Bacon—was the ill-starred alliance stricken between the old philosophy and the new faith.

In the temper of Bacon—we speak of Bacon the philosopher, not of Bacon the lawyer and politician—there was a singular union of audacity and sobriety.

NOTE. In modern practice, commas are rarely used in connection with dashes, although some stylebooks suggest the use of commas as well as dashes when a comma would normally be used if the dash were omitted. It is correct, however, to use dashes only, and as this is the simpler and the more common modern practice, it is recommended.

In printing, three dashes of varying length are used: the *en dash* between inclusive figures (1776–1789) and between elements that normally require a hyphen but have two or more words in one or both of the elements (the New Haven–New York run); the *em dash*, which is the normal dash used in most instances; and the *2-em dash* when a sentence is not finished. In typewritten manuscript the best practice is to use a hyphen to designate the en dash, two hyphens

to designate the normal dash, and four hyphens to designate the 2-em dash—without space before or after the hyphens; in handwriting, the different kinds of dash cannot be so clearly distinguished, but except for the en dash, the length should be at least a quarter of an inch to distinguish it from the hyphen.

The dash is a valuable mark of punctuation when it is used correctly. The indiscriminate use of the dash in the place of commas and periods not only indicates ignorance but is in poor taste.

PARENTHESES

Parentheses—sometimes called *curves*—have four uses.

57a. Use parentheses to inclose matter only indirectly related to the main thought of the sentence—matter that is irrelevant or purely explanatory or is more formal and less essential to the meaning than that for which dashes are used.

This rule applies particularly to examples, illustrations, definitions, and references when these are short (if they are long, it is better to give the information in a footnote).

The conjunctive adverb (see page 70) is used to link independent clauses.

At 3:30 a.m. (the time agreed upon at the conference the evening before) the attack on the fort began.

No one play could deal with a war in its entirety (even in Hardy's *Dynasts,* perhaps the most ambitious play ever written, the conflict is centralized in the characters of Napoleon, Wellington, and Nelson); therefore the playwright presents some phase of the greater conflict in the lesser conflicts that form his plot.—Milton Marx, *The Enjoyment of Drama.*

Yet for all their seeming lack of structure, the plays of Chekhov contain (or perhaps a better word would be conceal) the highest artistry. —*Ibid.*

57b. Use parentheses in personal letters and informal writing to inclose an aside which the reader is likely to know but may for the moment not recall.

My Uncle John Simpson (my mother's brother) came to see us last week.

57c. Use parentheses to inclose figures or letters that mark items in an enumeration. (For an example see rule 22, example 3.)

57d. Use parentheses to inclose signs, figures, and words when accuracy is essential.

Except in legal documents or when accuracy is vital, it is no longer considered necessary to use this rule.

The check should be made out for the exact amount ($19.98).

I am sending you fifty dollars ($50) to pay the rent for one month.

NOTE. *Before* a parenthesis within a sentence no punctuation mark is used. *After* a parenthesis within a sentence no mark is used unless it would be required if the parenthesis were removed; then whatever mark would be required normally, follows the parenthesis. *Within* a parenthesis inside a sentence, the punctuation is the same as if the matter were a separate sentence, except that when it is a complete sentence no capital is used at the beginning and no period at the end—though a question mark or an exclamation point is used if one is required. Parentheses may, of course, inclose a separate sentence, in which case the ordinary rules for using the capital and period apply.

57e. Do not use parentheses to emphasize a word (use italics instead), to indicate a title (use italics or quotation marks, according to the sort of title), or to cancel a passage (run lines through the passage).

Avoid using parentheses for other than the legitimate purposes discussed in this section.

BRACKETS

58a. The chief use of brackets is to inclose something—a correction, an addition, an explanation, or some comment—that a writer interpolates in matter he is quoting.

"In the collection are letters by E[dward]. L[ear]., Thomas Woolner, and [Edward] Fitzgerald."

"It [the acknowledgment of Henry VIII as head of the church] was the first step in a policy by which the Church was to be laid prostrate at the foot of the throne."—J. R. Green.

"In 1630 [a typographical error for 1603] James came to the throne."

"The song [Jesus, Lover of My Soul] has become a treasury of spiritual wealth."—J. B. Reeves.

In applying for the job, he wrote, "I am very good in atheletics [*sic*], and I can teach mathmatics [*sic*]."

NOTE. The term *sic*, Latin for *thus*, is inserted to show that a misspelling or some other error, as of a date, appeared in the original and is not an error by the one quoting.

58b. Use brackets to place a parenthesis within a parenthesis.

In general, however, avoid such complicated usages.

At 3:30 a.m. (the time agreed on the evening before [see the correspondence by Captain Williams, Letter X]) the attack on the fort began.

58c. Use brackets to inclose stage directions in plays.

Mrs. Annerly [sipping her coffee]. I don't wonder.

In the use of other punctuation marks with brackets, the same rules apply as with parentheses.

QUOTATION MARKS

59. The main function of quotation marks is to inclose matter quoted from any source; a subsidiary function is to inclose words used in a special manner and to inclose certain titles.

Normally in the United States, and occasionally in Great Britain, double quotation marks are used to mark quotations; hence in this section *quotation marks* will refer to double marks unless single marks are specified.

59a. Use quotation marks to inclose every quotation.

The only exception to this rule is in lengthy quotations, where the quotation marks may be omitted if some other means is employed to call attention to the passage as a quotation. Quotation marks are not used to inclose a summary of the ideas of another. There is no such thing as a halfway quotation: if the direct words of another are used, they should appear exactly as in the original and should be inclosed by quotation marks; if the source is not quoted exactly, do not use quotation marks, but state that the ideas in general are those of whatever source you are using. Indirect discourse is never inclosed in quotation marks.

59b. Use quotation marks to inclose the title of (a) a chapter in a book or (b) an individual poem, essay, or story.

For the title of the book or magazine, use italics. It is true that usage in this respect varies. Most newspapers and magazines, for instance, make no distinction between titles of whole volumes and single items in them. The reason for this is that changing fonts of type is expensive, and it is less important in journalistic style to maintain fine distinctions of style than to save expense. Those who are careful to observe the best rules of style make the distinction noted in this rule. Fortunately for students, it takes no more time or effort in longhand or typescript to be exact in applying the rule than to lump all

titles in one class; and since the rule is observed in all masters' and doctoral theses, in all formal papers, in all books that have pretensions to a literary style, and in the best magazines, it is highly recommended that students use the rule as stated.

Read the poems "Emerson" and "Lands End" in the volume *More People* by Edgar Lee Masters.

For information about the development of frequency modulation in radio, see "Revolution in Radio" in *Fortune*, October, 1939.

59c. Do not inclose the title of your own manuscript in quotation marks, unless it is a quotation.

Even when your title is a quotation, it need not be quoted. Such titles as *Look Homeward, Angel* and *Gone with the Wind*, for instance, are taken from the works of other authors and are used without quotation marks.

59d. Use quotation marks to inclose words used in a special manner or words coined for some special, limited use.

They were in close association with "bounty-jumpers," men who deserted as soon as the bounty was received and enlisted elsewhere under other names.—J. S. Bassett, *A Short History of the United States.*

If thousands were squandered on the subsidization of newspapers, were they not "loyal" newspapers? If unheard-of prices were paid in the furnishing of the State House, were not the purchases made of "Union men"?—C. G. Bowers, *The Tragic Era.*

NOTE. Authorities differ widely on the question of using quotation marks to inclose slang expressions, colloquialisms, newly coined technical terms, and the like. Good taste would indicate that the introduction of slang and colloquialisms in formal, dignified style is out of place. On the other hand to report a conversation between college students, carpenters, or oil-field workers in formal, grammatically correct sentences would give an air of unreality to the conversation. The best rule to adopt in this manner is to avoid using slang or colloquial expressions in formal writing, but, if it becomes essential to use such a term, to designate it by the use of quotation marks; and when reporting conversation or writing informally to use such expressions when it is natural to do so, and to omit the quotation marks. As to newly coined technical terms, if it is reasonably certain that readers in general will be unfamiliar with the terms, use quotation marks to suggest that their status in the language is tentative.

PUNCTUATING DIRECT QUOTATION

60a. When a directive element precedes the quotation, use a comma if the quotation is short, and a colon if the quotation is long or if it is introduced in a formal manner.

He called out, "What are you doing with my driver?"

He said hesitantly, "I don't see how I can do that."

Stephen Leacock, in his essay "American Humour," says: "It is perhaps not difficult to understand why so few writers have attempted a painstaking and scientific analysis of what is humorous. There appears to be a sort of intellectual indignity involved in the serious study of the comic."

60b. When the explanatory expression interrupts the quotation, a comma precedes it; a comma follows it if no punctuation mark or a comma would be employed were the interrupter omitted, and a semicolon or period if one were normally required in the absence of an interrupter.

"It is not," she interrupted, "my habit to change my mind so quickly."

"That is my idea," she declared; "therefore I won't have you stealing it."

"It is a fine day," John called. "Are you going to the game?"

60c. When the explanatory expression comes after the quotation, a comma

precedes it unless the quotation itself ends with a question mark or an exclamation point, in which case the comma is omitted.

"Well, that settles the matter," she said.

"What are you going to do about it?" she inquired.

"What a beautiful car!" she exclaimed.

60d. A comma and a period precede the closing quotation marks. A semicolon and a colon come after the closing quotation marks. A question mark and an exclamation point come before the quotation marks if the quotation itself is a question or an exclamation and after the quotation marks if the quotation itself is not interrogative or exclamatory but forms a part of an interrogative or exclamatory sentence.

He called out, "I shall not take a minute."

"That isn't the point," he said.

Yesterday we studied Milton's "Lycidas"; today we shall read Shelley's "Adonais."

In this essay, F. A. Woods defines "oily words"; they are words which "are difficult to handle," which "slip through the fingers like the long thin fish of three letters of a crossword puzzle."

"What a wonderful day!" she exclaimed.

"Are you coming?" he asked.

Have you ever heard her say, "I don't play bridge"?

Do you know the song "Did You Ever See a Dream Walking"?

How charming of her to say, "You may wear my hat"!

NOTE. When a question mark or exclamation point ends a quotation, no other punctuation mark is used. (Note the last four sentences above.)

When a question is asked about a quoted question, the question mark that would normally follow the quoted expression is omitted, and the final question mark does duty for both questions.

60e. **Observe also the special rules that follow.**

1. Do not use the comma to set off quotations built into a sentence.

> He said that his car would "do eighty miles an hour" and he was "going to let it out."
>
> This folder refers to Chicago as "The American Venice, where beautiful streets wind along twenty-five miles of lake front."

2. In a single quotation of several sentences without an interpolation, use quotation marks at the beginning and end only, not for each sentence:

> He said, "I don't believe that man's statement. I have evidence of my own to disprove it. I think he was just guessing."

3. When the remarks of several different speakers are reported in one sentence, each person's remarks are inclosed by quotation marks.

> John was the first to get back from the game, and everyone shouted questions at once: "Who won?" "What was the score?" "What did Jim do?" "Was there much passing?"

4. When quoting several paragraphs, use quotation marks at the beginning of each new paragraph, but at the end of only the final paragraph.

The purpose of this rule is to indicate to a reader at the beginning of each paragraph that the quotation continues, and at the end of each paragraph that it is not yet ended. If the quotation is very long, consisting of a long paragraph or several paragraphs, it is better to omit the quotation marks and to indicate the quotation by indenting about two inches on each margin when writing in longhand; and to indent and single space the lines in typescript.

5. When quoting a fragment, do not begin the quotation with a capital letter unless the quoted passage began with a capital.

> He said "the machinations of a corrupt political machine" would have to stop.

6. Do not use quotation marks for proverbs and phrases that are common knowledge.

> He said the devil would find no mischief for his hands to do.
>
> He was honest not because he believed that honesty is the best policy, but because honesty was inherent in his make-up.

7. Do not use quotation marks for statements that are not quoted from someone else, but are quotations in form only.

> He said to himself: I believe I am going to win this race.
>
> She thought, Shall I wear my new hat to the game?

8. For quotations within quotations use single quotation marks; then if a quotation is given within this quotation, use double quotation marks; and so alternate the double and single quotation marks with all matter quoted.

> In his letter, John wrote: "I have been following the example of my instructor, who said, 'When I decide to write something, I first sit down and read Wordsworth's "Ode to Duty" to give myself impetus to finish'; but I find it doesn't work for me."

9. In writing dialogue, put each speech in a separate paragraph and inclose it in quotation marks.

> "I doubt our being able to do so much," said Morland.
> "You croaking fellow!" cried Thorpe, "we shall be able to do ten times more. Kingsweston! aye, and Blaize Castle too, and anything else we can hear of; but here is your sister says she will not go."
> "Blaize Castle!" cried Catherine; "what is that?"
> "The finest place in England; worth going fifty miles at any time to see."
> "What, is it really a castle, an old castle?"
> "The oldest in the kingdom."
> "But is it like what one reads of?"
> "Exactly: the very same."—Jane Austen, *Northanger Abbey.*

10. Be careful to put quotation marks at the end of a quotation as well as at the beginning.

Omitting the final quotation mark is a common error in the manuscripts of students. It is the result solely of carelessness, and is inexcusable. There is no such thing as one quotation mark: use a pair—one at the beginning and one at the end of a quotation—or none.

THE APOSTROPHE

The apostrophe has three uses: (1) to form the possessive of nouns and indefinite pronouns, (2) to denote the omission of letters or figures, and (3) to form the plural of figures, letters, signs, and words to which special allusion is made.

61. Always use an apostrophe to designate the possessive case of nouns and indefinite pronouns.

Next to the incorrect use of the comma, the greatest number of errors in punctuation results from the omission of the apostrophe. The reason for most of these errors is carelessness. Watch possessives, and form the habit of inserting an apostrophe to denote a possessive, as in earlier years you formed the habit of dotting *i*'s and crossing *t*'s. And be certain that the apostrophe is placed properly. The rules about the position of the apostrophe are very definite.

1. To form the possessive of a noun or indefinite pronoun, singular or plural, which does not end in a sibilant sound (*s, x, z*), add an apostrophe and an *s:*

> dog's leash, horse's bridle, man's hat, men's hats, children's hats, William's hat, Marivaux's plays (*x* silent), one's hat

2. To form the possessive of a plural noun or indefinite pronoun ending in *s, x,* or *z,* add only an apostrophe:

> dogs' leashes, horses' bridles, girls' hats, the Smiths' dinner party, the Thomases' house, The Beaux' Stratagem, others' ills.

3. To form the possessive of a singular noun ending in a sibilant sound (*s, x, z*), add an apostrophe and an *s* except in one case: if the noun has two or more syllables and if the last syllable is not accented and is preceded by a sibilant sound, add only the apostrophe:

> Burns's poems, Jones's store, the fox's tail, Liz's idea, Moses' law, Ulysses' voyage, Jesus' sake, conscience' sake (the *ce* is a sibilant sound).

NOTE. The reason for the exception here is to prevent the disagreeable sound of too many sibilants in succession. The *s* when added to form the possessive is pronounced as a syllable. Such combinations of sound as *for Jesus-es sake, Moses-es law, for goodness-es sake* are not pleasant to the ear, hence the omission of the *s* to form the possessive of these words.

When forming the possessive of a word ending in *s,* be especially careful to place the apostrophe *after* the *s* which is a part of the word. Never write *Keat's* for John Keats, the poet, for instance. The *s* here is a part of his name, and it is as incorrect to write *Keat's* as *Ji'ms* for *Jim's.*

4. To denote joint possession, add the apostrophe or apostrophe and *s* after the second noun only:

> Harold and Templeman's Victorian prose collection, the Watfords and Tuckers' annual picnic, John and George's farm (they own the farm jointly). If they owned separate farms, the sign of the possessive would be used with each (*John's and George's farms*).

5. To form the possessive of compound nouns and indefinite pronouns, add the apostrophe or apostrophe and *s* after the last element of the compound:

> her daughter-in-law's opinion, the menservants' opinions, everyone else's opinion

6. Do not use an apostrophe to form the possessive of a personal pronoun—*his, hers, its, theirs, yours*—or the relative pronoun *whose.* These pronouns, since they retain the inflectional ending of an old genitive case, have the idea of possession inherent in them; hence no sign is necessary to denote the possessive.

NOTE. Do not confuse the pronouns *its* and *whose* with the contractions *it's* (for *it is*) and *who's* (for *who is*). Contractions of course take apostrophes. Each of the following is correct:

Who's going with me? It's his. Who's first? Whose shoes are these? Its fur is soft.

62. Use an apostrophe to denote the omission of letters or figures.

He *hasn't* been here today.

They *weren't* anxious to go.

The class of '25 had its reunion this year.

Meet me at two *o'clock*.

"Good *mo'nin'*," he drawled; "*I'm goin'* back to my *ol'* home.

NOTE. When using an apostrophe to denote the omission of a letter, be careful to put it where the letter is omitted. Careless students frequently put the apostrophe before the *n* in such contractions as *haven't* or *shouldn't*.

63. Use an apostrophe to designate plurals of figures, letters, signs, and words to which special allusion is made.

If there are no *6's* left in this type, use *9's* turned upside down.

Your *T's* and *F's* are too much alike, and your *v's* and *u's*.

Use *+'s* and *—'s* to denote whether the sentences are correct.

You are using too many *and's* and *the's*.

63a. Do not put an apostrophe in plurals (except the instances noted in rule 63) or in predicates ending in *s*.

THE HYPHEN

64. Use a hyphen to mark the division of a word that comes at the end of a line.

1. To divide a word between two lines, always place a hyphen at the end of the first line, never at the beginning of the second. Divide the word only between syllables; if you are not certain where to divide, consult a dictionary.

2. Never divide words of one syllable. This applies to words ending in *ed* but pronounced as one syllable—*e.g., called, spelled, bowled*—as well as to words like *brought, which,* and *world*.

3. In general avoid dividing words of more than one syllable, but if a considerable space remains to be filled at the end of a line, divide according to the following rules. Note the pronunciation, and do not divide words so that the different parts sound unnatural, as would be true in such divisions as *comparisons, und-erscoring, syllab-le*. When a consonant is doubled and stands between two vowels, divide between the consonants—*expres-sion, stab-bing, run-ning*. Divide between two vowels when each is sounded—*zo-ology, co-operate, sci-ence*. Divide between the body of a word and a prefix or a suffix—*dis-appear, con-struct, lead-ing, habit-able*. When a consonant stands between two vowels, usually the division is made between the first vowel and the consonant—*ame-nable, la-borer*. When two or more consonants stand between vowels, the division is usually made between the consonants—*sym-bolic, contentious;* but there are frequent exceptions to this rule, and it is well to consult a dictionary when you have to divide a word. Do not divide a digraph or trigraph (two or three letters representing a single sound, as *eau* in *beautiful,* or *ph* in *diphthong*).

65. Use a hyphen to designate certain compound words or phrases.

In forming compound words, ordinarily consult a dictionary, for there is wide variance in the use of hyphens in compounds. *Bedroom,* for instance, is written as one word, *dining room* as two words; *trade-mark* is hyphenated, *trade name* is written as two words. A few general rules, however, apply to the use of the hyphen in forming compounds.

65a. Use a hyphen between a prefix ending with a vowel and a root word beginning with the same vowel, though sometimes two dots—called a diaeresis—are placed over the second vowel to indicate that it is to be sounded separately:

co-operate, pre-eminent, re-elect, re-enforce

65b. Use a hyphen when a compound word would be confused with one spelled similarly but having a different meaning:

re-create, recreate; re-form, reform

65c. Use a hyphen between a prefix and a proper name:

post-Aristotelian, pre-Hoover, anti-Communist

65d. Use a hyphen in compounds formed of a noun or verb and a preposition:

set-to, head-on, house-to-house, passer-by

65e. Use a hyphen in compound numerals between twenty-one and ninety-nine, whether these are used singly or with larger figures:

thirty-three, one thousand and sixty-seven

65f. When two or more words precede a noun and have the force of a single adjective, preferably insert a hyphen between them:

a *long-established* custom, an *up-to-date* method, a *well-known* author

This usage, however, does not apply when one of the words is an adverb ending in *ly:*

a *highly paid* executive

nor when the words come after the noun:

The man is *well known.*

65g. Use a hyphen in writing out a fraction used as a single adjective before a noun, but not with a fraction consisting of an adjective plus a noun:

a *five-eighths-inch* bolt, a *one-fourth* share, *two thirds* of a mile, *three fourths* of a pie.

THE ELLIPSIS MARK

66. The ellipsis mark, consisting of three periods with a space between each, denotes an omission from a passage being quoted.

If the omitted passage comes at the end of a sentence a period is added, making four periods.

In his essay "Hebraism and Hellenism" Matthew Arnold says: "The final aim of both Hellenism and Hebraism . . . is no doubt the same: man's perfection. . . . The very language which they both . . . use . . . is often identical."

Among contemporary writers, particularly of fiction, the ellipsis mark is sometimes used to denote a brief passage of time, or in the stream-of-consciousness type of writing to denote the gliding of the mind from one fragment of thought to another.

THE CARET

67. The caret, an inverted v-shaped mark (∧), is put at the *bottom* of a line between two words where something has been omitted.

The omitted word or passage is then written above the line where the omission occurs. If the caret comes near the end of a line and the omitted passage is somewhat long, it is better to begin the omitted passage near the beginning of the left margin than to carry it over to the following line.

where
We were standing ∧ we could see the magician.

In the final revision of a manuscript, it is legitimate to add a brief omission rather than recopy the whole page; but if there are many omissions, rewrite the paper. Remember to place the caret so that its top is at the *bottom* of the line.

G. Mechanics

Rules concerning capitalization, italics, abbreviations, and the representation of numbers have evolved from practices that literate writers and printers have found economical and effective. Some have gradually developed from ancient practices; others have been established arbitrarily in modern times. The result is that all do not have the same degree of acceptance, and it is easy to find variations in usage regarding them. The following usages, however, are generally observed by good writers everywhere.

CAPITALS

68a. Capitalize the first word of a sentence, the first word of a direct quotation, and the first word of a line of poetry.

The rule that a capital should mark the first word of a sentence carries the implication that capitalizing some internal part of a sentence, unless of course it is a proper noun or adjective, is incorrect; and also that capitalizing a fragment not meant as an independent unit of thought is incorrect. Sometimes, however, single words or phrases used legitimately instead of complete sentences are capitalized.

> On the mark!
> "Ready?"
> "Yes."

Furthermore, the rule to begin each direct quotation with a capital implies that an indirect quotation should not be capitalized.

> He asked, "Are you ready to go?"
> He asked if we were ready to go.

As to the use of capitals to mark the first words of lines of poetry, the rule must be followed scrupulously when the poem being quoted follows this practice; but some recent poets capitalize the first word of those lines only that begin a sentence, and in these instances, the usage of the author should be followed.

This is the land of lost content,
 I see it shining plain,
The happy highways where I went
 And cannot come again.
   —A. E. HOUSMAN

Once Wonder dwelt here, child-wise and joyous, watching
through the five windows, through the open door;
saw all the pageant of life pass by, nor heeded the spiders, dim in the cornice, the sharp-toothed beetles under the floor.
   —HORACE SHIPP

1. When only part of a sentence is being quoted directly, do not capitalize the first word.

> He asked us to "row along the inlet as far as the Dahlman cabin."

> I felt as Lear did when he requested "an ounce of civet, good apothecary, to sweeten my imagination."

2. When quoting more than one line of poetry and not following the poet's own line arrangement, retain the capitals as in the original.

> She said I should remember Pope's words, "And yet believe me, good as well as ill, Woman's at best a contradiction still."

68b. Capitalize proper nouns and adjectives.

The following classes are capitalized:
1. Names and initials of individuals;
2. Nicknames and titles used as part of the name:

Blondy Johnson, Alexander the Great

3. Names referring to the Deity and to deities of all religions and times, and pronouns referring to God.
4. Names of months, days of the week, holidays, and holy days:

Epiphany, Fourth of July

5. Names of organizations, political parties, religious bodies:

Boy Scouts, the Democratic or Republican Party, Catholic Church, Methodist Church

6. Names of places, geographical sections, political divisions:

Lake Erie, Missouri River, Carson City, Pike's Peak, the Southwest, Second Precinct, First Ward

7. Names of countries, nationalities, races:

France, Canadians, Indians, Negroes, Jews, Gentiles, Caucasians

8. Names of specific historical events, specific laws, departments of government:

Magna Carta, Bill of Rights, Patent Office, Department of State

9. Names of divisions of a college or university:

Department of Chemistry, College of Arts and Sciences, School of Business Administration

10. Titles prefixed to the names of individuals and abbreviations after a name:

General John J. Pershing; Professor Harry Smith, Ph.D.; the Reverend James Thorne; Father O'Flynn; Sir Charles Tennyson, C.M.G.

11. Names of specific buildings, ships, trains, airplanes:

the *America,* Empire State Building, the *Spirit of St. Louis*

12. Personifications:

Tell me, Fancy, sweetest child.

Of the words in these classes, few will present difficulties if one bears in mind the rule that a specific person or thing is a proper noun, and adjectives derived from these are proper adjectives and should be capitalized, and that a reference to any one of a class of persons or things does not require a capital. Some special stumbling blocks among these are discussed below.

1. The words *father, mother, brother, sister,* and the like should be capitalized if used in direct address or if not preceded by a possessive pronoun.

I must tell you, Sister, of my new roommate.
Let's ask your mother if we may go.
Where is Father this morning?

2. In the use of such particles as *d', de, von, van, le* and *della* in proper names, usage in this country varies; and the only safe way is to take careful note of how an individual writes his name and extend him the courtesy of following his example. The same is true of the abbreviations *jr.* and *sr.* after a name, for despite categorical statements in some texts that these should or should not be capitalized, a careful check indicates that usage is almost exactly divided in this matter.

3. In the capitalization of the generic term that follows a proper name, usage varies, but the best practice is to capitalize the generic term:

the Ohio *River,* the Atlantic *Ocean,* Central *Park.*

4. Capitalize a section of the country but not a direction of the compass:

Birds that were in the *South* are flying *north.*

5. In referring to a specific department in a college, use capitals, but do not capitalize a subject unless it is derived from a proper noun.

I am majoring in mathematics; hence I know best the instructors in the Department of Mathematics. But as I am minoring in French and physics, I know several instructors in those departments too.

6. The words *honorable* and *reverend* are not really titles but are complimentary adjectives; hence when used they should be followed by the first name, the initials, or the appropriate title. When used in the body of a sentence, they should be capitalized and should be preceded by *the:*

the Honorable James A. Hill, the Reverend Dr. Jones.

7. Titles and places should not be capitalized when they are generic in reference, even when one refers to a specific person or thing:

I saw the *professor* coming from the *library* just now.
I saw *Professor* Pugh in the *Smith Library* just now.

He was on the way to the *theater*.

He was going to the *Majestic Theater*.

He graduated from *high school* but did not attend *college*.

He graduated from *East High School* and entered *Coe College*.

He served as *dean* for several years.

There is *Dean* Williams of the *School of Business Administration*.

8. Capitalize derivatives of proper nouns that are used as proper adjectives:

an *Elizabethan* play, *Mexican* music, an *Indian* arrowhead, a *Spanish* course, a *Papal* decree, a *Western* habit.

68c. In the titles of books, magazines, newspapers, articles, stories, poems, musical compositions, and the like, capitalize the first word and all other words except articles, conjunctions, and prepositions.

Consult the Book Review Section of this week's *New York Times*.

An Enquiry into the Nature of Certain Nineteenth Century Pamphlets, though concerned with bibliography, is a brilliant piece of detective work.

NOTE. The best modern practice is not to capitalize an article that begins the title of a newspaper or magazine unless it is the first word of a sentence, but to capitalize such an article in the title of a book: the Kansas City *Star* (newspaper), the *New Yorker* (magazine), *The Enjoyment of Drama* (book), *A Short History of the English People* (book).

68d. Capitalize the first and last words of a salutation, and the first word of the complimentary close of a letter.

Dear Sir, My dear Sir, Dear Mr. Birch, Yours truly, Yours very sincerely.

68e. Capitalize the words *Whereas* and *Resolved* in formal resolutions, and the first word following either of these.

68f. Capitalize the abbreviations A.D. and B.C., and I and O (but not *oh* unless it comes at the beginning of a sentence).

69. Do not use a capital letter unless you can state a rule for its use.

Note especially the following rules.

1. Do not capitalize for emphasis.

2. Do not capitalize the names of the seasons:

spring, autumn.

3. Do not capitalize (1) the names of college classes:

freshman, sophomore

unless the class is referred to as a specific organization, or (2) the name of a member of a college class.

4. Do not capitalize prefixes to proper names:

ex-President Hoover, *anti*-Nazi, *pre*-Revolutionary.

5. Do not capitalize *earth, sun, moon* (but capitalize the names of other planets, stars, and constellations).

6. Observe contemporary usage in the matter of capitalizing words that were once proper nouns but are in the process of becoming common nouns. When in doubt about such a word, do not trust your own judgment, but consult a dictionary. Note, however, that many such words have already become common nouns and should not be capitalized:

macadam, boycott, bowdlerize, venetian blinds, leghorn hat, scotch plaid, and many others.

ITALICS

To designate in manuscript that something is to be printed in italics, underline once.

70a. Use italics to emphasize a word.

This usage, however, is generally avoided by good writers, and it should be employed with great discretion.

70b. Use italics to refer to a word or letter taken out of its context.

Always dot your *i*'s and cross your *t*'s.

Do not write *and* and *the* slantwise across the line.

The word *thane* referred to one of superior rank.

70c. Use italics to designate a foreign word not yet anglicized.

Do you like potatoes *au gratin*?

The abbreviations *c.*, *loc. cit.*, *q.v.*, and the like, which are commonly used in footnotes, refer to Latin words, and should therefore be italicized. Such commonly used abbreviations as *etc.*, *i.e.*, and *e.g.*, although from Latin words, are frequently not italicized in current usage.

70d. Italicize titles of books, pamphlets, newspapers, magazines, dramas, and musical compositions.

Note that the titles of books and magazines are italicized, and parts of these, as chapters in a book and articles in a magazine, are designated by the use of quotation marks (see page 130).

NOTE. In designating the titles of magazines, the best contemporary practice is not to italicize an article that comes at the beginning of the title, and in the titles of newspapers not to italicize the article or the name of the city. The following are correct: I read good articles this week in the *Survey Graphic* and the Boston *Herald*.

70e. Use italics to designate the names of ships and airplanes:

the *Queen Mary*, the *Winnie Mae*.

70f. Use italics to mark the word *Resolved* in formal resolutions.

ABBREVIATIONS

Both courtesy and intelligence suggest to a writer the removal of every possible obstacle between himself and a reader. Abbreviations are likely to be such obstacles.

71. In all formal and most informal writing, avoid all abbreviations except a very few that are accepted universally.

Careful writers even avoid many abbreviations that a reader will have little trouble recognizing.

1. Do not abbreviate names of states, countries, and cities—even in informal letters and in addresses on envelopes.

2. Do not abbreviate names of months and days of the week.

3. Do not abbreviate given names, as *Chas.* for *Charles*, *Wm.* for *William*.

4. Do not abbreviate *etc.* for *and so forth* or *and the like*.

NOTE. When *etc.* is used, as in footnotes or lists, observe that it is the abbreviation for *et cetera*, meaning *and others*, and that the *t* precedes the *c*.

5. Do not abbreviate *co.* for *company*, except in lists, footnotes, or other places where abbreviations in general are permissible.

6. Do not abbreviate words such as *avenue*, *building*, *boulevard*, *court*, and *street* in addresses.

72. A few abbreviations are correct in formal usage.

1. *Mr.*, *Mrs.*, *Messrs.*, *Dr.*, and *St.* (Saint) in connection with proper names, whether initials or first names are included. Such abbreviations as *Rev.*, *Hon.*, *Prof.*, *Gen.*, *Col.*, *Capt.*, and *Lieut.*, are allowed when they precede the full name—surname and given name; when only the surname is used, however, these should be written out.

2. *Esq.*, *A.B.*, *A.M.*, *Ph.D.*, *LL.D.*, *Sr.*, *Jr.*, and the like when used after proper names. All titles, whether they precede or follow names, should be written in full unless they are used in connection with a given name. The following, for instance, are correct:

Prof. John Williams, A.B., Ph.D., will lecture here tonight.

Professor Williams, who has the degree of Doctor of Philosophy, will lecture.

The Hon. Joseph Green will speak at assembly tomorrow.

George Worth, Esq., is a grandson of a duke.

In England *Esquire* is a complimentary title used when writing to someone not of the nobility but above the class of artisan.

3. The sign $ for *dollars, B.C.* and *A.D., a.m.* and *p.m.,* and *No.* (for number) when used with numerals. In the most formal writing, however, these abbreviations except *B.C.* and *A.D.* are ordinarily avoided.

4. Such abbreviations as *e.g.* (*exempli gratia,* for example), *ibid.* (*ibidem,* in the same place), *i.e.* (*id est,* that is), and *viz.* (*videlicet,* namely) in footnotes and bibliographies; and abbreviations of many kinds in indexes, tables, lists, and so on, provided an explanation of all abbreviations is attached.

5. The names of some governmental agencies, such as TVA, FBI, WPA, or SEC. Only those agencies should be abbreviated which are very well known. If in doubt, always write out the name.

NOTE. A period almost always follows an abbreviation. The only exceptions are in some technical contexts where *rpm* or *mph* are accepted and in some of the better-known governmental agencies, such as NATO or WPA.

NUMBERS

73a. Use figures for dates, house numbers, telephone numbers, page numbers of books, decimals, and hours of the day when *a.m.* or *p.m.* is used.

The museum was opened in Charleston, South Carolina, on January 12, 1773.

He lives at 1447 Devon Avenue.

Call me at Argyle 2-3926.

You will find that quotation on page 637 of your text.

That was a .32 caliber revolver.

The *Mercury* arrives at Chicago at 4:45 p.m.

73b. Write out round numbers and numbers under a hundred when only one or two are given.

Use figures for numbers requiring more than one or two words, for several numbers close together or complicated sets of numbers, or in quoting statistics.

73c. Write out a fraction unless it follows a whole number, and write out a number used as part of a compound adjective.

A vote indicates that two thirds of the class will go.

I require these sizes: shoes, 8½; collar, 16¼; and hat, 7½.

He bought a ten-dollar hat.

73d. Write out a number at the beginning of a sentence.

73e. Observe the following special rules concerning numbers.

1. When writing out figures for dollars, do not use a decimal point and two zeros for cents when the amount is in even dollars, but write $15, $68, $125.

2. Except in legal papers or where great accuracy is essential, do not write out a number and then repeat it in figures in parentheses. In ordinary writing, use one method or the other, not both.

3. When a number has more than three figures, set off figures in groups of three by commas, except street numbers and years, which should be written without punctuation.

4. Designate volume and chapter numbers and the main divisions of outlines by Roman numerals:

Vol. III, ch. x.

5. In writing out compound numerals from twenty-one to ninety-nine, use hyphens:

The river is *eighty-seven* yards wide.

6. The convention of indicating a decimal point by *and* in mathematics sometimes leads a writer to omit the *and* in writing out such numbers as six hundred and sixty-seven, on the assumption that *and* here is incorrect.

The use of this *and* in mathematics, however, is special and technical, and has nothing to do with representing numbers in ordinary writing. The *and*, therefore, should be kept in such instances.

(See *Workbook,* Exercises 46 and 47.)

I Chose America[1]

PERCY WAXMAN

IT WAS NOT to escape tyranny or poverty that I became an American citizen. I was born in Australia, educated there in the traditional British manner. Up to my twenty-third year even the idea of renouncing allegiance to the Empire would have seemed sacrilege.

Then one day the opportunity came to take a trip around the world. I went first to the United States. After a brief stay in San Francisco I eagerly set out for Chicago, which I had been led by tourist literature to believe was a cross between Paris and Paradise. I arrived there on an April morning—and in the midst of a raging, subzero blizzard. That Arctic wilderness did not seem enticing to one who had never before seen snow. A train for New York was leaving in ten minutes; so I dashed aboard.

I immediately found myself confronted by an embarrassing situation. I had left the West Coast with only enough money to last until I reached Chicago, where I could use my letter of credit, for I had been warned that carrying money around America was highly hazardous. So after paying for ticket and berth to New York I was left with exactly 75 cents. It was a 28-hour run to New York, and I had the hollow prospect of going all that time without food.

I asked the porter to tell the dining-car conductor of my situation and find out if I might not open an account with him based on my letter of credit. A few minutes later a middle-aged man stopped where I was sitting.

"I overheard the porter telling the conductor that you were in need of money," he said, "and I thought I'd see if I could help out."

Considerably embarrassed, I sputtered forth the reasons for my predicament, and that man, a complete stranger, loaned me $10. When I asked him to come to the bank with me as soon as we reached New York he said:

"Oh, I get off at Cleveland. Here's my card. You can send me the money when you get settled."

The fact that the man had *sought me out* to render me a kindness impressed me tremendously. I concluded that a country where such things happen to a stranger was a country well-worth knowing. One year after this incident I returned to the United States to stay.

I have made my home here for over thirty years. During my first years in New York I took no steps to become naturalized. One day I received notice to serve on a jury. Not being a citizen, I ignored it. A few days later I was served with a summons to appear at City Hall. There I presented myself to a gentleman of the old dyed-mustache school of Tammany statesmen who menacingly demanded to know why I had paid no attention to the previous notice. Somewhat smart-alecky I asked: "What is the penalty for a British subject serving on an American jury?"

"Oh, that's it, is it?" he remarked with Irish fervor and across the face of my sum-

---

[1] From the *Reader's Digest,* XXXVII (December, 1940), 77-80. Reprinted by permission of the author and the *Reader's Digest.*

mons wrote "Alien" in big red letters, as if he wished to impress me with the full significance of that sinister designation.

On my way home I thought over this experience. At first with amusement, then more seriously. Here I was, living and working in America, enjoying its privileges but not sharing full responsibilities. I decided to be an alien no longer. And now after having been a citizen for almost twenty-five years I can honestly say that the longer I live here the better I like it. My love for America has nothing to do with that brand of patriotism which a cynical friend defined as "self-interest multiplied by population."

It has often been said that Americans are dollar-chasers. But it has been my experience that one of the characteristics of Americans is the casualness with which they regard money. No people are more generous or extravagant. After having lived in many different parts of the world, I can honestly say that if I were friendless, unemployed, and penniless I would rather take my chances asking for help on the corner of an American street than anywhere else on earth.

I can say these things openly where a born American might hesitate. The fact that I am naturalized gives me a sort of detached privilege to speak freely without seeming to talk about myself.

American hospitality is proverbial. Was there ever anything to compare with the open-hearted reception accorded a foreign visitor? Nothing is too good for him. No one bothers to inquire who his ancestors were. In spite of their reputed smartness, Americans are more liable to be swindled by foreigners than foreigners are by Americans.

As for sportsmanship, no people are more ready to give the competing foreigner a break. I have been a spectator several times during Davis Cup matches here and abroad. There is no comparison between the sportsmanlike attitude of the Forest Hills crowd and foreign spectators. At Wimbledon there is, to be sure, a certain aloof politeness toward American players, but at Auteuil I have

witnessed vociferous demonstrations against non-French contestants that made me wonder at what moment diplomatic relations would be broken off.

This is the only country I know where unsatisfactory performers in the theater are not loudly booed. And where else but in America could the following have occurred:

Some years ago a famous English vaudeville performer came to this country with tremendous advance publicity. New York's Palace Theater was packed the day he made his debut. But his material, so popular in England, failed to click with the American audience. After his third number the actor, tears streaming down his cheeks, stepped in front of the curtain and said: "Ladies and gentlemen, I am doing my best to entertain you, but apparently you do not like what I am offering. I am sincerely sorry." That audience, the so-called hardboiled New Yorkers, touched by such manifest sincerity, cheered him and from then on his act was a triumph.

These incidents may seem unimportant but it is the trivial happenings, the spontaneous daily incidents that reveal a nation's character. And the character of America is something of which to be proud. In the maintenance of American ideals we who are naturalized have our part to play in gratitude for benefits received. We must do more than wave flags and sing *God Bless America*. We who *chose* America must remember that if the privileges we enjoy are worth living for, they are also worth dying for.

I sometimes think that we who *chose* to be Americans and had to make some effort to achieve citizenship have the greatest appreciation of the true significance of our American heritage. In my own particular circle of friends I belong to the minority group who have read the Bill of Rights, have a nodding acquaintance with the Constitution, and don't have to fake along with "Da de da da de da" when *The Star-Spangled Banner* is being sung. Born Americans have more of a take-it-for-granted attitude than the naturalized, perhaps because most of the latter become Americans to escape unhappy conditions in their native land.

On the pedestal of the Statue of Liberty are inscribed the following words written by Emma Lazarus:

Give me your tired, your poor,
Your huddled masses yearning to breathe free,
The wretched refuse of your teeming shore,
Send these, the homeless, the tempest-tossed to
     me,
I lift my lamp beside the golden door.

As one of the 38,000,000 of "wretched refuse" (a rather unhappy phrase I think, Miss Lazarus) who have settled here in the past hundred years, I believe that every American should kneel daily and thank God for the privilege of living in the United States. And if this expression of gratitude applies to those *born* here it is at this fateful hour 50 times more applicable to naturalized Americans.

To me the name America symbolizes an idea and connotes a way of life. And the more I study its history the more significant becomes its genesis and the more far-reaching its destiny. It has become a trite saying that America is the land of opportunity. But it is too often forgotten that the opportunity sought by its original settlers had a spiritual, not a material, basis. This momentous fact has had an overwhelming influence in shaping the destiny of the United States. Despite temporary checks to our economic progress,

America can never fail so long as we preserve a free educational system, freedom of opportunity, a jealous regard for individual rights, and a constantly lessening sense of class distinction.

This matter of class distinction has always seemed to me one of the most important factors in the preservation of American ideals, a factor which distinguishes this country from all lands where hereditary privilege or a titular aristocracy exists.

In America we have a fervent loyalty to a way of life, to a kind of society that presents definite promises to the most humble of its citizens. In this free atmosphere is an electric sparkle that spells hope for every legitimate ambition. And a minimum of class distinction is our guarantee of maximum opportunity for each individual in each generation.

SUGGESTIONS FOR STUDY

1. What incident impelled the author to become a citizen?
2. List several American qualities which he finds noteworthy.
3. Of what may the naturalized citizen have greater awareness than the native American?
4. What ideals does the author deem necessary for the preservation of the country?
5. Study any well-written paragraph in the article for stylistic devices, especially sentence variety and emphasis.
6. Define the following words from the article: platitudinous, dynamism, imperialism, cardinal, fratricidal, viable.

The American Way of Life[1]

DOROTHY THOMPSON

THE POLITICAL SPEAKER ended his television address by saying, "We must be prepared to defend our American Way of Life."

The words, I thought, had become hack-

[1] From the *Reader's Digest* (July, 1952), condensed from the *Ladies' Home Journal* (April, 1952). Reprinted by permission of the *Reader's Digest*.

neyed. What, I wondered as I turned off the set, *is* the "American Way of Life"?

I knew what it meant to the man I had just heard. It meant production: steel and cement, wheat and corn, oil and machines, wages and salaries—"purchasing power." All these, the speaker indicated, were threatened—by Communism, by the fall of great Western empires in Asia, by the impoverishment of Europe, by inflation.

I knew what the American Way of Life meant to my European friends. "Frankly," a Norwegian woman had said in a letter, "I can hardly bear to look at your magazine advertisements—shining kitchens, wonderful cars, packaged foods, beautiful clothes— things nearly everybody seems to have in America and that only the very well-to-do have here."

But neither the speaker nor the correspondent from Norway touched what the American Way of Life means to me. It is none of those things.

Perhaps that is because I was born and grew up in a different America. Until I was 12 years old I had never lived in a house with a bathroom, never set foot in a movie, never seen a mechanical refrigerator, never sat in an automobile. Some of these things existed in the small towns where I lived, but not for professional people like my father, who was a clergyman.

My father was an English immigrant who had originally come to visit relatives here, been offered a church, and decided to stay. He was respected in the communities where he lived, but nobody thought it was beneath him to push a lawn mower, paint a wall, or empty the slops.

We had no servants—only an occasional hired girl, usually a farmer's daughter, going to high school and working for her keep. My mother and my aunts were women of gentle tastes, but they led, part of the time, the lives of charwomen. Monday washing, on a corrugated washboard, with yellow soap; Tuesday ironing, with irons heated on the kitchen stove; Wednesday baking; Thursday sewing or mending (except for overcoats, and not always then, we children never had "boughten" clothes); Friday polishing the silver; Saturday house cleaning—with all the children helping. And, on top of that, operating in season a home cannery to provide us with food for the winter. Yet these women

had time to participate in parish and village life; to sing in the choir, help organize suppers and "sociables," care for sick neighbors, have home parties for the children, and— like the rest of the family—read, for oneself or aloud.

After my father's death we found a diary he had kept during his early days in this country. One item concerned family suggestions that he return to England. He commented, "Life in America is often hard. But there is a security here that exists nowhere else, for nowhere are there such kind people, ever willing to help each other."

I think it was during a visit of some British relatives that I first began to realize that there was a distinctly *American* Way of Life, different from others.

My British relatives always gave a fine education to *one* of their sons—usually the eldest—at Oxford or Cambridge. That he should help work his way through was out of the question. Other sons would be taken into business and the daughters sent to finishing schools. From our childhood it was taken for granted that we would all go to college, *if* our school marks justified it. And it was also taken for granted that we would help earn our own way through college; otherwise college would have been impossible. I did some tutoring and some dressmaking and during every vacation worked, usually in summer resorts, waiting on table. My female English cousins would rather have lived on the margin of starvation than fall out of their class by engaging in manual work.

The American Way of Life was a social democracy that had nothing to do with "ideology." It opened greater opportunities and gave one confidence—in the country, in one's fellow Americans, and in oneself. One was not confident that there would be no hard times or that one would ever enjoy luxury. One was confident merely that there would always be *some* kind of opening for willing and competent hands and heads. Intuitively, one knew that one was part heir to a great estate, to a land of continental proportions and immense resources. Here was a society both individualistic and coöperative—and as long as it remained so, one felt that nothing permanently disastrous could happen to America or America's children.

The American Way of Life was patriotic, but not nationalist in the imperial sense. Its patriotism was expressed in doing the best job of work one could, in helping others, in determining not to be a burden to friend or country, but relying on both in times of crisis. (The notion of a special loyalty oath would have been as mystifying to me in my youth as the notion of asserting loyalty to one's family.)

The American Way of Life meant to have been born free, and to be so recognized—and therefore not to talk about it much. It meant to *live* democratically, in the simplest and most human sense of noticing, caring about, and encouraging people.

This is what the American Way of Life still means to me. It doesn't mean a 300-billion-dollar national income, or the statistics of production, or being the "leading world power." It doesn't mean "the world's highest standard of living." It means the most human standard of life and relationships; it means hard work—even, if it comes to it, austerity. It means belonging to a nation of friends, and doing as you would be done by.

And if this still *is* the American Way of Life, then God will save America—with the coöperation of Americans.

SUGGESTIONS FOR STUDY

1. State the meanings of the "American Way of Life" which the author rejects.
2. State the contrast between the activities of the author's family and those of her British relatives.
3. On what did the author's confidence in America rest?
4. State the distinction made between patriotism and nationalism.
5. State the thesis.
6. Compare the conception of America with that of Percy Waxman. Both writers speak of our way of life. In what do they agree concerning it?

Credo[1]

THOMAS WOLFE

I BELIEVE THAT WE are lost here in America, but I believe we shall be found. And this belief, which mounts now to the catharsis of knowledge and conviction, is for me—and I think for all of us—not only our own hope, but America's everlasting, living dream. I think the life which we have fashioned in America, and which has fashioned us—the forms we made, the cells that grew, the honeycomb that was created—was self-destructive in its nature, and must be destroyed. I think these forms are dying, and must die, just as I know that America and

the people in it are deathless, undiscovered, and immortal, and must live.

I think the true discovery of America is before us. I think the true fulfillment of our spirit, of our people, of our mighty and immortal land, is yet to come. I think the true discovery of our own democracy is still before us. And I think that all these things are certain as the morning, as inevitable as noon. I think I speak for most men living when I say that our America is Here, is Now, and beckons on before us, and that this glorious assurance is not only our living hope, but our dream to be accomplished.

I think the enemy is here before us, too. But I think we know the forms and faces of

[1] From Thomas Wolfe, *You Can't Go Home Again*, (copyright, 1940). Reprinted by permission of Harper & Brothers.

the enemy, and in the knowledge that we know him, and shall meet him, and eventually must conquer him is also our living hope. I think the enemy is here before us with a thousand faces, but I think we know that all his faces wear one mask. I think the enemy is single selfishness and compulsive greed. I think the enemy is blind, but has the brutal power of his blind grab. I do not think the enemy was born yesterday, or that he grew to manhood forty years ago, or that he suffered sickness and collapse in 1929, or that we began without the enemy, and that our vision faltered, that we lost the way, and suddenly were in his camp. I think the enemy is old as Time, and evil as Hell, and that he has been here with us from the beginning. I think he stole our earth from us, destroyed our wealth, and ravaged and despoiled our land. I think he took our people and enslaved them, that he polluted the fountains of our life, took unto himself the rarest treasures of our possession, took our bread and left us with a crust, and, not content, for the nature of the enemy is insatiate —tried finally to take from us the crust.

I think the enemy comes to us with the face of innocence and says to us:

"I am your friend."

I think the enemy deceives us with false words and lying phrases, saying:

"See, I am one of you—I am one of your children, your son, your brother, and your friend. Behold how sleek and fat I have become—and all because I am just one of you, and your friend. Behold how rich and powerful I am—and all because I am one of you—shaped in your way of life, of thinking, of accomplishment. What I am, I am because I am one of you, your humble brother and your friend. Behold," cries Enemy, "the man I am, the man I have become, the thing I have accomplished—and reflect. Will you destroy this thing? I assure you that it is the most precious thing you

have. It is yourselves, the projection of each of you, the triumph of your individual lives, the thing that is rooted in your blood, and native to your stock, and inherent in the traditions of America. It is the thing that all of you may hope to be," says Enemy, "for"—humbly—"am I not just one of you? Am I not just your brother and your son? Am I not the living image of what each of you may hope to be, would wish to be, would desire for his own son? Would you destroy this glorious incarnation of your own heroic self? If you do, then," says Enemy, "you destroy yourselves—you kill the thing that is most gloriously American, and in so killing, kill yourselves."

He lies! And now we know he lies! He is not gloriously, or in any other way, ourselves. He is not our friend, our son, our brother. And he is not American! For, although he has a thousand familiar and convenient faces, his own true face is old as Hell.

Look about you and see what he has done.

SUGGESTIONS FOR STUDY

1. Does Thomas Wolfe believe in a static America, content with its customs and institutions, or a dynamic America, willing and able to change to meet the future? Does he have faith in our people?

2. What true discovery does he envision lying ahead of us and forming our dream of the future?

3. What is our arch enemy? What is meant by its appearing before us "with a thousand faces"?

4. Were the Founding Fathers confronted by the enemy, or is it of modern origin?

5. What guise does it assume in deceiving us? What ideal of life does it demand that we follow blindly? What more fitting ideal does Wolfe suggest we follow?

6. Study the author's style with particular attention to his use of loose and periodic sentences and of parallelism.

7. Define the following words from the selection: catharsis, compulsive, insatiate, sleek, incarnation.

Where I Stand[1]

ELIA KAZAN

I WANT TO MAKE my stand clear:

I believe that Communist activities confront the people of this country with an unprecedented and exceptionally tough problem. That is, how to protect ourselves from a dangerous and alien conspiracy and still keep the free, open, healthy way of life that gives us self-respect.

I believe that the American people can solve this problem wisely only if they have all the facts about Communism.

I believe that any American who is in possession of such facts has the obligation to make them known, either to the public or to the appropriate Government agency.

Whatever hysteria exists—and there is some, particularly in Hollywood—is inflamed by mystery, suspicion and secrecy. Hard and exact facts will cool it.

The facts I have are 16 years out of date, but they supply a small piece of background to the graver picture of Communism today.

I have placed these facts before the House Committee on Un-American Activities without reserve and I now place them before the public.

Seventeen and a half years ago I was a 24-year-old stage manager and bit actor, making $40 a week when I worked.

At that time nearly all of us felt menaced by two things: the depression and the ever-growing power of Hitler. The streets were full of unemployed and shaken men. I was taken in by the Hard Times version of the Communists' recruiting technique. They claimed to have a cure for depressions and a cure for Nazism and Fascism. I joined the Party late in the summer of 1934. I got out a year and a half later.

I have no spy stories to tell, because I saw no spies. Nor did I understand, at that time, any opposition between American and Russian national interest. It was not even clear to me in 1936 that the American Communist Party was abjectly taking its orders from the Kremlin.

What I learned was the minimum that anyone must learn who puts his head into the noose of Party "discipline." The Communists automatically violated the daily practices of democracy to which I was accustomed. They attempted to control thought and to suppress personal opinion. They tried to dictate personal conduct. They habitually distorted and disregarded and violated the truth. All this was crudely opposite to their claims of "democracy" and "the scientific approach."

To be a member of the Communist Party is to have a taste of the police state. It is a diluted taste, but it is bitter and unforgettable. It is diluted, because you can walk out.

I got out in the spring of 1936.

Why did I not tell this story sooner? I was held back, primarily, by concern for the reputations and employment of people who may, like myself, have left the Party many years ago.

I was also held back by a piece of specious reasoning which has silenced many liberals. It goes like this: "You may hate the Communists, but you must not attack them or expose them, because if you do you are attacking the right to hold unpopular opinions and you are joining the people who attack civil liberties."

I have thought soberly about this. It is, simply, a lie.

[1] This article appeared originally as an advertisement in *The New York Times* (April 12, 1952), following the appearance of the author before the House Committee on Un-American Activities. From the *Reader's Digest* (July, 1952). Reprinted by permission of the *Reader's Digest*.

Secrecy serves the Communists. At the other pole, it serves those who are interested in silencing liberal voices. The employment of a lot of good liberals is threatened because they have allowed themselves to become associated with or silenced by the Communists.

Liberals must speak out.

I think it is useful that certain of us had this kind of experience with the Communists, for if we had not we should not know them so well. Today, when all the world fears war and they scream peace, we know how much their professions are worth. We know tomorrow they will have a new slogan. First-hand experience of dictatorship and thought control left me with an abiding hatred of Communist philosophy and methods, and with the conviction that these must be resisted always.

It also left me with the passionate conviction that we must never let the Communists get away with the pretense that they stand for the very things which they kill in their own countries.

I am talking about free speech, a free press, the rights of property, the rights of labor, racial equality and, above all, individual rights. I value these things. I take them seriously. I value peace, too, when it is not bought at the price of fundamental decencies.

I believe these things must be fought for wherever they are not fully honored and protected whenever they are threatened.

The motion pictures I have made and the plays I have chosen to direct represent my convictions.

I expect to continue to make the same kinds of pictures and to direct the same kinds of plays.

SUGGESTIONS FOR STUDY

1. What problem faces the American people as a result of Communist activity?
2. What does the author feel will allay hysteria?
3. Why did Communism win converts here in the 1930's?
4. What disillusioned the author concerning Communism?
5. What reasoning held him back from discussing his story earlier? Why does he now feel such reasoning false?
6. What does the author feel are the attributes of the "American Way of Life"?
7. Relate this declaration of belief directly to that of Thomas Wolfe. Study the similarity of ideas found in these two works.

How to Misunderstand the USA [1]

TIBOR KOEVES

ON A BRIGHT September day almost fifteen years ago, I was seated in the office of the US Consul in my native Budapest, and I was thoroughly puzzled. I had come on a routine errand—a foreign correspondent, I needed a visitor's visa for my passport—and I was promptly exposed to a twist of the American mind which struck me as utterly paradoxical. Little did I know then that this was only the

[1] From the *United Nations World* (July, 1952). Reprinted by permission of the *United Nations World*.

first one of innumerable similar experiences which were to dog me for so many years in the future.

My paper was the largest daily in Hungary. It had such good standing that when my editor decided to send me to New York, I was given an official *Demande de Visa*, a diplomatic request lavishly printed in French. I had taken it for granted that this polite note from the Hungarian Foreign Office would be the open sesame to all doors, but apparently I had not reckoned with one man: the young, tall and handsome vice-consul of the United States.

He scanned the document, put it down on his desk, then gave me a friendly smile.

"I'm not satisfied," he quietly said. "There's no guaranty here that your Foreign Minister would support you should you become a public charge."

I was startled. The argument impressed me as preposterous. And mainly, the vice-consul's offhand reference to one of our highest officials struck me as an insult to the whole Hungarian nation. I was thinking of an answer, when the vice-consul looked at my name again and asked if I were related to a man by the same name, owner of a well-known restaurant where he had eaten a few times. I told him this was my brother. The consul pondered.

"Well," he then looked at me, "your brother is an honest and hardworking Hungarian. I've often admired his diligence and efficiency. I guess I'm going to take it for granted that honesty runs in your family."

Presently I had my visa, but I was perplexed. The US government had given me permission to go to New York not because I was a bona fide newspaperman vouched for by highest authority, but because it presumed that I was an honest man.

I had had dealings with consuls of most European nations, but this was entirely different. Red tape and diplomatic niceties had taken the back seat as the endorsement of a businessman was given the edge over that of a cabinet minister.

At that time I attributed the incident to the quirk of an individual. Today I know better. I know it was the expression of a philosophy which exasperates so many outsiders, but is shared by most Americans. Perhaps because of the aristocratic traditions of their societies, most Europeans still take titles at their face value and are impressed by high officials. To the more realistic mind of the American, dignitaries, cabinet members, and the like have more glamor than substance. A businessman, however, who is on his job and makes a success of it, is quite another matter. He represents stability in a world of dreamers and schemers.

Today I understand this reversal of values, but my first years in this country were a chain of endless surprises. Ask any correspondent from abroad and he will tell you that the United States is the world's toughest assignment. He is up against it, he will say, because America is shot through and through with contradictions and paradoxes which he cannot fit into a clear pattern.

Correspondents will also tell you that their task is much simpler in most other countries. For one, they can indulge in useful generalizations. In England, for instance, a man may be able to interpret the meaning of the news by applying such key words as "insularism," "fair play," "ancient social conventions." In France he will remember that every Frenchman is the follower of the philosopher Descartes, who said, "I think, therefore I am." This will make him understand to what extent tight logic and clever formulae are the secret of success in public and private life alike.

In the US there seems to be no similar short cut. The newcomer has the impression that logic is turned topsy-turvy and things work out by some mysterious, unknown process. The craziest propositions get a hearing from the most serious people, and extremes meet on all levels. "I will try anything once," is a national slogan, but so is its opposite "show me." And who knows which one of them is more characteristic, who knows which is a more American quality—horse sense, or indulging in fantastic speculations? Who will ever be able to describe accurately the United States, and explain the paradoxes of the American mind?

Take the peculiar American attitude toward the highest dignitary in the land—the President. In so many cases there is an astounding mixture of respect and scorn, admiration and abuse—respect for the office, scorn for the man; admiration for the function, abuse of the individual.

The first time I heard an American mention the President in terms usually reserved for a shifty bum who is an imbecile to boot, my hair bristled with astonishment. A marvelous contradiction, however—the man who pours vitriol on the President is at the same time unswervingly loyal to him, for the President is his Commander-in-Chief under whose orders he is willing to lay down his life for his country's sake.

It takes time to understand the peculiar logic behind this situation. Since the President is both the head of a partisan government and the impartial Chief of the State and of the Armed Forces, the typical American simply splits the tenant of the White House in two, so that he may vent his spleen on one of the fragments.

Such recalcitrance and apparent cynicism go down the line of public life, and create another false impression which occasionally influences international policy even on the highest level.

The senators, representatives, government officials, heads of agencies, and even judges who don't come in for a drubbing in impatient and impassioned language are so few that the innocent observer jumps to an inevitable conclusion. He is apt to believe that Americans are fed up with their whole system, lock, stock, and barrel, and are eager for a change.

Those who are familiar with the American scene, of course, know much better that what lurks behind these loud gripes is nothing more serious than the American's inborn desire to sound off continuously at the expense of anyone lesser than God. Notwithstanding frequent appearances to the contrary, no one is more passionately sold on his form of government than the American—as Hitler found out, too late.

But don't scorn Hitler for his boner when he believed that the dissenting, raucous voices in the US spelled nothing less than the doom of this "decadent democracy." For too long before him most European states were of an authoritarian character and it was generally held that only people cowering before authorities made for stable society, while critical, outspoken citizens were a danger to its very existence. In this shuffle of generalizations only one thing was lost from sight; namely that it was the streets of the most "disciplined" imperial capitals—Berlin, Moscow, Vienna, Budapest—which witnessed bloodshed and barricades in civil strife, and not those of impertinent New York, Washington, or Chicago.

Independence astounds the foreigner most when he finds it rampant in the army itself, as I did one morning shortly after the outbreak of the second World War.

Anxious to enlist, although technically an enemy alien, I obtained a letter of recommendation from the then Undersecretary of War, and rushed with it to the New York induction and enlistment center. There a lean staff sergeant scanned the letter and shrugged his shoulders.

"You're out of luck. Foreigners can't enlist," he said.

I tried to explain that the Secretary thought something might be done about the situation, but the sergeant cut me short.

"He doesn't know what he's talking about. He should learn his business better!" he barked and then added with finality: "And you can tell him *I* told you so!"

Finally I got to see a captain and told him about the reception the sergeant extended to the Secretary and to me.

"Sorry, I can't help you," the captain answered coolly. "The sergeant is right."

I left in confusion. I just couldn't understand that these underlings could insult someone near the top command without being court-martialed.

A few nights later, an incident I witnessed completed the destruction of my faith in the discipline and morale of the US Armed Forces.

It took place in a steak and chop restaurant on First Avenue, so popular at that time that people willingly stood in line for a table. Among other customers, there were two colonels and two privates. Then suddenly it happened, and I could hardly believe my eyes.

A table had become vacant, the hostess beckoned, *and it was the privates—two kids of twenty or less—who went over and sat down while the colonels, who had arrived after them, continued to wait their turn, completely unconcerned.*

I still remember the chills that ran down my spine. Such utter disregard of rank and precedence staggered my imagination. I had never heard of a citizen's army, or that soldiers might be private individuals. A thousand years of militarism had sold me on the idea that on or off duty a soldier was subject to the drastic rules of subordination and that the fate of his country depended on his behaving like an automaton in all circumstances. That night I wouldn't have bet on the chances of America winning the war a hundred to one.

As to the political scene, for years I wondered what decided a man to vote for one rather than the other of the two national parties. Both parties had liberals, progressives, and conservatives in their ranks, and how could one tell a Democrat from a Republican when the parties were not based on *theories,* when they had never published their abstract political philosophy clearly printed black on white? Secretly, I was convinced that the voter simply flipped a coin and then voted: tails Democrat, heads Republican.

The labor movement was equally puzzling. Why, the workers had no political party! They weren't even represented in Congress. How absurd, I often thought. They're a hundred years behind the times.

And then one day I met a second-generation Hungarian, son of an immigrant mine worker. He was a salesman who came to my house on business. He had a big car and showed me a picture of his new house.

His name was Kiss. It's a good Hungarian name. It means Small, and hundreds of thousands of peasants and workers answer to it. Only, in Hungary I had never met the son of a worker or a peasant who had a big car and a new house and who wore an expensive suit and a silk necktie. Yet we had many political parties with well-defined theoretic programs—including a socialist one —but somehow the loftiest theories never seemed to avail or to benefit those who were in the greatest need.

Reluctantly I had to admit that although the American system of politics couldn't possibly work in theory, it managed somehow to work out successfully in practice. And for the first time it occurred to me that it might be exactly the other way around on the Continent.

One thing still bothered me: the national conventions, where Presidential candidates were nominated amid the restraint of Barnum and Bailey and the quiet decorum of Coney Island on the Fourth of July.

I watched some of the outstanding citizens of this country—bankers, lawyers, senators, society women—lose every inhibition and go completely berserk. I heard their shrieks and yells, I saw them indulge in wild Indian dances hours on end. I was perturbed. Somehow it seemed doubtful that this was an infallible way of choosing the wisest and most qualified man to lead a great nation in peace and war.

It dawned on me only much later, after years of living in this country, that there might be an unconscious wisdom behind this strange exhibition. This Mardi gras, together with so many other bewildering features of the American political folklore—baby-kissing, back-slapping, constant accent on a sense of humor, clambakes, of calling candidates by their first names—all have served the same purpose. They have prevented the formation of a pompous and ossified officialdom in every branch of the government.

To the mind of every European who has suffered from dehumanized and byzantine bureaucracies and that "insolence of office" of which Hamlet had already complained, this is a rare and happy achievement. Perhaps American habits were incongruous, and much less aesthetic than Spanish etiquette, but they certainly bred much less humiliation and discontent.

In the United States not even the august State Department lives in a rarefied atmosphere, far removed from the cares and worries of the citizen. As a rule, a Foreign Office is the haughtiest office of a government; but in America it is always at the service of the humblest individual. This is true not only in dramatic cases like those of an Oatis or Vogeler, whose arrest by totalitarian powers provoked strongest diplomatic action, but also in much more obscure instances, where there is no question of national interest. I can testify to this personally, for this spirit was the providential force which saved the life of the man who is nearest to my heart.

It happened when a cable from Budapest informed me that my father, gravely ill at the age of 80, urgently needed penicillin, a panacea that was unobtainable in a defeated country after the war.

I was in a quandary, for no commercial flights to Central Europe had been established as yet, and, furthermore, I needed a written export permit from the State Department.

I sent my letter to Washington, but I was worried. The State Department was winding up the war and was engaged in important business up to its neck. I was prepared to wait a week or ten days at least; but would my father still be alive?

Next morning my telephone rang.

"This is the State Department," a pleasant feminine voice announced. "Your request is granted. We realize the case is urgent, so I'm phoning you the permit number. Air mail the package right away to Army Transport Command, Westover, Mass. Give them the number and say the papers will be forwarded later."

Within 48 hours the penicillin arrived at Budapest. It saved my father's life; he is still alive and vigorous. It couldn't have happened anywhere else, and I was dizzy with joy and wonder.

How shall I ever be able to understand the Americans? I asked myself. They refused me permission to fight and perhaps die for their nation; but, regardless, they went to great expense and trouble, they used the state apparatus and army facilities in order to save the life of my father, an old man of whom they had never heard. And I wasn't even a citizen at that time. What was the logic behind all this, how could one explain and describe these people and their land?

I still don't know the answer. But this incident confirmed me in the belief that one simply cannot hazard a purely logical guess about the way an American will act. There's another element which comes into play—call it instinctive judgment, moral obligation, emotional impulse or what you like—which moves the typical American to action more promptly and naturally than any abstract idea or analytical operation of his mind.

And this is exactly why America cannot be described. In Europe, ever since Plato, at least, the fondest dream of philosophers and statesmen has been to invent a science of government and society, and establish strict rules for the behavior of the citizen. The latest form is found in the various totalitarian doctrines which tell a man what he must believe, where he must live, how he must behave to his superior, where his exact place is in the scheme of things, which, in fact, leave him hardly any liberty to judge or to follow his impulses.

In stark contrast, social and political life in America are akin not to science but to art. Americans play life by ear, by emotions, inspiration, imagination. In this sprawling country, as yet unfettered by tyrannical traditions and conventions, an unprecedented proportion of people are determined to choose their own style and obey nothing but the dictates of their conscience or their whims.

This collection of improvisers—guided only by their instinct, their dreams, their genius, their heart—how does one describe them?

A knotty question indeed! How do you describe art, how do you describe teeming, ever-growing life?

SUGGESTIONS FOR STUDY

1. State the clash of ideas between the author and the vice-consul as expressed in the opening incident.

2. Why is the correspondent's task harder in the United States than in England or France?

3. Summarize the author's conception of the American attitude toward the President.

4. What did Hitler fail to understand?

5. What amazed the author about our army? our political parties? our labor movement? our nominating conventions? our State Department?

6. State the thesis.

7. Define the following words used in this article: paradox, insularism, vitriol, recalcitrance, spleen, raucous, byzantine, panacea.

Suggestions for Writing

From this section on the American Way of Life, you should be able to find many subjects on which to write. Try a definition of what seems to you most distinctively American in your home town, much as Dorothy Thompson did. Or synthesize her discussion with that of Elia Kazan and Thomas Wolfe. You might try to explain American ways—customs, traditions, law, spirit—to a foreigner, though you must be sure to limit such a topic severely. From the articles by Percy Waxman and Tibor Koeves, select concepts of America which you can further illustrate or expand, or which you would take exception to; for instance, what do you think of Mr. Koeves's analysis of our attitude toward the President? In writing, pursue the same method which each of these writers has employed—be specific; use anecdotes from your experience or details of life to exemplify your generalities. Strive especially to use variety of sentence types and sentence beginnings; for a time avoid compound sentences, and rarely begin a sentence with the subject.

Parts of the Composition

ༀༀༀༀༀ

II. THE WORD

A. The Dictionary

THE APPROPRIATE PLACE to begin the study of the word is the dictionary, for here we learn the meanings, spellings, history, and levels of usage of our vocabulary. As the accurate use of words and the precise understanding of meanings are first requisites in both reading and writing, do not attempt to study long in college without a good dictionary. Do not be content with a small pocket dictionary, for these volumes are little more than spelling lists and do not contain the wealth of information of the more standard works; purchase one of the dictionaries mentioned in the following paragraphs, and then set yourself to learning what it contains and how it is to be properly used.

THE UNABRIDGED DICTIONARY

The unabridged dictionaries provide complete information and are the final authority on the spelling, pronunciation, etymology, meanings, and usage of words. Although these dictionaries are too large to carry about and too expensive for the ordinary student to purchase, consult them in the college library whenever you cannot answer a question by reference to a smaller desk dictionary.

The most common unabridged dictionaries are *Webster's New International Dictionary,* Funk and Wagnalls' *New Standard Dictionary, The New Century Dictionary, The Universal Dictionary, The Dictionary of American English,* and *The New English Dictionary.* The last of these—also called the *Oxford English Dictionary*—is the most pretentious; it is the result of over seventy years of labor by more than two thousand workers, and in listing over 400,000 words it tries to give the biography of every word used in English during the last eight hundred years.

THE ABRIDGED DICTIONARY

On the desk of every student during his years in college should be a standard abridged dictionary. Though it does not contain so many words as the unabridged dictionary nor have so many distinctions of meanings, so complete etymologies, or so exhaustive specialized information, it is quite as reliable and for day-to-day use is complete and practical.

The commonly used abridged dictionaries are *Webster's New Collegiate Dictionary, The American College Dictionary, Webster's New World Dictionary* (College Edition), Funk and Wagnalls' *New College Standard Dictionary, The Winston Simplified Dictionary* (Advanced Edition), *Macmillan's Modern Dictionary,* the *Concise Oxford Dictionary,* and the Thorndike-Barnhart *Comprehensive Desk Dictionary.* As these dictionaries compress their information by technical symbols and abbreviations, and as there is variation among them in the type of symbol used and the method of recording each entry, you must get to know your dictionary thoroughly before you will know precisely what an entry means.

Here are a few of the errors that students often make in using their dictionaries.

1. They misinterpret the diacritical marks which designate proper pronunciation. Such marks are explained in the introduction to the dictionary and frequently also for convenience at the bottom of each page.

2. They confuse the derivation of the word with its meaning. For instance, though the word *folio* derives from the Latin word meaning *leaf*, it no longer carries that same meaning for us today but signifies a book of the largest size.

3. They accept the first occurrence of a word in the dictionary without pausing to observe whether the word may be entered two or more times to show its various meanings. The sentence "A settee was plainly visible on the horizon" is manifestly ludicrous if one tries to understand it by means of the first entry of the word *settee*, which explains the significance of the word as a medium-sized sofa; only the second entry explains that a particular kind of nautical vessel is also called a settee.

4. They content themselves with the first meaning in a given entry, even though the dictionary may have listed a dozen or more shades of meaning of the word. For example, what does the word *dress* mean in the sentence, "After a ride in the country he dressed his horse"? In *Webster's New International Dictionary* no meaning clarifies this sentence until the ninth definition is reached, namely "to groom or curry." To confuse this matter further for some students, the order in which the various meanings of a word are entered is not standard among all dictionaries. In *Webster's Collegiate Dictionary*, for example, the first meaning given is historically the oldest, and the last meaning is the most recent; but in *The American College Dictionary* this order is reversed so that the first meaning is the most recent.

There are three parts of a dictionary which you must study carefully: the introduction, the dictionary proper, and the special features.

The introduction. All dictionaries have an introduction to explain to the reader the terminology used and to show him how to use the book most effectively. Here is found (a) a *guide to pronunciation,* in which is given the key to the diacritical marks; (b) an *example of a typical vocabulary entry,* with a careful explanation of every part; and (c) a *list of abbreviations used,* which you should study until familiar with the more common abbreviations, such as *OF., Lat., ML., MHG., AS., OE., ME., Mil., Naut., Gr.* This is probably the most important and useful part of the introduction. A short article on "Orthography" and "Rules for Spelling" is sometimes included in the introduction also.

The dictionary proper. This part, which contains an alphabetical list of the most important words in the English language, packs a great deal of material into a very small space. A typical entry in *Webster's Collegiate Dictionary* reads:

cal'lous (kăl'ŭs), *adj.* [L. *callosus,* fr. *callum, callus,* callous skin.] 1. Having a callus; hardened; indurated. 2. Hardened in sensibility, feeling, etc.; unfeeling.—**Syn.** Horny; pachydermatous, thick-skinned.—**Ant.** Soft, delicate; sensitive.—**cal'lous·ly,** *adv.*—**cal'lous·ness,** *n.* —*v.t. & i.* To make or become callous.

The word to be defined appears first, followed by the pronunciation (if there are two possible pronunciations, the preferred one is usually given first); the part of speech (adj.); then in brackets the etymology of the word (Latin from *callum, callus,* "callous skin"). After the derivation of the word has been properly discussed, the definition or definitions follow. (The primary meaning of *callous* is *hardened;* from this there has developed a secondary meaning, *hardened in sensibility* or *unfeeling.*) In the definitions, quotations are often cited from English authors to illustrate the usage. Abbreviations commonly appear here, referring to a special meaning that the word has, for example, in commercial language (Com.—commercial). Next the synonyms and antonyms are listed. Antonyms, words which have the opposite meaning from that of the word listed, are frequently as useful as synonyms in giving clues to exact usage.

Next after the antonyms are usually found the formations of the other parts of speech derived from the word in question, especially those which are in any way irregular. Thus, from *callous* we have the adverb *callously* and the noun *callousness;* also a verb which can be used both transitively and intransitively and which means "to make or become callous." If the word belongs to a level of diction other than standard, the status of the word is indicated by *colloq., slang,* etc.

All this information is compressed into an extremely small space. The key to effective use of an entry is a *knowledge of the abbreviations used* in the dictionary. Without this knowledge, much of the information becomes gibberish. Look in the front of your dictionary for the table of abbreviations.

The special features. Besides the introduction and the main body of the dictionary, there is a third section—the special features —with which the student should be familiar. The special features included in *Webster's New Collegiate Dictionary* are as follows:

Abbreviations Used in Writing and Printing
Arbitrary Signs and Symbols
Biographical Names
Pronouncing Gazetteer
Colleges and Universities in the United States
    and Canada
Pronouncing Vocabulary of Common English
    Given Names
Vocabulary of Rhymes
Orthography
Punctuation, Compounds, Capitals, etc.
Preparation of Copy for the Press

Actually a good desk dictionary is a small encyclopedia. It is the most practical, generally useful, and valuable textbook you can possess.

THE THESAURUS

Although all unabridged English dictionaries list some of the more common synonyms and antonyms, no attempt is made to do more than touch upon this important phase of vocabulary building. A thoroughgoing treatment is reserved for the thesaurus, which is a storehouse [fr. L. *thesaurus,* from Gr. *thēsauros, treasure*] of synonyms and antonyms. The best-known and most easily accessible thesauri are *Roget's Thesaurus of English Words and Phrases* (now printed in a cheap edition), *The Roget Dictionary of Synonyms and Antonyms* (ed. C. O. Sylvester Mawson), Crabb's *Dictionary of Synonyms,* Smith's *Synonyms Discriminated,* March's *Thesaurus Dictionary of the English Language,* Webster's *Dictionary of Synonyms,* and Fernald's *Funk and Wagnalls' Standard Handbook of Synonyms, Antonyms, and Prepositions.* A special sort of work is Fowler's *Dictionary of Modern English Usage,* which discusses shades of meaning of many words and also many other matters of usage that will interest serious students.

Using the Thesaurus for synonyms. A synonym is a word which has approximately the same meaning as another word. Very few pairs of exact synonyms exist; if two words mean exactly the same thing, one of them is likely to be discarded and forgotten. Therefore, to be precise in the use of words, you must discriminate carefully among synonyms, as you can readily understand if you open *Roget's Thesaurus* to the seventy-nine synonyms of the verb *think.*

When you study words which mean approximately the same thing, try to become aware of differences, of similarities, of the hundreds of very slight but nevertheless existing shades of coloring to be found in every word. For example, the verb *to eat* is a general word that has as synonyms *taste, nibble, dally with, gulp, bolt,* and *stuff.* In deciding which of these words to select for a particular purpose, examine the level of diction used in the paper and consider who is eating. A society matron or a college Dean of Women would scarcely *bolt* food at a formal sorority banquet, nor would a hungry athlete *nibble* his double steak smothered in mushrooms. In choosing a synonym of the verb *walk,* you can choose from *plod, trudge, tread, stride, saunter, meander, hike, tramp, stroll, march, mince, ramble, prowl, hobble,* and *sneak.* Looking over this list, realize how general is the meaning of *walk* and how much care should be taken in selecting a suitable synonym. Some of the words suggest leisurely movement (saunter, meander, stroll); others, furtive movement (sneak, prowl). Still others are suggestive of people's personalities: an effeminate person *minces,* a military man *marches,* a conceited individual *struts.* Thus a writer narrows the choice to one word which gives the meaning that he wants.

NOTE. The thesaurus does not usurp the place of the general English dictionary; each synonym should be checked with the dictionary to make sure that the shade of meaning is the one wanted.

Do not use a word because it is big, and do not use a new word just for the sake of using it. Do not use an unnecessary word. Above all, never use a word whose meaning you have not carefully checked.

Using the thesaurus for antonyms. An antonym is a word which has the opposite meaning from that of another word. Antonyms function by what psychologists call "the power of association," for when we see the word *love,* it is relatively simple to call to mind its opposite, *hate.* A great many meanings cannot exist without a conception of their opposites. For example, the word *light* has no meaning to the person who does not understand what is meant by *dark; long* and *short* and *fat* and *thin* are relative terms depending altogether on the understanding one has of each of them. Antonyms, therefore, are sometimes as useful as synonyms in determining the meaning of a word. In actual writing they are especially valuable in contrasts and comparisons. Of course, the same warning applies to the selection of antonyms as was given with regard to synonyms.

SUGGESTIONS FOR STUDY

Distinguish among the following synonyms by using each word correctly in a sentence.

1. pay, compensate, recompense, requite, reimburse, indemnify
2. proud, arrogant, presumptuous, haughty, supercilious, insolent, insulting
3. sin, vice, crime
4. impostor, mountebank, charlatan
5. good, serviceable, fit, excellent, sound, reliable
6. marriage, matrimony, wedlock, wedding
7. martial, warlike, military
8. old, ancient, antique, venerable, antiquated, archaic, obsolete
9. instrument, implement, tool, utensil, machine, apparatus, agent
10. ominous, portentous, sinister
11. interest, excite, entertain, engage, occupy, hold
12. rebellion, revolution, revolt, insurrection, mutiny
13. story, tale, anecdote
14. tear, rip, rend, cleave, split, rive
15. lessen, decrease, impair, weaken
16. irony, sarcasm, satire
17. walk, traverse, perambulate, meander, amble
18. flit, flutter, flicker, hover
19. talk, speak, converse
20. exceed, excel, surpass, transcend, outdo

(See *Workbook,* Exercises 1, 2, 3, and 4.)

Featherbeds and Parnassus[1]

CAROL HOVIOUS

PROBABLY something of the same spirit that impels small boys to tie tin cans to puppy-dogs' tails prompted me to this experiment on my college Freshmen. Certain it is that I tortured them unmercifully, stretching their tender minds upon the ruthless rack of knowledge and subsequently cracking open their pates to see what had happened. I looked upon myself, of course, as a scientist in search of truth; campus legend, I am told, has not been so kind.

It all came about as the result of a wager. I was sitting one day in the Union with a member of the history department of the university where I peddled English. Over our coffee we fell to ringing changes on that favorite pedagogical lament—the low estate of incoming Freshmen. My companion brought his fist down upon the table with a belligerent thump.

"I tell you," he exploded, "these Freshmen can't think! All they can do with an idea is ogle it!" He puffed his pipe reflectively for a moment and then added with a sidewise swipe at me, "Or maybe it isn't that they're fundamentally incapable of handling an idea, but that the English department hasn't equipped them with words to express it."

"Oh, come now," I protested defensively, rubbing the tender heel of my wounded professional pride.

"Listen," he interrupted, wagging a bony finger knowingly at me, "I'm willing to lay you 10 to 1 that at least—hm-m—at least 90 per cent of your Freshmen will not know the meaning of so common a word as—as—oh, well, say 'prodigal.'"

I had—or thought I had—no illusions about the verbal capacity of college Freshmen. But still—90 per cent! That was a bit steep; particularly since "prodigal" was such an ordinary word. It was not an academic word; one ran across it every day in magazines, in newspapers, in common speech.

"Done!" I answered, already savoring my triumph and already preparing the crushing little speech with which I should rebuke him for his impertinent reflections upon the purveyors of English, once I had good evidence at hand.

Since my bet had gone statistical, I was taking no chances with my evidence. I was getting it in irrefutable, incontrovertible black and white. The next day I wrote the word "prodigal" on the board and asked each of my fifty Freshmen to jot down on a slip of paper the best definition he could muster.

To make a sad story short, my historical friend won—by a generous margin of 6 per cent! He confessed then that he had already tried the experiment for himself with similar results, adding that to collect his bet was almost as heartless as to take candy from the baby. However, he collected it.

I went out to grieve and salt my wounds. Only two of my flock of fifty Freshmen had defined "prodigal" with reasonable accuracy as "wasteful." The other forty-eight miserable black sheep had gone variously astray, but their vagaries were of two general sorts. About one third of the miscreants confused "prodigal" with "prodigy" and hence informed me that the word meant "exceptional," "gifted," "a smart kid."

And would that the other two thirds had never heard the story of the prodigal son! With his ill-advised squanderings and wanderings in mind, they assured me that prodigal meant "one who returns after absence,"

[1] From the *English Journal*. Reprinted by permission of the author and of the *English Journal*, College Edition (now *College English*).

"sort of hitchhiker a long time ago," "one who has strayed away," "a good-for-nothing," "worthless," "wayward," "a mild form of sinner."

When, dismayed, I sought to bring them back to sanity by asking them what such an expression as "the prodigal hand of nature" would mean, they only looked at me with blank faces.

The next day, possessed of a sort of horrible curiosity to discover if I could what other monsters of misconception lurked in the minds of my innocents, I led them to a second and more dreadful slaughtering. Picking a dozen or so words at random from current magazines in order to have a fairly representative list, I asked each student to state briefly what the word meant to him, and then, as a check, to use the word in a sentence.

I reaped a whirlwind of ignorance for my folly. In view of the fact that my fifty Freshmen were something better than the average, I determined on one last try which should give them every opportunity to show what they knew. I selected words from their own text in Freshman English; I warned them far enough in advance so that they could check over any unfamiliar words; and, finally, I did not ask them to formulate their own definitions or to write illustrative sentences—I asked only that they select the correct definition from the list I furnished them. The results of this test were, if possible, even more shocking than those of my earlier probings.

Sobered and saddened by these researches into the ignorance of my own students, I sought consolation by inducing my colleagues to try the test on their students—on the principle, I suppose, that misery loves fellow sufferers. The results were always the same; the more papers I scored and tabulated— and there were hundreds before my courage failed—the sorrier became the spectacle of the Freshman mind.

As I worked over the test papers, the errors of definition began gradually to sort themselves into certain general categories which I have labeled "dogberrian," "tangential," "etymological," and "orthographical." The orthographical confusions such as "assent" for "ascent" and "principle" for "principal" we may dismiss summarily, since they form a relatively small and innocuous group. Such confusions as these are, I suppose, inevitable as long as the English language continues to have homonyms and the human mind continues fallible.

The student who falls afoul of the dogberrian vice is in much worse case than his brother who sins orthographically. It is one thing to confuse "principle" and "principal" and quite another to blur the distinction between "odious" and "odorous," as did Mrs. Malaprop in her famous "comparisons are odorous." Mrs. Malaprop, of course, traces her lineage directly to Shakespeare's loquacious old constable, Dogberry, in *Much Ado about Nothing*. The basis of the "malapropism" is an auditory or visual confusion of words: "odious" and "odorous" both look and sound somewhat alike; so do "prodigy" and "prodigal." But what is merely amusing in Mrs. Malaprop becomes maddening in a college student. Shakespeare and Sheridan amused themselves and delighted their audiences by this simple device because it manifested itself in illiterate people of whom one expected nothing better. But the dogberrian disposition of college students is at once exasperating and terrifying to the professor who must address them seriously upon serious subjects which they are supposed to comprehend.

Typical dogberrian confusions are: "impetuous" with "impetus," "precipitous" with "precipice," "imminent" with "eminent," "veracity" with "voracity," and "utilitarian" with "Unitarian."

Tangential errors spring from a partial understanding of a word and are mostly context derived; that is, meanings inferred—erroneously—by a student from reading a word in a given context and subsequently attaching that meaning to the word permanently. Thus, Freshmen who told me that "prodigal" meant "a wanderer," or "a sinner," or "a hitchhiker" had in mind the tangential meanings of the word in the story of the prodigal son. To be sure, the young man in the biblical legend was a wanderer and a mild form of sinner, but he was not therefore called "prodigal." Probably the student came to associate wandering and sinning with prodigality because the emphasis in the story is more upon the young scapegrace's peregrinations than upon his wasteful dissipation of his patrimony.

Thus, it will be seen that a tangential definition comes close to the real meaning of a word, yet misses it, flies off at a "tangent" from it. To define "avidity" as "speed" is to miss the central meaning of the word—"greed"—and to emphasize a tangential meaning which is subsidiary. To define "recumbent" as "still" is likewise to skirt the truth, to come close to the real meaning and yet to miss it.

The student who defined "scrupulous" as "criminal" fell doubly upon evil days, for his thinking was at once dogberrian and tangential. In the first place, with malapropian ineptness he confused "scrupulous" with its opposite, "unscrupulous." In the second place he attached to "unscrupulous" the tangential meaning "criminal," rather than the exact meaning, "unprincipled."

The most ludicrous boners, however, were not malapropian or tangential, but philological. Students who have had too light a draft from the Pierian Spring become giddy and fall headlong into the most amazing abysses. Some of these falls from grace result from "little Latin and less Greek." If *homo* is Latin for "man," why should not "homogeneous" mean "pertaining to man"? The student is mildly outraged to discover that his little Latin will not unlock the secret meaning of every word. Occasionally the student is even betrayed by his own language and defines "salutary" as "one who salutes."

I am now about to offer an explanation for this amazing chaos in the minds of our college students This explanation I realize is purely hypothetical. It is likely to be very unpopular with certain of our educationalists. Nevertheless, it is my best explanation, and I submit it.

Let us dismiss first of all the pseudoetymological errors. They come from a little learning, but even a little learning is not to be too lightly despised in these parlous times. They are to be regretted, but still forgiven. They are the ludicrous result of well-meaning Latinists who, intent upon salvaging Latin from the dead, have cried out insistently that Latin survives in the living speech. The Latinist may be forgiven much, for he has suffered much, but it might be wished that he preach his doctrine with a little caution.

More serious, however, is the malapropism. It is, I am convinced, an unwanted and unexpected child of the "configuration method" of teaching reading. No doubt the configurationists, who have flourished mightily in the last years, would disown the child I make so bold to lay upon their doorstep; whether they admit the parentage or not, the child has its father's eyes.

The configuration-taught child, it will be recalled, learns by wholes. He walks without bothering to creep or crawl; he builds glittering castles without any unpleasant digging in the basement; he reads right pop out of the box without any tedious fiddling with mere letters and their sounds.

All this is very gratifying to papas and mamas who adore being dazzled by their offspring. And no one can deny that children learn to read much more rapidly by this method. The theory is that having learned to read whole words, the child gradually, by some vague and subterranean process, learns to recognize letters and their sounds.

Aye, but there's the rub! For the child learns no such thing. Many a bewildered college student has come to me with groans and tears and begged me to teach him "how to sound out words the way mother does." And I—well, I give him a primer and let him sweat a bit over phonetics, for without a

groundwork in phonetics he cannot spell nor
can he sound out new and unfamiliar words.
It is this reading of words by their shape that
leads him to confuse such similars as "impetus" and "impetuous."

The attachment of tangential instead of
exact meanings to words, like the malapropism, is a Dead Sea apple of an unwise peda-
gogy. It is the result of substituting a guess
for the dictionary. The student is not to be
blamed too harshly for this practice; he had
been encouraged in it. Modern educational
theory preaches that a child's pleasure in a
book is chilled by the frigid breath of the
dictionary. One enthusiast opined—in print
—that it made no difference if the child who
heard *Lady of the Lake* read aloud thought
it was about a "staggit eve." If the child
caught the emotional lift of the poem, that
was enough.

In short, a child need not know what a
book is about. It is enough that his imagination should soar upward on "wings of book"
without any scholarly ballast. If only he will
read widely and rapidly, he will by some
inexplicable magic become a full man.

Such rhapsodists seem to overlook the cold
fact that one cannot enjoy what one does not
understand. They overlook, too, the fact that
children are not altogether fools. Students
learn early that a few round-eyed "oh's" and
beatific "ah's" judiciously placed will do more
to bring home an "A" than any amount of
grubbing. So with their tongues in their
cheeks they turn sycophant and settle back
to a life of intellectual ease. They are
pleased, of course, because they can be lazy
with impunity—but they are also secretly
contemptuous of the system that lets them
get by with it.

Although the exigencies of space prevent
an adequate elaboration of the point, I
should like to suggest in passing that the
schools are not primarily to blame for this
unfortunate situation. After all, the schools
merely pander to the public taste. One needs
but to scan the current magazines to discover
that we as a people are characterized by a

desire to get something for nothing—to acquire personal charm by perfume instead of
discipline, big salaries by techniques instead
of hard work, musical proficiency by charts
instead of practice. The schools with their
modern "get-smart-quick" schemes are
merely following the trend of the times.

The evil effects of this laxness are everywhere evident, but to me, specifically, as an
English teacher, painfully so in my students'
inability to deal with words. Without words
they walk in a world of textbooks they cannot read, professors they cannot understand,
misty ideas they cannot express. Words are
the bright coin with which they buy their
sheepskins, and they are paupers.

That students need not always remain in
this intellectual workhouse I have tried to
indicate by analyzing the sources of their
verbal—and therefore ideational—incompetence. If we know that they are betrayed by
our methods of teaching words by wholes
and our airy disregard of the dictionary, we
have at least a signpost pointing the road to
rehabilitation.

But one thing is certain—there is no royal
road to learning; there are no escalators up
Parnassus. Every student must mount under
his own power. If we carry him around on a
featherbed all the days of his youth we have
only ourselves to blame if he is not in trim
for the stiff climb up Parnassus.

SUGGESTIONS FOR STUDY

1. What rhetorical value does the introductory
anecdote have?
2. Explain what is meant by dogberrian, tangential, etymological, and orthographical.
3. State the reasons for the students' making
such blunders with words.
4. On whom can the blame be laid?
5. Is this lack of vocabulary serious for college
students engaged in the mastery of intellectual
subjects?
6. What suggestions are offered for remedying
the situation?
7. How is the title of the article derived?
8. Define the following words used in the
article: purveyors, irrefutable, incontrovertible,
homonyms, fallible, orthographical, odious, odorous, loquacious, auditory, illiterate, impetuous,

precipitous, imminent, veracity, utilitarian, context, scapegrace, peregrinations, patrimony, avidity, subsidiary, recumbent, scrupulous, ineptness, philological, Pierian Spring, homogeneous, salutary, etymological, parlous, salvage, subterranean, opined, sycophant, impunity, rehabilitation, Parnassus.

9. Using the tone employed by the author of the essay, write a paper on the same subject from your own point of view.

B. Spelling

Spelling is primarily a problem of the grade school and high school. At least it should be mastered there. The student who has entered college without the ability to spell is laboring under a handicap which only he can remedy. The ability to spell comes gradually as a result of extensive reading and the forming of correct habits. Rules exist, but for most rules there are exceptions, so that on the whole the easiest way to learn to spell is to master a few words each day. The following rules point the way to good spelling. Learn and apply them, but also use your dictionary conscientiously in order to impress upon your mind images of the words as they should appear, and thus make correct spelling a habit which cannot easily be broken.

74a. Rule for *ie* and *ei*.

To spell words like *believe* and *receive*, a help is to remember the jingle

i before *e* except after *c*,
or if sounded like *a*
as in *neighbor* and *weigh*.

1. *i* before *e*:

believe, relieve, achieve, siege, field, thief, grief, retrieve, mischief.

2. except after *c*:

receipt, deceive, perceive, ceiling.

3. or if sounded like *a* as in *neighbor* and *weigh*:

neigh, heinous, sleigh.

4. Exceptions:

seize, weird, leisure, either, neither.

74b. Rules governing prefixes and suffixes.

1. If the final consonant of the prefix is the same as the first consonant of the root word, both consonants are retained:

mis and *spell—misspell; un* and *necessary—unnecessary; dis* and *solve—dissolve; over* and *rate—overrate.*

2. If a suffix begins with a consonant and the root word ends in any letter except *y*, the two are simply written together:

fate and *ful—fateful; lone* and *ly—lonely.*

If the word ends in *y*, the *y* changes to *i*:

busy and *ness—business; lazy* and *ness—laziness.*

3. If a suffix begins with a vowel and the word is of one syllable or has an accented last syllable composed of a final consonant preceded by one vowel, the final consonant of the word is doubled:

drop and *ed—dropped; whip* and *ed—whipped; occur* and *ed—occurred; equip* and *ed—equipped.*

4. If a suffix begins with a vowel but the word has an unaccented last syllable, the final consonant does not double:

offer and *ing—offering; enter* and *ed—entered; benefit* and *ed—benefited.*

74c. Rules governing the spelling of the plurals of nouns.

1. Nouns which do not end in *s* or an *s* sound (*s, z, x, sh, ch*) regularly form the plural by adding *s* to the singular form: *hats, stores.*

2. Nouns which end in *s* or an *s* sound (*s, z, x, sh, ch*) form the plural by adding *es* to the singular form: *churches, glasses.*

3. Nouns ending in *y* form their plurals in two ways:

(a) If a consonant or *qu* precedes the *y*, the *y* is changed to *i* and *es* added:

lady—ladies, soliloquy—soliloquies.

(b) If a vowel precedes the *y*, *s* is added to the singular form:

dray—drays, day—days.

4. Nouns ending in *o* are divided into two major groups: those with a vowel before the *o*, and those with a consonant before the *o*.
    (a) If a vowel precedes the *o*, the plural is formed by adding *s* to the singular form: *embryos, radios*.
    (b) If a consonant precedes the *o*, the plural form usually ends in *es*:

heroes, potatoes.

There are many exceptions, however. All musical terms, for instance, end in *s*:

altos, banjos, sopranos, solos,

as well as many nonmusical terms: *curios, octavos*. Some words, moreover, have both endings:

cargos, cargoes; mottos, mottoes; zeros, zeroes.

5. Most nouns ending in *f* form the plural by changing the *f* to *v* and adding *es*:

leaf—leaves

(exceptions are *roof, chief,* and others).

6. Letters, figures, symbols, or words out of their normal context form their plurals by adding *'s*:
    Letters:

The *A's* are legible in this MS.

Symbols:

You have used two *5's* too many here.

Words:

The *and's* and *so's* are far too numerous in your paper.

7. Compound nouns form their plurals by adding *s* to the part of the compound which carries the meaning of the word; this part of the compound may be the first or the second element:

bookstores, steamboats, mothers-in-law, attorneys-general, passers-by.

Compounds with *ful* add *s* to the latter element:

spoonfuls, cupfuls.

8. Words borrowed from foreign languages usually retain the plural form of their own language.
    (a) Latin and Greek:

curriculum, curricula; stratum, strata; stimulus, stimuli; alumnus, alumni; alumna, alumnae; larva, larvae; crisis, crises; thesis, theses; appendix, appendices; phenomenon, phenomena; automaton, automata.

    (b) French:

beau, beaux; tableau, tableaux; madame, mesdames.

    (c) Hebrew:

cherub, cherubim; seraph, seraphim.

(See *Workbook*, Exercise 5.)

Words Frequently Misspelled. The words listed below are among those most frequently misspelled by college students.

In trying to master the spelling of these words, make sure that you learn the meaning of any with which you are not familiar.

absence	bachelor	conceit
accessible	believe	concise
accessory	benefited	confident
accidentally	biscuit	connoisseur
accommodate	Britain	conquer
accumulate	buoyant	conscience
accustom	business	conscientious
achieve	cafeteria	consistent
acquainted	captain	contemptible
across	carburetor	corroborate
aghast	category	courteous
all right	cede	criticism
amateur	cemetery	crystal
analyze	certain	dealt
annihilate	chamois	deceit
anxiety	changeable	decision
appropriate	chauffeur	definite
argument	colonel	descendant
arrival	colossal	describe
ascend	committee	desirable
asinine	comparative	despair
athletic	competent	desperate
attacked	completely	develop
attendance	concede	dilemma

disappear
disappoint
disastrous
disciplinary
discriminate
disease
dissatisfied
divine
dormitories
ecstasy
efficiency
eliminate
embarrass
emphasize
environment
equipped
especially
exaggerated
exceed
excellence
exercise
exhaust
exhilaration
existence
experience
familiar
fascination
February
fiery
financial
foreign
forcible
friend
fundamental
generally
ghastly
ghost
government
grammar
grievance
guarantee
guard
handkerchief
harass
height
heir
heroes
hindrance
humorous
hypocrisy
illiterate
immediately
incidentally
incredible
independence
indict
indispensable

inimitable
inoculate
insistent
intrigue
inveigle
irrelevant
irresistible
judgment
knowledge
laboratory
lacquer
leisure
lieutenant
literature
livelihood
loneliness
losing
maintenance
malign
maneuver
mathematics
medicine
merely
miniature
misspelled
moccasin
momentous
mortgage
necessary
negligible
nickel
noticeable
occasion
occurred
occurrence
omitted
opportunity
optimistic
original
oscillate
ostracize
pageant
pamphlet
panicky
parallel
paralyzed
participle
particularly
perceive
permanent
permissible
perseverance
persistent
persuade
physically
physiology
picnicking

plagiarize
playwright
plebeian
poignant
politician
practically
prairie
preference
prejudiced
preparatory
prestige
privilege
procedure
proceed
professor
propeller
psychology
pursuing
quizzes
recede
receive
recognize
recommend
reference
referred
rehearse
relieve
religious
repetition
reservoir
restaurant
rhetoric
rhythmical
ridiculous
righteous
sacrifice
scarcely
scene
schedule
scientific
secretary
seize
separate
sergeant
severely
shepherd
sheriff
shining
siege
sieve
similar
sincerely
soliloquy
sophomore
sovereign
specimen
stopping

strategic
strength
studying
succeed
suddenness
summarize
supersede
surprise
symbol
synonym
tariff
technical
temperament

tendency
toboggan
tragedy
tranquillity
transferred
truly
twelfth
tyrannize
unconscious
undoubtedly
unnecessary
unusual
usually

vacillate
vacuum
valuable
vegetable
veil
vengeance
villain
weather
weird
writing
yacht
yeast
zoology

C. Words Frequently Confused

Study the meanings and spelling of the following words. Those which are starred are described in the Glossary of Usage, but the others you must consider carefully in your dictionary.

abbreviated, abridged
ability, capacity
accede, cede
accept, except (verb)°
adapt, adopt
admit, confess
adverse, averse
advice, advise, inform
affect, effect°
affection, affectation
aisle, isle
allay, alley, ally
alleviate, relieve
allude, elude
allusion, illusion°
already, all ready°
altar, alter
altogether, all together
amateur, novice
amend, emend
among, between°
ancient, antiquated
angel, angle
anxious, eager
apt, likely, liable°
ascend, ascent, assent
avenge, revenge
avocation, vocation
bare, bear
baring, barring
bating, batting
beside, besides°
boarder, border
breath, breathe
bridal, bridle

can, may°
caning, canning
cannon, canon
canvas, canvass
capital, capitol
caring, carrying
casual, causal
censor, censure
censure, criticize
ceremonial, ceremonious
character, reputation
choose, chose
cite, sight, site
climactic, climatic
clothes, cloths
coarse, course
common, mutual
complement, compliment
comprehensible, comprehensive
comprise, compose
condemn, contemn
condescension, condensation
confidant, confident
conscience, conscientious, conscious
contemptible, contemptuous
continual, continuous
convene, convoke
council, counsel
credible, credulous

dairy, diary
deadly, deathly
debase, demean
decent, descend, descent, dissent
deference, difference
deprecate, depreciate
desert, dessert
detract, distract
device, devise
dining, dinning
disability, inability
discussed, disgust
disinterested, uninterested
distinct, distinctive
dual, duel
durable, endurable
effeminate, feminine
egoist, egotist
eight, eighth
elicit, illicit
emigrant, immigrant
eminent, imminent
equable, equitable
exceptional, exceptionable
faint, feint
famous, notorious
farther, further*
fatal, fateful
fewer, less*
filing, filling
finally, finely
formally, formerly
forth, fourth
furry, fury
gap, gape
genius, genus
genius, talent
gracious, kind
griping, gripping
hanged, hung
help, succor
historic, historical
hoping, hopping
human, humane
idle, idol, idyl
imply, infer
imposition, imposture
inaugurate, initiate, begin
incidence, incidents
ingenious, ingenuous
interest, intrigue
invaluable, valuable
judicial, judicious

juvenile, puerile
later, latter
laudable, laudatory
lay, lie*
lead, led
leave, let*
loath, loathe
loose, lose*
loses, losses
luxuriant, luxurious
majority, plurality
mating, matting
moping, mopping
moral, morale
moral, religious
morality, mortality
morn, mourn
musing, mussing
oblivious, unconscious
official, officious
oral, verbal
ordinance, ordnance
pastime, past time
peace, piece
persecute, prosecute
person, personage
personal, personnel
perspicacity, perspicuity
pining, pinning
plain, plane
planing, planning
practical, practicable
precede, proceed
prescribe, proscribe
presence, presents
principal, principle*
prophecy, prophesy
propose, purpose (verb)
puling, pulling
quiet, quite
rain, rein, reign
receipt, recipe
respectfully, respectively
riding, ridding
right, rite, write
sensible, sensitive
sensual, sensuous
scaring, scarring
set, sit*
sloping, slopping
sole, soul
specie, species
staring, starring
stationary, stationery

statue, stature, statute
stimulant, stimulus
taping, tapping
than, then*
their, there, they're*
to, too, two*
troop, troupe

vicious, viscous
weather, whether
who's, whose
willfully, willingly
wining, winning
woman, women
your, you're

(See *Workbook*, Exercises 5 and 6.)

D. The Appropriate Preposition

75. Choose the appropriate preposition.

An extremely vexatious matter in word usage is the correct use of prepositions, for in the English language have grown many idioms which sometimes have no apparent logic in their construction but must simply be learned for a writer to express himself accurately. For instance, we wait *for* a person, we wait *at* a place, and we wait *on* a customer; we agree *with* our friends in agreeing *on* a plan, agreeing *in* the necessity for a plan, and agreeing *to* their demands. An unabridged dictionary is one's guide through this jungle of usage, but among other books considering this subject H. W. Fowler's A *Dictionary of Modern English Usage* and Fernald's *Funk and Wagnalls Standard Handbook of Synonyms, Antonyms, and Prepositions* may prove the most helpful.

In the following list are a few of the idiomatic usages concerning prepositions which occur frequently. Call this particular matter of word selection to your attention by studying these usages carefully.

accuse by, of: He was accused *of* theft *by* the policeman.
adept in: He was extremely adept *in* skating.
angry at: My father was angry *at* the car; he was also angry *at* me.
angry with: My father was angry *with* me. (*Angry with* is generally preferred to *angry at* in reference to people.
apply for, to: Students should apply *to* the registrar *for* admission.
apropos of, to: His remarks apropos *of* the legislation were not apropos *to* the occasion.
argue against, for: He argues *against* the sales tax but *for* the seaway project.
argue with: He argued *with* me.

attitude toward: No one understands his attitude *toward* me.

capacity for: The teacher relished her capacity *for* retaining facts.

capacity of: The tank has a capacity *of* eighteen gallons.

center in, on: His interests center *in* (or *on*) photography. (Be sure to avoid the illogical *center around*.)

compare to: He tried to compare the crossbow *to* the slingshot.

compare with: He tried to compare the English crossbow *with* the French crossbow.
(*Compare to* designates an examination of objects to show both likeness and difference. *Compare with* refers essentially to the likeness between objects of very similar characteristics.)

conform to: You must conform *to* the regulations or be punished.

confidence in: The coach had great confidence *in* his ability.

consist in: Loyalty consists *in* lending arms and ammunition. (Notice that a definition is offered of loyalty.)

consist of: The solution consists *of* water, soda, and aspirin. (Notice that the ingredients are named.)

conducive to: Hot weather is not conducive *to* study.

correspond to: Shooting a spark across the gap corresponds *to* lighting a match.

correspond with: The secretary corresponded *with* me concerning my dues.

differ about: Let us differ openly *about* this legislation.

differ from: In what way does this plan differ *from* that one?

differ with: The Senator said he must differ *with* you about the plan.

distaste for: Bill has a strong distaste *for* modernistic design.

identical with: Your answer is identical *with* mine.

infer from: I infer *from* your remarks that you are irked.

inferior to: His plan is manifestly inferior *to* mine.

in search of: The coach is in search *of* a good quarterback.

involve in: He quickly became involved *in* campus activities.

jealous of: Others were jealous *of* his success.

liable for: Who is liable *for* damages in this accident?

liable to: You are liable *to* the plaintiff for $100.

negligent of: I wish he were not so negligent *of* his appearance.

peculiar to: This variety of flower is peculiar *to* our state.

prefer to: Do you prefer him *to* his brother?

prior to: Edison's invention was prior *to* all others.

proficient in: He is extremely proficient *in* diving.

sensible about: I hope you will be sensible *about* obeying.

sensible of: I cannot fail to be sensible *of* the debt of gratitude.

sensitive to: His skin was especially sensitive *to* heat.

superior to: Can his work be superior *to* mine?

worthy of: His gallant act is worthy *of* mention.

(See *Workbook*, Exercise 7A.)

E. Levels of Usage

Good writing demands not only an extensive vocabulary but also a nice sense of the appropriateness of words and phrases to various occasions, for words are like people in having their social levels. Many a word, like an old pair of tennis shoes, is comfortable and easy in an informal situation but sadly out of place when formality is demanded. The writer who remarks informally to his friends, "The news flabbergasted me," will write in a magazine article in accordance with good usage, "The news astounded me." Because a standard dictionary is a writer's guide to the level of usage of words, get into the habit of consulting the dictionary about words which puzzle you on this score. But you must also understand that words are constantly shifting from one level of appropriateness to another. Relative usefulness and color may raise a word from slang to standard speech. Great public interest in a technical process may bring a word from the jargon of scientists to the vocabulary of common intercourse. On the other hand, expressions may degenerate from good, meaningful usage and become unacceptable or forgotten.

As ordinarily conceived, there are six levels of usage: common, technical, literary, colloquial, slang, and illiterate.

THE COMMON LEVEL

This is the most extensive of all the levels of diction because here belong the words

LEVELS OF DICTION

LITERARY	COMMON DICTION	TECHNICAL
abortive	tree, day, night, house, building, weaken, straighten,	heliotropic
invidious	beautiful, energetic, finished	palimpsest
quintessence		orthodontic
insensible		pulmonary

COLLOQUIAL
flabbergasted, harum-scarum, blues, phone

SLANG
swell (adj.), stand the gaff, gadget, screwball, boy friend

ILLITERATE
ain't, youse, furriner, it don't, irregardless, those kind of

NOTE: This diagram represents the levels of usage of large groups of words; individual words are constantly shifting from one level to another, leaving the main structure, however, relatively constant.

used and understood by everybody. Words such as *hat, coat, table, day, night, chair, see, feel,* and *know* are parts of the active vocabulary of all people to whom the English language is a native tongue. They are used by children as well as adults, and constitute not only the first words which an English-speaking person learns but also the linguistic stock which serves him best in all ordinary affairs throughout his life.

While the common level of speech is recruiting unceasingly among words of other levels, it avoids terminology which is too formal or literary for easy conversation, too technical to be readily understood, or too lacking in dignity to be useful in serious communication. It prefers a short word to a long one, the homely Anglo-Saxon expression to its more elegant synonym of Latin derivation. With a good vocabulary of words in common usage you can always make yourself understood in a direct, forceful manner. Beauty and variety of expression, and sometimes exactness of expression, however, frequently require a command of all levels of diction except the illiterate.

THE LITERARY LEVEL

Words and expressions employed in formal writing but not commonly in ordinary speech belong to the literary level of diction.

Most of these words are of Latin or Greek derivation. A literary sentence, "A large proportion of current slang is vulgar," may be reduced to a colloquial level by taking out the Latin derivatives: "A lot of everyday slang is coarse."

Ordinarily your passive vocabulary (*i.e.,* the words that you recognize and understand in your reading, but which are not in your daily speech) comes under this heading. Literary diction is admirable and effective when used in ordinary speech by one thoroughly at home with it and to whom it comes as naturally as common diction does to most of us; but the person who uses literary diction for ordinary communication to produce an effect of culture lays himself open to ridicule. In formal writing and in public addresses, however, literary diction is usually preferred because it is more accurate and more subtle than our common stock of words.

THE TECHNICAL LEVEL

Technical words and phrases are the vocabulary of particular professions or branches of knowledge. In standard dictionaries technical words are marked by an abbreviation of the particular branch of knowledge to which they belong. Some examples are *ceiling, strut* (aviation), *gamete* (zoology), *iso-*

tope (chemistry), *stoma* (botany). Avoid words such as these in everyday writing if they have synonyms in common usage. They belong properly in special treatises and are understood only by a few people.

THE COLLOQUIAL LEVEL

As *colloquial* means conversational, the colloquial level of diction accordingly is the level of informal oral communication. It should be understood, however, that the term *colloquial,* as used by the dictionaries, refers to the conversational vocabulary of fairly well-educated people.

The fact that a word is marked *Colloq.* by a dictionary does not mean that it is not a useful or legitimate word. It means merely that it is useful at a certain time and place and not at all times or places.

76. *A colloquialism is out of place in formal writing, business letters, and most written exercises in college,* even as sport dress is out of place at a formal party. A generation or so ago, the distinction between formal and colloquial English was much more marked than it is now. Today a commencement speaker, a Phi Beta Kappa orator, and even the President of the United States are likely to make use of racy, pungent expressions taken from the conversation of commen men. In most respects this is an admirable tendency. We speak much more than we write; spoken English is the source of our language, and a wide separation of colloquial and formal diction can only be harmful to good expression. On the other hand, a person whose vocabulary is composed exclusively of colloquialisms cannot achieve the accuracy of expression characteristic of literary diction, the precision tool of communication.

A study of the Glossary of Usage (page 197) will help you in selecting the proper expression in formal writing.

77. THE SLANG LEVEL

Slang words and expressions are distinctly undesirable in formal writing. By slang is meant, according to the *American College Dictionary,* "1. language of a markedly colloquial character, regarded as below the standard of cultivated speech. 2. the jargon of a particular class, profession, etc. 3. the special vocabulary of thieves, vagabonds, etc.; argot." The first part of this definition refers to such obnoxious words and phrases as "He told some *corny* jokes," "Bill is a *screwball,*" or "Tom was *on the beam* today." The second part of the definition embraces words and phrases which are understood primarily by the members of one group and are generally unintelligible to others. Terms of this sort are the aviators' reference to helicopters as *eggbeaters,* the naval designation of destroyers as *tin cans* or of coffee as *jamoke,* or the musicians' use of *jive* for swing music. The third part of the definition refers to the language of the underworld, originally designed for purposes of secrecy, such terms as *copper* for policeman, *soup* for dynamite, or *punk* for a brash young hoodlum.

There are a number of very good reasons for avoiding the use of slang. The first is that it is ephemeral. Slang words are here today and gone tomorrow. Campus slang, for example, not only differs with geographical areas, but changes almost from one generation of students to the next. The person who writes or speaks with a serious purpose should desire to use language which will last at least throughout his lifetime.

The vagueness of many slang terms is another reason for their being inappropriate in careful writing. In recent years the word *swell* has become very popular as the lazy man's method of indicating any shade of commendation: a swell party, a swell guy, a swell view, a swell dinner, a swell compliment, a swell movie. *Swell* is applied so generally that it means almost nothing. But the language of an educated man should be exact. If you depend on such general terminology, not only do you not express yourself clearly, but you actually injure your mental processes. To a large extent the ability to think in terms of accurate distinctions depends on possessing in your vocabulary the words which express such distinctions. To fail to acquire or to forget sharp, incisive diction is to deprive your mind of indispensable tools of thought.

Finally, the connotations of slang are not suited to serious expression. With regard to the user, slang connotes extreme informality if not vulgarity; with regard to the occasion, casualness and lack of importance. An attempt to use slang to connote dignity and significance is doomed almost inevitably to failure.

This condemnation of slang in serious writing does not mean that slang expressions are without value to the English language. On the contrary, they play an important part in its development. A great many of our best words have come up to common diction from the level of slang. In general, such words have received their promotion for one or both of the following reasons: they expressed meanings for which there were no words in respectable diction, or they provided a vigorous figure of speech. Slang which creates metaphors is especially likely to achieve permanence—that is, if the comparison implied in the metaphor remains a part of general experience. When we call an ineffective person a *flat tire*, or a girl who is unable to attract men a *wallflower*, we employ graphic metaphors. Similarly, such terms as *snake in the grass* and *dud* create definite pictures. Words belonging in this group are the result of the free play of imagination, of originality among the English-speaking peoples. It is rather words like *lousy, swell, terrific, awful*, which are merely the generalizations of foggy minds, that have no legitimate place in good writing and speaking.

It follows, therefore, as a general principle that slang words should not be used in papers for college classes unless for a particular purpose, such as dialogue. Nor is it permissible to avoid this principle by placing the slang terms in quotation marks. If a slang word is actually the only one to convey a desired meaning and connotation, it is therefore, for the purpose in hand, a respectable word and should not be put in quotation marks.

THE ILLITERATE LEVEL

Here belong terms that occur commonly in the speech of those who have little or no education, and who therefore habitually violate grammatical rules and correct usages. Some of these expressions—*He don't talk like no furriner. I hain't seed him lately*—are unlikely to enter the speech of college students. Others, such as the double negative, *done* for *did, ain't, irregardless, seldom ever* for *rarely*, may persist into a student's college years, or longer, if he does not become aware of them and make a positive effort to eliminate them from his speech and writing.

These usages are classed in most dictionaries as *barbarisms, dialectal expressions, provincialisms*, and *illiteracies*. A barbarism is a word that was in good repute but has been corrupted through misuse, such as *disremember, unbeknownst*, light *complected*. A dialectal expression is one peculiar to a certain class, group, or race of people. A provincialism is a word or usage which is limited to a certain section of the country, as *tote* in the South, *calculate* for *think* in New England, and *sick to my stomach* in some sections of the Midwest.

78. Avoid illiteracies.

Form the habit of attending to the speech of cultured people, and when you hear a cultured person using a word unfamiliar to you, look it up in a dictionary and add it to your own vocabulary. Listen to the speech of other students, and if you hear one using a term that you suspect is incorrect, check upon it likewise by going to the dictionary. Look up terms you use yourself to see if they are marked as slang, colloquial, dialectal, or illiterate. In this way you establish an awareness of correct speech, and your own speech and writing will begin to improve.

(See *Workbook*, Exercise 7B.)

F. The Right Choice of Words

You will certainly be understood as a writer if you will follow the injunctions just enumerated and employ words which are in national use—not provincial or dialectal; in current use—not obsolescent; and in reputable use—favored by good writers and speakers. But if you are going to master a superior style, you must consider certain necessary refinements of language. You will not be content with the first word that comes to mind, but, using dictionary and thesaurus, will search for the exact word. You will not employ more words than are needed to express your meaning, you will prefer specific and concrete words to abstract ones, and you will learn to use words for their suggestiveness as well as for their meaning. The following sections will discuss these suggestions more fully.

1. ECONOMY OF DICTION

By failing to discriminate carefully among words and by supposing that two or three words, however vague, are to be preferred to one that is precise, most students manage to waste words. If you write, "I'd like to tell you about my case," just what does *case* mean? Is it a medical case (a patient), a case of merchandise, a problem, or an experience? Or if you say, "Our battle-scarred veterans of the gridiron wars romped through formations all afternoon on the greensward of the practice field," you mean simply, "The football team practiced all afternoon." That sentence is commendable in which each word bears the precise meaning which the author intends.

79. If some words have vague, hazy meanings, or can just as well be omitted, the sentence is guilty of wordiness and inexactness.

The following rules may help you to gain greater economy:

79a. Do not use too many simple sentences.

Such usage necessitates repetition of the subject and often of the verb. "John was a savage boy. He was always disobedient and revengeful. In addition he was cruel to his friends. For these reasons he had earned a bad reputation among his schoolmates." These short sentences can be thus economically telescoped: "John was a savage boy, always disobedient and revengeful, and, in addition, cruel to his friends. For these reasons he had earned a bad reputation among his schoolmates."

79b. Do not begin sentences unnecessarily with *it, it was, there is, there are,* or other impersonal expressions.

The sentence "There are many reasons which are given in defense of the superintendent's action" may be amputated to read, "Many reasons are given in defense of the superintendent's action."

79c. Do not use vague, stereotyped expressions.

They make sentences wordier and at the same time add to their ineffectiveness. The overuse of terms like *case, instance, factor, proposition, beg to reply, wish to state, along the line of, asset, the professional world, the business world, a new angle on, element, in the field of, development* is a sign of laziness. Sir Arthur Quiller-Couch, in *The Art of Writing*, labeled this kind of language *jargon* because many of the terms included in it are derived from the terminology of particular professions or occupations, but, when extended to general use, have lost their significance. Jargon is a crutch for the person with limited vocabulary, or the lazy person, or the person whose mind is too dull to perceive its lack of accuracy.

Mention has been made already of the meaninglessness of *case*. Some people think that by substituting *instance* for *case* they have somehow achieved better diction, but *instance* has very little more meaning. Note how the following sentences are improved by eliminating both of these words:

> Let me tell you of a case where a student corrected his instructor. (Let me tell you of a student's correcting his instructor; *or* Let me tell you about a student who corrected his instructor.)
>
> In the case of Richard Roe, the circumstances are different. (For Richard Roe the circumstances are different.)
>
> In case you want help, call me. (If you want help, call me.)

Do not try to find synonyms for *case* and *instance,* because words which have no meaning cannot have synonyms; revise the sentence in such a way as to communicate the meaning directly. *Factor* has been used so indiscriminately that its legitimate meaning has been blurred. "Health is an important factor in education" means no more than "Health is important in education." *Proposition* has a good meaning as "something which is proposed," but is out of place in "Getting the water out of the cellar was a difficult proposition." *In the field of* and *along the line of* are generally deadwood. "He is succeeding in the field of medicine" should be "He is succeeding in medicine." "He is good in the line of scholarship" is awkward when compared with "He is a good scholar." Why should one say "He is an asset to the business world" when "He is a good businessman" is shorter and more direct?

It is unnecessary to cite more examples. Economy and accuracy of diction are hard to master, but they pay well in effectiveness.

79d. Do not use unnecessary phrases or clauses.

The following are examples:

> My classmate wrote me that he would be here *at no great date in the future* (soon).
>
> My automobile operates *with a high degree of efficiency* (efficiently).
>
> One of the noblest qualities *which John possesses is unselfishness.* (One of John's noblest qualities is unselfishness.)

> At last the day dawned *in the east.* (Did it ever dawn in the west?)
>
> The books that he held were oblong *in shape.* (How else could they be oblong?)

79e. Do not repeat expressions that are already etymologically present in a word which has been used.

This error is largely due to ignorance of the meaning of words.

> He returned *back* to his home. (The prefix *re* means *back.*)
>
> Endorse this check *on the back.* (*Endorse* means *on the back.*)
>
> Some day I am going to write *my* autobiography. (An autobiography is the life history of oneself.)

79f. Do not sprinkle a sentence with modifiers which add nothing to the meaning.

In the following sentences, for example, the italicized words should be omitted.

> *Strict* accuracy requires that the *important* essentials be listed first.
>
> *Successful* achievement is necessary if a *joint* partnership is to enjoy *abundant* wealth.
>
> Her face was *just too* lovely; it was so *very* perfect that I thought she was *absolutely* the *most* unique girl at the party.

79g. Do not use ornamental phraseology, especially high-flown synonyms.

Percy Marks, novelist and author of *The Craft of Writing*, places the use of such synonyms next to the excessive use of modifiers as the most frequently occurring fault of affected writers. Many students think that words which are in daily use are not fit to express lofty ideas and universal truths. Literature (with a capital L) means to them something concocted in unusual, exotic, and grandiose diction. A versatile author does command a larger vocabulary than most of his readers, but his diction is likely to be more accurate rather than more ornamental. Consider the dignity and also the simplicity of the following incident as related in the King James translation of the nineteenth chapter of I Kings:

> And he arose, and did eat and drink, and went . . . unto Horeb the mount of God. And he came thither unto a cave, and lodged there; and, behold, the word of the Lord came to him, and he said unto him, "What doest thou here, Elijah?"
>
> And he said, "I have been very jealous for the Lord God of hosts: for the children of Israel have forsaken thy covenant, thrown down thine altars, and slain thy prophets with the sword; and I, even I only, am left; and they seek my life, to take it away."
>
> And he said, "Go forth, and stand upon the mount before the Lord."
>
> And, behold, the Lord passed by, and a great and strong wind rent the mountains, and brake in pieces the rocks before the Lord; but the Lord was not in the wind: and after the wind an earthquake; but the Lord was not in the earthquake: and after the earthquake a fire; but the Lord was not in the fire: and after the fire a still small voice. And it was so, when Elijah heard it, that he wrapped his face in his mantle, and went out, and stood in the entering of the cave.

The injunction against excessive ornamentation does not imply that only those words understood by uneducated people are permissible in good writing, or that student papers should be reduced to words of one syllable. Far from it. A good writer certainly should be given the freedom of the whole great treasure house which is the English language; but he knows that the *right* word brings with it its own weight, dignity, and beauty—qualities which cannot be achieved in any other way. Do not be satisfied with your present vocabulary: expand it; add new words every day—but do not use new words for the sake of making a show of them, and by all means possess an accurate understanding of them.

(See *Workbook*, Exercise 8.)

2. SPECIFIC AND CONCRETE WORDS

Words have one purpose only—to transmit images and ideas from one mind to another. If you have in your own mind a clear, un-blurred image or idea and care at all about transmitting it without distortion to someone else, seek the most specific terms you can find for communication.

80. Prefer concrete words to abstract ones.

Abstract words lack the power that concrete words have to transmit exact images.

A general word, as the term implies, refers to a whole group, class, or kind of objects or conditions. Since it includes many words in its meaning, it can transmit only a vague and indistinct image or idea. The general word *tree*, for example, refers to any one of a large class of woody plants ranging in size from a large shrub to the giant redwoods of California, and in shape from the slim poplar to the spreading banyan. The general word *laugh* refers to a way of showing mirth by certain facial expressions and guttural sounds, whereas the specific words *giggle, snicker, titter, chuckle,* and *guffaw* express a more precise sort of expression and sound. Likewise *cry* indicates a general state of unhappiness; *weep, sob, whine, whimper, howl, wail,* and *blubber* particularize the method of crying and transmit a more accurate image of the sort of unhappiness expressed. A general word, then, gives only a vague idea and indicates little concerning the particular characteristics of the object, act, or quality named; a specific word stands for a precise meaning different from all other meanings within the general class to which it belongs.

Abstract words refer to qualities apart from any objects, as *blackness, honesty, loyalty, patriotism.* Concrete words, on the other hand, refer to things that can be perceived by the senses, as *rock, coffee, thunder, velvet, perfume.* Any reference that arouses a sensory image (*i.e.,* an artificially stimulated experience of the senses: seeing, hearing, tasting, feeling, smelling) will have a more powerful appeal than one that does not.

Benjamin Franklin well illustrated these principles in his satirical essay, "Proposed New Version of the Bible," in which he used abstract diction to ridicule writers of his day by "modernizing" a few selections from the Book of Job, as these writers might do. For instance, the verse from Job, "Then Satan answered the Lord, and said, Doth Job fear God for naught?" became in Franklin's version, "And Satan answered, Does your Majesty imagine that his good conduct is the effect of mere personal attachment and affection?"; the selection from Job reading, "But put forth thine hand now, and touch all that he hath, and he will curse thee to thy face," is rendered by Franklin, "Try him;—only withdraw your favor, turn him out of his places, and withhold his pensions, and you will soon find him in the opposition." Notice how Franklin's abstract diction destroys both clarity and suggestiveness.

In *The Gilded Age*, Mark Twain and Charles Dudley Warner describe a room in these specific and concrete terms:

> A dreary old haircloth sofa against the wall; a few damaged chairs; the small table the lamp stood on; the crippled stove—these things constituted the furniture of the room. There was no carpet on the floor; on the wall were occasional square-shaped interruptions of the general tint of the plaster which betrayed that there used to be pictures in the house—but there were none now. There were no mantel ornaments, unless one might bring himself to regard as an ornament the clock which never came within fifteen strokes of striking the right time, and whose hands always hitched together at twenty-two minutes past anything and traveled in company the rest of the way home.

The effectiveness of this passage, with such specific touches as *haircloth* sofa, unfaded parts of the wall where pictures had hung, and the hitching together of the clock hands, becomes apparent by comparing it with such a general statement as the following:

> The furniture of the room comprised only the barest necessities. The floor was bare, no pictures were on the wall, and the mantel also was bare, except for a clock that was useless for telling the time.

A few short examples may complete these illustrations:

GENERAL: My brother was injured yesterday while playing in a game.

SPECIFIC: My brother broke his right ankle yesterday while playing left halfback against Oklahoma.

GENERAL: The woman went into the store to make a purchase.

SPECIFIC: Mrs. Trout went into Finn's hardware store to buy a paring knife.

GENERAL AND ABSTRACT: Good citizenship means being loyal and patriotic.

SPECIFIC AND CONCRETE: A good citizen supports and obeys his country's laws and institutions, votes at election time, and is willing to fight for his country and if need be die for it in time of war.

If you employ specific and concrete terms, readers not only understand what you have to say, but cannot misunderstand it. The words "a red pencil, three inches long, sharpened at one end, containing a soft black lead, and with an eraser worn to the metal cap" will evoke the same image in the mind of almost everyone who reads them, but the words "a virtuous and handsome man with a high code of honor" will not. What does the writer mean by virtue? What is a handsome man? What constitutes a high code of honor? All these need further explanation before writer and reader can be in complete accord.

General and abstract words have their place in language, of course, or they would not exist. Too many specific words may confuse a reader by focusing his attention too much on details. Topic sentences of paragraphs and summarizing sentences are often general. But a writer who aspires to exactness will use general and abstract words frugally.

(See *Workbook*, Exercise 9.)

Co-operation versus Competition

JOHN RUSKIN

WE CAN HARDLY arrive at a more absolute type of impurity than the mud or slime of a damp, overtrodden path in the outskirts of a manufacturing town. I do not say mud of the road, because that is mixed with animal refuse; but take merely an ounce or two of the blackest slime of a beaten footpath on a rainy day near a large manufacturing town.

That slime we shall find in most cases composed of clay (or brick dust, which is burnt clay) mixed with soot, a little sand, and water. All these elements are at helpless war with each other, and destroy reciprocally each other's nature and power, competing and fighting for place at every tread of your foot—sand squeezing out clay, and clay squeezing out water, and soot meddling everywhere and defiling the whole. Let us suppose that this ounce of mud is left in perfect rest, and that its elements gather together, like to like, so that their atoms may get into the closest relations possible.

Let the clay begin. Ridding itself of all foreign substance, it gradually becomes a white earth, already very beautiful; and fit, with help of congealing fire, to be made into finest porcelain, and painted on, and be kept in kings' palaces. But such artificial consistence is not its best. Leave it still quiet to follow its own instinct of unity, and it becomes not only white, but clear; not only clear, but hard; not only clear and hard, but so set that it can deal with light in a wonderful way, and gather out of it the loveliest blue rays only, refusing the rest. We call it then a sapphire.

Such being the consummation of the clay, we give similar permission of quiet to the sand. It also becomes, first, a white earth, then proceeds to grow clear and hard, and at last arranges itself in mysterious, infinitely fine, parallel lines, which have the power of reflecting not merely the blue rays, but the blue, green, purple, and red rays in the greatest beauty in which they can be seen through any fired material whatsoever. We call it then an opal.

In next order, the soot sets to work; it cannot make itself white at first, but, instead of being discouraged, tries harder and harder, and comes out clear at last, and the hardest thing in the world; and for the blackness that it had, obtains in exchange the power of reflecting all the rays of the sun at once in the vividest blaze that any solid thing can shoot. We call it then a diamond.

Last of all the water purifies or unites itself, contented enough if it only reach the form of a dewdrop; but if we insist on its proceeding to a more perfect consistence, it crystallizes into the shape of a star.

And for the ounce of slime which we had by political economy of competition, we have by political economy of co-operation, a sapphire, an opal, and a diamond, set in the midst of a star of snow.—*Modern Painters*.

SUGGESTIONS FOR STUDY

1. From the last paragraph of this selection, list the general words which the author wrote the article to clarify. Then list the specific words in the same paragraph which he used in making the clarification.

2. Having noted the important general and specific words, analyze each paragraph in turn for concreteness of diction. For example, in the first paragraph, which is more specific, *impurity* or *mud? type* or *slime?*

3. Do specific or general words predominate in the selection as a whole?

4. Explain Ruskin's purpose in this selection, and state his thesis.

Basic English for Science[1]

TOM BURNS HABER

THE FOLLOWING LETTER (evidently not written to be posted) I found in the English notebook of one of my students in Freshman Composition:

To THE AUTHORS OF *A Botany Textbook:*

As a student in the botany course which is given at our university, I have become familiar with your textbook and workbook which are used in connection with the course. I wish to inform you that I am having a great deal of difficulty with botany, and I believe your books are largely responsible.

The purpose of botany, I believe, is to acquaint the student with the different types of plant life and to help him understand the growth and structure of plants. In my estimation *A Botany Textbook* defeats that purpose. The average student is lost in the maze of difficult and highly technical language of your text and in the complexity of the demonstrations and problems in your workbook. For example, in describing the beginning of a leaf you state that "development of a leaf begins with the proliferation of a primordium"— without any previous hint of what a primordium is!

As a result of your heavy treatment of the subject, botany is dreaded and disliked by the majority of students on this campus. Many have failed the course because of this dislike —for which your boring textbook is largely responsible. You have, in the eyes of many students, attached a stigma to the useful science of botany.

The evident sincerity of this letter, I hope it will be agreed, entitles it to a fair hearing. What college freshman has not at some time or another felt a similar protest rising within him as he tried to advance through the maze of language between him and the subject he was studying? The writer of the above letter

may pass her course in botany and give the lie to her fears. She may even go on to like botany. But what a pity that she must arrive in spite of the language in which her textbooks are written. Much has been said on the teachers' side of the difficulty instructors of physics, of botany, and of chemistry have in getting their students interested in these branches of science. Perhaps the main reason lies not in the students' dislike for the subject itself but for the language in which the subject is presented to them.

Too many college texts in science are burdened with an unnecessarily heavy style. The use of essential scientific words makes for economy; certainly the author is not expected to eschew them to the point of repeating long definitions. But why cannot he use "growth" instead of his beloved "proliferation"? "Chain of events" instead of "series of concatenations"? "Scaling off" instead of "desquamation"? It would seem that some authors of secondary science texts think that unless they write in the style of Herbert Spencer's definition of evolution, they cannot impress their readers with the importance of their subjects; as if what is stated simply cannot be worth learning. Clear exposition is a craft which scientific writers ought to regard as highly as the validity of their ideas. Generally speaking, they seem not to be aware of its existence; or, if they are, acknowledge it by keeping as far as possible from it—after the example of Professor Longbore, who used to open his science lectures each quarter with this warning, the only intelligible sentence in his discourses: "I do not intend to make clear to you in twelve weeks what it took me fifty years to learn."

The style of Professor Longbore and his

[1] From the *Scientific Monthly*, LXII (March, 1946), 258-262. Reprinted by permission of the author and of the *Scientific Monthly*.

ilk is probably the result of a passive rather than an active state of mind. As one turns the pages of a ponderously written text in college zoology, for example, he begins to wonder whether the author may not have drifted into his style merely by following the course of least resistance. A polysyllabic style is a lazy style. It is easy to master the learned jargon of any science, and mastery of the jargon is too often mistaken by publishers' readers for mastery of the subject. "Easy writing makes cursed hard reading," observed Dick Sheridan; and although laborious writing is not guaranteed *per se* to make easy reading, it has a good chance to, if the writer knows what he wants to say and tries hard enough to say it. My point is that it is downright hard work to express scientific concepts in a clear, mature style. And yet texts written for college students ought to be worth that much effort.

For some writers, no doubt, there is a fascination in the weighty language of which my student complained. Thus the trap is baited and set for the author's complete undoing: he lets words take the place of thought. He has seen these splendid terms so often; they were right to him in the books he read. Are they not as good in his own? He does not stop to ask what the words really mean, how he expects his reader to interpret them. If by any chance a conscientious student narrows his eyes and carefully examines this lingo, the result is usually a feeling of dismay like that expressed in the letter at the beginning of this article.

Is there, for example, any reason why a book in psychology should be written in this style?——

The apperception of self-motivation is a psychological fact. A concomitant phenomenon is the consciousness that the origin of this motivation is internal and not external.

Is not this what the writer *means?*——

The mind is conscious that it is self-moving; and at the same time, that the motion comes from within itself.

The last sentence above is written in Basic English. This simplified English ought to have an especial appeal to scientific writers because its discovery was analogous to the procedure of the scientist seeking basic principles in the natural world. The originators of Basic English, sifting the thousands of words in our language, isolated 850 indispensable terms by which the meanings of the others could be expressed. For science an additional list of 100 words is provided.

The methods by which the Basic word list was determined can be tested by anyone who takes a dictionary in his hand. He will find in reading definitions that certain words keep returning time after time—usually little words such as *go, get, make, be, thing, name, true, good,* together with necessary conjunctions and prepositions. These words and others of their kind *are* the basic vocabulary of our language. They make a restricted common ground on which it is possible for writer and reader to meet with the least possible chance for confusion or mistake. In its inductive origin, as well as in its purposes, Basic English is scientific English.

It is not urged here that all writers of college texts in science adopt at once the Basic English vocabulary. The Spartan simplicity of Basic, though it is the handmaiden of truth, does not always serve other ideals as faithfully. Variety and subtlety, for example, are not main properties of Basic. These virtues and other qualities of a pleasing style ought not to be lacking from the books our science students read. Nevertheless Basic English could have a tonic effect upon these books. It could dispel much foggy thinking, which is the real cause of bad writing. If an author *thought* in Basic first, he would not write "heliotropic inclination toward the illuminating source." He would see that the meaning of his first word is repeated needlessly in the five that follow and might decide that his whole phrase could be put thus: "turning in the direction of the light"—which is good science and good Basic. No one can compose in Basic without having in his mind a pretty clear idea of what he wants to say. There are no superfluous terms in Basic to get between him and his manuscript. He will often be reminded that between his idea *A* and the words *B* that represent it there ought to be the same relation as between an object *a* held before a mirror and its reflection *b*. A true reflection requires a good mirror. Basic English has the makings of a good mirror because its vocabulary is level and impersonal—a plane reflector. Even though the scientific writer makes use of a larger vocabulary, if he keeps firmly in mind Basic equivalents as he composes his sentences, his writing will gain clearness, whatever words he finally chooses. And his readers—his students or his peers—will call him blessed.

But there is another field of scientific writing where the need for Basic English is far more pressing. I mean the scientific books and magazines printed in this country and Great Britain. A great many foreigners before World War II were coming into English via Basic. Now as an international language Basic is gaining steadily in general esteem everywhere. Public interest in it was greatly stimulated by Winston Churchill's ardent approval of Basic in his address at Harvard University, September 6, 1943. No artificial language can meet the stern needs of an international tongue as Basic English can. First, it has behind it the compelling prestige of the Anglo-Saxon tradition; it "looks" like English and it *is* English, the vital heart and core of the language of Shakespeare and Jefferson. Basic is easy for the non-English speaker to learn. A few weeks' steady effort under skilled direction can make an intelligent foreigner at home in written and spoken Basic. The demand for books in Basic, both here and abroad, is on the upswing. It is one sign of the world-hunger for unity and commonalty among the peoples of our shrinking planet.

In satisfying this hunger the place of science is nothing less than strategic. It remains for science to recognize some of the practical aspects of its position. Science, as an international agency, must create or adopt an international tongue. The scientist today is faced with the problems faced by English traders 500 years ago as they carried their goods and their language into the Seven Seas. Through necessity, between them and their brown-, black-, and yellow-skinned customers, a species of international language slowly developed. The barbarous pidgin ("merchant") English of the Far East is a natural phenomenon brought into being by the needs of men groping toward each other's minds. These needs are a hundred times more imperative today. The very existence of the race may depend upon our finding right answers to them. Science, like trade, now has the earth as its province. More fortunate than trade, science does not have to await the development of a crude, mass-made English. A scientifically evolved speech is at hand; in the words of Mr. Churchill, "a very carefully wrought plan for an international language, capable of very wide transactions."

It is a truism to say that the great impetus felt by scientific research during the past five years will continue and accelerate. Parallel with this step-up of activity in the ranks of the scientists is a keen public concern about what they are doing. Jet-propelled aircraft and atomic bombs have drawn the fearful attention of everyone to the laboratory of the technician. This public interest cannot be written off as mere curiosity. We are hearing it said on all sides: Why, if the scientist is so expert in devising the machines of death and destruction, why cannot he turn his talents as effectively to the service of humanity? This protest is admittedly naïve: Burbank and Edison were scientists. But the protest still stands. Its ultimate meaning is that everyone the world over wants to know what the scientist is about.

Modern science has therefore a vast new social responsibility which it cannot ignore.

The day of unadulterated "pure" research is about over. Even though the scientist may not, like Terence, agree that "Everyman's business is my business," Everyman is telling the world and himself that "the scientist's business is my business." And Everyman pays the taxes and makes the grants that keep the scientist going. Everyman is a Chinese farmer, a Chicago businessman, a French taxi driver, a Greek fisherman, a Russian fur dealer. All these are invading the hitherto sacred confines of the technician's laboratory. And they have a right to do so.

In practical terms this means that the findings of the technician must be put on paper. Books must be written, articles contributed to scientific and lay journals. At present the chances are twenty to one that the native tongue of our hypothetical scientist will be English. Why should he not address himself to his world-wide audience in a truly international language—Basic English?

Basic is surprisingly easy for the English user to learn. With a little experience a copy writer can translate a full-English draft into Basic about as rapidly as he can compose. It is most desirable, of course, that the scientific writer prepare his own Basic version of his books and articles. Thus the thoughts of such authorities as Sir James Jeans, J. B. S. Haldane, Walter S. Landis, and Sir Arthur Stanley Eddington could go directly to the minds of men all over the earth without the warped meanings and false emphases that lurk in translations.

In facilitating this direct communication between the writing scientist and his universal reader, the American and British scientific journals have a place of unique importance. Their large circulation is a token of the immense service they can render to science and to humanity. By the use of complete articles in Basic English and by special Basic editions and supplements, they can directly interpret the findings of modern science to a circle of readers that in a very true sense is world-wide. In so doing they will be assuming their share in the large responsibilities borne by science in the world today. . . .

SUGGESTIONS FOR STUDY

1. Why do many authors resort to excessively heavy diction?
2. Why do many readers admire such wording?
3. What is Basic English?
4. What purposes does it have?
5. What virtues are lacking in a style employing only Basic?
6. Study your own textbooks for examples of unnecessarily difficult passages. Copy several of these, and then state the same idea in simple, clear wording.
7. Employing the resources of your library, investigate more fully the subject of Basic, its nature, uses, and limitations.
8. Define the following words from this article: eschew, validity, ilk, analogous, truism, hypothetical, facilitating.

I Can't Quite Hear You, Doctor[1]

JOSEPH A. BRANDT

FOR SIXTEEN YEARS I was the publisher of the scholarship of three of our great universities. Frequently, in the books I published, I was called upon to accept without question scientific conclusions which I and millions of my fellow men did not, and could not, understand.

Of course, there are certain areas of pure scientific exploration where it would be ridiculous to try to reduce the terminology to such simple terms that the student of the

[1] From *Harper's Magazine*, CXCII (March, 1946). Reprinted by permission of the author and *Harper's Magazine*.

social sciences or of the humanities, or the ordinary literate man or woman, could understand. But it is equally true that all science is not pure mystery. At some stage, it must coincide with the needs and the comprehension of mankind.

Yet so impenetrable is the language in which most scientists speak that not only does the layman fail to understand it, but other scientists often are puzzled by it. A zoologist once complained to me that he was at a loss to understand the terms used by a colleague of his, a physical scientist. A few days later I had occasion to bring up this question, obliquely, with the physical scientist himself. I was delighted as well as amused to find that he, too, felt that science was becoming so specialized that it was impossible for him to keep abreast of the other disciplines—and the science he mentioned as having the vocabulary most incomprehensible to him was zoology!

It is difficult to tell which controls scholarship today, the scholar or the monstrous terminology which he has created. Terminologitis has swept, like an uncontrollable forest fire, from the pure sciences into the social sciences and even into the humanities. One of the most significant books published thus far in this century is one I had the privilege of publishing a number of years ago. Its field was social science. Its subject concerned every thinking American. My colleagues were as excited as I when the manuscript arrived, and as downcast after we had examined it. Who, we wondered, would be able to read it? Because of my sincere admiration for the content of the manuscript, I suggested to the author that he substitute lucidity for terminology. By return mail the author wrote me a blistering letter accusing me of wanting to commit intellectual mayhem. So the manuscript was published as written and found as its audience mainly the specialists in the man's own field. It was little satisfaction to us to have an acerbic reviewer, who wanted the author's message shouted from the housetops, suggest that the publishers bring out another edition—"in English"!

Why this insistence upon unintelligibility? I think the explanation lies in the fact that the scholar, by the very nature of his training, is taught to think of his work as something impersonal to everybody but himself, whose future career is at stake. He must be "objective." He must be colorless, lest he prove objectionable to the more conservative of the elder statesmen who will pass ultimately upon the quality of his work and determine whether he can be admitted to the greater glory of doctorhood. Rarely, during his training, is he taught to think of an audience. So, when he turns writer, it is small wonder that he writes for no audience; or, if he is aware of readers, he thinks of them either as members of his own cult, or else as people he must impress—or whom he instinctively fears. And, since his associations are almost exclusively with fellow scholars, he rarely is aware of the painful longing, among people beyond the academic pale, for some insight into the comforting realm of certainty which the scholar rules.

Many have been the long and apparently fruitless sessions that I as a publisher have been compelled to have with physical scientists in particular, as I argued that science, as a social instrument, should be concerned with the ultimate ends to which its discoveries would be used.

Why, I used to ask these men, do the scientists not only leave to the inventor and the business man the task of applying what they discover for the benefit of man, but also maintain an attitude of such studied unconcern as to how it is applied? The great Bell or Du Pont laboratories are truly governed by as impeccable a sense of scientific truth as any university scientific body; but science in the commercial laboratory is shaping the destiny of man, and shaping it consciously. Why, I would ask, does the academician not assume a responsibility to people as well as to learning? The usual reply to this question was that *pure* research should be an end in itself. True scientific triumph lay in pushing a search to its conclusion—in the form of an answer satisfactory to the scientist himself. He was under only one obligation: to satisfy himself intellectually.

The result of this deliberate aloofness has been a curious state of affairs. In our American society the engineer has served as butler at the feast which the inventors supplied from the fertile fields of scientific research. The scientists, particularly the physical scientists, have been a sterile priesthood in the society served by the butlers. Although their intellectual achievements have been the most brilliant in the history of man, knowledge of these has been confined among the priesthood. No public relations council has explained to the rest of us the ultimate meaning of their discoveries. The scientists have maintained their own societies, published their own magazines; they have been a world apart, regally oblivious to the feudal society below them.

For the truth is that, in the period of the most widespread education in the history of mankind, we have established a twentieth-century feudalism. The difference between it and medieval feudalism is that it is intellectual rather than economic. In the period of medieval feudalism, the gulf between the lord of the manor and the villein or the serf tied to the land was both intellectual and economic; but the principal characteristic of that gulf was economic. It is true, of course, that the serf had no intellectual freedom. But it is equally true today that the average citizen cannot speak intelligently about, or criticize constructively, the scientific age. The gulf between him and those who understand it is too great. And yet, as he has just discovered, he is tied to it inescapably, and the penalty for forgetting that fact is the same as in the Middle Ages—death.

Envious of the exploits of science, American higher education as a whole has sought to emulate the Brahmins, the physical sci-entists. It has tried to reduce unpredictable and immeasurable man to a science. Social study becomes social science. The humanities struggle in a maze, ignored, shunned, and even suspected. Economics becomes statistics. Humane history becomes a social science, the science of footnotes. Home economics is elevated to the level of philosophy, is given a curriculum all its own, and becomes domestic science.

There is scarcely any limit to the catalogue of this dangerous academic absurdity. At a certain university, when the faculty was confronted with a candidate for the degree of Doctor of Philosophy whose entire work for this degree was a statistical operation—adding and subtracting certain classified types of man-hours—it hurriedly instituted the degree of Doctor of Education. But the faculty was not trying to protect society against uneducated educators. It was acting for the less worthy purpose of protecting an academic monopoly.

The Big Three—engineering, law, and medicine—have been less imitative of scientism, but they have basked too long in the respect which the American instinctively pays to the so-called professions, and have paid too little attention to broadening their students as human beings. The engineering curriculum (which for almost all engineering students comprises the complete time they spend in a college or university) seldom contains any subjects having to do with society. Law and medicine have established prerequisite undergraduate training programs, but these in the main do little to prepare the future lawyer or doctor to assume a place of leadership in society except on the simple plane of professionalism. This absence of training in social thinking on the part of doctors is visibly placing the profession more and more in the unenviable position of being at war with the society it serves. The argument of most doctors against "socialized" medicine is not a social argument.

The higher learning in our country,

despite brilliant exceptions, seems to have become a form of self-worship, a series of rites performed by a priesthood which has left its congregation to be served, so far as discernible leadership is concerned, solely by the politician. This is unfortunate because the politician, however skillful he may be in the management of human affairs, is as much lost in a world of scientism—thanks to the isolating policy of science—as is the humblest precinct captain.

The people have been long-suffering with their politicians, largely, I suspect, because they speak the people's own language, are their own kind, do things which people can see and experience. Huey Long left good roads and magnificent buildings for the people he deceived. They could ride along the roads, their children could go to their new state university, and they could look in wonderment at the magnificence of their state capitol. The politician, because he sees people in their homes and knows their wants, realizes how thin is the thread by which democracy clings to the star of destiny. He knows that the children of democracy are still, despite our relatively high standard of living, the children of poverty, and that the average man's abiding fear, even as American democracy enters the atomic age, is still of the breadline.

Despite their imperfections, the politicians have been far more scientific socially than the scientists, however pure they may be. Government somehow has moved along, and the citizen has felt some sense and certainty about it. When he votes, he votes with the realization that the parties and candidates have "educated" him to the issues.

The educator, on the other hand, and particularly the scientific educator, has had no such liaison with the people—as he discovered to his dismay after Hiroshima. Not until science had brought about an immediate possibility of the end of the world did it realize that socially it had been going nowhere at all. It was going nowhere because society was as unaware of it in all of its

implications as an amoeba is of the niceties of a Tschaikovsky symphony.

Unless people understand, they cannot be led, except it be by the whip of fear. And frequently, when society does not understand, it destroys. How else can one explain the wanton destruction of the priceless Japanese cyclotrons? We ourselves are willing to destroy the science of another country if it frightens us.

Does this mean anything to the educator, the scientist? Yes. It means that the life of academic quietism is over. The man of learning, however ill-equipped he may be, must learn to become a man of action, a politician, a man of the people, speaking for people, leading people. Certainly, in my brief experience as a university administrator I never found any educator who was at all bashful about becoming an academic politician. The academician loves politics. The only trouble with him has been that he either fears people outside his academic world or is contemptuous of them.

The atomic bomb destroyed something more than Hiroshima and Nagasaki. It blew up the ivory tower. Ultimately, this may be the greatest gain we made by the conquest of the atom. Even when the physical scientists began their work on the atom bomb, they suddenly realized they had taken in their hands the fate of society, of a society which they had not prepared for the ultimate triumph of their scientism. Leaders among them, like Professor Harold C. Urey of Chicago, have gone to the people, to tell them about the fate which may be in store for us. And they are using simple, everyday language, such as the eloquent statement of Mr. Urey to *The New Yorker:* "I've dropped everything to try to carry the message of the bomb's power to the people, because, if we can't control this thing, there won't be any science worthy of the name in the future. I know the bomb can destroy everything we hold valuable and I get a sense of fear that disturbs me in my work. I feel better if I try to do something about it."

Perhaps the academic eclipse is over, an eclipse which Daniel Coit Gilman never intended when he established the modern American type of university at Johns Hopkins. We cannot expect all scholars to realize that the citadel which protected them from the people is gone. But we know now that the men most responsible for the kind of world in which we live are determined to reunite themselves with the people, and if possible to lead them.

This is pleasing to one who spent sixteen years trying to persuade scholars, scientists especially, to translate the translatable things they were doing. In far too many instances the scientist-scholar would reply, "Oh, I couldn't think of doing anything popular. Why, it would ruin me in the profession."

In all fairness, let me say that this attitude is not limited to scientism alone. I found it in all the academic disciplines. There was a fear, an unreasonable fear, of consequences among colleagues which constituted an unconscious condemnation of the entire academic profession.

Sometimes the youngsters were ready to go ahead but were held back by their older colleagues. I remember one young historian who had written a delightful and almost readable dissertation which, with some concessions to intelligibility, would have reached a large audience. The modifications I suggested to him had nothing to do with erudition or scholarship. They were concerned simply with pruning a too-lush thesis which had been designed to satisfy the vanity of a Ph.D. jury. With these modifications, the university, through its press, could have afforded to publish the dissertation and even pay the author royalties. But if the author, as I explained to him, insisted upon publishing a document designed for no audience, he would have to reimburse the university for the inevitable loss it would sustain.

The young scholar agreed heartily with my suggestions. "There's one thing I want to do, however," he said. "I think I should talk this over with the professor who directed my doctorial work."

"Well," I replied, "I know what the answer will be. I think you should keep in mind, however, that either you have been trained to be an independent thinker or you haven't been. Why should a single professor veto a real service which you can perform for the people?"

Nevertheless, the young man did consult the professor. My memorandum might be all right, the professor said. He didn't quarrel with it as a "commercial" proposition—I had written my memorandum from the point of view of a non-commercial institution, remember—but the young historian had better publish his dissertation just as he had written it. And the reason?

"You may want a job in another university some day," the professor told the young man. "You'll have to show some departmental chairman that you know how to do research. You may not get a job if you don't publish the thesis as you wrote it."

It is on that narrow plane, on that viciously anti-social plane, that we have been conducting the business of higher education. President Gilman's type of new university has degenerated through the years to become merely a super-employment service in the interest of scholars but not in the interest of society.

A young botanist I know had been doing fundamental research which he was translating for the benefit of the garden clubs of his state. Several magazines of general circulation asked him to write about his work, which he did and most successfully. It occurred to him that perhaps in view of this interest, he ought to write a book for the people. On his vacation, he went back to the university from which his doctorate had been awarded, to talk the matter over with the professor who had directed his work.

"Great heavens, man, why do you want to

waste time writing for the layman?" the professor demanded indignantly. "You've got such a fine start with those papers you've been doing for the scientific journals. Keep on with that. Forget about the garden clubs."

On the other hand, I well remember the day, during the height of the dust storms in Oklahoma, when Paul B. Sears, then chairman of the Botany Department at the University of Oklahoma, walked into my office and without preliminaries said, "Joe, how would you like to publish a book called *Deserts on the March?*"

Paul Sears had seen what man was doing to nature. As an undergraduate he had been shocked at the frightful waste caused by the Ohio River floods. However, he pursued the normal research which is expected of any faculty man if he is to have pay and promotion. He had brought this research to the point where he knew that he had to do something for society. In Oklahoma we were cowed by the calamity of witnessing millions of tons of precious earth being swept daily into the atmosphere. The only hope that the Chambers of Commerce could hold out was rain. Professor Sears knew that the answer lay not alone with nature but with man, who has to live in harmony with nature or perish, as the physical scientists have themselves since discovered.

So he wrote *Deserts on the March,* one of the most brilliant and beautifully written books in the field of science in our time. Paul Sears knew the people, he liked them, and he associated with them. And he knew how to write for them. Because the book depended upon an Anglo-Saxon style rather than scientific terminology to carry its message, some of Mr. Sears' colleagues dismissed it with the remark, "It isn't science, it's literature."

Finally, I asked one of these scientific critics the question: "Well, what is literature if it isn't the record of life as we live it? And isn't science a part of life?"

The people read the book and took it to heart. Something was done about the Dust Bowl. Perhaps Mr. Sears had discharged a scholar's obligation to the people by writing so clearly, so forcefully, that they could understand and take action. But he did not stop at this point. He had a total sense of society. Everyone was involved in the destruction of the land—farmers, bankers, utility magnates. So Paul Sears turned politician.

He met with bankers. They had lent money on farms and still carried at full value the amount of their loans. Sears, who had inspected much of the land being devastated, could tell a banker that a loan still valued at $4,000 was now worth only $400—and why this was so. He met with farmers and repeated the message which the agricultural experts should have been giving, in language which persuaded them. Even so, there were far too many farmers who said boastingly, "Why, I've worn out three farms already."

The utility people are powerful in the Middle Western states and rather skeptical of scholars. Sears went into the lions' den. He told them what was happening, how it could be stopped, and what would happen if destruction of the land was not halted. Who, he asked, would buy the electricity?

Sears was a one-man crusade. Oklahoma and America are richer today because *one* scholar knew that science, scholarship, and the people must prosper together—or die together.

The lesson is one that all members of the scientific and scholarly priesthood may well take to heart. I suggest that, as they prepare to leave their feudal citadel, they begin by purchasing a dictionary of the English language.

SUGGESTIONS FOR STUDY

1. According to the author, what are the causes of unintelligibility among writers in specialized fields, such as science and the social sciences? (Note the specific reasons given in the fifth paragraph.) What causes the unintelligibility in scholarly writing?

2. What is Dr. Brandt's chief charge against higher education in general? How do the various professional schools contribute to the conditions he attacks?

3. What is the abiding fear of the average man? Who has been the only one to realize this among those who serve the public?

4. What does the author think may have been the greatest gain we made by the conquest of the atom?

5. According to the author, on what narrow, viciously anti-social plane has the business of higher education been conducted? If you can locate three doctoral dissertations, examine them to see if you think he is fair and accurate in his statements.

6. What is the author's definition of literature?

7. What general principle did Paul Sears put into practice?

8. What specific suggestion does the author make to scholars? What is the point of the suggestion?

3. IMAGINATIVE WORDS

Connotation

The connotation of a word is its suggested or implied meaning, an overtone which has become attached to the word because of repeated use in the same context. It is complementary to denotation, the literal meaning of the word as given by the dictionary. *Steed* denotes *horse;* but it connotes *knights in armor, tournaments, chivalry,* and *dress parades.* Names of colors are rich in connotative power: *red,* for example, denotes a kind of visual experience; it connotes *blood, revolution, Communism, anger, frenzy, danger. Green* connotes *coolness, freshness, inexperience, youth, the outdoors.* Connotations appeal to the imagination. They arouse associations by stimulating half-forgotten recollections of previous experiences with the things that words denote. Certain words have greater connotative power than others because they denote things directly connected with the more powerful and permanent emotions. *House* denotes a moderate-sized structure with four walls and a roof, and for most people connotes very little more; but *home* is rich in connotation because it is associated with the family and family life. The connotations of words are harder to manage than denotations because they change rapidly.

Whereas denotations do change, connotations, being much more subtle, can alter completely in a few months. Depending upon the current amount of public sympathy with the worker's point of view in industry, the term *labor organizer* can imply a popular hero or a public menace. At present there seems to be an attempt on foot to supplant *capitalist* with *industrialist* because of the unfavorable connotations which cluster about the former term, just as *capitalist* once supplanted *rich man.* In the 1920's *collegiate* connoted long fur coats, hot jazz, horn-rimmed glasses, and a flask on every hip; the word has nearly passed out of the present college student's vocabulary. The connotations of words, therefore, cannot be studied and learned once for all, as one learns the multiplication table. To use the language of your contemporaries as effectively as possible, you must be forever a learner, alert to every syllable you read or hear.

Although as a student you can hardly be expected to achieve thorough mastery of connotative diction, you can learn to be aware of connotations which are not in the spirit of the context. The connotations of slang, for example, in a business letter or a formal address are as out of place as a pun in a prayer. The language of the editorial column, consisting of words chosen to arouse patriotic or civic emotion, is not appropriate for the research paper. An undignified word cannot rest peaceably in a dignified sentence, but confuses and misdirects the trend of the whole communication. A cold, lifeless word set in glowing poetic terminology is an intruder to be cast out lest it deaden the effect of the passage. "On that memorable night in August the gale trumpeted past the steeple of Weatherby Church and the rain, rather than falling steadily with a rhythmic tattoo, flung itself with sudden slops against the windows." Here, *slops* is out of place. It is a vigorous word, and would perform notably elsewhere, but its connotations are not those of steeples and church windows. In the following sentence from *Macbeth,* select the words and phrases which you think are the most suitable because of their connotations:

> (Any old day; tomorrow, and tomorrow, and tomorrow; day after day after day; throughout the whole future) creeps in this (daily chore; business of living; petty pace) from day to day to (the last syllable of recorded time; the bell ending the last round; the blast from the trumpet of Gabriel); and (all the days in the past; all our yesterdays; the innings that have been played) have lighted fools the way to (dirty, wormy, unlovely, dusty) death.

If you do not remember the terms Shakespeare chose, look up the passage in Act V of *Macbeth*. A comparison of Shakespeare's language with the other terminology suggested here may show the effectiveness of words chosen for connotations which fit the context.

Figures of Speech

The person who uses language imaginatively frequently has recourse to figures of speech, stated or implied comparisons between one set of experiences and another, or between an abstract idea and a sensory image. Figures of speech, if they are original and yet within the scope of common experience, add color and concreteness to writing. Following are the most common types.

a. *Simile*. A simile is a direct comparison between objects, experiences, or ideas of different classes; it is usually introduced by *like, as, as if,* or *as when.*

> Horatius stood *like a sturdy oak.*
> His smile was *as cold as ice water.*

b. *Metaphor*. A metaphor implies a similarity rather than stating it directly. It says that a thing *is* something else rather than that it is *like* something else. "He sped through the opposing team like a bullet" is a simile: "He was a human bullet that afternoon as he shot through the opposing team" is a metaphor.

> Methought I heard a voice cry, "Sleep no more!

Macbeth does *murder* sleep,"—the innocent sleep,
> Sleep that *knits up the ravel'd sleeve of care,*
> *The death of each day's life, sore labor's bath,*
> *Balm of hurt minds, great nature's second course,*
> *Chief nourisher in life's feast, . . .*

c. *Hyperbole*. A deliberate overstatement, not for the sake of misleading someone but for the sake of emphasis, is called hyperbole.

> Our neighbors cannot come to dinner; they say they have a *thousand* things to do.
> The terrace *bakes* in the mid-afternoon sun.

d. *Litotes*. A deliberate understatement for the sake of ironic emphasis is called litotes.

> That *wasn't a bad meal* for thirty-five cents.
> He is a person *of no little importance* in his home town.

e. *Personification*. Personification is the attribution of human qualities or characteristics to an inanimate object or an abstraction.

> The sun *showed his fiery face.*
> The moon *looked down* upon the quiet scene.
> *O Death,* where is thy sting?

When properly adjusted to the context, an original metaphor or simile may enliven an otherwise dull sentence. If figures of speech are to appear natural, however, you must exercise care in writing them. The best figurative language is suggested spontaneously by observation of the common elements of life. It results from the play of imagination on experience. If you deliberately invent figurative language, your writing will very likely show evidences of these laborious efforts. On the other hand, a spontaneous figure of speech should not be immune from a critical examination simply because it is spontaneous.

81. Avoid mixed figures.

The dangers of figurative language are the mixed figure error and triteness. A mixed figure is improperly adjusted to its context or to another figure of speech with the same reference. The classic example is "I smell a rat; I see it floating in the air; but we shall nip it in the bud." Others: "All students who come to college have a spark of originality, which their instructors should water and make grow"; "Your contribution will seem like a drop in the bucket in this large bundle of red tape."

82. Avoid trite expressions, or clichés, those expressions used so frequently that they have lost all their connotative force and have become threadbare.

They are the staple of those who lack imagination or who are too lazy to think of fresh, new expressions and figures of speech. In an article following this section, "The Cliché Expert Takes the Stand," Mr. Frank Sullivan satirizes those who employ such terms.

A list of trite expressions would run to many pages and still be incomplete. The following examples, however, will serve to illustrate what is meant: alluding to a person as being strong as an ox, weak as a kitten, pale as a ghost, or white as a sheet; to a girl as a member of the fair sex, a raving beauty, a blushing bride, or as entering upon the sea of matrimony; to someone as reclining in the arms of Morpheus, being hungry as a bear, making a Herculean effort, falling with a sickening thud, beating a hasty retreat, burning the midnight oil, or being sadder but wiser. Certain quotations and proverbs have become equally colorless from overuse: the exception proves the rule, great minds run in the same channels, it never rains but it pours, variety is the spice of life, ignorance is bliss, and many others. The one who first coined such expressions probably had a highly imaginative mind, but the one who continues to repeat them long after they have ceased to stimulate a mental image exemplifies, if not weakmindedness, at least a mind that has ceased to grow.

Euphemisms

To use language imaginatively, avoid euphemisms—pale synonyms or circumlocutions for common terms which allude usually to something unpleasant. Although euphemisms often become clichés, they are unlike clichés in that the latter are the product of a lazy mind, whereas euphemisms are the product of a timid mind. Reporters on small-town newspapers, for instance, fill their stories of births, marriages, and deaths with such words as *the grim reaper*, a man's *passing, Hymen, Cupid, the stork,* and *a little stranger being ushered into the world.* To the euphemist addict, *sweat* becomes *perspire, spit* becomes *expectorate, a drunken man* is *intoxicated,* no one ever *tells a lie* but *misrepresents the facts,* the *poor* are the *underprivileged,* an *undertaker* is a *mortician,* and *boarders* are *paying guests.* Ironically, euphemisms soon fall into disrepute and become more objectionable than the common word they try to displace. Thus their connotations become bad.

Words do not need to be new, exotic, or different to have the power to stimulate the imagination and to have rich connotations. Such words as *friend, brother, rose, girl, dog,* and a thousand others we use every day, never grow old or shopworn. The writer who uses them without affectation, who deals sparingly in ornamentation and flowery verbiage, and who avoids trite expressions and euphemisms will find the imaginative appeal for which he is seeking.

(See *Workbook,* Exercise 10.)

The Cliché Expert Takes the Stand[1]

FRANK SULLIVAN

Question—Mr. Arbuthnot, you are an expert in the use of the cliché, are you not?

Answer—Yes, sir, I am a certified public cliché expert.

Q.—In that case would you be good enough to answer a few questions on the use and application of the cliché in ordinary speech and writing?

A.—I should be only too glad to do so.

Q.—Your occupation?

A.—Well, after burning the midnight oil at an institution of higher learning, I was for a time a tiller of the soil. Then I went down to the sea in ships for a while, and later, at various times, I have been a guardian of the law, a gentleman of the Fourth Estate, a poet at heart, a bon vivant and raconteur, a prominent clubman, an eminent—

Q.—Just what is your occupation at the moment, Mr. Arbuthnot?

A.—At the moment I am an unidentified man of about forty, shabbily clad.

Q.—How do you cliché experts reveal yourselves, Mr. Arbuthnot?

A.—In our true colors, of course.

Q.—And you expect to live to . . .

A.—A ripe old age.

Q.—What do you shuffle off?

A.—This mortal coil.

Q.—What do you thank? *A.*—My lucky stars.

Q.—What kind of retreats do you like?

A.—Hasty retreats.

Q.—What do you do to hasty retreats?

A.—I beat them.

Q.—Regarding dogs, what kind of dog are you?

A.—A gay dog.

Q.—And how do you work? *A.*—Like a dog.

Q.—And you lead? *A.*—A dog's life.

Q.—So much for dogs. Now, Mr. Arbuthnot, when you are naked, you are . . .

A.—Stark naked.

Q.—In what kind of daylight?

A.—Broad daylight.

Q.—What kind of outsider are you?

A.—I'm a rank outsider.

Q.—How right are you?

A.—I am dead right.

Q.—What kind of meals do you like?

A.—Square meals.

Q.—What do you do to them?

A.—Ample justice.

Q.—What is it you do to your way?

A.—I wend my way.

Q.—And your horizon?

A.—I broaden my horizon.

Q.—When you buy things, you buy them for . . . *A.*—A song.

Q.—You are as sober as . . . *A.*—A judge.

Q.—And when you are drunk?

A.—I have lots of leeway there. I can be drunk as a coot, or a lord, or an owl, or a fool——

Q.—Very good, Mr. Arbuthnot. Now, how about the fate of Europe?

A.—It is hanging in the balance, of course.

Q.—What happens to landscapes?

A.—Landscapes are dotted.

Q.—What kind of precision are you cliché-users partial to?

A.—Clocklike precision.

Q.—And what kind of order?

A.—Apple-pie order.

Q.—When you watch a parade, you watch it from . . .

A.—A point of vantage.

Q.—And you shroud things . . .

A.—In the mists of antiquity.

Q.—What kind of threats do you make?

[1] From *The New Yorker*. Reprinted by permission of the author and *The New Yorker*.

A.—Veiled threats.

Q.—And what kind of secrets do you betray?

A.—Dark secrets.

Q.—How about ignorance?

A.—Ignorance is always abysmal.

Q.—When you travel, what do you combine?

A.—I combine business with pleasure.

Q.—And you are destined . . .

A.—To go far.

Q.—Thank you, Mr. Arbuthnot. What time is it? A.—High time.

Q.—How do you point?

A.—I point with pride, I view with alarm, and I yield to no man.

Q.—What do you pursue?

A.—The even tenor of my way.

Q.—Ever pursue the odd tenor of your way?

A.—Oh, no, I would lose my standing as a cliché expert if I did that.

Q.—As for information, you are . . .

A.—A mine of information.

Q.—What kind of mine?

A.—A veritable mine.

Q.—What do you throw?

A.—I throw caution.

Q.—Where? A.—To the winds.

SUGGESTIONS FOR STUDY

1. Examine the papers you have written so far in your composition course. Are you dependent on clichés, like those in this selection, for instruments of communication?

2. Make a list of clichés that you hear during one day, and note who uses them—another student, an instructor, and so on.

Emotional Meanings[1]

ROBERT H. THOULESS

WHEN WE USE a word in speech and writing, its most obvious purpose is to point to some thing, or relation, or property. This is the word's "meaning." We see a small four-footed animal on the road and call it a "dog," indicating that it is a member of the class of four-footed animals we call dogs. The word "dog" as we have used it there has a plain, straightforward, "objective" meaning. We have in no way gone beyond the requirements of exact scientific description.

Let us suppose also that one grandparent of the dog was a collie, another was an Irish terrier, another a fox terrier, and the fourth a bull-dog. We can express these facts equally scientifically and objectively by saying that he is a dog of mixed breed. Still we have in no way gone beyond the requirements of exact scientific description.

Suppose, however, that we had called that

[1] From *How To Think Straight* by Robert H. Thouless. (Copyright, 1932, 1939, by Simon and Schuster.) Reprinted by permission of Simon and Schuster and Hodder and Stoughton, the English publisher.

same animal a "mongrel." The matter is more complicated. We have used a word which objectively means the same as "dog of mixed breed," but which also arouses in our hearers an emotional attitude of disapproval towards that particular dog. A word, therefore, can not only indicate an object, but can also suggest an emotional attitude towards it. Such suggestion of an emotional attitude does go beyond exact and scientific discussion because our approvals and disapprovals are individual—they belong to ourselves and not to the objects we approve or disapprove of. An animal which to the mind of its master is a faithful and noble dog of mixed ancestry may be a "mongrel" to his neighbor whose chickens are chased by it.

Similarly, a Negro may be indicated objectively as a "colored man" or with strong emotional disapproval and contempt as a "nigger." The use of the latter word debases any discussion in which it is used below the level of impartial and objective argument.

Once we are on the look-out for this difference between "objective" and "emotional" meanings, we shall notice that words which carry more or less strong suggestions of emotional attitudes are very common and are ordinarily used in the discussion of such controversial questions as those of politics, morals, and religion. This is one reason why such controversies cannot yet be settled.

There is a well-known saying that the word "firm" can be declined as follows: I am *firm*, thou art *obstinate*, he is *pig-headed*. That is a simple illustration of what is meant. "Firm," "obstinate," and "pig-headed" all have the same objective meaning—that is, following one's own course of action and refusing to be influenced by other people's opinions. They have, however, different emotional meanings; "firm" has an emotional meaning of strong approval, "obstinate" of mild disapproval, "pig-headed" of strong disapproval.

In much the same way when, during the war, our thought was dominated by emotion, our newspapers contrasted the *spirit* of our heroic boys with the *mentality* of the *Huns,* and the *unquenchable heroism* of our troops with the enemy's *ponderous foolhardiness.* Now, with the more objective attitude which has been brought by the lapse of time, we can look back and see that a *spirit* and a *mentality* are objectively the same thing, only the one word has an emotional meaning of approval, the other of disapproval. We can see too that a soldier going forward under shellfire to probable death is doing the same thing whether he is a German or one of our own countrymen, and that to distinguish between them by applying the word *foolhardiness* to the action of the one and *heroism* to that of the other is to distort reality by using words to make an emotional distinction between two actions which are objectively identical.

Such thinking in war-time may do much harm by leading humane people to condone cruelty. When the ordinarily liberal-minded Swinburne wrote a poem during the Boer War on the death of a British officer who had been blamed for the bad condition of the camps in which the Boer women and children were interned, he said:

Nor heed we more than he what liars dare say
Of mercy's holiest duties left undone
Towards *whelps* and *dams* of *murderous* foes,
    whom none
Save we had spared or feared to starve and slay.

Whelps and *dams* clearly mean in objective fact *children* and *wives* with the added meaning of the emotional attitude adopted towards the females and young of wild beasts, while *murderous* means no more in objective fact than that our foes killed us when they could (as we also killed them), with the added emotional meaning of an attitude towards them which is our attitude to those who are guilty of murder.

The use of emotionally toned words is not, of course, always to be condemned. They are always harmful when we are trying to think clearly on a disputable point of fact. In poetry, on the other hand, they have a perfectly proper place, because in poetry (as in some kinds of prose) the arousing of suitable emotions is an important part of the purpose for which the words are used.

In *The Eve of St. Agnes,* Keats has written:

Full on this casement shone the wintry moon,
And threw warm gules on Madeline's fair breast.

These are beautiful lines. Let us notice how much of their beauty follows from the proper choice of emotionally colored words and how completely it is lost if these words are replaced by neutral ones. The words with strikingly emotional meanings are *casement, gules, Madeline, fair,* and *breast. Casement* means simply a kind of window with emotional and romantic associations. *Gules* is the heraldic name for red, with the suggestion of romance which accompanies all heraldry. *Madeline* is simply a girl's name, but one calling out favorable emotions absent from a relatively plain and straightforward name. *Fair* simply means, in objective fact, that her skin was white or uncolored—a necessary condition for the colors of the window to show—but also *fair* implies warm emotional preference for an uncolored skin rather than one which is yellow, purple, black, or any of the other colors which skin might be. *Breast* has also similar emotional meanings, and the aim of scientific description might have been equally well attained if it had been replaced by such a neutral word as *chest.*

Let us now try the experiment of keeping these two lines in a metrical form, but replacing all the emotionally colored words by neutral ones, while making as few other changes as possible. We may write:

Full on this window shone the wintry moon,
Making red marks on Jane's uncolored chest.

No one will doubt that all of its poetic value has been knocked out of the passage by these changes. Yet the lines still mean the same in external fact; they still have the same objective meaning. It is only the emotional meaning which has been destroyed.

Now if Keats had been writing a scientific description for a textbook on physics instead of a poem, it would have been necessary for him to have used some such coldly objective terms as those into which we have just translated his lines. Such emotionally charged phrases as *warm gules* and *fair breast* would only have obscured the facts to which the scientist exactly but unbeautifully refers when he speaks of "the selective transmission of homogeneous light by pigmented glass."

The purpose of the present essay is to deal with the kind of problem in which cold and scientific thinking is required. Most of the practical problems of life are of this order. The fact that I shall abuse the use of emotional thinking in connection with such problems as tariffs, prohibition, social ownership, and war does not mean that there is no place for emotional thinking. Poetry, romantic prose, and emotional oratory are all of inestimable value, but their place is not where responsible decisions must be made. The common (almost universal) use of emotional

words in political thinking is as much out of place as would be a chemical or statistical formula in the middle of a poem. Real democracy will come only when the solution of national and international problems is carried out by scientific methods of thought, purged of all irrelevant emotion. Into the action which follows decision we can put all the emotion which we have refused to allow in our thinking. Let us think calmly and scientifically about war, and then actively oppose it with all the passion of which we are capable.

The growth of the exact thinking of modern science has been very largely the result of its getting rid of all terms suggesting emotional attitudes and using only those which unemotionally indicate objective facts. It was not always so. The old alchemists called gold and silver "noble" metals, and thought that this emotionally colored word indicated something belonging to the metals themselves from which their properties could be deduced. Other metals were called "base." Although these terms have survived as convenient labels for the modern chemist they carry none of their old emotional significance.

In popular biological discussions, on the other hand, such words are still used with their full emotional meaning, as when the "nobility" of man is contrasted with his alleged "base" origin. In this respect, popular biological discussion differs from that of the textbook and the laboratory, in which are used terms almost as devoid of emotional meaning as those of physics or chemistry.

Psychology is still younger in the ranks of the sciences, and the clearing away from it of emotional words has not gone very far. "Passion," "emotion," "sex" are all terms of our science which carry strong emotional meanings, so that it is difficult to discuss a controversial matter in psychology without using words which rouse strong emotions and confuse all issues. A beginning is being made. "Intelligence" was a subject on which it was difficult to think clearly because it carried so much emotional meaning. Now Professor Spearman has replaced it by what he calls "g" (or the "general factor"), which is a conception derived from the statistical analysis of a large collection of figures, and yet which is in its essence all that was really scientific in the old conception of intelligence. Some day a psychological genius will give us X or Z to replace the old emotional conception of sex, and we shall be able to discuss psychoanalysis as objectively as a mathematical physicist can discuss the quantum theory.

When we turn to politics and international questions, we are still further from straight scientific thinking. Such words as "Bolshevik," "reactionary," "revolutionary," "constitutional," "national honor," etc., are all words used in national and international political thinking which carry more of emotional than of any other meaning. So long as such words are the ordinary terms of rival politicians, how can we hope to think straight in national and international affairs? If a chemist doing an experiment depended on such thought processes as a nation uses in selecting its rulers or in deciding on peace or war with other nations, he would blow up his laboratory. This, however, would be a trivial disaster in comparison with what may result from emotional thinking in politics. Better have a hundred chemical laboratories blown up than the whole of civilization!

We must look forward to and try to help on the day when the thinking about political and international affairs will be as unemotional and as scientific as that about the properties of numbers or the atomic weights of elements. The spirit of impartial investigation of facts unswayed by irrelevant emotions has given us great advances in the sciences. Its triumphs will be even greater when it is applied to the most important affairs of life. We look forward to the day when we shall be able to discuss and settle such questions as Tariffs, Prohibition, Public *vs.* Private Ownership, and Disarmament treaties as successfully as physicists have discussed and settled Einstein's theory of relativity.

Let us try to study a few more examples of the use of words with emotional meanings taken from various sources. Accounts of wars are rich sources of such material, so we are not surprised to find in a book on the French Commune the statement that large numbers of the regular troops were *assassinated* during the street fighting by the communards, while a much larger number of the latter were *summarily executed* by the regulars. In order to reduce this to a statement of objective fact it is clear that the one word "killed" should be used in place both of *assassinated* and *summarily executed*. We have already noticed how such a choice of words with the same objective but opposite emotional meaning can be used to make us feel sympathetic to one and hostile to the other of two sides in warfare. During the conflicts between Red and White forces in Russia and in China, our newspapers told us of the *atrocities* of the Bolsheviks and of the *wise severity* of the White commanders. Examination of the details (often possible only long afterwards) shows that the objective facts of an *atrocity* and of *wise severity* are much the same, and that they are not the kind of objective facts which will call out an emotion of approval in a humane person.

A similar choice of words will be noticed in political discussion. A fluent and forcible speech delivered by one of our own party is *eloquent,* a similar speech by one of the opposite party is *rhodomontade;* again two words with the same objective meaning but with the opposite emotional meanings of approval and strong disapproval. The practical proposals of the opposition, moreover, are *panaceas*—a highly emotional word calling out the strongly disapproving emotions which we feel for those quack patent medicines which make extravagant claims. Those who show enthusiasm in support of proposals with which a speaker disagrees are *extremists;* while those showing similar enthusiasm on his own side are called *staunch*. If a politician wishes to attack some new proposal he has a battery of these and other words with emotional meanings at his disposal. He speaks of "this suggested *panacea* supported only by the *rhodomontade of extremists*"; and the proposal is at once discredited in the minds of the majority of people, who like to think of themselves as moderate, distrustful of panaceas, and uninfluenced by windy eloquence. Also we may notice that it has been discredited without the expenditure of any real thought, for of real objective argument there is none, only the manipulation of words calling out emotion.

It is not, however, only in warfare and politics that such words are used in order to influence opinion more easily than can be done by words embodying real thought. Art criticism is also a good source for this kind of material. Ruskin said of Whistler's Nocturnes: "I have heard and seen much of *Cockney impudence* before now, but never expected to hear a *coxcomb* ask two hundred guineas for *flinging a pot of paint in the public's face*." As in earlier passages, I have italicized the words or phrases with strongly emotional meanings. Stripped of these and reduced to a statement of objective fact, the passage would have to be paraphrased in some such way as follows: "I have heard and seen much of the behavior of Londoners before now, but never expected to hear a painter ask two hundred guineas for painting a picture which seemed to me to have no meaning." Plainly not much is left of Ruskin's criticism after this operation has been performed on it.

As a last example, we may take a part of an attack made by a newspaper on a novel. This runs: "Its *vicious plea* for the acknowledgment and *condonation* of *sexual perversity*, and the grounds on which it is based, loosen the very *sheet-anchor of conduct*." This passage calls out such strong emotions of abhorrence that most readers will be content to condemn the novel without further inquiry. Yet the effect is gained entirely by the choice of words with emotional meanings. It happens to deal with a subject on which emotions are strong, so a dispassionate

examination is all the more necessary. We note that a *plea* is simply an argument, plus a suggestion of repugnance for the kind of argument used; that *condonation* is tolerance plus an emotional suggestion that such toleration is indefensible; that *sexual* means something in the life of love of which we disapprove, and that a *perversity* is an unusualness plus an emotional suggestion of abhorrence. The loosening of a *sheet-anchor* is a metaphor implying change and suggesting to a landsman the emotion of fear, while *conduct* is simply behavior of which we approve.

So reduced to its bare bones of statement of objective fact (ignoring for a moment the special difficulties raised by the word *vicious*) the passage becomes: "Its argument for the acknowledgment and tolerance of unusualness in the life of love, and the grounds on which it is based, change the principles of behavior." This clearly is an important statement if it is true, but is not enough in itself to condemn the book, because undoubtedly our principles of behavior do need changing from time to time. We can only decide intelligently whether or not they need changing in the particular case under discussion, when we have made a dispassionate statement of what the proposed changes are and why they are defended. As in all other cases, discussion of the question with emotionally charged words obscures the problem and makes a sensible decision difficult or impossible.

The word *vicious* has some special difficulties of its own. It arouses emotions of disapproval, but there is no word with the same objective meaning which would not. If we call the book bad, corrupt, or evil, the same emotions would be aroused. So we cannot perform the simple operation of replacing *vicious* by an emotionally neutral word with the same objective meaning. Can we then leave it out altogether, on the ground that it has no objective meaning, but that it is used merely to arouse emotion?

Here we are up against a problem about

which there has been much dispute. Some people consider that all such words as "good," "bad," "beautiful," "ugly," only indicate one's own emotional reactions towards actions or things and in no sense properties of the actions or things themselves. But when we see a man steal a penny from a child and we call his action "bad," we are in fact saying something meaningful about the action itself and not merely about our own feelings. As to what that something is we may leave the philosophers to dispute; it may only be that the man's action has subtracted from the total amount of human happiness. So to say a book is *vicious* is not the same kind of thing as contrasting the *assassination* of regular troops by communards with the *summary execution* of the communards by regular soldiers. The statement that the book is vicious has a meaning which is not merely emotional, although, of course, the statement may not be true.

On the other hand, it is clearly not quite the same kind of meaning as a simple statement of outside fact such as "This is a book." Whether the book is good or bad is a real question, but it is a question peculiarly difficult to decide. Our own statement one way or the other is likely to be nothing but a reflection of our own personal prejudices and to have, therefore, no sort of scientific exactness. At the same time, such words certainly arouse strong emotions and should, therefore, be used sparingly in honest argument. The use of words implying moral judgments in the course of argument is very generally an attempt to distort the hearers' view of the truth by arousing emotions.

If we are trying to decide a simple question of fact, such words should be left out, because it is easier to settle one question at a time. If a man is accused of poisoning his wife, the prosecuting attorney should not say, "This *scoundrel* who hounded his wife to her grave." The question to be decided is whether the man did poison his wife. If he did, he is a "scoundrel" undoubtedly, but calling him a scoundrel does not help to decide the question of fact. On the contrary, it makes a correct decision more difficult by rousing emotions of hatred for the accused in the minds of the jury. Another obvious objection to the use of the word "scoundrel" before the man is convicted, which puts it in the ranks of "crooked thinking," is that it "begs the question" or assumes what is to be proved. The man is only a scoundrel if he is guilty, and yet the word has been used in the course of an argument to prove that he is guilty.

These two objections can be urged against the word "vicious" in the condemnation of a book quoted above. It calls up strong emotions, making a just decision of the nature of the book difficult, and it assumes exactly what the article professes to prove—that the book is a bad one.

The aim of this essay has been to distinguish one kind of crooked thinking, in the hope that those who recognize how their opinions can be twisted away from the truth by the use of words with emotional meanings may be able to recognize this source of error and to guard themselves against it. Those of its readers who have found anything new to them in the ideas of this essay should not, I suggest, be content simply to read the essay, but should try to do some practical work on its subject-matter. If you were studying botany, you would not be content merely to read books on botany. If you were, that would not carry you far in botanical knowledge. Instead you would gather plants from the hedges and weeds from your garden, dissecting them, examining them with a microscope or magnifying glass, and drawing them in your note-book. Psychology too should be studied by practical methods. Emotional thinking (like most of the other kinds of crooked thinking) is as common as a weed. It is to be found in the leading articles of newspapers, in the words of people carrying on discussions on political, religious, or moral questions, and in the speeches made by public men when these deal with controversial matters. In order to understand it, we should collect specimens by putting them down on paper and then we should dissect them.

The practical exercise which I recommend is one which I have already performed on some passages in which truth seemed to be obscured by emotional thinking. I suggest that readers should copy out controversial passages from newspapers, books, or speeches which contain emotionally colored words. Then they should underline all the emotional words, afterwards rewriting the passages with the emotional words replaced by neutral ones. Examine the passage then in its new form in which it merely states objective facts without indicating the writer's emotional attitude towards them, and see whether it is still good evidence for the proposition it is trying to prove. If it is, the passage is a piece of straight thinking in which emotionally colored words have been introduced merely as an ornament. If not, it is crooked thinking, because the conclusion depends not on the objective meaning of the passage but on the emotions roused by the words.

When we condemn such a use of emotional words in writings and speeches, we must remember that this is a symptom of a more deep-seated evil—their prevalence in our own private, unexpressed thinking. Many of our highly-colored political speakers whose speeches stir us as we are stirred by romantic poetry show themselves unable to think calmly and objectively on any subject. They have so accustomed themselves to think in emotionally toned words that they can no longer think in any other way. They should have been poets or professional orators, but certainly not statesmen.

It really does not matter much if we sometimes use emotional words. We all do when we are trying to produce conviction. What does matter is that we should not lose the power to think without them. So a more important exercise than any we can perform on written material is one we can perform on our own minds. When we catch ourselves thinking in emotional phraseology, let us form a habit of translating our thoughts into emotionally neutral words. Thus we can guard ourselves from ever being so enslaved by emotional words and phrases that they prevent us from thinking objectively when we need to do so—that is, whenever we have to come to a decision on any debatable matter.

SUGGESTIONS FOR STUDY

1. List five words with an explanation of their objective and emotional meanings.

2. From current newspapers or magazines select ten words or phrases conveying emotional meanings intended to make us feel hostile or sympathetic toward one side or another of a discussion.

3. Under what conditions is the use of emotional meanings permissible? Substitute in a line or two of poetry an objective word for each emotional one, and analyze the result.

4. What problem does the psychologist face in using the terms of his science?

5. Under what conditions is the use of emotional meanings harmful?

6. State the thesis sentence of the article.

7. What relation does this discussion bear to that of Mr. Haber in "Basic English for Science"? What is its relation to the following article "On Word Magic" by Mr. Gardiner?

8. Define the following words from the article: controversial, humane, condone, homogeneous, dispassionate, prevalence.

On Word Magic[1]

A. G. GARDINER

I SEE THAT a discussion has arisen in the *Spectator* on the "Canadian Boat Song." It appeared in *Blackwood's* nearly a century ago, and ever since its authorship has been the subject of recurrent controversy. The author may have been "Christopher North," or his brother, Tom Wilson, or Galt, or the Ettrick Shepherd, or the Earl of Eglinton, or none of these. We shall never know. It is one of those pleasant mysteries of the past, like the authorship of the Junius Letters (if, indeed, that can be called a mystery), which can never be exhausted because they can never be solved. I am not going to offer an opinion; for I have none, and I refer to the subject only to illustrate the magic of a word. The poem lives by virtue of the famous stanza:

From the lone shieling of the misty island
  Mountains divide us, and the waste of seas—
Yet still the blood is strong, the heart is High-
    land,
  And we in dreams behold the Hebrides.

It would be an insensible heart that did not feel the surge of this strong music. The yearning of the exile for the motherland had never been uttered with more poignant beauty, though Stevenson came near the same note of tender anguish in the lines written in far Samoa and ending:

Be it granted me to behold you again, in dying,
  Hills of home, and to hear again the call,
Hear about the graves of the martyrs the pee-
    wees crying—
  And hear no more at all.

But for energy and masculine emotion the unknown author takes the palm. The verse is like a great wave of the sea, rolling in to the mother shore, gathering impetus and grandeur as it goes, culminating in the note of vision and scattering itself triumphantly in the splendor of that word "Hebrides."

It is a beautiful illustration of the magic of a word used in its perfect setting. It gathers up the emotion of the theme into one chord of fulfilment and flings open the casement of the mind to far horizons. It is not the only instance in which the name has been used with extraordinary effect. Wordsworth's "Solitary Reaper" has many beautiful lines, but the peculiar glory of the poem dwells in the couplet in which, searching for parallels for the song of the Highland girl that fills "the vale profound," he hears in imagination the cuckoo's call

Breaking the silence of the seas
Among the farthest Hebrides.

Wordsworth, like Homer and Milton, and all who touch the sublime in poetry, had the power of transmuting a proper name to a strange and significant beauty. The most memorable example, perhaps, is in the closing lines of the poem to Dorothy Wordsworth:

But an old age serene and bright,
And lovely as a Lapland night
Shall lead thee to thy grave.

"Lapland" is an intrinsically beautiful word, but it is its setting in this case that makes it shine, pure and austere, like a star in the heavens of poetry. And the miraculous word need not be intrinsically beautiful. Darien is not, yet it is that word in which perhaps the greatest of all sonnets finds its breathless, astonished close:

Silent—upon a peak—in Darien.

[1] From *Leaves in the Wind* by A. G. Gardiner, published and copyrighted by E. P. Dutton & Co., Inc.

And the truth is that the magic of words is not in the words themselves, but in the distinction, delicacy, surprise of their use. Take the great line which Shakespeare puts into the mouth of Antony—

I am dying, Egypt, dying.

It is the only occasion in the play in which he makes Antony speak of Cleopatra by her territorial name, and there is no warrant for the usage in Plutarch. It is a stroke of sheer word magic. It summons up with a sudden magnificence all the mystery and splendor incarnated in the woman for whom he has gambled away the world and all the earthly glories that are fading into the darkness of death. The whole tragedy seems to flame to its culmination in this word that suddenly lifts the action from the human plane to the scale of cosmic drama.

Words of course have an individuality, a perfume of their own, but just as the flame in the heart of the diamond has to be revealed by the craftsman, so the true magic of a beautiful word only discloses itself at the touch of the master. "Quiet" is an ordinary enough word, and few are more frequently on our lips. Yet what wonderful effects Wordsworth, Coleridge, and Keats extract from it:

It is a beauteous evening, calm and free;
The holy time is quiet as a nun,
Breathless with adoration.

The whole passage is a symphony of the sunset, but it is that ordinary word "quiet" which breathes like a benediction through the cadence, filling the mind with the sense of an illimitable peace. And so with Coleridge's "singeth a quiet tune," or Keats':

Full of sweet dreams and health and quiet
   breathing.

Or when, "half in love with easeful Death," he

Called him soft names in many a mused rhyme
To take into the air my quiet breath.

And again:

Far from the fiery noon and eve's one star
Sat grey-hair'd Saturn, quiet as a stone.

There have been greater poets than Keats, but none who has had so sure an instinct for the precious word as he had. Byron had none of this magician touch. Shelley got his effects by the glow and fervor of his spirit; Swinburne by the sheer torrent of his song, and Browning by the energy of his thought. Tennyson was much more of the artificer in words than these, but he had not the secret of the word magic of Shakespeare, Wordsworth, or Keats. Compare the use of adjectives in two things like Shelley's "Ode to the Skylark" and Keats' "Ode to the Nightingale," and the difference is startling. Both are incomparable, but in the one case it is the hurry of the song, the flood of rapture that delights us; in the other each separate line holds us with its jeweled word. "*Embalmed* darkness." "*Verdurous* glooms." "Now more than ever seems it *rich* to die." "Cooled a long age in the *deep-delved* earth." "*Darkling* I listen." "She stood in tears amid the *alien* corn." "Oh, for a beaker full of the *warm south*." "With beaded bubbles *winking* at the brim." "No *hungry* generations tread thee down." And so on. Such a casket of jewels can be found in no other poet that has used our tongue. If Keats' vocabulary had a defect it was a certain overripeness, a languorous beauty that, like the touch of his hand, spoke of death. It lacked the fresh, happy, sunlit spirit of Shakespeare's sovereign word.

Word magic belongs to poetry. In prose it is an intrusion. That was the view of Coleridge. It was because, among its other qualities, Southey's writing was so free from the shock of the dazzling word that Coleridge held it to be the perfect example of pure prose. The modulations are so just, the note so unaffected, the current so clear and untroubled that you read on without pausing once to think "What a brilliant writer this fellow is." And that is the true triumph of the art. It is an art which addresses itself to the mind, and not the emotions, and word magic does not belong to its true armory.

SUGGESTIONS FOR STUDY

1. What "place words" does the author think especially magical?

2. Since he gives no scientific proof that he is correct in attributing magic to these words, what does he assume concerning his reader? Has he a right to make such an assumption?

3. What does he say is necessary to bring out the "perfume of their own" which words possess? What instances does he give to illustrate his statement?

4. Where would word magic be employed? Why would it be out of place in much prose?

5. Define the following words from the article: recurrent, poignant, transmute, intrinsically, incarnated, benediction, cadence, modulations.

83. *G. Glossary of Usage*

A, an. *A* is used before words beginning with a consonant sound; *an* is used before words beginning with a vowel or a silent *h:* a car, a house, a gypsy, an ear, an honor.

Accept, except. *Accept* means *receive; except,* as a verb, means *omit* or *leave out:* He accepted our advice and excepted no one from his directive.

Accidently. Incorrect for *accidentally.*

Ad. Colloquial for *advertisement.*

Affect, effect. 1. *Affect,* as a verb, means *influence* and has no noun form except in a very technical usage in psychology: The war greatly affected our lives. 2. *Effect,* as a verb, means *accomplish* or *bring about despite obstacles* and, as a noun, means a *result:* Though the prisoners effected their escape, the effect of the confinement on them was extreme.

Aggravate. Colloquial for *irritate* or *annoy:* The pranks of the children annoyed me (not: aggravated me). *Aggravate* means *make worse:* Their noise aggravated my headache.

Alibi. Colloquial for an *excuse:* We had a good excuse for not attending the meeting (not: a good alibi for not attending the meeting). Use this word only in its legal meaning.

Allow. Provincial for *declare, assume, maintain:* I assume you are right (not: allow you are right). Use this word in the sense of *permit:* I allow you to go.

All ready, already. *All ready,* a phrase, means *completely ready; already,* an adverb, means *previously* or *by this time:* By the time the suitcases were all ready, the train had already left.

All the farther, all the higher. Incorrect for *as far as, as high as:* That is as high as we climbed (not: all the higher we climbed).

Allusion, illusion. 1. An *allusion* is a passing reference or an incidental mention of something: Pope's allusions to Horace are well known. 2. An *illusion* is a false impression or misconception: He was misled by illusions of grandeur.

Alright. Incorrect for *all right.*

Alternative. In strict usage *alternative* offers two things from which a choice must be made and only in looser usage more than two things: My alternative was to attend college or go to work. It is usually considered preferable to use the word *choice* for the possibility of selecting among three or more things: I was given a choice: to play the piano, the trumpet, or the cello.

Among, between. 1. *Among* designates a mingling with more than two objects: He stood among the people. 2. *Between,* in ordinary usage, refers to only two objects: He stood between the two houses. For the occasional exceptions in the use of *between,* consult a standard dictionary.

Any place, no place, some place. Colloquial for *anywhere, nowhere, somewhere:* I had nowhere to go (not: I had no place to go).

Anywheres, everywheres, nowheres, somewheres. Dialect forms. Drop the final *s.*

Apt, likely, liable. *Apt* and *likely* are often used synonymously. 1. More strictly, *apt* means *inclined* or *having an inborn disposition to:* An impulsive man is apt to become angry. 2. Strictly speaking, *likely* indicates probability: Our team seems likely to win tomorrow. 3. The word *liable,* loosely used, shares the idea of probability with *likely* but has its own strict meaning of *responsible* or *exposed to certain unfortunate consequences:* The boys are liable for the damage they did.

Around. Colloquial for *about, nearly:* We left about eight o'clock (not: around eight o'clock).

As. Incorrect when introducing a noun clause: I don't believe that it will rain (not: as it will rain).

As regards. See *in regard to.*

At. Redundant with *where:* Where is he? (not: Where is he at?)

At about. Unnecessary. Use *at* or *about:* We

went about eight o'clock (not: at about eight o'clock).

Awful, awfully. Colloquial for *unpleasant* or *very great:* It was an unpleasant party (not: an awful party); it was an extremely difficult lesson (not: an awfully difficult lesson). Use *awful* to mean *inspiring fear or reverential awe:* The storm broke with awful fury.

Beside, besides. 1. *Beside,* ordinarily a preposition, means *by the side of:* Tom walked beside Bill. 2. *Besides* as a preposition means *in addition to:* Besides Bill no one was walking beside Tom. *Besides* as a transitional word means *moreover:* The day, besides, was clear and bright.

Between. See *among.*

Blame it on. Colloquial: They blamed me for it, or They placed the blame on me (not: They blamed it on me).

Broke. Slang for *out of money:* I have no money today (not: I am broke today).

Burst. The correct past participle. Avoid *bust, busted, bursted.*

But what. Colloquial for *but that* or *that* in contexts like the following: I don't know but that you are right (not: but what you are right).

Calculate. Provincial in the sense of *intend, plan, suppose, think:* I intend to go tomorrow (not: I calculate on going tomorrow).

Can, may. Though sometimes used interchangeably, *can* is usually understood to denote the ability to do something, whereas *may* indicates permission, possibility, or probability: Can he lift the trunk? May we go home? He may remain with us.

Case. An overused word, often indefinite in meaning. Avoid using it excessively. For the construction *"In case we are not there,* go on ahead," substitute *"If we are not there,* go on ahead." For the phrase *"In the case of John* we made an exception," substitute *"For John* we made an exception" or *"John was an exception."* For the usage "I do not know of a *case* like his," substitute "I do not know of a *predicament* like his."

Complected. Colloquial or dialectal for *complexioned.*

Considerable. Colloquial for *much* or *a great deal:* He knows much about the subject (not: considerable about the subject).

Contact. Colloquial as a transitive verb. Use *write, telephone, call,* or the like: I will call him tomorrow (not: I will contact him tomorrow).

Could of. Illiterate for *could have.*

Crack. Slang for a *joke* or *jibe.* Colloquial in the sense of 1. *excellent:* He was an excellent marksman (not: a crack marksman) 2. *break*

into: He broke into the safe (not: cracked the safe) 3. *enforce discipline:* The police enforced the laws against gambling (not: cracked down on gambling).

Cut. Colloquial for *absent oneself from class:* He was absent from class (not: cut class).

Cute. Colloquial. In its stead use *dainty, attractive, pleasing, picturesque,* or the like.

Data. A plural word from the Latin *datum.* Students would do well to observe the traditional use of the word only as a plural, despite a growing feeling that a singular usage is justified in some instances: These data are correct.

Different than. Though widely used, this term is not accepted as standard usage by many people in this country. Preferably use the form *different from* and so make the usage like that of the verb *to differ from:* His book was different from mine.

Dove. Colloquial for *dived.*

Dreadfully. Colloquial for *extremely bad, ugly,* or *greatly:* He was extremely tired (not: dreadfully tired). Use the word in the sense of *terrible* or *inspiring terror:* At midnight the lightning was dreadful.

Due to. Though widely used as an adverbial construction, *due to* is not accepted as standard by many people in that usage. Reserve it preferably for adjective constructions: His illness is due to fatigue. Employ *because of* or *owing to* in adverbial constructions: Because of fatigue, he is ill.

Dumb. Colloquial for *stupid.* Use it to mean *lacking the power of speech.*

Effect. See *affect.*

Enthuse. Colloquial for *be enthusiastic.*

Etc. An abbreviation for *et cetera,* which means *and other things.* To write *and etc.,* therefore, is to repeat *and;* use simply *etc.* In formal usage *and so forth* or *and the like* is preferred to the abbreviation *etc.*

Every so often. Colloquial for *occasionally.*

Everywheres. Dialectal. Drop the final *s.*

Except. See *accept.*

Expect. Colloquial for *think, suppose, suspect:* I suppose this is the house (not: I expect this is the house). Use this word to mean *look forward to* or *anticipate:* I expect to enter the house.

Extra. Not acceptable in formal usage for *unusually:* It is an unusually hot day (not: an extra hot day).

Factor. An overused word, meaning an element that produces a result or helps to produce a result. Employ such words as *element, circumstance, constituent, influence* in its place.

Farther, further. Although sometimes used synonymously, *farther* ordinarily refers to space or distance, *further* to time, quantity, or degree: If we go farther up the mountain, we can make a further study of our problem.

Fellow. Colloquial for *person* or *man:* Do you see that man? (not: Do you see that fellow?)

Fewer, less. *Fewer* means *a smaller number; less* means *a smaller amount:* We paid less money this year to hear fewer concerts.

Fine. Often overused. Find a suitable synonym if you have the habit of using the word frequently. Use *admirable, distinguished, idealistic,* or the like.

Fix. Colloquial as a verb for *repair* and as a noun for *predicament:* We escaped from our predicament (not: fix) as soon as the garage man repaired (not: fixed) the car.

Folks. Colloquial for *members of one's own family:* I visited my parents (not: my folks).

Funny. Colloquial for *queer, odd.* It means *amusing* or *comical.*

Grand. Colloquial for *splendid, very good, exciting:* We had an exciting time at the party (not: a grand time). *Grand* means *imposing in size, lofty, dignified.*

Hardly, scarcely. Not to be used in addition to another negative, as each involves a negative idea: He could not find his way, or He could hardly find his way (not: He could not hardly find his way).

Help but. Not preferred after the adverb *not,* which expresses fully the negative and so renders *but* unnecessary: I cannot help thinking that you are correct (not: help but think that you are correct).

Hisself. Illiterate for *himself.*

In back of. Colloquial for *back of* or *behind.*

Inside of. Colloquial for *inside* or *within.*

Irregardless. Incorrect for *regardless.*

Its, it's. *Its* is a possessive pronoun meaning *of it; it's* is a contraction of *it is:* It's necessary to conceive its mighty power.

Kibitz, kibitzer. Colloquial in both the noun and the verb forms.

Kind, sort. When singular, these nouns should be modified by singular adjectives: This kind of glove is sold everywhere.

Kind of, sort of. Colloquial for *rather, somewhat:* He looked rather puzzled (not: sort of puzzled).

Lay, lie. *Lay* (principal parts: *lay, laid, laid*) is a transitive verb meaning *put* or *place; lie* (principal parts: *lie, lay, lain*) is an intransitive verb meaning *put oneself down* or *be in a horizontal position:* I laid the papers on the desk and then lay down for a nap. Error ordinarily occurs in the substitution of forms of *lay* for those of *lie* in such incorrect expressions as *he is laying down* or *he laid down.* Observe these correct sentences: The dog lying before the fire has often lain there. The dog, laying the bone in the hole, is trying to conceal the place where he has laid it.

Leave, let. *Leave* means *go away from* or *allow to remain; let* means *permit* or *permit to enter or leave:* I let him leave early. Error results ordinarily from substituting *leave* for *let* in such incorrect expressions as *leave us go, leave us be.*

Less. See *fewer.*

Liable. See *apt.*

Like. A preposition, not to be used for *as* or *as if* to link clauses: The coach, like many people this spring, looks as if he is tired (not: like he is tired).

Likely. See *apt.*

Line. Jargon in the sense of *business* or *profession:* What is your business? (not: your line)

Locate. Colloquial for *establish one's residence:* We settled in Grand Rapids (not: We located in Grand Rapids).

Loose, lose. *Loose* means *set free* or *loosen; lose* means *misplace, suffer the loss of,* or *fail to win:* He began to lose hope when he was not able to loose the bonds which bound him.

Lots of. Colloquial for *much* or *a great deal of:* We had a great deal of trouble (not: lots of trouble).

Lovely. Colloquial for *pleasing* or *delightful:* We had a delightful visit (not: lovely visit). *Lovely* means *exquisitely beautiful,* a term which conveys ordinarily the sense of moral, spiritual beauty as well as physical beauty.

Mad. Colloquial for *angry.* Use it to mean *insane.*

May. See *can.*

Mean. 1. Colloquial in the sense of *nasty, ill-tempered:* He is an ill-tempered man (not: a mean man). 2. Colloquial for *ashamed:* I felt ashamed after his rebuke (not: mean after his rebuke). 3. Slang for *formidable* or *extremely good:* He hits an extremely good one-iron shot (not: a mean one-iron shot). In standard usage this word signifies *ignoble, contemptible, of little importance:* He has a mean purpose in mind.

Might of. Illiterate for *might have.*

More so. Illogical as a substitute for a preceding adjective: He was slow, but she was slower (not: but she was more so).

Most, almost. *Most,* generally an adjective, means *nearly all* or *the greatest* (as an adverb, it means *in the greatest degree*); *almost,* an adverb, means *nearly:* Almost all men will agree on that subject, but most boys will disagree.

Nice. Overused. Substitute *agreeable, pleasant, kind,* and the like.

No-account. Dialectal for *worthless.*

No doubt but, no other but. Illogical. *But* is unnecessary after the negative force of *no doubt* and *no other:* As the voters wanted no other than Jim, there can be no doubt that he is elected.

No place. Colloquial for *nowhere.*

Nowheres. Dialectal. Drop the final *s.*

Off of. Dialectal. Drop the *of:* Keep off the porch (not: off of the porch).

OK, O.K., okay. Colloquial for *correct* or *all right.*

Outside of. Colloquial in the sense of *besides, except:* No one was there except us (not: outside of us).

Over with. Colloquial for *over, finished.*

Pass out. Slang for *faint* or *die.*

Percent, per cent, percentage. *Per cent* may be spelled as either one word or two. It is preferred when a number is used (as *three per cent*); *percentage* is preferred when no number is given (as *a low percentage*). Percentage is slang in the sense of *use* or *profit:* There was no use in our going (not: percentage in our going).

Plenty. Colloquial as an adverb: He was very sick (not: plenty sick).

Plug. Slang for *advertise* or *advertisement:* He advertised his product (not: He plugged his product).

Principal, principle. *Principal,* as an adjective, means *chief; principle* is not an adjective but a noun meaning *a basic law:* The principal reason for the mistake was their inability to grasp the principle of operation. *Principal,* however, may also be a noun meaning *a leader, the executive officer of a school,* or in finance *the sum from which interest is derived:* By drawing six percent interest on his principal, our high-school principal showed an astute knowledge of finance.

Put across. Slang in the sense of *convey a meaning* or *make clear:* The lecturer could not explain his ideas clearly (not: put across his ideas).

Put over. Slang in the sense of *get an acceptance for:* We gained acceptance for our plan (not: We put our plan over).

Proposition. Colloquial for *undertaking* or *situation requiring action:* Assembling a baseball team was a difficult undertaking (not: a difficult proposition). In standard usage *proposition* means *a proposal to be accepted or rejected:* He made us a fair proposition.

Quite. 1. Colloquial in the sense of *to a considerable degree:* She was rather attractive (not: quite attractive). 2. Colloquial in expressions such as *quite a little* and *quite a few,* although these are apparently approaching standard usage: I know several people like that (not: quite a few people like that). *Quite* signifies in standard usage *wholly, entirely:* She was quite wrong.

Real. Colloquial for the adverb *very:* She was very happy (not: real happy).

Regular. Colloquial for *complete, thorough, out-and-out:* He is a complete bookworm (not: a regular bookworm).

Right away. Colloquial for *immediately:* I shall come at once (not: come right away).

Said. Objectionable for *aforementioned* except in legal documents: We brought the book with us (not: We brought the said book with us).

Same. Jargon when used loosely for *it* or *they:* A carload of steel has been ordered; it will be sent immediately (not: the same will be sent immediately).

Scarcely. See *hardly.*

Seldom ever. Redundant. Omit *ever.*

Set, sit. *Set,* ordinarily a transitive verb (principal parts: *set, set, set*), means *put* or *place; sit,* ordinarily an intransitive verb (principal parts: *sit, sat, sat*), means *put oneself,* as in taking a seat: Maria sets the chair on the lawn so that Tom may sit down. Exceptions are found in rare expressions like *the setting sun* and *the setting hen.*

Should of. Illiterate for *should have.*

Show up. 1. Colloquial for *arrive:* We arrived on time (not: We showed up on time). 2. Colloquial for *expose:* We exposed his guilt (not: We showed him up to be guilty).

Size up. Colloquial for *estimate, judge:* We estimated the situation well (not: We sized up the situation well).

So. 1. Overused for *very* or *exceedingly:* I was very tired (not: so tired). 2. Improper for *so that:* I drove rapidly so that I could arrive on time (not: so I could arrive on time). 3. Frequently improper for introducing the second independent clause of a compound sentence; subordinating the first clause often lends a better emphasis: Because he told the truth, he was not punished (rather than: He told the truth; so he was not punished).

Soap opera. Colloquial for *radio serial.*

Socialite. Colloquial for *one socially prominent:* She was socially prominent (not: a socialite).

Some. 1. Colloquial for *somewhat* or *a little:* He studied a few minutes (not: studied some).

2. Slang for *to a great degree:* That was an excellent shot (not: That was some shot).

Sort, sort of. See *kind, kind of.*

Some place. Colloquial for *somewhere.* See *any place.*

Somewheres. Dialectal. Drop the final *s.*

Such. Overused as an intensive for *very:* It was a very hot day (rather than: such a hot day). Often *such* needs a completing clause: It was such a hot day that we went swimming.

Sure. Colloquial for the adverb *surely:* He surely played well at third base (not: He sure played well at third base). Use *sure* as an adjective: He was sure of success.

Suspicion. Dialectal as a verb: He suspected he would lose (not: He suspicioned he would lose). Use *suspicion* only as a noun: His suspicions were confirmed.

Swell. Slang for *excellent, grand, first rate:* He is an excellent golfer (not: a swell golfer).

Take and. Dialectal and redundant in compound verb forms: He hit the ball (not: He took and hit the ball).

Take off. Colloquial for *mimic* or *imitate.*

Terrible. Colloquial for *extremely bad* or *unpleasant:* He gave a poor speech (not: a terrible speech). *Terrible* means in standard usage *dreadful, fearful, severe:* The flood wrought terrible havoc.

Than, then. 1. *Than* is a conjunction. Observe that when it introduces an elliptical clause, it is followed by the nominative case: He is taller than I (elliptical for: He is taller than I am tall). 2. See *different from.* 3. *Than* should never be confused with *then,* an adverb expressing time: Then appeared those stronger than he.

Their, there, they're. 1. *Their* is the possessive case of *they:* They brought their books. 2. *There* is an expletive (there is, there are) or an adverb: There is evidence that the book lay there on the table. 3. *They're* is a con-

traction of *they are:* They're all coming to the dance tonight.

To, too, two. 1. *To* is a preposition in most usages: They went to class. 2. *Too* is an adverb meaning *extremely, excessively,* or *in addition:* We were too sick to go; the teacher was sick too. 3. *Two* is the cardinal number: Two students went to the lecture.

Used to could. Illiterate for *once could, used to be able.*

Want. Followed by an infinitive, not a clause: I want you to come (not: I want that you should come).

Way. 1. Singular in expressions of distance: It was a long way (not: a long ways). 2. Colloquial in reference to health: He is in poor health (not: in a bad way).

Where. Inadequate as a substitute for *that:* I read in the paper that he is coming (not: where he is coming).

While. Overused in the sense of *whereas,* and also felt by many people to be colloquial in that sense: Route 26 is narrow and winding, whereas Route 29 is wide and straight (rather than: while Route 29 is wide and straight). Notice also a possible ambiguity. Strictly speaking, *while* means *during the time that;* to write "Tom studied while Bill loafed" can really mean only that Tom was studying during the time that Bill was loafing. Contrast can better be stated by means of *but* or *whereas:* Tom studied but Bill loafed.

Without. Most commonly a preposition, not to be used as a substitute for the conjunction *unless:* He cannot go unless his mother approves (not: without his mother approves).

Worst way. Colloquial for *very much:* I want the book very much (not: I want the book in the worst way).

(See *Workbook,* Exercises 11, 12, and 13.)

Parts of the Composition

༈༈༈༈༈

III. THE PARAGRAPH

A. Definition

WITHOUT THE AID of any paragraph indentations a reader could follow the growth of thought in a well-written article or book, but obviously paragraphing greatly eases the task of understanding by marking transitions in thought, parts of the thesis idea, or steps in the development of the idea. Though paragraphs are of many different kinds, some long, some short, a paragraph may perhaps be defined most satisfactorily as a unit of the whole composition in which one single, main idea is developed by means of supporting details. Each paragraph has its own unit of thought and its own structure, but each is closely related to the paragraphs which precede and follow it, and is a vital part of the whole composition.

LENGTH

Paragraphs vary in length. Newspaper paragraphs usually have but a few sentences, whereas those in many books and magazines contain several hundred words. In general, however, you should build paragraphs of about one-hundred words. In the ordinary article very short paragraphs are so choppy that the reader cannot find the main ideas among these many small units; extremely long paragraphs of many hundreds of words incorporate so many ideas that he has difficulty here too in finding the key ideas. Considering adaptation to the audience, you will discover also that excellent readers deal easily with long paragraphs which confuse the inexperienced or immature reader.

THE TOPIC SENTENCE

84. **Almost all good paragraphs are built around a central idea.**

This is sometimes not directly stated but more often appears in what is known as the topic sentence. The paragraph is fundamentally the expansion of this sentence. Suppose, for instance, in writing about a baseball game, you wish to say, "We lost the game because of poor umpiring." The reader, however, will not be satisfied by that simple statement; he wants it clarified and proved—when did the faulty umpiring occur? under what circumstances? how did it occasion the loss of the game? You think of a decision at first base that prevented a run from scoring and of an apparent home run which was called a foul ball. Your paragraph now begins to take shape as the expansion of your original statement, the topic sentence:

> We lost the game because of poor umpiring. In the third inning, with Mike Jones on third and two out, Haines hit an infield ball which he clearly beat for a hit. He was, however, called out, and the tying run which Jones brought over the plate did not count. Again in the ninth inning Thomas hit a prodigious line drive over the left-field fence which was called foul, even though it was several feet in fair territory. Such poor umpiring is a disgrace to the league and an unfair handicap to the players.

In this manner a paragraph expands one central idea.

There is no rigid rule concerning the place of the topic sentence in the paragraph. Ordinarily it is found early—in the first or second sentence. Obviously if it is a question which the paragraph will answer or if it announces what the paragraph concerns, it will be near the beginning; but if it is a summarizing statement, it will of course conclude the paragraph. Sometimes, for emphasis, it occurs in both places.

Here is a sample of the sort of paragraph which begins with a question:

Probably the scholar should not be left standing here in a state of partial paralysis, yet what elixir will supple his joints and rejuvenate his mind? How can the lamb hope to lie down with the lions? Throughout the history of culture, learning and literature have generally gone hand in hand, but the spread of democratic literacy changed all that. Nowadays, especially perhaps in the United States, the scholar and the popular author bite their thumbs at each other. The latter's want of learning, as Witwoud said of his friend Petulant, is his happiness; it gives him the more opportunities to show his natural parts. The scholar, it seems, has no natural parts. This cleavage is bad for both, and for the public.

—Douglas Bush, "Scholars, Poor and Simple." [1]

A more usual kind of paragraph begins with a simple statement announcing what the paragraph concerns; such a statement assists the reader in following the orderly progress of the thought of the article:

The world expects scholars to get their reward in the discovery of truth, and it may be hoped the world is right, since they get nothing else. They toil for years, they scorn delights and live laborious days, and when they have written a book they are lucky if they can get it published. If they do they usually have to pay for it, though the professorial salary does not allow for subsidies to publishers. Sometimes a scholar has the superlative good fortune to get a book published for nothing. Sometimes the work of many years cannot get published at all. It is by no means a sufficient explanation to say that scholars can't write; many a scholar writes well, but if he objects to the cheaper arts of salesmanship the world will have none of him.—Douglas Bush, *op. cit.*[1]

[1] From the *Atlantic Monthly* (October, 1940). Reprinted by permission of the author and of the *Atlantic Monthly*.

Sometimes, however, an author who is sure that his readers follow him, places his topic sentence at the end of the paragraph for emphasis or summary:

A good story is told of an Irish gentleman—still known in London society—who inherited the family estates and the family banshee. The estates he lost—no uncommon circumstance in the history of Irish gentlemen,—but the banshee, who expected no favors, stuck to him in his adversity, and crossed the channel with him, making herself known only on occasions of deathbeds and sharp family misfortunes. This gentleman had an ear, and, seated one night at the opera, the *keen*—heard once or twice on memorable occasions—thrilled through the din of the orchestra and the passion of the singers. He hurried home of course, found the immediate family well, but on the morrow a telegram arrived with the announcement of a brother's death. Surely of all superstitions that is the most imposing which makes the other world interested in the events which befall our mortal lot.—Alexander Smith, *Dreamthorp.*

When special emphasis is required, an author sometimes places the topic sentence at both the beginning and the end of the paragraph. The following paragraph gains increased emphasis by the use of "genteel" in the opening lines and of "vulgar" in the last line:

But whatever we might do or leave undone, we were not genteel, and it was uncomfortable to be continually reminded that, though we should boast that we were the Great West till we were black in the face, it did not bring us an inch nearer to the world's West-End. That sacred enclosure of respectability was tabooed to us. The Holy Alliance did not inscribe us on its visiting list. The Old World of wigs and orders and liveries would shop with us, but we must ring at the area-bell, and not venture to awaken the more august clamors of the knocker. Our manners, it must be granted, had none of those graces that stamp the caste of Vere de Vere, in whatever museum of British antiquities they may be hidden. In short, we were vulgar.—James Russell Lowell, "On a Certain Condescension in Foreigners."

84a. As a general rule, place the topic sentence where it will be most readily noted.

Thus the reader can understand the paragraph quickly and easily.

TRANSITIONAL AND NARRATIVE PARAGRAPHS

To the preceding remarks, one must add two exceptions: the *transitional paragraph* and the *narrative paragraph.* The transitional paragraph is a bridge between large sections of a composition to note when a writer leaves one point and begins consideration of the next. The following paragraph forms a transition in Edmund Burke's *Speech on Conciliation with America:*

These, Sir, are my reasons for not entertaining that high opinion of untried force by which many gentlemen, for whose sentiments in other particulars I have great respect, seem to be so greatly captivated. But there is still behind a third consideration concerning this object, which serves to determine my opinion on the sort of policy which ought to be pursued in the management of America, even more than its population and its commerce —I mean its *temper and character.*

The narrative paragraph also has a specific purpose: to carry forward a story. It cannot be governed by our already formulated principle of a topic sentence supported by explanation or proof. As the narrative moves forward, the paragraphs must aid that movement. The use of long paragraphs, that is, the grouping of material into large units, aids the flow of a story; the use of short paragraphs puts emphasis upon bits, such as exciting action or vivid description or sharp dialogue. The writer therefore judges the length of a paragraph by the purpose which he has in mind. Observe how the following long paragraph forwards the action:

In about six weeks from the time when the *Pilgrim* sailed, we had all the hides which she left us cured and stowed away; and having cleared up the ground and emptied the vats, and set everything in order, had nothing more to do, until she should come down again, but to supply ourselves with wood. Instead of going twice a week for this purpose, we determined to give one whole week to getting wood, and then we should have enough to last us half through the summer. Accordingly we started off every morning, after an early breakfast, with our hatchets in hand, and cut wood until the sun was over the point— which was our mark for noon, as there was not a watch on the beach—and then came back to dinner, and after dinner started off again with our hand-cart and ropes, and carted and "backed" it down until sunset. This we kept up for a week, until we had collected several cords—enough to last us for six or eight weeks—when we "knocked off" altogether, much to my joy; for, though I liked straying in the woods and cutting very well, yet the backing the wood for so great a distance, over an uneven country, was, without exception, the hardest work I had ever done. I usually had to kneel down, and contrive to heave the load, which was well strapped together, upon my back, and then rise up and start off with it, up the hills and down the vales, sometimes through thickets—the rough points sticking into the skin and tearing the clothes, so that at the end of the week I had hardly a whole shirt to my back.—RICHARD HENRY DANA, JR., *Two Years before the Mast.*

In the following selection the short paragraphs emphasize details:

Presently the darkness thickened.

He was entering a great wood. Huge branches shot across the narrow road, and the benighted stranger groped his way in what seemed an interminable and inky cave with a rugged floor, on which he stumbled and stumbled as he went.

On, and on, and on, with shivering limbs, and empty stomach, and fainting heart, till the wolves rose from their lairs and bayed all round the wood.

His hair bristled; but he grasped his cudgel, and prepared to sell his life dear.

There was no wind; and his excited ear heard light feet patter at times over the newly fallen leaves, and low branches rustled with creatures gliding swiftly past them.—CHARLES READE, *The Cloister and the Hearth.*

In writing dialogue, make a separate paragraph of each speech and the directive element or explanatory matter that goes with it, as in the following example:

" 'Tis well!" said Eli; "but I am older than thou." Then he turned gravely to Margaret: "Wilt answer me a question, my pretty mistress?"

"If I may, sir," faltered Margaret.

"What are these marriage lines Gerard speaks of in the letter?"

"Our marriage lines, sir. His and mine. Know you not we are betrothed?"

"Before witnesses?"

"Ay, sure. My poor father and Martin Wittenhaagen."

"This is the first I ever heard of it. How came they in his hands? They should be in yours."

"Alas, sir, the more is my grief; but I ne'er doubted him: and he said it was a comfort to have them in his bosom."

"Y'are a very foolish lass."—CHARLES READE, *The Cloister and the Hearth*.

An exception to the foregoing is found when the quotation is relatively unimportant or through its brevity is contained within another sentence: "I rushed up the stairs and called out, 'Hello! Who's there?' as I flung open the door and burst into the room."

For instructions on the punctuation of the narrative paragraph, see p. 132.

B. Unity, Coherence, and Emphasis

UNITY

Whenever a whole composition or paragraph follows but one progression of thought, which it expands fully and completely to the reader's satisfaction, it is said to have unity. But whenever it rambles from the subject, it violates this principle of good writing.

85. **To observe the unity of a paragraph, keep strictly to the topic idea.**

Repress all other ideas, no matter how attractive in themselves. By such restraint you assure the unity of the whole composition, for if each paragraph develops but one idea, and if each topic sentence pertains directly to the main idea of the whole composition, unity of the whole must result.

The following paragraph lacks unity. It begins perfectly properly, but the mention of the name of Smollett sends the writer rambling in the last two sentences into ideas that do not pertain to the topic sentence:

> The novel *Mr. Midshipman Easy,* written by Captain Marryat, is one of the best sea stories of the nineteenth century. It narrates the adventures of Jack Easy, son of a crack-brained philosopher, an easy-going lad who lands in a thousand scrapes while in the service of the British navy. The vigorous action and infectious humor are reminiscent of the novels of Smollett, written in the previous century. Smollett was one of a group of four—Fielding, Richardson, and Sterne were the others—who were responsible for giving the novel a strong start in English literature. Fielding was especially successful, as the plot of his *Tom Jones* is sometimes called one of the finest plots ever created.

COHERENCE

86. **You must also make paragraphs coherent—that is, arrange ideas in a clear, logical order.**

Avoid jumps in thought and gaps between sentences. If inexperienced, you might begin a paper thus: "The rain was falling fast outside. Tom was reading the latest novel. He knew that if he did not get downtown soon, he would miss his appointment." But the ideas are so widely separated here that a reader must fill in the gaps for himself in order to fashion a continuous narrative. Such weak writing may be avoided in several ways.

86a. **Present the ideas in a logical order.**

Perhaps the best device by which to secure such unity and coherence is the outline. Imagine for a moment that you are writing a report on how to make a workable budget plan for the family. As an automobile is usually a large item of expense in the average family, you decide that at least one paragraph of the report should be devoted to the place of the automobile in the budget plan. Hence for one paragraph your topic sentence might be: "It is advisable to carry an account book in the dash compartment of your auto-

mobile." You may then expand this suggestion by indicating the best method for keeping such an account. The little outline for
your paragraph might develop into the following form:

1. *It is advisable to carry an account book in
   the dash compartment of your automobile.*
   a. To record gas expenditure
      (1) The date of purchase
      (2) The amount of gas purchased
      (3) The cost
      (4) The mileage on the car at the time
          of the purchase
   b. To record oil and other lubrication ex-
      penditures
      (1) The date of purchase
      (2) The amount purchased
      (3) The cost
      (4) The mileage on the car
   c. To record miscellaneous expenditures
      (1) Insurance costs
      (2) Tires
      (3) Automobile club fees
      (4) Repairs

Your paragraph could then be put together
very quickly somewhat as follows:

It is well to assist your keeping of an accurate
budget by carrying an account book in the
dash compartment of your automobile. There
each item of cost for your automobile can be
listed at the time that the expenditure is
made. In one column of the book you can
place the amount spent for gas, noting for
your convenience such details as the date of
the purchase, the amount of gas purchased,
the cost of the purchase, and the mileage recorded on the speedometer at the time of the
purchase. Likewise in another column may
well be kept the expenditures for oil and
other lubricants, with again a listing of the
date of purchase, the amount, the cost, and
the mileage on the car. In a third column can
be put the miscellaneous expenditures such
as those for insurance, tires, automobile club
fees, and repairs. In this way you will be able
to compute easily at the end of each month
the operating cost of your automobile and be
able to make allowances for that cost in your
budget.

Such an outline keeps one to his topic sentence and prevents him from discussing any
subject but the pertinent one. Of course, an
outline as elaborate as this is rarely com-

posed for one paragraph by an experienced
writer, as he has trained himself to set up an
equally orderly scheme in his own mind; but
an inexperienced writer may well use such a
method.

86b. **Use transitional words and phrases
to link closely associated ideas.**

The following list classifies a few of these
to show their use in the sentence:

To carry forward the same progression of
thought from one sentence to the next:
*also, besides, especially, finally, for exam-
ple, furthermore, in addition, indeed, in
fact, in other words, likewise, moreover,
namely, next, similarly, that is, then.*
To show how one statement is the result of
the preceding statement:
*accordingly, as a result, consequently, for
this reason, hence, inevitably, so, therefore,
thus.*
To present a contrast between ideas:
*however, nevertheless, on the contrary, on
the other hand, still, yet.*

To illustrate the value of transitional
words, the following paragraph is shown first
without such words, then with them. Note
in the first how disconnected the ideas seem,
but in the second how the addition of a few
transitional expressions promotes smoothness
and meaning:

In the summer all the snow above the snow
line does not melt. The exact position of this
line is not fixed. The line is lower in cold
latitudes and higher in warm latitudes. Temperature appears to be important in determining its position. Other conditions enter, for
a low snow line may sometimes be found in
a warm climate.

In the summer all the snow above the snow
line does not melt. The exact position of this
line, however, is not fixed. Ordinarily the line
is lower in cold latitudes and higher in warm
latitudes. Therefore, temperature appears to
be important in determining its position. Yet
other conditions occasionally enter, for a low
snow line may sometimes be found in a warm
climate.

Transitional expressions not only show the
connection between ideas inside the para-

graph, but also serve as links between paragraphs. The use of such expressions, for instance, as *in addition to this fact, as a consequence, as stated above, most important of all, on the whole, secondly, these circumstances being true,* obviates sudden jumps, and aids the reader in seeing the structure of the whole paper. He needs these guideposts if he is to grasp the argument of the paper fully and quickly.

86c. Avoid shifts of subject, voice, and tense in consecutive clauses (see pages 113-115).

86d. Repeat important constructions in consecutive sentences.

This repetition may be effected by selecting the outstanding word or idea from one sentence to begin the following sentence (as in this very sentence the word "repetition" harks back to its verb form "repeat" in the preceding sentence) or by using pronouns to refer frequently to the important word in the paragraph, as "The chairman is all important. He must not be fettered, or he will lose his forcefulness. He must be given freedom to exercise his initiative and assistance in the completion of his ambitious enterprises."

86e. Use parallelism.

Parallelism is repetition in consecutive words, phrases, clauses, or sentences of identical or similar word order and form to express ideas of nearly equal importance. Parallelism of single words of like part of speech is found in a sentence like this: "Our candidate is honest, brave, and resolute." Parallel phrases are exemplified here: "From the villages of New England, from the plantations of the South, and from the dense forests of the frontier came delegates to the convention." The following are parallel clauses: "The prisoner declared that he had no criminal record, that he was ignorant of the charges brought against him, and that

on the night in question he was at home asleep." Parallel sentences, most important of the group for binding together a paragraph, are seen here: "Whenever Antony was gloomy, Cleopatra was gay. Whenever he was merry, she was sad." Parallelism thus not only indicates to the reader which ideas balance but also promotes an orderly arrangement of topics. Study carefully the parallelism in the following famous paragraph from Lincoln's Gettysburg Address. The parallelism exists both within and between sentences:

> But, in a larger sense, we cannot dedicate— we cannot consecrate—we cannot hallow— this ground. The brave men, living and dead, who struggled here, have consecrated it far above our poor power to add or detract. The world will little note nor long remember what we say here, but it can never forget what they did here. It is for us, the living, rather, to be dedicated here to the unfinished work which they who fought here have thus far so nobly advanced. It is rather for us to be here dedicated to the great task remaining before us— that from these honored dead we take increased devotion to that cause for which they gave the last full measure of devotion; that we here highly resolve that these dead shall not have died in vain; that this nation, under God, shall have a new birth of freedom; and that government of the people, by the people, for the people, shall not perish from the earth.

EMPHASIS

87. Emphasis is secured in the paragraph by essentially the same means as in the sentence: the first and the last are the important positions.

For that reason the topic sentence normally should be located in one of these two positions, according to the principles already formulated. Special emphasis is gained by putting the topic sentence in both positions. Inside the paragraph other devices such as the frequent use of transitional expressions and of parallelism will promote emphasis by breaking the monotony of excessively regular sentence structure.

SUGGESTIONS FOR STUDY

1. Using parallelism of structure, develop one of the following topic sentences into a paragraph of approximately 125 words.

Clothing styles for young people are likely to change from year to year.

Television reception is not good in some areas.

What is the one most important attribute of a good teacher?

As football is played today, a fourteen-point lead does not assure victory.

There are many types of news commentators on the radio.

Basketball rules have undergone many changes through the years.

The autumn foliage was especially vivid this year.

Students can concentrate better in some classrooms than in others.

A fighter plane must have several special characteristics.

Cigarette advertisements are sometimes misleading.

2. Using as many transitional words and phrases as you can, develop one of the following topic sentences into a paragraph of approximately 125 words; underline each transitional expression.

Some courses demand more study than others.

A longer (or shorter) spring vacation would be advantageous.

The off-campus student misses many features of campus life.

The comedian who is a success on radio may fail in television.

Summer vacation is best spent at a cottage on a lake.

Long trips for athletic contests may seriously affect a student's academic work.

Who is the best outfielder in baseball today?

What is the most popular fashion magazine with college students?

College students should beware of hasty marriages.

Traveling by bus can be fun.

3. The following paragraphs are lacking in unity. Strike out the passages which are extraneous.

(a) Jacques was extremely limited in his interests. So far as anyone knew, he cared for only one thing—the steam locomotive. Perhaps he had never been introduced to any other subject, but no one knew about that, for he spoke but seldom and had no intimates. Only to his engines did he speak in a kindly tone of voice. And he was never known to show affection for any engine but the steam engine. Diesels he snorted at in disgust, even though the diesel locomotive is one of the smoothest and most economical performers in the business. Just within the last five years the railroads, particularly those of the West, have installed diesel locomotives, not only for passenger traffic but for freight hauls as well. But Jacques hated them. All he knew and all he wanted to know was the old iron horse.

(b) Several years ago an unusual competition arose among the leading colleges of America. These institutions, mostly private, were not particularly concerned with getting enough students to meet their quotas but with getting students of a high quality to set good standards on their campuses. Each institution, therefore, set up a series of scholarships to be awarded to select students, and each institution sent out representatives in the spring to visit the leading preparatory and high schools all over America. Inducements were not being offered to athletes, as most of these universities were sincere in their attempt to curb the evils known to accompany such practices. Some colleges have been known to put eleven hired men on the football field in the fall, men who could not meet the scholastic requirements but who were given special considerations because of their athletic ability. The feeling which such action aroused on the campus was not altogether desirable. These institutions in question, however, gave no inducements to high-school athletes, but sought men who were excellent students and who had well-rounded personalities. So from Washington to Florida, from Maine to California, their representatives toured the country each spring.

The Author's Account of Himself

WASHINGTON IRVING

(1) I WAS ALWAYS fond of visiting new scenes, and observing strange characters and manners. (2) Even when a mere child I began my travels, and made many tours of discovery into foreign parts and unknown regions of my native city, to the frequent alarm of my parents, and the emolument of the town-crier. (3) As I grew into boyhood, I extended the range of my observations. (4) My holiday afternoons were spent in rambles about the surrounding country. (5) I made myself familiar with all its places famous in history or fable. (6) I knew every spot where a murder or robbery had been committed, or a ghost seen. (7) I visited the neighboring villages, and added greatly to my stock of knowledge by noting their habits and customs, and conversing with their sages and great men. (8) I even journeyed one long summer's day to the summit of the most distant hill, whence I stretched my eye over many a mile of *terra incognita,* and was astonished to find how vast a globe I inhabited.

(9) This rambling propensity strengthened with my years. (10) Books of voyages and travels became my passion, and, in devouring their contents, I neglected the regular exercises of the school. (11) How wistfully would I wander about the pierheads in fine weather, and watch the parting ships, bound to distant climes; with what longing eyes would I gaze after their lessening sails, and waft myself in imagination to the ends of the earth!

(12) Further reading and thinking, though they brought this vague inclination into more reasonable bounds, only served to make it more decided. (13) I visited various parts of my own country; and had I been merely a lover of fine scenery, I should have felt little desire to seek elsewhere its gratification, for on no country have the charms of nature been more prodigally lavished. (14) Her mighty lakes, like oceans of liquid silver; her mountains, with their bright aërial tints; her valleys, teeming with wild fertility; her tremendous cataracts, thundering in their solitudes; her boundless plains, waving with spontaneous verdure; her broad deep rivers, rolling in solemn silence to the ocean; her trackless forests, where vegetation puts forth all its magnificence; her skies, kindling with the magic of summer clouds and glorious sunshine—no, never need an American look beyond his own country for the sublime and beautiful of natural scenery.

(15) But Europe held forth the charms of storied and poetical association. (16) There were to be seen the masterpieces of art, the refinements of highly cultivated society, the quaint peculiarities of ancient and local custom. (17) My native country was full of youthful promise: Europe was rich in the accumulated treasures of age. (18) Her very ruins told the history of times gone by, and every moldering stone was a chronicle. (19) I longed to wander over the scenes of renowned achievement—to tread, as it were, in the footsteps of antiquity—to loiter about the ruined castle—to meditate on the falling tower—to escape, in short, from the commonplace realities of the present, and lose myself among the shadowy grandeurs of the past.

(20) I had, beside all this, an earnest desire to see the great men of the earth. (21) We have, it is true, our great men in America: not a city but has an ample share of them. (22) I have mingled among them in my time, and been almost withered by the shade into which they cast me; for there is

nothing so baleful to a small man as the shade of a great one, particularly the great man of a city. (23) But I was anxious to see the great men of Europe; for I had read in the works of various philosophers, that all animals degenerated in America, and man among the number. (24) A great man of Europe, thought I, must therefore be as superior to a great man of America as a peak of the Alps to a highland of the Hudson; and in this idea I was confirmed by observing the comparative importance and swelling magnitude of many English travelers among us, who, I was assured, were very little people in their own country. (25) I will visit this land of wonders, thought I, and see the gigantic race from which I am degenerated.

(26) It has been either my good or evil lot to have my roving passion gratified. (27) I have wandered through different countries, and witnessed many of the shifting scenes of life. (28) I cannot say that I have studied them with the eye of a philosopher, but rather with the sauntering gaze with which humble lovers of the picturesque stroll from the window of one print shop to another, caught sometimes by the delineations of beauty, sometimes by the distortions of caricature, and sometimes by the loveliness of landscape. (29) As it is the fashion for modern tourists to travel pencil in hand, and bring home their portfolios filled with sketches, I am disposed to get up a few for the entertainment of my friends. (30) When, however, I look over the hints and memorandums I have taken down for the purpose, my heart almost fails me at finding how my idle humor has led me aside from the great objects studied by every regular traveler who would make a book. (31) I fear I shall give equal disappointment with an unlucky landscape painter, who had traveled on the continent, but, following the bent of his vagrant inclination, had sketched in nooks, and corners, and by-places. (32) His sketchbook was accordingly crowded with cottages, and landscapes, and obscure ruins; but

he had neglected to paint St. Peter's, or the Coliseum; the cascade of Terni, or the bay of Naples; and had not a single glacier or volcano in his whole collection.

SUGGESTIONS FOR STUDY

1. What is the thesis sentence of this article? The purpose? Where is the thesis stated?
2. What is the topic sentence of paragraph one? What transition is to be found in sentence two? In sentence three? What device binds together sentences five, six, seven, and eight?
3. What is the topic sentence of paragraph two? What words link paragraph two to paragraph one? What device aids clarity and binds together the independent clauses of sentence eleven?
4. What is the topic sentence of paragraph three? Does the opening sentence contain a link to carry the thought from paragraph two? What is the effect of the list of items in paragraph three?
5. Does paragraph four attach itself clearly to paragraph three in any way as a development of the main idea of paragraph three? Does it have a topic idea of its own? What device do you find in sentence nineteen to promote concreteness, clarity, and emphasis?
6. What transitional words carry the thought from paragraph four to paragraph five? What is the topic sentence of paragraph five? What pronoun binds sentence twenty-three to sentence twenty-two? What word sets off the contrast beginning in sentence twenty-three? What is the transitional word in sentence twenty-four? What transitional expression follows the semicolon in sentence twenty-four? In sentence twenty-five, what is the linking word?
7. What links paragraph six with the preceding paragraphs? What is the purpose of paragraph six? Point out the parallelism in this paragraph. What end does it serve? What transitions are to be found in sentences thirty and thirty-two? What is the topic idea of this paragraph?
8. Define the following words from the article: emolument, propensity, wistfully, gratification, verdure, moldering, chronicle, baleful, picturesque, vagrant, cascade.

C. Paragraph Development

In building a composition, you do well to start thinking about the structure and substance of the body of your paper by listing the topic sentences which you desire to use and then arranging them in a logical order.

These will suffice for the moment in place of a more elaborate outline to insure orderliness in presenting your ideas.

For illustration, suppose the composition is intended as an article for a wide-circulation magazine on the thesis, "Contrary to popular opinion, professors are of many types and temperaments." Confined by limitations of space to discussing but four types in detail, you might break this thesis into such topic sentences as these:

1. Some professors are hard-headed realists.
2. Other professors are most strikingly jovial, hearty, and expansive.
3. Others impress by their sharp, cold efficiency.
4. Still others are lavish in their way of life.

Having stated these points in brief, an immature writer often thinks no more can be said about them, but listing the topic sentences is really only the beginning.

88. Good writing demands that each generalized topic sentence be developed clearly and fully.

No reader can know specifically what is meant by any one of the general terms used above—*realists, expansive, efficiency, lavish,* and the others. The only way in which precise meaning can be carried into the reader's mind is by a list of details—that is, concrete, specific nouns, adjectives, verbs—to raise an image of the attributes of these men.

DEVELOPMENT BY DETAIL

A first way to effect this end is to itemize these details as specifically as possible:

Contrary to the popular notion of the professor as a thin, emaciated individual, undernourished, impoverished, disreputable in the car he drives and the home he owns, some professors are lavish in their way of life. Collegewood Drive, one of the most exclusive residential sections of town, is studded with the homes of professors. The Lincoln, Packard, and Cadillac dealers testify that a fair proportion of their most faithful clientele consists of professors. The label of Brooks Brothers and other fashionable clothiers appears on their clothing, and the delicacies of the finest groceries—the imported cheeses, the caviare and *pâté de foie gras*—go to the professor's table as to the business man's.

Development of the topic sentence by detail can take several forms. The paragraph used above employs *analysis;* that is, it breaks the topic sentence into its parts in answer to the reader's question, "What do you mean by *lavish?*"

The following paragraph uses another arrangement of the details, a *cause and effect* relationship, to answer another possible question of the reader, "What enables the professor to live lavishly?"

Some professors are indeed lavish in their way of life. Because few enjoy salaries above $10,000, they must have additional means to support a high standard of living. Some are themselves scions of wealthy families or have married wives who enjoy large incomes from hereditary wealth. Another small group has been able to double or treble its income by wise investment in the stock market. An even smaller group has performed the miracle of academic life by writing one or more books which have met popular taste and reached the golden land of the best-seller lists.

Another method of arranging the details might afford *proof* to meet the reader's remark, "I don't believe it." But there are many other arrangements. The writer must choose that which best meets the imagined questions of the reader and answer those questions as fully as space permits.

Study the following paragraph as one further example of development by detail:

The real film *raconteur* will turn his camera on the detailed rather than the general. His film will not show "a woods," but rather a tall, stately tree with sunlight shafting through the leaves; a cluster of violets at the base of a rotted stump; a ripple on the brook and the water bubbling over into a quiet pool disturbed only by leaves falling quietly on the surface of the water; a butterfly nervously hovering above a flower; the tiny handprints made by a raccoon the night before; a squirrel, undecided whether to run or stay, peering around the trunk of a tree. Our cameraman will not see "a field." Instead, he will photograph the way the tall grass ripples in the wind; the grouse scuttling out of the hedge; the tattered scarecrow with sparrows teetering impertinently on the broomstick arms.— ROBERT W. WAGNER, "Man with Camera." [1]

DEVELOPMENT BY ILLUSTRATION

Though every good paragraph is developed by details, certain special uses of detail add clarity and variety to an article. The use of illustration means telling a little story or anecdote about the topic idea or following a chronological, narrative series of events which reveals the topic idea in action, as shown here:

> Some professors are indeed lavish in their way of life. Professor Jones is typical of this group. He rises in the morning in his sumptuous, spacious, rambling ranch-type home on exclusive Collegewood Drive. Finishing his breakfast, he leaves for the campus in a Cadillac sedan and as usual on his arrival flutters pulses with the casual correctness of his English tweeds. In class, so it is said, the co-eds are more smitten with the variety and excellence of his ties than with the ease and profundity of his lectures. Returning home in the evening, he becomes the genial and urbane host, discourses with his guests on the vintage of his amontillado, and presents them to a table laden like that in Keats's "The Eve of St. Agnes," "With jellies soother than the creamy curd, and lucent syrops, tinct with cinnamon."

A second example of development by illustration employs an incident to clarify the topic sentence, which is the first sentence of the paragraph:

> Slade was a matchless marksman with a navy revolver. The legends say that one morning at Rocky Ridge, when he was feeling comfortable, he saw a man approaching who had offended him some days before—observe the fine memory he had for matters like that— and, "Gentlemen," said Slade, drawing, "it is a good twenty-yard shot—I'll clip the third button on his coat!" Which he did. The bystanders all admired it. And they all attended the funeral, too.—MARK TWAIN, Roughing It.

[1] From the News Letter, XI (1946), No. 6 (an organ of the Ohio State University). Reprinted by permission of the author.

DEVELOPMENT BY COMPARISON

Though less frequently used perhaps than illustration, development by comparison is a major device whereby the topic idea can be clarified by its likeness to an idea supposedly better known to the reader or its parts analyzed by a demonstration of the likeness among them:

> Think, for the moment, of the typical, wealthy American, the business tycoon. He lives in an exclusive residential area in a mansion of Colonial or perhaps Georgian or Gothic design; from the house extend in all directions spacious, well-clipped lawns, attractive flower gardens; high, neat hedges or a stone wall bounds the property to give him peace and privacy. The garage houses a station wagon, a Cadillac, a Lincoln, and a Ford convertible. He steps out to his lawns with an air of assurance, bred from the confidence of success and from his realization that not only his residence but his clothing, his speech, his connections, and his general air are all what they should be. Though few college professors can aspire to such wealthy elegance as this, yet many in a smaller way, blessed by the resources from private means, live the same life of luxury and ease, quite contrary to the popular notions of the indigence of the professor.

For a second example of comparison, study the following paragraph:

> Thus it becomes obvious that one must be wary in attributing scientific discovery wholly to any one person. Almost every discovery has a long and precarious history. Someone finds a bit here, another a bit there. A third step succeeds later and thus onward till a genius pieces the bits together and makes the decisive contribution. Science, like the Mississippi, begins in a tiny rivulet in the distant forest. Gradually other streams swell its volume. And the roaring river that bursts the dikes is formed from countless sources.— ABRAHAM FLEXNER, "The Usefulness of Useless Knowledge." [2]

DEVELOPMENT BY CONTRAST

A method closely associated with comparison is that of contrast, which clarifies a topic

[2] From Harper's Magazine (October, 1939). Reprinted by permission of the author.

idea by setting it against a quite different idea with which the reader may be familiar or by setting in opposition for striking effect the differing parts of the topic idea:

> Some professors are indeed lavish in their way of life. They are not like the outcast dog of society, begging his bone at a stranger's door, sleeping in what forlorn nook presents itself at eventide, cringing in fear of rebuke, and arousing pity by the desolate sight of his ribs showing plainly through his mangy coat. No, these professors are not the outcasts of society. They live in richly carpeted homes, dress in gay apparel, and eat at the banquet tables of the mighty.

The following paragraph by John Ruskin uses contrast among the parts of the total idea:

> Your power over the rain and river-waters of the earth is infinite. You can bring rain where you will, by planting wisely and tending carefully;—drought where you will, by ravage of woods and neglect of the soil. You might have the rivers of England as pure as the crystal of the rock; beautiful in falls, in lakes, in living pools; so full of fish that you might take them out with your hands instead of nets. Or you may do always as you have done now, turn every river of England into a common sewer, so that you cannot so much as baptise an English baby but with filth, unless you hold its face out in the rain; and even *that* falls dirty.—*Fors Clavigera.*

DEVELOPMENT BY ELIMINATION

By this means erroneous or irrelevant ideas are eliminated from the reader's mind in order that precise ideas may remain. This device is especially helpful in definitions or careful distinctions of concept:

> Some professors are lavish in their way of life. By "lavish" I do not mean that they enjoy such boundless wealth as to be able to endow great foundations or libraries. They cannot cover the walls of their homes with paintings of the Old Masters or cruise in their yachts to winter mansions on the ocean front at Palm Beach. But they do live in the better residential sections of their towns, drive their Cadillacs and Lincolns, and send their children to the more exclusive finishing schools.

In the ensuing paragraph Lincoln uses this device to delineate more clearly what he understands by the famous assertion that all men are created equal:

> I think the authors of that noble instrument intended to include *all* men, but they did not intend to declare all men equal *in all respects.* They did not mean to say all were equal in color, size, intellect, moral developments, or social capacity. They defined with tolerable distinctness in what respects they did consider all men created equal—equal with "certain inalienable rights, among which are life, liberty, and the pursuit of happiness." This they said, and this they meant. They did not mean to assert the obvious untruth that all were then actually enjoying that equality, nor yet that they were about to confer it immediately upon them. In fact, they had no power to confer such a boon. They meant simply to declare the right, so that enforcement of it might follow as fast as circumstances should permit.—ABRAHAM LINCOLN, Speech at Springfield, Illinois, June 26, 1857.

DEVELOPMENT BY QUESTIONS

In this type of development the thought of the paragraph is carried forward by a series of aptly proposed questions. If used sparingly, this device will promote a pleasing variation in sentence structure and paragraph construction.

> Do we call this the land of the free? What is it to be free from King George and continue the slaves of King Prejudice? What is it to be born free and not to live free? What is the value of any political freedom, but as a means to moral freedom? Is it a freedom to be slaves, or a freedom to be free, of which we boast? We are a nation of politicians, concerned about the outmost defenses only of freedom. It is our children's children who may perchance be really free. We tax ourselves unjustly. There is a part of us which is not represented. It is taxation without representation. We quarter troops, we quarter fools and cattle of all sorts upon ourselves. We quarter our gross bodies on our poor souls, till the former eat up all the latter's substance.—HENRY THOREAU, "Life without Principle."

DEVELOPMENT BY A COMBINATION OF METHODS

Although attention has been centered thus far on the development of the paragraph by a single method, you should not suppose that only one means can be used in each paragraph. Most paragraphs, in fact, are a combination of several methods. The following paragraph illustrates the combination of methods. It employs detail and cause and effect as its general devices, but also comparison and a slight amount of contrast and elimination to establish the cause and effect.

Still, we do not think that the blame of Burns's failure lies chiefly with the world. The world, it seems to us, treated him with more, rather than with less kindness than it usually shows to such men. It has ever, we fear, shown but small favor to its teachers: hunger and nakedness, perils and reviling, the prison, the cross, the poison-chalice have in most times and countries been the marketprice it has offered for wisdom, the welcome with which it has greeted those who have come to enlighten and purify it. Homer and Socrates, and the Christian Apostles, belong to old days; but the world's martyrology was not completed with these. Roger Bacon and Galileo languish in priestly dungeons; Tasso pines in the cell of a madhouse; Camoens dies begging on the streets of Lisbon. So neglected, so "persecuted they the Prophets," not in Judea only, but in all places where men have been. We reckon that every poet of Burns's order is, or should be, a prophet and teacher to his age; that he has no right to expect great kindness from it, but rather is bound to do it great kindness; that Burns, in particular, experienced fully the usual proportion of the world's goodness; and that the blame of his failure, as we have said, lies not chiefly with the world.—THOMAS CARLYLE, "Burns."

SUGGESTIONS FOR STUDY

1. Identify the topic sentence and the most important means of development in each paragraph:

(a) Man is timid and apologetic; he is no longer upright; he dares not say "I think," "I am," but quotes some saint or sage. He is ashamed before the blade of grass or the blowing rose. These roses under my window make no reference to former roses or to better ones; they are for what they are; they exist with God today. There is no time to them. There is simply the rose; it is perfect in every moment of its existence. Before a leaf bud has burst, its whole life acts; in the full-blown flower there is no more; in the leafless root there is no less. Its nature is satisfied and it satisfies nature in all moments alike. But man postpones or remembers; he does not live in the present, but with reverted eye laments the past, or, heedless of the riches that surround him, stands on tiptoe to foresee the future. He cannot be happy and strong until he too lives with nature in the present, above time.—RALPH WALDO EMERSON, "Self-Reliance."

(b) A tree is an underground creature, with its tail in the air. All intelligence is in its roots. All the senses it has are in its roots. Think what sagacity it shows in its search after food and drink! Somehow or other, the rootlets, which are its tentacles, find out that there is a brook at a moderate distance from the trunk of the tree, and they make for it with all their might. They find every crack in the rocks where there are a few grains of the nourishing substance they care for, and insinuate themselves into its deepest recesses. When spring and summer come, they let their tails grow, and delight in whisking them about in the wind, or letting them be whisked about by it; for these tails are poor passive things, with very little will of their own, and bend in whatever direction the wind chooses to make them. The leaves make a deal of noise whispering. I have sometimes thought I could understand them, as they talk with each other, and that they seemed to think they made the wind as they wagged forward and back. Remember what I say. The next time you see a tree waving in the wind, recollect that it is the tail of a great underground, many-armed, polypuslike creature, which is as proud of its caudal appendage, especially in summertime, as a peacock of his gorgeous expanse of plumage.—OLIVER WENDELL HOLMES, *Over the Teacups.*

(c) Meanwhile Byron had again retired to Newstead, where he invited some choice spirits to hold a few weeks of farewell revel. Matthews, one of these, gives an account of the place, and the time they spent there— entering the mansion between a bear and a wolf, amid a salvo of pistol shots; sitting up to all hours, talking politics, philosophy, poetry; hearing stories of the dead lords, and the ghost of the Black Brother; drinking their wine out of the skull cup which the owner had made out of the cranium of some old monk dug up in the garden; breakfasting at two, then reading, fencing, riding, cricketing, sailing on the lake, and playing with the bear or teasing the wolf. The party broke up without having made themselves responsible for any of the orgies of which Childe Harold raves, and which Dallas in good earnest accepts as veracious, when the poet and his friend Hobhouse started for Falmouth on their way *"outre mer."*—JOHN NICHOL, *Byron.*

(d) Women are more quick-sighted than men; they are less disposed to confide in persons upon a first acquaintance; they are more suspicious as to motives; they are less liable to be deceived by professions and protestations; they watch words with a more scrutinizing ear, and looks with a keener eye; and, making due allowance for their prejudices in particular cases, their opinions and remonstrances, with regard to matters of this sort, ought not to be set at naught without great deliberation. Louvet, one of the Brissotins who fled for their lives in the time of Robespierre, . . . relates that being on his way to Paris from the vicinity of Bordeaux, and having no regular passport, fell lame, but finally crept on to a miserable pot-house in a small town in the Limosin. The landlord questioned him with regard to who and what he was, and whence he came, and was satisfied with his answers. But the landlady, who had looked sharply at him on his arrival, whispered to a little boy, who ran away and quickly returned with the mayor of the town. Louvet soon discovered that there was no danger in the mayor, who could not decipher his forged passport, and who, being well plied with wine, wanted to hear no more of the matter. The landlady, perceiving this, slipped out and brought a couple of aldermen, who asked to see the passport. "Oh yes, but drink first." Then there was a laughing story to tell over again at the request of the half-drunken mayor; then a laughing and more drinking; the passport in Louvet's hand, but never opened, and while another toast was drinking, the passport slid back quietly into the pocket, the woman looking furious all the while. At last, the mayor, the aldermen, and the landlord, all nearly drunk, shook hands with Louvet, wished him a good journey, and swore he was a true *sans culotte;* but he says that the "sharp-sighted woman, who was to be deceived by none of his stories or professions, saw him get off with deep and manifest disappointment and chagrin." I have thought of this many times since, when I have had occasion to witness the quick-sightedness and penetration of women.—WILLIAM COBBETT, *Advice to Young Men.*

(e) Another distressing phobia that often embarrasses me in public is "prodigal's paralysis." When I am dining at a restaurant with a group of friends and the waiter puts the check on the table, I find it physically impossible to reach out and pick it up. The other members of the party may scramble for it with mock belligerence, crying, "Drop that, you son-of-a-gun!" "Let me take it!" "No, this is on me!" But although longing to join in their good-natured rivalry, somehow I can neither move nor speak. For rigor mortis sets in as soon as I hear the waiter tear the check from his book, and continues until after the check has been paid.—WEARE HOLBROOK, "You Know Me, Allergy." [1]

(f) If then a practical end must be assigned to a University course, I say it is that of training good members of society. Its art is the art of social life, and its end is fitness for the world. It neither confines its views to particular professions on the one hand, nor creates heroes or inspires genius on the other. Works indeed of genius fall under no art; heroic minds come under no rule; a University is not a birthplace of poets or of immortal authors, of founders of schools, leaders of colonies, or conquerors of nations. It does not promise a generation of Aristotles or Newtons, of Napoleons or Washingtons, of Raphaels or Shakespeares, though such miracles of nature it has before now contained within its precincts. Nor is it content on the other hand with forming the critic or the experimentalist, the economist or the engineer, though such too it includes within its scope. But a University training is the great ordinary means to a great but ordinary end; it aims at raising the intellectual tone of society, at cultivating the public mind, at purifying the national taste, at supplying true principles to popular enthusiasm and fixed aims to popular aspiration, at giving enlargement and sobriety to the ideas of the age, at facilitating the exercise of political power, and refining the intercourse of private life.—JOHN HENRY NEWMAN, "The Aim of a University Course."

(g) I believe that, year in and year out, no other part of speech has so keen a sense of humor as the participle (*participium ridiculosum*). In an example from Washington Irving's *Life and Voyages of Christopher Columbus* we find a corpse reluctant to cease worldly activities: "Alas! while writing that let-

[1] New York *Herald Tribune.* Reprinted by permission of the New York *Herald Tribune.*

ter his noble benefactress was a corpse." Transplanted participles also may be mirthful: "Until then the infection had been handled by those in charge, and being considered of no consequence I was not informed"; "As applied to Mud Lake, the writer finds difficulty in accepting this explanation"; "Being the belle of the town, he lost no time in making Miss McCarthy's acquaintance." The last example is from a Harvard theme written over a half century ago. The name of the student, unlike that of the crank who, in order to immortalize himself, set fire to the temple of Diana at Ephesus on the night Alexander was born, is unknown, although his words have doubtless already survived him.—EUGENE S. MCCARTNEY, "Some Participles I Have Met." [1]

(h) The title *wise* is, for the most part, falsely applied. How can one be a wise man, if he does not know any better how to live than other men?—if he is only more cunning and intellectually subtle? Does Wisdom work in a treadmill? or does she teach how to succeed *by her example*? Is there any such thing as wisdom not applied to life? Is she merely the miller who grinds the finest logic? It is pertinent to ask if Plato got his *living* in a better way or more successfully than his contemporaries—or did he succumb to the difficulties of life like other men? Did he seem to prevail over some of them merely by indifference, or by assuming grand airs? or find it easier to live, because his aunt remembered him in her will? The ways in which most men get their living, that is, live, are mere makeshifts, and a shirking of the real business of life—chiefly because they do not know, but partly because they do not mean, any better.—HENRY THOREAU, "Life without Principle."

(i) Sometimes, but rarely, one may be caught making the same speech twice over, and yet be held blameless. Thus, a certain lecturer, after performing in an inland city, where dwells a *Littératrice* of note, was invited to meet her and others over the social teacup. She pleasantly referred to his many wanderings in his new occupation. "Yes," he replied, "I am like the Huma, the bird that never lights, being always in the cars, as he is always on the wing."—Years elapsed. The lecturer visited the same place once more for the same purpose. Another social cup after the lecture, and a second meeting with the dis-

tinguished lady. "You are constantly going from place to place," she said.—"Yes," he answered, "I am like the Huma,"—and finished the sentence as before.

What horrors, when it flashed over him that he had made this fine speech, word for word, twice over! Yet it was not true, as the lady might perhaps have fairly inferred, that he had embellished his conversation with the Huma daily during that whole interval of years. On the contrary, he had never once thought of the odious fowl until the recurrence of precisely the same circumstances brought up precisely the same idea. He ought to have been proud of the accuracy of his mental adjustments. — OLIVER WENDELL HOLMES, *The Autocrat of the Breakfast-Table.*

(j) For the scholar is a less noxious kind of parasite than the popularizer. At his worst the scholar, like John Earle's plodding student, brings to his task nothing but patience and a body, and he does no harm to his subject and his few readers. The popular writer, at his worst, brings nothing but impatience and a temperament, and he often gives a distorted picture of his subject to a multitude of readers. One pernicious thing about popular books on literary figures is that they enable people to feel that they have read a great author's works without the trouble of doing it. Of the thousands who read *Ariel*, how many were moved to read Shelley? Perhaps it would have been odd if they had been.—DOUGLAS BUSH, "Scholars Poor and Simple." [2]

D. Introduction and Conclusion

Even for the experienced writer two sections of the composition are especially difficult: the introduction and the conclusion. The one must generate momentum for the reader; the other must check the momentum. The introduction in particular is likely to cause trouble because the writer has not yet warmed to his subject and his thoughts will not flow easily. Nevertheless, some few principles and some examples of introductions and conclusions may help to make the writing of these sections of the paper somewhat easier.

[1] From *Michigan Alumnus Quarterly Review.* Reprinted by permission of the author and of the *Michigan Alumnus Quarterly Review.*

[2] From the *Atlantic Monthly.* Reprinted by permission of the author and of the *Atlantic Monthly.*

THE INTRODUCTION

The introduction is not just a preliminary flourish which the writer makes before settling down to the task of presenting his subject.

89. It has a definite function: to attract the attention of the reader, and to put him in possession of whatever is needed to make an intelligent approach to the body of the material.

1. *Attracting attention.* If the reader has a previously acquired interest in the subject matter, you can best attract his attention by an immediate statement of the thesis or of the problem which the thesis will ultimately solve. Such a beginning is also forceful. Francis Bacon begins an essay with his thesis sentence in this manner: "Houses are built to live in, and not to look on; therefore let use be preferred before uniformity, except where both may be had." Poe illustrates how the problem may be stated in the opening paragraph:

> The natural scenery of America has often been contrasted in its general features, as well as in detail, with the landscape of the Old World —more especially in Europe—and not deeper has been the enthusiasm, than wide the dissension, of the supporters of each region. The discussion is one not likely to be soon closed, for although much has been said on both sides, a word more yet remains to be said.— "The Elk."

If, however, the reader has no special interest in the subject, you must attract his attention by other means. A little story or anecdote will often suffice. For example, Stevenson begins thus his essay "The English Admirals":

> There is one story of the wars of Rome which I have always very much envied for England. Germanicus was going down at the head of the legions into a dangerous river—on the opposite bank the woods were full of Germans —when there flew out seven great eagles which seemed to marshal the Romans on their way; they did not pause or waver, but disappeared into the forest where the enemy lay

concealed. "Forward!" cried Germanicus, with a fine rhetorical inspiration, "Forward! and follow the Roman birds." It would be a very heavy spirit that did not give a leap at such a signal, and a very timorous one that continued to have any doubt of success.

An attractive question, an apt saying, an unusual or startling statement may turn the trick, provided that you are not forced and unnatural so that the introduction does not fit the body of the paper. Mark Twain begins a humorous sally against chambermaids with this opening exclamation: "Against all chambermaids, of whatsoever age or nationality, I launch the curse of bachelordom!" Reinhold Niebuhr stimulates attention with this catching statement: "The political situation and problem of America in world affairs can be put in one sentence: America is at once the most powerful and politically the most ignorant of modern nations." (The *Atlantic Monthly,* January, 1932.) Robert M. Gay begins an article this way: "Some dogs are christened in jest, some in earnest, and some with malice aforethought, but the Boojum was christened by inspiration." (The *Atlantic Monthly,* January, 1932.)

2. *Providing necessary information.* The other function of the introduction is to provide whatever knowledge is needed for comprehension of the body of the article. One requirement is an indication of what the paper is to be about, a necessity which requires the immediate statement of the problem to be discussed or of the thesis. The problem may be stated first if you feel that you wish to withhold the thesis until certain facts, essential for its comprehension, have been discussed. But from the outset the nature of the material to follow must be clearly indicated. To make doubly sure that the reader will follow the discussion, you can not only state the thesis but briefly outline the paper by stating the major points to be considered.

Sometimes you may wish to explain why you are writing the paper and so make an introductory statement of purpose. Josiah

Royce begins *The Spirit of Modern Philosophy* in this way:

> In the following course of lectures I shall try to suggest, in a fashion suited to the general student, something about the men, the problems, and the issues that seem to me most interesting in a limited but highly representative portion of the history of modern philosophy. I undertake this work with a keen sense of the limitations of my time and my powers. I plead as excuse only my desire to interest some of my fellow students in the great concerns of philosophy.[1]

Notice how the author has limited his subject and makes no pretense at covering the whole of modern philosophy. To limit the subject to any one point for discussion is very acceptable in the introduction so that the reader is not led to expect more than he gets. Josiah Royce also establishes a fine tone in his introduction by making no claims to universal knowledge. The reader immediately feels more confidence in him. A skillful writer may also find it useful to bring out at the beginning in what way he is qualified to write on his subject, to establish himself as an authority, or to explain how he happens to be writing. Stevenson says in the first paragraph of his article on the Japanese reformer, Yoshida-Torajiro:

> I wish to say that I am not, rightly speaking, the author of the present paper: I tell the story on the authority of an intelligent Japanese gentleman, Mr. Taiso Masaki, who told it me with an emotion that does honor to his heart; and though I have taken some pains, and sent my notes to him to be corrected, this can be no more than an imperfect outline.

The importance of the topic may also be established at the start in order that the reader's interest may be quickened. This introduction is particularly fitting where the reader is not well acquainted with the subject matter. John Nichol begins a chapter on the ancestry of Byron in this way:

[1] From Josiah Royce, *The Spirit of Modern Philosophy* (Boston). Reprinted by permission of Houghton Mifflin Co.

> Byron's life was passed under the fierce light that beats upon an intellectual throne. He succeeded in making himself—what he wished to be—the most notorious personality in the world of letters of our century. Almost every one who came in contact with him has left on record various impressions of intimacy or interview. . . . All concur in the admission that Byron was as proud of his race as of his verse, and that in unexampled measure the good and evil of his nature were inherited and inborn. His genealogy is, therefore, a matter of no idle antiquarianism.—*Byron*.

The introduction is also a good place in which to define any terms with which the reader may be unacquainted or which need to be sharply defined for purposes of discussion. Argument is dependent on an accurate knowledge of the implications of the terms used. Here is Poe's beginning to "The Rationale of Verse":

> The word "Verse" is here used not in its strict or primitive sense, but as the term most convenient for expressing generally and without pedantry all that is involved in the consideration of rhythm, rhyme, meter, and versification.

THE CONCLUSION

90. **A short composition does not require a special concluding paragraph.**

In a short composition which contains in all probability an obvious set of ideas and a clear organization, to use a whole paragraph for summary is a waste of words, and to indulge in an emotional appeal to arouse the reader's feelings is absurd. Such conclusions as the latter are useful only on special occasions, as possibly in Fourth-of-July addresses. Usually all that a paper needs is a final sentence, perhaps a restatement of the thesis, introduced by a transitional expression such as "in the end," "finally," "therefore," "after all," "in the last analysis."

In long papers with complex material the conclusion is usually a summary. It reemphasizes the thesis idea or restates the major points very briefly so that they stand out sharply and their relationships are made clear. Henry Fielding ends his essay "On the Knowledge of the Characters of Men" with this conclusion:

> Thus I have endeavored to show the several methods by which we can purpose to get any insight into the characters of those with whom we converse, and by which we may frustrate all the cunning and designs of hypocrisy. These methods I have shown to be threefold, viz., by the marks which nature hath imprinted on the countenance, by their behavior to ourselves, and by their behavior to others. On the first of these I have not much insisted, as liable to some uncertainty; and as the latter seem abundantly sufficient to secure us, with proper caution, against the subtle devices of hypocrisy, though she be the most cunning as well as malicious of all the vices which have ever corrupted the nature of man.
>
> But, however useless this treatise may be to instruct, I hope it will be at least effectual to alarm my reader; and sure no honest, undesigning man can ever be too much on his guard against the hypocrite, or too industrious to expose and expel him out of society.

He thus summarizes his major points and brings out the importance of his subject once again for the reader.

SUGGESTIONS FOR STUDY

1. From selections given in any part of this textbook, select five introductory and five concluding paragraphs, and be ready to state the method used in each.

2. Write a composition. After the completion of it, underline topic sentences once, transitional words and phrases twice, and list in the margin of the paper the means of development used in any three paragraphs.

College Football "Expendable" [1]

ROBERT M. HUTCHINS

IT IS COMMONLY SUPPOSED that I abolished intercollegiate football at the University of Chicago.

I wish that I could take the credit for this action, for it was one of the few unqualifiedly successful changes that occurred at the university during my administration.

Candor compels me to state, however, that the board of trustees abolished football. The board of trustees consisted of 35 men, none of them educators, many of them alumni, and a few of them former football players.

It all came about because the university was going to celebrate the 50th anniversary of its foundation and planned to do what all universities do on such occasions: It planned to have a money-raising campaign.

John Nuveen, an investment banker in Chicago, who was a trustee and alumnus of the university, had the responsibility for the campaign among the alumni.

He reported that they did not care for the results that the university's representatives were achieving on the gridiron.

In the last game with Michigan, Chicago was defeated, 85 to 0, and every time a Chicago student was tackled by a Michigan player there was a serious question as to whether he would ever get up.

This was a sad change from the good old days. When Amos Alonzo Stagg journeyed from Yale to Chicago in 1892, he knew more about football than anybody west of the Alleghenies.

The other Midwestern universities were small and, athletically speaking, unsophisticated.

Mr. Stagg's initial successes attracted to the university men like Walter Eckersall, one of the greatest natural athletes that ever lived.

[1] From the Chicago *Daily News.* Reprinted by permission of the author and of the Chicago *Daily News.*

The result was that for almost 30 years, until football became big business, Chicago, which had been the principal organizer of the Big Ten, had little trouble in maintaining its position in it.

After the First World War the Midwestern universities expanded at an incredible rate, and intercollegiate athletics expanded even faster.

This was the age of stadium building, in which almost all universities loaded themselves with debt in order to provide seats for the large number of cash customers that watched their games and for the still larger numbers they hoped to attract. In this period football became big business.

The University of Chicago expanded like all other universities, though it did not borrow money to erect its stadium.

The increasing size of its student body was not helpful to it from the athletic point of view, because the expansion took place chiefly in the graduate and professional schools, the members of which were ineligible to play.

The university had achieved an unfortunate reputation. It had made the mistake of letting it be known that it was an educational institution. It would not buy players or knowingly permit its alumni to do so.

It had no school of physical education, from which the student could graduate by getting passing marks in elementary, intermediate, and advanced exercise. The University of Chicago began to lose.

Mr. Nuveen said that the alumni did not like this. He thought they would not participate enthusiastically in a financial campaign unless the athletic situation was remedied. He asked what the remedy was.

The usual remedy was to fire the coach. Here it was suggested that the coach accounted for about 15 per cent of the success of the team and that with a perfect coach Chicago might hope to lose to Michigan, 72 to 0, instead of 85 to 0.

When football was abolished at Chicago, the coach went to Stanford and took the team to the Rose Bowl in his first year.

The problem was the material. The only way Chicago could obtain the material was to buy it. This the board was unwilling to do.

Could the university have withdrawn from big-time football and continued in the game, playing institutions that had the same attitude toward athletics and a male population of the same size?

Johns Hopkins has taken the money out of football—it charges no admission to its games—it plays the small colleges in the neighborhood.

But Johns Hopkins has no great athletic past to contend with. It never defeated Yale, Harvard and Princeton as Chicago defeated Michigan, Illinois and Purdue.

The constituency of the University of Chicago preferred to have it out of football altogether rather than see it risk defeat at the hands of Knox, Kenyon or Oberlin.

When the board of trustees unanimously decided to abolish intercollegiate football, a sigh of relief went up from the students, alumni, and faculty.

Although the sports writers freely predicted the decay and collapse of the university, it has grown in reputation and resources since that day.

Julius Rosenwald used to say that the secret of business success was, when you have a lemon, make a lemonade out of it.

Intercollegiate football was an activity in which the University of Chicago could not hope to excel without compromising its principles.

It was an irrelevant activity that diverted attention from the real purposes and accomplishments of the university. By abandoning it the university established itself at one stroke as an independent institution seriously devoted to the advancement of learning.

SUGGESTIONS FOR STUDY

1. Who abolished football at the University of Chicago?

2. What success had its football teams formerly enjoyed? Why had this situation changed?

3. Why did the alumni not favor competing with smaller colleges?

4. What was the effect of abolishing football?

5. What is the essential purpose of a university?

6. The paragraphs in this article are very short in accordance with newspaper practice. As an exercise in writing for more advanced readers, group these paragraphs into larger units developing a single topic sentence each. For instance, can the first three paragraphs properly form one satisfactory introductory paragraph?

7. Define these words from this article: candor, unsophisticated, constituency, compromising, irrelevant.

My America[1]

JOHN BUCHAN (LORD TWEEDSMUIR)

I FIRST DISCOVERED America through books. Not the tales of Indians and the Wild West which entranced my boyhood; those seemed to belong to no particular quarter of the globe, but to an indefinable land of romance, and I was not cognizant of any nation behind them. But when I became interested in literature, I came strongly under the spell of New England. Its culture seemed to me to include what was best in Europe's, winnowed and clarified. Perhaps it was especially fitted to attract youth, for it was not too difficult or too recondite, but followed the "main march of the human affections," and it had the morning freshness of a young people. Its cheerfulness atoned for its occasional bleakness and anemia. Lowell was the kind of critic I wanted, learned, rational, never freakish, always intelligible. Emerson's gnomic wisdom was a sound manual for adolescence, and of Thoreau I became—and for long remained—an ardent disciple. To a Scot of my upbringing there was something congenial in the simplicity, the mild austerity, and the girded discipline of the New England tradition. I felt that it had been derived from the same sources as our own.

Then, while I was at Oxford, I read Colonel Henderson's *Stonewall Jackson* and became a student of the American Civil War. I cannot say what especially attracted me to that campaign: partly, no doubt, the romance of it, the chivalry and the supreme heroism; partly its extraordinary technical interest, both military and political; but chiefly, I think, because I fell in love with the protagonists. I had found the kind of man that I could whole-heartedly admire. Since those days my study of the Civil War has continued, I have visited most of its battlefields, I have followed the trail of its great marches, I have read widely in its literature; indeed, my memory has become so stored with its details that I have often found myself able to tell the descendants of its leaders facts about their forebears of which they had never heard.

My interest soon extended from the soldiers to the civilians, and I acquired a new admiration for Abraham Lincoln. Then it was enlarged to include the rest of America's history—the first settlements, the crossing of the Appalachians, the Revolution, the building of the West. Soon America, instead of being the unstoried land which it appears to most English travelers, became for me the home of a long tradition and studded with sacred places. I dare to say that no American was ever more thrilled by the prospect of seeing Westminster Abbey and the Tower, Winchester and Oxford, than I was by the thought of Valley Forge and the Shenandoah and the Wilderness.

[1] From *Pilgrim's Way* (published in England under the title of *Memory Hold the Door*) by John Buchan (Lord Tweedsmuir). (Copyright 1940 by the Houghton Mifflin Company.) Reprinted by permission of the Houghton Mifflin Company, Lady Tweedsmuir, and Hodder and Stoughton, the English publisher.

I came first into the United States by way of Canada—a good way to enter, for English eyes are already habituated to the shagginess of the landscape and can begin to realize its beauties. My first reflection was that no one had told me how lovely the country was. I mean *lovely*, not vast and magnificent. I am not thinking of the Grand Canyon and the Yosemite and the Pacific coast, but of the ordinary rural landscape. There is much of the land which I have not seen, but in the East and the South and the Northwest I have collected a gallery of delectable pictures. I think of the farms which are clearings in the Vermont and New Hampshire hills, the flowery summer meadows, the lush cow-pastures with an occasional stump to remind one that it is old forest land, the quiet lakes and the singing streams, the friendly accessible mountains; the little country towns of Massachusetts and Connecticut with their village greens and elms and two-century-old churches and court houses; the secret glens of the Adirondacks and the mountain meadows of the Blue Ridge; the long-settled champaign of Maryland and Pennsylvania; Virginian manors more Old-England perhaps than anything we have at home; the exquisite links with the past like much of Boston and Charleston and all of Annapolis; the sunburnt aromatic ranges of Montana and Wyoming; the Pacific shores where from snow mountains fishable streams descend through some of the noblest timber on earth to an enchanted sea.

It is a country most of which I feel to be in a special sense "habitable," designed for homes, adapted to human uses, a friendly land. I like, too, the way in which the nomenclature reflects its history, its racial varieties, its odd cultural mixtures, the grandiose and the homespun rubbing shoulders. That is how places should be named. I have no objection to Mechanicsville and Higginsville and Utica and Syracuse. They are a legitimate part of the record. And behind are the hoar-ancient memorials of the first dwellers, names like symphonies—Susquehanna, Ticonderoga, Shenandoah, Wyoming.

"Ah, my cabbages!" Henry Adams wrote, "when will you ever fathom the American? Never in your sweet lives." He proceeds in his genial way to make epigrams about his own New Englanders: "Improvised Europeans we were and—Lord God!—how thin!" —"Thank God I never was cheerful. I come from the happy stock of the Mathers, who, as you remember, passed sweet mornings reflecting on the goodness of God and the damnation of infants." Where an Adams scrupled to tread it is not for a stranger to rush in. But I would humbly suggest a correction to one reading which, I think, has the authority of Robert Louis Stevenson. America is, no doubt, a vast country, though it can be comfortably put inside Canada. But it is not in every part a country of wide horizons. Dwellers on the Blue Ridge, on the prairies, and on the western ranges may indeed live habitually with huge spaces of land and sky, but most of America, and some of its most famous parts, is pockety, snug and cozy, a sanctuary rather than a watch-tower. To people so domiciled its vastness must be like the mathematician's space-time, a concept apprehended by the mind and not a percept of the eye. "The largeness of Nature and of this nation were monstrous without a corresponding largeness and generosity of the spirit of the citizen." That is one of Walt Whitman's best-known sayings, but let us remember that the bigness of their country is for most Americans something to be learned and imaginatively understood, and not a natural deduction from cohabiting with physical immensities.

Racially they are the most variegated people on earth. The preponderance of the Anglo-Saxon stock disappeared in the Civil War. Look today at any list of names in a society or a profession and you will find that, except in the navy, the bulk are from the continent of Europe. In his day Matthew

Arnold thought that the chief source of the strength of the American people lay in their homogeneity and the absence of sharply defined classes, which made revolution unthinkable. Other observers, like Henry James, have deplored the lack of such homogeneity and wished for their country the "close and complete consciousness of the Scots." (I pause to note that I cannot imagine a more nightmare conception. What would happen to the world if a hundred and thirty million Scotsmen, with their tight, compact nationalism, were living in the same country?) I am inclined to query the alleged absence of classes, for I have never been in any part of the United States where class distinctions did not hold. There is an easy friendliness of manner which conceals a strong class pride, and the basis of that pride is not always, or oftenest, plutocratic. Apart from the social snobbery of the big cities, there seems to be everywhere an innocent love of grades and distinctions which is enough to make a communist weep. I have known places in the South where there was a magnificent aristocratic egalitarianism. Inside a charmed circle all were equal. The village postmistress, having had the right kind of great-great-grandmother, was an honored member of society, while the immigrant millionaire, who had built himself a palace, might as well have been dead. And this is true not only of the New England F.F.M.'s and the Virginian F.F.V.'s, the districts with long traditions, but of the raw little townships in the Middle West. They, too, have their "best" people who had ancestors, though the family tree may only have sprouted for two generations.

No country can show such a wide range of type and character, and I am so constituted that in nearly all I find something to interest and attract me. This is more than a temperamental bias, for I am very ready to give reasons for my liking. I am as much alive as anyone to the weak and ugly things in American life: areas, both urban and rural, where the human economy has gone rotten; the melting-pot which does not always melt; the eternal colored problem; a constitutional machine which I cannot think adequately represents the efficient good sense of the American peoples; a brand of journalism which fatigues with its ruthless snappiness and uses a speech so disintegrated that it is incapable of expressing any serious thought or emotion; the imbecile patter of high-pressure salesmanship; an academic jargon, used chiefly by psychologists and sociologists, which is hideous and almost meaningless. Honest Americans do not deny these blemishes; indeed they are apt to exaggerate them, for they are by far the sternest critics of their own country. For myself, I would make a double plea in extenuation. These are defects from which today no nation is exempt, for they are the fruits of a mechanical civilization, which perhaps are more patent in America, since everything there is on a large scale. Again, you can set an achievement very much the same in kind against nearly every failure. If her historic apparatus of government is cranky, she is capable of meeting the "instant need of things" with brilliant improvisations. Against economic plague-spots she can set great experiments in charity; against journalistic baby-talk a standard of popular writing in her best papers which is a model of idiom and perspicuity; against catchpenny trade methods many solidly founded, perfectly organized commercial enterprises; against the jargon of the half-educated professor much noble English prose in the great tradition. That is why it is so foolish to generalize about America. You no sooner construct a rule than it is shattered by the exceptions.

As I have said, I have a liking for almost every kind of American (except the kind who decry their country). I have even a sneaking fondness for George Babbitt, which I fancy is shared by his creator. But there are two types which I value especially, and which I have never met elsewhere in quite the same form. One is the pioneer. No doubt the physical frontier of the United States is apges.

now closed, but the pioneer still lives, though the day of the covered wagon is over. I have met him in the New England hills, where he is grave, sardonic, deliberate in speech; in the South, where he has a ready smile and a soft, caressing way of talking; in the ranges of the West, the cowpuncher with his gentle voice and his clear, friendly eyes which have not been dulled by reading print—the real thing, far removed from the vulgarities of film and fiction. At his best, I think, I have found him as a newcomer in Canada where he is pushing north into districts like the Peace River, pioneering in the old sense. By what signs is he to be known? Principally by the fact that he is wholly secure, that he possesses his soul, that he is the true philosopher. He is one of the few aristocrats left in the world. He has a right sense of the values of life, because his cosmos embraces both nature and man. I think he is the most steadfast human being now alive.

The other type is at the opposite end of the social scale, the creature of a complex society who at the same time is not dominated by it, but, while reaping its benefits, stands a little aloof. In the older countries culture, as a rule, leaves some irregularity like an excrescence in a shapely tree-trunk, some irrational bias, some petulance or prejudice. You have to go to America, I think, for the wholly civilized man who has not lost his natural vigor or agreeable idiosyncrasies, but who sees life in its true proportions and has a fine balance of mind and spirit. It is a character hard to define, but anyone with a wide American acquaintance will know what I mean. They are people in whom education has not stunted any natural growth or fostered any abnormality. They are Greek in their justness of outlook, but Northern in their gusto. Their eyes are shrewd and candid, but always friendly. As examples I would cite, among friends who are dead, the names of Robert Bacon, Walter Page, Newton Baker, and Dwight Morrow.

But I am less concerned with special types than with the American people as a whole. Let me try to set down certain qualities which seem to me to flourish more lustily in the United States than elsewhere. Again, let me repeat, I speak of America only as I know it; an observer with a different experience might not agree with my conclusions.

First I would select what, for want of a better word, I should call homeliness. It is significant that the ordinary dwelling, though it be only a shack in the woods, is called not a house, but a home. This means that the family, the ultimate social unit, is given its proper status as the foundation of society. Even among the richer classes I seem to find a certain pleasing domesticity. English people of the same rank are separated by layers of servants from the basic work of the household, and know very little about it. In America the kitchen is not too far away from the drawing-room, and it is recognized, as Heraclitus said, that the gods may dwell there. But I am thinking chiefly of the ordinary folk, especially those of narrow means. It is often said that Americans are a nomad race, and it is true that they are very ready to shift their camp; but the camp, however bare, is always a home.[1] The cohesion of the family is close, even when its members are scattered. This is due partly to the tradition of the first settlers, a handful in an unknown land; partly to the history of the frontier, where the hearth-fire burnt brighter when all around was cold and darkness. The later immigrants from Europe, feeling at last secure, were able for the first time to establish a family base, and they cherished it zealously. This ardent domesticity has had its bad effects on American literature, inducing a sentimentality which makes a too crude frontal attack on the emotions, and which has produced as a reaction a not less sentimental "toughness." But as a social cement

[1] In the Civil War homesickness was so serious a malady that the "printed forms for medical reports contained an entry for nostalgia precisely as for pneumonia."—Douglas Freeman, *The South to Posterity*, p. 4.

it is beyond price. There have been many to laugh at the dullness and pettiness of the "small town." From what I know of small-town life elsewhere, I suspect obtuseness in the satirists.

Second, I would choose the sincere and widespread friendliness of the people. Americans are interested in the human race, and in each other. Deriving doubtless from the old frontier days, there is a general helpfulness which I have not found in the same degree elsewhere. A homesteader in Dakota will accompany a traveler for miles to set him on the right road. The neighbors will rally round one of their number in distress with the loyalty of a Highland clan. This friendliness is not a self-conscious duty so much as an instinct. A squatter in a cabin will share his scanty provender and never dream that he is doing anything unusual.

American hospitality, long as I have enjoyed it, still leaves me breathless. The lavishness with which a busy man will give up precious time to entertain a stranger to whom he is in no way bound remains for me one of the wonders of the world. No doubt this friendliness, since it is an established custom, has its fake side. The endless brotherhoods and sodalities into which people brigade themselves encourage a geniality which is more a mannerism than an index of character, a tiresome, noisy, back-slapping heartiness. But that is the exception, not the rule. Americans like company, but though they are gregarious they do not lose themselves in the crowd. Waves of mass emotion may sweep the country, but they are transient things and do not submerge for long the stubborn rock of individualism. That is to say, people can be led, but they will not be driven. Their love of human companionship is based not on self-distrust, but on a genuine liking for their kind. With them the sense of a common humanity is a warm and constant instinct and not a doctrine of the schools or a slogan of the hustings.

Lastly—and this may seem a paradox—I maintain that they are fundamentally modest. Their interest in others is a proof of it; the Aristotelian Magnificent Man was interested in nobody but himself. As a nation they are said to be sensitive to criticism; that surely is modesty, for the truly arrogant care nothing for the opinion of other people. Above all they can laugh at themselves, which is not possible for the immodest. They are their own shrewdest and most ribald critics. It is charged against them that they are inclined to boast unduly about those achievements and about the greatness of their country, but a smug glorying in them is found only in the American of the caricaturist. They rejoice in showing their marvels to a visitor with the gusto of children exhibiting their toys to a stranger, an innocent desire, without any unfriendly gloating, to make others partakers in their satisfaction. If now and then they are guilty of bombast, it is surely a venial fault. The excited American talks of his land very much, I suspect, as the Elizabethans in their cups talked of England. The foreigner who strayed into the Mermaid Tavern must often have listened to heroics which upset his temper.

The native genius, in humor, and in many of the public and private relations of life, is for overstatement, a high-colored, imaginative, paradoxical extravagance. The British gift is for understatement. Both are legitimate figures of speech. They serve the same purpose, for they call attention to a fact by startling the hearer, since manifestly they are not the plain truth. Personally I delight in both mannerisms and would not for the world have their possessors reject them. They serve the same purpose in another and a subtler sense, for they can be used to bring novel and terrible things within the pale of homely experience. I remember on the Western Front in 1918 that two divisions, British and American, aligned side by side, suffered a heavy shelling. An American sergeant described it in racy and imaginative speech which would have been appropriate to the

Day of Judgment. A British sergeant merely observed that "Kaiser 'ad been a bit 'asty." Each had a twinkle in his eye; each in his national idiom was making frightfulness endurable by domesticating it.

The United States is the richest, and, both actually and potentially, the most powerful state on the globe. She has much, I believe, to give to the world; indeed, to her hands is chiefly entrusted the shaping of the future. If democracy in the broadest and truest sense is to survive, it will be mainly because of her guardianship. For, with all her imperfections, she has a clearer view than any other people of the democratic fundamentals.

She starts from the right basis, for she combines a firm grip on the past with a quick sense of present needs and a bold outlook on the future. This she owes to her history; the combination of the British tradition with the necessities of a new land; the New England township and the Virginian manor *plus* the frontier. Much of that tradition was relinquished as irrelevant to her needs, but much remains: a talent for law which is not incompatible with a lawless practice; respect for a certain type of excellence in character which has made her great men uncommonly like our own; a disposition to compromise, but only after a good deal of arguing; an intense dislike of dictation. To these instincts the long frontier struggles added courage in the face of novelties, adaptability, enterprise, a doggedness which was never lumpish, but alert and expectant.

That is the historic basis of America's democracy, and today she is the chief exponent of a creed which I believe on the whole to be the best in this imperfect world. She is the chief exponent for two reasons. The first is her size; she exhibits its technique in large type, so that he who runs may read. More important, she exhibits it in its most intelligible form, so that its constituents are obvious. Democracy has become with many an unpleasing parrot-cry, and . . . it is well

to be clear what it means. It is primarily a spiritual testament, from which certain political and economic orders naturally follow. But the essence is the testament: the orders may change while the testament stands. This testament, this ideal of citizenship, she owes to no one teacher. There was a time when I fervently admired Alexander Hamilton and could not away with Jefferson; the latter only began to interest me, I think, after I had seen the University of Virginia, which he created. But I deprecate partisanship in those ultimate matters. The democratic testament derives from Hamilton as well as from Jefferson.

It has two main characteristics. The first is that the ordinary man believes in himself and in his ability, along with his fellows, to govern his country. It is when a people loses its self-confidence that it surrenders its soul to a dictator or an oligarchy. In Mr. Walter Lippmann's tremendous metaphor, it welcomes manacles to prevent its hands shaking. The second is the belief, which is fundamental also in Christianity, of the worth of every human soul—the worth, not the equality. This is partly an honest emotion, and partly a reasoned principle—that something may be made out of anybody, and that there is something likeable about everybody if you look for it—or, in canonical words, that ultimately there is nothing common or unclean.

The democratic testament is one lesson that America has to teach the world. A second is a new reading of nationalism. Some day and somehow the peoples must discover a way to brigade themselves for peace. Now, there are on the globe only two proven large-scale organizations of social units, the United States and the British Empire. The latter is not for export, and could not be duplicated; its strength depends upon a thousand-year-old monarchy and a store of unformulated traditions. But the United States was the conscious work of men's hands, and a task which has once been performed can be performed again. She is the supreme example of a federation in being, a federation which recognizes the rights and individuality of the parts, but accepts the overriding interests of the whole. To achieve this compromise she fought a desperate war. If the world is ever to have prosperity and peace, there must be some kind of federation—I will not say of democracies, but of states which accept the reign of Law. In such a task she seems to me to be the predestined leader. Vigorous as her patriotism is, she has escaped the jealous, barricadoed nationalism of the Old World. Disraeli, so often a prophet in spite of himself, in 1863, at a critical moment of the Civil War, spoke memorable words:

> There is a grave misapprehension, both in the ranks of Her Majesty's Government and of Her Majesty's Opposition, as to what constitutes the true meaning of the American democracy. The American democracy is not made up of the scum of the great industrial cities of the United States, nor of an exhausted middle class that speculates in stocks and calls that progress. The American democracy is made up of something far more stable, that may ultimately decide the fate of the two Americas and of "Europe."

For forty years I have regarded America not only with a student's interest in a fascinating problem, but with the affection of one to whom she has become almost a second motherland. Among her citizens I count many of my closest friends; I have known all her presidents, save one, since Theodore Roosevelt, and all her ambassadors to the Court of Saint James's since John Hay; for five years I have been her neighbor in Canada. But I am not blind to the grave problems which confront her. Democracy, after all, is a negative thing. It provides a fair field for the Good Life, but it is not in itself the Good Life. In these days when lovers of freedom may have to fight for their cause, the hope is that the ideal of the Good Life, in which alone freedom has any meaning, will acquire a stronger potency. It is the task of civilization to raise every citizen above want, but in so doing to permit a free development and avoid the slavery of the beehive and the antheap. A humane economic policy must

not be allowed to diminish the stature of man's spirit. It is because I believe that in the American people the two impulses arc of equal strength that I see her in the vanguard of that slow upward trend, undulant or spiral, which today is our modest definition of progress. Her major prophet is still Whitman. "Everything comes out of the dirt—everything; everything comes out of the people, everyday people, the people as you find them and leave them; people, people, just people!"

It is only out of the dirt that things grow.

SUGGESTIONS FOR STUDY

1. What is the tone of the article? Would the tone appeal most to Americans, to Englishmen, or to both equally?

2. Cite several instances to show that the author was writing for British readers in order to dispel erroneous ideas about America.

3. The author was a Scot, a novelist, and a statesman who traveled extensively in the United States. Do you think his observations accurate and just? Consider closely the list of "weak and ugly things in American life": are his statements here true and apt? Be prepared to discuss these weaknesses and to write a paper concerning them. Note also all the virtues which he lists. Did he miss any important ones? Is he correct in attributing these virtues to Americans?

4. Do you know any people who exemplify his two outstanding American types—the pioneer and the truly cultured man? If so, write a character sketch of one of them (for instructions on writing a character sketch, see the section in this book under Biography).

5. Name the three characteristics which Lord Tweedsmuir says are special with the American people. Do you agree with him? If you know the people of any foreign country well, try to enumerate characteristics of them that will distinguish them as well as Lord Tweedsmuir does.

6. What does he mean by the statement that democracy is a negative state which "provides a fair field for the Good Life, but is not in itself the Good Life"? What does he mean by "the Good Life"?

7. Analyze any three paragraphs in the article which you consider to be especially well written, and note down all the stylistic devices used in them, such as parallelism, loose and periodic sentences, transitional words and phrases, variation of sentence types and of sen-

tence beginnings, repetition for emphasis, and the like.

8. Select a paragraph from the first five which is especially distinguished for its details; itemize at least ten of these. Also find in the article examples of comparison, contrast, and illustration.

9. Compare the length of these paragraphs with those in the preceding article. What would result in this article if each sentence were made a separate paragraph? Does the long paragraph assist a good reader to understand better the organization of difficult material? As an experiment here, read the first sentence of each paragraph. Can you follow the course of the thought?

10. Define the following words in the article: recondite, winnowed, gnomic, austerity, protagonist, aromatic, nomenclature, sanctuary, homogeneity, plutocratic, egalitarianism, extenuation, obtuseness, sodalities, gregarious, ribald, testament, deprecate.

Topics for Writing

The following list is given merely to suggest topics on which a student may write. The individual items are not meant to serve as titles.

I. *Concerning college life*

The failure of high school to prepare me for college

What my goal is in college

The value of good grades

Are the classical languages worth studying?

Are any foreign languages worth studying?

How much rhetoric should students be required to take?

Should all students be required to take literature courses?

The ideal college instructor

Common faults of college instructors

What constitutes a good college course?

Are daily quizzes desirable?

Should mid-semester examinations be abolished?

Are final examinations justified?

Should examinations be essay-type or objective?

Is the honor system desirable during examinations?

Can fraternities justify their existence?

What qualities should a fraternity look for

in freshmen whom it might wish to pledge?

Is it worth while to belong to a fraternity?

Should initiates to a fraternity be hazed?

Should freshmen have to undergo hazing of any sort?

Are freshman caps justifiable?

What is the proper dress to wear to class?

Should girls wear slacks on campus?

The value of intramural sports

How essential is a winning football team to an institution?

Should coaches be appointed on long-term contracts?

Methods of playing various sports well

Should students pay large sums to "name" bands for college dances?

Should colleges be coeducational?

Preparing for examinations

Proper methods of studying

Dormitory life

Possible jobs for college students

Should all college students work their way through college?

Are marking systems fair?

How should marks in college be compiled?

Should attendance at class be required?

Should the student council punish students for infractions of the rules of the institution?

Campus politics

Do intercollegiate athletics actually promote good sportsmanship?

Do some sports encourage fair play more than others?

What architecture is best adapted to collegiate buildings?

What code of morals is prevalent for students on campus?

What vacations are essential during the college year?

Are college entrance requirements too high?

What type of news should appear in the college newspaper?

Should the newspaper be strictly censored?

Should football teams play postseason games?

Is it desirable that athletic teams go on long trips?

Are athletes good scholars?

Should athletic scholarships be given by the college?

Does the library staff co-operate with students?

What makes a good textbook?

Should students keep their textbooks after finishing a course?

What situations need attention in your institution?

II Concerning reading

What constitutes a good novel?

Are book clubs worth joining?

The value of poetry

What is necessary to gain a large circulation for a magazine?

A magazine that I like

Types of poetry

What the average American reads

A consideration of comic strips

The different editorial policies of various newspapers

The difference between the tabloids and other types of newspapers

What constitutes good sports writing for a newspaper?

III. Concerning politics and government

The salaries of public officials

The control of strikes

Should the term of office of the President be limited to two terms?

Government control of broadcasting

Is the sales tax a fair method of taxation?

What are the most desirable forms of taxation?

Are there inadequacies in our present income-tax system?

What are the virtues of a unicameral legislature?

What qualifications should a congressman have?

How can good men be induced to enter politics?

Should automobile insurance be required by law?

Should gasoline taxes be used for purposes other than highway maintenance?

Should the government operate the railroads?

What limits should be imposed upon freedom of speech?

Is socialized medicine advisable?

For what does each of our political parties stand?

Is our party system desirable?

Should the electoral college be abolished?

Should the legal voting age be lowered to eighteen?

How to reduce international animosity

Methods of curbing child delinquency

Programs of law enforcement

The value of patriotic symbols such as the flag

IV. Concerning the definition of difficult terms

A liberal education	Religion
Superstition	Immortality
Progress	Evolution
Rights of man	Introverts
Propaganda	Cowardice
Heroism	Democracy
Liberalism	Radicalism
Good morals	Respectability
Reds	Genius
Patriotism	Hypocrisy
Agnosticism	Cheating

"All men are created equal"

V. Concerning miscellaneous topics

The curtailment of radio advertising

Recent marvels of surgery

Diesel versus steam locomotives

How old should one be before marrying?

The case against suicide

Philately

Interior decorating problems

The scientific method

Operas in English

The values of classical music

What is jazz music?

Should capital punishment be abolished?

Fads in clothing styles

Movies or the legitimate stage?

The evils of gambling

Drug addiction in America

How to train a dog

Should women smoke?

Why I attend church

Methods of preventing seasickness and airsickness

Air travel as opposed to train travel

Is flying safe?

Love at first sight

Simplified spelling

Women as business executives

What is a high standard of living?

Causes of war

Superhighways

Desirability of billboards along the highways

Applying for a job

Is compulsory military training desirable?

Planning a new home

The latest devices to aid the housewife

The Whole Composition

I. BASIC PRINCIPLES AND ORGANIZATION

THE GOAL of a student in composition is the acquiring of such mastery of skills and techniques as will enable him to organize a series of related ideas into a unified and coherent whole, and to write a manuscript of some scope that will show evidence of this mastery. The preceding sections of this text have dealt with parts of the composition: words, sentences, paragraphs. How these parts combine in the best way to form essays, articles, stories, biographies, letters, and the like is the purpose of the remaining sections of the text.

A. Three Basic Principles: Unity, Coherence, Emphasis

Three time-honored principles which form the basis of clear and correct writing are those of unity, coherence, and emphasis; and these apply to the total unit no less than to such parts as the sentence and the paragraph. Despite fads and varying styles and new methods, the primary aim of writing still is to convey ideas from one mind to another; and as aids in accomplishing this aim, these principles are of paramount importance.

Unity is the principle of oneness: oneness of theme, of purpose, of tone. To possess unity, a composition must have one aim, one recognizable point of view, and definite limits. Any matter which does not contribute to a unified total effect, which is not part of the writer's aim as stated in his specific purpose, must be rigidly excluded, however interesting it may be in itself. Thus a student who knows what is meant by the principle of unity, and applies it in his writing, will avoid long, rambling introductions before he comes to the main point under discussion; he will likewise avoid lingering, trailing conclusions after he has finished what he had to say; and along the way he will avoid detours, however alluring the by-roads, and will stick to the main route as charted in the statement of his specific purpose and in his thesis sentence. A composition will have unity if a writer chooses one main idea to develop, begins without preamble with a consideration of this idea, and when he has finished with the development of his main idea, stops. It is the lackadaisical approach to a subject, without plan or chart, that makes for lack of unity in writing.

Coherence is the principle of order and arrangement applied to composition. It means a steady progress toward a definite goal. It involves the arrangement of ideas in a clear order, so that first things come first, co-ordinate ideas are clearly indicated by their position as being co-ordinate, subordinate details are given their proper place and clearly shown to be subordinate, and related ideas are grouped according to a definite pattern. The pattern may be that of a natural order, an order according to time, an order according to proximity and position, or an order of increasing importance; but whatever the pattern chosen, it should be followed throughout the composition without any deviation, and it should be fixed clearly in the writer's mind from his first sentence to his last in any given piece of writing. Observing the principle of coherence will save a writer from backing up to develop some point that belonged elsewhere, but which he forgot to take up at the proper place, from shifting his point of view unnecessarily, and from other practices which scatterbrained writers all too frequently fall into.

Emphasis is the principle of placing stress on the most important ideas in a composition, and making this stress obvious to a reader. It involves ordering ideas in such a way that the importance of a certain point or idea will stand out clearly. In short papers two or three points at most should be emphasized, and even in long papers it is best to limit the number of points on which one lays stress. The two chief ways of showing emphasis are by position and by proportion. As in the sentence and the paragraph, the most emphatic positions in the whole composition are at the beginning and the end. Whatever stands first or last in an article is likely to attract special notice. In arranging his ideas, therefore, a writer should develop a plan whereby ideas he wishes to stand out will come at the beginning or the end of a composition. Another way of securing emphasis is to give more space to an idea the writer deems important, since it is true that the devotion of considerable space to some idea will indicate that the writer considers it more important than an idea to which he gives little space. This method is called emphasis by proportion.

B. The Outline

An important step in planning the composition so that it will have unity, coherence, and emphasis is to construct an outline before the actual writing is done, as an aid to both you and the reader. It will enable you to organize your thoughts before committing them to paper. It will enable him to follow the progress of your thought more easily.

THE MECHANICAL FORM

The purpose of the outline is to present the structure of a whole work at a glance. To accomplish this end, it must have an orderly appearance on the page.

1. *Use a consistent system of notation.* The most usual system employs Roman numerals to indicate main points, and in descending order of importance, capital letters, Arabic numerals, small letters, Arabic numerals in parentheses (1), and small letters in parentheses (a).

2. *Indent each subdivision clearly.*

3. *Place divisions of equal importance directly under each other.*

4. *Capitalize the first word in each point.* The outline will then take this form:

   I.
      A.
      B.
         1.
         2.
   II.   etc.

This form indicates that *I* and *II* are of nearly equal importance—that is, they are *co-ordinate. A* and *B* are of less importance than *I* and *II*, they are parts of *I*, and they are co-ordinate. *1* and *2* are of even less importance, are parts of I.B., and are equal to each other.

THE COMPOSITION OF THE OUTLINE

91. **The major principle of the outline is division.**

91a. **Each major point is a subdivision of the thesis of the paper.**

If an outline has four main headings, the thesis, therefore, has four parts. Likewise, point *I* has two parts if *A* and *B* are listed under it. *Never try to make an outline by adding A and B to I;* they can only be parts of *I*, not additions to it.

91b. **Each section which is divided must have at least two parts.**

It is obviously impossible to divide anything into less than two parts. So the outline must have at least two main headings, and any subsection which you choose to divide must have at least two subheadings.

Suppose, for example, that you are making an outline for a paper on roofs. The first main point is "Fireproof roofs"; if slate is the only kind of fireproof roofing which occurs to you, do *not* begin your outline this way:

    I. Fireproof roofs
      A. Slate
    II. . . .

The single subdivision is illogical. If slate is the only kind of fireproof roof, slate is not a subdivision of the main point; it *is* the main point, and the outline should read: I. Fireproof roofing: slate. Of course, many times further reflection will provide a real subdivision of a heading, as here tile and metal would soon suggest themselves as additional kinds of fireproof roofing.

91c. **Do not allow co-ordinate points to contain material in common.**

The following division is illogical:

    I. Shingle roofs
    II. Slate roofs
    III. Durable roofs

Points two and three overlap. Slate roofs are durable roofs. Between points I and II, however, the division is clean and the outline correct.

The cure for overlapping is to establish a *basis of classification.* In classifying roofs, decide whether you wish to consider them according to cost or durability or composition or some other basis; then adhere strictly to that one method. Your outline might take any one of the three following forms:

    I. Shingle
    II. Slate
    III. Thatch
    IV. Tile

    I. Roofs with short life
    II. Durable roofs

    I. Expensive roofs
    II. Medium-priced roofs
    III. Inexpensive roofs

91d. **Do not number the introduction and conclusion to your paper.**

You could classify the main points on the basis of structure—I. Introduction, II. Body, III. Conclusion—but that is unnecessary. Subdivide the thesis directly on the basis of content. If you wish to include an introduction and conclusion in your outline, use this form:

Introduction: . . .
    I. . . .
    II. . . .
Conclusion: . . .

Never write down just the word *Introduction* or *Conclusion.* If these are worth including in your outline, they deserve to be accompanied by a statement of what each is to contain.

Here are a few other cautions about this process of division. Use only a few main headings or overlapping will result. Also, as a general practice, leave no heading undivided which is designated by a Roman numeral, as such topics are ordinarily so important as to require further explanation by division. Further, do not encumber the outline with excessive detail or with examples or illustrations, although, of course, you should organize fully all essential material.

THE TOPIC OUTLINE

Although there are many kinds of outlines, two are in common use: the topic and the sentence. The topic outline expresses each point by means of a phrase or a catchword without trying to convey the full meaning of each point. Because each point is brief, the topic outline is useful in organizing material, for the topics can be shifted around readily and their relationship quickly perceived. Its brevity, however, may make it obscure at a later date or to some other person.

92a. State each point carefully.

Do not try to make a topic by cutting the subject from a sentence, by omitting part of the verb, or by omitting articles. Restate the point entirely. If you wish to convey the idea that "Material is needed for the work to continue," do not write "Material needed for work to continue," nor "Need material for work to continue," but restate the point concisely as "The urgent need for material."

92b. Use parallel structure for co-ordinate headings.

It will enable you to organize your ideas more logically. Roman numerals should be parallel, points *A* and *B* under *I* should be parallel, and so on. *A* and *B* under *I* need not, however, be parallel with *A* and *B* under *II*, as each group is subdividing a different main heading. The following outline on the subject of pruning fruit trees lacks parallelism:

I. Proper time of year
  A. Late fall
    1. To prevent "bleeding"
    2. Insects
  B. etc.

The writer of this outline cannot be sure that heading 2 is logical. What does "insects" mean? If the point were stated "To guard against insects," the writer could be sure that it was properly classified.

92c. Phrase the subpoints so that they read clearly from the main points.

If the points *1* and *2* in the above outline had read "bleeding" and "insects," their relation to the main point "Late fall" would not have been clear. The infinitives "to prevent" and "to guard" made that logical relationship apparent.

Placing a thesis sentence at the top of the outline is an excellent practice. Such a sentence will keep your thinking directed on the problem at hand.

EXAMPLE OF A TOPIC OUTLINE

THESIS: *College English should increase a student's ability to understand and use the English language.*

I. His ability to read
  A. To comprehend the printed page
  B. To understand the qualities of good writing
II. His ability to express himself
  A. In speech
    1. By instruction in correct forms
    2. By practice
      a. In informal recitation
      b. In oral recitation
  B. In writing
    1. By drill on mechanical details
    2. By the study of correct models
    3. By practice in writing
III. His ability to think clearly
  A. To construct a logical train of thought
    1. By the study of instructions in the text
    2. By the study of his instructor's comments
      a. Oral
        (1) In class
        (2) In conference
      b. Written: comments on assigned papers
  B. To be intelligently critical of the ideas of others

THE SENTENCE OUTLINE

The sentence outline is made up of complete sentences rather than phrases or catchwords. For purposes of suggesting your organization to someone else or of keeping a plan of organization lucid in your own mind over a long period of time, it is superior to the topic outline. The same principles govern it that have just been applied to the topic outline.

EXAMPLE OF A SENTENCE OUTLINE

THESIS: *College English should increase a student's ability to understand and use the English language.*

I. College English should increase his ability to read.
  A. It should give him power to comprehend the thought of the printed page.
  B. It should give him an understanding of the qualities of good literature.

II. It should increase his power of expression.
  A. It should improve his habits of speech.
    1. It should teach him what good speech is.
    2. It should give him mastery of it by constant practice.
      a. It should provide instruction through informal recitation.
      b. It should provide instruction through formal talks.
  B. It should improve his written expression.
    1. It should provide benefits by drill on mechanical details.
    2. It should provide benefits by the study of correct models.
    3. It should provide benefits by constant practice in writing.
III. It should increase his ability to think clearly.
  A. It should enable him to construct a logical train of thought.
    1. The textbook should offer instructions on logical presentation.
    2. The instructor should offer comments on logical presentation.
      a. The instructor should offer oral comments.
        (1) These comments should be given in class.
        (2) These comments should also be given in conference.
      b. The instructor should give written criticism in his comments on assigned papers which the student submits.
  B. It should enable him to be intelligently critical of the ideas of others.

SUGGESTIONS FOR STUDY

A

Immediately following are three lists of words. Without adding or subtracting words from any list, rearrange the words according to their proper classification and importance into a topic outline form with correct outline numbering.

EXAMPLE:

Large blackboards	I. Poor classrooms
Good classrooms	A. Hot
Poor classrooms	B. Ill-lighted
Hot	II. Good classrooms
Ill-lighted	A. Large blackboards

Good illumination	B. Good illumination
Good ventilation	C. Good ventilation

1.

Winter sports	Swimming
Tennis	Football
Skating	Cross-country running
Summer sports	Tobogganing
Boating	Soccer
Hockey	Skiing
Fall sports	Golf

2.

Social studies	American literature
History	American history
Economics	Money and banking
English	Shakespeare
Corporation finance	French
German	Spanish
Foreign languages	Modern European history

3.

Denotation	Indirect object
Sentence structure	Colloquialisms
Uses of the objective case	Opening prepositional phrases
Grammar	Variety in sentence beginnings
Noun	Opening gerund phrases
Direct object	Adjective
Complex sentence	Adverb
Types of sentences	Opening participial phrases
Compound sentence	Object of a preposition
The word	Verb
Levels of usage	Pronoun
Parts of speech	Slang
Preposition	Simple sentence
Economy of wording	

B

Each of the following outlines is defective in some way. Revise each in such a way as to make it conform to the principles in the preceding chapter. The first four outlines are to be topic outlines; the fifth is to be a sentence outline.

1. *The diet prevented my eating many foods.*
  I. Condiments
    A. Relishes were forbidden.
    B. Avoiding sauces of all sorts
    C. Spices
  II. Sweets were also not to be eaten.
    A. Candy especially bad
    B. Soft drinks also
  III. Starches forbidden
    A. Bread

B. Pastry not allowed
  1. Cake
  2. Pie, not even in small slices

2. *Driving our own car offered us two main advantages.*
  I. We could visit points of interest.
    A. Natural landmarks which attracted us
      1. We wanted to see Lake George.
      2. Nearby is Ausable Chasm.
      3. The Adirondacks
    B. Historical landmarks
      1. Visiting the battlefield of Saratoga
      2. There is the fort at Ticonderoga too.
      3. The fortifications at Crown Point
  II. To renew acquaintances
    A. Among relatives
      1. We could visit my brother.
      2. We could visit my uncle.
    B. Visiting among friends

3. *In playing long shots in golf, choose your club with care.*
  I. Playing off the tee
    A. For long holes
      1. Use the driver for greatest distance.
      2. The brassie
    B. For shorter holes
      1. The spoon is used.
      2. The long irons are useful but do not carry as far as the spoon.
  II. Off the fairway
    A. Shooting from over 200 yards from the green
      1. The brassie for greatest distance
      2. The spoon
    B. Over 150 yards from the green
      1. No. 1 iron for low shots into the wind
      2. Using the No. 2 iron
      3. No. 3 iron has greater loft.

4. *A poet can vary the motion of a line of verse at will.*
  I. For slower motion
    A. Accented syllables
      1. The spondee: two accented syllables
      2. The iambic is faster but has a moderate motion.
    B. He can use long vowels.
    C. Using mute consonants
  II. If he wishes more rapid motion
    A. Unaccented syllables
      1. The anapestic foot has two unaccented syllables.
      2. The dactylic foot
    B. Short vowels are read rapidly.
    C. Liquid consonants readily pronounceable.

5. *A course in composition is valuable to every college student.*
  I. The objections to college composition are based on a misunderstanding of its aims.
    A. It does not aim to produce professional writers.
      1. It could not if it would.
        a. Most composition teachers are not trained for such a function.
        b. Composition teachers realize that such a purpose would be foolish.
    B. It does not put emphasis on style rather than on content.
      1. Style and content are considered inseparable.
      2. Content should determine style.
  II. College composition does not teach an impracticable kind of English.
    A. Modern textbooks stress current usage.
    B. Many colleges try to employ teachers who are themselves writers.
  III. The composition course helps the student in his other courses.
    A. It trains him in the techniques of reading.
    B. It trains him to express what he knows.
      1. In written reports.
      2. Examinations.
      3. Recitation.
    C. It helps the student to write better term papers.
    D. It helps the student to write better reports on outside reading.
  IV. The composition course broadens the student's interests.
    A. It makes him more broadminded.
    B. It introduces him to subject matter he is not familiar with.
      1. Through readings.
      2. He writes on diversified topics.
    C. He becomes familiar with many new words.
  V. A composition course trains the student to be more critical of the language he hears.
    A. He is less susceptible to propaganda.
      1. He is discriminating about words.
      2. He is not overpowered by gorgeous, vague terminology.
      3. He acquires an admiration for specific words.
  VI. The composition course helps a student after he graduates.
    A. It equips him with the means of communicating with people of culture and importance.
    B. The writing of a formal letter does not frighten him.

C. It provides him with the means of becoming an appreciative reader.

C

From each of the following paragraphs, select the topic sentence and write it down. Then below the topic sentence, write a topic outline of the material in the paragraph.

1. One of the first English dictionaries was that by Henry Cockeram, printed in 1623. It had three parts: the first contained difficult words with an explanation of their meaning; the second contained easy words translated into hard words; the third was a key to classical and mythological terms to be found in the best reading of the day.

2. The year 1837 was an interesting year in the literary world. In England Dickens published *Oliver Twist,* Carlyle published the *French Revolution,* Lockhart the *Life of Scott,* and Browning *Strafford.* In America Whittier produced *Poems,* Hawthorne *Twice-Told Tales,* and Emerson delivered his address "The American Scholar."

3. All baseball players should be able to bunt. The bunt can frequently produce a hit for a swift runner and when used as a surprise move can yield a hit for almost any runner. It is more valuable, however, for sacrifice purposes to advance a runner one base and occasionally to squeeze a run home from third base.

4. The sonnet has long been an important literary form. Its history traces back to an origin in Italy, where it was developed probably in the thirteenth century and was perfected by Petrarch in the fourteenth century. It spread throughout England in the sixteenth century after its introduction by Wyatt and Surrey and was soon brought to perfection in the sonnets of Shakespeare. It has customarily taken two forms in English. The more popular form has been the Italian, composed of an octave and a sestet; the other form is the English, or Shakespearean, composed of three quatrains and a closing couplet.

5. To be successful in a large business firm, young people must observe many principles of conduct. They must first show loyalty to the firm. It is very easy to grouse about the job they hold, about the efficiency of the firm's operation, and about their fellow workers or the employers, but they must refrain from such complaints. They must also refrain from circulating rumors and gossip about the firm or its employees. They must secondly show initiative concerning their positions. This can take the form of offering constructive suggestions, of rendering their assistance in carrying out the projects of their superiors or fellow employees, or of assuming responsibilities when the opportunity offers. They must also remember to conduct themselves modestly. It behooves them to admit their errors frankly, to accept criticism cheerfully, and to work hard in what jobs are offered them.

6. The Imagists were a group of British and American poets who flourished about 1912. Their group included such prominent poets as Amy Lowell, Hilda Doolittle, Ezra Pound, J. G. Fletcher, and D. H. Lawrence. The aims they chose for their verse were to present clear images, to preserve freedom in the choice of subject matter, to create appropriate new rhythms, and to gain great concentration of expression.

7. One of the most important dictionaries was that written by Samuel Johnson in the middle of the eighteenth century. His dictionary was inadequate in that it contained inexact quotations, it revealed his personal prejudices (such as his dislike of the Scots), and it sometimes defined words in language too difficult to be readily comprehended. But it had many desirable features that stamp it as a great dictionary. Johnson studied a great many writings to get accurate definitions, he made more exact the specific meanings of many words, he entered more words than previous lexicographers had, and he gave fuller information about each word. His dictionary stands as a great work for its time.

8. Perhaps the greatest of modern dictionaries is the Oxford English Dictionary. It contains over 400,000 words, and has nearly 2,000,000 illustrations to show their meanings in the writings of standard authors. But it is great in other ways than size. It is complete in furnishing information about every word used in the language for the last eight hundred years. It is scholarly, for each word is traced through its various changes of meaning, and the time of its entrance into or exit from the language is stated. It is also scholarly in its use of fresh quotations for study to derive exact meanings.

9. The Transcendentalist movement in America produced many reforms. Some of the reformers wished to stay in the world and make their changes from within. They thought that through the agency of the churches and schools society could be bettered. Others, however, withdrew in despair from the world and turned to the life of the country. A few, like Thoreau, were solitary hermits, but many congregated in ideal communities. Fruitlands and Brook Farm and the Oneida Community were communities formed by the Transcendentalists in the search for perfect human societies.

10. James Burbage had quite a problem in

selecting a place for a theater in Elizabethan London. He had to find a spot which was outside the jurisdiction of the city authorities, for they were puritanical and hated the drama. But at the same time he had to be near the center of activity so that people could attend his performances and so that he could make a profit from his venture. The solution was found in the plots of land once owned by different monasteries. The monasteries situated in London had been from olden time free from molestation by city authorities, and when Henry VIII had abolished them as monasteries, he had not removed their special privilege. So by building his theater upon one of these plots, Burbage solved his problem.

D

1. Write down the names of a dozen or so members of your high-school graduating class. Arrange these people in classifications on the basis of what they are doing at the present time. Make a topic outline which will represent these classifications. Arrange subordinate divisions which will state the particular occupation of each person.

2. Convert the topic outline made for Exercise 1 into a complete sentence outline.

3. Ask eight or ten students their opinions as to the best way to prepare for final examinations. Organize and outline their opinions.

4. Read the editorial opinions of several newspapers in your college library concerning some recent event of national importance. Make an outline which would serve as a guide for a paper on "The Stand Certain Newspapers Are Taking on . . ."

5. Make an outline for a paper on types of music (or books, pictures, girls, boys, neckties, and so forth) which you like and which you do not like, with your reasons.

6. Classify the instruments in a symphony orchestra, those in a college band, the players on an athletic team, the members of a newspaper staff, or the student organizations on your campus, in at least three different ways. Make an outline of each method of organization.

The Conditions of Art

JOHN RUSKIN

BEAUTIFUL ART can only be produced by people who have beautiful things around them, and leisure to look at them; and unless you provide some elements of beauty for your workmen to be surrounded by, you will find that no elements of beauty can be invented by them.

I was struck forcibly by the bearing of this great fact upon our modern efforts at ornamentation, in an afternoon walk last week, in the suburbs of one of our large manufacturing towns. I was thinking of the difference in the effect in the designer's mind, between the scene which I then came upon, and the scene which would have presented itself to the eyes of any designer of the middle ages when he left his workshop. Just outside the town I came upon an old English cottage, or mansion, I hardly know which to call it, set close under the hill, and beside the river, perhaps built somewhere in the Charleses'

time, with mullioned windows and a low arched porch; round which, in the little triangular garden, one can imagine the family as they used to sit in old summertimes, the ripple of the river heard faintly through the sweet-brier hedge, and the sheep on the far-off wolds shining in the evening sunlight. There, uninhabited for many and many a year, it had been left in unregarded havoc of ruin; the garden gate still swung loose to its latch; the garden, blighted utterly into a field of ashes, not even a weed taking root there; the roof torn into shapeless rents; the shutters hanging about the windows in rags of rotten wood; before its gate, the stream which had gladdened it now soaking slowly by, black as ebony, and thick with curdling scum; the bank above it trodden into unctuous sooty slime; far in front of it, between it and the old hills, the furnaces of the city foaming forth perpetual plague of sulphurous darkness; the volumes of their storm clouds coiling low over a waste of grassless fields, fenced from each other not by hedges but by slabs of square stone, like gravestones, riveted together with iron.

That was the scene for the designer's contemplation in his afternoon walk at Rochdale. Now fancy what was the scene which presented itself, in his afternoon walk, to a designer of the Gothic school of Pisa—Nino Pisano, or any of his men.

On each side of a bright river he saw rise a line of brighter palaces, arched and pillared, and inlaid with deep red porphyry, and with serpentine; along the quays before their gates were riding troops of knights, noble in face and form, dazzling in crest and shield; horse and man one labyrinth of quaint color and gleaming light—the purple, and silver, and scarlet fringes flowing over the strong limbs and clashing mail, like sea waves over rocks at sunset. Opening on each side from the river were gardens, courts, and cloisters; long successions of white pillars among wreaths of vine; leaping of fountains through buds of pomegranate and orange; and still along the garden paths, and under and through the crimson of the pomegranate shadows, moving slowly, groups of the fairest women that Italy ever saw—fairest because purest and thoughtfulest; trained in all high knowledge, as in all courteous art—in dance, in song, in sweet wit, in lofty learning, in loftier courage, in loftiest love—able alike to cheer, to enchant, or save, the souls of men. Above all this scenery of perfect human life, rose dome and belltower burning with white alabaster and gold: beyond dome and belltower the slopes of mighty hills hoary with olive; far in the north, above a purple sea of peaks of solemn Apennine, the clear, sharp-cloven Carrara mountains sent up their steadfast flames of marble summit into amber sky; the great sea itself, scoring with expanse of light, stretching from their feet to the Gorgonian isles; and over all these, ever present, near or far—seen through the leaves of vine, or imaged with all its march of

clouds in the Arno's stream, or set with its depth of blue close against the golden hair and burning cheek of lady and knight—that untroubled and sacred sky, which was to all men, in those days of innocent faith, indeed the unquestioned abode of spirits, as the earth was of men; and which opened straight through its gates of cloud and veils of dew into the awfulness of the eternal world—a heaven in which every cloud that passed was literally the chariot of an angel, and every ray of its Evening and Morning streamed from the throne of God.

What think you of that for a school of design?

I do not bring this contrast before you as a ground of hopelessness in our task; neither do I look for any possible renovation of the Republic of Pisa, at Bradford, in the nineteenth century; but I put it before you in order that you may be aware precisely of the kind of difficulty you have to meet, and may then consider with yourselves how far you can meet it. To men surrounded by the depressing and monotonous circumstances of English manufacturing life, depend upon it, design is simply impossible. This is the most distinct of all the experiences I have had in dealing with the modern workman. He is intelligent and ingenious in the highest degree—subtle in touch and keen in sight; but he is, generally speaking, wholly destitute of designing power. And if you want to give him the power, you must give him the materials, and put him in the circumstances for it. Design is not the offspring of idle fancy; it is the studied result of accumulative observation and delightful habit. Without observation and experience, no design—without peace and pleasurableness in occupation, no design—and all the lecturings and teachings and prizes and principles of art in the world are of no use, so long as you don't surround your men with happy influences and beautiful things. It is impossible for them to have right ideas about color, unless they see the lovely colors of nature unspoiled; impossible for them to supply beautiful incident and action in their ornament, unless they see beautiful incident and action in the world about them. Inform their minds, refine their habits, and you form and refine their designs; but keep them illiterate, uncomfortable, and in the midst of unbeautiful things, and whatever they do will still be spurious, vulgar, and valueless.—*The Two Paths*, Lecture 3.

SUGGESTIONS FOR STUDY

1. In what two parts of the article do you find the thesis stated? Formulate that thesis in your own words.

2. What means of paragraph development is used in paragraphs two and four? State the topic sentence of each paragraph. What means is used for the presentation of the composition as a whole?

3. In Ruskin's estimation, is the modern craftsman lacking in intelligence and artistic ability? What then does he lack?

4. Make an outline of this selection. Limit the number of main headings which you employ; preferably do not use more than two here. State the thesis before you begin to outline; then consider what parts of the composition are subdivisions of the thesis, and what parts serve only to introduce or summarize it. Do not use numerals for the latter parts, as they are the thesis itself, not parts of it.

5. Define the following words from the selection: mullioned, ebony, unctuous, porphyry, serpentine, pomegranate, alabaster, amber, renovation, destitute, accumulative, spurious.

Skiing[1]

STRAND MIKKELSEN

As far as I know, skiing is the simplest sport to learn—provided you get the right start. Naturally, everyone who wants to ski would like to jump and experience the thrill of flying through the air with a white world beneath him. But in skiing you cannot begin by jumping any more than you can run before you walk. The great mistake of young skiers in this country is that they try to jump before being able to walk and slide on skis.

The first essential is to have the right equipment. Get good skis, and be sure that, when upended, they stand as high as you can reach. In other words, if you, for instance, are five feet ten inches tall and you can reach one foot above your head, your skis should be six feet ten inches long. Then buy a pair of good ski boots.

The most important item, however, is the fastenings, which should be strong and heavy and correctly fit the boots. Remember this, for not having proper bindings will set you back in skiing, and you never can learn to jump with poor bindings. One of the main reasons for the prowess of Norwegian, Swedish, and Swiss ski runners is that, no matter how young they were when they began, their ski-wise parents provided them with good fastenings from their very start in the sport.

Assuming that you have the proper outfit, you now are ready to learn walking or sliding on level ground. Here we go! Lunge forward on one foot, keeping the weight well on the front ski. Before the skis stop, lunge forward again and slide on the other ski, transferring your weight. The chief points to remember are: Never lift the skis from the ground, and *keep sliding*.

Propel your skis with easy, dipping motions of the legs and manage your weight with corresponding balancing motions of the arms. The action somewhat resembles skating, except that the feet are not turned sideways to make a forward push, but are kept in a straight line.

The next thing to master is sliding downhill. This is where the fun begins. I can give you only one rule for sliding, but that one is

[1] This selection is an excerpt from a longer article in which the author also describes how to ski jump. From *Popular Science Monthly*, CXVIII (January, 1931), 38. Reprinted by permission of *Popular Science Monthly*.

important: Don't bend either the body or the knees, but keep perfectly straight. The rest is a matter of practice and achieving form. No two skiers ride downhill in the same way; neither do they jump in the same fashion. Start with low hills that have level slopes. Then take steeper hills. After those, try hills with bumps. All this is easy, and should take no longer than two or three weeks.

As a majority of ski runners make curves on level ground with the momentum attained by sliding downhill, you now are ready to try your hand at curves. There are several kinds of turns, but the principal types are the Christiania swing and the Telemark swing. The Christiania is the easiest.

Move the left foot forward so that the heel of the left foot is even with the toe of the right, and keep your body weight on the left ski. Steer to the left with your weight, and make the right ski follow by a slight dipping motion of the knees to produce the necessary slide, holding the arms out straight to maintain balance. Continue again with the left ski, twisting the body to keep the weight on the left foot, but holding back a little for the sake of balance. Repeat these steps until the curve is achieved. In making the turn to the right, it is necessary to reverse the process.

The Telemark is the prettiest and most popular of the curves, and expert skiers often use it as a finish to a perfect ski jump. In this curve you turn to the left by pushing the *right* ski two feet ahead of the left. Then stretch the arms out straight. Bend the left knee way down and the right knee a little, meanwhile twisting the right ankle to the left and leaning in toward the left until the swing is completed. Here, as you see, the right ski is the steering ski.

If the Telemark is made to the right, the entire action is, of course, reversed. But since with most people the right leg is stronger than the left, the curve usually is executed to the left. I make the Telemark both ways, but something tells me that it will take you quite a little while to do this.

Sliding downhill is great fun and almost anyone can do it in some fashion, but going uphill is not so easy. The main thing in hill climbing is to make a quick study of each hill as you come to it. Carefully observe its shape and the character of the upgrade, and map out a little campaign as to how to reach the top.

If the hill is low and of gentle slope, walk straight up with the aid of your two poles. All skiers use two poles, except the Lapps, that strange race of Mongolian people who inhabit the northern parts of Norway, Sweden, and Finland. They are the only skiers who never use more than one pole. The reason is that they utilize it as a weapon in their frequent fights with the wolves that attack their reindeer herds. In such a battle, a second pole would be a severe handicap.

To climb steep hills, you must resort to side-stepping, half-side-stepping, and herringboning. In side-stepping you simply turn your profile to the hill and walk sideways. It is used in tramping the ski hill below the take-off. In the half-side-step, you push one ski forward diagonally, at the same time making sure to bring up the heel of the ski in such a way that the ski in its new position is parallel to but ahead of the other ski. Then lift up the lower ski to take its place beside the other.

The half-side-step is the least fatiguing and most useful of all hill-climbing steps. The herringbone, used to climb steep, short, narrow trails and to negotiate hilltops quickly, is much more difficult and a considerable strain on the leg muscles. Face straight up the hill. Keep the feet apart and turn your toes out as far as convenient. Then walk uphill Charlie Chaplin fashion.

The next trick to learn is the kick-turn. This is almost indispensable in hill climbing, and especially useful in reversing your position on steep slopes. Let us suppose you want to make a kick-turn to the right. Lift the right foot as high as you can, twist it to the right, and bring it down with the ski in a horizontal position, so that it clears the toe of the left ski. Now, shifting your weight to the right and lifting the left foot, turn it and then bring it down beside the right. The kick-turn is used only on steep hills, or when going over a fence.

As for braking, snow-plowing is the easiest method, especially if you have no poles. It is best to try the snow-plow when not under too much speed. Straddle the legs wide apart, force the heels out, and bring the points of the skis as close together as possible. The skis, in this position, will be forced half sideways instead of end on through the snow. To make the snow-plow still more effective for braking, edge the skis by making yourself knock-kneed. When under great speed, snow-plowing is better as a preventive than as an actual means of stopping, because when you are coming down very fast all your strength may not be sufficient to hold the skis apart. Stemming is half snow-plowing. To stem, simply run one ski straight ahead and force the other partly sideways through the snow.

Just a few words about handling the poles. On level ground, they may be used effectively in two ways. One is to propel yourself by alternate downward punches of the left and right pole, using your arms much in the same way as when climbing a steep stairway with the aid of two banisters. The other method somewhat resembles rowing. Hold the poles behind you, swing both forward simultaneously, punch the spikes into the ground, and literally pull yourself through between the poles.

SUGGESTIONS FOR STUDY

1. Under what circumstances is skiing the simplest sport to learn?
2. What equipment is essential?
3. What is the first step in learning to ski?
4. What is the second step?
5. What are the two methods of hill climbing?
6. How does one brake his speed?
7. What methods of using poles are effective?
8. Having answered these questions, construct an outline of this article.

Types of Industrial Organization[1]

WILLARD L. THORP

THERE ARE a number of different ways in which business enterprises may be organized. The most important are: individual ownership, the partnership, the corporation, and the co-operative society. The businessman must operate through one or another of these forms of organization.

More establishments of the United States are operated by individuals than in any other way. The figures for 1919 for manufacturing concerns are as follows:

[1] From Willard L. Thorp, *Economic Institutions* (New York, 1930). Reprinted by permission of The Macmillan Company.

	Number of Establishments	Per Cent
Individuals	138,112	47.6
Corporations	91,517	31.5
All others	60,476	20.8
Total	290,105	100.0

These figures without further interpretation do not give an accurate picture. They must be supplemented by the following:

	Number of Employees	Per Cent
Individuals	623,469	4.0
Corporations	7,875,132	86.0
All others	597,771	10.0
Total	9,096,372	100.0

From these two tables it appears that although corporations number less than one third of the establishments, they employ more than six sevenths of the wage earners. Furthermore, they produce more than seven eights of the total value of all products. This situation is also found in the mining industries. But in agriculture, and, until recently, in retail trade, the corporate form of organization has made little headway.

Nearly one half of the manufacturing concerns in the country and the bulk of agricultural and mercantile enterprises are operated by individuals. These enterprises start usually without formality or legal permission. One person assumes all responsibility. In some cases, he may be required to obtain a license, as in restaurants, or pass examinations, as with doctors and lawyers.

In such a concern, control is concentrated in the hands of one person. This saves much red tape and routine, and is desirable where the business is one which cannot be systematized. The fact that the business rests on one individual, however, limits it in many respects. The most direct limitation is in the amount of money which a single person can borrow. It should be noted that, in case of failure, the individual is liable not only for the amount he has put into the business but to the extent of all his assets.

Individually-owned concerns are seldom long-lived. Beginning and ending their existence is an easy matter. Retail stores sometimes change hands several times in one year. The owner may sell out, the store may go bankrupt, or, more happily, it may grow into a corporation or partnership.

When one man finds that he cannot satisfy his business ambitions alone, one way out is to take one or more partners into his business. Each partner invests a certain sum, not necessarily equal in amount, and a contract is signed, which is legally binding. This definitely states the purposes of the organization and the rights and duties of the partners.

Although the exact nature of the partnership may vary according to the conditions of the contract, certain advantages are common to all. A partnership puts at the disposal of the business a larger amount of capital than any one partner could advance alone. Each partner is liable for the entire debt of the firm. If the firm runs heavily into debt, the creditors may collect all that is owed from any of the partners. Obviously, such a condition necessitates the greatest care in selecting partners, and prevents the formation of partnerships with many members.

Since each partnership is based upon a contract between several persons, it automatically ends when one member withdraws or dies. If the business is to continue, a new partnership must be formed. Partnerships are found chiefly in mercantile undertakings, small manufacturing concerns, and in the professions, especially the law.

In recent years, a new form of business organization has greatly overshadowed all others. Upon request of a prescribed number of individuals and the passing of certain formalities, a state government creates a corporation. This corporation is legally an individual, behaving in the eyes of the law as if it were a person. It may commit a crime, may be sued for damages, and the like. The capital, or money with which it begins business, is supplied by persons who receive shares, commonly called stock, in exchange for a sum invested. The possession of these shares gives them a proportion of the total ownership in accordance with the relative amount of stock each owns. The owners of shares elect directors who guide and operate the business. The policies of the corporation are determined by this board of directors. They presumably keep in close touch with the business, though generally engaging competent individuals to make and carry out decisions of minor importance.

The corporation differs vitally from the forms of business organization already discussed. In the first place, it is permanent. Its charter may run for a limited time but can usually be easily renewed. Ownership may be transferred from one person to another; even though all the original incorporators die, the corporation still lives. In the second place, the liability of each individual is limited. Quite different from the individual enterprise, or partnership, he may lose only what the share of stock has cost him. Beyond that he is not liable, no matter how much his corporation owes. One of the few exceptions to this rule is a national bank, in which each stockholder is liable for an additional sum equal to his original investment. In the third place, there is no limit to the amount of capital such a concern may obtain, if it can persuade persons to invest. It may issue stock and thereby gather capital from thousands of stockholders. This may all be done, however, without losing centralized control, vested in the directors.

The corporate form also has certain disadvantages. In the first place, it is difficult to fix responsibility. There are many persons partly responsible for anything that may be done. No one individual feels that concentrated responsibility which exists in the case of a single owner or a partner. In the second place, ownership is almost wholly separated from management. The firm is actually run by managers or engineers under salary. The owners are far away, many of them having no knowledge of the business, and little interest beyond the scale of dividend payments. In the eyes of the law, an act by the manager, such as entering an unlawful combination, is punished by fining the corporation. The distant stockholders bear the burden for acts, the responsibility for which is certainly far from theirs. In the third place, this "absentee ownership of capital" leaves the chief responsibility in the hands of a small group. There can be concentration of control in very few hands, despite widespread ownership. The corporation is operated in accordance with the mandates of the holders of a majority of the stock. The small stockholders, who may be many, have really no control. In the fourth place, any corporation is an impersonal organization. Loyalty or co-operation between employer and employed is difficult to stimulate. Perhaps the prejudice which so many persons feel against corporations is caused by their impersonality.

Incorporation may be used as a method whereby an energetic promoter can obtain money from individuals without pledging himself that they will receive any return. In many corporations the stockholder has no intelligent understanding of the real activity of the enterprise of which he is part owner. On the other hand, he feels no responsibility since no one thinks of identifying him as one of the owners of the U.S. Steel Corporation unless he has a very large block of the stock. At the beginning of 1925 the U.S. Steel Corporation had 96,285 stockholders, the Pennsylvania Railroad 145,174, and the American Telephone and Telegraph Company 345,133. These figures represent large increases over the prewar distribution of holdings. . . .

Co-operative societies are organizations formed by a group of producers or consumers for joint economic action. The most important types are societies for co-operative handling and marketing of products, societies for co-operative buying, and societies for co-operative credit.

The societies for co-operative handling and marketing of products are, in many cases, well known. In 1925 the United States Department of Agriculture reported that there were 10,803 such societies, grouped as follows:

Industries	Number of Societies
Grain	3,338
Dairy products	2,197
Livestock	1,770
Fruits and vegetables	1,237
Cotton and cotton products	121
Tobacco	24
All others	2,116
Total	10,803

The estimated membership of these organizations is 2,450,000 farmers. These organizations are engaged in providing elevators and storehouses, shipping, advertising, and the actual marketing of products. The farmer is generally far from market, unacquainted with market conditions, and unable to sell his product to his best advantage. By organizing co-operative societies, he is able to reduce the expense of selling his crop, as well as to do it more conveniently.

The United States Department of Agriculture reports 1,217 societies among farmers for co-operative purchasing. These include general purchasing associations, co-operative stores, lumber yards, fuel yards, and the like. Their purpose is two-fold: they save by purchasing in large quantities; and they avoid the necessity of paying a profit to middlemen. They must meet the costs of their enterprise, but they can keep the profits in their own pockets.

The co-operative credit societies most often take the form of building and loan associations. There were 10,000 such organizations in the United States in 1923, with a membership of nearly seven million persons. Their assets were $3,342,000,000.

The co-operative movement has not made so rapid an advance in this country as in Europe. The lack of experience among the members and their failure to select competent managers have hindered their expansion. Recent legislation has encouraged the formation of co-operative organizations, and the Department of Agriculture openly supports the movement.

SUGGESTIONS FOR STUDY

1. Of what rhetorical use is the enumeration, in the introduction, of the major points of the article?
2. What statistics indicate the strength of the corporations?
3. State the advantages and limitations of individual concerns.
4. State the differences between the individual concern and the partnership.
5. What major risk is involved in forming a partnership?
6. In what way does the law regard a corporation?
7. How are shares important in a corporate organization? Who determines the policies of the corporation?
8. State three major differences between the corporation and the two preceding types.
9. State four disadvantages of the corporation.
10. Define a co-operative society.
11. For what reader is this selection written?
12. Make an outline to show in diagrammatic form the analysis of this subject.
13. Define the following words from this selection: mercantile, prescribed, liability, vested, dividend, mandates, competent.

C. The Précis

At one time the précis was a very practical exercise demanded of European students, especially those in England; it was expected of these students that later in life, to save time for their superiors in public office, they would have to summarize accurately and well any long detailed documents that their superiors did not need to read in entirety. The values of such training, however, were so apparent that the précis has since become recognized as a form of writing which can profitably be practiced by most young people.

When writing a précis well, you are practicing several important skills. You are sifting fundamental ideas from lesser considerations and so practicing a very valuable part of good reading. You are further assisting yourself to become a good reader by reproducing ideas with exactitude and following the growth of an author's ideas. You are mastering a form which will aid you in taking lecture notes and notes on assigned reading. Furthermore, all the while you are sharpening your own powers of expression. The précis is a form well worth your closest attention.

In writing a précis, you are indeed making a summary, but more than that you are expressing in your own words the essential ideas of the original. To understand this form more thoroughly and to master it, practice the following steps. First, read the given selection to gain some idea of its organization. Then reread the selection with great care, marking on an extra sheet or even in the book itself what you consider the important ideas. Base your judgment on your knowledge of rhetorical principles. For instance, you have studied about the thesis and topic sentences—how these contain the major idea of the composition and the important subdividing ideas. These are, so to speak, the generalities of the composition which you must be sure to have in your précis. But supporting these are details and illustrations. Choose from the details the most important or summarize the meaning of several, and in general avoid reproducing an anecdote or other illustrative story. In the first illustrative example below, the details about the Emperor Alexander's court are summarized in the précis in one sentence for contrast with the important idea about Napoleon. In the second example, the topic idea about our vulgarity, contained in the opening and closing sentences of the paragraph, forms the basis for the précis, which omits the intervening details. Some passages, of course, will contain many important ideas; others will have few. Do not expect any given number of ideas per page. You may find, by the way, that reading some passages aloud will help you to understand them better.

Now begin to write the précis. Do not rearrange the order of the author's ideas, but follow his organization exactly. Do not copy his wording.

93. Translate his ideas into your own words, so that they have clear meaning for you.

Be very careful to transcribe these ideas accurately; add nothing of your own, and do not change any emphasis in the original. The usual practice also is to keep to the author's point of view; if he uses, for instance, the "I" point of view ("I lectured that day"), use "I" also in the précis. Preserve his tone—serious, comic, whimsical, ironic, or whatever it may be. In this way you keep both the tone and the idea of the selection. If you have

done a good précis, it will usually be about a quarter or third the length of the original, but there is no exact principle to guide you on this score.

Before you make the final draft of your précis, study the rough draft to make sure it is not only exact but rhetorically excellent. Paragraph it properly, improve the diction, grammar, or sentence structure wherever needed, and make sure that you have not wasted any words in your own sentences. Now make the final draft.

To assist you further in learning to write a précis, study the following three précis carefully.

1. *Original:* The Emperor Alexander and a Countess Wierbord, or some such name, have had a dressing match. They met, and by a signal left a common room. The Countess returned fresh-dressed in one minute and twenty-five seconds, the Emperor in one minute and fifty seconds. General Czernichef and Sophie Zichy had another match. Whilst these mummeries are performing, Napoleon puts his foot on the French shores and exclaims, *"Le Congrès est dissout."*—LORD BROUGHTON, *Recollections of a Long Life.* [71 words]

Précis: While the Emperor Alexander and his court are engaging in frivolous contests to see who can change clothing most quickly, Napoleon has landed in France and orders Congress dissolved. [29 words]

2. *Original:* But whatever we might do or leave undone, we were not genteel, and it was uncomfortable to be continually reminded that, though we should boast that we were the Great West till we were black in the face, it did not bring us an inch nearer to the world's West-End. That sacred enclosure of respectability was tabooed to us. The Holy Alliance did not inscribe us on its visiting-list. The Old World of wigs and orders and liveries would shop with us, but we must ring at the area-bell, and not venture to awaken the more august clamors of the knocker. Our manners, it must be granted, had none of those graces that stamp the caste of Vere de Vere, in whatever museum of British antiquities they may be hidden. In short, we were vulgar.—JAMES RUSSELL LOWELL, "On a Certain Condescension in Foreigners." [135 words]

Précis: No matter how much we boasted of

our greatness and resented our treatment, the aristocratic nations of Europe regarded us as tradesmen and sneered at our manners as vulgar. [29 words]

3. *Original:* The slaughter lasted three hours; when, at length, the survivors, as if impelled by a general impulse, rushed tumultuously from the place of carnage, and with dastardly precipitation fled across the Monongahela. The enemy did not pursue beyond the river, flocking back to the field to collect the plunder and gather a rich harvest of scalps. The routed troops pursued their flight until they met the rear division of the army under Colonel Dunbar; and even then their senseless terrors did not abate. Dunbar's soldiers caught the infection. Cannon, baggage, provisions and wagons were destroyed, and all fled together, eager to escape from the shadows of those awful woods, whose horrors haunted their imagination. They passed the defenceless settlements of the border and hurried on to Philadelphia, leaving the unhappy people to defend themselves as they might against the tomahawk and scalping-knife.—FRANCIS PARKMAN, *The Conspiracy of Pontiac.* [142 words]

Précis: After three hours of carnage the remnants fled across the Monongahela, unpursued by the plundering enemy; they threw panic into the rear division, and destroying their matériel in the terrifying woods, all hastened back to Philadelphia, leaving the frontier undefended. [40 words]

SELECTIONS FOR PRÉCIS WRITING

1. The period for a new election of a citizen to administer the executive government of the United States being not far distant, and the time actually arrived when your thoughts must be employed in designating the person who is to be clothed with that important trust, it appears to me proper, especially as it may conduce to a more distinct expression of the public voice, that I should now apprise you of the resolution I have formed to decline being considered among the number of those out of whom a choice is to be made.—GEORGE WASHINGTON, "Farewell Address." [95 words]

2. Since his death the popularity of his works —the "Lives of the Poets" and, perhaps, the "Vanity of Human Wishes," excepted—has greatly diminished. His *Dictionary* has been altered by editors till it can scarcely be called his. An allusion to his *Rambler* or his *Idler* is not readily comprehended in literary circles. The fame even of *Rasselas* has grown somewhat dim. But though the celebrity of the writings may have declined, the celebrity of the writer, strange to say, is as great as ever. Boswell's book has done for him more than the best of his own books could do. The memory of other authors is kept alive by their works. But the memory of Johnson keeps many of his works alive.—THOMAS MACAULAY, "Essay on Johnson." [123 words]

3. The proper force of words lies not in the words themselves but in their application. A word may be a fine-sounding word of an unusual length and very imposing from its learning and novelty, and yet in the connection in which it is introduced, may be quite pointless and irrelevant. It is not pomp or pretension, but the adaptation of the expression to the idea that clenches a writer's meaning:—as it is not the size or glossiness of the materials but their being fitted each to its place that gives strength to the arch; or as the pegs and nails are necessary to the support of the building as the larger timbers, and more so than the mere showy, unsubstantial ornaments. I hate anything which occupies more space than it is worth. I hate to see a load of band-boxes go along the street, and I hate to see a parcel of big words without anything in them.—WILLIAM HAZLITT, "On Familiar Style." [135 words]

Woodchuck Therapy[1]

ROBERT PEEL

AFTER A DAY spent in a steaming office—where the wallpaper should be asbestos—

[1] From *Nature Magazine*, XLII (August-September, 1949). Reprinted by permission of *Nature Magazine*.

and a forty-five-minute drive home through blatant traffic, a man is ready for either the laundry or a psychiatrist. If it were not for the woodchuck colony on the hillside of my farm, I might have ended up as a steady customer of the latter.

My car would deliver me, a soaked and weary mess, at the door about 5:30 every weekday evening. Supper was planned for seven, and I had to find an appetite for it, and a cooling-off process for myself. A change of clothes and a climb over the back fence, and I was well on my way to finding both.

Our farm straddles one of the high ridges that run north and south through the central New York dairy land. Scattered stands of maple and birch hang over the top of the ridge, and barley and corn fields flank the western side all of the way down to the house. On the eastern slope, the far side that first sees the morning sun, and also cools in the evening shadows, the woodchucks have colonized a twenty-acre pasture.

After I climb that back fence, I go through my wife's manicured truck patch. With each step on the soft, rich soil the fatigue of the day seems to drain away and be soaked up by the warm earth. Blaring automobile horns and broken air-conditioning systems are forgotten. One begins walking on tiptoes when the rows of sweet corn are reached.

On the other side of the head-high corn a pile of uprooted stumps and battered fence rails, ten feet high, is the private domain of the biggest woodchuck on the farm. His fur is hoary with age, but his senses are still razor sharp. He likes to climb to the topmost jutting fence rail and survey the scenery.

Will I be able to surprise him this time, perhaps catch him 'chuck-napping atop his perch? I inch forward to the last rows of corn and peer between the stalks. My approach has been noiseless, and maybe this time . . . but—z-i-i-i-p—there he goes!

Scuttling down from the rails, he ripples with fat. At the bottom of the heap, where his den entrance is located, he stops for an instant before disappearing—turns to glare at the cause of this disturbance. I feel as if I should apologize to him.

As I leave the cover and skirt a field of bearded barley, I note that the grade becomes steeper. Then I climb through another fence and am at the top of the ridge. On the other side of an elderberry thicket is the pasture with the woodchuck colony.

At this point I drop to my knees and crawl to the brow of the hill. From behind a thick clump of grass I raise my head. There, fifty feet downhill, is a pair of 'chucks in the middle of a clover patch. Farther downhill a fat rascal is stretched out on a rock, dozing in the last rays of the sun.

Crawling out a little farther, like a big measuring worm, I find a more comfortable spot. Over on the left, where several sumacs have ventured out from the wood's edge and have gotten themselves lost in the pasture, a woodchuck is standing at attention on his doorstep. On his hind legs, as erect and motionless as a West Point Cadet, he is making sure there are no enemies in sight. For almost five minutes he holds his pose; then, not having seen me, he drops to all fours and waddles to his feeding patch.

Resting my eyes for a minute, I admire the panoramic view from the ridge. On the far side of the valley the farms, with their neat quiltwork fields, look like those miniature scenes often set up under Christmas trees. To the north, clear as crystal in the evening air, lies pale-blue Oneida Lake. That water is twenty miles away, but it seems close enough for one to hear the rippling waves as the breeze ruffles them.

But look! Only ten feet away a woodchuck, up on his haunches, is staring right at me. He must have been feeding in the deep grass as he moved uphill. Now that he has seen me, he is a nervous mixture of fright and curiosity.

His eyes are beady with excitement, his stubby ears are twitching, and that moist little nose is doing its darnedest to try to figure me out; I do not move a muscle; maybe he will come closer.

Oh, oh! He finally added everything up and decided that I was not welcome. That shrill whistle he gave just before he turned pale and rocketed downhill will spread the alarm to every 'chuck within a quarter mile. All over the field they are scooting for their holes—the pair in the clover patch, the fat fellow on the rock, the cadet over by the sumacs. And there are two more I had not seen.

Well, the game is over for tonight, and I might as well stand up and head for home myself. But on the way back, near the elderberries, I have a stop to make. There is a woodchuck den here, and I have not seen its roly-poly occupant for almost a week. Just to see if he is still at home, I get down and, putting my face placed close to the hole, make a chirping noise.

The chirp is nothing like woodchuck talk —it sounds more like a strangling canary— but it does attract the ever-curious fellow. One can hear him scuffling toward the entrance; then he rounds the last turn and there he is. Blinking his eyes for a moment, he surveys my face, only a foot from his own. Finally he stamps his forefeet and, snorting with disgust, backs down the tunnel. Both curiosities have been satisfied.

Then I go down the hill to the house with a healthy appetite under my belt. A soothing closeness to Nature has stilled the triphammers in my head, and tomorrow is something to be anticipated, not feared.

Suppose that I had carried a rifle up to the ridge? In two or three nights of slaughter I could have eliminated the source of a summer's pleasure. But, my way, I learn something new every night; like the time I watched a 'chuck climbing a scrubby, wild cherry tree.

Here is the back fence by the truck patch, and I scamper over like a chipmunk. The therapeutic values of that woodchuck colony of mine are truly amazing.

SUGGESTIONS FOR STUDY

1. Make a topic outline of this selection so that you will be sure to have studied the organizational pattern.

2. Write the précis. As this selection is a narrative experience, you should be able to condense it considerably. Your précis probably should not exceed a fourth of the length of the original.

Nobel Prize Acceptance Speech

WILLIAM FAULKNER

I FEEL THAT this award was not made to me as a man but to my work—a life's work in the agony and sweat of the human spirit, not for glory and least of all for profit, but to create out of the materials of the human spirit something which did not exist before. So this award is only mine in trust. It will not be difficult to find a dedication for the money part of it commensurate with the purpose and significance of its origin. But I would like to do the same with the acclaim too, by using this moment as a pinnacle from which I might be listened to by the young men and women already dedicated to the same anguish and travail, among whom is

already that one who will some day stand here where I am standing.

Our tragedy today is a general and universal physical fear so long sustained by now that we can even bear it. There are no longer problems of the spirit. There is only the question: When will I be blown up? Because of this, the young man or woman writing today has forgotten the problems of the human heart in conflict with itself which alone can make good writing because only that is worth writing about, worth the agony and the sweat.

He must learn them again. He must teach himself that the basest of all things is to be afraid; and, teaching himself that, forget it forever, leaving no room in his workshop for anything but the old verities and truths of the heart, the old universal truths lacking which any story is ephemeral and doomed— love and honour and pity and pride and compassion and sacrifice. Until he does so, he labors under a curse. He writes not of love but of lust, of defeats in which nobody loses anything of value, of victories without hope and, worst of all, without pity or compassion. His griefs grieve on no universal bones, leaving no scars. He writes not of the heart but of the glands.

Until he relearns these things, he will write as though he stood among and watched the end of man. I decline to accept the end of man. It is easy enough to say that man is immortal simply because he will endure; that when the last ding-dong of doom has clanged and faded from the last worthless rock hanging tideless in the last red and dying evening, that even then there will still be one more sound: that of his puny inexhaustible voice, still talking. I refuse to accept this. I believe that man will not merely endure: he will prevail. He is immortal, not because he alone among creatures has an inexhaustible voice but because he has a soul, a spirit capable of compassion and sacrifice and endurance. The poet's, the writer's, duty is to write about these things. It is his privilege to help man endure by lifting his heart, by reminding him of the courage and honour and hope and pride and compassion and pity and sacrifice which have been the glory of his past. The poet's voice need not merely be the record of man, it can be one of the props, the pillars to help him endure and prevail.

SUGGESTIONS FOR STUDY

1. To whom is the author addressing his remarks?
2. What does he believe our modern tragedy to be?
3. What alone can make good writing? What must be the subjects for the writer?
4. What does the author believe concerning the immortality of man?
5. State the thesis.
6. Use your answers to these questions as guides for your précis. You will not be able to condense this article as much as you did the previous one.

Technology—Hope or Hobgoblin?[1]

HENRY B. du PONT

THERE HAVE BEEN times in the past when fears were expressed that widespread unemployment would result from technological advances. But today few are deluded by the myth that technology will make displaced persons of our industrial population. If the buggy whip and the livery stable have become extinct, they cannot be mourned by a society that employs 12,000,000 people to make and service the automobile. Today, after the most intensive technological pro-gram in history, we have the largest employment force in history.

Yet occasionally there have been those who actually called for a moratorium on research and invention. You will recall that such outcries were popular during the Thirties. But let us suppose that all research and development had somehow been halted arbitrarily at some given point in history. Without tractors and machinery and chemical fertilizers, our farms could not have supported our growing population and soon we would have stagnated into a nation of paupers and peasants like India or China, always at the edge of famine. With our food prob-

[1] This article forms one part of an address by Mr. Henry du Pont before the Association of Land-Grant Colleges and Universities, November 11, 1952, in Washington, D.C. Reprinted by permission of the author.

lem solved, people were able to turn their attention to other activities. It is estimated that fully half of the American working population now earns its living producing things unknown in 1902. And even since 1930 we have seen huge gains in employment opportunities—to indicate the fields that new technology has opened we need only to mention such things as air-conditioning, television, synthetic fibers, home freezers, and frozen foods.

It is quite true that technology creates problems. No one denies that. And obviously it creates change, like nothing else. It is the greatest revolutionary in history, for it has had a more profound effect upon social custom and social reform than any legislation or any code of law. Let me cite just one example:

A hundred years ago, the average American workman had a few simple hand tools, and for power he was limited to his own muscles, plus the help of domestic animals and water wheels. He worked from the time he was through with his elementary schooling until he died. Assuming that he survived for the Biblical three-score-years-and-ten, he probably spent a total of 56 years on the job, 72 hours a week, 52 weeks a year. Add this up, it comes to something like 180,500 hours of his life.

The average workman today, with modern machinery and equipment, probably works from the age of 19 to the age of 65, or 46 years. He works only 40 hours a week, and has at least two weeks' vacation. When you total this, you find he works over his productive life less than 90,000 hours—or about half of the time put in by the 1852 worker, and he performs his duties in greater ease, safety and comfort.

The reason, of course, is advancing technology. It has been estimated that every horsepower of mechanical or electrical or chemical energy put at his disposal multiplied his own efforts 22 times. He doesn't work shorter hours because some benevolent

law permits it. He works less hours only because with modern machinery he can outproduce his grandfather many times over.

There has also been a remarkable readjustment of the American workman's living pattern. Fifty years ago, the difference in living standards between the wage-roll man and the manager or owner of a plant was very great. They lived in different neighborhoods, wore different kinds of clothes, and had a widely different degree of comforts and diversions.

This picture has changed completely. There may be a difference in income between the workman and his boss, but the difference in their living patterns is small. Each drives to work in a comfortable, dependable automobile—the difference between them is only one of degree. One may drive a Chevrolet, one a Buick—both can and do travel well. Either may spend his vacation in Florida or in traveling through the Rockies. Their homes may differ in size; they differ little in comforts for the family —both have automatic heating units and modern equipment of all kinds in the laundry, the kitchen, and the bathroom. Their own clothing and that of their wives suffer little by comparison. Both see the same TV programs on the same kind of set, attend the same concerts, art galleries, and theaters. This is the only country in the world where this situation exists.

Technology is everybody's rich uncle. But the benefactions of this generous relative will continue only so long as he is alive and healthy; when he dies he takes it with him.

It seems to me if technology should be developed throughout the world to a point approaching our own, many of the causes of conflict between peoples would disappear. There is no doubt in my mind that if the Russian people, for example, knew the facts about what an applied technical program could do for them they would soon deal appropriately with the leaders who stand in the way. There is no doubt that technology could produce in most countries of the world a standard of living quite comparable to our own.

But it could be done, of course, only by adopting the same conditions that have kept our technology alive and progressive—the atmosphere of free development, the incentives that make it grow. By this, of course, I mean the incentives for the inventor to invent, the investor to invest, the manager to manage, the worker to work.

It seems to me that the colleges can perform a great service in helping to dispel the confusion that exists about technological development. Perhaps one way to do so is to widen the base of both the scientific and liberal arts curricula. I would not think it amiss, in this technical age, to require each of our students in the arts and social sciences to have some background of technical study as well—at least enough to understand our dependency on technical advances. I would

urge that this be as much a part of his educational equipment as for the engineer to have some background of literature and the humanities. To misjudge technology, the most significant force of the age, is to turn our backs on the future.

SUGGESTIONS FOR STUDY

1. What attitude toward technology does the author fear his audience may have? What parts of the article reflect his concern?
2. What effect has technology had on employment? on working conditions? on the workman's pattern of living?
3. What would greater technology mean internationally if other countries could approach our level?
4. What can colleges do to dispel the misunderstandings concerning technology?
5. State the thesis of the selection.
6. These questions should assist you in finding the key ideas in this article. Make sure that you have answered them all before you begin to write your précis.

Humor and America[1]

MAX EASTMAN

ONCE I CALLED on a famous psychologist in Europe, and in the course of a not too psychological conversation received some advice.

"I want you to go home," he said, "and write a book on America, and I will tell you what to call it. *Misgeburt*—what is that word in English? No, not *monster*. *Miscarriage*—that's it. The *Miscarriage of American Culture*—that shall be the title of your next book, and you will tell the truth about the whole awful catastrophe."

We laughed, somewhat unsymmetrically, at this jest and I asked:

"What makes you hate America so?"

"Hate it?" he said. "I don't hate America,

I regret it. I regret that Columbus ever made the mistake of discovering it!"

It happens that I am as a patriot rather slow to boil. I think of myself instinctively as a citizen of the world and have the habit of discussing the defects and merits of my native land—except for its plumbing conveniences, about which I brook no two opinions—in a mood of cool appraisal. Therefore this violence of idea, in a great authority on the manner in which violent ideas are formed, stimulated rather than incensed me. America *has* failed to shine in most branches of human culture which transcend the mood of the matter-of-fact. We are a hard-surfaced folk, or have been. Our serious culture is like one of those modernist plays enacted on a bare stage with no backdrop and no scenery

[1] From *Scribner's Magazine,* C (July, 1936), 9. Reprinted by permission of the author.

—and withal a sentimental play. We have used our brains well, but not our imaginations, not our emotional perceptions. We lack "depth"—whatever depth is—and we lack fineness.

I recognize all these facts and sense a validity in the viewpoint of the old-world critic. And yet as I left his study I settled back with a very comfortable feeling into being an American, and being part of the process of creating an American culture. My feeling was not only comfortable, but also a little gleeful, a little on the laughing side. It was as though I had said to the old man: "It is just as well you don't understand our system—wait till the homestretch and we'll show you."

The basic thing historically is that America was born late, and spent her youth with grown-up brothers and sisters. She is precocious—or she is "old-wise," to translate a better German term. I mean in so far as she is wise at all, and not like all other countries full of dead men and clods. Our earliest heroes—Franklin, Jefferson, Washington, Tom Paine—were disbelievers in the legends in which all other early heroes lived and breathed. They were heroes of the matter-of-fact, and of will and resolution based upon a knowledge of it. A lot of religious and cultural top hamper that came over with us on the ships, and then the long and pious effort of our second-rate geniuses to imitate it, has obscured this fact. Where other "national minds" were born in an atmosphere of imaginative belief, ours was born in an atmosphere of skeptical common sense. It was born with the industrial revolution and with modern science.

"Poets," said Benjamin Franklin, in a poem almost bad enough to prove it, "are the mere *wastepaper* of mankind."

This does not mean that we are standing still at a goal. It means that we are moving in a different direction. We started in fact and are moving toward imagination; other cultures have moved the other way. I have no assurance where we shall come out. It may be impossible to work this process backward. But if it is not, then those other more imaginative cultures will fade out and die. For facts *are* facts, and once they are known you cannot with inward dignity deny them. I think and hope that American poets will find a way to unleash the imagination, and cultivate subtleties of feeling, without losing that inestimably precious sense of hard fact which is instinctive with us and not a thing that we have slowly had to learn. Nothing could be more interesting than to try to do this. No national mission, or adventure, could be more exciting.

That is why I felt comfortable in returning to my own nest of Americanness, after agreeing with so much that the great man in Europe said. Why I felt like laughing is not so easy to tell. It may be that I was retreating into the fastnesses of our own cultural territory. I was running up the flag on our sole impregnable fortress. For America *has* unleashed imagination and cultivated feelings in the one realm where, held down by that harsh sense of fact, she instinctively could—the realm of humor. "You may laugh at our crudity and make jokes about Columbus, but we could make a better joke and laugh with more imagination." That is perhaps what I was saying to the old man. That is what I want to say here.

It is no accident that Mark Twain and Abraham Lincoln—both men in whom humor took the place of ideological anchorings—became and have remained in the world's eyes the representative Americans. Their headstrong sensibleness, their steadfast confrontation of fact, and their adjustment through humorous emotion to the predicament in which facts, steadfastly confronted, place the wishful heart of man, is the keynote of our culture if we have one.

There was hardly a bolder and lonelier thing a man could do in Lincoln's place than crash through military discipline with acts of human mercy. There, if anywhere, he needed the support of angels or ideas. "Well, I don't believe shooting will do him any good," he would say to the indignant military. Or: "I put it to you to decide for yourself; if God Almighty gives you a cowardly pair of legs, how can you help their running away with you?" And in this acceptance with a quizzical playful emotion of life's ultimate predicament, his mind would find rest, his will the requisite support. It is not a trivial or incidental thing to be as humorous as Lincoln was.

"I'm quite sure," said Mark Twain, "that . . . I have no race prejudices, and I think I have no color prejudices nor caste prejudices nor creed prejudices. Indeed, I know it. I can stand any society. All that I care to know is that a man is a human being—that is enough for me; he can't be any worse."

In that, it seems to me, you have the whole temper and equilibrium of Mark Twain's mind, the ruthless vision—out of those hawk's eyes—and the laughter. You cannot separate the two as solemn critics do, and arrive at something called "Mark Twain's philosophy." Facts are awful, but you can be honest if you laugh—that was his "philosophy."

I am not saying that these attitudes are final, but just the opposite, that they are the starting point of a distinctively American culture, and that nothing is final. In order to see them so, however, it is necessary to disregard most of what has been done by the historians, for they call American culture everything that developed on this continent. I can find roots running back, but I think American culture as a distinct entity began not so very early in the nineteenth century. And it has its natural beginning, just as all national cultures have, in a mythology—a mythology which has been described, rather unfortunately, as the "tall talk" of the western frontier. If you want to see how much more it is than that, you should read a few pages of Lowell Thomas's sapless collection of "Tall Stories," and compare it with a page of Constance Rourke's chapter on "The

Gamecock of the Wilderness" in her book about *American Humor*. I spare you the sample from Lowell Thomas, but here is a page from Constance Rourke's rich book. She is describing the legends which grew up around the historic figure of Davy Crockett.

The story of his life in one of the almanacs began by picturing him as a baby giant planted in a rock bed as soon as he was born and watered with wild buffalo's milk. Another declared that as a boy he tied together the tails of two buffaloes and carried home five tiger cubs in his cap. In another he wrung the tail off a comet, and announced that he could "travel so all lightnin' fast that I've been known to strike fire agin the wind." . . . On one of his adventures he was barred by an "Injun rock so 'tarnal high, so all flinty hard, that it will turn off a common streak of lightnin' and make it point downward and look as flat as a cow's tail." Once he escaped up Niagara Falls on an alligator. "The alligator walked up the great hill of water as slick as a wild cat up a white oak."

In the end he became a demigod, and spoke in his own person:

One January morning it was so all screwen cold that the forest trees were stiff and they couldn't shake, and the very daybreak froze fast as it was trying to dawn. The tinder box in my cabin would no more ketch fire than a sunk raft at the bottom of the sea. Well, seein' daylight war so far behind time I thought creation war in a fair way for freezen fast: so, thinks I, I must strike a little fire from my fingers, light my pipe, an' travel out a few leagues, and see about it. Then I brought my knuckles together like two thunderclouds, but the sparks froze up afore I could begin to collect 'em, so out I walked, whistlin' "Fire in the mountains!" as I went along in three double quick time. Well, arter I had walked about twenty miles up the Peak O'Day and Daybreak Hill I soon discovered what war the matter. The airth had actually friz fast on her axes, and couldn't turn round; the sun had got jammed between two cakes o' ice under the wheels, an' thar he had been shinin' an' workin' to get loose till he friz fast in his cold sweat. C-r-e-a-t-i-o-n! thought I, this ar the toughest sort of suspension, an' it mustn't be endured. Somethin' must be done, or human creation is done for. It war then so anteluvian an' premature cold that my upper and lower teeth an' tongue war all collapsed together as tight as a friz oyster; but I took a fresh twenty-pound bear off my back that I'd picked up on my road, and beat the animal agin the ice till the hot ile began to walk out on him at all sides. I then took an' held him over the airth's axes an' squeezed him till I'd thawed 'em loose, poured about a ton on't over the sun's face, give the airth's cog-wheel one kick backward till I got the sun loose— whistled "Push along, keep movin'!" an' in about fifteen seconds the airth gave a grunt, an' began movin'. The sun walked up beautiful, salutin' me with sich a wind o' gratitude that it made me sneeze. I lit my pipe by the blaze o' his top-knot, shouldered my bear, an' walked home, introducin' people to the fresh daylight with a piece of sunrise in my pocket.

Is it any wonder that this childlike and savage imaginative explosion, crashing in on the refined habits of English literary humor of the genteel tradition, gave rise to the idea that exaggeration is the sole thing at which Americans laugh? Expressing, as Miss Rourke says, "an exhilarated and possessive consciousness of a new earth and even of the wide universe," these legendary heroes found no room to exist in British drawing rooms of the Victorian era. They were indeed too big for that. But among their own companions— and the companions of Davy Crockett are Theseus and Hercules, Thor and Baldur— these American heroes are not distinguished by size but by humor. All mythical heroes have been exaggerations, but they have been serious ones. America came too late for that. Her demigods were born in laughter; they are consciously preposterous; they are cockalorum demigods. That is the natively American thing—not that her primitive humor is exaggerative, but that her primitive exaggerations were humorous.

I am not very strong in history—it is one of the things I have put off writing until I should have time to read up on it. But it seems to consist of riding some idea through a morass of facts that would bog you down and drown you if you were not mounted. And I should like to propose a brief history of American literature, of American imaginative culture, in which the idea would be that it is only about one hundred years of age, and is not to be regarded as a gradual deposit of calcium in the backbone and vision in the eyes of nice, white-handed New England teachers and preachers, mastering a graceful penmanship and learning to write almost as well as the English poets, but as a rough, laughing growth springing up out of the struggles of the pioneers, and having its background in a humorous mythology, in legendary heroes taken as a joke.

If imagination is what we failed of in our belated infancy, it is in this humorous mythology rather than our sober poets that we began vigorously to have it. And it is in the humorists, rather than the poets, that, up to recent times at least, this vigor of imagination flourished. This was what made them something of a sensation in the world. They did of course exaggerate. Imaginative humor runs out automatically into exaggeration. How could you play laughing havoc with the qualities of things, and not pile them up into quantities that also overwhelm the mind? The two things go together like size and shape—the inordinate quantity and the preposterous image. Ring Lardner said that "if the penalty for selling honest old beer to minors was a $100 fine why two to fourteen years in a meat grinder would be mild for a guy that sells white pop on the theory that it is a drink." As a modification of the penal code that is indeed extreme, but it is also—is it not—fantastic? And the fantasy, not the extremeness, is what makes Ring Lardner's hand unmistakable in the writing of it.

> At high noon the wind was blowing a 2 inch gale backwards and neither scow would move, so the starter postponed it till along came a breath of fresh air, which was a ¼ to 2″. Then away went the two sloops like a snail with paralysis.

> They were in Brock's inner office, the walls of which were adorned with autographed pictures of six or seven of the more celebrated musical comedy stars, and a too-perfect likeness of Brock's wife, whom he had evidently married in a dense fog.

She smiled and Rita noticed her teeth for the first time. Most of the visible ones were of gold, and the work had evidently been done by a dentist for whom three members of a foursome were waiting.

"Does she think," said Stu, "that just because she comes from the golden State she has to run around with a mouthful of nuggets?"

That is the way Ring Lardner exaggerates. And here is Mark Twain:

"Kings" and "kingdoms" were as thick in Britain as they had been in little Palestine in Joshua's time, when people had to sleep with their knees pulled up because they couldn't stretch out without a passport.

I own millions and millions of feet of affluent silver leads in Nevada—in fact the entire undercrust of that country nearly, and if Congress would move that State off my property so that I could get at it, I would be wealthy yet.

Twenty-four years ago, I was strangely handsome. . . . In San Francisco, in the rainy season I was often mistaken for fair weather.

Pa's got a few buck-shot in him, but he don't mind it 'cause he don't weigh much anyway.

You can find all the exaggerations you want in Baron Munchausen, but you cannot find a phrase to match those in any writer of English before Mark Twain. Even Lord Byron's wit was not lighted with these exploits of poetic humor. In Charles Dickens you could search all day for a phrase to print on the page with them. "Mark Twain can be quoted in single sentences," says Stephen Leacock, "Dickens mostly in pages." But all vigorously imaginative minds can be quoted in sentences—all of the tribe of Shakespeare. And American humorists, casual and unsustained as their flights are, belong to the tribe of Shakespeare. It is as though that revival of an Elizabethan gleam and range of vision which we call the romantic movement, and which occurred in poetry in England at the beginning of the nineteenth century, occurred a half century later in the United States and in humor instead of poetry.

Comic imagination, then, or what I prefer to call poetic humor, would stand not only at the beginning but close to the center of my briefer history of America's imaginative culture. Another feature of my history would be our humor troubadours. For America has not only a comic mythology; she has had her minstrelsy of laughter too, her jesting tramps or gleemen, who got about by making people smile instead of singing to them. Artemus Ward was the prince of this tribe, a travelling printer who could write "copy," and subsequently a platform entertainer. And he brought something from his Eastern home that was not to be found at all in that loud humor of the pioneers. It was not exactly what we call a "dry New England wit," and I am not sure but he got it out of his own bosom rather than out of some abstraction called New England. It was what underlies that dry wit in a laughter-loving rather than a caustic mind—a taste for pure absurdities. Artemus Ward liked to speak out before the public the kind of "foolishness" that is indulged at home. Phrases like "of the same similarness," or "Why is this thus? What is the cause of this thusness?" acquired a delicious drollness on his lips. He made people laugh by saying things that made absolutely no sense, or which there was absolutely no sense in saying.

I was born in the state of Maine of parents.

One of the peculiarities of my lecture is that it contains so many things that haven't anything to do with it.

He used to have with him when lecturing on the Mormons a panorama representing what he saw in Utah. In his picture the lion on Brigham Young's gate had a ridiculously elongated tail. He would point to it and say: "Yonder lion, you will observe has a tail. It will be continued a few evenings longer." It appears that his British audience could hardly hold their joy when he pointed to one of the Nevada mountains and said in a modestly informing tone: "The highest part of that mountain is the top."

It is of course impossible to revive the alluring plausibility which his presence could impart to such a statement, how he could make the whole mortal being of a listener move with breathless playful expectation to this simple fall. We merely know that it was true. When it came to making humor humorous—and it very often does—Artemus Ward seems to have had no equal among men. No man on the platform was ever more successful or more loved.

I think the unique quality of his humor can be conveyed, after a fashion, by saying that his jokes were almost always blunt. If they had a point, he would slur it in the utterance so that you could hardly catch the gleam. And frequently they had no point. And frequently they would seem to lose their point, or forget all about it, and go wandering off in search of some ludicrous situation or image.

> "Does this railroad company allow passengers to give it advice, if they do so in a respectful manner?"
> The conductor replied in gruff tones that he guessed so.
> "Well, it occurred to me that it would be well to detach the cowcatcher from the front of the engine and hitch it to the rear of the train, for you see we are not liable to overtake a cow, but what's to prevent a cow from strolling into this car and biting a passenger?"

Artemus Ward was not perhaps more gifted than other American humorists, but his gift was more unusual. He was, like Poe among our poets, a prodigy. And like Poe he was so recognized in Europe as well as in America. After his first London lecture in 1866, *Punch*, in an editorial ovation, advised "funny men on or off the stage to hear Artemus Ward 'speak his piece' at the Egyptian Hall, and then, in so far as in them lies, to go and do likewise.

"To be sure Artemus Ward's delivery of fun is 'un-English.' But there are a good many things English one would like to see un-Englished. Gagging, gross, overdone low comedy is one of them. Snobbishness is another. The two go hand in hand. One of the best of many good points of Artemus Ward's piece is that it is quite free from all trace of either of these English institutions."

Those who think that British humor is a very subtle fluid whose quiet stream has been disturbed by the coarse, loud guffaws of the Americans, may learn something from these lines. The fact is that Artemus Ward so surprised London with the possibility of a gentle grace and mental quietness in platform humor, that all English society was excited about it. Even the heavy-sitting queen was lifted by the general wave of enthusiasm.

"The most delightful fooling," she said, "that it has ever been our good fortune to hear. During his extraordinary prologue the audience fairly laughed till they could laugh no more, for the strange, quaint, quiet, gentlemanly humor of the lecturer was irresistible."

"Never was an American in London so beloved," said Moncure D. Conway, and Charles Reade nicknamed him "Artemus the delicious." "His jokes," said the *London Times*, "are of the true transatlantic type to which no nation beyond the limits of the States can offer any parallel."

It would be easy, with such a lead, to exaggerate Artemus Ward's Americanness. In his love for pure absurdity, he must take his place with Lewis Carroll as an event in world literature rather than an American event. Chesterton has said that the Victorians "discovered nonsense," and it is true that they were first in the pure love of it. But their nonsense derives some sense from the fact that it was designed for the entertainment of children. Their pointless jokes have always that point. That serious thought sustains many a true lady and gentleman in the indignity of enjoying them. It gives moreover a flavor of condescension, almost a baby-talk flavor, to some of their finest foolishness. Artemus Ward's delicious absurdities were for grown-up minds. He loved nonsense with a manly and mature love.

Unfortunately for the world, he died in the midst of those lectures in London, when he had barely become conscious of his powers. No literary monument exists to perpetuate his rare spirit. Only in the testimony of those who heard him, and in collected fragments—here too like the poetry of Edgar Allan Poe—is the original quality of his mind to be perceived. But almost as Poe stands at the source of a tendency toward "pure poetry," or poetry as an art and not a preachment, so Artemus Ward stands at the source of a tendency toward pure humor—toward the cultivation of absurdity so exquisitely that it is treasured without condescension for its own sake.

It is the blending of these two strains—the primitive vigor of imagination and the mature enjoyment of nonsense—that gives its distinct flavor to American humor. Both Mark Twain and Josh Billings were aware of this flavor, and tried to identify it by isolating the word "humor" for the purpose. Mark Twain said that the art of telling a "humorous," as opposed to a "comic," or a "witty" story, "was created in America and has remained at home." And Josh Billings apologized for the failings of this art by explaining that "Americans haven't had time yet to bile down their humor and git the wit out ov it."

Josh Billings was a crude character in comparison to Mark Twain—a "cracker-box philosopher," and on some subjects rather more of a cracker-box than a philosopher. But he possessed these two gifts, the comic vision and the liberated taste for foolishness, in a degree that enabled him to create a new artistic form. He would appear in our brief and reckless history as the father of imagism. For he was the first man in English literature to set down on his page, quite like a French painter reared in the tradition of art for art's sake, a series of tiny highly polished verbal pictures, and leave them there for what they might be worth.

The crane is neither flesh, beast, nor fowl, but a sad mixtur ov all theze things.
He mopes along the brinks of kreeks and wet places, looking for sumthing he haz lost.
He haz a long bill, long wings, long legs, and iz long all over.

When he flies thru the air, he is az graceful az a windmill broke loose from its fastenings.

The gote is a koarse wollen sheep.
They have a good appetite, and a sanguine digestion.
A maskuline gote will fite ennything, from an elephant down to his shadder on a ded wall.
They strike from their but-end, instead ov the shoulder, and are as liable to hit as a hammer is a nail-hed.
They kan klime ennything but a greast pole, and know the way up a rock, az natral az a woodbine. . . .

The Duk iz a kind ov short-legged hen.
They kan sale on the water as eazy as a grease spot.
Duks hav a broad bill which enables them tew eat their food without enny spoon.
Thare ain't any room on the outside of a duk for enny more feathers.
The duk don't kro like a rooster, but quacks like a duk.

There is little in New England poetry up to that date as graphic as some of this Poughkeepsie auctioneer's metaphors—nothing quite comparable to his statement that goats "know the way up a rock as natural as a woodbine," which is Homeric. Our history would make much of the originality of Josh Billings, and also of his crudity—for our whole history would be of something crude.

We should also devote a considerable and animated section to the great American art of laughing at oneself—that "humor of discomfiture written in the first person," which Leacock again says "absolutely distinguishes" Mark Twain from Dickens. It was not original with us, nor with anyone in history. But with us, I think, it first became a humorous convention. It first seemed the natural and appointed way to engage a reader in the joys of ridicule. One of the most interesting processes in cultural history, and most indisputable, has been the steady playing down of cruelty, and playing up of sympathy, in laughter. And this tendency of American humor stands at the height of that curious, and seemingly almost Christian, development. When you have taken upon your own person a defect or misfortune with which you propose to invite laughter, you are surely not inviting sneers. That is what Constance Rourke means, perhaps, by attributing to American humor as a whole a quality of "tenderness." A more complete and universal understanding of the mood of play would probably describe it better.

We hold ourselves up to laughter because we believe in laughter. We understand it, and know how to distinguish it from snarling and showing of teeth. We believe in being humorous. We believe in it more with our souls than most civilized folk. And this, if my hypothesis about our general culture is correct, is because we have had the energy and the abounding spirits of a young nation, and yet our childhood fell in a day of skepticism instead of animal faith. We have made more of humor because deprived in infancy of serious childish fancies.

Such in outline would be my chapter on humor as the origin and almost the central stem of America's distinctly own imaginative culture. It would go on to tell, of course, how this native tree of laughter, rooted in a humorous mythology, grew to its height in Mark Twain and his contemporaries, and then about the time of his death suddenly burgeoned out all over the sky and with a violent hilarity, and a certain thinning of the life sap, blossomed. We might call our chapter *The Root, Stem, and Petals of American Humor*. It would not agree with the prevailing opinion that this recent phenomenon, this still continuing shower of arrantly hilarious laughter, known variously as The Newer Nonsense, the Larger Lunacy, the Higher Goofyism—or "Humor Gone Nuts," as Donald Ogden Stewart calls it—is an essentially new departure. It is the natural bloom of the tree. It was all foretold and predestined in the riotous mythology of the pioneers and in Artemus Ward's consecration of absurd nonsense—two things which might almost exon-

erate Columbus for his little mistake, a natural one after all when sailing west for India, in discovering America.

That would not be the whole of our history. It would say much of Edgar Allan Poe, stifled in this cold climate of fact because he lacked the gift of laughter. And it would say more of Walt Whitman, so like Mark Twain in his passion for democracy and fact, and yet unlike him as another world because instead of humor he relied on mystical belief. And with these strands to weave, it would say something about the future—about what might be done by a mind, trained in fact and true to it, equipped as such a mind must be with humor, and yet not ill at ease in deeps of feeling and among fervent ventures of imagination, not ill at ease among revolutionary ideas, not condemned to make a final resting place of fact and laughter.

SUGGESTIONS FOR STUDY

1. How much of this article may be regarded as introductory? What rhetorical function is performed by that introduction? State the major idea contained in it.

2. In what does the author find consolation amid the jibes at America?

3. In what way are Mark Twain and Lincoln representative Americans?

4. What is the English conception of American humor?

5. State the three qualities of American humor which Eastman presents.

6. Characterize Artemus Ward.

7. What basis of classification does the author use in his main points? Is there any shift in his subpoints?

8. Define the reading group, the purposes, and the thesis of this article. Then make an outline of it.

9. Define the following words from the article: unsymmetrically, appraisal, incensed, impregnable, ideological, entity, morass, troubadours, caustic, elongated, plausibility, prologue, perpetuate, animated, burgeoned, exonerate.

10. Write a précis of the article. Make sure that you paragraph your précis carefully so that the organization of the original will be clear.

The Whole Composition

ʊʊʊʊʊ

II. THE FOUR FORMS OF WRITING

WHATEVER YOU WRITE may be loosely classified under one of the general forms of exposition, argumentation, description, or narration. In general, exposition informs or clarifies, argumentation persuades, description presents a picture, and narration tells a story. Of course, in one piece of writing these four forms are usually mixed. In exposition many passages may be descriptive or narrative, or in narration many passages may be expository. But in each piece of writing one form will be dominant. As a writer you must be perfectly clear as to your chief aim each time you compose.

A. Exposition

You will constantly be asked to define, explain, or interpret something: How is that made? What does the term mean? What are the facts of this matter? What are the aims of the organization? You make use of exposition in answering such questions.

Exposition, then, tries to give a reader a perfect understanding of some matter and does not seek to persuade or amuse, though by chance it may do both or either. Obviously you must have a perfect understanding of the matter before you can explain it to others, and obviously too you must keep to the stated purpose or you will violate the principle of unity.

DEFINITION

Definition tries to make essential terms clear to avoid misconceptions and so is one of the most important forms of exposition. Writing definitions should make you more aware of the exact meaning of words and help train you to make distinctions of meaning.

Some definitions can be made very simply and yet be completely clear. Verbs, adjectives, and adverbs, for example, can ordinarily be defined just by a synonym, as *to expedite* means *to hasten*. These definitions will cause little trouble if you are careful to define a word by another which is the same part of speech—an adjective by another adjective, an adverb by another adverb, and so on.

> *To frown* is *to scowl.*
> *Martial* means *warlike.*
> *Often* means *frequently.*

Other words, however, nouns in particular, cannot be defined so easily. These need more extended consideration.

Intensive Definition

You can best define the meaning of a noun by placing it in a certain classification and then distinguishing it from all the other terms in the same classification. To examine this procedure, consider first not the expository composition devoted to definition, but the intensive, logical definition of the kind found in the dictionary. This latter kind contains the essentials of any type of definition; it also offers the clearest illustration because of its limited scope.

Classification. By classification is meant

the inclusion of a term in the general group to which it belongs by its characteristics. To begin the definition of the word "barometer," you might classify it as an instrument. The first part of the definition would read: "The barometer is an instrument." In like fashion, a bicycle is classified as a vehicle, a manse as a residence, and filtration as a process. The reader is thereby given his first clue as to the meaning of the word. How ably he is assisted by the classification is perhaps best illustrated by the consideration of a word that may be unfamiliar to most people. What is a "nepman"? Does the word refer to a person or a thing? If it refers to a person as the suffix of the word would seem to indicate, what kind of person is meant? These questions are immediately answered by the classification. A nepman is "one who engages in private trade." The first limits are thus imposed upon the word.

Differentiation. Very obviously, however, the explanation is not completed by the classification of the word. To say merely that a barometer is an instrument is not to distinguish it from other instruments. The second part of the definition, that known as the differentiation, has as its purpose the explanation of how the term differs from all other terms in the same classification. *Webster's New International Dictionary* differentiates the barometer from all other instruments in this manner: a barometer is an instrument "for determining the pressure of the atmosphere and hence for judging of the probable changes of weather, for ascertaining the height of any ascent, etc." Thus the limitations of the word are clearly marked. A bicycle is "a light vehicle having two wheels one behind the other. It has a steering handle, and a saddle seat or seats, and is propelled by the feet acting upon treadles connected with cranks or levers." A manse is "the residence of an ecclesiastic." Filtration is the process of separating a fluid from the solids suspended in it by straining them out. A nepman is "one who engages in private trade as permitted by the Nep [the New

Economic Policy]. *Russia.*" The technique of definition, therefore, consists in making a classification and following it with a sharp differentiation.

Precautions. To employ this technique to advantage, *use clear, simple terms that will be understood by the reader.* Samuel Johnson's often-quoted definition of a network as "anything reticulated or decussated with interstices between the intersections" is of scant assistance to most readers. Even in the definition of the manse, as given above, the word "ecclesiastic" might occasion difficulty for some readers. A simplified explanation might substitute "a member of the clergy," or, more loosely, "a minister."

Second, *do not employ any derivative of the word being defined.* The statement that filtration is the process of filtering or that division is the process of dividing tells nothing.

Third, *do not make the definition too broad or too narrow.* It should never be so broad that it embraces more than the one word, and never so narrow that it fails to give a complete explanation. For example, if a revolver is defined as a portable firearm, the definition is too inclusive because rifles, shotguns, and other portable firearms could be contained in it equally well. On the other hand, if rhetoric is defined as the art of writing well, the definition is too narrow, for rhetoric also includes the art of speaking well. The explanation must, therefore, be of just the right scope. Of some assistance in securing such precision is a careful limitation of the classification. The definition of a revolver can be made through the use of the term "weapon" as the classifying word, but the definition is greatly simplified by the use of a more specific term, "firearm." This latter word includes weapons which discharge a shot by explosion and has in addition specific reference to small arms. Thus, the more the classification can be restricted without damaging the meaning, the more effective will be the explanation.

Fourth, *make a real classification.* The most common error in definition is the use of "is when" and "is where" in place of a classification: filtration is when a liquid is separated from the solids suspended in it; a nepman is where a Russian engages in private trade according to the regulations of the New Economic Policy. Obviously, filtration is not a "when," nor is a nepman a "where."

Extensive Definition

The extensive definition is simply a broader application of the technique of the intensive definition. As a grown plant is the expansion of the parts found in a seed, so is an extensive definition the amplification of the elements found in an intensive definition. The value of such amplification is that some definitions can be made more significant by fuller treatment. The explanations of the barometer, the bicycle, and the nepman, for example, seem to call for amplification. This can come through discussion of either the classification or the differentiation. The reader desires more knowledge of the differentiae of the barometer and the bicycle, but he might be curious about private trade in Russia and so demand more about the classification of the nepman.

Extensive definitions can be of two kinds. Some can be made absolutely comprehensive—the treatment of the barometer, for example—but others can never reach such perfection, and so make no pretense at completeness. No definition of abstract terms— such as romanticism or democracy—can be completely satisfying. Each reader has certain conceptions of the term which he would like to see added, and few readers would agree on certain inclusions.

The means of expansion for the extensive definition are those studied in connection with the development of the topic sentence of the paragraph: detail, illustration, comparison or contrast, division, elimination, and cause and effect. The definition of the revolver or bicycle would lend itself to development by detail, as the parts and operation of these would be enumerated. A more general term, however, such as patriotism, is more suitable for illustration; the writer can draw freely upon history or fiction for examples of patriotic deeds. Comparison or contrast is valuable to explain an unfamiliar term by linking it with a term known to the reader. Comparison aids particularly in establishing the classification; contrast aids in marking the differentiae. For example, if you were attempting to explain an automobile to a South Sea islander, the classification might be created by comparing the automobile to a vehicle of the islanders, some kind of cart. The differentiae could be shown by the contrast of the automobile and the cart.

Division is useful for developing a subject that can be reduced to its component parts. The best definition of narrative poetry, for example, would probably divide this subject into the metrical tale, popular and literary ballads, the metrical romance, the mock epic, the literary epic, and the heroic epic. Elimination is also useful, for it rules out of consideration those members of a classification group which are not meant. An explanation of the Elizabethan meaning of the word "humour" might begin by the elimination of the modern meaning of that term, or the definition of democracy could be made through the elimination of other forms of government, such as the monarchy, the aristocracy, the theocracy, and the communalistic society. Having established these limitations to the term democracy, you could then proceed to more positive assertions. Cause and effect, as used in relation to definition, is a statement of the origin and growth of the meaning of a word. To take a simple example, the word "familiar" assumes fresh meaning when it is seen in reference to the word from which it stems, the word *familiaris* meaning "belonging to the *familia* or household." In this way the meaning of certain words may be clarified and given added significance.

Definition then merits close study and further use by most writers. Every discussion involving a possible ambiguity of meaning should begin by a definition of terms. Otherwise reader and writer will not progress along the same paths. Moreover, definition is valuable for placing one on guard against inexactness of usage in the writing of others and in offering training in logical analysis.

SUGGESTIONS FOR STUDY

1. Define each of the following words by means of an intensive definition; underline the classification term of each word:

> haberdasher, orphan, pen, lake, bookplate, installment, inventory, Mocha, pun, saxophone, sauerkraut, coloratura, hydrogen, lagniappe, pier, plane, plaid, equilibrium, index, palanquin, corbel, bellows, saw, target, filigree, micrometer, metronome, aisle, blockhouse, phonograph, philology, unicorn, whirlpool, zombi, yard.

2. Ascertain the error in each of the following definitions, and then write a correct definition:

A memoir is a history or narrative.

A propitiator is one who propitiates.

Proximity is a close propinquity in time.

Pseudonymous is using a pseudonym.

Theism is a religious belief.

A sacristy is a room in a church.

Caliph is the title of the former spiritual rulers of Turkey.

A didapper is a dabchick.

An entr'acte is when one takes an intermission between two acts of a play.

A pastiche is a pasticcio.

3. Define one of the following words first by means of an intensive definition, and then by means of an extensive definition of a paragraph in length:

> sonnet, thermodynamics, thermometer, carburetor, hemstitch, innuendo, nebula, snaffle, mashie, lob, monarchy, lyric, transept, frieze, galley, carbine, diamond, element, paragraph, cathedral.

4. By means of a careful intensive definition, distinguish between the meanings of the words in any five of the following groups:

mansion, dwelling, cottage

pork, ham, bacon

mare, filly, colt

river, stream, creek

mountain, hill

ocean, sea, lake

tree, shrub

mist, vapor, cloud

sloop, dinghy, schooner

star, planet

book, volume

periscope, telescope, microscope

acquaintance, friend

mashie, brassie, putter

orchestra, band

hamlet, town, village, city

street, highway, boulevard

delusion, allusion

sarcasm, irony

earnings, winnings

arrogance, insolence, superciliousness, haughtiness

event, occurrence

pity, sympathy, compassion, commiseration, condolence

contemplation, anticipation

condonement, excuse, pardon

interrogation, question

discrimination, promiscuousness

litigation, jurisdiction

5. Write an extensive definition of one of the following words:

> romance, heroism, democracy, patriotism, citizenship, honor, virtue, folly, understanding, Nazism, Americanism, religion, atheism, agnosticism, criticism, home, charity, friendship, progress, culture, education, socialism, communism, literature.

Donjon[1]

THE STRONGEST PART of a strong castle of the European Middle Ages. It was usually a tower more or less completely separated from the other works and defenses, but always capable of prolonged defense after the rest of the castle had been mastered by the assailants. The earlier donjons were usually round towers, but in the fourteenth century and later they were often square or of irregular outline. Originally, the apartments of the lord of the castle and his family were in the donjon, but this ceased when the desire became manifest for much more spacious and comfortable rooms, and when, at the same time, the entire circuit of the walls became an organized whole, capable of defense, every part in harmony with and assisting every other. From both these causes, the peculiar importance of the donjon disappears as early as 1350, although there still remains an exceptionally strong tower or group of towers which can be called by that name.

SUGGESTIONS FOR STUDY

1. State the intensive definition. Distinguish the classification and the differentiation.
2. Trace the changes in meaning of the word *donjon*. Why is such a word history often necessary in definition?

Bathtub[1]

W. P. GERHARD

A RECEPTACLE OF sufficient size and of proper shape to enable a person to immerse the body in water, for washing and bathing purposes, and, in modern buildings, a stationary plumbing fixture, generally provided with waste and overflow pipes, hot and cold water supply pipes, plug and chain or waste valve, and single or combination bibbs. . . . The fixture is either set on the floor, or raised from it on legs, or sunk into the floor.

Examples of fine monolithic Roman bathtubs cut out of large blocks of granite or marble are on exhibition in some of the museums of Europe. Similar marble baths of great splendor were constructed for the French kings. It was usual to place in the tub a linen sheet, as the sides were cold, and this custom has remained in France up to the present day. Marble tubs being costly and cold, bathing tubs were subsequently made of wood and of sheet metal. Some curious varieties, like the "sofa" baths . . . were designed by the French furniture makers of the past centuries. A "mechanical" bathtub, the invention of a certain French count, is mentioned, in which the water was constantly kept in motion to imitate the effect of a river or surf bath. A similar device, called a *"Wellen"* or *"Schaukel-bad"* has attained some popularity in Germany at the present day. Another curious out-of-date form of bathtub, the so-called "slipper bath," consisted of a tub in the shape of a shoe, and partly covered, in which the bather sat erect with his feet in the toe of the slipper. The object of the covering was to prevent the spilling of water, to protect the bather, and to enable a person to take a long soaking bath, as required by some medical practitioners. In some of the towns of Provence in the south of France slipper baths may be found at this day. In England, the

[1] From Russell Sturgis, *et al., Dictionary of Architecture and Building* (New York, 1901). Reprinted by permission of The Macmillan Company.

modern tub baths are sometimes designated as "slipper baths." . . . The modern bathtub, as used in private houses, is manufactured of wood lined with zinc or with copper; of heavy copper; of cast iron or sheet iron, painted, galvanized, or enameled; or porcelain or stoneware, and, quite recently, of glass. In the older patterns the long sides are tapering in plan and also from the top toward the bottom; all recent tubs have parallel sides which make the tub more roomy. The head end of the tub is semicircular in plan and commonly sloped; sometimes both ends are sloped and built symmetrical. The length of tubs varies from 4 feet to 6 feet 6 inches; the width varies from 22 inches to 32 inches; according to the inside depth the bath is called either a shallow or a deep tub.

Special forms of tubs, for bathing only parts of the body, are the sitz bath . . . , the foot bath, the bidet, and the cleansing tubs arranged in modern swimming baths for bathers to take a thorough ablution with soap and warm water before they are permitted to enter the swimming pool.

SUGGESTIONS FOR STUDY

1. State the intensive definition of a bathtub. Distinguish the classification and the differentiation. Name several other items from which the bathtub is differentiated.
2. List several different types of bathtubs. Why was it necessary for the author to discuss these in his definition?
3. Make a topic outline of this definition.
4. Define the following words from this selection: immerse, bibbs, monolithic, practitioners, galvanized, ablution.

Radicalism and Conservatism[1]

ARTHUR M. SCHLESINGER

WHAT DO THE terms "conservative" and "radical" mean? Popular usage has tended to rob these expressions of exact meaning and to convert them into epithets of opprobrium and adulation which are used as the bias or interest of the person may dictate. The conservative, having mapped out the confines of truth to his own satisfaction, judges the depravity and errors of the radical by the extent of his departure from the boundaries thus established. Likewise the radical, from his vantage-point of truth, measures the knavery and infirmities of his opponents by the distance they have yet to travel to reach his goal. Neither conservative nor radical regards the other with juidicial calm or "sweet reasonableness." Neither is willing to admit that the other has a useful function to perform in the progress of society. Each regards the other with deep feeling as the enemy of

everything that is fundamentally good in government and society.

In seeking a workable definition of these terms, the philosophic insight of Thomas Jefferson is a beacon light to the inquirer. When Jefferson withdrew from active political life at the close of his presidency in 1809, he left behind him the heat and smoke of partisan strife and retired to a contemplative life on his Virginia estate, where his fellow-countrymen learned to revere him as the "Sage of Monticello." The voluminous correspondence of these twilight years of his life is full of instruction for the student of history and politics. His tremendous curiosity caused him to find an unfailing source of speculation in the proclivity of mankind to separate into contrasting schools of opinion. In one luminous passage, representative of the bent of his thought, he declared: "Men, according to their constitutions, and the circumstances in which they are placed, differ honestly in opinion. Some are Whigs, Liberals, Demo-

[1] From A. M. Schlesinger, *New Viewpoints in American History* (New York, 1922). Reprinted by permission of The Macmillan Company.

crats, call them what you please. Others are Tories, Serviles, Aristocrats, etc. The latter fear the people, and wish to transfer all power to the higher classes of society; the former consider the people as the safest depository of power in the last resort; they cherish them, therefore, and wish to leave in them all the powers to the exercise of which they are competent."

In this passage Jefferson does not use the expressions "conservative" and "radical"—indeed, those words had no place in the American political vocabulary until Civil War times—but his penetrating analysis throws a flood of light on the significance of those terms nevertheless. The Tory who fears the people and the Whig who trusts them are equivalent to our own categories of "conservative" and "radical." Thus Jefferson finds the vital distinction between the two schools of opinion in their respective attitudes toward popular government.

But before accepting Jefferson's classification as correct, what shall we do with the common notion that the conservative is a person who opposes change and that the earmark of the radical is his liking for innovation? This does not seem to be a fundamental distinction. If a difference of opinion concerning the need of change were the basic difference between the two, then Americans who advocate a limitation of the suffrage to male property-owners may properly be regarded as radicals, for they advocate an alteration in the established order; and French patriots of today opposing the reestablishment of the Orleanist monarchy are to be classed as conservatives, for they would keep things unchanged. Few people would be willing to follow the logic of their premises to such conclusions. On the other hand, it cannot be denied that history has generally shown the radical in the role of an active proponent of change and has cast the conservative for the part of the stalwart defender of things as they are. Is such evidence to be dis-

missed as a coincidence oft-repeated, or has there been behind the actions of both radical and conservative some self-interested purpose which has determined their respective attitudes toward the established order?

The very question perhaps suggests the answer. Broadly speaking, all history has been an intermittent contest on the part of the more numerous section of society to wrest power and privilege from the minority which had hitherto possessed it. The group which at any period favored broader popular rights and liberties was therefore likely to find itself as a contender for the new and untried, leaving to its antagonists the comfortable repute of being the conservators of the *status quo* and the foes of change. But, though the historical conditions influenced the character of the contest, such conditions were, after all, merely the stage setting of the struggle. Advocacy of change should, under such circumstances, be regarded merely as the means employed to attain an end and, in no sense, as an end in itself. Recurring now to Jefferson's definition, the goal sought by each group—whether it be in the direction of greater or less democracy—would appear to constitute the real difference between the two.

SUGGESTIONS FOR STUDY

1. In what light do conservatives and radicals commonly regard each other?
2. State Jefferson's distinction between the Whigs and the Tories.
3. Does the term "conservative" find an adequate counterpart in Jefferson's term "Tory"?
4. Is it advisable to base the distinction between the conservative and the radical just on their opposition to or liking for change?
5. Using your own words, frame an intensive definition of each of the two terms "conservative" and "radical."
6. Define the following words used in the article: opprobrium, adulation, depravity, knavery, infirmities, partisan, proclivity, luminous, depository, innovation, suffrage, intermittent, advocacy.

A Gentleman

JOHN HENRY NEWMAN

IT IS ALMOST a definition of a gentleman to say he is one who never inflicts pain. This description is both refined and, as far as it goes, accurate. He is mainly occupied in merely removing the obstacles which hinder the free and unembarrassed action of those about him; and he concurs with their movements rather than takes the initiative himself. His benefits may be considered as parallel to what are called comforts or conveniences in arrangements of a personal nature: like an easy chair or a good fire, which do their part in dispelling cold and fatigue, though nature provides both means of rest and animal heat without them. The true gentleman in like manner carefully avoids whatever may cause a jar or a jolt in the minds of those with whom he is cast—all clashing of opinion, or collision of feeling, all restraint, or suspicion, or gloom, or resentment; his great concern being to make every one at their ease and at home. He has his eyes on all his company; he is tender towards the bashful, gentle towards the distant, and merciful towards the absurd; he can recollect to whom he is speaking; he guards against unseasonable allusions, or topics which may irritate; he is seldom prominent in conversation, and never wearisome. He makes light of favors while he does them, and seems to be receiving when he is conferring. He never speaks of himself except when compelled, never defends himself by a mere retort, he has no ears for slander or gossip, is scrupulous in imputing motives to those who interfere with him, and interprets everything for the best. He is never mean or little in his disputes, never takes unfair advantage, never mistakes personalities or sharp sayings for arguments, or insinuates evil which he dare not say out. From a long-sighted prudence, he observes the maxim of the ancient sage, that we should ever conduct ourselves towards our enemy as if he were one day to be our friend. He has too much good sense to be affronted at insults, he is too well employed to remember injuries, and too indolent to bear malice. He is patient, forbearing, and resigned, on philosophical principles; he submits to pain, because it is inevitable, to bereavement, because it is irreparable, and to death, because it is his destiny. If he engages in controversy of any kind, his disciplined intellect preserves him from the blundering discourtesy of better, perhaps, but less educated minds; who like blunt weapons, tear and hack instead of cutting clean, who mistake the point in argument, waste their strength on trifles, misconceive their adversary, and leave the question more involved than they find it. He may be right or wrong in his opinion, but he is too clear-headed to be unjust; he is as simple as he is forcible, and as brief as he is decisive. Nowhere shall we find greater candor, consideration, indulgence: he throws himself into the minds of his opponents, he accounts for their mistakes. He knows the weakness of human reason as well as its strength, its province and its limits. If he be an unbeliever, he will be too profound and large-minded to ridicule religion or to act against it; he is too wise to be a dogmatist or fanatic in his infidelity. He respects piety and devotion; he even supports institutions as venerable, beautiful, or useful, to which he does not assent; he honors the ministers of religion, and it contents him to decline its mysteries without assailing or denouncing them. He is a friend of religious toleration, and that, not only because his philosophy has taught him to look on all forms of faith with an impartial eye, but also from the gentleness and effeminacy of feeling, which is the attendant on civilization.

Not that he may not hold a religion too, in his own way, even when he is not a Christian. In that case his religion is one of imagination and sentiment; it is the embodiment of those ideas of the sublime, majestic, and beautiful, without which there can be no large philosophy. Sometimes he acknowledges the being of God, sometimes he invests an unknown principle or quality with the attributes of perfection. And this deduction of his reason, or creation of his fancy, he makes the occasion of such excellent thoughts, and the starting point of so varied and systematic a teaching, that he even seems like a disciple of Christianity itself. From the very accuracy and steadiness of his logical powers, he is able to see what sentiments are consistent in those who hold any religious doctrine at all, and he appears to others to feel and to hold a whole circle of theological truths, which exist in his mind no otherwise than as a number of deductions.

Such are some of the lineaments of the ethical character, which the cultivated intellect will form, apart from religious principle. They are seen within the pale of the Church and without it, in holy men, and in profligate; they form the *beau idéal* of the world; they partly assist and partly distort the development of the Catholic. They may subserve the education of a St. Francis de Sales or a Cardinal Pope; they may be the limits of the contemplation of a Shaftesbury or a Gibbon. Basil and Julian were fellow students at the schools of Athens; and one became the Saint and Doctor of the Church, the other her scoffing and relentless foe.—*Idea of a University*, Discourse 8.

SUGGESTIONS FOR STUDY

1. State five or six general propositions to embrace the attributes of the gentleman, as given in the first paragraph.
2. What is the classification term in the essay, and from whom is the gentleman being differentiated?
3. Give an intensive definition of a gentleman, as defined in this article.

4. Define the following words from the article: concur, unseasonable, scrupulous, insinuate, affronted, bereavement, irreparable, misconceive, lineaments, pale, profligate, subserve.

THE PROCESS

The expository form known as *the process* is devoted to explaining how to make or do something. Processes are very frequently written, for such manuals as cookbooks, textbooks on rhetoric or engineering or accounting, pamphlets on the care of automobiles or refrigerators or typewriters, are all processes.

General Principles

Be simple and clear. That is the cardinal principle for writing a process. Such advice demands, of course, that you keep the reader constantly in mind, for if he is immature or has little technical knowledge, the explanation must proceed slowly and employ elementary terminology, but if he is more advanced, then the process may move forward swiftly. Nevertheless, it is perhaps better to err on the side of being too simple than of being too advanced. It is also well to define at the outset any terms likely to occasion difficulty, and to hold technical terminology to a minimum. Of course, technical terminology is often required by the subject matter, but if you wish to be understood, use popular phraseology wherever you can.

A good process also never takes too much for granted. If you possess a thorough command of a subject, you often assume that certain essentials of that subject are common knowledge and hence fail to mention or explain them, much to the reader's bewilderment. If an explanation of how to play football failed to mention the system of four downs, the reader would lack so vital a piece of information that his comprehension of the game would be slow indeed. And, of course, one of the stock complaints of students against their teachers is that the subject matter is presented so rapidly or with so little consideration of the actual knowledge possessed by students that learning is difficult. One of the qualities of a good teacher is an understanding of the problems of the beginner; the same might be said of the writer of the process.

Specific Considerations

Generally speaking, there are two kinds of processes—simple and complex. The simple process is an elementary explanation such as directing a stranger to a particular city street, explaining how to make a dish of junket, how to milk a cow, or how to buy a savings bond. The method used in the explanation is chronological; that is, the process is followed step by step from the beginning as if one were actually performing it. If the process requires the use of several pieces of equipment or ingredients, as in a laboratory experiment or a cooking recipe, these had better be listed before the chronological relation is begun. Also, in your zeal to tell the reader what to do, do not forget to tell him how to do it. In an explanation of how to drive a car, it is not enough to tell a novice to shift gears from low to high after the car is started; he must be told how to perform that act. The simple process is then but a matter of arranging all the necessary steps carefully in chronological order before the account is begun, and thereafter presenting these with constant attention to how each step is managed.

The second type of process is complex, involving the explanation of a complicated procedure: how to repair a typewriter, how to clean a watch, how to build a radio. Obviously you must exercise more skill here than in the simple process. The best advice is to proceed from the general to the particular. That is, at the beginning of the account, give the reader a general view of what he is to do, its purpose, the materials employed, the relationship of these materials in the process, and any points of special difficulty in the performance. To realize the value of such a procedure, think of such an example as that of the French soldiers during the first World War, who were praised for the intelligent manner in which they carried out assignments; part of their success undoubtedly lay in the procedure of their superiors who considered them not as automatons but as human beings, and accordingly outlined to them the general plan of each battle. In seeing how their individual assignments fitted into the general action, the soldiers were able to perform them more successfully.

Thus a reader needs to be oriented somewhat before he is plunged into a mass of details. Suppose that you are explaining how to print handbills or the like, a process which is relatively simple for an experienced printer but difficult for a beginner. Assuming that a novice has access to suitable equipment, you might begin by identifying several of the materials for him, such as the type and its frame, the composing stick, the galley, and so on, with a brief word as to their relationship in the process. To discuss the details, which would come next, divide the subject into convenient units. A first unit of this subject might be on the different kinds of type, their identification by the point system and perhaps the differences between them as they appear on the printed page. The following unit might be on the method of composition, with explanation of such topics as the arrangement of type cases, the use of the composing stick, the problem of making the lines fall evenly on the margins, and the transference of the type to the galley. A final section could explain how to lock up the galleys for printing. In this way, a complex subject can be reduced to its parts and so made intelligible to the learner. The steps in the explanation are, therefore, a brief, general description of the process, a statement of the equipment needed, and a division of the subject into logical units for detailed presentation.

You will undoubtedly find it advisable to avoid trying the complex process until you have mastered the technique of the simple process. Then address your article to a reader who has little or no knowledge of the subject. In making the explanation clear to him, do not be afraid to use diagrams or charts, for they will give him a pictorial representation and avoid many complicated descriptions. As a final word, do not be too dull. A touch of humor or of human interest will do much toward making the process both instructive and appealing.

SUGGESTIONS FOR STUDY

Write a process explaining how to do one of the following:

Drive a car
Operate a bookstore (or other store)
Write a composition
Play golf (or other game)
Build a bookcase (or other article of furniture)
Change a tire
Make a dress
Play jazz
Write an advertisement
Plant a garden
Make pottery
Tie knots
Sail a boat
Watch a football game
Conduct a track meet
Operate a machine (of any type)
Get a job
Typewrite
Paint a picture
Model a statue
Give a party
Knit
Engrave
Take photographs
Read a newspaper
Break in a horse
Cure a cold
Teach an animal tricks
Serve a meal
Sell a car (or other product)
Write a song lyric
Play a musical instrument
Form a band
Decorate a room
Study
Build an outdoor fireplace
Make camp for the night
Build a fire
Make a telescope
Drill a well
Lay a concrete walk
Pledge a freshman to a fraternity
Choose an apartment
Solder
Perform a laboratory experiment
Paint a house
Climb a mountain
Ride a horse
Give first aid to someone

How to Write a Book[1]

HAROLD NICOLSON

IN SLOANE SQUARE the other day I met a friend who had just been demobilized. I asked him what he meant to do now. "Well," he answered, "as a matter of fact, I was thinking of writing a book. Tell me, since you know about these things, how does one write a book?"

I gazed across that ungainly Square towards the bright façade of Peter Jones. "Many years ago," I said, a trifle sententiously perhaps, "I asked Somerset Maugham how one wrote a play. He gave me excellent advice."

"And what was that advice?" my friend asked me.

"He said, 'Well, you get an idea; and then you write a p-p-p-play about it.'"

"Yes, I see," my friend murmured, and thereat we went our different ways across pavements glistening in September rain.

[1] From the *Atlantic Monthly*, CLXXVII (January, 1946), 111. Reprinted by permission of the author and the *Atlantic Monthly*.

I realized, as I walked, that I had not been helpful. I realized that having written books myself, I should have asked the man to luncheon and explained at length to him how the thing is done. I realized that on that afternoon of all afternoons I should have been in a mood of philanthropic helpfulness, since on that very morning I had typed the last words of the final chapter of a book on which I had been engaged for two years. I should have been filled with a mood of achievement and lassitude, of melancholy and delight, such as assailed Gibbon on the night of June 27, 1787, when he paced his acacia walk having just blotted the last words of the *Decline and Fall*.

I should have been more communicative and less selfish. I should have told him that the first essential is to know what one wishes to say; that the second essential is to decide to whom one wishes to say it. Once one has chosen the theme and selected the audience, then the book more or less should write itself. But would that have been helpful to a young officer recently demobilized? And how, after all, does one really write a book?

I am not thinking, of course, about creative writing. I am well aware that the poets and the novelists do not, as Aristotle observed, "create what they create by taking thought; but owing rather to natural temperament and in a mood of ecstasy." I am thinking rather of those who, being gifted with average industry and certain powers of narrative, wish to record in written form either their own experiences or the experiences of others.

The creative writers stand in a class apart. They possess a special gift, such as that which enables a painter to paint or a pianist to play; they are driven by some inner daemon who afflicts them with strange spasms of intuition interspersed with long blanks of discouragement. Their days and nights are disturbed by the conflict between their sense of power and their consciousness of powerlessness; they "learn in suffering what they teach in song."

The ordinary writer, the man who "thinks of writing a book," lives in a more equable climate, and remains unaffected by the typhoons and the doldrums of genius; he can, with ordinary skill and attention, navigate his little ship through quiet seas. If he has a good story to tell, whether it be firsthand or secondhand, his task is almost mechanical. It is as if he were building a house. He must start with some idea of the size and proportion of the house he wants to build; he must have some conception of the relation between surfaces and decoration; he must remain constantly aware of the purposes for which the house is intended; and thereafter he must assemble his material in the right order and fit it neatly and efficiently into place.

If he starts with the intention of building a bungalow and then determines that he will turn it into a hotel, the resultant effect is likely to be confused. If he begins in lath and plaster and later decides to try a little brick-

work, the ultimate impression will not be orderly. Yet with ordinary sense and prevision he should be able to avoid such discrepancies. And there are, I suppose, certain suggestions which one can make to him which may save undue wastage of energy and time.

The man who sets out to "write a book" about his own experiences may imagine that the problem of proportion, the actual plan, will be determined by the chronological sequence. This is an incorrect assumption. Only those who possess an acute sense of audience realize that those passages of time which interest them personally are not necessarily the passages which will interest their readers.

Most adults, for instance, have a nostalgic affection for their own childhood which is rarely communicable to those whose associations have been different. Many autobiographical writers tend to dwell lovingly and at length on passages of time which for them are illumined by an experience which they are too reticent to relate; their readers, being ignorant of the significant event, fail to be warmed by the required glow of reminiscence.

It often occurs, moreover, that a man who is recounting his own adventures is unduly interested in the mood of anticipation which surrounded him before the adventures began; he will thus tend to devote disproportionate space to his prelude, to "the journey out," without realizing that the reader is becoming impatient. The purely chronological method, moreover, unless it is firmly controlled, is apt too accurately to reflect the intermittences of actual life.

It is seldom that adventure moves in a continuous curve from prelude, through climax, to solution; there is liable to occur a suspension or, what is worse, a repetition of climax. That in itself may prove an interesting theme; but it requires skill and management on the part of the writer to convince the reader that these gaps and repetitions are due to competence rather than to incompetence.

The man who writes the narrative of his own experiences should thus realize that time is measured, not by the amount of seconds it absorbs, but by the intensity of experience it contains; and that unless he can communicate to his readers an intensity of experience similar to his own, he will find that the chronological method complicates his proportions, instead of simplifying them.

On the other hand, the man who writes the story of other men's experiences (the man, that is, who writes biography or history) is less exposed to such subjective dislocations; for him the time-sequence does in fact constitute a useful blueprint. His task is to arrange and to interpret a vast mass of material in such a manner as to provide a true and lucid narrative; and as such his difficulty is almost wholly one of preparation and arrangement. The beginner who decides to write a history or a biography should realize that his main difficulty will not be the actual writing of the narrative but the previous absorption and arrangement of his material.

I recommend, for what it is worth, the following procedure. The intending biographer or historian should first purchase a very large and, if possible, loose-leaved notebook. He should then acquire the most detailed standard work upon his subject. He should then devote much time and trouble to summarizing in his notebook the facts and comments contained in the standard work. If he does this carefully, legibly, and methodically, if he above all leaves himself a large amount of space for subsequent additions, he will then after much toil have before him the main outlines of the narrative to which he wishes to give his personal interpretation.

Thereafter he will read all available works or documents bearing on his subject, and will insert in his notebook all the additional material he acquires. He must have the energy and the patience to write out these references in full, so that in the end his notebook contains, correctly arranged, far more material than he can possibly use. He can then discard all works of reference and use his notebook as the sole quarry from which to build his house.

Had I said all this to my demobilized friend in Sloane Square should I have encouraged or discouraged him? There are other things I might have said. I might have warned him of the dark days when his book would grow stale to him as the sound of his own voice. I might have warned him that there would come moments when his material, however carefully arranged, would become disorganized and flap round him in confusion like a colony of rooks. I might have warned him that there would come a time when he would hate his characters and his narrative with a wearied loathing. And I could have told him that the morning would come when he would write the last word of the last chapter and walk elatedly thereafter upon pavements glistening in September rain.

SUGGESTIONS FOR STUDY

1. How much of this article can properly be called introduction? Why is such an introduction a necessary part of the presentation?

2. To what reader are these remarks addressed? What kind of book does the author presume that the reader wishes to write?

3. What is the "chronological sequence" of organizing materials? What dangers are inherent in its use? To what sort of writing is it well adapted?

4. Summarize the author's advice both to the writer of autobiography and to the writer of history or biography.

5. Define the following words from this article: philanthropic, lassitude, intuition, interspersed, nostalgic, reticent.

How to Detect Propaganda[1]

IF AMERICAN CITIZENS are to have clear understanding of present-day conditions and what to do about them, they must be able to recognize propaganda, to analyze it, and to appraise it.

But what is propaganda?

As generally understood, *propaganda is expression of opinion or action by individuals or groups deliberately designed to influence opinions or actions of other individuals or groups with reference to predetermined ends.* Thus propaganda differs from scientific analysis. The propagandist is trying to "put something across," good or bad, whereas the scientist is trying to discover truth and fact. Often the propagandist does not want careful scrutiny and criticism; he wants to bring about a specific action. Because the action may be socially beneficial or socially harmful to millions of people, it is necessary to focus upon the propagandist and his activities the searchlight of scientific scrutiny. Socially desirable propaganda will not suffer from such examination, but the opposite type will be detected and revealed for what it is.

We are fooled by propaganda chiefly because we don't recognize it when we see it. It may be fun to be fooled but, as the cigarette ads used to say, it is more fun to know. We can more easily recognize propaganda when we see it if we are familiar with the seven common propaganda devices. These are:

1. The Name Calling Device
2. The Glittering Generalities Device
3. The Transfer Device
4. The Testimonial Device
5. The Plain Folks Device
6. The Card Stacking Device
7. The Band Wagon Device

[1] From *Propaganda Analysis* (November, 1937). The devices for propaganda analysis were worked out at Teachers College, Columbia University, and were made available to the Institute for Propaganda Analysis by Professor Clyde R. Miller, by whose permission the article is here reprinted.

Why are we fooled by these devices? Because they appeal to our emotions rather than to our reason. They make us believe and do something we would not believe or do if we thought about it calmly, dispassionately. In examining these devices, note that they work most effectively at those times when we are too lazy to think for ourselves; also, they tie into emotions which sway us to be "for" or "against" nations, races, religions, ideals, economic and political policies and practices, and so on through automobiles, cigarettes, radios, toothpastes, presidents, and wars. With our emotions stirred, it may be fun to be fooled by these propaganda devices, but it is more fun and infinitely more to our own interests to know how they work.

Lincoln must have had in mind citizens who could balance their emotions with intelligence when he made his remark: ". . . but you can't fool all of the people all of the time."

NAME CALLING

"Name Calling" is a device to make us form a judgment without examining the evidence on which it should be based. Here the propagandist appeals to our hate and fear. He does this by giving "bad names" to those individuals, groups, nations, races, policies, practices, beliefs, and ideals which he would have us condemn and reject. For centuries the name "heretic" was bad. Thousands were oppressed, tortured, or put to death as heretics. Anybody who dissented from popular or group belief or practice was in danger of being called a heretic. In the light of today's knowledge, some heresies were bad and some were good. Many of the pioneers of modern science were called heretics; witness the cases of Copernicus, Galileo, Bruno. Today's bad names include: Fascist, demagogue, dictator, Red, financial oligarchy, Communist, muckraker, alien, outside agitator, economic royalist, Utopian, rabble-rouser, troublemaker, Tory, Constitution wrecker.

"Al" Smith called Roosevelt a Communist by implication when he said in his Liberty League speech, "There can be only one capital, Washington or Moscow." When "Al" Smith was running for the presidency, many called him a tool of the Pope, saying in effect, "We must choose between Washington and Rome." That implied that Mr. Smith, if elected President, would take his orders from the Pope. Likewise Mr. Justice Hugo Black has been associated with a bad name, Ku Klux Klan. In these cases some propagandists have tried to make us form judgments without examining essential evidence and implications. "Al Smith is a Catholic. He must never be President." "Roosevelt is a Red. Defeat his program." "Hugo Black is or was a Klansman. Take him out of the Supreme Court."

Use of "bad names" without presentation of their essential meaning, without all their pertinent implications, comprises perhaps the most common of all propaganda devices. Those who want to *maintain* the status quo apply bad names to those who would change it. For example, the Hearst press applies bad names to Communists and Socialists. Those who want to *change* the status quo apply bad names to those who would maintain it. For example, the *Daily Worker* and the *American Guardian* apply bad names to conservative Republicans and Democrats.

GLITTERING GENERALITIES

"Glittering Generalities" is a device by which the propagandist identifies his program with virtue by use of "virtue words." Here he appeals to our emotions of love, generosity, and brotherhood. He uses words like truth, freedom, honor, liberty, social justice, public service, the right to work, loyalty, progress, democracy, the American way, Constitution defender. These words suggest shining ideals. All persons of good will believe in these ideals. Hence the propagan-

dist, by identifying his individual group, nation, race, policy, practice, or belief with such ideals, seeks to win us to his cause. As Name Calling is a device to make us form a judgment to *reject and condemn,* without examining the evidence, Glittering Generalities is a device to make us *accept and approve,* without examining the evidence.

For example, use of the phrases, "the right to work" and "social justice," may be a device to make us accept programs for meeting the labor-capital problem which, if we examined them critically, we would not accept at all.

In the Name Calling and Glittering Generalities devices, words are used to stir up our emotions and to befog our thinking. In one device "bad words" are used to make us mad; in the other "good words" are used to make us glad.

The propagandist is most effective in use of these devices when his words make us create devils to fight or gods to adore. By his use of the "bad words," we personify as a "devil" some nation, race, group, individual, policy, practice, or ideal; we are made fighting mad to destroy it. By use of "good words," we personify as a godlike idol some nation, race, group, etc. Words which are "bad" to some are "good" to others, or may be made so. Thus, to some the New Deal is "a prophecy of social salvation" while to others it is "an omen of social disaster."

From consideration of names, "bad" and "good," we pass to institutions and symbols, also "bad" and "good." We see these in the next device.

TRANSFER

"Transfer" is a device by which the propagandist carries over the authority, sanction, and prestige of something we respect and revere to something he would have us accept. For example, most of us respect and revere our church and our nation. If the propagandist succeeds in getting church or nation to approve a campaign in behalf of some program, he thereby transfers its authority, sanction, and prestige to that program. Thus we may accept something which otherwise we might reject.

In the Transfer device, symbols are constantly used. The cross represents the Christian Church. The flag represents the nation. Cartoons like Uncle Sam represent a consensus of public opinion. Those symbols stir emotions. At their very sight, with the speed of light, is aroused the whole complex of feelings we have with respect to church or nation. A cartoonist by having Uncle Sam disapprove a budget for unemployment relief would have us feel that the whole United States disapproves relief costs. By drawing an Uncle Sam who approves the same budget, the cartoonist would have us feel that the American people approve it. Thus, the Transfer device is used both for and against causes and ideas.

TESTIMONIAL

The "Testimonial" is a device to make us accept anything from a patent medicine or a cigarette to a program of national policy. In this device the propagandist makes use of testimonials. "When I feel tired, I smoke a Camel and get the grandest 'lift.'" "We believe the John L. Lewis plan of labor organization is splendid; C.I.O. should be supported." This device works in reverse also; counter-testimonials may be employed. Seldom are these used against commercial products like patent medicines and cigarettes, but they are constantly employed in social, economic, and political issues. "We believe that the John L. Lewis plan of labor organization is bad; C.I.O. should not be supported."

PLAIN FOLKS

"Plain Folks" is a device used by politicians, labor leaders, business men, and even by ministers and educators to win our confidence by appearing to be people like ourselves—"just plain folks among the neighbors." In election years especially do candidates show their devotion to little children and the common, homey things of life. They

have front porch campaigns. For the newspaper men they raid the kitchen cupboard, finding there some of the good wife's apple pie. They go to country picnics; they attend service at the old frame church; they pitch hay and go fishing; they show their belief in home and mother. In short, they would win our votes by showing that they're just as common as the rest of us—"just plain folks,"—and, therefore, wise and good. Business men often are "plain folks" with the factory hands. Even distillers use the device. "It's our family's whiskey, neighbor; and neighbor, it's your price."

CARD STACKING

"Card Stacking" is a device in which the propagandist employs all the arts of deception to win our support for himself, his group, nation, race, policy, practice, belief, or ideal. He stacks the cards against the truth. He uses under-emphasis and over-emphasis to dodge issues and evade facts. He resorts to lies, censorship, and distortion. He omits facts. He offers false testimony. He creates a smokescreen of clamor by raising a new issue when he wants an embarrassing matter forgotten. He draws a red herring across the trail to confuse and divert those in quest of facts he does not want revealed. He makes the unreal appear real and the real appear unreal. He lets half-truth masquerade as truth. By the Card Stacking device, a mediocre candidate, through the "build-up," is made to appear an intellectual titan; an ordinary prize fighter a probable world champion; a worthless patent medicine a beneficent cure. By means of this device propagandists would convince us that a ruthless war of aggression is a crusade for righteousness. . . . Card Stacking employs sham, hypocrisy, effrontery.

THE BAND WAGON

The "Band Wagon" is a device to make us follow the crowd, to accept the propagandist's program en masse. Here his theme is: "Everybody's doing it." His techniques range from those of medicine show to dramatic spectacle. He hires a hall, fills a great stadium, marches a million men in parade. He employs symbols, colors, music, movement, all the dramatic arts. He appeals to the desire, common to most of us, to "follow the crowd." Because he wants us to "follow the crowd" in masses, he directs his appeal to groups held together by common ties of nationality, religion, race, environment, sex, vocation. Thus propagandists campaigning for or against a program will appeal to us as Catholics, Protestants, or Jews; as members of the Nordic race or as Negroes; as farmers or as school teachers; as housewives or as miners. All the artifices of flattery are used to harness the fears and hatreds, prejudices, and biases, convictions and ideals common to the group; thus emotion is made to push and pull the group on to the Band Wagon. In newspaper articles and in the spoken word this device is also found. "Don't throw your vote away. Vote for our candidate. He's sure to win." Nearly every candidate wins in every election—before the votes are in.

PROPAGANDA AND EMOTION

Observe that in all these devices our emotion is the stuff with which propagandists work. Without it they are helpless; with it, harnessing it to their purposes, they can make us glow with pride or burn with hatred, they can make us zealots in behalf of the program they espouse. As we said at the beginning, propaganda as generally understood is expression of opinion or action by individuals or groups with reference to predetermined ends. Without the appeal to our emotion—to our fears and to our courage, to our selfishness and unselfishness, to our loves and to our hates—propagandists would influence few opinions and few actions.

To say this is not to condemn emotion, an essential part of life, or to assert that all predetermined ends of propagandists are "bad." What we mean is that the intelligent citizen does not want propagandists to utilize his emotions, even to the attainment of "good"

ends, without knowing what is going on. He does not want to be "used" in the attainment of ends he may later consider "bad." He does not want to be gullible. He does not want to be fooled. He does not want to be duped, even in a "good" cause. He wants to know the facts and among these is included the fact of the utilization of his emotions.[1]

Keeping in mind the seven common propaganda devices, turn to today's newspapers and almost immediately you can spot examples of them all. At election time or during any campaign, Plain Folks and Band Wagon are common. Card Stacking is hardest to detect because it is adroitly executed or because we lack the information necessary to nail the lie. A little practice with the daily newspapers in detecting these propaganda devices soon enables us to detect them elsewhere—in radio, news-reel, books, magazines, and in expression of labor unions, business groups, churches, schools, political parties.

SUGGESTIONS FOR STUDY

1. Distinguish the aims of the propagandist from those of the scientist.
2. Why do the devices of the propagandist deceive us?
3. Be prepared to define each of the seven devices of the propagandist. State an example of each drawn from your own experience or reading.
4. Compare this investigation of propaganda with the study made by R. H. Thouless in his article "Emotional Meanings."
5. The usual process organizes its material in a chronological sequence, following regularly from the first act to be performed to the last act. Why is an alternation of this plan necessitated by this subject?
6. Define the following words from this article: dispassionately, heretic, sanction, titan, effrontery, espouse, gullible.

[1] For better understanding of the relationship between propaganda and emotion see Chapter One of *Folkways* by William Graham Sumner. This shows why most of us tend to feel, believe, and act in traditional patterns. See also *The Mind in the Making* by James Harvey Robinson. This reveals the nature of the mind and suggests how to analyze propaganda appealing to traditional thought patterns.

Be Your Own Weatherman[1]

CARL WARDEN

RAINBOW AT NIGHT is the shepherd's delight. . . . Red sky at morning is a sailor's sure warning. . . . The higher the clouds, the finer the weather. . . .

For centuries, sayings such as these have been part of the folklore of the sky. Modern science has proved the truth of many of these beliefs concerning clouds and winds as weather prophets. By understanding a few simple facts about the whys and wherefores of changes that take place over your head, you can foresee, with reasonable accuracy, the coming of storms and rapid shifts in temperature. You don't have to know anything about aneroid barometers or wind gauges. It doesn't make any difference if you can't tell an isobar from an iceberg. With two eyes as your only equipment, you can read the weather from the sky.

Take the clouds, for instance. Divided into four general types—nimbus, cirrus, stratus, and cumulus—they form one of the most important sources of clues to weather. Nimbus clouds are the thick banks, sometimes with ragged edges, from which rain or snow is falling. Cirrus clouds, consisting of ice crystals, are the thin, feathery wisps that glide across the sky at high altitudes. Stratus clouds, as the name implies, collect in layers and often thicken into an unbroken, leaden mass without form or structure, while the fluffy, cottonlike billows that appear during clear weather are the familiar cumulus variety.

Other important clouds are either variations or combinations of these four basic types. Cirro-cumulus, for example, the sailor's "mackerel sky," a good-weather cloud, is a combination of cirrus and cumulus. Cumulo-nimbus, combining cumulus and nimbus, is the awesome "thunderhead" that occurs in spring and summer. Rising like huge mounds of white smoke from the dark base of a gigantic fire, they tower up to tremendous heights and often hold millions of gallons of rain. When the prefix "alto" or "fracto" is included in the name of a cloud, remember that the former merely means high, and the latter broken. Alto-stratus clouds, therefore, are high stratus, and fracto-cumulus are wind-broken cumulus.

In general, the cumulus and the cirrus clouds are classified as fair-weather types, while the stratus and nimbus are associated with rain or snow. Rain generally falls from the gray nimbus clouds, but it may also occur with cumulo-nimbus and sometimes with strato-cumulus. In winter, alto-stratus clouds may produce snow, but only on rare occasions will rain fall from them.

However, a better guide to weather changes is found in the sequence of the clouds—since, as bad weather approaches your locality, the clouds normally form in a definite order. First to appear after a period of good weather are the cirrus clouds. Blown along at speeds that sometimes exceed 200 miles an hour, and at heights as great as 50,000 feet, they often precede the center of an approaching storm by several days. If the wind is blowing thin cirrus wisps from the northwest or the west and the sky is a bright blue, look for fair weather to continue for twenty-four hours or more; but if the cirrus clouds are developing into a translucent blanket, rain or snow generally follows.

Trailing cirrus in this parade of the clouds is the stratus variety, the commonest of all. When these clouds form their gray cover

[1] From *Popular Science Monthly*, CXXXVI (March, 1940), 65. Reprinted by permission of *Popular Science Monthly*.

over the sky, it is usually a sure indication that a storm is on its way toward you. Eventually, unless the wind shifts into the west, they normally thicken to form nimbus or rain clouds.

As the storm center progresses and passes over you, the nimbus formation will break up and the skies will clear. The next morning probably will be cloudless. Soon, however, the fourth basic type, cumulus clouds, will begin to form against the bright, blue sky to complete one cycle of the clouds from fair weather through rain or snow and back to fair weather again.

Cirrus, stratus, nimbus, cumulus—knowing this normal sequence of the clouds gives you a good start in learning to predict the weather. For if you see stratus clouds forming, you know that nimbus or rain clouds are generally next in line. And when nimbus clouds begin to break up, and you sight cumulus puffs through the holes the wind has torn, it's a good bet that clear weather is on the way. However, there are exceptions to every rule, and if you see huge mounds of cumulus clouds lying close to the horizon in the direction from which the wind is blowing, expect a storm within a comparatively short time.

But clouds can serve the amateur weather forecaster in other ways. They may give you tips about what the temperature will be. For example, if clouds disappear from the sky at nightfall, the temperature probably will drop during the night. And if thin cirrus clouds, nicknamed "mare's-tails," are blowing across the sky from the north, fair and warmer weather is on the way.

The clouds can also serve as a weather vane to tell you the direction of the winds, which form another important factor in weather prediction. To use them for this purpose, always look at them in relation to some object on the ground—a church steeple, a tall tree, or the corner of a building. Observe those flying directly overhead, for perspective may fool you if you concentrate on the clouds near the horizon. And if cloud move-

ments are very slow, support your head firmly against a solid object to make sure that it is the *clouds* that are moving in a certain direction, and not your own eyes.

In general, north and west winds are associated with fair weather, and south and east winds with rain and squalls. An enduring southeast wind, particularly on the east coast, is a sure sign of rain. But the shifting of the wind from one direction to another is the important point for a weather forecaster. For when gentle westerly winds begin to swing around into the south and east, it is a fairly reliable indication that a storm center is on the way. Conversely, a shift in the opposite direction is a good sign, for if the wind is blowing from almost any direction and then shifts into the west, the approach of a period of good weather is practically an assured fact.

But why does the shifting of the wind have a bearing on weather changes? To understand that, first glance at the weather map . . . issued daily by the U.S. Weather Bureau and . . . mailed to anyone for a nominal sum. You will notice certain areas marked "high" and others marked "low." As the Bureau points out in its weather-map explanation pamphlet, "lows" indicate areas where the atmospheric pressure, or weight of the air, is low because of warm, rising currents of air. These "lows" mark the center of general storms, which may cover an area as wide as 1,000 miles. "Highs," on the other hand, indicate areas of high atmospheric pressure and are generally the centers of fair weather. The arrows on the map, which fly *with* the wind—not into it—and show its direction at various observation stations, demonstrate the shifting of the wind.

In the northern hemisphere, winds blow in a general counterclockwise direction toward and around the center of a "low," and clockwise around a "high." Moreover, these pressure centers move across the United States roughly from west to east, traveling at an average rate of about 500 miles a day in summer and over 700 miles a day in winter, the "lows" normally preceded by warmer temperatures and the "highs" by colder, though not invariably.

Therefore, the wind in your locality is likely to shift into the south or east as a "low," or storm center, approaches you from the west. And when the storm has passed, and a period of good weather is on its way, the wind will tend to shift into the west or northwest.

Generally, rain is most prevalent in the southeast section of these circular storm centers. A daily weather map will tell you pretty accurately whether your locality lies in this southeast sector, but you can establish the fact roughly without this printed aid by applying a law worked out by Buys Ballot, a famous Dutch meteorologist: When you stand with your back to the prevailing wind, atmospheric pressure will generally be lower toward your left and higher toward your right. That means that if a "low" is approaching and you are standing with your back to a southwest wind, the center of the "low," or storm area, will be toward your left, and you will therefore be in the "low's" southeast sector where rain is more prevalent.

Numberless variations on this sequence of clouds, winds, and temperatures are possible, of course, but figuring them out forms part of the duties of the professional and much of the fun of the amateur weather forecaster. The official weather experts have the advantage of long years of scientific training, plus a host of valuable meteorological instruments, such as barometers, wet- and dry-bulb thermometers, automatic weather balloons, and theodolites. But from accurate observations of the clouds, in addition to wind directions and temperature changes, you can sometimes make a better prediction for your immediate locality than the U.S. Weather Bureau, although their batting average over a long period and over wider areas is bound to be better.

As you become more and more proficient in your forecasting, buy a small pocket note-book and keep an accurate day-to-day log of your observations. Make notes on the cloud formations, the temperature, the direction of the wind, and the amount of rain, snow, and hail. After a period of a year or so, your log will provide you with a complete history of the weather in your locality and, by allowing you to compare present conditions with past performances, will help you to read weather clues more accurately.

Don't expect to gain fame as a weather prophet the first week you make predictions. For, in addition to a good working knowledge of the whys and wherefores of weather, you must learn to make accurate observations and then draw the correct conclusions from this evidence you find in the sky. That takes practice—but so does everything else. Good luck to you as a weather forecaster!

SUGGESTIONS FOR STUDY

1. Define each of the four types of clouds. What two are fair-weather clouds? What two are rain or snow clouds?
2. In what three ways do clouds aid in forecasting the weather?
3. How do shifting winds affect weather?
4. How does the author attract the reader's attention at the beginning of the article? What does the introduction tell you concerning the intended reader for the article? Is the article adapted well to this reader?
5. State the general divisions of subject matter. Does this plan of organization promote ease of comprehension?
6. What person (first, second, third) is used for the point of view in this process? How does the author keep this point of view from becoming monotonous through excessive use?
7. Define the following words from the article: isobar, translucent, conversely, prevalent, barometer.

MECHANISMS AND ORGANIZATIONS

A common and important type of exposition concerns mechanisms and organizations, that is, how mechanisms operate, how organizations function, how scientific experiments have been performed, how laws of nature operate, how natural phenomena like volcanic explosions or disastrous storms happened. In these explanations you must, of course, remember that you are not giving instructions to be followed by a reader (as in the process) but are promoting understanding of an operation of some sort.

The starting point for such description is a general statement of what the mechanism purports to do, what it looks like, what its important parts are, and what the relationship of the parts is. In this way the reader builds a general plan in his mind into which he can fit the later details. For example, if you wish to tell of the operation of an oil well, the first step would be to explain that the oil pressure in the rock far below the surface is so great that it forces the oil to the surface through pipes and thence to the separators and the field storage tanks. The equipment consists generally then of a pipe sunk anywhere from a few hundred feet to two and one-half miles into the earth, a system of valves at the top of the pipe to regulate the flow of oil, a conduit line to the separators, and a further conduit to the field storage tanks. The reader can accordingly see the basic principle upon which the mechanism works and the relationship of the primary parts.

Having established a general picture of the operation, you can then explain the details. Observe, however, that you cannot describe every detail in the mechanism, unless the details are very few. A writer endeavoring to explain the operation of an automobile by such methods would become hopelessly involved. The methods of arranging the details are two: either they can follow a chronological sequence, or they can follow from an important or striking part of the mechanism. The chronological method would probably be better to describe bringing oil to the surface. You might begin with the situation of the oil underground, imprisoned in a trap or pocket of the rock, with some explanation of the geologic formation of these traps. The oil would then be traced as it is forced from the trap through the pipe. The tubing and the casing around it would

be described, and the system of valves at the top of the pipe explained in relation to its function of regulating the flow of oil. The account would continue to the separators where the crude oil is removed for piping to the storage tanks, and where the by-products are handled. This is the chronological method.

On the other hand, in describing the drilling of the well, you might begin with the derrick as the most conspicuous and striking feature of the scene, even though chronological order would call for following the transmission of power from the operating machines to the turntable which revolves the rotary drill so often used in modern well-digging. But whatever procedure is employed, be sure to observe an orderly progression adapted to the reader's ability.

All the general principles stated in connection with the process must again be observed here. The reader and his knowledge of the subject matter need to be carefully ascertained, and the purpose must be analyzed in terms of the reader. For example, a paper on the oil fields might be on many different subjects: on the location of oil to interest financiers, on a new drilling rig to interest the drillers, on the operation of wells to instruct engineering students, or on methods of determining the location of oil to instruct geology students. The reader and the purpose must, therefore, be closely analyzed.

Thus far the illustrations have dealt exclusively with writing the mechanism, but the principles for describing other operations are the same. An account of the United States Senate would introduce first a brief sketch of the Senate and its place in the national government. The details of the operation of the Senate could then be given through such a device as following the passage of a bill from the time it is introduced until it becomes law.

The tendency of unskilled writers is to make the account of the mechanism or organization very dull. It is perhaps better to be dull and accurate than lively and inaccurate, but better still is to be lively and accurate. The introduction of diagrams or charts may help to ease the task of describing with the written word and so add interest to the writing. Bits of humor, vivid diction, analogies, and human interest may also make the paper pleasant as well as instructive.

SUGGESTIONS FOR STUDY

Explain the production or operation of a mechanism or organization suggested by one of the following general subjects:

Steel mills
Farm equipment
Road making
Cotton gins
Radio construction
Automobile construction
Sports equipment
Electrical apparatus, as

the dynamo or transformer
Dictionaries
Filing systems, such as the Library of Congress system
Musical instruments
Summer camps
City government

Typewriters
Tobacco products
Stock exchanges
Clearing houses
Dress designs
Shoes
Bookmaking
Paper
Cotton thread
Plastics
Photography
Glass
Metals or alloys, such as steel, copper, aluminum
Mines, as coal or copper mines
Locomotives
Newspapers
Telegraphy
Streamlining
Airplanes

Plumbing systems
Pumps
Lumbering
Geologic formations
Timepieces
Explosives
Permanent waves
Marketing a popular song
Presentation of a radio program
Church services
Traffic control
Lens grinding
City planning
Blueprints
House construction
Interior decoration
Lawmaking
Smoke elimination
Optical work

Under Mobile River[1]

R. G. SKERRETT

MOBILE, ALABAMA, on the much-traveled old Spanish Trail, has built, at a cost of $4,000,-000, a different type of subaqueous tunnel for the convenience of automotive traffic. The tunnel will shorten the east and west route by 7½ miles, and will materially reduce heavy traffic congestion.

Mobile is at the mouth of Mobile River and at the head of Mobile Bay at a point 30 miles inland and north of the Gulf of Mexico. The city is Alabama's historic and only seaport. It is on the west bank of the stream, opposite Blakely Island.

Work on the Bankhead Tunnel, as the river underpass is called, was started in July of last year. It links Mobile with Blakely Island and connects with a 10½-mile causeway extending eastward from the island and spanning several narrow water gaps.

The underwater sections of the tunnel were built at a local shipyard, launched one by one, towed to a nearby slip on the west side of Blakely Island, and there brought to a stage of near completion before being moved to and sunk in a deep trench dug in the river bed. Five of the seven sections are each 298 feet long, and the two other sections are each 225 feet long. The under-river structure has a total length of 2,000 feet; and near each shoreward end there is a transition section which connects with a rectangular or box-like section of the tunnel. At the Mobile end, an open ramp approach extends downward from the street level to the portal of the western section. On Blakely Island, the steel box section runs right up to the ground surface, and is equipped with a steel gate which may be closed, in time of hurricanes, against water piled up on the island. The Bankhead Tunnel has a total length of nearly 3,390 feet between grade levels, and its roadway is 21 feet wide for two traffic lanes—eastbound and westbound.

[1] From the Scientific American, CLXIII (September, 1940), 135. Reprinted by permission of the Scientific American.

The Bankhead Tunnel is similar in principle to the Detroit Tunnel, built in 1930, but differs in a number of particulars which represent engineering advances. Each tubular section of the under-river divisions is made up of an inner steel cylinder 30 feet in diameter surrounded by an octagonal steel tube that has a minimum diameter of 34 feet. The two concentric tubes were tied together by equidistant radial ribs, and the spaces between the two tubes filled with concrete before the tubes were finally sunk in the trench and covered. The inner tube of each section is lined with reinforced concrete not less than 18 inches thick. The top of the tunnel, in mid-channel, is about 46 feet below the level of mean low water.

Each end of each tube was sealed temporarily with a watertight steel bulkhead before launching; and concrete was poured into the intertubular space to a height of 10 feet to give each section stability when it was first launched. Steelwork was put together by welding; and, before launching, each tube was coated with soapy water and subjected to internal air pressure—any leak promptly blew tell-tale bubbles.

At Blakely Island, openings were cut in the top plates of each inner tube to give temporary access to the inside of a section so workmen could place the concrete lining, the conduits for power, lighting, and telephone circuits, the roadway slabs, and the ventilating duct beneath the mid-section roadway for a distance of 400 feet. That done, the access hatchways were sealed, and the sections, starting at Blakely Island, were floated to the trench and sunk.

At the trench, the last of the concrete was poured into the spaces between the inner and outer shells until a section lost its buoyancy. It was held suspended in a sling and lowered deliberately. Succeeding sections were brought together by pulling the newly laid section, with ratchet turnbuckles, snugly against one already installed. A projecting ring on one fitted into an annular recess filled with a rubberized gasket on the other. Divers did this work. Later, the joint was covered on the outside with concrete poured underwater. Finally, when bulkheads were cut away, adjacent inner tubes were tied together by a welded ring of steel.

One ventilation building, on Blakely Island, is equipped with exhaust fans only which suck vitiated air into ports on both sides of the roadway level for 400 feet in the mid-section of the river part. No fresh air is blown into the tunnel, but the action of the fans at the low point is counted upon to draw fresh air inward and downward from both portals and maintain proper circulation. This arrangement is based upon experimental work of the U.S. Bureau of Mines. An unusual feature of the illumination is that, while lights are arranged to give proper illumination at all points in the tunnel, special additional lights are installed near each portal. These latter lights burn only during the day, their purpose being to make the transition more gradual for the eyes of the driver as he enters from the strong outside sunlight.

SUGGESTIONS FOR STUDY

1. What is the function of the first four paragraphs?

2. Describe the construction of each tube. What are the different layers that compose each?

3. What ingenious device was used to test for air leakage?

4. Describe the method of laying the tube.

5. What new feature characterizes the ventilation system?

6. Describe the reader for whom the author was writing. How much technical knowledge does he have? Cite specific points to illustrate your answer.

7. What plan does the author use to organize his material? Make a topic outline of the article.

8. Define the following words from the selection: subaqueous, slip, ramp, tubular, equidistant, radial, bulkhead, stability, conduits, ratchet, turnbuckles, annular, gaskets, vitiated.

Earthquakes[1]

REV. JOSEPH LYNCH, S.J.

A STORY IS TOLD of a night watchman who was watching an astronomer making some observations through a large telescope. Suddenly, in the region of the sky towards which the telescope was pointing, a star fell—a shooting star. The watchman whistled in amazement and exclaimed to the astronomer, "Gee, Mister, that was some shot!"

Our watchman gave the astronomer credit for far more than he was able to do, and in the study of earthquakes we seismologists too are often given credit for far more than we are able to do. People have often expressed surprise that we are able to record an earthquake here that is occurring thousands of miles away. The fact is, we don't record it—the earthquake is obliging enough to record itself for us. It does not require the talent of a Sherlock Holmes to find the name of a friend who has called to see us during our absence, if the caller has been thoughtful enough to leave his visiting card under our door. So it does not require the talent of a Sherlock Holmes to find out what earthquake is visiting the earth if the quake is obliging enough to leave its visiting card under our seismic observatory door—which is what every earthquake does. True, sometimes it is difficult to make out the writing on the card, but most quakes write their names sufficiently legibly for us to make them out. We have to supply the pen and ink and even the card, but the quake does the rest. On Monday, January 15, at 3:43 A.M. New York time, a violent earthquake visited northeastern India, and some ten minutes later its visiting card was under our observatory door.

[1] From the *Scientific American*, CL (May, 1934), 246. Reprinted by permission of the author and the *Scientific American*.

But what is the signature of a quake and how does it write its name?

Before discussing the signature of a quake let us see what an earthquake is. An earthquake may be described as a sudden slipping of a portion of the earth's crust—a readjustment of the crust to a change of forces. A landslide is a readjustment of the crust on a small scale. A snowslide on a sloping roof is an example on a still smaller scale. When the underneath part of the snow melts, the snow begins to slide down the roof, and blocks of it fall with a thud to the ground. The force holding the snow to the roof, causing it to stick to the roof, is lessened considerably and the slipping is a readjustment to this change of force—the snow moves until it finds a force which will hold it in place. A slight readjustment of the earth's crust is going on nearly all the time at Niagara. From time to time huge boulders of rock fall into the water. The softer rocks underlying the overhead rock become washed away by the spray of the falls. The supporting force is thus removed from under this overhead rock, and boulders of it fall in readjustment. The rock readjusts itself to the forces present.

An earthquake is such a readjustment to changes of pressure, but a readjustment on a much larger scale. It is a readjustment taking place deep in the earth's crust, down to the depth of a hundred miles or so. The changes of pressure on such earth blocks may be due to a multiplicity of causes—erosion and deposition; tidal forces; centrifugal force (indicated by the fact that earthquakes are more or less confined to the equatorial belt); and numerous others beyond the scope of this short article. Briefly then, an earthquake is a sudden movement of a portion of the earth's crust.

This sudden movement causes the whole earth to quiver. This quiver travels through the earth as ripples through a pond, only much faster. It is not very noticeable, but it has been noticed on the surface of mercury levels and still ponds. But, while not noticeable as a rule by our unaided senses, it may be made noticeable by a seismograph, the microscope of the geophysicist.

The seismograph is the fountain pen used by the earthquake to write its signature. Its essential part is a delicately supported pendulum, something like a clock pendulum, the tip of the pendulum being equivalently the penpoint. When the earthquake occurred in India the whole earth quivered and, as the quiver passed through the ground under our delicately suspended pendulum, it made our pendulum quiver, and this quivering was traced out by the pen on our paper record underneath it, giving us the signature of the quake.

We said the pendulum quivered—actually, the pendulum did not quiver. The observatory and the paper record and everything in contact with the earth quivered under the pendulum while the latter alone remained still. Hence, relative to the paper, we say the pendulum quivered, just as we say the sun rises when really it is the earth that is in motion and not the sun. Because it stays still while ground and observatory move underneath it, the pendulum is able to trace out for us the motion of the ground and to give us the signature of the earthquake. The pendulum stays still, while all around it quivers, because of its inertia—literally laziness. It will not respond to the earth's quiver for the same reason that none of us care to respond to the alarm clock in the morning. All bodies possess this inertia or laziness of motion. If a careless chauffeur starts a car suddenly, the passengers are thrown backward. Actually, they do not move, but refuse to move; they do not respond to the quick motion of the car because of their inertia, and are left behind

—that is, stay still—while the car moves forward; hence they are equivalently thrown backward in the car. Similarly, if the chauffeur jams on the brakes suddenly, the passengers are thrown forward. Because of their inertia they refuse to have their motion stopped; so they continue forward while the car stops—hence they lurch forward in the car. We show this inertia in a personal way: we hate to go to bed, but once there we hate to get up. When the earth moves suddenly, then, under a delicately suspended pendulum, the pendulum lurches backward or forward, depending on the motion of the ground. We say it lurches—actually it stays still while the ground underneath it lurches.

This slight motion of the pendulum can be magnified in many ways: mechanically by a system of levers, electrically by winding a coil round the pendulum and setting the latter up between the poles of a strong magnet—the slight motion of the coil across the magnetic field generates a current which can be magnified in many ways. The most sensitive seismographs we have at Fordham University magnify the motion of the ground about 2,000 times. This magnified motion is recorded on paper by attaching a pen to the pendulum or its lever system. To lessen friction and increase magnification, on the more sensitive instruments the motion is recorded on photographic paper by a beam of light reflected from a mirror attached to the pendulum in place of a pen. Such a seismograph set up anywhere on the globe will be set in motion by the quivering of the earth due to an earthquake and will faithfully record the latter's signature.

But how can we tell the signature of one quake from that of another? Just as we have the Christian name and the surname or family name in any signature, so we have, as it were, a Christian name and family name in every quake signature. The quiver that is sent out through the earth from every quake is a double quiver. The first pushes or compresses the earth ahead of it and is called a compressional quiver and travels five miles a second. The second quiver is a twist quiver, twisting or shaking the earth from side to side as it travels. It travels more slowly than the first, averaging only three miles a second. The farther an observatory is from the scene of a quake the longer will be the interval between the arrival of these two quivers, and the more drawn out will be the signature of the quake.

We recognize the signature of the quake from this double signature. If it is a long drawn out signature it is a distant quake. If the two names—that is, if the two quivers—are recorded close together it is a close quake, the exact distance being told at once by measuring carefully just how far apart the two quivers are on our record, which is kept moving at a constant rate under our pendulum, the time being marked on it automatically every second by the clock.

These two quivers or waves are due to the elasticity of the earth. The "push wave" is due to the elasticity of volume of the earth, the "shake wave" to its elasticity of shape. We have something similar in the case of a lightning bolt—an earthquake in the sky if you wish. We have two distinct waves sent out—a lightning wave which we see, and a thunder wave which we hear. The lightning wave travels much faster than the thunder wave; hence we always see the lightning before we hear the thunder. In fact we can estimate the distance of the lightning bolt by the number of seconds that elapse between the arrival of the lightning and the arrival of the thunder—each second putting the bolt a fifth of a mile away. In a similar way we can estimate the distance of an earthquake from a seismograph by measuring the number of seconds that elapse between the arrival of the "push wave" or primary wave and the arrival of the "shake wave" or secondary wave. A set of tables has been compiled giving the distance of the quake for each time interval in seconds. In addition to the push and shake waves, a third wave, a combination of the two, travels around the outside of the earth and arrives much later. It is not necessary for the computation of the quake's distance, but it acts as a useful check since its speed is likewise known.

I can imagine your saying that this explains how we can tell the distance of a quake from its signature, but it does not tell us just where the quake is. The long-drawn-out signature of the Indian quake could tell us it was a quake 7,600 miles away, but could not tell us whether it were in India or Chile because both are about 7,600 miles away. How can we tell the direction from the signature? If we had only one seismograph we could not tell the direction, but we have a whole family of seismographs, and the quake obligingly writes its name under each one. Three seismographs of any one type are required if we are to be able to tell not only the distance but also the direction of the quake from its signature. One seismograph is set so as to respond only to motions from the north or south, another seismograph is set so as to respond only to motions from the east or west, and a third seismograph has the weight of its pendulum suspended by a coiled spring so as to respond only to an upward push or a downward pull of the ground. It tells us whether the ground is first pushed up or pulled down under it as a result of the quake. If we piece together all three motions, the first two tell us whether the quake is, say, from the northeast or the southwest. The third or vertical instrument tells us whether the ground was being pushed from the north-east or pulled from the south-west.

Hence with three instruments we can tell both distance and direction. Moreover, we have the addresses of nearly all quakes that are likely to call at any time, and if we have the distance and probable direction of a quake that has called we can usually say, "That is that South Mexican quake calling again," or "That is that Aleutian Island quake calling again." Both of these were frequent callers during the past year; nine calling from the Aleutian Islands and six from South Mexico.

Often, of course, the signature of the quake is a poor one—very illegible. Legible enough to tell us the distance but not the direction. In that case we consult two other stations and, knowing the distance of the quake from three stations, we draw three circles on our globe with the three stations as centers and the three distances as radii. The three circles can intersect only in one point, and that point is the scene of the quake.

We said we had a whole family of seismographs—at Fordham University we have eight in operation. Three of these are very sensitive and magnify about 2,000 times. For a very large quake, however, they are sometimes too sensitive and magnify the motion too much. So we have a pair of less sensitive instruments to give us the signatures of the larger quakes. Then again we sometimes have little baby quakes that are felt only locally. They are not only much feebler than the larger quakes but they quiver more rapidly—the baby takes shorter and quicker steps than its parents, and we have to have a more rapidly quivering pendulum to be able to write down these quick baby steps. We have two so-called short-period seismographs for near and baby quakes.

With regard to the frequency of quakes: During the past ten months nearly 300 quakes called on us—more than one a day. Of these, about 50 left signatures sufficiently legible for us to recognize and locate definitely. Few of these did any serious damage until the last Indian quake, which destroyed about 5,000 people.

But of what practical use is an earthquake observatory? The new seismology, or the scientific study of earthquakes, since its birth around 1895, has busied itself mainly with four lines of investigation: What can seismology tell us about the nature of the earth's interior; how can seismology be used in prospecting for oil, coal, and such materials; how can we construct buildings that will withstand earthquake shocks; and, lastly, how can we foretell when an earthquake is due in any given locality?

Much progress has been made along all four lines. We have now a fairly accurate picture of the internal structure of the earth. Seismology has, as it were, let down its camera into the interior of the earth and photographed it for us, and we find it to be a solid sphere with a dense core probably of nickel or iron, starting about halfway down like the core of a baseball. For many years the interior of the earth was thought to be liquid, but a liquid core does not fit in with the findings of seismology. The existence of the core is deduced from the fact that earthquake waves are refracted or bent as they pass through the earth, much as light waves are refracted as they pass through glass or water. From the amount of refraction we can argue to the depth of the refracting surface. The twist or shake or secondary wave is due to the elasticity of shape and can exist only in a medium which has a shape of its own; namely, a solid. Since the twist wave passes through the core, we conclude that the core is solid, since only a solid can transmit a twist wave.

With regard to the prediction of earthquakes, seismology has not yet reached the stage where we can foretell quakes, but investigations in this direction which are being carried out in Japan give hope that the time is not far distant when such prediction will be possible. It has been noticed that in earthquake regions the earth shows evidence of tilt or gradual rising for some years before the quake occurs, much as the inner tube of a tire or the bladder of a football rises gradually through a tear in the cover before finally bursting. The tilt of the ground is being carefully observed and measured, and it is hoped that it will finally give the clue to the forecasting of earthquakes.

Seismology has been used successfully in prospecting for oil and coal. An artificial earthquake is set up in the ground to be prospected by setting off an explosive in the ground, portable seismographs being set up at known distances from the center of this artificial quake. The time of the arrival of the earthquake waves from the artificial quake is carefully observed on these instruments, and this time gives a clue to the structure of the ground through which the waves have passed.

In the matter of building, much has been accomplished. The data on seismology given to the engineers have enabled the latter to revise the building codes in California and Japan considerably, and these codes offer a basis for safer construction in other earthquake regions. According to the late Professor Suyehiro, even in the violent Japanese earthquake, buildings which had been designed to resist a horizontal force of one-tenth of their weight successfully withstood the shock. The increased building cost necessary to provide this resistance to earthquake shock has been carefully figured and is ridiculously small—about fifteen per cent. Quakes can, with a little forethought and a little extra trouble in building construction, be effectively provided against.

Seismology has also shed light on earthquake insurance. The late Dr. Freeman has shown that earthquake risk has in the past been enormously exaggerated. Even in the most disastrous quakes, the actual damage has always been confined to a comparatively small area, and careful analysis reveals the assuring fact that the actual loss seldom exceeds five per cent of the structural value. Were the full facts made clear, both to the public and to the insurance companies, each would be better served; premiums would be reduced, helping the insured, and insurance would be more generally taken out, helping the companies.

In conclusion we might say that earthquakes are nature's safety-valve, wisely arranged by Divine Providence for our greater protection. They come for the most part in uninhabited regions, but if at times they cause sorrow and hardship, perhaps those beautiful lines of Father Tabb will come to our aid in viewing them in the light of blessings in disguise:

My life is but a weaving between my God and
 me.
I offer Him the threads, He weaveth steadily.
Full oft He weaveth sorrow and I in foolish
 pride
Forget He sees the upper and I the under side.

SUGGESTIONS FOR STUDY

1. Define an earthquake. What are some causes of earthquakes?

2. Explain the principle of operation of the seismograph. What is inertia?

3. What are the three kinds of quake waves? What are their relative speeds?

4. How do these waves enable the seismologist to determine the location of the quakes? What further aids are there in determining locations?

5. Of what use is the work done in seismology?

6. How can seismology determine the internal structure of the earth?

7. What methods are being used in the endeavor to predict quakes?

8. With what added cost can buildings be made shock-proof?

9. State the rhetorical function of the opening anecdote of the article.

10. Define the reader. Cite six or seven points of adaptation to this reader. What means are used to make the mechanism of interest?

11. What are the three major divisions of the explanation?

12. Define the following words from the article: seismologist, legibly, erosion, centrifugal, geophysicist, compressional, elasticity, illegible, refraction, portable.

The Struggle for Existence[1]

HENSHAW WARD

THIS CHAPTER is the first step in describing evolution. It is a description of the fundamental fact—never understood a century ago—that the life of every plant and animal is a struggle in a fierce competition for a chance to exist and propagate. If nature had caused all her creatures to live by a policy of "give the weak ones a chance," there never would have been any development of such adaptations as were described in the previous chapter.

Early in every man's life there comes a time when he hears the story of the blacksmith who offered to shoe a farmer's horse for some grains of wheat—thus: one grain for the first nail, two for the second, four for the third, and so on. Of course the farmer was pleased with such a price. The driving of the fifth nail cost him only sixteen grains, and the total wages for putting on the first shoe were only two hundred fifty-five grains. The farmer kept tally: two hundred fifty-six grains for the ninth nail, five hundred twelve for the tenth, one thousand twenty-four for the eleventh. He was amused, and the more so because his wheat was small; it took five hundred of the grains to fill a cubic inch, and a million of them to make a bushel. The last nail of the second shoe cost him not much over a quart. He lighted his pipe and smoked contentedly, reflecting that he was paying hardly anything for the labor and nothing for the material.

The trouble began while the third shoe was going on; the twentieth nail cost 524,288 grains—half a bushel; the twenty-first a bushel, the twenty-second two bushels, the twenty-third more than four bushels; the

total for the third shoe amounted to sixteen bushels. The thirty-first nail cost over a thousand bushels; the total price for the job was 4,256 bushels.

When we tell this story to children, we are amused at their skepticism and pleased with our effort to show them the difference between adding two and multiplying by two. We do not realize that we need the lesson for ourselves when we consider successive generations of animals. The rate of increase is not found by *adding* to their number each time, but by multiplying. Most animals tend to increase by a factor larger than two, and it does not require a long stretch of years to include thirty-two generations. Even a seasoned mathematician is rather startled when he figures the number of descendants that one pair may produce in no long while.

The largest and most slow-breeding kind can furnish amazement if we grant them a few centuries. Suppose that the average pair of elephants produces only four children that live to have grandchildren, and suppose that there are only three generations in each century, and suppose that the parents die as soon as they have brought up their last child. Under these conditions one pair will have sixteen great-grandchildren in the world after a century, one hundred twenty-eight descendants after two centuries, and one thousand twenty-four after three centuries. The rate of increase may seem as insignificant as it did to the guileless farmer. But in five hundred years there will be sixty-six thousand descendants; in six hundred years there will be over half a million, and after another century over four million. Now the numbers roll up. In the thirty-second generation of descendants there will be eight billion five hundred million—that is, five times

---

[1] Chapter 6 from Henshaw Ward, *Evolution for John Doe*, (New York, 1925). Reprinted by special permission of The Bobbs-Merrill Company.

the human population of the globe. After seven more centuries of increase there would not be standing room for the elephants if they were packed closely on every acre of land surface from pole to pole. Does seventeen centuries seem a long while? It is not the thousandth part of the centuries during which elephants have been breeding on our earth.

There is no trick in this reckoning; the figures do not lie; they give a conservative estimate of the way elephants actually would have increased if they had had a chance. We know as a matter of history that a few horses, left by the Spanish conquerors of Mexico to run wild, must have increased on our western plains for a century or more at a rate that doubled their numbers in each generation.

As soon as we deal with smaller and more short-lived animals, the normal rate of increase is prodigious. In 1860 a few rabbits were carefully conveyed to Australia and tenderly nourished there with the hope that a few of them might be able to live and propagate. Never was a hope more abundantly fulfilled. So rapidly did they multiply that within twenty years they were a pest; rabbit-drives had to be organized, and such heaps of the animals were slaughtered that it was difficult to dispose of the carcasses. A fence of wire mesh was run clear across the continent in order to head off this prairie-fire of life.

Any animal that bears several young in one litter and breeds several times a year can soon make a counting-machine weary. In two years of the World War the rats multiplied enormously along the battle line—amid all the destruction of artillery and poison gas, in spite of the utmost efforts to hold them in check. Against the unremitting warfare of man, rats have always increased wherever there is food. One estimate of their fecundity in England is that, even if ninety-five per cent of them died without breeding, they could quadruple their numbers in a year. If they had food and room, and were not opposed, their skins could make a carpet for the earth in a few decades.

Some similar computation would be true of any animal that is normally adapted to hold its own in the world. It is fitted to increase in swarms, and ever multiplying swarms; and whenever it has opportunity, it infallibly lives up to the predictions about its fertility, actually does propagate in overwhelming numbers. The English sparrow was brought to our shores in 1851 and promptly set to work producing every season several large broods. Within twenty years it had become more numerous than any native bird. The point of this story is not that a certain sparrow is an undesirable citizen, but that any bird in a favorable environment will unfailingly produce astounding numbers in a few years. A very moderate estimate will show that a pair of blackbirds could easily become ten millions in ten years, and that many ordinary birds could have two billions of descendants in fifteen years—would unquestionably have that many in favorable surroundings. When the Ohio Valley was being settled, the pigeons used to be seen in such numbers that we gasp as we read the naturalist Wilson's account of what he saw in Kentucky. "They were flying with great steadiness and rapidity, at a height beyond gunshot, in several deep strata. From right to left, as far as the eye could reach, the breadth of this vast procession extended, seeming everywhere equally crowded. It was then half past one. About four o'clock in the afternoon the living torrent above my head seemed as numerous and extensive as ever." Wilson reckoned that in this one "torrent" there were two-billion pigeons; and this was "only one of several aggregates known to exist in various parts of the United States." Yet these pigeons hatched *only two eggs at a time.*

Every form of plant or animal life has some similar ability to multiply its numbers. Until we hear that statement repeated, and repeatedly emphasized with examples, we cannot have any conception of the prolific power of all life. For even observant people have very little opportunity to realize the abounding vitality of all animate nature. And most of us are not observant. I, for example, hardly see one rat a year, hardly know an English sparrow by sight, am much impressed by the way my trees and shrubs tend to die. I always see, year after year, the same number of crows or buzzards or woodchucks. What do I know about the power of life to multiply? . . .

It is easy enough to see why an animalcule does not continue its rate of increase—there is not space for it in the universe. It is clear why no fish has packed the ocean full and why elephants are not standing five hundred thick on every acre of land. The reproduction of every species—even if it were the only one in the world—is limited by the supply of food. And since there are half a million species of animals, each of which would like to fill the earth and would be quite able to do so, there must be a severe pressure upon every species by all the other species that are tending to swell in numbers and to occupy the same territory. Such a pressure must cause intense rivalry; it must restrict, must strongly check, the increase of each individual. This check upon the increase of numbers causes the "Struggle for Existence."

As soon as we hear that ominous phrase, we naturally begin to think of warfare, of bloody design. Indeed the literature of evolution is dotted with hints of this sort, and of late years the story-writers have given us many pictures of the world of nature as a battle-ground where all feet are swift to shed blood, a cruel place where venom and claw make way with enemies, where "nature is red of tooth and fang," where life is a "gruesome cockpit." This horrible notion[1] is so generally

[1] William J. Long in his *Mother Nature* has done good service by denouncing this notion as "an appalling and degrading superstition" (though his own notion is not one that many naturalists endorse). The ideas of "cruelty" and "terror" are not to be found in Darwin. Long's book is only an amplifying of the description that Darwin gives as a summary at the close of Chapter III of the *Origin of Species:* "When we reflect on this struggle, we may console

held that it has been used to justify human warfare. The German Bernhardi actually argued as crudely as this: "Wherever we look in nature, we find that war is a fundamental law of evolution. This great verity, which has been recognized in past ages, has been convincingly demonstrated in modern times by Charles Darwin."

In the main all such ideas are false. To compare the struggle of nature with human warfare is absurd. Because we human beings are cruel to one another, because *we* plunge into ruthless wholesale killing, because *we* have tortured and enslaved and exterminated one another in our struggles for *domination,* we cannot assume that the struggle for existence is similar. Only a gorilla has a right to such an argument. Before any one can have a true view of evolution, he must thoroughly purge his mind of this common and deep-seated error. Before we go on in this chapter to picture the struggle for existence as it is, we must take time to see what it is not.

It is not what our sentimental human minds would suppose. If we conceive it as cruel, as fierce-minded, as warlike, we are making the old mistake of having the great sun of nature revolve around our little mental sphere. Nature is not bitter with human hate. Nor, on the other hand, is nature sweet with human sentimentality. Nature is as different from a man as the starry heavens are from their reflection in a pool. "Nature" is simply a name for The Way Things Are. In this great scheme of things we cannot detect any plotting of altruism nor any exercise of cruelty, neither sympathy nor jealousy. To our poor senses nature may seem like a loving mother, or like a stern inexorable stepmother; but the beauty and the harshness alike are flimsy imaginings; they are not nature.

The struggle for existence does not invite men to go to war nor certify that might

ourselves with the full belief that the war of nature is not incessant, that no fear is felt, that death is generally prompt, and that the vigorous, the healthy, and the happy survive and multiply."

makes right nor discourage charity. It is not hideous, but partakes of the beauty of all truth. It contains no cruelty unless all facts are cruel.

In the whole long history of false reasoning there is no funnier chapter than the record of how man has sentimentalized the struggle for existence. He has shuddered at the fierceness of the tiger while digesting the beefsteak of a slaughtered cow. He has written poetry about "the pious robin"; yet for every kill of a tiger a robin will slay his hundreds. The only relentless and unreasonable slaughterer on earth is man. No wonder that man, who exterminates moose and bison while he tolerates the marriage of idiots, is quite unable to comprehend the wisdom and purity of the struggle for existence that is decreed by nature.

The struggle for existence is a contest in which there is no motive of cruelty, no lust for power over others, no desire to do harm to another creature. It is an effort by every creature to do his best, his utmost, to live and have young. Every force of his being is animated by these two elemental instincts: (1) he must live according to the law that nature has planted in him, and (2) he must obey the primal commandment to be fruitful. Every act in the natural struggle for existence is entirely innocent and wholesome.

In another way the struggle is unlike what we might assume. It is not a universal combat in which every creature's weapons are turned against other creatures. In a great variety of ways animals and plants are useful to each other, confer benefits on others in the course of seeking their own welfare —as when birds remove caterpillars from leaves. Success in the struggle often comes from avoiding competition—as when the sagebrush grows on the desert where other plants cannot live.

In another and more important way the struggle differs from what we have so far dwelt on. It is to a large extent not a set of duels between individuals; the contest is often impersonal, unfelt, unsuspected. Perhaps an illustration from human life will be useful here: if an actor or an author pleases the public, his work may be highly paid for, and the income of some other actors or authors be reduced. Stevenson says that a successful author—who may be a shrinking, affectionate person—stabs other authors with his pen as surely as if he used a dagger. So impersonal and unsuspected may the struggle for existence be at times in human affairs. Much more is it true that the unreasoning lives of a large part of the animal kingdom may be passed without any consciousness of rivalry, in peaceful success. Success need not depend on the ability to kill. All through the millions of years of the geologic ages the armored fighters have perished; today one of the most prolific animals is the least offensive—the rabbit. The rats and beetles have not conquered in the strife by slaughter. Some of the most successful animals are those that organize a society, like the ants and bees, in whose colonies there is no individualism but only a ceaseless, unstinted labor for the whole group.

But the struggle, for all kinds alike, is none the less fierce and unremitting because it is indirect and unknown. It is pitiless. If a communistic society of bees cannot find nectar in competition with other societies, it will fail to leave offspring as surely as the lonely pair of eagles that fail to strike enough victims in their wide domain of sixty square miles. When any kind of organism cannot produce enough seed, or suck enough water from the ground, or resist a plague of fungus, or withstand a change of climate, it dies. There is no more tragedy about this for the individual than there is about the most successful life, for every individual, weak or strong, must die. The only difference is that, in the long run, the weak leave few offspring; the earth is peopled by those who leave most offspring. "Reproduce or perish" is the eternal necessity. In this struggle to propagate, the mushroom feeds upon decaying matter, the condor wheels its lonely flight above the mountains, the fish feels its sightless way in caves and ocean depths, the mosquito swarms beyond the arctic circle, the snow-plant spreads its abundant red upon the ice-fields of cold heights, the beaver builds his dam. High and low, everywhere under the whole heavens, in every cranny of space, with every imaginable adaptation, the urge of life compels every individual to seek out a living and have young.

Though we can learn very little about the adjustments in nature, we can guess at them to some extent by what we see when man disturbs any balance. As soon as the dry valleys of California were set to orchards about fifty years ago, the cottony cushion scale multiplied upon them at such a rate that destruction was in sight. The orchards were rescued [1] by studying nature's adjustments in Australia, the home of the scale. It was found that there the scale was kept in bounds by ladybird beetles; some of these were imported, bred and turned into the orchards; they promptly and completely played their expected part in the struggle for orchards. The cantaloupes were saved from a pest by a similar army of ladybirds brought by the bushel from the high Sierras. Man's best, and often the only, way of coping with the multitudes of nature is to employ the troops of nature, as in fighting the gypsy moth, the Hessian fly, and the grain aphis. We are in a perpetual contest with the hordes of life that swarm against our interests.

Some such gross examples are about all that man can learn of the interplay of forces that work in the struggle for existence. If we look at any landscape, we see that all forms of life are fitted into a mosaic where each can thrive to a certain extent, thus far and no farther. Each is, in the ordinary course of the seasons, checked from dominating over others. Grass and spruce trees and violets and robins exist in abundance, and now one and now another may fluctuate somewhat in its numbers; but as the decades pass, the balance only swings to and fro about a cen-

ter. Each plant and animal is severely restrained by the whole competition. Year after year we look upon the same peaceful assemblage, hear the same songs, see the same bright blossoms, exclaim with the same satisfaction at the restful peace of it all.

But there is no peace. In any landscape each leaf and beak and fin is tirelessly at work to keep up its numbers. Every plant bears seeds in prodigious quantity; every animal's body is a factory of countless eggs or sperms. With all the power of every mother's being there is effort to rear young. Every pair of individuals is doing its best to leave descendants that would spread over the whole region. With what result? Only this: that next year, and ten years hence, and fifty, and a hundred, there will probably be the same number of descendants. All this ceaseless power is somehow held in check by the competition of powers. Of all the seeds that are formed by a plant with such lavish extravagance only a few sprout. "There is a British starfish which produces at least two hundred millions of eggs, *and yet it is not what one would call a common animal.*" [1] There is something fearsome about such tremendous possibilities that accomplish no more than just to keep the numbers of this starfish from decreasing. Many of the lower animals hatch a thousand eggs to insure one offspring. And only a small fraction of the young can grow up. The rearing of all the offspring with such intense devotion has only one result, that when the years have passed and the parents have died, there are two other members of the species to take their places.

Here is a fact to which the ordinary citizen never gives a thought. The pretty scene that he surveys from a porch or a canoe is a cemetery for the young that never mature. We need not weep their fate, but we observe the fact. This is the struggle for existence.

SUGGESTIONS FOR STUDY

1. Is the potential rate of increase of animals a matter of addition or multiplication?

[1] Elizabeth A. Ward, "Mustering Nature's Mercenaries," *Forum* (October, 1915).

[1] J. A. Thomson, *The System of Animate Nature.*

2. Have there been instances when animals did increase in keeping with their potential rate of propagation?

3. Why do not all animals increase according to their potential rate?

4. Can the struggle for existence in nature be used properly as a justification for human warfare? Explain.

5. Is nature cruel, kindly, or neither?

6. Do creatures invariably kill off one another, or are there instances in which they are useful to each other?

7. Is it accurate to say that success in the struggle for existence depends upon the ability to kill?

8. Even with a tremendous potential power to increase their kind, what is the net result of the striving of creatures to reproduce?

9. Analyze carefully the reader addressed by Mr. Ward in this article, and cite several ways in which he adapted his writing to that reader.

10. Outline the article so that you will be well aware of the divisions of the subject matter. Then observe how each major unit of subject matter slowly and clearly advances the thought for the intended reader's easy assimilation.

11. Define the following words used in the article: propagate, prolific, inexorable, unstinted, prodigious.

ANALYSIS

Another highly important type of exposition is analysis. It is the resolution of a subject into its parts to see of what it is made. The small boy who takes apart a watch to discover what makes it tick is employing a rudimentary form of analysis. On a higher plane, a chemist analyzes a solution to determine its ingredients, an engineer analyzes a river bed and the river banks to decide if a new bridge would be practicable, a major-league manager analyzes his team to learn who is deserving of an increase in salary, an architect analyzes the needs of a family and the characteristics of a community before he designs a new dwelling. Analysis is therefore a common and important procedure.

Formal Analysis

The first kind of analysis—often called formal analysis—is an exhaustive, impersonal division of a subject until every aspect of it has been considered. The method is essen-

tially scientific, as it accounts for all known evidence. It may constitute a *partition,* that is, the analysis of an individual person or object, or a *classification,* the analysis of a group of people or objects.

To observe the method used in formal analysis, let us consider a classification of rocks.[1] The primary division of this subject —and remember that analysis is division— produces three main parts: sedimentary, igneous, and metamorphic rocks. Each of these parts is capable of further division. The sedimentary rocks, when analyzed, prove to be of two kinds: the major rock masses of conglomerate, sandstone, shale, and limestone, and the minor rock deposits of coal, iron ore, rock salt, gypsum, and chert or flint. For each of these minor parts further divisions are demanded. The conglomerates, for example, are typical conglomerates, breccia, and arkose; shale is laminated shale or mudstone. Thus an outline of this analysis would take the following form:

I. Sedimentary rocks
  A. Major rock masses
    1. Conglomerate
      a. Typical conglomerate
      b. Breccia
      c. Arkose
    2. Shale
      a. Laminated shale
      b. Mudstone
    3. Sandstone
      a. Even-grained varieties
      b. Hybrid varieties
        (1) Verging on conglomerate
        (2) Verging on shale
    4. Limestone
      a. Chalk
      b. Coquina
      c. Dolomite
  B. Minor Rock deposits
    1. Coal
    2. Iron ore
    3. Rock salt
    4. Gypsum
    5. Chert
II. Igneous rocks
III. Metamorphic rocks

[1] The classification used here is that of *A Textbook of Geology,* Part I, by Louis V. Pirsson, revised by William Agar *et al.,* third edition.

Actually, of course, this outline stops short of a complete treatment of the subject as the points under *I.B.* are not divided, nor are the main points *II* and *III*, but the method shown will illustrate how an analysis of these points could be made in order to render this a truly formal analysis. The type of paper written from such an analysis has therefore the intent of presenting an impersonal, complete report.

Informal Analysis

Also in common use is the informal analysis. It differs in purpose from the formal analysis in that it tries to be not complete but selective. Just as in definition certain words were noted to be so general as not to admit of complete delineation, so in analysis certain topics do not admit of complete division. The analysis of a contemporary world problem, for example, cannot be exhaustive, for no one and no group has all the facts needed to make the formal analysis. It takes many years before the causes of a war can be fully ascertained and a complete analysis made of them. Thus many of the articles appearing in our modern news magazines and journals on contemporary affairs are informal analysis. They endeavor to present certain aspects of their subject which seem of primary importance without making a pretense of completeness. The term "informal" describes their method in so far as the judgment of the writer is exercised when a selection is made. In addition, the writer is given greater freedom of presentation. In keeping with his subject, his writing may be as satirical, humorous, or serious as he wishes. The formal analysis, on the other hand, makes a more impersonal presentation.

The following brief illustration may perhaps depict the method of the informal analysis. An educator, requested to write an article for a publication read by high-school teachers, chose as his subject the qualities of a good teacher. If he had filled a volume with his observations, it is doubtful if he could have exhausted this subject, but with only a few hundred words at his disposal, he was severely limited. He therefore chose four points which he believed to embody the chief characteristics of the good teacher: a cheerful devotion to the tasks facing the teacher, a knowledge of subject matter, skill in classroom presentation, and an understanding, pleasant personality. Such points, for example, as the relation of the teacher to the community or to the high-school faculty were disregarded, and all the skill of the educator was thrown into presenting the four divisions of the subject as clearly, forcefully, and entertainingly as possible.

Precautions

A first precaution is to *realize clearly the problem being analyzed and the persons for whom the analysis is being made*. If the general subject is the playgrounds in a certain city, the exact problem in that extensive topic must be ascertained. An analysis might be made of the need for new playgrounds, of the expense involved in the upkeep of existing playgrounds, of the benefits of the existing playgrounds, of the supervision to be found on them, or of many similar problems. So first determine exactly what you are analyzing. Having made a selection, then decide to whom you are addressing your remarks. A report to the Chamber of Commerce would demand one technique, a talk to the Rotary Club another, and a letter to the newspaper still a third. The reader, purpose, thesis, and principle of unity thus deserve careful attention.

As the division of the subject is begun, *a basis of classification must be formulated immediately*. For example, the buildings on a campus might be classified according to their style of architecture; some might be Gothic, others colonial, and others Georgian. Style of architecture would thus be the basis of classification. It is apparent, however, that many other bases of classification would be available for an analysis of the buildings: beauty of appearance, suitability for classroom purposes, age, cost of erection or maintenance, function, and so on. The precaution is that only one such basis should be established for the main points of the outline. Only in the subpoints can a different basis be used. For example, the table of classification of igneous rocks in *A Textbook of Geology* by L. V. Pirsson employs texture of the rock as the basis of classification. The main division thus employs such headings as granular, glassy, and fragmental and thereby includes all igneous rocks in the classification. To insert any other basis would break the classification and introduce confusion by the overlapping of points. The insertion of such a heading as "granite" would shift the basis of classification to mineral composition and so remove granite from its proper position as a subdivision of "granular." However, in the subdivisions a new basis may sometimes be established, although such a shift is not necessary in all analyses. In the classification of igneous rocks, the mineral composition is made the basis of the subpoints; granular is divided into granite, diorite, gabbro, dolerite, and peridotite. The basis must be closely adhered to, however, once it has been chosen in the subdivision. One basis of classification must be formulated for all co-ordinate points.

As another precaution, *each heading must have at least two subpoints if it is to be divided at all.* Analysis is division. Thus it is as impossible to divide any topic into less than two parts as it is to cut an apple into fewer than two pieces. If in the above outline, "granite" had seemed to be the only type of granular rock, the classification would *not* read:

I. Granular
    A. Granite
II. Granular and porphyritic, etc.

Such an arrangement would be logically impossible because granite would be the equivalent of the main heading "granular" and so would not be a part of that heading. No division would take place, and the form should read:

I. Granular: Granite
II. Granular and porphyritic, etc.

Actually, of course, in this classification, there were types of granular rocks other than granite, and a fuller division could be made. Such is usually true of any main heading.

From this discussion it follows that *the sum of the subdivisions must equal the main heading.* When added to one another, granite, diorite, gabbro, dolerite, and peridotite constitute exactly the class of granular igneous rocks. So in a complete analysis the sum of the minor points equals the main point. Arithmetically this process would read:

I. 4
    A. 1
    B. 1
    C. 1
    D. 1

By observing the principle of division and by employing but one basis of classification for co-ordinate points, you should be able to construct a satisfactory analysis. For other principles, refer to the section in this textbook on outlining.

SUGGESTIONS FOR STUDY

1. Criticize and reconstruct the following outlines.

a. THESIS: *All kinds of people play golf.*
    I. Duffers
        A. Those who are beginners
        B. Those who have played long but who play poorly
    II. Experts
        A. Amateurs who play well
        B. Professionals
    III. People of all ages
        A. Young people
        B. Old people
    IV. Men
        A. Office workers
        B. Manual workers
    V. Women

b. THESIS: *A good room is essential for effective studying.*
    I. Proper lighting
        A. Large windows
        B. A good desk lamp
    II. Good ventilation
        A. Plenty of fresh air

III. Comfort
   A. A large desk
   B. A comfortable chair
   C. Convenient bookcases
   D. Quiet
IV. Good technique of study
   A. A well-planned program of study hours
   B. The ability to read well
   C. The ability to outline well
   D. Skill in taking notes

c. THESIS: *Certain economies are possible under a large-scale operation of business.*

I. The economy in producing goods
   A. Purchasing in large quantities
   B. Specializing through the use of large plants
   C. Making use of by-products
II. The economy in marketing goods
   A. Shipment in large quantities
   B. Maintenance of selling agencies
   C. Loss of contact between producer and consumer
III. The economy in administering the plant
   A. Comparatively low fixed charges
   B. Comparatively low office charges
   C. Comparatively low cost of advertising because of large volume

D. Piling up of financial reserves in case of emergency
IV. The economy in regulating industrial finance
   A. Availability of lower rates of interest on loans

2. For the same limited aspect of one of the following general subjects, construct two outlines to illustrate the analysis of the subject upon two different bases of classification:

teachers, colleges, trees, automobiles, the engineering profession, radios, rhetoric, lyrical poetry, railroading, insects, types of architecture, bridges, shoes, furniture, doctors, orchestras, clocks, cameras, houses, hobbies, operas, paintings, golf clubs, schools, food, the errors in your compositions of this year.

3. Write an article which makes an analysis of a limited aspect of one of the following subjects:

college students, magazines, newspapers, sports, guns, pumps, oil, oceans, lakes, mountains, airplanes, balloons, ships, harbors, canals, swamps, diseases, scientists, rivers, dogs, watches, any industry, a zoo, brushes, Congress.

The Business Type[1]

JAMES TRUSLOW ADAMS

FIRST LET US analyze the businessman himself. Is there such a thing as a business "type"? Thinking of all the variations among those one knows, much as one thinks of one's varied French friends, one may think it impossible to classify them under one head; but just as, contrasting one's French friends with English or Russian, a French type does emerge, so contrasting a man who is in business all his life with those engaged in other pursuits, a business type does also take form. Apart from initial tastes and nature, a man is bound to be molded by the aims, ideas,

ideals, and whole nature of the career to which he devotes practically his entire energies and time. It is obvious that a poet or musician will react to the facts of existence differently from the way a steel manufacturer, an admiral, a high ecclesiastic, a politician, or a Supreme Court judge would do. All of them naturally have to provide themselves with a living, but the fundamental facts that regulate their reactions to the world about them are different.

For a businessman that fundamental fact is, and is bound to be, *profit*. Having made money, the businessman may be, as he often is, more generous and careless with it than an aristocrat or a churchman; but that does

[1] From James Truslow Adams, *Our Business Civilization* (New York, 1929). Reprinted by permission of Albert & Charles Boni, Inc.

not alter the fact that the main function of
his work, his main preoccupation, and the
point from which he views everything connected with his work is that of a profit. For
one thing, all men, whether they be poets,
soldiers, diplomats, or department-store owners, crave, as we have said, success and
recognition in their chosen field. The hall-
mark of success in business is the extent of
profit a man gets out of it. An artist may find
no public for his wares, but, if he is doing
great work, he will be supported by the
opinion of his peers. A doctor may struggle
in a country village with nothing but a
pittance, but he has the satisfaction of a
noble work nobly done. A man like Asquith
may spend his whole life in the service of
his country and yet retire as prime minister
with the income of a bank clerk. But a man
who spends his life in business and ends no
wealthier than he began is voted a failure
by all his fellows, even though he may have
personal qualities that endear him to his
friends.

This fundamental preoccupation with
making a profit has been much emphasized
by the shift of business from the individual
to the corporate form. A man may do what
he likes with his own, and if he chooses to be
quixotic he can be; but in the new triple relationship of workmen, executives, and stockholders in the modern corporation there has
ceased to be personality anywhere. The
American is a great believer in the magical
power of words. The bare facts of business
are now being covered over by the new
American gospel of "service"; but when we
analyze this, does it not merely come down
to the obvious facts that the businessman
performs a highly useful function in society
and that, so far as he can, he should see that
the public gets its full money's worth? The
fundamental need of profit remains. The professional classes—doctors, artists, scholars,
scientists, and others—may, as they often do,
work for little or nothing at all, but, except
in the rarest of personal instances, the businessman is precluded from doing so. What

stockbroker, manufacturing company, railway, or electric light corporation, with all
their talk about service, would ever consider running their business at a voluntary
loss in order to render greater service or tide
the public over a crisis? It cannot be done. It
is profit first, and then, perhaps, as much
service as is compatible with profit.

Now this primary and essential preoccupation with making a profit naturally tends to
color a businessman's view of his entire
world, and is what, in my opinion, mainly
differentiates business from the professions.
Nor do I speak as an impractical intellectual.
Of the last thirty years I have spent about
one half in business and half in professional
work, and I realize the great difference, having paid my monthly bills, between concentrating primarily on the work rather than the
profit.

Moreover, dealing inevitably with material
things and with the satisfying of the world's
material wants, the businessman tends to
locate happiness in *them* rather than in the
intellectual and spiritual unless he constantly
refreshes his spirit away from business during his leisure. When the pressure of business
on his time, or his concentration on it, becomes so great as to preclude his reasonable
use of leisure for the development of his
whole human personality, he is apt to become a complete materialist even if, as is
now frequently not the case, he ever had it
in him to become anything else. He may live
in a palace, ride in the most luxurious cars,
and fill his rooms with old masters and the
costliest manuscripts which his wealth can
draw from under the hammer at Christie's,
but if he cares more for riches, luxury, and
power than for a humanely rounded life he
is not civilized but what the Greeks properly
called a "barbarian."

Aside from narrowness of interests, the
businessman, from the nature of his major
occupation, is apt to have short views and
to distrust all others. It was once said, as
superlative praise, of the late J. P. Morgan,
one of the most public-spirited and far-

sighted businessmen we have had, that he "thought in ten-year periods." Most businessmen think—and do well to do so as businessmen—in one- or two-year periods; the businessman cares nothing for the tendency of what he is doing. This has been emphasized in the American businessman by the vast extent of the natural resources with which he has had to deal and the recuperative powers of an active people in a half-settled continent. If, as he did in the northern Mississippi Valley, he can make his personal profit by ripping the forests off the face of half a dozen states in a decade, he is content to let those who come later look after themselves.

Nor is he any more solicitous about the social results of his activities. Obviously, what interests the businessman as a businessman is a free hand to gather wealth as quickly as may be, combined with a guarantee that society shall protect him in that wealth once he has gathered it. He may steal the water resources of a dozen states, but, once they are stolen, he is a defender of the Constitution and the sanctity of contract. It is not hard to understand why the United States is the most radical country in the world in its business methods and the most conservative in its political!

Preoccupation with profit, again, tends to make a businessman, as businessman, blind to the aesthetic quality in life. A beautiful bit of scenery, such as Montauk Point, is for him merely a good site for a real-estate development; a waterfall is merely waterpower. America's most successful businessman, Mr. Ford, while rolling up millions by the hundreds in profits, was content to turn out what was, perhaps, the ugliest car on the market. It was only when his profits were threatened that he turned to the consideration of beauty, and he would not have done so had it not promised profit. No sane businessman in charge of a large business would do so. It is much the same with the cultivation of the businessman's mind. Time is money, and anything which takes time and does not give

business results is waste. But if you tell him that if he shows an interest in Keats he can probably land Smith's account—Smith being a queer, moony guy—or that if he will go to hear the "Rheingold" he can make a hit with that chap he has long been after, the effect will be magical. Innumerable advertisements of books on teaching of foreign languages will easily illustrate what I mean.

These and other qualities of the businessman are his qualities *as* a businessman. They are qualities that are bred in him by his occupation. Plenty of businessmen are much more than businessmen and outside of their offices and business hours have other qualities and other interests. But there is this to be said. Society at large, including the businessman himself, owes its opportunity for a fully rounded life mainly to those who have not been businessmen. What will be the effect on all of us of the growing dominance of the business type and of the hold which the businessman and business ideals have attained upon our civilization?

SUGGESTIONS FOR STUDY

1. What is the aim of the businessman? By what is he tested as a success or failure?

2. What distinguishes business from the professions?

3. What qualification does the author have to be writing on this subject?

4. In what does the businessman seek to find happiness? What is narrow about this conception?

5. Why will he be nothing more than a "barbarian" if he puts his trust in riches, luxury, and power?

6. What is the second great weakness of the business type?

7. What weakness in the business type explains why the United States is radical in business methods and conservative in politics?

8. What attitude does the business type take toward the aesthetic quality in life? What will serve to stimulate his interest in the aesthetic?

9. Is this analysis a partition or a classification? Is it a formal or an informal analysis?

10. Define the following words from the analysis: ecclesiastic, crave, pittance, quixotic, precluded, compatible, differentiate, humanely, recuperative, solicitous, sanctity, preoccupation.

You Are One of These[1]

VERGIL D. REED

FEW THINGS are more firmly imbedded in our minds than our mental image of the typical American—our picture of ourselves: We are a young people. Most of us live in a growing city, or on a farm in a growing state. Most of us work in a factory or on a farm. We are of the melting pot, partaking of all the races and nationalities; likely as not, our parents were born in Europe. These are some generally held impressions.

But not one of these statements is true! The average age of Americans today is 30; it used to be 16—another way of saying we are rapidly getting to be a nation in which old folk predominate. Most of our cities are not growing, and most of our states are losing population. Twice as many persons are employed in the service industries—trade, transportation, communications—as in factories or on farms. And we are getting to be as American as corn on the cob or ham and eggs. Half the babies born in the United States in 1915 had one parent at least who was foreign born. Now nine out of ten babies have two American-born parents.

Census figures tell us a great deal more than the mere size of New York and Walla Walla. Carefully studied, they reveal themselves to be packed with drama—the drama of a changing America. To begin with, our country will not continue to grow as it did formerly. By 1980 we probably shall have reached our peak population, about 150,000,-000. From then on, population figures will remain stationary or show a slight decline. This is quite natural in a maturing industrial nation and does not mean that our standard of living need decline.

But while the population is growing more slowly than in past decades, the number of *families* is increasing faster than ever. In the ten years between the last two censuses, population increased only 7.2 per cent while the number of families increased 16.6 per cent. That meant, of course, that the size of the average family was decreasing (from 4.1 persons to 3.8 persons). This increase in the number of families is more important to many industries than the increase in population, for the sale of refrigerators, kitchen ranges, automobiles, and many other things depends upon the number of families rather than the number of individuals. It is the increase in the number of families that intensifies our present headache, the housing shortage.

We start founding families a little earlier than we used to. The average age of the bridegroom in 1940 was 24.3 years; in 1890, 26.1. The 1940 bride was 21.6 years old; her grandmother married at 22. The war years, for which statistics are not yet available, undoubtedly brought the age of first marriage even lower.

Our birth rate, taking the long view, is declining; it fell from 25 births per thousand persons in 1915 to a low of 16.6 in 1933. But there is a great wave, or hump, on this long-term downward curve. The birth rate rose to 17.6 in 1940 and to 21.5, its wartime peak, in 1943. The decline has started again, and the baby boom will be over in 1947. When these babies reach childbearing age, their babies will cause another, but smaller wave, and it, too, will slide down the declining trend. Each generation, that wave will recur on smaller scale until it finally disappears.

In 1947 the babies born in 1941 will begin to flood our schools. We will find ourselves

[1] From the *Nation's Business* (June, 1946), and the *Reader's Digest* XLIX (July, 1946) 77. Reprinted by permission of the author and the *Reader's Digest*.

short of schoolrooms and teachers. That seven-year wave will later on pass through each grade, through elementary and high schools and into the colleges. Aside from the war wave, the fact that far more young people are going through high school and college than in the past will add to the troubles of school officials.

After the seven-year wave passes, many school boards and superintendents will be surprised at the sudden drop in enrollments —and the vacant space left. Manufacturers and retailers of children's goods will be in for similar surprises, unless they know the nature of this "bonus," which will not occur again for a generation. The baby boom will have passed.

Speaking of babies, there are 106 boys born for every hundred girls, and this approximate figure prevails the world over. However, males continue to die off faster than females all through life, in peace as well as in war. So the ladies finally prevail by a considerable margin.

There will be no shortage of husbands, except among the elders. When Miss America reaches her 20th birthday her chances of marrying within the year are 15.5 out of 100, and her normal chances of ever marrying are 92 out of 100. Eleven out of every 12 persons reaching the age of 15 will eventually marry.

America is aging. Almost a fourth of our people are over 45 already. Between 1930 and 1940 those over 65 rose about 35 percent. There will be three times as many people over 65 years of age in 1980 as there were in 1930.

From birth rates to taxes this increasing proportion of elders will influence our future. People are living longer. The old do not bear children. This cuts the birth rate further and decreases the proportion of the young. There will be more old people to be supported by fewer young ones. This will raise taxes to provide old-age pensions, social-security benefits, institutions, and medical care. For better or for worse, there will

be enough voting elders "to do something about it."

The increase in the aged will have many other effects, too.

An unusually large proportion of our people is *now* in the employable range of 20 to 59 years of age. More jobs have to be found *now*. But because fewer persons are approaching 20 and more persons are passing 59, this large wave of extra workers will ultimately decrease.

Industry's own retirement, benefit, and employe-relations plans will be greatly affected and undoubtedly liberalized. Elders will have more leisure time, and more assured incomes with which to enjoy it. Conservatism in politics will probably increase. Many changes in tastes, preferences, and needs for goods and services will develop. Geriatrics, the study and treatment of the ailments of old age, will be a promising field of medicine for our future doctors.

Recreation and amusement will have to take account of the habits and preferences of the elders. Many will move to warmer climates or spend their winters there. There will be more travel, both at home and abroad.

The rate of growth of our urban population has been slowing up since 1910. Large cities have practically ceased to grow within their corporate limits, with few and temporary exceptions. Their suburban areas, however, are growing rapidly and will continue to grow. Half of us now live in 140 metropolitan districts made up of cities of over 50,000 population and adjoining townships. Industry is already beginning to decentralize, with more but smaller factories outside the big cities.

As decentralization continues there will be more and better shopping centers in the suburbs; suburban land values will increase while urban values decrease, or increase at much slower rates.

The proportion of our population on farms was standing still before the war at 23.1 per cent. Every basic trend is against a back-to-the-farm movement. Better methods, better seeds, mechanization, and the wider use of fertilizers make possible vast increases in production on fewer acres and with fewer workers. The standard of living of those who remain on farms will increase if these better methods and means are used. The number of farms is decreasing, their size increasing.

The proportion of our labor force employed in trade, transportation, and the service "industries" has been increasing for more than a hundred years. These fields, excluding government, accounted for 45.8 per cent of our civilian employed persons in 1940. Manufacturing employed 23.4 per cent, while agriculture, forestry, and fisheries combined accounted for only 18.8 per cent.

Two definite mass migrations have taken place in recent years: the "Grapes of Wrath" depression migration in the '30's, and the late war-boom migration. The West Coast states were big gainers in population, along with Florida. A solid tier of states, from North Dakota to Oklahoma, were the big losers. Substantial increases in Maryland and Virginia really represent the growth of Washington, which has spilled over its own boundaries.

This pattern of migration is a long and basic one. For example, there is no reason to look for a net reverse migration from the West Coast. New factories, more favorable freight rates, climate, and future trade with the Orient are among the factors favoring further growth there. By 1950 the population of the Pacific states will probably exceed its war peak by a considerable margin. The West and Southeast will continue to gain, largely at the expense of the North and Northeast.

During the war years the number of women in rural-farm areas decreased 11.3 per cent but increased in cities. Of this female migration cityward, 665,000 were between 14 and 24 years of age. These younger women have acquired new wants, tastes, and standards which will greatly affect their future outlook on life.

Our long-run prospects are excellent. These people—of whom you are one—have what it takes. What we do with it is up to us.

SUGGESTIONS FOR STUDY

1. What percentage of babies are born of two American-born parents?
2. This was written in 1946. Check present population figures and see if the author's prophecy as stated in paragraph 3 has turned out to be true. This might lead you to check other prophecies of ten years ago and provide material for a series of papers on the validity of prophecy based on statistics.
3. How has the number of families increased in ratio to the number of individuals?
4. Do young people marry, on an average, at an earlier age than their grandparents did?
5. Explain how the wave of births in 1941-1947 will create problems in our school systems.
6. Explain what is meant by "America is aging."
7. Is the general trend toward living in large cities or in suburban areas? Is there a back-to-the-farm movement?
8. What sections of the country are growing?
9. Make an outline of this analysis to indicate clearly into what divisions the subject of population has been broken.

Let's Join the Human Race[1]

STRINGFELLOW BARR

OUR BASIC FOREIGN policy since World War II has been to oppose Russia. But that is a negative policy, and, deep down underneath, most Americans know it. Now we are slowly discovering that we need a positive policy. We are discovering we need a positive policy because we are slowly discovering what the world's basic problem is.

The world's basic problem was recognized by Secretary of State Acheson in his speech to the United Nations on September 20, 1950, and by President Truman, speaking to the same body on October 23, 1950. But unless American public opinion also recognizes that problem, these two speeches will of course remain just speeches.

We have been sadly agreeing that this is no longer what Wendell Willkie called "one world" but that we are living in two worlds —the Communist world and the non-Communist. And now we are beginning to learn that Willkie was right. It is still one world, a world torn by tension between its two most powerful states, a world rising against inequality whether of race or of economic opportunity, but still one world inhabited by one human race. What will happen to this world will depend, not just on us, or on Russia, but on what the human race does. What should they do? If the American government is to find a foreign policy, a policy that is constructive and realistic, we American citizens had better have a good realistic look at the human race.

But this is hard for us to do. In terms of food to eat and clothes to wear and houses to live in, the United States is a rich suburb, surrounded by slums. Some of the slums, like western Europe, were once elegant suburbs themselves, controlling every other continent on our planet. Some, like India, have not been powerful or elegant for hundreds of years. For a long time their citizens have been hungry, naked, and without decent shelter.

It is not easy for people who live in rich suburbs to understand the needs of people who live in slums. No bread? Why don't they eat cake? No money to buy clothes? Why don't they charge them? No roof on the house? They ought to phone a reliable contractor! Sick? They ought to call a doctor. Out of work? No real hustler stays out of work very long.

But a few of our economists and engineers, and a lot of our G.I.'s, have seen the staggering human misery of Asia, of Africa, of Latin America. The rest of us must just try to imagine it. Otherwise we won't understand the actual problems of the human race. And until we begin to understand those problems, our foreign policy will go on being unrealistic, and we Americans will ourselves seem less and less real to the two billion human beings who are not Americans. They may learn to fear us, but they won't understand us.

I believe there is a trick by which we Americans can understand these two billion men, women, and children scattered all over the globe. Will the reader play "Let's pretend" with me, the way children do? Let's pretend that you have not yet been born but will be born this year, somewhere on the planet, somewhere in this Mighty Neighborhood. And let's try to estimate your chances

[1] This article is the opening portion of the author's pamphlet *Let's Join the Human Race* (Chicago, 1950), which argues for a new foreign policy for the United States. Reprinted by permission of the University of Chicago Press.

of living a happy, healthy, decent, and useful life.

If you are born this year, then on the same day more than 200,000 other babies will be born, all over the world.

You will have less than one chance in twenty of being born in the United States. Your chance of being born in the Soviet Union will be not much better. These countries may be heavily armed, but most people just don't live in them.

You will probably be colored. Remember that you and the 200,000 other squawking brats who will be the day's baby crop are going to be born all over the planet and that there are just not many openings in the places where the white race lives. You must take your chances with the other babies. And the chances are, you will be colored—colored black, or colored brown, or colored yellow.

Your chances of being born white this year are not more than one in three. Your chances of being Chinese are one in four; of being born in India, better than one in nine.

If you are born colored, you will probably be born either among people who have recently revolted and thrown out the white folks who used to govern them or else in a country that is still trying to throw the white folks out. If you are born in Africa, you are likely to learn the maxim: "Never trust a white man."

You have only about one chance in four of being born a Christian. It is far more likely that you will be born a Confucian or a Buddhist, a Mohammedan or a Taoist.

If you are born in the United States—and, remember, that's quite an *if*—you will probably live longer than a year. But if you are born in India, which is more likely, you have only a little better than a one-to-four chance of living more than a year. But cheer up! your chances in some places would be worse; and, besides, even if you survive babyhood in India, you have only a fifty-fifty chance of growing to maturity.

If you are born colored, the chances are overwhelming that you will be chronically sick all your life—from malaria, or intestinal parasites, or tuberculosis, or maybe even leprosy. And even if you are not chronically sick, you are likely to be weak from hunger. You have about a two-to-one chance of suffering from malnutrition, either from too little food or from food that is not a balanced or nourishing diet. You have a reasonably good chance of experiencing real famine—to the point where you will be glad to eat the bark off a tree. But this chance is extremely hard to calculate.

Again, if you are born colored, you have only a one-to-four chance of learning to read. And since you almost certainly will not own a radio, you will be pretty well cut off from that part of the human family that has enough to eat and that is reasonably healthy. You will most likely live in a mud hut, with a dirt floor and no chimney, its roof thatched with straw. You will almost certainly work on the land, and most of what you raise will go to the landlord. In addition, you are likely to be deeply in debt to the local money-lender, and you may have to pay him annual interest of anywhere from 30 to 100 per cent.

But enough of this "Let's pretend." No need to be quaint about it. What I am describing is the actual condition of mankind in the middle of the twentieth century. To explain how it got there would involve a good deal of history for which we have no time here. The point is, that is where it got. Many millions of these sick, hungry, illiterate, and oppressed people belong to "the free nations" we propose to lead in a crusade against communism. We had better take a good look at the real world we live in before we lead much further. We had better base American foreign policy on real facts.

SUGGESTIONS FOR STUDY

1. For clarification of our international situation, to what is our nation compared in the fourth paragraph?

2. At what point in the article does the analysis begin?

3. What different bases of classification does the author use to analyze mankind?

4. For what audience is this analysis intended? Study especially the attitude of mind which the author anticipated.

5. Make a sentence outline of the article.

B. Argumentation

The aim of argumentation is to convince a reader of the truth of a conclusion. It may try to stimulate an audience which is but lukewarm in its acceptance of an idea or which has yet been unable to make up its mind at all; more difficult to accomplish, it may also try actually to reverse the judgment of an audience which shows an aggressive hostility to a measure. An engineer's report to a city manager on the feasibility of establishing new water mains is an example of addressing an undecided reading group; in Shakespeare's *Julius Caesar* the speech of Mark Antony in defense of Caesar is an example of changing the mind of a hostile audience.

The general problem, then, is to present a set of facts in such a manner psychologically that they will insinuate themselves into a reader's mind and cause him to act as you desire. The first step, of course, in achieving that aim is to collect pertinent facts, complete enough so that you will not have overlooked any important consideration. But before you begin to write your paper, you must subject these facts to a logical analysis, for the arguments which you are preparing are very slippery and your reasoning can easily go awry. Such an analysis should begin with a scrutiny of the thesis which you are defending, usually termed a *proposition* in argument. Next it must examine the major *issues* which you must prove to win your point. Once the proposition and issues are decided upon, you are in a position to construct an outline and write your argumentative paper.

THE PROPOSITION

The first step in argument is to define the proposition. By a proposition is meant the point which is being argued. Every word in

the proposition must be clearly defined before any logical arguing can be done. For example, a discussion of the proposition, "Poetry is a type of reading which most students dislike," could never reach any satisfactory conclusions. The terms are too vague. Poetry embraces a wide variety of materials; some people might enjoy lyrics but dislike epics; others might like ballads but dislike ballades. The term "poetry" would quickly turn out to be too general to suffice in a logical argument without careful definition. The proposition also contains another troublesome word—"most." If a more specific word such as "majority" were substituted, a poll of students might be undertaken to establish the proposition. But what kind of students? Grade-school pupils are students. Thus every word in the proposition must be closely scrutinized for ambiguity or looseness.

THE ISSUES

The next step in the argument, once the point has been clearly defined, is to formulate the specific issues which must be settled in the course of the discussion. In order to be convinced, a reader must have certain questions concerning the proposition answered to his satisfaction. For example, suppose that a salesman is trying to sell a house to a prospective buyer. He praises the beauty of the location, the attractiveness of the grounds surrounding the house, the pleasing appearance of the exterior, the satisfactory arrangement of rooms, and so on. The buyer courteously listens to the eloquent plea but asks one question: What does the house cost? That to him is a major issue. If it is answered to his satisfaction, then he is willing to be convinced on other issues. But if the price is too high, then all the other pleading has no effect on him.

The salesman might proceed in the following manner in preparing his argument. First, he might list all the questions that need to be answered in order to make the sale. These would be purely temporary:

What will it cost?

How can it be financed?

What will be the tax rate?

What kind of furnace has it, and how much will fuel cost?

Is it cool in summer and warm in winter?

Will the grounds afford space for children to play?

Is there room for a garden?

Are the neighbors congenial?

Is the community a desirable one?

Many such questions would occur to him. He could then condense these to a few so that he could answer them effectively. One question would deal with the cost and financing of the house; a second with the upkeep; a third with the condition of the house and grounds; and a fourth with the community. The revised list would then read:

What will it cost, and how can it be financed?

What will be the cost of upkeep?

What is the condition of the house and grounds for comfort, convenience, and attractiveness?

What is the nature of the community?

By analyzing these issues, the salesman can convince his customer, but by the neglect of almost any one, he may lose the sale. Thus it is in any argument.

THE METHODS OF REASONING

For the construction of a logical argument revolving round a definite proposition and comprehensive issues, two methods of reasoning may be employed: *inductive* and *deductive*. The former is a derivation of a conclusion from the observation of a group of facts; the latter is a derivation of a conclusion by the application of a general principle to an isolated fact.

Inductive Reasoning

A student walking across the campus in spring notices that the girls are wearing their new spring attire. One girl after another passes him, dressed in brightly colored sweaters, peasant skirts, and saddle shoes.

After some time, the student concludes: the spring fashions for college women demand brightly colored sweaters, peasant skirts, and saddle shoes. He is reasoning inductively. From a set of facts which he has observed, he has drawn a conclusion. This method of reasoning has been made more famous as the scientific method. Laboratory technique to establish a hypothesis, theory, or law from the observation of a multitude of facts is inductive.

Causes of error in inductive reasoning. In employing inductive reasoning, be careful to avoid certain causes of error. *A first cause is faulty observation.* A color-blind student might well come to the wrong conclusion about the colors of the spring attire. Those pseudo scientists who believe that a hair when placed in water will metamorphose into a snake are guilty of the same mistake. Perhaps the most universal errors of this kind were the beliefs that the world is flat and that the sun revolves about the earth. It is essential to guard against superficial observation.

A second cause of error is the derivation of a conclusion too hastily. Most of us tend to state a conclusion without having accumulated enough evidence. One or two girls dressed in a particular manner would not present enough evidence for one to derive a satisfactory conclusion concerning the fashions; only the observation of a great many girls can lead to a tenable conclusion. Students at classification time often err in enrolling for courses because of this logical error. They accept the word of a classmate that a particular course is easy, only to find later to their dismay that it is very difficult for them. They fail to accumulate sufficient evidence.

A second human tendency is to state a conclusion without having accumulated pertinent facts. If fifty girls who care nothing for their manner of dress should troop across the campus, one might conclude hastily that no new spring fashions had been created. The conclusion would be unwarranted only because the facts were not representative. This error is the one which all pre-election and other straw polls endeavor to avoid. The famous poll conducted by the *Literary Digest* magazine which predicted the easy victory of Alfred Landon over Franklin Roosevelt erred because its sampling of the voting public was not a representative sampling; the facts were not pertinent.

A *third cause of error lies in the source of the facts*. Some facts we can amass ourselves; others we can gather only at second hand. Thus a reliance upon inaccurate sources of information can produce error. The source must first be checked for its timeliness. In wartime, facts concerning the imports and exports of European nations are nearly useless if they are much more than a month old. Likewise, an argument concerning present policy toward Japan would err if the writer employed for his information on Japan solely the writings of Lafcadio Hearn dated fifty years ago. The timeliness of the facts must therefore be ascertained. The latest material, of course, is not always the best. On the character of Shakespeare, for example, one would rather accept the testimony of a contemporary who knew him well than to accept the conjectures of a later critic or biographer.

The source of information must also be checked for its authority. If we are to accept a man's word as fact, we must first ask, what authority has he for making this statement? A general rule is *never accept as fact the testimony of a man when he is speaking outside his special study*. For example, when Bill Jones who operates a machine in a local factory states that the machines in that factory are unsafe for use, he may well be believed, with certain reservations. But when the same Bill Jones declares that the last ruling of the Supreme Court was erroneous, his word is subject to error. Or when Professor Calkins of the mathematics department speaks on the teaching of mathematics, his words carry weight; when he speaks on the teaching of history, his authority is

immediately diminished. Or when Senator Sorghum advises on his special study of taxation, he is more significant than when he expresses an opinion on international trade agreements.

Having ascertained a man's authority, you may next ask, did he actually say this? If his remark has been repeated at second, third, or fourth hand, it has probably been altered materially. A girl involved in an accident while swimming escaped unscathed; soon after, her parents received the crushing news that she was drowned. Such is the fallacy of hearsay evidence. Each recipient of the evidence is very likely to interpret it to suit his own liking or to be sensational.

Next we may ask: is the authority prejudiced? The testimony of those who are in a perfect position to speak authoritatively is often worthless because of their bias. The shopkeeper who is paying tribute to gangsters for "protection" will not speak truly to the police because he fears for the lives of his wife and children. Many times, the bias is purely unintentional. The United States is full of people who affirm sincerely that the locality in which they live is the most beautiful in the land. Thus it behooves one to determine whether a prejudice exists, and to make due allowance for it.

A *fourth cause of error is the derivation of an unwarranted conclusion from accurate facts*. Error is likely to occur in any statement of cause and effect. One common assumption is that because two events happen in close proximity, the one causes the other. On a sullen day a small patch of blue appears in the sky; the sun shines through it; soon the whole sky has cleared up. Therefore, the sun cleared away the cloud masses. Such a conclusion is unwarranted. Because the clouds were clearing up, the sun was able to shine through them. People often reason rather superstitiously in this manner. Last Thursday I was going to take out insurance on my automobile, but I forgot; on Friday, I was in an accident and my car was smashed beyond repair. Therefore, the failure to take out the policy occasioned the accident. Political reasoning often follows similar channels. President Hoover was in office when the depression of 1929 broke; therefore he was responsible for it and must be defeated at the polls. President Roosevelt and the New Dealers were in office during the 1930's; therefore they are responsible for all the ills of that decade. This is often called *post hoc propter hoc* reasoning, in which a purely time sequence is mistaken for a cause and effect sequence.

Sometimes, too, an effect is attributed to a cause which is too slight to have produced it. This fallacy is frequently responsible for the dismissal of athletic coaches. When a team falls into a losing streak, the coach is usually blamed. A football coach is but one man; on the field are eleven men who do the actual playing, and on the bench are perhaps sixty more. Yet the coach alone is held responsible for the games which are lost.

The apparent cause and effect may also be invalid through the operation of a more powerful yet hidden cause. For example, if the nephew of a prominent governmental official were appointed to an important post, the usual comment would be, "Well, he's the nephew, you know; he has the pull that the rest of us lack." But if the nephew had passed a civil service examination with the highest possible grade, his appointment would be on sheer merit and the obvious cause would be entirely inoperative.

These errors—faulty observation, insufficient evidence, faulty sources, and the illogical derivation of cause and effect—will suffice to show how careful you must be in the pursuance of inductive argument. If you fall into errors such as these, your argument may prove fallacious.

Deductive Reasoning

Instead of proceeding from particulars to a generalization, deductive reasoning proceeds from a generalization to the particular. A statement which is assumed to be true is made as a general classification; a particular fact is then classified under that generalization, and a conclusion is drawn as a consequence. Reduced to its logical elements, this process is known as the *syllogism*, the three parts of which are called the major premise, the minor premise, and the conclusion. Here is a typical syllogism:

MAJOR PREMISE: All students in this class are over seventeen years of age.

MINOR PREMISE: Bill is a student in this class.

CONCLUSION: Bill is over seventeen years of age.

A general classification of students is made in the major premise; a particular student is placed in this group by means of the minor premise; the conclusion is then drawn that as long as the student belongs in this classification, its characteristics belong to him as well as to the other members of the group.

It will be clear that the generalization to be found in the major premise is the result of inductive reasoning. From the examination of many individual instances, certain general laws of the world have been derived. That is the inductive process. But once these laws have been established, they can be used to interpret any number of individual instances that come within their scope. That is the deductive process.

Causes of error in deductive reasoning. Every member of the syllogism must be accurately stated if the conclusion is to be true. *First be sure that the major premise is sound,* for obviously, if it is faulty, no true conclusion can be drawn.

All radios cost more than thirty dollars.
This is a radio.
Therefore, it costs more than thirty dollars.

The fact that some radios cost as little as ten dollars invalidates the major premise and hence the conclusion also. Especially dangerous are unwarranted generalizations, such as "All the good fellows on campus are fraternity members" or "All the great industrialists in the world are Americans."

The minor premise must also be true. For example, a chemist might fall into error by reasoning this way:

Sodium sulphate when added to barium chloride produces a barium sulphate precipitate.

This is sodium sulphate.

Therefore, when added to barium chloride, it will produce a barium sulphate precipitate.

Failing to get the desired precipitate, he analyzes the supposed sodium sulphate and finds it to be another compound. The classification of the minor premise was inaccurate and the conclusion therefore erroneous.

The conclusions must also arise logically from the premises. Error may first come from a failure to make a classification in the minor premise.

Outdoor sports provide good exercise.
Basketball provides good exercise.
Therefore, basketball is an outdoor sport.

There is, of course, no classification in this syllogism. Error may also come from the use of more than three terms in the syllogism. In the proper syllogism, two terms are given in the major premise (as *Conscientious students* study their *lessons*), an additional term is added in the minor premise (*John* is a conscientious student), but the conclusion adds no new term (Therefore, *John* studies his *lessons*). If a fourth term is given in the conclusion, error will result, as in the following:

Iced drinks are cooling in summer.
This grape juice is an iced drink.
Therefore, it should be pleasing.

Patriotic deeds are greatly in demand.
John's deed was patriotic.
Therefore, John is much in demand.

APPLICATION OF REASONING TO THE WRITING OF ARGUMENT

The two major processes of reasoning which have just been considered have a direct application to the writing of argument. If the argument is presented inductively, a statement at the beginning of the paper establishes the subject which is being discussed, the facts are then presented, and the conclusion is finally drawn from these facts. This method is especially desirable for persuading a hostile reader. If the argument is well presented, he finds that he cannot escape the conclusion which follows from the facts.

Deduction is no less useful but calls for more practice. If the writer can present a sound generalization in his paper and have the minor premise correctly classified under it, then the reader must accept the conclusion which follows logically from the premises. Suppose that the president of a state university is arguing before the budget committee of the state legislature that his institution needs a new physics building. His aim is to get the committee by its vote to appropriate the necessary funds. He must establish therefore as his major premise what the general principle of voting is as applied to this situation. He decides that this generalization should read: All needs of a state institution should be met by your appropriation of necessary funds. If he deemed it necessary, he might then establish more fully this concept of the legislator's duty. Having fortified the major premise, he might frame the minor premise: Our need of a physics building is a need of a state institution. His task would clearly be to prove the minor premise. To make the proof, he might again have recourse to syllogisms: Physicists can carry on modern research only with proper equipment and building facilities; we have on our campus a whole department of physicists; therefore, they can carry on modern research only with proper equipment and building facilities. Poor buildings and equipment are detrimental to the work of both students and faculty; our present physics building is poor; therefore, it is detrimental to the work of both students and faculty. Through such a process of reasoning the minor premise might well be proved. Therefore, the legislators would logically have to accept the conclusion:

All needs of a state institution should be met by your appropriation of necessary funds.

Our need of a physics building is a need of a state institution.

Therefore, our need of a physics building should be met by your appropriation of necessary funds.

Although this argument has been in general conducted by deductive reasoning, inductive reasoning may be employed at any point to support the truth of any major or minor premise. Thus the two are not exclusive but may be used in conjunction with each other.

FINAL PRECAUTIONS

As you may mislead both the reader and yourself in the course of an argument—and we are assuming here that you wish to be scientifically accurate, and not to resort to propagandist devices intended to mislead the reader—you must guard against certain human weaknesses that may destroy the force of your logic. Some of these precautions have been stated already, but others are of such importance that they need to be mentioned also.

Analogy. Reasoning is sometimes conducted by means of analogy. That is, a writer argues that because two objects are alike in one respect, they must be alike in other respects. Suppose that you were arguing that college freshmen should not be subjected to a close discipline in grammar and sentence structure, but should spend their time in mastering various subjects so that they would have something to say in their papers. You might offer an analogy. If a man cannot handle an ax, you would not spend hour after hour teaching him how to grasp it and swing it and make a clean cut; on the contrary, you would give him a few words of instruction as you led him to the woodpile, and then you would let him start chopping wood. Soon by trial and error and by experience, he would chop well because once he saw his goal and what he had to do to achieve it, he would quickly find the means. So, you argue, it is in rhetoric. Give the student a goal that he can see and a mastery of content so that he can achieve it, and he will find the suitable means of expression.

That argument sounds very good; indeed argument by analogy is one of the most persuasive means of reasoning—to the unwary. *Actually, analogy carries no proof.* The best it can do is to indicate that *perhaps* some point may be true. In the analogy given above, there is no essential similarity between the two processes; they are both learning processes, but the one is a relatively simple physical process, whereas the other is a very difficult mental process. It may be true that rhetoric students should be given such leeway, but the analogy does not prove that proposition. A writer should therefore use analogy only with the intent of clarifying. It is an excellent means whereby a difficult point may be explained. Lincoln once spoke of his administration during the Civil War as being similar to a tight-rope walker crossing Niagara Falls on a tight wire. No one would think for a moment of interfering with that performer for fear that he should fall. In like manner no one should interfere with the administration of the government which was passing through equally perilous times. Thus Lincoln made clear what he meant—but he proved nothing.

Rationalizing. Justifying an action by a *post facto* chain of reasoning is called "rationalizing." A man wishes to play golf when he knows he should attend to his business; at the links he meets a man whose good will may help him in his business. He then convinces himself that his decision to play golf was an excellent business stroke. Akin to this is "wishful thinking." We should like to have easy victories and quick success in time of war; hence we interpret each action of the enemy as a sign of weakness. The skilled logician, however, does not blind himself to essential facts, but he analyzes basic motives and facts to arrive at truthful conclusions.

The argument against the man. An old trick of the propagandists which one must guard against in his own thinking is the direction of the argument against a man rather than against the cause which he advocates.

To praise or condemn the New Deal, one does not praise or condemn the character of Mr. Roosevelt. An argument concerns the issues of a question and not the men involved.

The argument to the people. The appeal to the emotions rather than to the intellect is known as the argument to the people. It is extremely pleasing to all of us and hence very dangerous. Through its force a generalization is accepted without being sufficiently examined. Many times have bad leaders of nations struck up the band, waved the flag, shouted about the nation's honor, and so marched the people off to war without their stopping to consider whether the war was well justified. Such emotionalism is, to be sure, often used by writers to further a worthy cause, but you must be very careful to distinguish in your own mind between the moment when you are indulging in emotionalism and the moment when you are on the solid ground of fact and logic.

The red herring. A remark which is drawn across the main path of the argument and so turns it into by-paths is known as a red herring. During the course of an argument to prove that the university needs a new stadium, it might come to light that forty years ago old President Whitebeard declared that the university had no need for a stadium of large proportions. The argument might well be switched off into a discussion of the president and his statement, the whole discussion being quite beside the point, as conditions have changed materially in the forty-year period. Thus the writer must keep to the main issues and not be led into by-paths by a red herring.

Ignoring the issues. Once an argument has been started, the main issues must be fully analyzed. Many arguments founder because only minor issues are settled or because the ground of the argument is shifted. Comparing football scores to indicate the relative strength of teams often fails as a true basis. Just because Yale defeated Princeton, and Princeton defeated Cornell, one cannot argue that Yale will necessarily defeat Cornell. The scores are but one issue. One must analyze further the size of the scores, the weather conditions during the games, the physical conditions of the teams, the heaviness of the respective schedules, and many other factors before any logical argument can be made.

Many people shift so rapidly from one point to the next that none is settled completely. A student talking to his adviser expressed difficulty in securing a good mark in chemistry. Suspecting that poor reading was a major cause of the boy's trouble, the adviser placed an English book before him and asked him to read a passage and tell exactly what it said. The student was unable to do so. The adviser counseled him thereupon to adopt sounder methods of reading, but the student, shifting the ground, urged that reading from an English book has little in common with reading from a chemistry book. The instructor produced a chemistry book, and the experiment was repeated with a similar result. The student again shifted the ground by declaring that he could not read with the instructor watching him but that in his own room he had no difficulty in mastering the chemistry text, and that his trouble was caused by the chemistry instructor's dislike for him. Thus the discussion would have ended in an argument against the man had the adviser allowed it to continue far along that path. Each issue must therefore be adhered to and completely settled before the argument proceeds to the next.

The argument must proceed in carefully planned steps from a clear and definite proposition. In the course of the argument no rash generalizations may be indulged in, no facts may be disregarded, and the writer must be very sure when he is being intellectually logical and when he is being emotional.

SUGGESTIONS FOR STUDY

1. State a proposition and the subsequent issues for one of the following general subjects:

Rationing of goods, the tariff, my home town as a place favorable for business establishments, the national debt, honor systems in college, required freshman courses, fraternities, crop control, proration of oil, a platform of a political party, drivers' licenses, income taxes, radio advertising, surrealism, All-American football teams, hitch-hiking, divorces, speed limits, admission to college.

2. An enthymeme is an abbreviated syllogism. Construct the syllogism contained in each of the following enthymemes:

Because we have been playing tennis lately, we are physically fit.

I got less than eight hours' sleep last night and therefore feel very tired.

Golf playing will be difficult today because of the strong wind.

Because the morale of our team is high today, we are likely to win.

Calculus, as it is a mathematics course, is difficult for me.

3. Examine each of the following statements for any possible error in reasoning:

The people in the Middle West are friendlier than those anywhere else in America.

My teacher, I am sure, must have been good, or she would not have been in the school.

Students who work must watch their pennies and cannot spend money foolishly for such things as fraternities.

The population of a city cannot be placed successfully upon an honor system; therefore, no better results will come from placing their children on an honor system in school.

I know that she plays the piano beautifully; her mother has told me so many times.

Chadwick has no right to be on the committee to study conditions in the colleges of the state. He has never been to college.

He no sooner sold his stocks than their price fell twenty points; whereupon he bought in again. He must have been responsible for engineering a coup so that he could sell profitably.

You have no right to bring a lie detector to work on this case; it's un-American.

Joe forgot to tap the plate as he came to bat; so, of course, he struck out.

Jumbo is so big that he can beat anyone in wrestling.

No one will ever pole vault over sixteen feet.

Her new pillow causes her hay fever; she never had hay fever until she purchased it.

He must be the best doctor in town. He cured Bill's sore throat very quickly.

I'm not going to vote for any political party that Josephson belongs to.

Of course Jack is intelligent; he graduated from the University last month.

Smoke Tabasco cigarettes. Rudolpho Weatherbanks, the famous movie actor, says they are the best.

Lightning automobiles are the finest on the market. Just last year a stock model won the Guadalupe Mountain hill-climbing test.

In this crisis, vote again for our party; don't change horses in the middle of the stream.

Si Maglie, who runs a shop on 33rd street, says that there is no racketeering going on in that district.

College professors should not be used in a governmental brain trust. They are all just theorists.

4. In each of the following statements, accept the major premise as true. Then examine the reasoning for accuracy as it proceeds from that premise. If you are in doubt about the accuracy of any reasoning, reduce it to its syllogistic form:

(a) A legal principle which has been evolved in our history is that any enterprise which engages in interstate commerce should be subject to regulation by the federal government. The operators of long-distance moving vans are protesting against federal regulation, but as they are engaged in interstate commerce, they should be so regulated.

(b) It has been shown that engineers in modern locomotives are seldom responsible for accidents in which their trains are involved. It is clear, therefore, that engineer Casey was not responsible for the accident in which his train was involved at Centerville last night.

(c) A controversial question for many years has been the socialized control of medicine. Certainly governmental support of individuals is likely to undermine their initiative and so produce inefficiency. Socialized medicine, of course, involves the governmental support of doctors, and so must fail by undermining the doctors' initiative and producing medical inefficiency.

(d) The radio industry since its inception has guarded against taking sides in debatable political or social arguments. It has been right in taking this stand, for any industry which affects large masses of people should avoid the attempt to sway the populace on controversial issues.

(e) The national debt which a country bears is not necessarily an economic evil. During the depression the United States added materially to its debt by spending freely for relief works. The conclusion which we see, therefore, is that the country has not erred in establishing relief works.

(f) Educational institutions of higher learning, if they are to be of value, should teach only those students who are capable of mastering advanced and complex subject matter. The State University was quite within its province therefore in rejecting those applicants who showed inability to master their high-school subjects.

(g) Our forefathers decided long ago that no American citizen of a certain age and fitness should be denied the right to vote. Sweeney is no American citizen and therefore must be denied the right to vote.

(h) Any instrument which produces greater ease and speed of writing is likely at the same time to encourage haste and slovenliness of rhetoric. In the hands of even an inexperienced operator, the modern typewriter increases the speed of writing nearly fifty per cent, and with an experienced operator, it increases the speed several hundred per cent. Writing with a typewriter thus has the danger of producing writing which is careless and inexact.

(i) It is better to raise public money directly by taxation than to try to float bond issues and so add to the public debt. The recent increase in taxation is therefore commendable.

(j) I think that my poor vision is attributable to a cramp of the eye muscles, for such a cramp often produces poor vision.

(k) The United States should maintain the freedom of the worker to strike whenever conditions imposed upon him become too severe. The recent strikes because of low wages and poor working conditions were therefore justified.

(l) The average adult in the United States has a mentality of fourteen years of age. Bert Robinson, who is an adult, has therefore a mental age of fourteen years.

(m) The telephone company customarily cuts off the service of any customer who does not pay his bill. Jack had his service cut off last week, and so we may assume that he did not pay his bill.

(n) The physical education department of a university should have as its duty the maintenance of good health among the undergraduates. The physical education department of the State University is accordingly obligated to give free health inspection to all students.

(o) The word "propaganda" has taken on a bad connotation, but actually propaganda which is skillful often aids a worthy cause. The propaganda which we are issuing is highly skillful and therefore is aiding a worthy cause.

Work Your Way Through College?[1]

RALPH COOPER HUTCHISON

THERE ARE great values to be had from the experience of earning one's way through college. There would be great values for my physician if he would close his office and build an automobile by hand. There would be great values for the leading lawyer in my community if he would build a barn, doing all the work with his own hands. But there

[1] From the *Rotarian* (August, 1940). The author, then president of Washington and Jefferson College, wrote the article as an answer to one which argued the advantages of working one's way through college. Reprinted by permission of the *Rotarian*.

are still higher values for these men if they will stay at their first tasks.

The physician might learn a lot about iron, steel, motors, and the composition of rubber, but it would be better for him to restore health and save lives. The lawyer would learn a great deal about bricks, woodwork, and construction, but there are higher values if he will perform his function in society. Surely a college student gains much when he sweeps floors in the Elks Hall, washes dishes at the dormitory, shovels coal in the professor's house, or acts as bellhop at the hotel. But there are higher values which he should be gaining and serving with every minute of his time and every ounce of strength. If these menial functions have such high value, why go to college? A boy can sweep floors, press suits, drive delivery wagons and shovel coal without going to college and paying for the privilege.

Yes, working one's way through college has its values. It is better than not going to college. It is also better than playing one's way through college. But it is not better than studying one's way through college.

The widespread illusion on this subject is due to several misconceptions. The first of these is the popular idea that the great objective is "to get through college." Getting through college is of no value whatsoever. Many men have "gotten through" college who would be better off if they had never seen a college. So would society. Which is to say that there are many ways of getting through college and some of them mean nothing. What counts is what a man gets out of college as he goes through. If he gets what he should, he will be immediately enriched and society will be blessed by his ability and his service. But if he does not get these proper values, he has nothing. The fact therefore that a man earned his way through college means nothing unless the man got something as he went through. Many of the earning men get little or nothing. They are in some cases like the playboys. In one case play interferes with education. In the other, menial, driving, all-absorbing remunerative work does the same.

What are the values of a college education in general terms? Well, men come to college having never used 70 per cent of their mental "muscles." They have never had to use them. Mentally they are as soft as a fat baby is physically. The college begins the process of exercising the unused and flabby 70 per cent. It is a long, slow, difficult process, much slower than the training of the

physical muscles in athletics. New academic tasks and achievements, advanced problems and speeds, are used to bring into play mental muscles, abilities, and capacities heretofore only suspected in the mind of the student. To succeed under this training requires the most prodigious effort of the student's life, and that effort is mental in the highest degree. His failure or success depends on whether he makes that effort consistently and earnestly until he gets results.

Waiving aside this sentimental bosh about college jobs, we must recognize the fact that 90 per cent of the jobs available to college men make little or no contribution to this intellectual achievement characterizing the college experience. Most of the jobs are menial, requiring abilities which are elementary. Some require a certain commercial ability, but, even so, are no serious contribution to the intellectual training of college. Students themselves are under no illusion on this subject. The jobs they get in college are to earn money, not to develop their mental abilities, train their minds, or open the windows of their souls, and well they know it.

The second great value of the college is social, in the higher meaning of the term. The college man is concentrating into four years a social experience and training which he might possibly obtain in twelve years outside. By the benefit of the phenomenon known as the college, he is placed in a peculiar society. This society is a complete world in itself. Superficial educational writers regret this, but it is one of the chief values of college. Here is created for a student a concentrated world, an epitome of life, isolated from general society to a degree, complete in itself. The citizens are his contemporaries, but they are picked by that eliminating and sifting process which college is. These contemporaries are strong men from the best homes with rich heritage and the highest purposes.

In a world of such men he must make his way. Here he must learn the **art** of following or of leading. He must choose friends and develop friendships. He must match wits, struggle for recognition, protect his rights, serve those in need—keep pace with these eager men, physically, mentally, and spiritually. The vastly complicated activities of the college campus are not a happenstance. They are an achievement. They constitute a complete little world, and in it the student begins to learn that which takes much longer outside. He learns to walk upright among men and make his way.

If he is to succeed in this social problem and training, he will need every ounce of strength, every vestige of enthusiasm, and every moment of time. Everything which draws him out of his college world is an interference and relatively a loss. Earning his way through college does two wrongs. It takes his time and strength from this larger experience. Secondly, it frequently puts him out into the other world. The transition from the college world to that of the downtown hotel or the filling station is not a helpful event in this peculiar social experience. It is right if he has to, wrong if he does not have to do it. It has values which he can get all the rest of his life. College has values which he can never get again.

The second popular illusion in this matter is to the effect that the men who work their way through are the men who are subsequently successful. This is an optical illusion. We have talked so proudly of those who have earned their way and who have made good that we have overlooked those who earned their way and didn't amount to the proverbial row of pins. We do not count them and I hope we never shall. Nor, on the other hand, do we make special note of the fact that many of our finest and greatest college men are men who did not earn their way, who fully appreciated the values of college, who made distinguished records, and who have been giants subsequently. As a matter of fact, there are no scientific statistics which prove that those who earn their way do better than those who study their way. The

chances are the second group would show the higher score. Both would score, of course, over those who "play their way."

Take again these men who earn their way and then make fine records in life. There is yet another optical illusion as we look at them. We say he is a success because he had to earn his way. No, all too often the reverse is true. He earned his way because he was a success before he started. That's why some go to college when others don't go. That's why they work like slaves to get through college. That's why they go hungry for an education. That's why they stick when others quit. They are the kind of people that make good, anytime, anywhere, college or no college.

When such a determined, able person does go to college, earns his way through, makes good in life, then a great chorus of praise is raised as to the virtues of dishwashing in the collegiate years. No, with such a man the dishwashing was a means to an end, the way to earn money. So far as the education he was seeking, the necessity was an interference, and he would of all men most thank God had he been able to put all that indomitable determination, all that time and strength into the larger opportunities for which he was fighting.

And such persons do more with those opportunities if they have them, do even better if they do not have to earn. Such persons invariably determine later that their sons, if qualified, shall not be tied down to such stern necessities, but shall go a step further and put all their strength into the herculean task of becoming educated for the exactions of life.

Finally, no man who does not have to earn his way has a right to earn his way. We have plenty of students who work in college and do not need to do so. In the first place, they take jobs which others should have. In the second place, they are self-deluded. They have been inculcated with the idea of working their way through college. They get this from storybooks and from well-intentioned parents. They work at their jobs with such a sense of satisfaction that they neglect their social development or their mental equipment. They make earning achievements an alibi for intellectual mediocrity. In their reverence for financial earnings they become intellectual sluggards. Their hard outside work exalts the ego while the mind atrophies. Slovenly workmanship in studies is accepted imperturbably because of the manly satisfaction of working half the night in the local steel mill.

Earning work in college is like many other things in life—a virtue only when a necessity. Robinson Crusoe did some remarkable things on that lonely island. Hollowing out a log for a canoe was magnificent. But to have done the same thing in London would have been an absurdity. So in college there are immeasurable opportunities for the development of the mind and the enrichment of the soul, for the growing of the bigger man. Let no student be denied these privileges save by stern necessity.

SUGGESTIONS FOR STUDY

1. Is proof or illustration offered in the opening paragraph?
2. Is it well in argument to offer such admissions to the opposition as are offered in paragraph 2?
3. How does definition aid President Hutchison's argument? Exactly what does he mean by a student who benefits from not working his way?
4. State the syllogisms contained in paragraphs 4, 5, and 6.
5. Test the statements in paragraph 6 by your own experience.
6. What social experience does college give?
7. State the syllogism employed in paragraphs 8 and 9.
8. Could the argument in paragraph 10 be strengthened in any way?
9. What is the effect of the word "invariably" in paragraph 13?
10. How effective is the analogy in the final paragraph?
11. Make an outline of President Hutchison's argument.
12. Define the following words from the article: menial, remunerative, prodigious, epitome, vestige, indomitable, imperturbably, atrophies.

Should Students Study?[1]

WILLIAM TRUFANT FOSTER

"Do NOT LET your studies interfere with your college education." This motto adorns the walls of many a student's room. It is his semihumorous way of expressing his semiconviction that studies do not count—that the thing to go in for is—"College Life." This thing, made up of intercollegiate athletics and lesser diversions, is spelled with capitals—with big capitals in the student's mind. This frequenter of college walks and halls and tombs and grandstands I call a "student" for want of a safer term, though it sometimes does him injustice. He has sundry answers to the question whether students should study.

In academic circles, this is not merely

[1] Reprinted by permission of *Harper's Magazine*.

an academic question. The boy who goes to college faces it, in one form or another, again and again. Indeed, before he dons his freshman togs, his father has told him to get an all-round education, and may even have given him to understand that deficiencies in scholarship which do not end his college career will be overlooked if he makes the football team. He observes the boys who return from college; he finds that their language and their clothes bear marks of a higher education. He hears accounts of initiations and celebrations. His chum's big brother takes him aside and tells him confidentially just how he must conduct himself in order to be rushed for the right fraternity. Everybody tells him he must be a "good fellow"; few discourse upon the joys of the curriculum. Whether students should study may remain with him an open question, but he begins to doubt whether students do study.

With his mind set on going to college, he reads all that comes to hand on the subject. The newspapers give him vivid details of the games, big and little, with full-page pictures of the heroes. They report nightshirt parades, student riots, dances, beer nights—anything but studies. Now and then they do give space to a professor, if he has been indiscreet, or has appeared to say something scandalous, which everybody in college knows he did not say, or if he is sued for divorce. They even spare him an inch or two if he is awarded a Nobel prize.

The lad reads stories of College Life. How they glow with escapades! His mind becomes a moving picture of thrilling escapes, of goats enthroned on professorial chairs, of freshies ducked in chilling waters, of battalions of rooters yelling with the precision of a cash register. Now and then there is mention of lectures and examinations, for it appears that the sophisticated youth knows many devices for "getting by" these impediments to the unalloyed enjoyment of College Life. Surely the high school teacher who spoke with such enthusiasm about the lectures of "Old Socrates" must be hopelessly behind the times. Surely nobody goes to college nowadays for lectures.

After entering college the boy continues his studies in the philosophy of education under the tutelage of a sophomore. His tutor informs him that the object of education is the all-round man. The faculty and the curriculum, he explains, are obstacles, but the upper classes rescue the poor freshman from pentagonal and other primitive shapes and round him out with smokers, hazing, initiations, jamborees, and visits to the big city, where he makes the acquaintance of drinks and ladies far more brilliant-hued than those of his somber native town. He is told that he is "seeing life," and that college will make an all-round man of him yet, if the faculty do not interfere with his education.

If this sophomoric philosophy leaves any doubts to puzzle the freshman, they may be cleared away by the alumni who return to warm up the fraternity house with stories of the good old days. And, of course, the lad joins a fraternity before giving his course of study a thought. For what is college to a non-fraternity man? Merely an institution of learning. To the man with the Greek-lettered pin the fraternity is the *sine qua non* of higher education, the radiant whole of which the college is a convenient part, providing for the fraternity a local habitation.

And so the undergraduate stretches his legs before the hearth and hears the wisdom of the "Old Grad." In his day, it seems, things were different. The students were not such mollycoddles, the beer flowed more freely, and the faculty did not try to run things. No, sir, in the good old days the faculty did not spoil College Life. What a glorious celebration after that 56 to 0 game, when every window in old West Hall was broken and the stoves were thrown downstairs!

"I tell you, boys," cries the Old Grad, warming his feet by the fire and his imagination by the wonder of the freshman, "it is not what you learn in your classes that counts. It is the College Life. Books, lectures, recitations—you will forget all that. Nobody cares after you graduate whether you know any Latin or algebra, unless you are a teacher, and no man can afford to be a teacher nowadays. But you will remember the College Life as long as you live."

Some of the alumni would have a different story to tell, no doubt, but they do not get back often for fraternity initiations. Perhaps they are too busy. And, again, they may have been nothing but "grinds" during their college days. . . .

Is high scholarship worth the effort? In other words, have colleges devised courses of study which bear any relation to the probable careers of their students? Is there any evidence that a man who attains high marks is more likely to achieve success after graduation than a man who is content with passing marks?

If there is any such connection between success in studies and success in life, it should be possible to measure it by approved statistical methods, and thus arrive at conclusions of more value as guidance to the undergraduate than the opinion of any man. Both the professor and the sport are in danger of arguing from exceptional instances— each is likely to find striking cases in proof of his preconceived notions; each is inclined to scorn the opinion of the other.

But conclusions drawn from large numbers of cases, not subject to invalidating processes of selection, and employing terms that are adequately defined for the purpose at hand, must command the respect of all men. If such conclusions do not support the contention that it pays to study, there is something radically wrong with the professor's part of college affairs; different kinds of achievement should receive academic distinction and new tests should be devised. If, on the other hand, present standards for rating students predict their future success with any degree of accuracy, the facts should be discovered and used everywhere to combat the prevalent undergraduate opinion. Whatever the outcome of such studies, we should have them in larger numbers, in many places, protected by every safeguard of scientific method. We may well ask, first, whether promise in the studies of one period becomes performance in the studies of a later period.

Are good students in high school more likely than others to become good students in college? Prof. Walter F. Dearborn tried to answer that question for the State of Wisconsin. He compared the records of hundreds of students at the University of Wisconsin with their records in various high schools. He found that above eighty per cent of those who were in the first quarter of their high school classes remained in the upper half of their classes throughout the four years of their university course, and that above eighty

per cent of those who were in the lowest quarter in their high school classes failed to rise above the line of mediocre scholarship in the university. The parallelism is so striking that we are justified in concluding that, except in scattering cases, promise in the high school becomes performance in the college. Indeed, only one student out of nearly five hundred in this investigation who fell among the lowest quarter in the high school attained the highest rank in the university. Of course, a boy may loaf in high school and take his chance of being the one exception among five hundred. But he would hardly be taking a sporting chance; it would be rather a fool's chance. The risk should be less in going over Niagara Falls in a barrel.

The University of Chicago found that high school students who failed to attain an average rank higher than the passing mark, by at least twenty-five per cent of the difference between that passing mark and one hundred, failed in their college classes. The faculty therefore decided not to admit such students. Exceptions were made of the most meritorious cases, but few of these exceptions made satisfactory records in the college.

Basing its policy upon such evidence as this, Reed College, at the beginning of its work five years ago, decided to admit, as a rule, only students who ranked in the first third of their preparatory-school classes. Some exceptions have been made. Twenty per cent of those admitted were known to be below the first third, and two per cent below the median line. In all cases these candidates were regarded as the most promising of those who fell below the first third in high school rank, yet almost without exception they have failed to rise above the lowest quarter of their college classes. Thus, it appears that in Oregon, as in Wisconsin and Illinois, those who get the best start in the lower schools maintain their advantage in the upper schools; few of their classmates overtake them.

But why strive for high rank in college? Why not wait for the more "practical" studies of the professional school? Hundreds of boys the country over declare today that it makes little difference whether they win high grades or merely passable grades in the liberal arts, since these courses have no definite bearing on their intended lifework. Almost invariably they are ready to admit that they must settle down to serious effort in the studies of law, medicine, engineering—that is to say, in professional schools. Even the sport who makes the grade of mediocrity his highest aim as a college undergraduate, fully intends to strive for high scholarship in his professional studies. Does he often attain that aim? That is the question.

And that, fortunately, is a question we may answer with more than opinions. We may take, for example, all the students who graduated from Harvard College during a period of twelve years and entered the Harvard Medical School. Of the 239 who received no distinction as undergraduates, 36 per cent graduated with honor from the Medical School. Of the 41 who received degrees of A.B. with high honor, more than 92 per cent took their medical degrees with honor.

Still more conclusive are the records of the graduates of Harvard College who during a period of twenty years entered the Harvard Law School. Of those who graduated from college with no special honor, only 6½ per cent attained distinction in the Law School. Of those who graduated with honor from the college, 22 per cent attained distinction in the Law School; of those who graduated with great honor, 40 per cent; and of those who graduated with highest honor, 60 per cent. Sixty per cent! Bear that figure in mind a moment, while we consider the 340 who entered college "with conditions"—that is to say, without having passed all their entrance examinations—and graduated from college with plain degrees. Of these men, not 3 per cent won honor degrees in law.

If a college undergraduate is ready to be honest with himself, he must say, "If I am content with mediocre work in college, it is likely that the men in my class who graduate with honor will have three times my chances of success in the Law School, and the men who graduate in my class with highest honor will have nearly ten times my chances of success." So difficult is it for a student to change his habits of life after the crucial years of college that not one man in twenty years—not one man in twenty years—who was satisfied in Harvard College with grades of "C" and lower gained distinction in the studies of the Harvard Law School.

The same relation appears to persist between the promise of Yale undergraduates and their performance in the Harvard Law School. If we divide the 250 graduates of Yale who received their degrees in law at Cambridge between 1900 and 1915 into nine groups, according to undergraduate scholarship, beginning with those who won the highest "Senior Appointments" at Yale and ending with those who received no graduation honors, we find that the first group did the best work in their studies of law, the second group next, the third group next, and so on, in the same order, with but a single exception, to the bottom of the list. The performance at Harvard of each of the eight groups of Yale honor graduates was in precise accordance with the promise of their records at Yale.

Apparently the "good fellow" in college, the sport who does not let his studies interfere with his education, but who intends to settle down to hard work later on, and who later on actually does completely change his habits of life, is almost a myth. At least his record does not appear among those of thousands of students whose careers have been investigated under the direction of President Lowell and others. It seems that results are legal tender, but you cannot cash in good intentions.

"Dignified credit to all," cries the billboard. "Enjoy your new suit now, and pay for it later." Many a boy, lured by the installment plan, expects to get an education on deferred payments in effort, only to find that there is no credit for him, dignified or otherwise.

What his honest effort has paid for in full is his today; nothing more by any chance whatever.

But why strive for the highest standing in professional school? Let us pursue the inquiry one step further. Let us ask whether success in studies gives promise of success in life. As far as the study of law is concerned, we may anwer at once that the known success of the honor graduates of the Harvard Law School is one reason why even college undergraduates at Cambridge believe that law students should study law—hard and seriously. For the same reason, leading law offices the country over give preference to honor graduates of law schools.

But what is success in life? That is the first problem. It is one difficulty that confronts everyone who attempts to speak with certainty about the meaning of education. There is no accepted definition of the aim of education. The philosopher has been likened to a blind man in a dark cellar hunting for a black cat that isn't there. The aim of education seems as elusive as the proverbial black cat. Nevertheless, we do not close our schools. We strive for concrete ends, such as proficiency in handwriting, aware that any particular end may soon be regarded as not worth the effort to attain it. Until recently we could not say even what we meant by proficiency in handwriting, for we had not attempted to define our aim or devise a measure of our progress toward it. We still speak of educational processes and results about as accurately as the Indians spoke of temperature. We still speak of the science of education without seeming to understand that there is no science without precise measurement. From our fragmentary beginnings to an adequate science of education is a long journey, and the road is beset with difficulties. While we struggle along this road, generations will come and go. We will help them to attain what seem, for the time, the proper aims of education. And each individual will strive for what seems to him success in life.

As one measure of success in life, we may take the judgment of certain men. In so far as we accept their judgment our findings concerning the relation between college studies and this kind of success will seem important to us. Here, as in most questions of educational aim, we can do no better for the present than take the consensus of opinion of competent judges.

Using this measure for success, I endeavored to find out whether the members of the class of 1894 of Harvard College who had become notable in their life work had been notable in their studies. I therefore asked three judges to select, independently, the most successful men from that class. I chose as judges the dean of the college, the secretary of the Alumni Association, and a professor in Columbia University who is a member of the class, because I thought that these men came nearer than any others to knowing all members of the class. I left each judge free to use his own definition of success, but I asked them not to select men whose achievements appeared to be due principally to family wealth or position. The judges agreed in naming twenty-three successful men. I then had the entire undergraduate records of these men accurately copied from the college records and compared with the standing of twenty-three men chosen at random from the same class.

The result was striking. The men who were thus named as most successful attained in their college studies nearly four times as many highest grades as the random selection. To the credit of the successful men are 196 "A's"; to the credit of the other men, only 56.

Following a similar plan, three judges selected the most successful men among the graduates of the first twenty-four (1878-1901) classes from the University of Oregon. An examination of the scholarship records of these men showed that 53 per cent had been good students and 17 per cent had been weak students. Of the graduates who were not regarded as successful, 52 per cent had been weak students and only 12 per cent had been good students.

Similar results have been found by Prof. A. A. Potter, Dean of the Kansas State Agricultural College, in an unpublished study of the relationship between superiority in undergraduate scholarship and success in the practice of engineering as indicated by salaries received. The Director of the School of Forestry of Yale University has collected evidence of the same kind in an unpublished study of the graduates of the Yale School of Forestry. It appears that about ninety per cent of the men who have had conspicuous success in the field of forestry were among the better students in their professional studies. President Thwing of Western Reserve University, the historian of higher education in America, says that he has found no exception, in the records of any American college, to the general rule that those who achieve most before graduation are likely to achieve most after graduation.

The list of the first ten scholars of each of the classes that graduated from Harvard College in the sixth decade of the last century, as presented by William Roscoe Thayer, is a list of men eminent in every walk of life. Indeed, it is likely that the first quarter in scholarship of any school or college class will give to the world as many distinguished men as the other three quarters.

What can we say in this connection of the 420 living graduates of the ten Wesleyan University classes from 1890 to 1899? Just this: Of the men in that group who graduated with highest honors, 60 per cent are now regarded as distinguished either by *Who's Who in America* or by the judgment of their classmates; of those who were elected to Phi Beta Kappa—the scholarship society—30 per cent; of those who won no superior honors in scholarship, only 11 per cent. Of the men now living who graduated from Wesleyan University between 1860 and 1889, 16 per cent are listed in *Who's Who;* of those who received high honors in scholarship during this period, 50 per cent; of those who attained no distinction as scholars, only 10 per cent.

From the records of 1,667 graduates of Wesleyan University, Professor Nicholson concludes that of the highest-honor graduates (the two or three leading scholars of each class) one out of two will become distinguished; of Phi Beta Kappa men, one out of three; of the rest, one out of ten.

Concerning the value of *Who's Who* as a criterion of success in life, we may say at least this, that it is a genuine effort, unwarped by commercial motives, to include the men and women who have achieved most worthy leadership in all reputable walks of life. Whatever flaws it may have, it is acknowledged to be the best list of names for such uses as we are now making of it—and such changes in the list as any group of competent judges might make would not materially affect the general conclusions we have drawn. . . .

In much that I have said about success I have used the mathematical term "chance," a term as far removed as any term could be from the popular notion of luck. If all these studies prove anything, they prove that there is a long chain of causal connections binding together the achievements of a man's life and explaining the success of a given moment. That is the nonskid chain that keeps him safe in slippery places. Luck is about as likely to strike a man as lightning, and about as likely to do him any good. The best luck a young man can have is the firm conviction that there is no such thing as luck, and that he will gain in life just about what he deserves, and no more. The man who is waiting around for something lucky to turn up has time to see a preparedness parade pass by him—the procession of those who have formed the habit of turning things up. In a saloon at a prairie station in Montana I saw the sign, "Luck beats science every time." That is the motto of the gambler and of every other fool. But all men who have won durable distinction are proof that science beats luck—science operating through the laws of heredity and habit. . . .

Ruskin had no patience with people who

talk about "the thoughtlessness of youth" indulgently. "I had infinitely rather hear of thoughtless old age," he declared, "and the indulgence due to *that*. When a man has done his work, and nothing can any way be materially altered in his fate, let him forget his toil, and jest with his fate, if he will; but what excuse can you find for willfulness of thought at the very time when every crisis of future fortune hangs on your decisions? A youth thoughtless! when all the happiness of his home forever depends on the chances or the passions of an hour! A youth thoughtless! when the career of all his days depends on the opportunity of a moment. A youth thoughtless! when his every act is a foundation stone of future conduct, and every imagination a fountain of life or death! Be thoughtless in *any* afteryears, rather than now."

Now let the student profit by the experiences of the thousands who have gone before and greet his next task with the words of Hotspur before the battle of Shrewsbury:

Oh, gentlemen, the time of life is short;
To spend that shortness basely were too long,
If life did ride upon a dial's point,
Still ending at the arrival of an hour.

SUGGESTIONS FOR STUDY

1. Where does the introduction end?
2. State the evidence concerning the relationship of achievement in undergraduate colleges and achievement in high school, and the conclusion drawn from the evidence. Is inductive or deductive reasoning being used?
3. Cite the conclusion concerning the relation of success in college and success in professional school. Does the author use inductive or deductive reasoning?
4. What problem in definition faces him on seeking to determine the relation of success in college and success in life? How does he solve this problem? State his conclusion about this relationship.
5. State the thesis. State also the main issues which he decides he must argue to if he is to establish his thesis.
6. Define these words from the article: curriculum, tutelage, sophomoric, meritorious, criterion.

World Government or World Destruction?[1]

STEPHEN KING-HALL

THE DROPPING OF atomic bombs on Hiroshima and Nagasaki was a fearful business, but it may be that never in all the long history of human slaughter have lives been lost to greater purpose. For now it is evident that every human being has a stake in the conduct not only of national affairs but of world affairs.

You are a unit of *humanity*, linked to all your fellow human beings, irrespective of race, creed, or color, by bonds which have been fused unbreakably in the diabolical heat of those explosions. The atomic bomb has made political and economic nationalism meaningless, and so has abolished large-scale national war.

Yet the fact that large-scale national or "total" war is obsolete, along with the nation-state, is still not fully realized. It is said that to every means of offense a defense can be provided. This is still true, but what must be understood is that the defense against the atomic bomb is unlikely to be found in the material sphere. It is no use having better bombs or more of them; it is no use going underground and thinking in terms of the old-fashioned war of 1939-45, which is now as out of date as the Battle of Hastings. The only defense against atomic bombs is the creation of a world in which no one has

[1] From the *National News-Letter* (of England), (August 16, 1945) and the *Reader's Digest,* XLVII (November, 1945), No. 283. Reprinted by permission of the *Reader's Digest* and of the author.

the slightest desire to drop atomic bombs on anyone else.

Today, for instance, we Britons know that the U.S.A. possesses atomic bombs and also the planes to carry them over London between sunset and dawn. Yet, we do not go about our business in the shadow of the valley of death. We are hardly conscious of the fact that we are potentially at the absolute mercy of the Americans. Can we honestly say that we should feel quite so comfortable if we heard that General Franco had a bagful of atomic bombs?

Look at it from another angle. It is a fair assumption that at least three great powers, the U.S.A., Great Britain, and Russia, will soon be able to make atomic bombs; they will be joined by France, Sweden, and others. The manufacture of atomic bombs will become easier. What then? It is impossible to imagine that the masses will tolerate a situation in which every time the papers report a ruffle on the waters of international politics people will say, "Suppose they send over 100 atomic bombs tonight!"

No country will ever again dare issue an ultimatum to another with a time limit of even six hours, because the reply in five hours might be a shower of atomic bombs. It is obvious that the national sovereign state, in its political and economic manifestations (as opposed to its very necessary and useful cultural existence) finds itself in a dilemma. The only way out is the creation as rapidly as possible of a world state. There is *no* other way out, except to get out of this world via a series of terrific explosions.

The emergence of a world state as a consequence of natural evolution would probably not have come for another century or two. The League of Nations was a successor of many similar attempts, yet the nations could not bring themselves to bend their proud necks under the relatively light yoke of the Covenant. Twenty-five years later, at San Francisco, an even feebler attempt to rationalize national sovereignty for the good of all men was adopted in an atmosphere of

cynicism. All this humbug is blown away in an instant by two bombs and a few young men in a couple of B-29 planes.

Yes or No? Life or Death? Get together or blow yourselves to hell? Those are the brutal questions put by the mighty ultra-microscopic atom released by the brain of man from the natural bonds of its balanced existence.

Consider the problem in greater detail. Of what use now are battleships, aircraft carriers, cruisers, submarines? The tank, the flame-thrower join on the scrap heap the myriads of batteries of guns, great and small. The vast and ponderous apparatus of combined operations, such as were being prepared for the invasion of Japan, are junk. Arguments for and against conscription are meaningless. For the atomic bomb enables its user to strike suddenly and with devastating effect at the whole of the enemy's civil population. Whoever uses it first does not necessarily win the war, because the atomic-bombers of nation A may be on their way to bomb nation B while their own homeland is being turned into a crematorium.

The statesmen of the Great Powers now find themselves obliged to grapple with the postwar problems of Europe, the Middle East, and the Far East at a moment when the atomic bomb has blown the normal standards of power politics to smithereens.

If we attempt to grapple with these tremendous matters with the thought that they are only more complex reproductions of problems which have plagued us since 1914, we shall fail. If we are so mistaken as to imagine that we can overcome the world's troubles inside the framework of and with the tools provided by the United Nations' Charter, Bretton Woods, and the Foreign Secretaries' Conference in London, we shall deceive ourselves. I say this for two reasons:

First, because our present-day problems are *not* reproductions of old ones. They are in principle a new kind of problem. They are not merely national problems with world implications. They are indisputably *world problems* and *humanity problems*.

Secondly, because the organizations and instruments mentioned above are based on the assumption that *national sovereign rights* are the foundations on which we must build. These organizations are like monkeys hanging head down from their national tails. We must have organizations which are like men sitting on their tails with their heads together.

If we are to solve these problems we must not be afraid to admit that world government is no longer merely a vision held by a few idealists. *World government has now become a hard-boiled, practical, and urgent necessity.*

If it is to be created quickly enough to avoid disaster, men in government must be bold in action. It is not enough, now, to have consultations at irregular intervals. The heads of states—using the machinery of the United Nations Security Council if nothing better is available—must meet regularly and become in effect a world executive committee. "Security" has almost overnight assumed a far more comprehensive meaning than was attached to it when the Council was established at San Francisco. This World Council must issue decisions and see that they are carried out.

We need not despair of human ability being capable of extracting a real peace and a new world from these seething difficulties. The mere fact that, through the workings of men's minds, events have occurred which have brought the world face to face with the greatest crisis in its history also shows that we are capable of thinking out the answer and taking appropriate action. It can be done. It must be done.

SUGGESTIONS FOR STUDY

1. Why does the author declare that the atomic bomb has made political and economic nationalism meaningless?

2. What is the only possible defense against the atomic bomb?

3. Is the United Nations' Charter sufficient in itself to solve the situation? Why?

4. What proposition does Mr. King-Hall argue for here?

Suggestions for Writing

1. Write a composition presenting an inductive argument suggested by one of the following statements or sets of statistics:

(a) Recent figures on education in the United States were:
1. College graduates: 2,380,000
   Those with some college work: 4,600,000
   Per cent of population: 9
2. High-school graduates: 6,400,000
   Per cent of population: 8
3. Those with some high school training: 15,130,000
   Those with grammar-school training or less: 49,590,000
   Per cent of population: 78
4. Illiterate: 4,100,000
   Per cent of population: 5

(b) A governmental bureau published a survey revealing the mental age of the average radio listener as fourteen years.

(c) In the same general period of years, the employees of a street railway company prepared a report that the minimum wage on which they could live decently was $1900 a year; but the average wage for clergymen was $735 a year, for country schoolteachers in the Middle Atlantic states was $870 a year, for village teachers was $1244 a year, for instructors, assistant professors, associate professors, and full professors on university faculties was $2958, for railway freight conductors was $3570 and for railway freight engineers was $4700.

(d) In 1929, the United States was paying 11 pensions as a result of the War of 1812, 849 as a result of the war with Mexico, 272,906 as a result of the Civil War. The total payments for pensions resulting from the Revolutionary War was $70,000,000; for the War of 1812 was $46,198,000; for the Mexican War was $59,073,000; for the Civil War was $7,244,677,000. To 1929, the cost of World War I to the United States was $37,573,960.

(e) In 1910, 45.8 per cent of the total population was urban (that is, was found in urban centers with 2,500 population and higher) and 54.2 per cent was rural; in 1930, 56.2 per cent was urban, and 43.8 per cent was rural.

(f) The number of horses, colts, and mules on farms decreased from 26,500,000 in 1915 to 15,182,000 in 1939; the period from 1930 to 1940 showed an increase of 746,000 tractors. In 1935 the WPA estimated that the tractor, motortruck, and automobile saved the labor in agriculture of 345,000 persons for one year.

(g) In 1939 automobile registration dropped slightly to 29,425,000 vehicles, but gasoline consumption increased 4.8 per cent to 20,-600,000,000 gallons. Deaths as a result of automobile accidents increased to 31,500 for the year.

(h) Industrial output for 1939 was 23 per cent higher than that of 1938. Unemployment was reduced by an estimated 1,000,000, but another 8,000,000 were left unemployed; factory employment increased by 8 per cent, and factory wages by approximately 16 per cent. Labor strikes and disputes in 1939 lost nearly 18,000,000 man days of labor, a sum about twice the loss in 1938.

2. Write a composition based on deductive principles; choose any aspect of one of the following subjects:

The persuasion of a high-school student to attend your college.

The improvement of one of your college courses.

The statement by Dr. Compton in favor of governmental support of research work: "There is a peculiarity of pure research, inherent in its nature, which gives a logical basis for this conclusion."

The addition of a new course to the curriculum.

The appropriation of funds to build a municipal golf course.

The adoption of daylight saving time in your home town.

The adoption or abolition of parking meters in the city.

The selection of movies shown in the local theater.

The rigorous enforcement of the state speed limit.

The establishment of a new factory in your home town.

Night baseball games.

Changes in requirements for graduation.

Reduction in prices of athletic contests.

The machine as an aid or detriment to industrial employment.

Changes in tuition for resident and out-of-state students.

A centralized school in your rural district.

Teachers' salaries in rural schools.

Industrial strikes.

Socialized medicine.

The study of foreign language.

3. After reading the article on the postwar organization of world government, read the latest articles on the same subjects in current periodicals to bring yourself up to date on these problems. After you have completed your reading, write an argument on some matter connected with this subject.

C. Description

The purpose of description is to reproduce for the reader a clear, vivid impression of a scene, a person, a sensation, an emotion, or other image that exists in the writer's own consciousness. Obviously, no one can transmit a clear, vivid impression of something that is blurred or distorted in his own mind. The first requisite of good description, therefore, is to perceive clearly and accurately what you wish to describe. The second is to find words that will reproduce the image as faithfully as language can do it. The third is to utilize certain techniques that insure logical development—consistency of point of view, transmission of the dominant impression, and the choice and arrangement of details.

ACCURATE OBSERVATION

Ability to observe accurately, to take in details readily, to catalogue impressions correctly and quickly comes of attention and practice. Because most people are content with general or hazy impressions, their senses grow dull through disuse. Yet the senses respond amazingly to demands upon them. The cotton buyer merely by feeling a sample of cotton can tell the length of the staple. The cattle judge can tell at a glance the weight of a steer. The good conductor can detect a sour note amid the sounds of a hundred-piece orchestra. Long and continual practice, however, is necessary to reach such adeptness. Back of the vivid images in the work of great writers is long effort. The comment of de Maupassant[1] is pertinent in this connection, as he relates what he learned as a novice from his master Flaubert:

Talent is long patience. It is a question of looking long enough and with enough attention at everything you want to express to discover a facet of it that no one else has seen and expressed. There is in everything something of the unexplored, because we are accustomed to using eyes only in the light of what has been expressed before about whatever we observe. The least thing contains a bit of the unknown. Let us find it. To describe a flaming fire and a tree on a plain, let's stand looking at this fire and this tree until, so far as we are concerned, they no longer resemble any other tree or any other fire.

That is the way you become original.

Besides, having stated this truth, that in the whole world there are not two grains of sand, two flies, two hands, or two noses exactly alike, he [Flaubert] used to make me express in a few sentences a being or an object in such a way as clearly to individualize it, to make it distinct from all other objects of the same race or the same species.

"When you pass by a grocer seated in his doorway," he used to tell me, "before a janitor smoking his pipe, before a cab-parking station, show me that grocer and that janitor, their posture, their whole physical appearance, containing also, indicated by the skill of the depiction, their whole moral nature, so that I cannot confuse them with any other janitor; and with a single word make me see how a cab horse is different from the fifty others who follow or precede him."

. . . Whatever you wish to say, there is only one word to express it, one verb to animate it, one adjective to qualify it. So you must keep looking for this word, this verb, this adjective until you have found them, and never be satisfied with an approximation.

De Maupassant states the goal: to isolate and animate an object in such a way as to distinguish it from all others. Ability to do this comes only of practice. From what de Maupassant says, it is clear that his own skill at depiction was an acquisition, not an endowment. Your inability to equal the skill of a great writer in making a scene or sensa-

[1] In the introduction to his *Pierre et Jean.* The whole of this introduction is worth close study.

tion come to life is no cause for discouragement. The remedy is to start practicing, it doesn't matter at what. Begin with buildings and landscapes, with dogs or faces or flowers, with postures or tones. Note exact shades of color, precise shapes and contours, arrangement of objects in a room. In all this, effort and persistency are the virtues to cultivate; the results will accrue.

CHOICE OF WORDS

Selecting the exact word to convey an idea is important to good writing of any sort; it is a necessity in writing good description. A painter with a few strokes of his brush can suggest the appearance of a skyscraper, or he can mix his paints to reproduce the precise shade of color in a dress or landscape. An orchestra performing Beethoven's *Sixth Symphony* can give a remarkable approximation of the rolling of thunder and the pouring of rain. What the painter or musician does by means of brush or instrument, the writer must accomplish with words. Since the best he can do will not reproduce an image with absolute fidelity, he must use the utmost care in selecting words that give exact impressions if he expects a reader to have even a fair approximation of what is in his own mind. One of the best means of reproducing an image faithfully is to use specific and concrete words rather than general or abstract ones.

Run is a general word; *dash, scramble, scurry, jog* are specific words. "Hearing the siren, Bill ran to the window" gives a more vivid picture than "went to the window" would give, but "Bill dashed to the window" gives a still more accurate picture of the action. "Frightened by the stranger, the little dog scrambled under the steps" evokes a more vivid picture of the dog's way of going than would "ran under the steps." "He was dressed in a slovenly fashion" is too general a statement to give a vivid, clear image of the man; but "His grease-spotted suit was baggy at the knees and elbows, and his collar and cuffs were gray with sweat stains and grime" projects a picture that is sharp and accurate and therefore forceful. Specific and concrete words force the reader to see, hear, smell, taste, touch, and because the senses are the most powerful stimulators of the imagination, the reader's natural indolence is overcome, and he becomes interested enough to participate in making the picture come to life.

Another gain in using specific and concrete words is that they are more suggestive than general and abstract terms. They connote as well as denote. *Scramble*, for instance, connotes a lack of dignity, an overtone of meaning that adds much to the image of the frightened dog. *Grease-spotted* and *sweat stains* mean not only carelessness in dress (slovenliness), but also physical repulsiveness. Attention to these overtones of connotation enables you to say a great deal with a few words. It imparts a richness of familiar experience. Notice the connotative power of the concrete terminology in the following selection from Thomas Wolfe's *Look Homeward, Angel*. The author does little other than give the names of things; yet the senses, particularly the sense of smell, are excited in an extraordinary way.

> He remembered yet the East India House at the Fair, the sandalwood, the turbans, and the robes, the cool interior and the smell of India tea; and he had felt now the nostalgic thrill of dew-wet mornings in Spring, the cherry scent, the cool clarion earth, the wet loaminess of the garden, the pungent breakfast smells, and the floating snow of blossoms. He knew the inchoate sharp excitement of hot dandelions in young Spring grass at noon; the smell of cellars, cobwebs, and built-on secret earth; in July, of watermelons bedded in sweet hay, inside a farmer's covered wagon; of cantaloupe and crated peaches; and the scent of orange-rind, bitter-sweet, before a fire of coals. He knew the good male smell of his father's sitting-room; of the smooth worn leather sofa, with the gaping horsehair rent; of the blistered varnished wood upon the hearth; of the heated calf-skin bindings; of the flat moist plug of apple tobacco, stuck with a red flag; of wood smoke and burnt leaves in October; of the brown tired autumn earth; of honeysuckle at night; of warm nasturtiums; of a clean ruddy farmer who comes weekly with printed butter, eggs, and milk; of fat limp underdone bacon and of coffee; of a bakery oven in the wind; of large deep-hued stringbeans smoking hot and seasoned well with salt and butter; of a room of old pine boards in which books and carpets have been stored, long-closed; of Concord grapes in their long white baskets.
>
> Yes, and the exciting smell of chalk and varnished desks; the smell of heavy bread sandwiches of cold fried meat and butter; the smell of new leather in a saddler's shop, or of a warm leather chair; of honey and of unground coffee; of barreled sweet-pickles and cheese and all the fragrant compost of the grocer's; the smell of stored apples in the cellar, and of orchard-apple smells, of pressed-cider pulp; of pears ripening on a sunny shelf, and of ripe cherries stewing with sugar on hot stoves before preserving; the smell of whittled wood, of all young lumber, of sawdust and shavings; of peaches stuck with cloves and pickled in brandy; of pine sap, and green pine needles; of a horse's pared hoof; of chestnuts roasting, of bowls of nuts and raisins; of hot cracklin, and of young roast pork; of butter and cinnamon melting on hot candied yams.
>
> Yes, and of the rank slow river, and of tomatoes rotten on the vine; the smell of rain-wet plums and boiling quinces; of rotten lily-pads; and of foul weeds rotting in green marsh scum; and the exquisite smell of the South, clean but funky, like a big woman; of soaking trees and the earth after heavy rain.[1]

In addition to choosing specific and concrete words, use modifying words with discretion and be chary in the use of figures of speech. Many students, attempting to write effective description, think too much of the power of modifying words, adjectives and adverbs, and so overburden their style with them. But often choosing a more specific noun or verb is preferable to using a noun and modifying adjective or a verb and modifying adverb. Superfluous modifiers will weaken your style.

Figures of speech, though among the most useful instruments for a writer of description, should also be used with discretion. Over-ornamentation of style is like wearing an ex-

[1] From Thomas Wolfe, *Look Homeward, Angel* (New York, 1929). Reprinted by permission of Charles Scribner's Sons.

cessive amount of jewelry. Too many similes, especially, are a mark of awkward elaboration. Metaphors are usually more vigorous than similes, as "The ruby burned on the jet black dress" is stronger than "The ruby looked like a coal of fire on the jet black dress." Figures of speech should bring clearness through adding concrete experience to a meaning which would otherwise be abstract, but if they confuse or repeat unnecessarily a perfectly clear meaning, they become useless ornamentation.

POINT OF VIEW

As the arrangement of details is as important in a written description as composition in a painting, you must organize details so as to stimulate images in an orderly fashion. Chaotic scrambling of images will defeat your purpose. Accordingly, you must assume a certain point of view in dealing with your material.

The physical point of view will determine the order in which to present images and the perspective in which to draw them. When a painter has chosen the best view of a landscape and started his picture, he does not paint one portion of a landscape from one point of view and another portion from another. He avoids meaningless distortion by a perspective in which objects appear smaller or larger depending on their distance from him. Similarly, in written description you must establish yourself in a certain physical relation to a scene and present the details as they would appear to a reader were the scene actually before him. If possible, explain this position in the opening sentence; do not change it without warning. Do not give a pilot's-eye view of a wheat field, and then without notice shift to the scene as it appears to a farmer riding a combine harvester.

If you observe the normal processes of perception, you will notice that the eye transmits to the brain certain parts of a scene before others. Large masses are seen before small, bright colors before dull, distinct differences of light and shade before

subtle. If the scene is extensive, a dominant central figure or mass is perceived before subordinate details. To take in a panorama, the eye may travel from right to left, left to right, or up and down. Written description, likewise, should present images in such a normal sequence. A farmhouse and barn sitting in the middle of a bleak prairie should certainly receive attention before a rooster strutting in the barnyard. The general characteristics of a milling horde of Christmas shoppers should be presented before Mary Smith is singled out as she buys a necktie from a drooping clerk. Remember too the principle of perspective. If you describe a lumberjack clearing the top from a redwood tree as he is seen from a person on the ground, do not mention that the hands of his wrist watch point to one o'clock.

You may, of course, shift the point of view if you inform the reader of the shift. To describe the Palisades of the Hudson as seen from the deck of a river steamer, you must tell the reader that the boat is moving at a certain speed. You must also indicate changes of time, as when you describe a body of water first at sunset and then at dusk.

A consistent mental point of view, moreover, is as important as the physical. Though a view through a glass-bottomed boat of a tropical ocean bed may impress an ordinary tourist with color, luxuriance, and strangeness, the same scene to a marine biologist reveals hundreds of fascinating species of plants and animals. A little red schoolhouse on a country road may look like scores of others to a passing motorist, but to a man who learned his three R's there and perhaps courted his first sweetheart behind his geography book, the building is invested with sentiment and beauty. An adult who goes to a circus sees the bored, set expressions of the performers, the tarnished costumes, and the wash strung between the wagons behind the main tent; but the child sees only glamorous people wearing wonderful clothes, animals captured at the risk of the lives of daring men in far corners of the earth, and clowns who do things sidesplittingly funny. The atmosphere, tone, and mood of the description depend on the mental point of view.

DOMINANT IMPRESSION

Dominant impression, closely related to the point of view, can be determined only after the point of view is established. It is that feature or quality of whatever is being described which a writer emphasizes in such a way that it dominates the whole. The dominant impression of Uriah Heep in *David Copperfield* is that of hypocritical " 'umble-ness." In his description of the House of Usher on a "dull, dark, and soundless day in the autumn of the year," Poe establishes a feeling of gloom which pervades the whole story. The person who visits the Lincoln Memorial in Washington at dusk comes away remembering best the quietness and dignity of the huge statue of Lincoln.

You should therefore study the subject of your description to determine what should receive the greatest emphasis. Is it to be some physical quality, a mood, or an interpretation? Whatever it is, it will serve to co-ordinate the parts of the description and give meaning to it. Without a dominant impression, a description may be truthful, but it will be flat. It will lack the emphasis and point that make the difference between a reader's remembering something important from a description and his recalling only scattered fragments.

As illustration of the principle of the dominant impression, think back to some scene of your childhood. Do you remember distinctly all the details? Do you not rather recall vividly some detail, when nearly everything else has faded? And does not some feeling about that scene recur whenever you recollect it? This is dominant impression in retrospect. The artist in description focuses attention on the most important element of his subject and subordinates other information to give the reader just such an impression as yours from childhood. Notice how Washington Irving in the physical description of Ichabod Crane in "The Legend of Sleepy Hollow" makes every detail contribute to an impression of ungainly angularity.

> The cognomen of Crane was not inapplicable to his person. He was tall but exceedingly lank, with narrow shoulders, long arms and legs, hands that dangled a mile out of his sleeves, feet that might have served for shovels, and his whole frame most loosely hung together. His head was small and flat at top, with huge ears, large green glassy eyes, and a long snipe nose; so that it looked like a weathercock perched upon his spindle neck, to tell which way the wind blew. To see him striding along the profile of a hill, with his clothes bagging and fluttering about him, one might have mistaken him for the genius of famine descending upon the earth, or some scarecrow eloped from a cornfield.

This description, of course, is a caricature rather than an exact portrait. No man ever had "hands that dangled a mile out of his sleeves" or "feet that might have served as shovels." Irving, knowing that his story is grotesque, wants to create a character to fit the atmosphere. Yet the exaggeration illustrates how the principle works.

CHOICE OF DETAILS

The choice of details is dependent on the dominant impression. In a way, the dominant impression acts in description as the thesis sentence acts in exposition; it serves as the central core which the details amplify. The details exist for the sake of supporting the main idea. No image is allowed to intrude that does not contribute to the unity of the whole impression.

Unity demands that you choose carefully the details you introduce into a description. Intelligent selection is a basic principle in all art. The painter who portrays a log cabin would never think of drawing each log minutely or making an arresting detail of every shingle. Having determined the general effect he wants to produce, he scans his subject for details that will contribute and rejects those that are irrelevant. The writer of description, also, presents only the significant portions of his subject. He knows it is impossible for him to tell everything that the closest scrutiny would disclose; furthermore, point of view and perspective automatically eliminate a great deal. The literary artist who produces a pen portrait of Abraham Lincoln selects details that create an image of a very tall, gaunt, stooped, kindly, sadly humorous man. The number of buttons on his coat or the glint of light from his watch chain would hardly be included.

In the following paragraphs Dickens characterizes Mr. and Mrs. Tibbs in different ways. Little is said about Mrs. Tibbs herself, but the description of her house implies so much about the one who runs it that the reader constructs a definite image of her. All we are told about Mr. Tibbs pertains to his size, legs, long face, and habit of speaking, but, again, we know Mr. Tibbs pretty well as the result. Details have been chosen very effectively.

> Mrs. Tibbs was, beyond all dispute, the most tidy, fidgety, thrifty little personage that ever inhaled the smoke of London; and the house of Mrs. Tibbs was, decidedly, the neatest in all Great Coram Street. The area and the area steps, and the street door and the street door steps, and the brass handle and the door-plate, and the knocker, and the fanlight were all as clean and bright as indefatigable white-washing and hearthstoning and scrubbing and rubbing could make them. The wonder was that the brass doorplate, with the interesting inscription "Mrs. Tibbs," had never caught fire from constant friction, so perseveringly was it polished. There were meat-safe-looking blinds in the parlor windows, blue and gold curtains in the drawing-room, and spring-roller blinds, as Mrs. Tibbs was wont in the pride of her heart to boast, "all the

way up." The bell lamp in the passage looked as clear as a soap bubble; you could see yourself in all the tables, and French-polish yourself on any one of the chairs. The banisters were beeswaxed; and the very stair wires made your eyes wink, they were so glittering.

> Mrs. Tibbs was somewhat short of stature, and Mr. Tibbs was by no means a large man. He had, moreover, very short legs, but by way of indemnification, his face was peculiarly long. He was to his wife what the 0 is in 90 —he was of some importance *with* her—he was nothing without her. Mrs. Tibbs was always talking. Mr. Tibbs rarely spoke; but if it were at any time possible to put in a word when he should have said nothing at all, he had that talent. Mrs. Tibbs detested long stories, and Mr. Tibbs had one, the conclusion of which had never been heard by his most intimate friends. It always began, "I recollect when I was in the volunteer corps in eighteen hundred and six,"—but, as he spoke very slowly and softly, and his better half very quickly and loudly, he rarely got beyond the introductory sentence. He was a melancholy specimen of the storyteller. He was the Wandering Jew of Joe Millerism.—*Sketches by Boz.*

Descriptive writing is rare apart from one of the other forms of discourse. A writer has little occasion to describe something unless he is explaining it, arguing about it, or using it in a story. The most common use of description is in narration. Practice in writing description is useful, however, especially for what it can teach you about the choice of words and the logical arrangement of images. The examples that follow, most of them taken from narratives, illustrate some of the more common uses of description.

SENSE IMPRESSIONS

On Observing Colors

JOHN RUSKIN

IF YOU WANT to color beautifully, color as best pleases yourself at *quiet times*, not so as to catch the eye, nor to look as if it were

clever or difficult to color in that way, but so that the color may be pleasant to you when you are happy or thoughtful. Look much at the morning and evening sky, and much at simple flowers—dog-roses, wood hyacinths, violets, poppies, thistles, heather, and such like—as Nature arranges them in the woods and fields. If ever any scientific person tells you that two colors are "discordant," make a note of the two colors and put them together whenever you can. I have actually heard people say that blue and green were discordant; the two colors which Nature seems to intend never to be separated, and never to be felt in either of them in its full beauty without the other!—a peacock's neck, or a blue sky through green leaves, or a blue wave with green lights through it being precisely the loveliest things, next to clouds at sunrise, in this colored world of ours. If you have a good eye for colors, you will soon find out how constantly Nature puts purple and green together, purple and scarlet, green and blue, yellow and neutral gray, and the like; and how she strikes these color concords for general tones, and then works into them with innumerable subordinate ones; and you will gradually come to like what she does, and find out new and beautiful chords of color in her work every day. If you *enjoy* them, depend upon it you will paint them to a certain point right: or, at least, if you do not enjoy them, you are certain to paint them wrong. If color does not give you *intense* pleasure, let it alone; depend upon it, you are only tormenting the eyes and senses of people who feel color, whenever you touch it; and that is unkind and improper.—*Elements of Drawing.*

Water

JOHN RUSKIN

OF ALL INORGANIC substances, acting in their own proper nature, and without assistance or combination, water is the most wonderful. If we think of it as the source of all the changefulness and beauty which we have seen in clouds; then as the instrument by which the earth we have contemplated was modeled into symmetry, and its crags chiseled into grace; then as, in the form of snow, it robes the mountains it has made with that transcendent light which we could not have conceived if we had not seen; then as it exists in the foam of the torrent—in the iris which spans it, in the morning mist which rises from it, in the deep crystalline pools which mirror its hanging shore, in the broad lake and glancing river; finally, in that which is to all human minds the best emblem of unwearied, unconquerable power, the wild, various, fantastic, tameless unity of the sea; what shall we compare to this mighty, this universal element, for glory and for beauty? or how shall we follow its eternal changefulness of feeling? It is like trying to paint a soul. . . .

To paint the actual play of hue on the reflective surface, or to give the forms and fury of water when it begins to show itself—to give the flashing and rocketlike velocity of a noble cataract, or the precision and grace of the sea wave, so exquisitely modeled, though so mockingly transient—so mountainous in its form, yet so cloudlike in its motion—with its variety and delicacy of color, when every ripple and wreath has some peculiar passage of reflection upon itself alone, and the radiating and scintillating sunbeams are mixed with the dim hues of transparent depth and dark rock below—to do this perfectly is beyond the power of man; to do it even partially has been granted to but one or two, even of those few who have dared to attempt it. . . .

The fact is that there is hardly a roadside pond or pool which has not as much landscape *in* it as above it. It is not the brown, muddy, dull thing we suppose it to be; it has a heart like ourselves, and in the bottom of that there are the boughs of the tall trees, and the blades of the shaking grass, and all manner of hues, of variable, pleasant light out of the sky; nay, the ugly gutter that stagnates over the drain bars in the heart of the foul city is not altogether base; down in that, if you will look deep enough, you may see the dark, serious blue of far-off sky, and the passing of pure clouds. It is at your own will that you see in that despised stream either the refuse of the street or the image of the sky— so it is with almost all other things that we unkindly despise.—*Modern Painters*, I, 5, 1.

Christmas Tree[1]

HERMAN SMITH

I HAVE SEEN many a Christmas tree . . . in far places on land and sea and at home, but never such a tree as that of my childhood. There it stood, tall and straight and green, a noble young hemlock filling the air with fragrance. Its lacy branches were aglitter with wax candles of every hue, each in a holder that ended with a gold or silver star, each with its halo of rainbowed light, such as must have surrounded that small and sacred head on the first Christmas in the Bethlehem stable.

No modern tree with silvered or gilded bough, no tree of ostrich plumes hung with pearls, no tree hung with jeweled flowers and ablaze with electric lights in varicolored forms, can ever equal the tree that was disclosed to our gaze on Christmas Eves. Strings of popcorn and cranberries, oranges and crimson apples, gilded nuts, cornucopias of isinglass filled with anise and caraway drops, gold and silver stars, and suspended over its spear-crowned tip was a fat wax angel with shining quivering wings.

[1] From Herman Smith, *Stina: The Story of a Cook* (New York, copyright, 1942, by Herman Smith). Reprinted by permission of M. Barrows and Company, Inc.

Water Hyacinths[1]

HARNETT T. KANE

THE CAPTAIN frowned and pointed. "Maybe you wouldn't believe it, but that's our worst trouble." His finger was directed at a narrow line of fragile green and lavender flowers on each side of the canal, that bobbed lightly as we passed—water hyacinths, "orchids of the bayou." Somewhere behind us, on the route, one or two had crept into the scene almost unnoticed, and now they were thickening and widening as we went, reaching toward the center of the channel. A few yards forward was a circular mat of the plants, a floating garden of tight-packed, waxlike leaves. From the glistening bulbous centers protruded upthrust blossoms, pale bunches of delicate, perfumeless bloom. I managed to reach below the rail and catch a handful. They were easily crushed, more water than green cells. Below each plant extended light, colorless strings of roots, for several feet. The flowers faded quickly; in a few minutes they were limp on the wet deck. It was hard for

[1] From Harnett T. Kane, *The Bayous of Louisiana* (New York, copyright, 1943, by Harnett T. Kane). Reprinted by permission of William Morrow & Company, Inc.

me to realize that I held in my hand a major threat to navigation over most of South Louisiana.

This beauty is in heavy over-production and must literally be plowed under. Wherever there are bayous, the hyacinths intrude, an ever-invading, advancing army—a fragile subversive. Lakes, bays, small waterways and large ones are entered and overgrown almost in a season. Unless something is done, within the next few years they will be impassable. The matted leaves can cover a spread of water so completely that it seems like land. The man with the paddle finds passage impossible; even a heavy motorboat can be stopped by this flowered barrier, its propeller hopelessly enmeshed. The wise pilot does not attempt to penetrate a waterway so blanketed.

Rain in Mexico[1]

GERTRUDE DIAMANT

WHILE WE ARGUED the rain came, the thunderous drumming incontinent downpour which may last ten minutes or the whole afternoon. This is the spring of Mexico, the rainy season that ends the long golden monotony of the dry months. But it is no pleasant spring of burgeoning trees and greening lawns. It is not a season for a poet, but one for priests and a primitive religion; for the rains come with elemental force, scourging the earth wrathfully each day.

If you must be caught in the rain, be caught in the market place. It is like seeing the approach of doom. The peddlers wait until the last minute under the livid sky, and their cries sound far away and faint against the roll of thunder. Then the first drops fall, and there is a frantic rout, a folding of tents, dumping of vegetables, and scurrying away, and in the next minute nothing but the empty streets awash like a ship in a storm, and desolate as if humanity had never been there.

Or watch the rain from under a tree on the Reforma, where you will be thoroughly drenched but unable to move, because the rain is an impenetrable wall around you. It thunders down in white spears, with a roar of wind in which the palm trees flail like straws; and blots out the world, and there is only a solitary charro on horseback, a black silhouette against the rain. He sits under his poncho, becalmed, and you think the rain must have beaten horse and rider to death. But then the white spears thin out, the air grows lighter and the rain darker, the sun appears, and the charro rides away, his wet poncho shining.

I liked the rainy season better than the dry, because I like weather better than climate. The dry season is a golden vacuum; but the rainy season has change, which is weather. And while climate may create a race, weather creates the temper and sensibility of the individual. Most mornings were still clear, with a blue sky more brilliant than ever. But there were some that were dull and pleasantly clouded with premonition of the rain. And the skies that came before and after each day's cloudburst were, so to speak, not of this earth.

Perhaps it is the rarefied atmosphere that gives the clouds their solidity, their depth and effulgence of color. They rise from the mountains in the early afternoon and fill the sky, inexhaustible as chaos, sweeping the earth with a splendor of shafted light. Slowly the hot white masses and purple depths begin to lose color. A livid gray suffuses and melts them, and then the rain rips from a sky grown hard and opaque as metal.

[1] From Gertrude Diamant, *The Days of Ofelia* (Boston, copyright, 1942, by Gertrude Diamant). Reprinted by permission of Houghton Mifflin Company.

The Merry-Go-Round[1]

STEPHEN CRANE

WITHIN THE Merry-Go-Round there was a whirling circle of ornamental lions, giraffes, camels, ponies, goats, glittering with varnish and metal that caught swift reflections from windows high above them. With stiff wooden legs, they swept on in a never-ending race, while a great orchestrion clamored in wild speed. The summer sunlight sprinkled its gold upon the garnet canopies carried by the tireless racers and upon all the devices of decoration that made Stimson's machine magnificent and famous. A host of laughing children bestrode the animals, bending forward like charging cavalrymen, and shaking reins and whooping in glee. At intervals they leaned out perilously to clutch at iron rings that were tendered to them by a long wooden arm. At the intense moment before the swift grab for the rings one could see their little nervous bodies quiver with eagerness; the laughter rang shrill and excited. Down in the long rows of benches, crowds of people sat watching the game, while occasionally a father might arise and go near to shout encouragement, cautionary commands, or applause at his flying offspring. Frequently mothers called out: "Be careful, Georgie!" The orchestrion bellowed and thundered on its platform, filling the ears with its long monotonous song. Over in a corner, a man in a white apron and behind a counter roared above the tumult: "Popcorn! Popcorn!"

[1] From Stephen Crane, "The Pace of Youth" in *Men, Women, and Boats* (1921). Reprinted by permission of Alfred A. Knopf, Inc.

Sounds in Late Summer

RICHARD JEFFERIES

THE LOUDEST SOUND in the wood was the humming in the trees; there was no wind, no sunshine; a summer day, still and shadowy, under large clouds high up. To this low humming the sense of hearing soon became accustomed, and it served but to render the silence deeper. In time, as I sat waiting and listening, there came the faintest far-off song of a bird away in the trees—the merest thin upstroke of sound, slight in structure, the echo of the strong spring singing. This was the summer repetition, dying away. A willow-wren still remembered his love, and whispered about it to the silent fir tops, as in after days we turn over the pages of letters, withered as leaves, and sigh. So gentle, so low, so tender a song the willow-wren sang that it could scarce be known as the voice of a bird, but was like that of some yet more delicate creature with the heart of a woman. . . .

Next morning the August sun shone, and the wood was all a-hum with insects. The wasps were working at the pine boughs high overhead; the bees by dozens were crowding to the bramble flowers; swarming on them, they seemed so delighted; bumble-bees went wandering among the ferns in the copse and in the ditches . . . and calling at every purple heath-blossom, at the purple knap-weeds, purple thistles, and broad handfuls of yellow-weed flowers. Wasplike flies barred with yellow suspended themselves in the air between the pine-trunks like hawks hovering, and suddenly shot themselves a yard forward or to one side, as if the rapid vibration of their wings while hovering had accumulated force which drove them as if discharged from a crossbow. The sun had set all things in motion.

There was a hum under the oak by the hedge, a hum in the pine wood, a humming among the heath and the dry grass which heat had browned. The air was alive and merry with sound, so that the day seemed quite different and twice as pleasant.—From "The Pine Wood," in *The Open Air*.

Early Morning[1]

SIEGFRIED SASSOON

I CAN ALMOST re-smell the early autumn air, while the musical cry of hounds goes swinging round the covert, and the voices of the hunt-servants are heard with "Tallyo bike" and other cub-scaring exhortations, varied by saddle-rappings and rebukes of "Ware rabbit" to members of the young entry. An indignant cock-pheasant whirrs upward from the undergrowth and skims away across a stubble field. A hound lollops past me and plunges through the brambly hedge into the wood, while I wonder how long it will take me to learn all their names.

[1] From Siegfried Sassoon, *The Weald of Youth* (New York, copyright, 1932, by Siegfried Sassoon). Reprinted by permission of The Viking Press, Inc.

Making Tortillas[2]

GERTRUDE DIAMANT

SLEEP WAS only a small moment before the sun sprang up from the mountains, and I heard the women making tortillas—the steady slap-slap as they tossed the dough between their palms.

It is the sound of Mexico, as the blue of the sky is its color. And the cold of the mountain night is still in the air when it begins. I would rise and draw the curtains, and see the sun low and clear on the level white buildings. From the huts came a haze of smoke and the morning noises—chopping of wood, water splashing, and the pigs squealing; and Ofelia's little sister singing shrilly over and over, "To heaven, to heaven let me go, to receive the blessed crown, the blessed crown." And through it all the insistent slap-slap of tortilla-making, a rhythmic sound like part of a ceremonial, and one seems to hear far off the accompanying beat of feet in some primitive dance.

I could see the women working in the smoky huts where the night still lingered, their hands twinkling in the obscure light, their faces bronze and shadowy as if emerging from a dark canvas. Outside the men were washing, dousing their heads in the dirty water in the barrels; and then, drying their faces, they went into the huts to eat. They squatted on the dirt floor, and took many tortillas at a time, and folded them and downed them with black coffee.

[2] From Gertrude Diamant, *The Days of Ofelia* (Boston, copyright, 1942, by Gertrude Diamant). Reprinted by permission of Houghton Mifflin Company.

The Wind[1]

R. C. HUTCHINSON

CHIEFLY THE change was for my skin and lungs. This was a lane where the wind would meet you in both directions, and had rubbed my face with a harshness no more disagreeable than your own dog's tongue. It was a cold wind still, but the harshness had all gone; it was a parting instead of a slapping wind, quietened by the sun which showed now and again between the high fast convoy of white clouds. It bore damp odors, as the autumn wind had, but of a homelier kind; not of the high bogs and salty, mountain mists, but of water trickling through stone and moss, of valley ferns and faintly, with the farmstead smells from Randall's Gift, of cowslip and hyacinth. This richness of sensation, born of moss and stippled cloud with the quick green light on Nelden, possessed me by degrees as the bus's exhaust was brushed away.

[1] From R. C. Hutchinson, *Interim* (New York, copyright, 1945, by R. C. Hutchinson). Reprinted by permission of the author.

Apples

JOHN BURROUGHS

Is THERE any other fruit that has so much facial expression as the apple? . . . The swaar has one look, the rambo another, the spy another. The youth recognizes the seek-no-further, buried beneath a dozen other varieties, the moment he catches a glance of its eye, or the bonny-cheeked Newtown pippin, or the gentle but sharp-nosed gilliflower. He goes to the great bin in the cellar and sinks his shafts here and there in the garnered wealth of the orchards, mining for his favorites, sometimes coming plump upon them, sometimes catching a glimpse of them to the right or left, or uncovering them as keystones in an arch made up of many varieties.

In the dark he can usually tell them by the sense of touch. There is not only the size and shape, but there is the texture and polish. Some apples are coarse-grained and some are fine; some are thin-skinned and some are thick. One variety is quick and vigorous beneath the touch, another gentle and yielding. The pinnock has a thick skin with a spongy lining; a bruise in it becomes like a piece of cork. The tallow apple has an unctuous feel, as its name suggests. It sheds water like a duck. What apple is that with a fat curved stem that blends so prettily with its own flesh—the wine-apple? Some varieties impress me as masculine—weather-stained, freckled, lasting, and rugged; others are indeed lady apples, fair, delicate, shining, mild-flavored, white-meated, like the egg-drop and the lady-finger. The practiced hand knows each kind by the touch.—*Winter Sunshine,* published by Houghton Mifflin Company.

Christmas Breakfast[1]

HERMAN SMITH

WHAT A GAY breakfast table was ours on Christmas morning, with all of us, my brothers with their wives and broods, cousins, uncles, and aunts, crowded about the table extended to its full length with a smaller one for the children. How we ate of Stina's homemade sausage, eggs fried in rosemary butter, apple pancakes dripping with buckwheat honey, and winding up with her *tarte à la crème avec les mirabelles,* a tart made of raised sweet dough, filled with thick cream, dotted with yellow plums, dusted with sugar and cinnamon, and baked. With all of this there were endless cups of coffee from what must have been the grandmother of all the coffee pots on earth. Even I was allowed to have *café au lait,* and I drank it proudly from a cup decorated with a wreath of roses and the words "For a Good Boy" in letters of gold luster around the brim. Beside me sat my elephant sagely nodding his head, and in the pocket of my jacket the last battered banana awaited some moment of hunger later in the day.

My sisters flew from kitchen to dining room replenishing plates and cups, and over all beamed Stina in her red woolen hood. . . .

[1] From Herman Smith, *Stina: The Story of a Cook* (New York, copyright, 1942, by Herman Smith). Reprinted by permission of M. Barrows & Company, Inc.

Dinner at Cousin Lil's[1]

HERMAN SMITH

MY SISTERS, in the best and stiffest of Victorian tradition, did not admire Cousin Lil. In shocked confidence they whispered that she not only used too much powder and perfume, but that she actually painted—a thing no lady of impeccable reputation might dare to do. But of all my more distant relatives I liked Cousin Lil the most. She was big and generous and gay, full of jokes and laughter and broad-minded far beyond her time. . . .

What a thrill it was to turn into Uncle Fred's unbarred gateway and to see the low rambling farmhouse, rosy welcoming light streaming through its windows, with Cousin Lil's Amazonian figure framed in the open doorway. She wore a red merino dress. Her booming welcome rose above the whistling of the wind. When I was far enough unwound, warming up beside the shining kitchen range, she gave me a resounding and highly perfumed smack.

But other and more enticing smells greeted our half-frozen noses as they emerged into that grateful scented warmth, when Cousin Lil from time to time lifted a pot cover or opened the oven door. I could not wait for the formality of the others in presenting their gifts, but promptly offered my own. Never, said Cousin Lil, in all her born days had she seen such a valentine, such fat and dimpled cupids, such lifelike doves, so many bleeding hearts. Why, you could almost smell the red

[1] From Herman Smith, *Stina: The Story of a Cook* (New York, copyright, 1942, by Herman Smith). Reprinted by permission of M. Barrows & Company, Inc.

roses and the violets, and she didn't know but what she'd have it framed. She exclaimed equally over the oysters, her enthusiasm and praise completely thawing the Victorian ice from my sister's hearts. . . .

The table was spread in the low-ceilinged dining room which had a latticed wall paper of red and blue morning glories. A lamp with a pink china shade painted with bluebirds and butterflies hung from chains by which it could be raised or lowered at will. Its roseate glow disclosed in the center of Aunt Mary's best white damask cloth a gigantic five-layered fresh coconut birthday cake, towering high on the cake-stand. . . .

In addition to that miraculous combination which comprised her famous potato soup and the oysters brought from our home, which were enough for the lustiest of appetites, there were platters of crisp fried chicken with a garnish of crescent-shaped turnovers filled with spicy country sausage. Accompanying them were feathery potatoes mashed with green onion tops and beaten eggs, with little indented lakes of sweet butter on the top. There were flat yellow bowls of cole slaw made with tart apples and sour cream. There were hot biscuits, "rizen" rolls and homemade bread, tomatoes stewed with corn, and homegrown celery crunchy and sweet.

Around the table in leaf-shaped dishes of pressed glass moved a procession of jams, jellies, pickles, and preserves—their reds, yellows, greens, purples, and golden browns flashing back from the iridescent prisms of the hanging lamp. Flanking the cake were glass compotes, one holding strawberries, the other peaches, grown and canned on the farm.

PLACES

Mexico City[1]

GERTRUDE DIAMANT

AN AMERICAN city may be an ugly hodge-podge. It may have its slums close to rich sections, and its unemployed idle in the shade of busy factories. But all its contradictions are part of one age, part of its industrial growth. But Mexico City is different. For all the shining new cars that rush so wildly through the streets, and the modern hotels proudly advertising "Stean [sic] Heat," and the skyscrapers built on special foundations on the swampy ground, the modernism of the city is only the thinnest veneer over all its past. It is still a village, part of the primitive countryside around it and the primitive Indian life. It is still the colonial city of the Spaniards, and the romantic nineteenth-century city of Porfirio Díaz; it is only super-ficially of this century and the things of this century. It is like a fresco in which there is no perspective to make things recede in time and space. Everything is of the present, jumbled together. One remembers the words of Bernal Díaz del Castillo, who was one of the soldiers who followed Cortés, and who in his old age sat down to write "the true history of the conquest," very indignant over the lies that had been told about it. ". . . For in a manner of speaking all that I tell happened only yesterday." He wrote that four centuries ago, and one still feels that all that has happened in Mexico was only yesterday.

I think the markets have not changed much. When the Spaniards had come to the city, by perilous marches over the mountains from the seacoast, and after they had met Montezuma with great ceremony and received lodgings in the palace, they sallied

[1] From Gertrude Diamant, *The Days of Ofelia* (Boston, copyright, 1942, by Gertrude Diamant). Reprinted by permission of Houghton Mifflin Company.

forth like good tourists to see the market. And it must have been very much like those that tourists see today.

"And when we had come to the Grand Plaza, as we had never beheld such a thing, we were astonished at the multitude of people and the abundance of merchandise, and the order and arrangement that there was in everything. And I will mention first the vendors of gold and silver and precious stones, and feathers and robes and embroidered things.[1] Then there were other vendors who sold cloth and ropes of hennequen, and sandals, which are the shoes that they wear, and everything was in one part of the Plaza in its appropriate place. Let us go and talk of those who sold beans and herbs and other vegetables. Let us go to those who sold chickens and rabbits and hares and other things of the sort. Let us speak of those who sold pottery made in a thousand different ways from big basins to little pitchers, which were by themselves apart, and also of those who sold honey and sweetmeats, and wood and firewood and resinous pine strips."

The list gets so long that he adds rather testily: "What more do you want me to say?" Naturally he could not mention the ugly lithograph calendars (made in Japan) which are now sold in the markets and which Mexicans buy for their gorgeous color, though they may be unable to read the days of the month; or the glittering pins with false stones (made in the United States), which Mexicans prefer to their own silverwork. The resinous pine strips that he mentions are still used for a quick fuel; and because they are so much used, together with charcoal, the land around Mexico City has been denuded of its forests. But now the Government is talking of using its newly recovered oil for making gas, which is still a luxury in Mexico. And the little pitchers that were by themselves apart, are still the chief kitchenware. They are made of mud and sell for a

centavo. One need stand on the streets only three minutes to see a cargador pass with a huge pile of them on his back.

But the Spaniards seem to have suffered the usual tourist difficulties, for as Bernal Díaz says, "the Plaza was so big and full of people it was impossible to see everything in one day." And so they left the market and went to see the great temple, ascending the hundred and fourteen steps with the aid of two priests, whom Montezuma sent to help them so that they should not get tired.

"And as we climbed to the top of the grand temple, we came to a platform covered with stones, where they placed the sad Indians for sacrifice. . . ."

Then Montezuma took Cortés by the hand and told him to look at the great city and all its environs, and it was very easy to see everything. . . . And they saw the three great highways leading into the city, and all the canals and the great lake of Texcoco crowded with canoes coming and going. The highways are still the same, but few of the canals are left now, and those near the city are muddied with pestilential drainage waters. And the great lake of Texcoco is dry, a tiny Sahara from which dense yellow clouds of dust rise in the rainy season to envelop the city. And all the glory of Tenochtitlan, the city that Cortés gazed on from the temple, is gone too. It withstood the siege of the Spaniards and their Indian allies for sixty-five days—a siege by land and water, for Cortés ordered ships built and launched them on the lake, and from them discharged the big guns on the city. And whatever the fighting did not destroy, the Spaniards destroyed when they entered the city again. . . .

The great Indian city is gone, but the sad Indians remain. One is curious to know whether Bernal Díaz found all the Indians sad, or only those who were about to be sacrificed, in which case it is very understandable. But it is certain that the Indians of today are sad. It may be racial, or it may be a sadness that comes from the conditions of their life. In the four centuries following the

[1] All these things, however, have since moved into the tourist stores, where they command a better price.

conquest nothing was added to the life of the Indians, everything was taken away. The Indians lived, and still live, under the most primitive conditions—a degraded form of the primitive because it is not a cultural stage, but a total deprivation of all that human beings should have. Only since the Revolution have the Indians been counted as part of the population of Mexico, and they are, whether pure-blooded or mixed, a good three fifths of it. But the work of the Revolution can better their lives only slowly, but that is its chief task, and it is the future of Mexico. The sad Indians had the first word, and they will probably have the last.

And they come to the city as though it were only a big village, and they never take the streets seriously, but sit down to rest or eat their tortillas in front of the modern buildings. Groups of campesinos come in their white smocks and white trousers, sandaled or barefoot, with leather bags slung over their shoulders, on pilgrimage to the Virgin of Guadalupe or to see about their lands. And they gape up at the big buildings, or look into the store windows where there are displays of modern farm machinery, or stand listening to a gramophone bawling American jazz. I think it is this constant reminder of the primitive in a modern setting that gives Mexico its quality of excitement. And it makes for comedy too.

I remember one day in the Alameda. It is a park in the center of town, bosky and well-treed like all the parks of the city, but cluttered with bad statues. At the end near the Palace of Fine Arts, the Inquisition used to burn its victims. Later it became a fashionable promenade. Now it is a pleasant place to read the paper, to have your shoes shined, to pass the siesta hours while you wait for the city to come to life again. I was reading the paper near one of the statues— a whipped-cream female nude—when the sound of suppressed laughter made me look up. A man and a woman, barefoot and very ragged . . . , were looking at the statue, nudging each other, laughing with their hands to their mouths, finding it indescribably funny. It was the most forthright piece of art criticism I have ever seen, and I enjoyed that statue with them, as I have enjoyed few works of art. Later a campesino came to have his picture taken. There are photographers in the Alameda who give you a donkey to sit on, or a sarape to drape over your shoulder, or a big oleograph of the Cathedral of Guadalupe for a background. This photographer happened to have a huge bull fiddle, and the campesino posed himself with it, and everyone stopped to watch in utter solemnity. Only the gringa laughed and went off in disgrace, but with a feeling that the day had been well spent.

Farmhouse Cellar[1]

HERMAN SMITH

A FARMHOUSE cellar is not to be confused with what is known as a basement. Our cellar was of stone and extended under practically the entire house. Its floor was of red brick, and its walls were freshly whitewashed every

[1] From Herman Smith, *Stina: The Story of a Cook* (New York, copyright, 1942, by Herman Smith). Reprinted by permission of M. Barrows & Company, Inc.

spring. There was a special room under the west wing for the apples, pears, turnips, carrots, cabbages, parsnips, and beets, which were to supply us with food while we waited for spring.

In shallow trenches—made of boards and filled with sand—celery, endive, chicory, and leeks made rows of summery green in the dim light which filtered through the little frosted windows set high in the walls. In summer, in that cellar I could see and smell the lilies-of-the-valley which grew and bloomed all around the foundation of our house. But to a small and ever hungry boy the winter sights and smells were best.

In the cupboards of whitewashed pine, tier on tier, stood the result of the summer labor of my sisters—for canning was the one work which Stina was willing to share with them. Every known kind of jelly, pickle, conserve, and jam, with preserved cherries, peaches, pears, plums, raspberries, strawberries, gooseberries, and blackberries from our own trees and vines, stood in shining jars. There were gallon jars of huckleberries, purple black and sweet, from our marshes along the creek. . . . Great stone jars as large as small barrels held cucumbers pickled with dill, sauerkraut and grape leaves, and cuts of home-corned beef, tangy with garlic, bay leaves, and peppercorns. . . .

Also in our cellar, resting on a platform of oak beams, were small barrels of homemade wine of various kinds, and of cider, often drawn upon by Stina for use in dishes in which to her, as to all supercooks, the use of wine is imperative.

The Furnished Room[1]

O. HENRY

THE GUEST reclined, inert, upon a chair, while the room, confused in speech as though it were an apartment in Babel, tried to discourse to him of its divers tenantry.

A polychromatic rug like some brilliant-flowered, rectangular, tropical islet lay surrounded by a billowy sea of soiled matting. Upon the gay-papered wall were those pictures that pursue the homeless one from house to house—The Huguenot Lovers, The First Quarrel, The Wedding Breakfast, Psyche at the Fountain. The mantel's chastely severe outline was ingloriously veiled behind some pert drapery drawn rakishly askew like the sashes of the Amazonian ballet. Upon it was some desolate flotsam cast aside by the room's marooned when a lucky sail had borne them to a fresh port—a trifling vase or two, pictures of actresses, a medicine bottle, some stray cards out of a deck.

One by one, as the characters of a cryptograph become explicit, the little signs left by the furnished room's procession of guests developed a significance. The threadbare space in the rug in front of the dresser told that lovely woman had marched in the throng. The tiny fingerprints on the wall spoke of little prisoners trying to feel their way to sun and air. A splattered stain, raying like the shadow of a bursting bomb, witnessed where a hurled glass or bottle had splintered with its contents against the wall. Across the pier glass had been scrawled with a diamond in staggering letters the name "Marie." It seemed that the succession of dwellers in the furnished room had turned in fury—perhaps tempted beyond forbearance by its garish coldness—and wreaked upon it their passions. The furniture was chipped and bruised; the couch, distorted by bursting springs, seemed a horrible monster that had been slain during the stress of some grotesque convulsion. Some more potent upheaval had cloven a great slice from the marble mantel. Each plank in the floor owned its particular cant and shriek as from a separate and individual agony. It seemed incredible that all this malice and injury had been wrought upon the room by those who had called it for

[1] From O. Henry, *The Four Million* (New York, 1905, 1933). Reprinted by permission of Doubleday & Company, Inc.

a time their home; and yet it may have been the cheated home instinct surviving blindly, the resentful rage at false household gods that had kindled their wrath. A hut that is our own we can sweep and adorn and cherish.—"The Furnished Room."

PERSONS

Captain Ahab

HERMAN MELVILLE

THERE SEEMED no sign of common bodily illness about him nor of the recovery from any. He looked like a man cut away from the stake, when the fire has overrunningly wasted all the limbs without consuming them, or taking away one particle from their compacted aged robustness. His whole high, broad form seemed made of solid bronze and shaped in an unalterable mold, like Cellini's cast of Perseus. Threading its way out from among his grey hairs and continuing right down one side of his tawny scorched face and neck, till it disappeared in his clothing, you saw a slender rodlike mark, lividly whitish. It resembled that perpendicular seam sometimes made in the straight, lofty trunk of a great tree, when the upper lightning tearingly darts down it. . . .

So powerfully did the whole grim aspect of Ahab affect me, and the livid brand which streaked it, that for the first few moments I hardly noted that not a little of this overbearing grimness was owing to the barbaric white leg upon which he partly stood. It had previously come to me that this ivory leg had at sea been fashioned from the polished bone of the sperm whale's jaw. "Aye, he was dis-

masted off Japan," said the old Gay-Head Indian once; "but like his dismasted craft, he shipped another mast without coming home for it. He has a quiver of 'em."

I was struck with the singular posture he maintained. Upon each side of the *Pequod's* quarterdeck and pretty close to the mizzen shrouds, there was an auger hole, bored about half an inch or so into the plank. His bone leg steadied in that hole, one arm elevated, and holding by a shroud, Captain Ahab stood erect, looking straight out beyond the ship's ever-pitching prow. There was an infinity of firmest fortitude, a determinate, unsurrenderable willfulness, in the fixed and fearless, forward dedication of that glance. Not a word he spoke; nor did his officers say aught to him, though by all their minutest gestures and expressions they plainly showed the uneasy, if not painful, consciousness of being under a troubled master eye. And not only that, but moody, stricken Ahab stood before them with an apparently eternal anguish in his face, in all the nameless, regal overbearing dignity of some mighty woe.— *Moby Dick.*

Eustacia Vye

THOMAS HARDY

EUSTACIA VYE was the raw material of a divinity. On Olympus she would have done well with a little preparation. She had the passions and instincts which make a model goddess, that is, those which make not quite a model woman. Had it been possible for the earth and mankind to be entirely in her grasp for a while, had she handled the distaff, the spindle, and the shears at her own free will, few in the world would have noticed the change of government. There would have been the same inequality of lot, the same heaping up of favors here, of contumely there, the same generosity before justice, the same perpetual dilemmas, the same captious alternation of caresses and blows that we endure now.

She was in person full-limbed, and somewhat heavy; without ruddiness, as without pallor; and soft to the touch as a cloud. To see her hair was to fancy that a whole winter did not contain darkness enough to form its shadow; it closed over her forehead like nightfall extinguishing the western glow.

Her nerves extended into those tresses, and her temper could always be softened by stroking them down. When her hair was brushed, she would instantly sink into stillness and look like the Sphinx. If in passing under one of the Egdon banks, any of the thick skeins were caught, as they sometimes were, by a prickly tuft of the large *Ulex Europœus*—which will act as a sort of hairbrush—she would go back a few steps and pass against it a second time.

She had Pagan eyes, full of nocturnal mysteries. Their light, as it came and went, and came again, was partially hampered by their oppressive lids and lashes; and of these the under lid was much fuller than it usually is with English women. This enabled her to indulge in reverie without seeming to do so: she might have been believed capable of sleeping without closing them up. Assuming that the souls of men and women were visible essences, you could fancy the color of Eustacia's soul to be flamelike. The sparks

from it that rose into her dark pupils gave the same impression.

The mouth seemed formed less to speak than to quiver, less to quiver than to kiss. Some might have added, less to kiss than to curl. Viewed sideways, the closing line of her lips formed, with almost geometric precision, the curve so well known in the arts of design as the cima-recta, or ogee. The sight of such a flexible bend as that on grim Egdon was quite an apparition. It was felt at once that that mouth did not come over from Sleswig with a band of Saxon pirates whose lips met like the two halves of a muffin. One had fancied that such lip curves were mostly lurking underground in the South as fragments of forgotten marbles. So fine were the lines of her lips that, though full, each corner of her mouth was as clearly cut as the point of a spear. This keenness of corner was only blunted when she was given over to sudden fits of gloom, one of the phases of the night side of sentiment which she knew too well for her years.

Her presence brought memories of such things as Bourbon roses, rubies, and tropical midnights; her moods recalled lotus-eaters and the march in "Athalie"; her motions, the ebb and flow of the sea; her voice, the viola. In a dim light, and with a slight rearrangement of her hair, her general figure might have stood for that of either of the higher female deities. The new moon behind her head, an old helmet upon it, a diadem of accidental dewdrops round her brow, would have been adjuncts sufficient to strike the note of Artemis, Athena, or Hera respectively, with as close an approximation to the antique as that which passes muster on many respected canvases.—*The Return of the Native.*

Stina[1]

HERMAN SMITH

I CAN SEE HER now—small, almost elfin—with the brightest, blackest, wisest eyes I have ever seen. Her face was crisscrossed with innumerable wrinkles which broke into sunbursts when she smiled. A despot she was—not always amiable—but a cook whom I know now to have been deserving of the *cordon bleu*. She slept in a small, cold, immaculate chamber not far from mine, but all her waking hours were spent in the kitchen which was her pride. . . .

In winter she wore a full-gathered skirt of dark-brown wool, a waist buttoned to the brooch of tiny, gold-clasped hands at her throat. A voluminous apron of blue, white-sprigged calico was tied about her waist. Upon her head, which was only slightly gray, she wore a little knitted hood of dark red wool; and often in the morning before the kitchen was warmed up, she wore a sleeveless, knitted woolen vest of the same dark red.

Sharp-eyed, sometimes sharp-tongued—though never to me—she concocted the most heavenly dishes with the ease and pride of the artist, for she was a genius in that most intimate of all the arts—the art of cookery.

[1] From Herman Smith, *Stina: The Story of a Cook* (New York, copyright, 1942, by Herman Smith). Reprinted by permission of M. Barrows & Company, Inc.

CHANGING POINT OF VIEW

A Road in England[1]

R. C. HUTCHINSON

A ROAD'S EXCELLENCE lies in its power to yield the unexpected; and this lane concealed its riches until you were right upon them. It took you for half a mile as straight and respectably as the lanes of Lincolnshire; you thought you could see ahead how it would curve to manage the rising ground. Then, when it had bent a little, it dodged abruptly to avoid a house that stood in its way and became immediately the high road of a village. I do not know if it has a name, this place; "yonder over edge" was how I had heard it called, as if the world ended there; it was a rhombic green, shaved close by goats and fenced with beeches, on which a dozen

[1] From R. C. Hutchinson, *Interim* (New York, copyright, 1945, by R. C. Hutchinson). Reprinted by permission of the author.

cottages stood at independent angles like children at the beginning of a party. Instead of taking the obvious course, the lane suddenly wheeled right again and squeezed between two granaries. You were in a beechwood now, where the breeze was oddly stilled and the day seemed to have strode forward into evening. And now, as the road dipped sharply, the fence of brush gave place to rock; you smelt and heard the flow of water over rock before you found it running beside you. For perhaps twelve minutes, at our pace, the lane tried to edge away from the beck; but the wall of rock, now sloped to carry little oaks, now moistly bare and vertical, would nudge it in again; until, squeezed hard by the narrowing gorge, it boldly turned to step across the beck, rose in one leap upon a gentle slope it found there, and broke away and up to the freedom of Pitch-nose Fell. Again you had made landfall on a foreign soil. The smell of moss and the stream's rustle fell away; all the rock you saw was the giant boulders that lay dry amidst the broom. Like small beasts born prisoner, we had been content with a prospect stretching to forty feet on either hand, with the gush and trickle of white water through hanging ferns, fragmented light on the marriage of cliff and green. We emerged in a land whose only boundary was the sky and the sky-toned hills, where the eye's convenient mark was the thrust of Skiddaw twenty miles away.

The wind here was fresh, but duller-edged than you would hope for in this season, for the sun had been clear all day to tame it. Strangely, it did not seem to blow from any quarter, and it stirred the bracken hardly at all; you felt its motion rather as the movement of the crowd about you watching a procession, a constant, not unfriendly pressure on all your sides. And the light was strange: pale and constant like summer eve-

ning's light reflected from a calm sea. I had thought this country had no new colors to show me; I knew the whole range of its grays, the bracken's luster, and the mournful shades of peat and dying heather. And now they came as if the eyes I used were subtler than my own, tones more translucent, more sensitively joined. About the level of the road a film of mist spread flat to the nearer hills. I saw it not as a cloud but rather as if a watered brush had been drawn across my view. Within this band the colors of moor and hill were paled, so that they seemed not Nature's but a romantic painter's reverie; and all the shades below and above, to where the sky held constant sympathy, were changed and softened to keep it in communion. Our chatter faded there; we walked beside the road and our shoes on the resilient turf were almost silent. From very far we heard an engine whistle as it scuttled into the Red-knock tunnel. But that was another world, and this we saw, fastened in stillness, was a new creation for ourselves.

A Steamboat Landing at a Small Town

MARK TWAIN

ONCE A DAY a cheap gaudy packet arrived upward from St. Louis, and another downward from Keokuk. Before these events, the day was glorious with expectancy; after them, the day was a dead and empty thing. Not only the boys but the whole village felt this. After all these years I can picture that old time to myself now, just as it was then: the white town drowsing in the sunshine of a summer's morning; the streets empty, or pretty nearly so; one or two clerks sitting in front of the Water Street stores, with their splint-bottomed chairs tilted back against the wall, chins on breasts, hats slouched over their faces, asleep—with shingle-shavings enough around to show what broke them

down; a sow and a litter of pigs loafing along the sidewalk, doing a good business in water-melon rinds and seeds; two or three lonely little freight piles scattered about the "levee"; a pile of "skids" on the slope of the stone-paved wharf, and the fragrant town drunk-ard asleep in the shadow of them; two or three wood flats at the head of the wharf, but nobody to listen to the peaceful lapping of the wavelets against them; the great Missis-sippi, the majestic, the magnificent Missis-sippi, rolling its mile-wide tide along, shining in the sun; the dense forest away on the other side; the "point" above the town and the "point" below, bounding the river-glimpse and turning it into a sort of sea, and withal a very still and brilliant and lonely one. Presently a film of dark smoke appears above one of those remote "points"; instantly a negro drayman, famous for his quick eye and prodigious voice, lifts up the cry, "S-t-e-a-m-boat a-comin'!" and the scene changes! The town drunkard stirs, the clerks wake up, a furious clatter of drays follows, every house and store pours out a human contribution, and all in a twinkling the dead town is alive and moving. Drays, carts, men, boys, all go hurrying from many quarters to a common center, the wharf. Assembled there, the people fasten their eyes upon the coming boat, as upon a wonder they are seeing for the first time. And the boat *is* rather a handsome sight too. She is long and sharp and trim and pretty; she has two tall fancy-topped chimneys, with a gilded device of some kind swung between them; a fanciful pilot-house, all glass and "gingerbread," perched on top of the "texas" deck behind them; the paddle boxes are gorgeous with a picture or with gilded rays above the boat's name; the boiler deck, the hurricane deck, and the texas deck are fenced and ornamented with clean white railings; there is a flag gallantly flying from the jack staff; the furnace doors are open and the fires glaring bravely; the upper decks are black with passengers; the captain stands by the big bell, calm, imposing, the envy of all; great volumes of the blackest smoke are rolling and tumbling out of the chimneys—a husbanded grandeur created with a bit of pitch pine just before arriving at a town; the crew are grouped on the forecastle; the broad stage is run far out over the port bow, and an envied deckhand stands picturesquely on the end of it with a coil of rope in his hand; the pent steam is screaming through the gauge cocks; the captain lifts his hand, a bell rings, the wheels stop; then they turn back, churning the water to a foam, and the steamer is at rest. Then such a scramble as there is to get aboard, and to get ashore, and to take in freight, and to discharge freight, all at one and the same time; and such a yelling and cursing as the mates

facilitate it all with! Ten minutes later the steamer is under way again, with no flag on the jack staff and no black smoke issuing from the chimneys. After ten more minutes the town is dead again and the town drunkard asleep by the skids once more.—*Life on the Mississippi.*

SUGGESTIONS FOR STUDY

1. Study the selections under "Sense Impressions" and for each selection state which sense is chiefly appealed to. If the selection appeals to more than one sense, list the senses appealed to, beginning with the sense to which the greatest appeal is made.

2. State the dominant impression which each selection gives.

3. State the specific purpose for each of the selections by Ruskin.

4. For each of the selections beginning with "Christmas Tree" through "The Furnished Room," give the exact setting and the position of the speaker in that setting.

5. If you were an artist, which of the selections could you illustrate most faithfully? Which would be more difficult to illustrate? State the reasons for your opinion.

6. Study the three selections under "Persons": What is the dominant impression in each? Compare the descriptions of actual physical features of the three. Of each, state whether the author was trying to transmit an impression of the whole character or a photograph of the exterior appearance.

7. Of the selections under "Changing Point of View," state concerning each whether the changing point of view is one of place or time or both.

8. Answer the following specific questions on the selections:

"On Observing Colors": (a) In what mood should the artist be when he is trying to color? Would the same hold true for one trying to transmit a picture by words instead of by brush? (b) According to Ruskin, what is the most beautiful thing in the world? the next most beautiful? (c) What advice does he give about putting colors together?

"Water": (a) How many different forms in which water may be observed does he mention? (b) To whom is the selection addressed primarily? Does it have value for those who depict through words? Explain your answer.

"Christmas Tree": (a) What date would you give to this Christmas tree? Why? (b) Mark any words in the selection which you could not define and look them up in a dictionary. Does this make the focus more sharp? (c) What do you deduce about the author from this selection?

"Water Hyacinths": (a) Could you draw a water hyacinth from the author's description? (b) What exact information about the water hyacinth does the selection give? (c) Do the flowers have an odor? (d) Why did the captain frown when he pointed to them?

"Rain in Mexico": (a) What does the author mean by the rainy season's not being for the poet but for the priest? (b) State in your own words what takes place as the rain approaches. (c) What distinction does the author make between climate and weather? (d) Look up the following words: incontinent, burgeoning, livid, charro, poncho, rarefied, effulgence.

"The Merry-Go-Round": (a) List the words that denote movement. (b) List all the sounds mentioned in the selection.

"Sounds in Late Summer": (a) What is the chief difference between the two scenes in the selection? (b) What differences in the sounds does the author note between the two scenes? (c) Try to find a single word that will best give the impression on the listener in each scene.

"Early Morning": (a) What is the occasion for this bit of description? (b) Explain the meaning of the last clause in the first sentence. (c) What adjectives and verbs seem well chosen to give an accurate impression with the fewest words?

"Making Tortillas": (a) List separately all the sounds and sights mentioned in the selection. (b) What is the dominant impression?

"The Wind": (a) What is the time of year? (b) What senses are appealed to? Which dominates? Which is next? (c) Try to locate the setting—general and specific.

"Apples": (a) Does the author's use of fantasy in any way vivify the description? (b) Which paragraph gives you the best impression? Which sense is appealed to in each?

"Christmas Breakfast": (a) What special privilege was given the author at Christmas breakfast? (b) Who were present? (c) Who assumed the duties of waiting table? (d) Consider the selection very carefully; then tell which of the senses is appealed to most.

"Dinner at Cousin Lil's": (a) Why did the author's sisters disapprove of Lil? (b) What date would you assign to the occasion? (c) Describe Cousin Lil—physical appearance and character. (d) What was the time of year and what the specific occasion for the dinner?

"Mexico City": (a) What contrast exists between Mexico City and an American city? (b) What changes have taken place in Mexico City in 400 years? What conditions persist? (c) According to the author, what gives Mexico its quality of excitement? (d) Who was the gringa? Why did she go away from the park in disgrace?

"Farmhouse Cellar": (a) In which season did the author most enjoy the cellar? (b) Describe the cellar in your own words. (c) List the contents of the cellar.

"The Furnished Room": (a) List the principal words which give the selection its dominant tone. (b) What specific clues indicated some of the past tenants of the room? (c) To what does the author attribute the treatment of the room by its tenants? (d) Which is important—physical or mental point of view?

"Captain Ahab": (a) In what order are the details of Ahab's appearance presented? (b) Is the omission of details of facial features bad? (c) What three figures of speech in the first paragraph dominate the description?

"Eustacia Vye": (a) Why do the last three sentences return to the idea of the first paragraph? (b) Are the reference to the Sphinx and the adjective *Pagan* in tone with the rest of the description? Why does he use the latter word instead of "peculiar"? (c) What hint does the description of Eustacia's hair give to her character? What other hints are present in the selection? (d) In the last paragraph, what do the attributes of her presence, moods, and voice have in common?

"Stina": (a) List the attributes of Stina as given in the selection. (b) Does her physical description harmonize with what the author says of her character?

"A Road in England": (a) In what does a road's excellence lie? (b) What was the shape of the village? What was it called? (c) List the main views a traveler along the road would have. (d) Make a list of words in the selection which are unfamiliar to you and look them up. Does knowing the words bring the picture into sharper focus? (e) List the terms that indicate a changing point of view.

"A Steamboat Landing": (a) Are the images produced by the description general or specific? (b) What point of view does the author assume in his description? Where would he have to be to see all that he describes? Is the changing point of view one of place, time, or tone?

Suggestions for Writing

1. Observe one of your college buildings from a distance of a block or two. Make a list of details in the order that they would appear in a description of the building from that point of view. State the dominant impression. Then approach to within twenty paces of the main entrance and make another list. Is the dominant impression the same?

2. Write a description of the classroom to which you go for freshman composition. Assume the point of view of yourself as you sit in your accustomed seat.

3. Using one of the topics suggested below, write a description of five hundred words or more. State at the top of your paper your point of view and dominant impression.

A familiar landmark on your campus

A country store

A third-rate movie house

A modern filling station

A favorite picture

A piece of antique furniture

A room in a historic house

A blizzard

A room in a broadcasting station

The community Christmas tree

A streamlined train

The house you would like to live in

A favorite camping spot

A stage setting for a play or opera

Backstage in a theater

A hotel or theater doorman

Some notable person in your home town

The janitor of a college building

4. Write a description in which the point of view changes or which involves the passing of time. Suggestions:

A trip up an elevator in a department store

The characteristic countryside seen by a motorist in some part of the country

The banks of a river as seen from a canoe

An airplane passenger's view of the country below

The crowd before and after a football game

The appearance of your room before and after your friends come in to investigate a box from home

5. Write a description which includes a wide sweep of vision—a panorama, in other words. Suggestions:

The audience which comes to witness free movies in a small town

A tourist camp

An airport

A city as seen from the top of a tall building

A crowd gathered to witness the departure of a steamship

The crowd at a professional baseball game

An automobile dump

A large industrial plant

6. Write a description which emphasizes the experiences of one sense only. Suggestions:

A "hamburger joint"

What a ball game sounds like to a person outside the fence

The noise of a carnival

The locker room of the gymnasium

A night in a Pullman berth

A roller coaster ride

The bodily sensations experienced when one is frightened while following a dark path at night

How to distinguish different kinds of cloth by the sense of touch

Riding in a rumble seat

7. Describe the auditory sensations you experience when listening to a certain piece of music in terms of images involving the other senses. If the piece of music tells a story, that can be part of your description, but do not be content with the story only. What pictures or other sensations does the music create?

D. Narration

Narration is the reporting of a series of happenings. It deals with *action* and the *passing of time*. The action may be single or multiple, the passing of time a moment or many years; but whether in a brief anecdote or a novel, the parts are arranged in such a way as to supply a succession of answers to the question, "What happened next?" The storyteller, in response to a reader's (or auditor's) interest, relates one after another a sequence of actions, incidents, or episodes, all leading to a conclusion that finally satisfies the reader's curiosity. The emphasis in narration, then, is on the *result* of a sequence of events rather than on the *manner* in which they take place, as in exposition. In exposition, for instance, a writer discussing a change of automobile casings explains what tools to use and how to manipulate them to get the old tire off and the new one on without damage to the rim or tire; in narration, he reports in sequence the actions of the one attempting to change the casings, makes the most of the conflict between him and his job, and leads up to a climax when the new tire is on or the worker throws down his tools in disgust and calls a garage.

The technique of narration involves the arrangement of characters and incidents in a way best designed to focus the attention of a reader on a sequence of events and to keep him interested in what is going to happen next. There are many ways of doing this. In *Tom Jones*, perhaps the first great English novel, Fielding begins with the finding of Tom as a baby at Squire Allworthy's and follows his fortunes till he is married. The same method was often used by Dickens and other nineteenth-century novelists. Some modern novels and motion pictures begin at a point near the end of a chain of events and by a system of flash backs fill in the past action. In short narratives and the short story, most writers begin at just the point when something is about to happen to the main character to effect some change in him. Whatever method is employed, a well-constructed narrative has three basic parts—the *initial situation,* the *action,* and the *conclusion*—and three qualities—*unity, suspense,* and the *illusion of reality.*

THE INITIAL SITUATION

The initial situation should contain the germ of everything that comes afterward. This does not mean, of course, that you must begin by giving away your ending; but it does mean that you should include in the initial situation the elements on which the subsequent action and conclusion are based. Once the initial situation is established, what follows should come as an almost inevitable corollary of this situation. In other words, the initial situation does not merely start the ball rolling, but it states the nature of the ball, provides it with motive power, and limits the direction in which it will be allowed to roll. Obviously, therefore, in a short narrative you cannot imagine an initial situation and then ramble along at will, letting the action take whatever turn it may. Instead, you have in mind from the first what you intend to produce as action and conclusion, and create an initial situation from which the subsequent events will proceed in the most natural way.

Conflict

The opening paragraphs of the narrative will, of course, present the setting and the important characters; but, even more important, they will indicate the basis for the conflict that is waged in the action and resolved in the conclusion. Conflict, or struggle, is an indispensable element of good narration, for without conflict there can be no suspense, and without suspense the narrative loses force. Because there are as many kinds of conflict as there are possibilities for stories, as a narrator you must from the very start have a clear concept of the conflict with which you will deal in a specific narrative. The struggle of a pursuit flyer against an enemy bomber, of a prize fighter against his opponent, of an expert fisherman against a particularly wily fish is a fairly easy kind of conflict to imagine and to control in writing. More subtle kinds of struggle—a contest between a man and his conscience, between the two parts of a split personality, between a man and his environment, between a woman and social conventions—require much deeper penetration on your part and much greater care in setting up the initial situation and tracing the conflict.

Tone

The initial situation is important also in setting the tone of the narrative—the emotional atmosphere that envelops the story and extends to the reader. Is the narrative to be a colloquial, tall story, like Mark Twain's "Baker's Blue-Jay Yarn"; a light, almost frivolous, treatment of some serious matter, like H. H. Munro's "Laura"; or a serious story, like James Gould Cozzens' "Foot in It"?[1] Whatever tone you employ, you should indicate it almost in the opening words of the narrative, certainly in the first few sentences. A story that begins, "Once upon a time, in a beautiful palace, there lived . . ." acquires a definite tone immediately, just as one does that begins, "Jack Roper zoomed his pursuit plane sharply upward, just in time to catch a glimpse of the bomber sliding into a cloudbank."

Point of View

Another important matter to decide before you begin writing and to indicate in the initial situation is the point of view from which as the author you will tell the story. You may identify yourself with one of the characters and tell the story in the first person; you may create a spokesman who will then tell the story in the first person but be outside the action; or you may tell the story in the third person, as a mere reporter of the events. The latter has some advantages. It permits you to assume an omniscient attitude towards your characters and the situation, so that you can report not only what actions occur but the thoughts and motives of the actors. A special adaptation of the third-person method is to emphasize the point of view of one of the characters, as Dickens does in *Oliver Twist*.

The chief advantage of telling the story

in the first person is that this increases the illusion of reality. A narrative told in the first person establishes an intimate narrator-to-reader contact. The story of Robinson Crusoe, told by the castaway himself, is undoubtedly more effective than if Defoe had thrust himself between the actor and the reader as the storyteller. The authenticity of Huckleberry Finn's experiences on the Mississippi is due in part to Huck's telling the story in his own way. Some readers, however, dislike the first-person technique because of what seems to be egotism on the part of the narrator. This is true especially if the narrator has to report heroic actions in which he wins against heavy odds. A more important disadvantage is that, since the story is limited to what the narrator can see and hear, the author sometimes finds it hard to avoid unnatural and unconvincing maneuvering to acquaint the reader with some essential detail. In *Moby Dick*, for instance, after describing the sinking of the *Pequod* and the death of the crew, Melville has to explain the rescue of one of the sailors, the man who tells the story.

The third method—that of having the story told by a first-hand narrator who is not himself implicated in the events of the story—has the advantage of giving the illusion of reality without the effect of egotism. This method is used in many of the short stories of Lord Dunsany, the Irish storyteller, and in many of the novels of Joseph Conrad. Conrad's mouthpiece, Marlowe, is an inquisitive and philosophical observer who gathers from numerous sources the details of a series of events that happened to someone and then relates them with enough documentation to make them seem authentic. The inherent difficulties in the method are shown when Conrad is forced at times to introduce scenes and conversations that Marlowe had no means of knowing about.

SUGGESTIONS FOR STUDY

Following are the opening paragraphs of two well-known stories. With regard to each of them, (1) enumerate four possible sequences of events

[1] Turn to these stories at the end of this section, and for the moment read only the first dozen lines or so of each to see how the tone is indicated at the very beginning of the story.

which can progress naturally from the initial situation, (2) describe the tone which has been set, and (3) state the point of view.

1. The "Red Death" had long devastated the country. No pestilence had ever been so fatal, or so hideous. Blood was its avatar and its seal— the redness and the horror of blood. There were sharp pains, and sudden dizziness, and then profuse bleeding at the pores, with dissolution. The scarlet stains upon the body, and especially upon the face, of the victim were the pest ban which shut him out from the aid and from the sympathy of his fellow men. And the whole seizure, progress, and termination of the disease were the incidents of half an hour.

But the Prince Prospero was happy and dauntless and sagacious. When his dominions were half depopulated, he summoned to his presence a thousand hale and light-hearted friends from among the knights and dames of his court, and with these retired to the deep seclusion of one of his castellated abbeys. This was an extensive and magnificent structure, the creation of the Prince's own eccentric yet august taste. A strong and lofty wall girdled it in. This wall had gates of iron. The courtiers, having entered, brought furnaces and massy hammers, and welded the bolts. They resolved to leave means neither of ingress nor egress to the sudden impulses of despair or of frenzy from within. The abbey was amply provisioned. With such precautions the courtiers might bid defiance to contagion. The external world could take care of itself. In the mean time it was folly to grieve, or to think. The Prince had provided all the appliances of pleasure. There were buffoons, there were improvisatori, there were ballet-dancers, there were musicians, there was Beauty, there was wine. All these and security were within. Without was the "Red Death."—EDGAR ALLAN POE, "The Masque of the Red Death."

2. As Mr. John Oakhurst, gambler, stepped into the main street of Poker Flat on the morning of the 23d of November, 1850, he was conscious of a change in its moral atmosphere since the preceding night. Two or three men, conversing earnestly together, ceased as he approached, and exchanged significant glances. There was a Sabbath lull in the air, which, in a settlement unused to Sabbath influences, looked ominous.

Mr. Oakhurst's calm, handsome face betrayed small concern in these indications. Whether he was conscious of any predisposing cause, was another question. "I reckon they're after somebody," he reflected; "likely it's me." He returned to his pocket the handkerchief with which he had been whipping away the red dust of Poker Flat from his neat boots, and quietly discharged his mind of any further conjecture.

In point of fact, Poker Flat was "after somebody." It had lately suffered the loss of several thousand dollars, two valuable horses, and a prominent citizen. It was experiencing a spasm of virtuous reaction, quite as lawless and ungovernable as any of the acts that had provoked it. A secret committee had determined to rid the town of all improper persons. This was done permanently in regard of two men who were then hanging from the boughs of a sycamore in the gulch, and temporarily in the banishment of certain other objectionable characters. I regret to say that some of these were ladies. It is but due to the sex, however, to state that their impropriety was professional, and it was only in such easily established standards of evil that Poker Flat ventured to sit in judgment.

Mr. Oakhurst was right in supposing that he was included in this category. A few of the committee had urged hanging him as a possible example, and a sure method of reimbursing themselves from his pockets of the sums he had won from them. "It's agin justice," said Jim Wheeler, "to let this yer young man from Roaring Camp—an entire stranger—carry away our money." But a crude sentiment of equity residing in the breasts of those who had been fortunate enough to win from Mr. Oakhurst overruled this narrower local prejudice.

Mr. Oakhurst received his sentence with philosophic calmness, none the less coolly that he was aware of the hesitation of his judges. He was too much of a gambler not to accept fate. With him life was at best an uncertain game, and he recognized the usual percentage in favor of the dealer.

A body of armed men accompanied the deported wickedness of Poker Flat to the outskirts of the settlement. Besides Mr. Oakhurst, who was known to be a coolly desperate man, and for whose intimidation the armed escort was intended, the expatriated party consisted of a young woman familiarly known as "The Duchess"; another, who had won the title of "Mother Shipton"; and "Uncle Billy," a suspected sluice-robber and confirmed drunkard. The cavalcade provoked no comments from the spectators, nor was any word uttered by the escort. Only when the gulch which marked the uttermost limit of Poker Flat was reached, the leader spoke briefly and to the point. The exiles were forbidden to return at the peril of their lives.—BRET HARTE, "The Outcasts of Poker Flat."

ACTION

Concerning the three parts of a narrative—initial situation, action, and conclusion—it is by no means always easy to state that a particular part begins precisely here and ends there. Children's stories and most fiction written for adults until fairly recent times follow a conventional pattern in which the initial situation (containing the germ of the action and establishing the tone and point of view), action, and conclusion are easily distinguishable. Many modern story-writers, however, start with action, making use of a technique that gradually brings to light the elements usually constituting the initial situation. The purpose of a technique of this kind is to establish an illusion of reality and create suspense as quickly as possible by plunging the reader into an interesting conversation or an exciting incident, the complete meaning of which will not be clear until he reads further.

Suspense

Regardless of whether the action of a narrative represents a solid mid-section or is extended in the manner just mentioned, the main problem is to create and maintain suspense. The familiar formula of the English writer, Wilkie Collins, "Make 'em laugh, make 'em cry, make 'em wait," is good in any place or age. Whether a person is composing scenarios for "to be continued" Saturday night movie thrillers or preparing an anecdote for an after-dinner speech, the success of his narrative rests largely on his skill in dosing out to his audience, minute by minute, exactly the right proportions of information. Even when the reader or the audience knows what the end of the story is going to be (as in a narrative which begins, "Let me tell you how I caught my first big fish"), curiosity can be aroused concerning other elements.

The length of a narrative depends, of course, on how much material is to be covered; but, from the point of view of technique, make the narrative as long as you can maintain suspense without sacrificing unity — exactly no longer and no shorter. If you draw out the action to the extent that the reader loses his grasp on the whole narrative and becomes involved in incidents only loosely related to the whole, you lose unity and should prune the narrative. However, most student narratives are not developed enough. When a student is told that he should make more of his material, he complains that he cannot do so without padding; but judicious padding is an essential part of any art. It becomes objectionable only when it is not related to the main issue or when it deadens suspense rather than enhances it.

Consider, for example, the excerpt, "The Duel in the Long Shrubbery," from Robert Louis Stevenson's novel, *The Master of Ballantrae.*

> Mr. Henry laid down his cards. He rose to his feet very softly, and seemed all the while like a person in deep thought. "You coward!" he said gently, as if to himself. And then, with neither hurry nor any particular violence, he struck the Master in the mouth.
>
> The Master sprang to his feet like one transfigured; I had never seen the man so beautiful. "A blow!" he cried. "I would not take a blow from God Almighty."
>
> "Lower your voice," said Mr. Henry. "Do you wish my father to interfere for you again?"
>
> "Gentlemen, gentlemen," I cried, and sought to come between them.
>
> The Master caught me by the shoulder, held me at arm's length, and still addressing his brother: "Do you know what this means?" said he.
>
> "It was the most deliberate act of my life," says Mr. Henry.
>
> "I must have blood, I must have blood for this," says the Master.
>
> "Please God it shall be yours," said Mr. Henry; and he went to the wall and took down a pair of swords that hung there with others, naked. These he presented to the Master by the points. "Mackellar shall see us play fair," said Mr. Henry. "I think it very needful."
>
> "You need insult me no more," said the Master, taking one of the swords at random. "I have hated you all my life."
>
> "My father is but newly gone to bed," said Mr. Henry. "We must go somewhere forth of the house."

"There is an excellent place in the long shrubbery," said the Master.

"Gentlemen," said I, "shame upon you both! Sons of the same mother, would you turn against the life she gave you?"

"Even so, Mackellar," said Mr. Henry, with the same perfect quietude of manner he had shown throughout.

"It is what I will prevent," said I.

And now here is a blot upon my life. At these words of mine, the Master turned his blade against my bosom; I saw the light run along the steel; and I threw up my arms and fell to my knees before him on the floor. "No, no," I cried, like a baby.

"We shall have no more trouble with him," said the Master. "It is a good thing to have a coward in the house."

"We must have light," said Mr. Henry, as though there had been no interruption.

"This trembler can bring a pair of candles," said the Master.

To my shame be it said, I was still so blinded with the flashing of that bare sword that I volunteered to bring a lantern.

"We do not need a l-l-lantern," says the Master, mocking me. "There is no breath of air. Come, get to your feet, take a pair of lights, and go before. I am close behind with this—" making the blade glitter as he spoke.

I took up the candlesticks and went before them, steps that I would give my hand to recall; but a coward is a slave at the best; and even as I went, my teeth smote each other in my mouth. It was as he had said, there was no breath stirring: a windless stricture of frost had bound the air; and as we went forth in the shine of the candles, the blackness was like a roof over our heads. Never a word was said; there was never a sound but the creaking of our steps along the frozen path. The cold of the night fell about me like a bucket of water; I shook as I went with more than terror; but my companions, bareheaded like myself and fresh from the warm hall, appeared not even conscious of the change.

"Here is the place," said the Master. "Set down the candles."

I did as he bade me, and presently the flames went up as steadily as in a chamber in the midst of the frosted trees, and I beheld these two brothers take their places.

"The light is something in my eyes," said the Master.

"I will give you every advantage," replied Mr. Henry, shifting his ground, "for I think you are about to die." He spoke rather sadly than otherwise, yet there was a ring in his voice.

"Henry Durie," said the Master, "two words before I begin. You are a fencer, you can hold a foil; you little know what a change it makes to hold a sword! And by that I know you are to fall. But see how strong is my situation! If you fall, I shift out of this country to where my money is before me. If I fall, where are you? My father, your wife who is in love with me—as you very well know—your child even who prefers me to yourself: how will these avenge me! Had you thought of that, dear Henry?" He looked at his brother with a smile; then made a fencing-room salute.

Never a word said Mr. Henry, but saluted too, and the swords rang together.

I am no judge of the play, my head besides was gone with cold and fear and horror; but it seems that Mr. Henry took and kept the upper hand from the first engagement, crowding in upon his foe with a contained and glowing fury. Nearer and nearer he crept upon the man till, of a sudden, the Master leaped back with a little sobbing oath; and I believe the movement brought the light once more against his eyes. To it they went again, on the fresh ground; but now methought closer, Mr. Henry pressing more outrageously, the Master beyond doubt with shaken confidence. For it is beyond doubt he now recognized himself for lost, and had some taste of the cold agony of fear; or he had never attempted the foul stroke. I cannot say I followed it, my untrained eye was never quick enough to seize details, but it appears he caught his brother's blade with his left hand, a practice not permitted. Certainly Mr. Henry only saved himself by leaping on one side; as certainly the Master, lunging in the air, stumbled on his knee, and before he could move, the sword was through his body.

I cried out with a stifled scream, and ran in; but the body was already fallen to the ground, where it writhed a moment like a trodden worm, and then lay motionless.

"Look at his left hand," said Mr. Henry.

"It is all bloody," said I.

"On the inside?" said he.

"It is cut in the inside," said I.

"I thought so," said he, and turned his back.

I opened the man's clothes; the heart was quite still, it gave not a flutter.

"God forgive us, Mr. Henry!" said I. "He is dead."

"Dead?" he repeated, a little stupidly; and then with a rising tone, "Dead? dead?" says he, and suddenly cast his bloody sword upon the ground.

Almost any reader would agree that this is an absorbing incident. When asked to give a reason for its being such, he might say, "Well, it tells about a duel, and violent action is always interesting." This is true enough, but a person with an eye for good storytelling technique will discover that an extraordinarily fine use of suspense enabled Stevenson to make the most of his subject matter. Notice how skillfully and unobtrusively he interposes obstacle after obstacle between his initial situation (the difficulty over cards and the blow) and his conclusion (the death of the Master).

The opening sentences act swiftly and briefly to arouse curiosity. Is there actually going to be a duel, and if so, who is going to be killed? But no sooner has Mr. Henry insulted the Master than Mackellar interrupts and tries to pacify the brothers. He is swept aside, and the action proceeds as the challenge is confirmed and the swords are taken from the wall. An inexperienced writer would now have the brothers fall to at once —but not Stevenson. The situation is too good to finish it so quickly. So there is dialogue concerning the best place for the duel; but again, when the men have decided to fight in the long shrubbery, the action is delayed by Mackellar's protest. Mackellar is cowed by the sight of the Master's sword, and the way is left clear for advancing the action, only to be blocked for another moment by the question of lights. At last, the men leave the house. Mackellar's description of the cold, dark night follows, not only for the sake of providing a stage setting for the approaching climax, but also to prolong the suspense. Having at last arrived at the dueling ground, the Master, with his complaint about the light, is made use of to present another obstacle; again, his speech to Mr. Henry adds another moment or two to the timing of the climax. Finally, the duel itself, while not described in great detail, is told at sufficient length to keep the reader waiting through another rather long paragraph. The thrusting of Mr. Henry's sword through the body of the Master is postponed to the latest possible moment. The important thing is that the timing is so good, and the choice of obstructions to place in the path of the action is so interesting, that the reader is pleased, rather than annoyed, at being delayed. The climax carries more weight and importance because the path to it has been prepared so carefully.

Characterization

Having read this episode from *The Master of Ballantrae*, ask yourself whether you are pleased at the outcome. Which man did you favor to win? Undoubtedly Mr. Henry. Why? Examine the selection again. From the beginning, Mr. Henry acts and speaks like a sober, quiet, responsible person who has been provoked beyond endurance, whereas the Master shows himself a braggart and a bully, possibly a coward. His first words are, "A blow! I would not take a blow from God Almighty"—rash words, to say the least. He threatens poor Mackellar with his sword, insists on having the advantage of the light before he will fight, and taunts his brother with his having won for himself the affections of Mr. Henry's wife and child. We have no physical description of either of the brothers; not once does the author step in to tell us what to think of either one (except as his mouthpiece, Mackellar, gives us one or two hints); yet our sympathies are focused from the beginning.

This, of course, is important. As it would be unfortunate if the reader sympathized with the wrong person, you must be on guard to see that this does not happen. Manufacturers of comic strips for newspapers depend almost entirely on the physical appearance of their characters to elicit sympathy or antagonism. A square jaw for a man and eyes large as turkey eggs for a woman are undeniable essentials among "good" people of the comic-strip world. A beard or even the most immature mustache seldom mars the physiognomy of a hero unless he is in disguise. To give him a foreign accent would be fatal. You can, of course, make use of these conventions also; but, if your purpose is at all serious, you will depend much less on physical description than on the impression formed by what the character says and does. The modern reader is likely to object seriously if the author, obviously and artificially, interposes himself and his views between the reader and the story. If, therefore, you wish to give the impression that a character is honorable, make him act honorably and speak honorably; do not pin a label on him: "This is an honorable man."

Foreshadowing

Turning again to the episode from *The Master of Ballantrae*, let us take note of one more thing, the foreshadowing of events. What is the effect of Mr. Henry's exclamation, "You coward!" and of his later remark, "Mackellar shall see us play fair. I think it very needful"? Do not both speeches drop a hint that the Master may resort to trickery or foul play, and does not the Master's act, grasping his opponent's sword in his left hand, verify that suspicion? In other words, the climax of the episode is foreshadowed by these bits tucked away in the earlier part so that they are almost overlooked.

The knack of clever foreshadowing is also an important part of the storyteller's technique. It is frequently an essential element in the action, heightening the force of the conclusion and emphasizing the quality of inevitability that is necessary if the illusion of reality is to be maintained. Heavily underscored foreshadowing that discloses too much or is too obviously the voice of the author speaking from behind the scenes is bad. It insults the intelligence of the reader, who feels that the author is treating him as a child when he says, in effect, "Look out, reader! Remember that Desperate Joe has a knife in his boot. He's the kind of person who would stick Honest James in the back if he cared

to. Be prepared for what is coming." However, the observant reader takes satisfaction in recognizing a hint dropped unobtrusively, and is pleased with himself when the conclusion bears out his suspicions. Remember, a complete surprise is seldom pleasant; it is more likely to be overwhelming or bewildering. On the other hand, half-formed suspicions or anticipations may be made sources of pleasure when they are wholly or partially verified.

CONCLUSION

If a narrative is adequately planned, writing the conclusion should be a comparatively easy task; yet both critics and the reading public are likely to find fault with the conclusion of a story more quickly than with the other parts. A story should build up to the conclusion with all the cumulative power that suspense and the illusion of reality can generate, and if the conclusion, when it is reached, is unsatisfactory, a great deal of time has been wasted. It is well, therefore, to consider the virtues of a good conclusion. These are clearness, inevitability, and aesthetic satisfaction.

Clearness

A writer who has planned his narrative in his head before he has put much of it on paper and may therefore be familiar with it to the point of boredom should be quite sure that he has not omitted some small detail without which the conclusion lacks meaning. Clearness is doubly necessary at that point of the story at which the reader's emotions have reached the highest pitch, where an interruption is comparable to the intensely irritating moments moviegoers used to experience when the operator had to shut off his machine to change reels. The conclusion should by all means be brief, but not so brief as to be cryptic. It is possible to say or imply a great deal with a few words and still be as lucid as if pages had been covered.

Inevitability

In the section on the initial situation it was said that the beginning of a story should contain the germ of all that develops later. The conclusion, therefore, should seem to be the natural result of forces set in motion in the initial situation and brought into conflict during the action. At this point experience with life and insight into human nature is of utmost importance to you. You are concerned with a character or characters upon whom certain influences have been brought to bear. What will be the effect of these influences? The interplay of character and character, or character and environment, or character and circumstances, is a fascinating study, and the results are to a certain extent unpredictable. However, no matter what he experiences, a character must remain himself; and it is necessary that you understand the essential nature of the character you are dealing with and remember that although it may suffer superficial alterations, it must remain fundamentally the same.

Tim McCarty, who after many years of successfully picking pockets was sent to prison, is released, and becomes a trusted clerk in a jeweler's store. Is he going to be steadfastly honest, or is he merely waiting his chance to make the greatest haul of his career? The answer involves a knowledge of just who Tim McCarty really is, the fundamental traits of character with respect to which his actions or occupations are symptoms or results. If the writer who uses Tim as a character wishes to make him turn out an honest man, he will have to indicate that when Tim was a pickpocket, he considered his occupation a regrettable but necessary evil; or he will have to show that Tim has undergone a recognizable and understandable change, *one which the conditions of Tim's own nature make possible.* Having chosen his characters, the writer must live with them, study them, and be true to them.

Nothing will destroy the illusion of reality more effectively than what appears to be a manipulated plot—a sequence of incidents that seem to have their origin in the writer's laboratory rather than in his observation of probable situations from life. Roman dramatists, having succeeded in getting their plots snarled hopelessly, sometimes in the last act introduced a god who, with his supernatural power, cleared up everything and made possible a happy ending. Folk tales and fairy stories frequently make use of a pixie or fairy godmother or guardian angel who appears unexpectedly in the nick of time to set right what otherwise would be a calamity. The same technique might be used in the story of Tim, the pickpocket-jeweler. Tim has lived a life of crime and has been hardened further by his time in prison. He gets his job in the jeweler's store and makes plans for burglary on a large scale. But, just as he is throwing the last sterling spoon in his bag before making off with his loot, he hears, from the church across the street, the organ playing and the choir singing (it is Christmas Eve, of course), and he is so affected that he puts everything back in the glass cases and runs across the street through the softly falling snow to pray at the altar.

A reader would have a right to be disgusted with the narrator, because the story has been manipulated to achieve a happy result. Is this the first time in his life that Tim has heard church music? Certainly not. Then why should he succumb to it now? We have been given no opportunity to note anything in Tim's nature that would make him respond in such a way, and therefore we condemn the author for either failing to give us necessary information about Tim or deliberately falsifying the story for the sake of a "happy" ending.

"But," someone might argue, "is it not possible for something that would make Tim respond to Christmas Eve and religious music to have been buried so deeply in his character that it has never been noticeable? After all, human nature is the most unpredictable thing we know." True enough; but an artistic story should have a *probable* development rather than just any possible development. Since a story is something composed, there must be a logical relationship among the parts. Every artist follows a pattern of some kind, and the pattern of the artist in narration is derived from probable experience. If a storyteller wishes us to recognize a certain element as being a legitimate part of his pattern, the least he can do is to acquaint us with its presence.

Before leaving the discussion of inevitability in a narrative, we should take some note of the "trick" or "snap" ending that has been used effectively by such authors as O. Henry and Leonard Merrick. This type of ending, by giving a quick twist to the sequence of events in the story, leaves the reader pleasantly surprised. In an O. Henry story, "Soapy," a bum, concludes that because cold weather is coming he should do whatever is necessary to be sentenced to a nice, warm jail. But after committing several offenses and remaining strangely immune to the penalties of the law, he passes a church and, reminded of home and mother, decides to get a job and become a decent citizen. At that moment he feels the firm hand of a policeman on his shoulder, and he is given ninety days for vagrancy. This is an unanticipated ending; but notice that the materials for this ending were inherent in the story from the beginning, and that the surprise is not due to the introduction of a new element. Thus, a "trick" ending may be used legitimately if it does not contradict the rest of the story and does not introduce new elements.

Aesthetic Satisfaction

You must end a narrative in a way that gives the reader aesthetic satisfaction. This you can do only by making the end a logical and necessary one in the light of the character of the actors and the influences to which they have been subjected. Many popular periodicals will use no story that does not end "happily," regardless of the aesthetic requirements of the story. Intolerance of this prac-

tice has led some writers to go to the other extreme and end all their stories "unhappily," even when the character of the actors and the incidents of the story do not demand it. Both attitudes are wrong. A reader derives aesthetic satisfaction from a story only when the end is a natural and inevitable result of preceding events and is true to the participants in the action. Any manipulation of the final action to give a different result is bad art. From an artistic point of view a happy ending may be as satisfying as an unhappy one, or the opposite may be true. What is necessary for an aesthetically satisfying ending is for the reader to feel that the events, actions, and result are all essentially true to the life being portrayed—that they are not merely possible but altogether probable.

ESSENTIAL QUALITIES OF GOOD NARRATION

A well-constructed narrative, as was said earlier, must have unity, suspense, and the illusion of reality. Something has already been said of these requirements, but they are of such importance as to merit special emphasis.

Unity

Perhaps even more than in other forms of writing, unity is important in narration. A narrator depends for his effect on holding the interest of his reader. Any deviation from his straight course is likely to lose this interest. Description is often necessary in a narrative, but it must be brief and must be worked into the fabric of the material rather than tacked on as mere embroidery. The same can be said of exposition when it becomes necessary to explain something. In short narratives an author almost never inserts a comment that does not bear directly on his story, and in novels it has not been the custom since Thackeray's day for the author to step out of his role as narrator and address the reader directly. Unity of tone throughout is also a requisite. A light passage in a deeply serious narrative is as out of place as jests in a funeral oration. Again, only those incidents and actions necessary to explain the characters and further the action have any place in the story. No matter how interesting an incident may be in itself, if it helps in no way to explain a character or to further the plot, and especially if you have to hold up the action of the story while you tell it, you have but one course—omit it. It hardly needs saying that the structure of the narrative should have unity and that one point of view must be maintained throughout the story. As in other forms of writing, an outline can be of great value in helping you achieve and maintain unity in narration.

Suspense

Suspense is the essence of good narration. If you have had the misfortune to listen to someone who always begins a joke by telling the point and then goes back to the details leading up to the point, you know how important suspense is in even the slightest form of narration. Except when using a different method for some specific purpose— as Thornton Wilder does in *The Bridge of San Luis Rey*—a narrator is careful always to keep the end of each action and the concluding action hidden till the last possible moment. The born storyteller, whether a novelist or a raconteur, is always a master of suspense. Till you have had much practice, you will miss many chances to add suspense to your writing, but awareness of the importance of this element in narration and a conscious effort to build suspense on every possible occasion will assuredly aid you to become a better storyteller.

Illusion of Reality

Fiction is not life, but the more closely it approximates life the more successful it will be. Any newspaper will demonstrate the old saw that truth is stranger than fiction. You could hardly imagine a situation that has not actually existed somewhere at some time; but in the realm of literary art you may not treat topics that are so unusual they make the front page of every newspaper. Unless you are writing for the most sensational pulp magazines, you are restricted to the normal occurrences of life and must leave those that are "impossible" to news reporters. Even in pulp fiction that deals with what at least for the present are impossible happenings, writers use every means possible to give the illusion of reality. The more accurately the fiction you write mirrors life, the more successful it will be.

In only two kinds of writing, farce and fantasy, may you depart to some extent from what has just been said. Farce is like caricature in drawing: it exaggerates actions and peculiarities of character and holds up the actors to good-natured ridicule. The reader accepts this situation and surrenders his normal critical faculties to the author in order to enjoy the exaggerated depiction of actions and characters. Even in farce, however, there must be a basis of reality, for as a caricature fails in its purpose if the artist exaggerates to such an extent that no one can identify his subject, so farce that departs from normal human actions so far that a reader loses all sense of probability will fail to satisfy any save the most immature minds.

Fantasy likewise deals with the improbable, but in a more imaginative, delicate, and whimsical way than does farce. In fantasy, the writer assumes a reader who, like himself, is interested in the purely imaginative and who, as in farce, is willing to surrender his everyday notions of reality and follow the author into an imaginative world of fancy. Yet successful creators of fantasy are careful to use basic elements of character, actions, and scenes that are familiar enough to the reader to make the supernatural or purely imaginative elements they introduce seem plausible.

TYPES OF NARRATION

Narrative ranges from such simple forms as the fable, the parable, the anecdote, and the incident to long novels. For the freshman composition course, it seems sufficient to differentiate two types—the short informal narrative, which of course has a plan and is well built structurally but lacks a carefully designed plot, and the carefully plotted narrative we call a short story.

Simple Narrative

Simple, informal narration is perhaps the most common form of writing in which the average person engages. Virtually everyone who writes a friendly letter writes narrative, for it is a natural impulse to report events one has witnessed or experiences in which one has participated. Yet few writers make the most of their chances to recreate events and experiences so vividly that these live for their readers. To do this requires a writer to plan the structure of his narrative so that (1) it has a carefully considered beginning, middle, and end, (2) the details are selected and arranged with care, and (3) the whole piece conveys to the reader a dominant impression. The simple narrative usually lacks the sort of suspense we associate with the short story, though suspense in some degree is a part of nearly all good narrative; and it lacks a well-developed plot. There is usually a steady progression of events of somewhat equal intensity, each following the others in some normal manner, usually chronological, but all so fitted together as to give a single dominant effect.

Such writing may range from a report of a single incident to a number which together form one unified event or experience. The incident relates a single occurrence. When we speak of the incidents of a day's fishing or a trip to the city or country, we mean the individual small happenings that may be interesting or even important in themselves, but that do not constitute for us the chief interest of the day or the trip. If one of these should be lifted out of the day's happenings and related without reference to the other events of the day, it would constitute the most simple form of narrative writing. The "Adventure of a Turtle" at the end of this section, for example, is inserted as a separate chapter by John Steinbeck in his *Grapes of Wrath*. Although it has a purpose in the whole novel, it could be omitted without detracting from the story. The incident, then, is a single action, event, or occurrence, of probably minor general significance, but possessing some inherent interest in character, local color, peculiarity of action, or the like, that makes it worth relating.

If several incidents are joined or a succession of actions are depicted, all of which relate to the same scheme but do not arouse high suspense and progress to a climax, the resulting piece of writing is usually termed a sketch. In the sketch, the narrative, if graphed, would appear as a relatively even plateau instead of climbing in a series of foothills and peaks as in the short story. This unemphatic structure tends to give the sketch an impromptu effect. That does not mean, of course, that informal writing of this sort is carelessly done, but that the organization appears informal because suspense is of secondary importance or may be absent altogether.

The writer of the simple narrative is less interested in creating suspense than in depicting character, portraying local color, recreating an experience or action. While he describes events as they take place, selecting of course only those that relate to his theme or that help to create the dominant impression he expects to convey, his tempo remains substantially the same throughout the narrative. He is thus perhaps nearer the informal essayist than the short story writer. The inexperienced writer needs to exercise great care, however, lest his narrative become merely a string of generalized statements which lack internal relationship and give no dominant impression—except one that the author is a lazy, careless person who was merely bent on filling some pages with dull and pointless matter. Like all good composition, the simple narrative has unity—unity of tone and unity of purpose. There must be a thesis sentence, a specific purpose; and all the parts of the narrative must contribute to the creation of a dominant impression. The mere piecing together of incidents that hap- pened to one person does not in itself pro- duce unity.

Finding a Room[1]

GERTRUDE DIAMANT

THE STREET BEHAVED just like a river. It ram- bled through empty lots and circled a field of corn, and then it disappeared. There was a high white wall where it disappeared, but not a sign or a person to tell me where the street had gone. Presently a boy on a bicycle came by, and seeing me standing in perplex- ity, he waved and called: "Follow the wall." I followed it, and there was the street again.

I was looking for Atoyac number 82, where the morning paper said there was a furnished apartment—cheap, comfortable, decent, ideal for an American. And I was in that part of Mexico City where all the streets bear the names of rivers. Already I had crossed the Tiber, the Rhine, and the River Po, old favor- ites familiar from high-school days. But what of the River Atoyac? Nobody knew where it was, and nobody seemed to have heard of it. The sun was high and the sidewalk burned my feet, and I wandered on, hoping that the street would not disappear again. For I was carrying the two big valises which I had brought with me to Mexico, and which now contained all that I owned in the world.

It was a way of burning my bridges behind me. I was tired of living in boarding-houses (those beautiful old colonial mansions of the guidebooks) with their damp dark rooms, slippery floors, and dreadful furniture. I had vowed never to enter another old colonial mansion, but to leave them all to their decay- ing splendors and to the Spartan Mexicans. And if there was no place in the city with an easy-chair and a comfortable bed and dry and sunny, then I would go back to the

States. But I did not want to go back, either. There are three hundred thousand Otomí Indians in Mexico, and I had tested a mere one hundred. I must test another two hun- dred at least to prove—but no, it is not scien- tific to know in advance what one is going to prove.

I put my valises down, flexed my arms, and looked around. There were houses now, but not a sign to tell me if I had come to the River Atoyac. To know where you are in Mexico City, you must look at the corner houses; and with luck you will see a tiny plaque which bears the name of the street. But usually it isn't there at all, and the Mexi- cans have a sweet reasonableness when they cannot enlighten you. "Pues . . . you see, señorita, the signs are missing which should bear the names of the streets. So I cannot tell you, señorita, forgive me." It was Sunday and the stores were closed and the street de- serted. I left my valises standing and walked until I came to where a man was sitting on the curb. He looked up from under a wide sombrero. "No, señorita," he said, "really I cannot tell you. I have little time here." "Time!" I thought scornfully. "What time do you need to tell me the name of a street?" And then I remembered my still meager Spanish. It is an idiom meaning that one has only just come to a place. "But if you ask the señor at the little stand over there," he went on, "possibly he can tell you. He has much time here." So I crossed to the little stand.

"Atoyac!" mused the man of much time. "Atoyac!" He smiled engagingly. "Forgive me, señorita, but I am unable to say. I do not concentrate on the names of the streets. However, if you should wish for the Street of

[1] From Gertrude Diamant, *The Days of Ofelia* (Bos- ton, copyright, 1942, by Gertrude Diamant). Re- printed by permission of Houghton Mifflin Company.

the River of the Plata"—he pointed with an exquisite grace—"it is over there, señorita, just two blocks over there." "Thank you," I said, "I do not wish for the Street of the River of the Plata." And I went back and gathered my valises and wandered on. There were empty lots again and many blocks where the houses were still being built. Soon I would come to the city limits. I could see fields of corn and beyond them the mountains, splendidly luminous in the afternoon light. But at the last corner before the fields began I came to a house that miraculously bore the number 82. Five little girls sat on the doorstep.

"Is there a furnished apartment here?"

They chorused raggedly, pointing. "Arriba . . . upstairs." And I saw that they all had the same shade of brown-green eyes. Then they rose in a body and we all went up.

SUGGESTIONS FOR STUDY

1. Analyze the structure of this selection to determine how much is beginning, middle, and end.

2. Write a thesis sentence for the piece. What is its dominant impression?

3. List the separate incidents which make up the episode.

4. These are the opening paragraphs of *The Days of Ofelia.* How much do we learn about the speaker from this selection? Try your hand at writing a brief character sketch of her, basing your conclusions on the style and mental point of view as well as on the descriptive details.

5. Write a sequel to this episode, telling what you think occurred when the author arrived upstairs; then procure a copy of the book and compare your account with the author's.

Adventure of a Turtle[1]

JOHN STEINBECK

THE SUN LAY on the grass and warmed it, and in the shade under the grass the insects moved, ants and ant lions to set traps for them, grasshoppers to jump into the air and flick their yellow wings for a second, sow bugs like little armadillos, plodding restlessly on many tender feet. And over the grass at the roadside a land turtle crawled, turning aside for nothing, dragging his high-domed shell over the grass. His hard legs and yellow-nailed feet threshed slowly through the grass, not really walking, but boosting and dragging his shell along. The barley beards slid off his shell, and the clover burrs fell on him and rolled to the ground. His horny beak was partly open, and his fierce, humorous eyes, under brows like fingernails, stared straight ahead. He came over the grass leaving a beaten trail behind him, and the hill, which was the highway embankment, reared up ahead of him. For a moment he stopped, his head held high. He blinked and looked up and down. At last he started to climb the embankment. Front clawed feet reached forward but did not touch. The hind feet kicked his shell along, and it scraped on the grass, and on the gravel. As the embankment grew steeper and steeper, the more frantic were the efforts of the land turtle. Pushing hind legs strained and slipped, boosting the shell along, and the horny head protruded as far as the neck could stretch. Little by little the shell slid up the embankment until at last a parapet cut straight across its line of march, the shoulder of the road, a concrete wall four inches high. As though they worked independently the hind legs pushed the shell against the wall. The head upraised and peered over the wall to the broad smooth plain of cement. Now the hands, braced on top of the wall, strained and lifted, and the shell came slowly up and rested its front end on the wall. For a moment the turtle rested.

[1] From John Steinbeck, *The Grapes of Wrath* (New York, copyright, 1939, by John Steinbeck). Reprinted by permission of The Viking Press, Inc.

A red ant ran into the shell, into the soft skin inside the shell, and suddenly head and legs snapped in, and the armored tail clamped in sideways. The red ant was crushed between body and legs. And one head of wild oats was clamped into the shell by a front leg. For a long moment the turtle lay still, and then the neck crept out and the old humorous frowning eyes looked about and the legs and tail came out. The back legs went to work, straining like elephant legs, and the shell tipped to an angle so that the front legs could not reach the level cement plain. But higher and higher the hind legs boosted it, until at last the center of balance was reached, the front tipped down, the front legs scratched at the pavement, and it was up. But the head of wild oats was held by its stem around the front legs.

Now the going was easy, and all the legs worked, and the shell boosted along, waggling from side to side. A sedan driven by a forty-year-old woman approached. She saw the turtle and swung to the right, off the highway, the wheels screamed and a cloud of dust boiled up. Two wheels lifted for a moment and then settled. The car skidded back onto the road, and went on, but more slowly. The turtle had jerked into its shell, but now it hurried on, for the highway was burning hot.

And now a light truck approached, and as it came near, the driver saw the turtle and swerved to hit it. His front wheel struck the edge of the shell, flipped the turtle like a tiddly-wink, spun it like a coin, and rolled it off the highway. The truck went back to its course along the right side. Lying on its back, the turtle was tight in its shell for a long time. But at last its legs waved in the air, reaching for something to pull it over. Its front foot caught a piece of quartz and little by little the shell pulled over and flopped upright. The wild oat head fell out and three of the spearhead seeds stuck in the ground. And as the turtle crawled on down the embankment, its shell dragged dirt over the seeds. The turtle entered a dust road and jerked itself along, drawing a wavy shallow trench in the dust with its shell. The old humorous eyes looked ahead, and the horny beak opened a little. His yellow toe nails slipped a fraction in the dust.

SUGGESTIONS FOR STUDY

1. Note especially the adjectives and verbs. Are there too many of either? See how many words could be omitted in the first paragraph without appreciably changing a reader's understanding of the events.

2. What is the point of including the incident of the head of wild oats?

3. Note that the author does not presume to attribute the ability to think to the turtle. Does the depiction of action alone interest you in the turtle? If you answer yes, list the details that aid in this.

4. Is the author successful in giving the point of view of both a human observer and the turtle? How is this done?

5. Are the details arranged in an effective sequence? Would the omission of the incident of the first driver detract in any way from the sketch?

Baker's Blue-Jay Yarn

MARK TWAIN

ANIMALS TALK to each other, of course. There can be no question about that; but I suppose there are very few people who can understand them. I never knew but one man who could. I knew he could, however, because he told me so himself. He was a middle-aged, simple-hearted miner who had lived in a lonely corner of California, among the woods and mountains, a good many years, and had studied the ways of his only neighbors, the beasts and the birds, until he believed he could accurately translate any remark which they made. This was Jim Baker. According to Jim Baker, some animals have only a limited education, and use only very simple words, and scarcely ever a comparison or a flowery figure; whereas certain other animals have a large vocabulary, a fine command of language and a ready and fluent delivery; consequently these latter talk a great deal; they like it; they are conscious of their talent, and they enjoy "showing off." Baker said, that after long and careful observation, he had come to the conclusion that the blue-jays were the best talkers he had found among birds and beasts. Said he:

"There's more *to* a blue-jay than any other creature. He has got more moods, and more different kinds of feelings than other creatures; and mind you, whatever a blue-jay feels, he can put into language. And no mere commonplace language, either, but rattling, out-and-out book-talk—and bristling with metaphor, too—just bristling! And as for command of language—why *you* never see a blue-jay get stuck for a word. No man ever did. They just boil out of him! And another thing: I've noticed a good deal, and there's no bird, or cow, or anything that uses as good grammar as a blue-jay. You may say a cat uses good grammar. Well, a cat does—but you let a cat get excited, once; you let a cat get to pulling fur with another cat on a shed, nights, and you'll hear grammar that will give you the lockjaw. Ignorant people think it's the *noise* which fighting cats make that is so aggravating, but it ain't so; it's the sickening grammar they use. Now I've never heard a jay use bad grammar but very seldom; and when they do, they are as ashamed as a human; they shut right down and leave.

"You may call a jay a bird. Well, so he is, in a measure—because he's got feathers on him, and don't belong to no church, perhaps; but otherwise he is just as much a human as you be. And I'll tell you for why. A jay's gifts, and instincts, and feelings, and interests, cover the whole ground. A jay hasn't got any

more principle than a Congressman. A jay will lie, a jay will steal, a jay will deceive, a jay will betray; and four times out of five, a jay will go back on his solemnest promise. The sacredness of an obligation is a thing which you can't cram into no blue-jay's head. Now on top of all this, there's another thing: a jay can out-swear any gentleman in the mines. You think a cat can swear. Well, a cat can; but you give a blue-jay a subject that calls for his reserve-powers, and where is your cat? Don't talk to *me*—I know too much about this thing. And there's yet another thing: in the one little particular of scolding—just good, clean, out-and-out scolding—a blue-jay can lay over anything, human or divine. Yes, sir, a jay is everything that a man is. A jay can cry, a jay can laugh, a jay can feel shame, a jay can reason and plan and discuss, a jay likes gossip and scandal, a jay has got a sense of humor, a jay knows when he is an ass just as well as you do—maybe better. If a jay ain't human, he better take in his sign, that's all. Now I'm going to tell you a perfectly true fact about some blue-jays.

"When I first begun to understand jay language correctly, there was a little incident happened here. Seven years ago, the last man in this region but me, moved away. There stands his house—been empty ever since; a log house, with a plank roof—just one big room, and no more; no ceiling—nothing between the rafters and the floor. Well, one Sunday morning I was sitting out here in front of my cabin, with my cat, taking the sun, and looking at the blue hills, and listening to the leaves rustling so lonely in the trees, and thinking of the home away yonder in the States, that I hadn't heard from in thirteen years, when a blue-jay lit on that house, with an acorn in his mouth, and says, 'Hello, I reckon I've struck something.' When he spoke, the acorn dropped out of his mouth and rolled down the roof, of course, but he didn't care; his mind was all on the thing he had struck. It was a knothole in the roof. He cocked his head to one side, shut one eye and put the other one to the hole, like a 'possum looking down a jug; then he glanced up with his bright eyes, gave a wink or two with his wings—which signifies gratification, you understand,—and says, 'It looks like a hole, it's located like a hole,—blamed if I don't believe it *is* a hole!'

"Then he cocked his head down and took another look; he glances up perfectly joyful, this time; winks his wings and his tail both, and says, 'O, no, this ain't no fat thing, I reckon! If I ain't in luck!—why, it's a perfectly elegant hole!' So he flew down and got that acorn, and fetched it up and dropped it in, and was just tilting his head back, with the heavenliest smile on his face, when all of a sudden he was paralyzed into a listening attitude and that smile faded gradually out of his countenance like a breath off'n a razor, and the queerest look of surprise took its place. Then he says, 'Why, I didn't hear it fall!' He cocked his eye at the hole again, and took a long look; raised up and shook his head; stepped around to the other side of the hole and took another look from that side; shook his head again. He studied a while, then he just went into the *details*— walked round and round the hole and spied into it from every point of the compass. No use. Now he took a thinking attitude on the comb of the roof and scratched the back of his head with his right foot a minute, and finally says, 'Well, it's too many for *me*, that's certain; must be a mighty long hole; however, I ain't got no time to fool around here, I got to 'tend to business; I reckon it's all right— chance it, anyway.'

"So he flew off and fetched another acorn and dropped it in, and tried to flirt his eye to the hole quick enough to see what become of it, but he was too late. He held his eye there as much as a minute; then he raised up and sighed, and says, 'Consound it, I don't seem to understand this thing, no way; however, I'll tackle her again.' He fetched another acorn, and done his level best to see what become of it, but he couldn't. He says, 'Well, *I* never struck no such a hole as this, before;

I'm of the opinion it's a totally new kind of a hole.' Then he begun to get mad. He held in for a spell, walking up and down the comb of the roof and shaking his head and muttering to himself; but his feelings got the upper hand of him, presently, and he broke loose and cussed himself black in the face. I never see a bird take on so about a little thing. When he got through he walks to the hole and looks in again for half a minute; then he says, 'Well, you're a long hole, and a deep hole, and a mighty singular hole altogether— but I've started in to fill you, and I'm d—d if I *don't* fill you, if it takes a hundred years!'

"And with that, away he went. You never see a bird work so since you was born. He laid into his work like a nigger, and the way he hove acorns into that hole for about two hours and a half was one of the most exciting and astonishing spectacles I ever struck. He never stopped to take a look any more—he just hove 'em in and went for more. Well, at last he could hardly flop his wings, he was so tuckered out. He comes a-drooping down, once more, sweating like an ice-pitcher, drops his acorn in and says, '*Now* I guess I've got the bulge on you by this time!' So he bent down for a look. If you'll believe me, when his head come up again he was just pale with rage. He says, 'I've shoveled acorns enough in there to keep the family thirty years, and if I can see a sign of one of 'em I wish I may land in a museum with a belly full of sawdust in two minutes!'

"He just had strength enough to crawl up on the comb and lean his back agin the chimbly, and then he collected his impressions and begun to free his mind. I see in a second that what I had mistook for profanity in the mines was only just the rudiments, as you may say.

"Another jay was going by, and heard him doing his devotions, and stops to inquire what was up. The sufferer told him the whole circumstance, and says, 'Now yonder's the hole, and if you don't believe me, go and look for yourself.' So this fellow went and looked, and comes back and says, 'How many did you say you put in there?' 'Not any less than two tons,' says the sufferer. The other jay went and looked again. He couldn't seem to make it out, so he raised a yell, and three more jays come. They all examined the hole, they all made the sufferer tell it over again, then they all discussed it, and got off as many leather-headed opinions about it as an average crowd of humans could have done.

"They called in more jays; then more and more, till pretty soon this whole region 'peared to have a blue flush about it. There must have been five thousand of them; and such another jawing and disputing and ripping and cussing, you never heard. Every jay in the whole lot put his eye to the hole and delivered a more chuckle-headed opinion about the mystery than the jay that went there before him. They examined the house all over, too. The door was standing half open, and at last one old jay happened to go and light on it and look in. Of course that knocked the mystery galley-west in a second. There lay the acorns, scattered all over the floor. He flopped his wings and raised a whoop. 'Come here!' he says, 'Come here, everybody; hang'd if this fool hasn't been trying to fill up a house with acorns!' They all came a-swooping down like a blue cloud, and as each fellow lit on the door and took a glance, the whole absurdity of the contract that that first jay had tackled hit him home and he fell over backwards suffocating with laughter, and the next jay took his place and done the same.

"Well, sir, they roosted around here on the house-top and the trees for an hour, and guffawed over that thing like human beings. It ain't any use to tell me a blue-jay hasn't got a sense of humor, because I know better. And memory, too. They brought jays here from all over the United States to look down that hole, every summer for three years. Other birds too. And they could all see the point except an owl that come from Nova Scotia to visit the Yo Semite, and he took this thing in on his way back. He said he couldn't see anything funny in it. But then he was a good deal disappointed about Yo Semite, too."—*A Tramp Abroad*.

SUGGESTIONS FOR STUDY

1. This belongs to a special *genre* of American literature known as the "tall tale." Does it gain in effectiveness by being attributed to Jim Baker?
2. What sort of person is Jim Baker? Describe him in your own words as you conceive him from the narrative.
3. What words would you use to describe the jay who tried to fill the hole? What quality does he have in common with the owl?
4. If you assume this to be a fable, in the manner of Aesop, what "moral" would you write for it?
5. Do the opening sentences help to make the story seem plausible? If the first paragraph were omitted, would the story be as interesting?

The Dinner Party[1]

MONA GARDNER

THE COUNTRY is India. A large dinner party is being given in an up-country station by a colonial official and his wife. The guests are

[1] From the *Saturday Review of Literature* (January 31, 1942). Reprinted by permission of the author and the *Saturday Review of Literature*.

army officers and government attachés and their wives, and an American naturalist.

At one side of the long table a spirited discussion springs up between a young girl and a colonel. The girl insists women have long outgrown the jumping-on-a-chair-at-sight-of-a-mouse era, that they are not as fluttery as their grandmothers. The colonel says they are, explaining that women haven't the actual nerve control of men. The other men at the table agree with him.

"A woman's unfailing reaction in any crisis," the colonel says, "is to scream. And while a man may feel like it, yet he has that ounce more of control than a woman has. And that last ounce is what counts!"

The American scientist does not join in the argument, but sits watching the faces of the other guests. As he looks, he sees a strange expression come over the face of the hostess. She is staring straight ahead, the muscles of her face contracting slightly. With a small gesture she summons the native boy standing behind her chair. She whispers to him. The boy's eyes widen: he turns quickly and leaves the room. No one else sees this, nor the boy when he puts a bowl of milk on the verandah outside the glass doors.

The American comes to with a start. In India, milk in a bowl means only one thing. It is bait for a snake. He realizes there is a cobra in the room.

He looks up at the rafters—the likeliest place—and sees they are bare. Three corners of the room, which he can see by shifting only slightly, are empty. In the fourth corner a group of servants stand, waiting until the next course can be served. The American realizes there is only one place left—under the table.

His first impulse is to jump back and warn the others. But he knows the commotion will frighten the cobra and it will strike. He speaks quickly, the quality of his voice so arresting that it sobers everyone.

"I want to know just what control everyone at this table has. I will count three hundred —that's five minutes—and not one of you is to move a single muscle. The persons who move will forfeit 50 rupees. Now! Ready!"

The twenty people sit like stone images while he counts. He is saying ". . . two-hundred and eighty . . ." when, out of the corner of his eye, he sees the cobra emerge and make for the bowl of milk. Four or five screams ring out as he jumps to slam shut the verandah doors.

"You certainly were right, Colonel!" the host says. "A man has just shown us an example of real control."

"Just a minute," the American says, turning to his hostess; "there's one thing I'd like to know. Mrs. Wynnes, how did you know that cobra was in the room?"

A faint smile lit up the woman's face as she replies: "Because it was lying across my foot."

SUGGESTIONS FOR STUDY

1. This is not an original story. In sending it to the publisher, Miss Gardner explained that she had heard it many years before and was sending it to be reprinted in the hope of learning who the author was. This accounts for her telling the story in the present tense and as briefly as possible. Does this increase the effectiveness of the narrative, or would it be better if told in the past tense and if more details were added?

2. What part does the bowl of milk play?

3. What is the purpose of the argument at the start of the narrative?

4. Is the end a surprise? Qualify your answer. Would this be different if the original author were telling the story?

The Evening Service[1]

R. C. HUTCHINSON

YES, I KNOW now it was three nights that Eadell spent with us. I remember for some reason that he came on a Friday, and he was with Bernard and me when we went to Dubbledale on the Sunday evening. . . .

The road goes through Isaiah's Drinkle, and the Ordnance surveyors, with their egregious breadth of mind, have colored it as second-class. I found it first when we traversed it in convoy, cursing its awkward dips and turns and the cottages which leaned across it at the sharpest corners: a tedious twenty minutes of clouding dust and jacitation and incessant change of gears. A scrabble of wide ruts was left on the verge where our quads had been slackly steered, here and there the banks were breached; but the dust had settled, the reek and rattle were long absorbed in the sanitary tides of wind. Curious, the diverse records that the same pair of eyes will make. I had noted the route carefully, matching ground to map, on the chance that I might have to pick it up by night. So the aspects were familiar, the very shape of the buildings had stayed on my mind's plate as solid pointers for a doubtful fork or obscure turn. But those pictures were like passport photographs in their likeness to what I saw this evening. A white cottage, which had merely shown itself more trim than its neighbors, was revealed now as a Georgian manor in perfect miniature. The granary beside Wisk Fall was no longer a rectangle of stone but a work of faultless grace in the fit of height to length, in the pitch of its stone roof, an artist's narrowing of the muscular steps which rose to the attic door. I had remarked a little bridge to have in mind that the road went over the Toin there; I had never seen how sensitively its parapets were curved. And the half-wit urchins who had darted in front of our wheels had grown through a month or two into fair and smiling images of God. . . .

At Drinkle we left the road and took the bridle path which is said to save you nearly half a mile; it does, perhaps in terms of distance. It may have been habit which sent Bernard that way; it was a deviltry (or I am astigmatic to human foible) which made him leave the bridle for a cut of his own over Wirrup Crag. He had led us all the way, at least a pace ahead on the flat; the shackles of rheumatism seemed to have no power against the ferocious energy with which he walked. I had run a steady second, with Eadell panting a pace or two behind, short legs and tiny feet moving like a barber's scissors to carry his vast bulk forward. And they had argued almost incessantly about the teaching of August Comte. . . .

The path had become a chute of boulders, and I was dripping with sweat when Bernard, as one who boards the 8:45 at Woking, took a handful of briar and hoisted himself on to a shelf of rock. I followed, and by the time I had landed there he was thirty feet higher, plowing like a bulldozer through the gorse towards the naked scree. Eadell came after us, but his dialectic powers were stifled at last. . . .

[1] From R C. Hutchinson, *Interim* (New York, copyright, 1945, by R. C. Hutchinson). Reprinted by permission of the author and Rinehart & Co.

The excerpt here reprinted is from chapter 11 of the novel. Father Eadell, a Jesuit priest, is visiting an old college friend, Bernard Quindle, a medical missionary in China, whom the war had forced home to England. Quindle, an Anglican, takes a service occasionally when the vicar is away. The two old collegemates are on intimate terms despite their theological differences. The scene is Cumberland in northern England. The narrator, who purports to be the author, is a soldier stationed near the Quindle home.

By way of a knife's-edge bridge of rock we reached the southern shoulder-blade of Wirrup and rounded it crabwise, clinging and sliding on the scree. From the other side you looked straight down into St. Bridget's tarn, shaped almost as perfectly as a church's font, and saw to your right the ladder of Seven Tarns reaching down to Clouden Mere. The wind was mettlesome here, cold with the coming nightfall, pleasant to our hot faces. In these few minutes the light had dropped in tone, and the birds' voices quieted. Towards the Clucker range the mist had formed to snowy hills with green lakes in between, and on the greening sky a shoal of narrow clouds had gathered to build up a floating landscape with its own soft hills and plateau and lake. So real that land seemed, and so ethereal the misted country beneath, the eye lost power to mark reality; I felt the strip of land we walked on was a vessel slumbering in unknown seas, that the seas would presently engulf it. The wind pouring in my ears strengthened this feeling of detachment; unreasonably, it increased our stillness and repose. We found Bernard waiting where a sheep-track started; he was standing against the wind as a sailor does and smelling it with an epicure's nose. He asked, as we came level, "Did you bust a bootlace or something?" He gave Eadell the coat he had been carrying. "Here, lad, you'd better put this on now." And presently, as we began the descent, he stopped again. "I find it almost intolerable," he said, gathering in his eyes the tarns and the Clucker hills with the clouds' grace and opalescence, "to have all this when men are being burnt and torn to bits." We slithered downwards on shallow turf, scattering the amazed sheep, came into gorse again and rejoined the bridle.

Dubbledale clings to the steep side of Cleat Rigg; its alleyways and gardens are put where nature allows them, the farms spread in the easier slopes above. Its one cartworthy street goes below it, sharing a narrow gully with a racing beck. Except for a pair of brawling dogs the street was lifeless when we came there; in the retreating light the houses looked to have shut as flowers do; fresh from the hills, we were like discoverers of a place long lost from human sight. A slab of stone took us over the beck; a flight of steps wedged narrowly between two cottages brought us up to the level of the lowest roofs. There were lights in the window here; on one side you saw a child being undressed for bed, from the other you got the smell of ham cooking. The church, still high above us, was a pattern of black and silver planes in the horizontal light of the falling day. . . .

At the sexton's cottage we were greeted by a tough, small woman, with a man's muscles in hand and arm. Chidroach was in bed with the bronchitty, she told us. She had the misfortune of a diagonal squint; she seemed to be gazing alternately at the top of the Church and down into the village. No, the church boiler had not been attended to since yesterday forenoon, she said, with sibylline relish, neither were the lamps dressed; a flock of sheep astray had chewed up a number of the prayerbooks, and the organist had broken her leg. Would Chidroach like to see Dr. Quindle? Well, to say truth, Chidroach was in a powerful humor, not caring for the fiery poultice which had been slapped on his chest by Mr. Partiquer the vet; and had sworn to break the nose of the next doctor who came inside the house.

I sigh even now when I think of Eadell's sufferings. Bernard, I suppose, would have left him out of the evening's labor; but the sexton's wife had gathered from his peculiar clothes that he was some kind of servant; it was he whom she commanded to clear up what the sheep had left in the chancel, he who caught the thong of her sarcasm when we tried to reanimate the stove. Having the will of a man and the strength of two, she held the sex in small esteem. "Well, you can help so long as you don't get in my way!" When Eadell staggered into the boiler house with a bucket he'd filled from the wrong coke-stack she seized it roughly from his hands, took it back, and emptied it. Heroically, in the semi-darkness, he put a shovel-full on the fire as it began to blaze. "If you want to put the fire out," she said, "you may as well use water."

"You know, Mrs. Chidroach," Bernard said, "my friend here is one of the most learned men in England." She snorted. "You," she said, with her eyes swivelling from heaven to hell, but apparently meaning me, "you'd better do the lamps. Unless you're a college lad as well."

That picture has stayed clearer than so many more important ones: the bald, distinguished Eadell, half-paralyzed with exhaustion and mirth, trying to nourish the Protestant boiler; Mrs. Chidroach on his one side, like a tigress ready to spring; on the other Bernard pincered between embarrassment and his palate for the absurd, muttering, "Leave it to me, lad, for heaven's sake leave it! Go and ring the bell if it won't ruin your conscience. For heaven's sake leave this to me." And a little afterwards Eadell, with the sly face of Naaman in the house of Rimmon, tugging awkwardly at the Protestant bell.

Of the service I remember little, for I had been detailed to play the organ and was wholly occupied by the anxieties of that employment. Only when Bernard began his sermon had I time to relax and to let my eyes wander about the miniature church; to see, among its infinite small beauties, the tablet commemorating "Master Edward Hake, who, in his Forty-Ninth Year, at God's Call, was Trampled by the Nearside Horse of the London Coach and Entered into Rest." With its light from four small lamps in the nave and one in the chancel the building had a Josef Israels quality; pillars and hammerbeams emerged from a suspended lake of darkness, the faces of children shyly herded in the rearmost pews were flakes of paleness in the shadow; only within an armspread of the lamps were features deeply etched. There, encompassed by a trio of plump dalesmen's wives, an ox-jowled youth in the weekly anguish of collar and tie stared far

ahead with his fine, Cumbrian eyes. An Australian corporal sat bolt upright like one on horseback, and as if to point the anchylosis of his face the squat couple who shared his pew had faces like butter soaking into toast. In the second pew a very small, hunched woman with a widow's bonnet sat by herself. I suppose she had passed her ninetieth year, but she did not look as if age had brought her face to this nobility: the deep and regular creasing in her forehead and the margins of her eyes, the way the shrunk, almost transparent flesh was stretched upon its frame, seemed rather the achievement of a deliberate artist than any overripeness in her body's evolution. I turned my head a little to get a sidelong view of Bernard, who stood on the lower chancel step with his knuckles wedged between chest and chin. He was smiling faintly, in the way of one recounting an adventure he has undergone some time before. He spoke as he always did, slowly, as if he would give way to anyone who wished to take the company's ear; and I noticed that a Derbyshire inflexion which one sometimes heard very faintly in his voice was near to its surface now. . . .

A farmer who had said all the wrong responses was now stertorously asleep; his anemic daughter still gazed with bovine fascination at the boa in the adjoining pew. But the corporal's face was of one who sees from a train window some patch of country he once found pleasure in; and on the mouth of the sexton's wife, who had dumped her little body in a rearward corner, I saw with astonishment the daybreak of a smile. It was a company which reminded me of provincial auction rooms, outmoded pieces gathered from old attics, the erroneous ardor of cottage dressmakers brought dreadfully to public view. But the measured light enclosed them in its own pattern; it found even a point of gallantry in the white of an old man's head above the dullness of his coat, in a girl's red scarf against the shadowed stone. And the voice, now hesitant, now eager, made us a circle no less intimate than any which formed in the Orchilly dining-room. Perhaps my emotions were warmed by the closeness of the air, the heat which grew from our breathing, and from the odorous lamps. I know that I felt myself in the very weft of these strangers, and discovered pride in feeling so, and would have kept this plot of time for ever lingering. . . .

At some point Eadell had stolen back into the church. I had not seen him come; I noticed suddenly the shape of his head far back in the darkness by the door. I smiled to him. But it was the pollard farm lad nearer to me who caught and answered my smile. The speaker's voice fell quieter still; it was no more public than the voice he used across the Orchilly table; but in the stillness it had won, the chiselled words were like small fires that leap in a darkened countryside. Eyes which had strolled about the pews came back to rest upon his face; I had the sense of dreams in which the surge and conquest depend upon your utter stillness. From that tranquillity my own eyes turned to search for Eadell again. But the place he had sat in was empty; like a shadow at nightfall he had slipped away.

I should not find again the cottage we went to afterwards. I reached it in the moving disc of light from someone's lamp; we seemed to go up and down many steps and across the yard of a public-house. In the little, crowded room we reached, the people who had been only clothes and faces turned into individuals. The old woman from the front pew became a gay and rather flirtatious creature; the man who had slept through half the sermon was volubly persuading me to try his home-brewed beer. Yet I do not think of that evening as falling into separate parts. The smiles, the squeezing of elbows which I took part in, now were rather a flowering of what had gone before; and this Bernard who was talking to a child with his mouth full while he bandaged her arm, who scolded the Australian corporal for the size of his feet, was in every part

identical with the one who had stood on the chancel step and mastered us with his quietness. An unusual meal we had, some standing and some at the table. I ate about a quartern of Grasmere cheese, while a man in a corduroy suit told me how his uncle had died of it. The woman I took to be our hostess gave me pink blancmange in a breakfast cup, and directly afterwards I had to take potato broth from a milk-jug, using a gravy spoon.

It was not, I think, a healthy room to sleep in, as a little boy was trying to do in a truckle bed behind the sofa; for from beneath the surface-odors of onion and hot linen there rose at intervals the indubitable smell of sewage. Nor had it any kind of comfort. Edging my way between the sewing machine and a laden piano, sitting on the arm of a broken chair and then leaning against the mangle, I thought I saw a clue to the many small infirmities discovered here; for of ten or twelve in the room there were few who did not suffer from deafness, or the pallor of some pulmonary disorder, or a nervous twitch. Yet as I saw them now, encompassed by the flow of Bernard's laughter, they were radiant with content; and I have found no group of people more generous to one who, with my total ignorance of beasts and grain, must have seemed to them not far removed from dementia. I remember the charm of a squirrel-like man who told me in hoarse whispers, continuously smiling, about the intestinal problems of a certain Mrs. Richardson; and the lovely, childlike eyes of a gaunt spinster who repeated many times, breathing chutney into my face, "But Government can't raise dead men any road, no matter what tax they put on t' brewing, no more than sow in farrow can skippit through daisy-chain." I was sorry when we had to go.

SUGGESTIONS FOR STUDY

1. In your own words give a brief character sketch of the three friends who make the trip.
2. What is the purpose of the trip?
3. What do you gather about the speaker as

a result of the change he has undergone towards the scenery?

4. Is the character of Mrs. Chidroach over-drawn?

5. The author is handling a situation that contains inherent elements of sentimentality (this is especially true in the book itself in which part of Bernard's sermon—omitted here because although it has a place in the entire book, it is not an essential part of this sketch—is given). How does he keep the story from crossing the borderline into sentimentality?

Suggestions for Writing

1. All parents are fond of relating amusing or frightening incidents that happened to their children when they were small. Write one such incident which you have heard told about you.

2. Isolate from the rest of the trip some happening that occurred on a camping trip, hitch-hiking expedition, or other journey, and relate it as an independent episode. If introductory material is needed, remember to make it as brief as possible.

3. Read carefully an incident in the Bible. Try to understand the full meaning of the occurrence for each of the people concerned. Reconstruct and amplify the incident, using modern English instead of Biblical English. If you wish, choose the point of view of one of the characters and tell the story in the first person.

4. Write an account of some historical incident from the point of view of an unimportant witness. (For example, the signing of the Magna Carta as told by a retainer of one of the barons; the assassination of Lincoln as told by an actor other than John Wilkes Booth; a visit by Walt Whitman to a Washington hospital, as told by a wounded soldier.)

5. Scan the newspapers for a brief story which you can rewrite as an incident. Do not try to rewrite a story with big headlines; look for short articles on the inside pages—even in the "want ad" and "personals" columns.

6. Write an episode that actually occurred or that you imagine as occurring in some place familiar to you but unfamiliar to your readers. Put enough information into it to give your readers a good idea of the place and of those participating in the action.

7. Write a sketch of the most exciting (or humorous or embarrassing or happy) event in your own life. Use all your skill to make it interesting to a reader.

8. Write a sketch which makes use of some interesting custom or recurring event in your home town or neighborhood.

9. Take a day of college life and see if, by selecting and arranging the details in such a way as to secure unity, you can make an interesting narrative.

10. By means of a narrative sketch, make a character study of an individual so that the person lives for the reader by what he says and does rather than by direct description.

THE SHORT STORY

By drawing on experience or observation or by the exercise of a moderate imagination, any student, with some care and practice, should be able to write interesting simple narrative. To write good short stories, however, demands mature skills; for in addition to the requirements for simple narrative, the short story must have plot, intensity and compression of style, and mounting suspense. The chief difference, in fact, between simple narrative and the short story lies in the greater intensity of struggle in the latter and in the dramatic arrangement of details in such a way as to create growing suspense.

A short story must have plot—a situation involving conflict and struggle and reaching some aesthetically satisfactory conclusion. Starting from an equilibrium, the action goes through a series of oscillations of growing intensity until another state of equilibrium, different from that at the start, is reached. To have conflict there must be opposing forces: hero–villain, protagonist–antagonist. The hero or protagonist should be animate—a person or animal—but the antagonist may be either animate or inanimate, and if inanimate, it may be some objective force like a mountain or desert, or be subjective. (In the examples at the end of this section, the antagonist in "The Color of Mama Josefina's Life" is objective—the drab village.) The conflict, however, need not be obvious at a glance—as it is in "Brandy for Breakfast" and "That Greek Dog"; some of the best short-story writers suggest the conflict so adroitly and subtly that to a casual reader it may not be at once apparent wherein the conflict lies.

Other elements that need your attention are setting, characters, and atmosphere. You need not lay the setting of a story in some distant, romantic spot; an intense drama may occur anywhere, as O. Henry demonstrated in his story, "A Municipal Report." But you must have the setting clearly in mind, and in harmony with the action. It is possible, of course, to write a story without a specific setting, but frequently the setting can be used advantageously; and since the short story must move at a much swifter pace than a novel, you must take account of every element that will aid you.

Since short stories generally depend more on plot and incident than on character, the characters need not be so fully drawn as in the novel. Yet they must be well enough depicted and differentiated that what they do matters to a reader; and, as was said earlier in this chapter, their character and actions must be in harmony: no one in the story must perform an action out of keeping with his character.

Because of the brevity of the short story, make every use possible of atmosphere, or tone. Poe, who was adept in the use of atmosphere, is not, however, the best guide, for an inexperienced writer using him as a guide may overdo the matter and create a mere parody. It is better to suggest the atmosphere by a word here and a phrase there, or to create the desired effect through conversation or obliquely by the association of ideas in the reader's mind. Yet you must be intensely aware of the atmosphere you wish to establish, and must be constantly alert to insinuate this atmosphere into the story.

For the successful development of a short story, arrange the incidents so that each grows naturally out of the preceding incident and leads inevitably to the next one. Thus throughout the action there is a growing intensity until the climax is reached. This is usually followed in the modern short story by a swift conclusion. In this regard, your chief care must be to see that each incident actually furthers the action and increases the interest of the reader. If it does not do this, it has no part in the story and must be omitted.

One other characteristic of the short story is compression. Once you have defined the situation and determined the line of action, cut away everything that does not pertain directly to the matter in hand. Condense to a page incidents which in a novel would occupy a chapter. Seldom attempt to portray a character completely; state concisely whatever about the character is pertinent to the story, but omit the rest. Unless for some reason the writer of the short story is striving consciously for another effect, the technique of his medium demands swift, absorbing movement.

Finally, the short story possesses unity of effect. Probably more frequently than not a story writer starts with something he has observed, an anecdote, or a newspaper clipping —in other words, the nucleus of the story itself rather than the effect he wants the story to produce. Nevertheless, even if a story does not produce a unified emotional effect, it possesses a singleness of purpose which may serve quite as well. If the story has as its core a theme—a comparison, contrast, or philosophical judgment—the theme is supported by the full weight of the narrative. The energy of the story is not dissipated upon other ideas. The force which is directed upon the reader is united.

The short stories that follow are included here for study and analysis; therefore they purposely vary in quality. In analyzing them, keep in mind the statements of the preceding section.

The Apparition

GUY DE MAUPASSANT

THE CONVERSATION concerned the process of sequestration in regard to a recent law suit. It was toward the end of a sociable evening in an old mansion in the Rue de Grenelle, and each had told his story, a story which he affirmed true.

Then the aged Marquis de la Tour-Samuel, eighty-two years old, rose and went to lean upon the mantelpiece. He said in a voice which trembled a little:

"I too, I know a strange affair, so strange that it has been the obsession of my life. It is now fifty-six years since that adventure happened to me, but a month does not pass without my seeing it again in a dream. From that day there has been stamped on me a mark, an imprint of fear, do you understand? Yes, for ten minutes I suffered a dreadful terror, so extreme that from that hour a sort of constant fear has lain on my soul. Unexpected noises make me tremble deep inside; objects which I can distinguish only poorly in the shades of evening arouse in me a foolish desire to escape. In fact, I have a fear of the night.

"Oh! I should never have admitted this before arriving at an advanced age. Now I can say all. To be afraid in the face of imaginary dangers is permitted when one is eighty-two years old. Before real dangers I have never recoiled, *mesdames*.

"This affair has so disturbed my spirit, has aroused in me a turmoil so profound, so mysterious, so horrible, that I have never even spoken of it. I have guarded it in the intimate depths of my being, in that recess where one hides bitter secrets, shameful secrets, all the unutterable weaknesses which we all have in our lives.

"I am going to tell you the adventure as it occurred without trying to explain it. With-out doubt it can be explained, unless I experienced an hour of madness. But no, I was not mad, and I shall offer you proof. Imagine what you wish. Here are the simple facts.

"It was in July, 1827. I found myself at Rouen in garrison.

"One day, as I was walking on the quay, I met a man whom I thought I recognized without recalling exactly who he was. Instinctively, I made a motion to stop him. The stranger perceived the gesture, looked at me, and fell into my arms.

"It was a friend of my youth whom I had loved dearly. During the five years since I had seen him, he seemed to have aged a half century. His hair was all white, and he stooped as he walked, as if exhausted. He understood my surprise and told me of his life. A terrible unhappiness had broken him.

"Fallen madly in love with a young girl, he had married her in a sort of ecstacy of joy. After a year of divine happiness and of deep passion she had died suddenly of an illness at the heart, without doubt slain by love itself. He had left his château the very day of the funeral and had come to live in his hotel in Rouen. He was still living there, alone and desperate, harrowed by sorrow, so miserable that he could think only of suicide.

" 'Now that I have found you thus,' he said to me, 'I shall ask you to render me a great service. It consists of going to my château and getting from the secretary of my room, of our room, some papers of which I have an urgent need. I cannot entrust this task to a servant or a business man, for I demand perfect discretion and absolute silence. As for me, I would not enter that house again for anything in the world.

" 'I shall give you the key to this room,

which I closed myself on leaving, and the key to my secretary. In addition, you shall bear a word from me to my gardener who will open the château for you. But have breakfast with me tomorrow, and we shall chat about that.'

"I promised to perform this slight service for him. It was but an excursion for me, his domain lying only five leagues from Rouen. I could get there in an hour on horseback.

"At ten o'clock the next morning I was at his house. We ate breakfast together, but he did not say twenty words. He begged me to forgive him; the thought of the visit which I was going to make to that room where his happiness expired was upsetting him, he said. Indeed I thought him singularly agitated and preoccupied, as if he were experiencing a mysterious struggle in his soul.

"Finally he explained to me exactly what I should do. It was very simple. I must take two packages of letters and one bundle of papers from the first drawer on the right of the desk to which I had the key. He added, 'I need not ask you to refrain from examining them.'

"I was nearly wounded by this remark, and I told him so a little hotly. He stammered, 'Pardon me, I am suffering too much.'

"And he began to weep.

"I left him about one o'clock to perform my mission.

"It was brilliant weather, and I trotted rapidly toward the fields, listening to the song of the larks and the rhythmical beat of my sabre against my boot.

"Then I entered the forest and allowed my horse to walk. The branches of the trees caressed my face; sometimes I would catch a leaf in my teeth and chew it avidly, in one of those moments of joy at being alive which fill you, you know not why, with a tumultuous and almost elusive happiness, with a sort of powerful intoxication.

"On approaching the château, I sought in my pocket the letter which I had for the gardener and perceived with astonishment that it was sealed. I was so surprised and irritated that I was tempted to return without executing my mission. I reflected, however, that in doing so I would be guilty of a certain bad taste. Moreover, in the midst of his troubles, my friend might have sealed the note unconsciously.

"The manor looked as if it had been abandoned for twenty years. The gate, open and rotten, held up one knew not how. Grass filled the walks; the borders of the lawn were not distinguishable.

"At the noise which I made on kicking a shutter, an old man came out of a side door and appeared stupefied at seeing me. I leaped to the ground and delivered my letter. He read it, reread it, turned it round, looked at me askance, put the paper in his pocket, and declared:

"'Well, what do you want?'

"I answered sharply: 'You ought to know, since you have received there the orders of your master; I wish to enter the château.'

"He seemed overwhelmed. 'So, you are going into . . . into his room?'

"I was beginning to be impatient. 'Parbleu! But do you by chance intend to interrogate me?'

"He stammered: 'No . . . monsieur . . . but only . . . only it has not been opened since . . . since the . . . death. If you will wait five minutes, I will go . . . go to see if . . .'

"I interrupted angrily: 'Aha! are you toying with me? You cannot enter there, for I have the key.'

"He had nothing more to say.

"'Then, monsieur, I will show you the way.'

"'Show me the staircase, and leave me alone. I will find it well enough without you.'

"'But . . . monsieur . . . however . . .'

"This time I flew into a fury: 'Now be quiet, do you understand, or you will have to answer to me.'

"I brushed him violently aside and marched into the house.

"I crossed first the kitchen, then two little rooms where this man lived with his wife. I traversed next a great hall, climbed the stair-way, and recognized the door indicated by my friend.

"I opened it without trouble and entered. The room was so dark that at first I could scarcely distinguish anything. I hesitated, struck by that moldy, lifeless odor of unin-habited, condemned rooms, these dead chambers. Then, little by little, my eyes be-came accustomed to the dark, and I saw clearly enough a great room all in disorder, containing a bed without sheets but with mattress and pillows, one of which bore a deep imprint of an elbow or a head as if someone had just lain on it.

"The chairs seemed in confusion. I noticed that a door, that of a closet no doubt, had remained half open.

"I went first to the window to let in some light and opened it, but the iron fastenings of the shutters were so rusty that I could not make them give. I even tried breaking them with my sabre, but without success. As I was becoming irritated by these useless efforts, and as my eyes had finally accus-tomed themselves perfectly to the gloom, I renounced the hope of seeing more clearly and went to the secretary.

"I seated myself in an armchair, lowered the lid of the desk, and opened the indicated drawer. It was full to the top. I needed only three packets, which I knew how to recog-nize, and I set myself to looking for them.

"I was straining my eyes to decipher the inscriptions when I thought I heard or per-haps felt a rustle behind me. I paid no at-tention, thinking that a breath of air had made the drapery move. But, after a minute, another movement, almost imperceptible, caused a singular, slight, but disagreeable shiver to pass over my skin. It was so stupid to be even a trifle nervous that I would not turn around, being ashamed of myself. Just then I happened to find the second of the bundles which I needed, and even as I found the third, a great and painful sigh, breathed against my shoulder, startled me

into giving one mad leap full two yards away. In my fright I had turned around, hand on sabre, and indeed had I not felt it by my side, I should have fled like a coward.

"A tall woman, dressed in white, stared at me from behind the armchair where I had been sitting a second before.

"Such a shudder coursed through my limbs that I almost fell backward! Oh, no one who has not experienced it can understand this frightful, unreasoning terror. The soul melts; the heart ceases to beat; the whole body be-comes as soft as a sponge; one might say the inner being is crumbling.

"I do not believe in ghosts; but I was faint-ing under the hideous fear of the dead, and I suffered, oh, I suffered in a few moments more than in all the rest of my life from the irresistible anguish of supernatural dread.

"If she had not spoken, perhaps I would have died! But she spoke. She spoke in a sweet and dolorous voice that made my nerves quiver. I dare not say that I became master of myself and recovered my reason. No. I was so frightened that I did not know what I was doing; but this kind of private dignity which I have within me, and also a little professional pride, enabled me to keep almost in spite of myself an honorable coun-tenance. I posed for myself, and without doubt for her, for her whatever she was, woman or spectre. I took account of all this later, for I assure you that in the instant of the apparition I thought of nothing. I was afraid.

"She said, 'Oh, monsieur, you can do me a great service!'

"I tried to answer, but I could not utter a word. Only a vague noise issued from my throat.

"She continued, 'Will you do it? You can save me, cure me. I suffer frightfully. I suffer, oh, I suffer!'

"And she seated herself gently in my arm-chair. She looked at me.

"'Will you do it?'

"I nodded 'yes,' my voice still paralyzed.

"Then she held out to me a tortoise-shell comb and murmured, 'Comb my hair, oh, comb my hair! That will cure me; someone must comb my hair. Look at my head. How I suffer, and my hair, how it makes me wretched!'

"Her unbound hair, which seemed to me very long and very black, hung down over the back of the chair and touched the floor.

"Why did I do this? Why did I, shivering, take the comb, and why did I take into my hands the long hair which gave my skin a feeling of atrocious coldness as if I were touching serpents? I do not know.

"This sensation has remained in my fingers, and I still tremble when I think of it.

"I combed her hair. I touched, I know not how, that icy hair. I twisted it, I bound it, I unbound it; I plaited it as one plaits the mane of a horse. She sighed, bent her head, and seemed happy.

"Suddenly she said, 'Thank you,' snatched the comb from my hands, and fled through the door which I had noticed half open.

"Left alone, I experienced for several seconds that wild dismay which comes on awakening from a nightmare. Then finally I recovered my senses; I rushed to the window and broke the shutters with a violent onslaught. A flood of daylight entered. I sprang to the door through which she had disappeared. I found it shut and immovable.

"Then a desire to flee swept over me, a panic, the real panic of the battlefield. I seized roughly the three packets of letters on the open secretary; I bounded across the room, leaped down the stairs four at a time, found myself outside I know not how, and perceiving my horse ten paces from me, hurled myself into the saddle at one bound and departed at a full gallop.

"I did not stop until I reached my own lodgings in Rouen. Throwing the reins to my orderly, I escaped to my room where I locked myself in to reflect. For an hour I kept asking myself anxiously if I had not been the victim of an hallucination. Certainly I had undergone one of those incomprehensible nervous shocks, one of those affections of the brain which dwarf the miracles to which the supernatural owes its power.

"I was about to believe it all a vision, an error of my senses, when, as I approached the window, my eyes by chance fell on my breast. My uniform was covered with the long hairs of a woman which had entwined themselves about the buttons!

"I seized them one by one, and threw them outside with trembling fingers.

"Then I called my orderly. I felt too nervous, too troubled, to go near my friend that day. And then I wished to reflect carefully on what I should say to him. I had the letters taken to him, for which he gave a receipt to the soldier. He inquired a good deal about me. The soldier told him that I was ill, that I had received a sunstroke, some tale I know not what. He seemed disturbed.

"I visited him the next day, early in the morning, resolved to tell him the truth. He had gone out the evening before and had not returned. I called again during the day; no one had seen him. I waited a week. He did not reappear. Then I informed the police. They searched everywhere without discovering a trace of his passing or of his whereabouts.

"A minute inspection was made of the abandoned château. Nothing suspicious was discovered. The inquiry having been fruitless, the search was discontinued.

"And for fifty-six years I have learned nothing. I know nothing more."

SUGGESTIONS FOR STUDY

1. Study the character of the Marquis de la Tour-Samuel. What kind of man does he seem to be? Irresolute? Cowardly? Proud? What authenticity does his character provide for the events of the tale? What "proof" does he offer that the events really occurred? What is the result of showing him filled with happiness as he rides to the château? Why is the gardener made so hesitant about admitting him?

2. Analyze the details that make the apparition unearthly. What is unusual about her be-

havior? What relation do the mysterious papers and the disappearance of the friend have to this unearthly effect?

3. The Marquis makes no attempt to explain the mystery. What does the author gain by such a device?

•

Foot in It[1]

JAMES GOULD COZZENS

THERE WERE three steps down from the street door. Then the store extended, narrow and low between the book-packed walls, sixty or seventy feet to a little cubbyhole of an office where a large sallow man worked under a shaded desklamp. He had heard the street door open, and he looked that way a moment, peering intently through his spectacles. Seeing only a thin, stiffly erect gentleman with a small cropped white mustache, standing hesitant before the table with the sign "*Any Book 50 Cents,*" he returned to the folded copy of a religious weekly on the desk in front of him. He looked at the obituary column again, pulled a pad toward him and made a note. When he had finished, he saw, upon looking up again, that the gentleman with the white mustache had come all the way down the store.

"Yes sir?" he said, pushing the papers aside. "What can I do for you?"

The gentleman with the white mustache stared at him keenly. "I am addressing the proprietor, Mr. Joreth?" he said.

"Yes sir. You are."

"Quite so. My name is Ingalls—Colonel Ingalls."

"I'm glad to know you, Colonel. What can I—"

"I see that the name does not mean anything to you."

Mr. Joreth took off his spectacles, looked searchingly. "Why, no sir. I am afraid not. *Ingalls.* No. I don't know anyone by that name."

Colonel Ingalls thrust his stick under his arm and drew an envelope from his inner pocket. He took a sheet of paper from it, unfolded the sheet, scowled at it a moment, and tossed it onto the desk. "Perhaps," he said, "this will refresh your memory."

Mr. Joreth pulled his nose a moment, looked harder at Colonel Ingalls, replaced his spectacles. "Oh," he said, "a bill. Yes. You must excuse me. I do much of my business by mail with people I've never met personally. 'The Reverend Doctor Godfrey Ingalls, Saint John's Rectory.' Ah, yes, yes—"

"The late Doctor Ingalls was my brother. This bill is obviously an error. He would never have ordered, received, or wished to read any of these works. Naturally, no such volumes were found among his effects."

"Hm," said Mr. Joreth. "Yes, I see." He read down the itemized list, coughed, as though in embarrassment.

"I see. Now, let me check my records a moment." He dragged down a vast battered folio from the shelf before him. "*G, H, I—*" he muttered. "*Ingalls.* Ah, now—"

"There is no necessity for that," said Colonel Ingalls. "It is, of course, a mistake. A strange one, it seems to me. I advise you strongly to be more careful. If you choose to debase yourself by surreptitiously selling works of the sort, that is your business. But—"

Mr. Joreth nodded several times, leaned back. "Well, Colonel," he said, "you're entitled to your opinion. I don't sit in judgment on the tastes of my customers. Now, in this case, there seems unquestionably to have been an order for the books noted from the

[1] From the *Redbook Magazine* (December, 1935), 146. Reprinted by permission of the author and of *Redbook Magazine*.

source indicated. On the fifteenth of last May I filled the order. Presumably they arrived. What became of them, then, is no affair of mine; but in view of your imputation, I might point out that such literature is likely to be kept in a private place and read privately. For eight successive months I sent a statement. I have never received payment. Of course, I was unaware that the customer was, didn't you say, deceased. Hence my reference to legal action on this last. I'm very sorry to have—"

"You unmitigated scoundrel!" roared Colonel Ingalls. "Do you really mean definitely to maintain that Doctor Ingalls purchased such books? Let me tell you—"

Mr. Joreth said: "My dear sir, one moment, if you please! Are you in a position to be so positive? I imply nothing about the purchaser. I mean to maintain nothing, except that I furnished goods, for which I am entitled to payment. I am a poor man. When people do not pay me, what can I do but—"

"Why, you infamous—"

Mr. Joreth held up his hand. "Please, please!" he protested. "I think you are taking a most unjust and unjustified attitude, Colonel. This account has run a long while. I've taken no action. I am well aware of the unpleasantness which would be caused for many customers if a bill for books of this sort was made public. The circumstances aren't by any means unique, my dear sir; a list of my confidential customers would no doubt surprise you."

Colonel Ingalls said carefully: "Be good enough to show me my brother's original order."

"Ah," said Mr. Joreth. He pursed his lips. "That's unfair of you, Colonel. You are quite able to see that I wouldn't have it. It would be the utmost imprudence for me to keep on file anything which could cause so much trouble. I have the carbon of an invoice, which is legally sufficient, under the circumstances, I think. You see my position."

"Clearly," said Colonel Ingalls. "It is the position of a dirty knave and a blackguard,

and I shall give myself the satisfaction of thrashing you." He whipped the stick from under his arm. Mr. Joreth slid agilely from his seat, caught the telephone off the desk, kicking a chair into the Colonel's path.

"Operator," he said, "I want a policeman." Then he jerked open a drawer, plucked a revolver from it. "Now, my good sir," he said, his back against the wall, "we shall soon see. I have put up with a great deal of abuse from you, but there are limits. To a degree I understand your provocation, though it doesn't excuse your conduct. If you choose to take yourself out of here at once and send me a check for the amount due me, we will say no more. If you prefer to wait for the arrival of an officer—"

Colonel Ingalls held the stick tight in his hand. "I think I will wait for the officer," he said with surprising composure. "I was too hasty. In view of your list of so-called customers, which you think would surprise me, there are doubtless other people to be considered—"

The stick in his hand leaped, sudden and slashing, catching Mr. Joreth over the wrist. The revolver flew free, clattered along the floor, and Colonel Ingalls kicked it behind him. "It isn't the sort of thing the relatives of a clergyman would like to have made public, is it? When you read of the death of one, what is to keep you from sending a bill? Very often they must pay and shut up. A most ingenious scheme, sir."

Mr. Joreth clasped his wrist, wincing. "I am at loss to understand this nonsense," he said. "How dare you—"

"Indeed?" said Colonel Ingalls. "Ordinarily, I might be at loss myself, sir; but in this case, I think you put your foot in it, sir! I happen to be certain that my late brother ordered no books from you, that he did not keep them in private or read them in private. It was doubtless not mentioned in the obituary, but for fifteen years previous to his death, Doctor Ingalls had the misfortune to be totally blind. . . . There, sir, is the policeman you sent for."

SUGGESTIONS FOR STUDY

1. This narrative is what in recent years has come to be called a short short story. On the basis of this story can you draw some conclusions concerning some of the problems which this type of writing places before the writer?

2. Is this a story of character, plot, or situation?

3. Are the elements of the story realistic or romantic?

4. On what element does the story chiefly depend for its interest?

The Happiest Man on Earth[1]

ALBERT MALTZ

JESSE FELT READY to weep. He had been sitting in the shanty waiting for Tom to appear, grateful for the chance to rest his injured foot, quietly, joyously anticipating the moment when Tom would say, "Why, of course, Jesse, you can start whenever you're ready!"

For two weeks he had been pushing himself, from Kansas City, Missouri, to Tulsa, Oklahoma, through nights of rain and a week of scorching sun, without sleep or a decent meal, sustained by the vision of that one moment. And then Tom had come into the office. He had come in quickly, holding a sheaf of papers in his hand; he had glanced at Jesse only casually, it was true—but long enough. He had not known him. He had turned away. . . . And Tom Brackett was his brother-in-law.

Was it his clothes? Jesse knew he looked terrible. He had tried to spruce up at a drinking fountain in the park, but even that had gone badly; in his excitement he had cut himself shaving, an ugly gash down the side of his cheek. And nothing could get the red gumbo dust out of his suit even though he had slapped himself till both arms were worn out. . . . Or was it just that he *had* changed so much?

True, they hadn't seen each other for five years; but Tom looked five years older, that was all. He was still Tom. God! was *he* so different?

Brackett finished his telephone call. He leaned back in his swivel chair and glanced

[1] From *Harper's Magazine*, CLXXVII (June, 1938), 74. Reprinted by permission of the author.

over at Jesse with small, clear blue eyes that were suspicious and unfriendly. He was a heavy, paunchy man of forty-five, auburn-haired, rather dour-looking; his face was meaty, his features pronounced and forceful, his nose somewhat bulbous and reddish-hued at the tip. He looked like a solid, decent, capable businessman who was commander of his local branch of the American Legion—which he was. He surveyed Jesse with cold indifference, manifestly unwilling to spend time on him. Even the way he chewed his toothpick seemed contemptuous to Jesse.

"Yes?" Brackett said suddenly. "What do you want?"

His voice was decent enough, Jesse admitted. He had expected it to be worse. He moved up to the wooden counter that partitioned the shanty. He thrust a hand nervously through his tangled hair.

"I guess you don't recognize me, Tom," he said falteringly, "I'm Jesse Fulton."

"Huh?" Brackett said. That was all.

"Yes, I am, and Ella sends you her love."

Brackett rose and walked over to the counter until they were face to face. He surveyed Fulton incredulously, trying to measure the resemblance to his brother-in-law as he remembered him. This man was tall, about thirty. That fitted! He had straight good features and a lank erect body. That was right too. But the face was too gaunt, the body too spiny under the baggy clothes, for him to be sure. His brother-in-law had been a solid, strong young man with muscle and beef to him. It was like looking at a faded, badly taken photograph and trying to recognize the subject: the resemblance was there but the difference was tremendous. He searched the eyes. They at least seemed definitely familiar, gray, with a curiously shy but decent look in them. He had liked that about Fulton.

Jesse stood quiet. Inside he was seething. Brackett was like a man examining a piece of broken-down horseflesh; there was a look of pure pity in his eyes. It made Jesse furious. He knew he wasn't as far gone as all that.

"Yes, I believe you are," Brackett said finally, "but you sure have changed."

"By God, it's five years, ain't it?" Jesse said resentfully. "You only saw me a couple of times anyway." Then, to himself, with his lips locked together, in mingled vehemence and shame, What if I have changed? Don't everybody? I ain't no corpse.

"You was solid-looking," Brackett continued softly, in the same tone of incredulous wonder. "You lost weight, I guess?"

Jesse kept silent. He needed Brackett too much to risk antagonizing him. But it was only by deliberate effort that he could keep from boiling over. The pause lengthened, became painful. Brackett flushed. "Jiminy Christmas, excuse me," he burst out in apology. He jerked the counter up. "Come in. Take a seat. Good God, boy"—he grasped Jesse's hand and shook it—"I *am* glad to see you; don't think anything else! You just looked so peaked."

"It's all right," Jesse murmured. He sat down, thrusting his hand through his curly, tangled hair.

"Why are you limping?"

"I stepped on a stone; it jagged a hole through my shoe." Jesse pulled his feet back under the chair. He was ashamed of his shoes. They had come from the relief originally, and two weeks on the road had about finished them. All morning, with a kind of delicious, foolish solemnity, he had been vowing to himself that before anything else, before even a suit of clothes, he was going to buy himself a brand-new strong pair of shoes.

Brackett kept his eyes off Jesse's feet. He knew what was bothering the boy and it filled his heart with pity. The whole thing was appalling. He had never seen anyone who looked more down and out. His sister had been writing to him every week, but she hadn't told him they were as badly off as this.

"Well now, listen," Brackett began, "tell me things. How's Ella?"

"Oh, she's pretty good," Jesse replied absently. He had a soft, pleasing, rather shy voice that went with his soft gray eyes. He was worrying over how to get started.

"And the kids?"

"Oh, they're fine. . . . Well, you know," Jesse added, becoming more attentive, "the young one has to wear a brace. He can't run around, you know. But he's smart. He draws pictures and he does things, you know."

"Yes," Brackett said. "That's good." He hesitated. There was a moment's silence. Jesse fidgeted in his chair. Now that the time had arrived, he felt awkward. Brackett leaned forward and put his hand on Jesse's knee. "Ella didn't tell me things were so bad for you, Jesse. I might have helped."

"Well, goodness," Jesse returned softly, "you been having your own troubles, ain't you?"

"Yes." Brackett leaned back. His ruddy face became mournful and darkly bitter. "You know I lost my hardware shop?"

"Well sure, of course," Jesse answered, surprised. "You wrote us. That's what I mean."

"I forgot," Brackett said. "I keep on being surprised over it myself. Not that it was worth much," he added bitterly. "It was running downhill for three years. I guess I just wanted it because it was mine." He laughed pointlessly, without mirth. "Well, tell me about yourself," he asked. "What happened to the job you had?"

Jesse burst out abruptly, with agitation, "Let it wait, Tom, I got something on my mind."

"It ain't you and Ella?" Brackett interrupted anxiously.

"Why no!" Jesse sat back. "Why however

did you come to think that? Why Ella and me—" He stopped, laughing. "Why, Tom, I'm just crazy about Ella. Why she's just wonderful. She's just my whole life, Tom."

"Excuse me. Forget it." Brackett chuckled uncomfortably, turned away. The naked intensity of the youth's burst of love had upset him. It made him wish savagely that he could do something for them. They were both too decent to have had it so hard. Ella was like this boy too, shy and a little soft.

"Tom, listen," Jesse said, "I come here on purpose." He thrust his hand through his hair. "I want you to help me."

"Damn it, boy," Brackett groaned. He had been expecting this. "I can't much. I only get thirty-five a week and I'm damn grateful for it."

"Sure, I know," Jesse emphasized excitedly. He was feeling once again the wild, delicious agitation that had possessed him in the early hours of the morning. "I know you can't help us with money! But we met a man who works for you! He was in our city! He said you could give me a job!"

"Who said?"

"Oh, why didn't you tell me?" Jesse burst out reproachfully. "Why as soon as I heard it I started out. For two weeks now I been pushing ahead like crazy."

Brackett groaned aloud. "You come walking from Kansas City in two weeks so I could give you a job?"

"Sure, Tom, of course. What else could I do?"

"God Almighty, there ain't no jobs, Jesse! It's slack season. And you don't know this oil business. It's special. I got my Legion friends here but they couldn't do nothing now. Don't you think I'd ask for you as soon as there was a chance?"

Jesse felt stunned. The hope of the last two weeks seemed rolling up into a ball of agony in his stomach. Then, frantically, he cried, "But listen, this man said *you* could hire! He *told* me! He drives trucks for you! He said you *always* need men!"

"Oh! . . . You mean *my* department?" Brackett said in a low voice.

"*Yes,* Tom. That's it!"

"Oh no, you don't want to work in my department," Brackett told him in the same low voice. "You don't know what it is."

"Yes, I do," Jesse insisted. "He told me all about it, Tom. You're a dispatcher, ain't you? You send the dynamite trucks out?"

"Who was the man, Jesse?"

"Everett, Everett, I think."

"Egbert? Man about my size?" Brackett asked slowly.

"Yes, Egbert. He wasn't a phony, was he?"

Brackett laughed. For the second time his laughter was curiously without mirth. "No, he wasn't a phony." Then, in a changed voice: "Jiminy, boy, you should have asked me before you trekked all the way down here."

"Oh, I didn't want to," Jesse explained with naïve cunning. "I knew you'd say no. He told me it was risky work, Tom. But I don't care."

Brackett locked his fingers together. His solid, meaty face became very hard. "I'm going to say no anyway, Jesse."

Jesse cried out. It had not occurred to him that Brackett would not agree. It had seemed as though reaching Tulsa were the only problem he had to face. "Oh no," he begged, "you can't. Ain't there any jobs, Tom?"

"Sure, there's jobs. There's even Egbert's job if you want it."

"He's quit?"

"He's dead!"

"Oh!"

"On the job, Jesse. Last night if you want to know."

"Oh!" . . . Then, "I don't care!"

"Now you listen to me," Brackett said. "I'll tell you a few things that you should have asked before you started out. It ain't dynamite you drive. They don't use anything as safe as dynamite in drilling oil wells. They wish they could, but they can't. It's nitroglycerin! Soup!"

"But I know," Jesse told him reassuringly.

"He advised me, Tom. You don't have to think I don't know."

"Shut up a minute," Brackett ordered angrily. "Listen! You just have to *look* at this soup, see? You just *cough* loud and it blows! You know how they transport it? In a can that's shaped like this, see, like a fan? That's to give room for compartments, because each compartment has to be lined with rubber. That's the only way you can even *think* of handling it."

"Listen, Tom—"

"Now wait a minute, Jesse. For God's sake just put your mind to this. I know you had your heart set on a job, but you've got to understand. This stuff goes only in special trucks! At night! They got to follow a special route! They can't go through any city! If they lay over, it's got to be in a special garage! Don't you see what that means? Don't that tell you how dangerous it is?"

"I'll drive careful," Jesse said. "I know how to handle a truck. I'll drive slow."

Brackett groaned. "Do you think Egbert didn't drive careful or knew how to handle a truck?"

"Tom," Jesse said earnestly, "you can't scare me. I got my mind fixed on only one thing: Egbert said he was getting a dollar a mile. He was making five to six hundred dollars a month for half a month's work, he said. Can I get the same?"

"Sure, you can get the same," Brackett told him savagely. "A dollar a mile. It's easy. But why do you think the company has to pay so much? It's easy—until you run over a stone that your headlights didn't pick out, like Egbert did. Or get a blowout! Or get something in your eye, so the wheel twists and you jar the truck! Or any other God damn thing that nobody ever knows! We can't ask Egbert what happened to him. There's no truck to give any evidence. There's no corpse. There's nothing! Maybe tomorrow somebody'll find a piece of twisted steel way off in a cornfield. But we never find the driver. Not even a fingernail. All we know is that he don't come

in on schedule. Then we wait for the police to call us. You know what happened last night? Something went wrong on a bridge. Maybe Egbert was nervous. Maybe he brushed the side with his fender. Only there's no bridge any more. No truck. No Egbert. Do you understand now? That's what you get for your God damn dollar a mile!"

There was a moment of silence. Jesse sat twisting his long thin hands. His mouth was sagging open, his face was agonized. Then he shut his eyes and spoke softly. "I don't care about that, Tom. You told me. Now you got to be good to me and give me the job."

Brackett slapped the palm of his hand down on his desk. "No!"

"Listen, Tom," Jesse said softly, "you just don't understand." He opened his eyes. They were filled with tears. They made Brackett turn away. "Just look at me, Tom. Don't that tell you enough? What did you think of me when you first saw me? You thought: 'Why don't that bum go away and stop panhandling?' Didn't you, Tom? Tom, I just can't live like this any more. I got to be able to walk down the street with my head up."

"You're crazy," Brackett muttered. "Every year there's one out of five drivers gets killed. That's the average. What's worth that?"

"Is my life worth anything now? We're just starving at home, Tom. They ain't put us back on relief yet."

"Then you should have told me," Brackett exclaimed harshly. "It's your own damn fault. A man has no right to have false pride when his family ain't eating. I'll borrow some money and we'll telegraph it to Ella. Then you go home and get back on relief."

"And then what?"

"And then wait, God damn it! You're no old man. You got no right to throw your life away. Sometime you'll get a job."

"No!" Jesse jumped up. "No. I believed that too. But I don't now," he cried passionately. "I ain't getting a job no more than you're getting your hardware store back. I lost my skill, Tom. Linotyping is skilled work. I'm rusty now. I've been six years on relief. The only work I've had is pick and shovel. When I got that job this spring I was supposed to be an A-1 man. But I wasn't. And they got new machines now. As soon as the slack started they let me out."

"So what?" Brackett said harshly. "Ain't there other jobs?"

"How do I know?" Jesse replied. "There ain't been one for six years. I'd even be afraid to take one now. It's been too hard waiting so many weeks to get back on relief."

"Well you got to have some courage," Brackett shouted. "You've got to keep up hope."

"I got all the courage you want," Jesse retorted vehemently, "but no, I ain't got no hope. The hope has dried up in me in six years' waiting. You're the only hope I got."

"You're crazy," Brackett muttered. "I won't do it. For God's sake think of Ella for a minute."

"Don't you *know* I'm thinking about her?" Jesse asked softly. He plucked at Brackett's sleeve. "That's what decided me, Tom." His voice became muted into a hushed, pained whisper. "The night Egbert was at our house I looked at Ella like I'd seen her for the first time. *She ain't pretty any more*, Tom!" Brackett jerked his head and moved away. Jesse followed him, taking a deep, sobbing breath. "Don't that tell you, Tom? Ella was like a little doll or something, you remember. I couldn't walk down the street without somebody turning to look at her. She ain't twenty-nine yet, Tom, and she ain't pretty no more."

Brackett sat down with his shoulders hunched up wearily. He gripped his hands together and sat leaning forward, staring at the floor.

Jesse stood over him, his gaunt face flushed with emotion, almost unpleasant in its look of pleading and bitter humility. "I ain't done right for Ella, Tom. Ella deserved better. This is the only chance I see in my whole life to do something for her. I've just been a failure."

"Don't talk nonsense," Brackett com-

mented without rancor. "You ain't a failure. No more than me. There's millions of men in the identical situation. It's just the depression, or the recession, or the God damn New Deal, or . . . !" He swore and lapsed into silence.

"Oh no," Jesse corrected him in a knowing, sorrowful tone, "those things maybe excuse other men. But not me. It was up to me to do better. This is my own fault!"

"Oh, beans!" Brackett said. "It's more sun spots than it's you!"

Jesse's face turned an unhealthy mottled red. It looked swollen. "Well I don't care," he cried wildly. "I don't care! You got to give me this! I got to lift my head up. I went through one stretch of hell but I can't go through another. You want me to keep looking at my little boy's legs and tell myself if I had a job he wouldn't be like that? Every time he walks he says to me, ' I got soft bones from the rickets and you give it to me because you didn't feed me right.' Jesus Christ, Tom, you think I'm going to sit there and watch him like that another six years?"

Brackett leaped to his feet. "So what if you do?" he shouted. "You say you're thinking about Ella. How's she going to like it when you get killed?"

"Maybe I won't," Jesse pleaded. "I've got to have some luck sometime."

"That's what they all think," Brackett replied scornfully. "When you take this job your luck is a question mark. The only thing certain is that sooner or later you get killed."

"Okay then," Jesse shouted back. "Then I do! But meanwhile I got something, don't I? I can buy a pair of shoes. Look at me! I can buy a suit that don't say 'Relief' by the way it fits. I can smoke cigarettes. I can buy some candy for the kids. I can eat some myself. Yes, by God, I want to eat some candy. I want a glass of beer once a day. I want Ella dressed up. I want her to eat meat three times a week, four times maybe. I want to take my family to the movies."

Brackett sat down. "Oh, shut up," he said wearily.

"No," Jesse told him softly, passionately, "you can't get rid of me. Listen, Tom," he pleaded, "I got it all figured out. On six hundred a month look how much I can save! If I last only three months, look how much it is —a thousand dollars—more! And maybe I'll last longer. Maybe a couple of years. I can fix Ella up for life!"

"You said it," Brackett interposed. "I suppose you think she'll enjoy living when you're on a job like that?"

"I got it all figured out," Jesse answered excitedly. "She don't know, see? I tell her I make only forty. You put the rest in a bank account for her, Tom."

"Oh, shut up," Brackett said. "You think you'll be happy? Every minute, waking and sleeping, you'll be wondering if tomorrow you'll be dead. And the worst days will be your days off, when you're not driving. They have to give you every other day free to get your nerve back. And you lay around the house eating your heart out. That's how happy you'll be."

Jesse laughed. "I'll be happy! Don't you worry, I'll be so happy, I'll be singing. Lord God, Tom, I'm going to feel *proud* of myself for the first time in seven years."

"Oh, shut up, shut up," Brackett said.

The little shanty became silent. After a moment Jesse whispered: "You got to, Tom. You got to. You got to."

Again there was silence. Brackett raised both hands to his head, pressing the palms against his temples.

"Tom, Tom—" Jesse said.

Brackett sighed. "Oh, God damn it," he said finally, "all right, I'll take you on, God help me." His voice was low, hoarse, infinitely weary. "If you're ready to drive tonight, you can drive tonight."

Jesse didn't answer. He couldn't. Brackett looked up. The tears were running down Jesse's face. He was swallowing and trying to speak, but only making an absurd, gasping noise.

"I'll send a wire to Ella," Brackett said in the same hoarse, weary voice. "I'll tell her you got a job, and you'll send her fare in a couple of days. You'll have some money then—that is, if you last the week out, you jackass!"

Jesse only nodded. His heart felt so close to bursting that he pressed both hands against it, as though to hold it locked within his breast.

"Come back here at six o'clock," Brackett said. "Here's some money. Eat a good meal."

"Thanks," Jesse whispered.

"Wait a minute," Brackett said. "Here's my address." He wrote it on a piece of paper. "Take any car going that way. Ask the conductor where to get off. Take a bath and get some sleep."

"Thanks," Jesse said. "Thanks, Tom."

"Oh, get out of here," Brackett said.

"Tom."

"What?"

"I just—" Jesse stopped. Brackett saw his face. The eyes were still glistening with tears, but the gaunt face was shining now with a kind of fierce radiance.

Brackett turned away. "I'm busy," he said.

Jesse went out. The wet film blinded him but the whole world seemed to have turned golden. He limped slowly, with the blood pounding in his temples and a wild, incommunicable joy in his heart. "I'm the happiest man in the world," he whispered to himself. "I'm the happiest man on the whole earth."

Brackett sat watching till finally Jesse turned the corner of the alley and disappeared. Then he hunched himself over, with his head in his hands. His heart was beating painfully, like something old and clogged. He listened to it as it beat. He sat in desperate tranquillity, gripping his head in his hands.

SUGGESTIONS FOR STUDY

1. What constitutes the conflict in this story? Name the protagonist and the antagonist.

2. What would you say is the purpose of this story? What would you expect other stories by the same author to be like?

3. Upon what elements in the story do you base your opinion of Tom Brackett? Does your

opinion of him remain fixed from the moment he is introduced, or does it change? If it changes, point out the factors which cause the change.

4. Is the point of view completely consistent throughout the story?

5. Do the things that Jesse wants to buy with his money seem trivial (shoes, clothes, candy, cigarettes, beer, meat four times a week)? What do these things indicate concerning Jesse's psychology?

6. Is Jesse's desire to earn money at the risk of his life made believable? Give your reasons.

7. Is this story basically one of plot or of character?

8. Are the elements of the story realistic or romantic?

9. Is sentiment held sufficiently in restraint? If so, how does the author achieve this?

Brandy for Breakfast[1]

LAURENCE W. MEYNELL

TOWARDS THE END of October a well-knit figure, with a pleasant air of vagabondage about it, was climbing the slopes of the Long Mynd.

"If you are on one of your insane walking tours, do come over our way," Hilary had written. "You will find Overley full of rather noisy people, but we shall all be delighted to see your serious old face." And a postscript had been added in an only too familiar scrawl, "Especially me—Anne."

Anne and Hilary and Overley House, a great, rambling thing, full of places where your head bumped and your feet stumbled, and quite completely full of an atmosphere in which your heart rejoiced—all excellent reasons (thought Roger Ascham) why a man should leave his chambers in Lincoln's Inn and set his face to that part of England which lies on the west of the Severn.

Shropshire was new country for Roger to walk in. When he had been to Overley before, it had been by train; and he was increasingly glad of his new approach there. He was as fit and youthful a forty as you could find (in spite of Hilary's rude remarks about his "serious old face"), and his long, athletic legs had brought him ahead of his schedule.

All day long he had been walking on the bare hills, those slopes as old as England that carry across them the very first tracks made by human feet on English soil. All day long he had had the sheep-nibbled, springy turf under him, and such names as Squilver, Stedment, Stiperstones, and Stent for companions. By nine o'clock at night he reached as lonely a wayside inn as even that bare countryside could show, where—for all the loneliness of the place—was a jewel of a woman who fried him such a plate of ham and eggs as he had never hoped to taste.

Roger ate his meal in the bar at an oaken table that was old when Trafalgar was fought, and afterwards he sat on there, sipping a pint of excellent beer and studying his map. Three other men were in the bar, of the dark and wiry sort that have been in these hills since time was.

They were uncommunicative at first, but thawed a little after a round of drinks, and Roger listened delightedly to the broad, unhurried dialect. Two of them were old and one was young, but they had all come out of the same mold and, in a way, were much alike.

The inn had only one drawback—it could not put him up; on the other hand, the Fates had provided a glorious full moon, and Roger had no doubts about what he would do. There was a hamlet some six miles ahead where he felt certain a bed of some sort could be obtained, and he intended to push on

[1] From Laurence W. Meynell, *Story Teller* (1936). Reprinted by permission of the author.

there in the moonlight as rapidly as was reasonably possible.

It seemed to him that the map offered a choice of two ways: the highroad; and, what was at least a mile shorter, a track up the hill and over the side. Wisely he sought local confirmation concerning his route.

"Road 'll tak' 'ee straight theare, sir," he was assured.

"Follow 'un aäl the way and 'ee's bound to come to 'un."

Roger nodded. "But can't I cut up over the hill?" he asked. There was a moment's silence.

"Up the Old Traäck?" someone queried.

"Yes, if that's what it's called."

Again there was that momentary silence, and for the first time it struck Roger that there was something odd about it. One of the old men broke it to say, "Anyone can go on the Old Traäck as 'as got a mind to. But maybe the road's the better way in the moonlight."

Roger folded his map up and laughed at rustic reasoning. If there was one time when the track was better than the road, he argued, it must be by moonlight when it could be seen easily.

He drained the last drop of his beer, set his tankard down noisily, and with a cheery "Good night" to everybody went out into the darkness.

"Good night, sir." Three men answered him, and not one of them looked at him as they did so; nor, after he had left, did they look for a minute or two directly at each other. Roger was swinging along the road, and in the nature of things he could not hear the remarks that followed his departure.

The moon was rising rapidly, and there was no difficulty in seeing where the track led off the road. Roger turned up it whistling and tackled the long climb with a light heart. It was a track first made no one knew when and since trodden by countless generations of feet and almost equally countless generations of wheels. As Roger climbed, the countryside fell away from him on either side, bare

and beautiful under the silver moonlight. Far away on the right, perhaps a mile away, a single light moved unevenly along the valley road, and its presence there seemed to Roger somehow friendly and reassuring. When the first crest of the hill was gained he saw, quite unexpectedly, a big farmhouse and its buildings lying amid trees on the left. The straight roofs of the house and the rounded tops of the barns glinted in the moonlight, but there was little light, and the pine trees behind rose dark and still and almost sinister. "A lonely place," Roger thought as he swung along, and on the instant, as though to contradict his verdict, a figure came out of the dark shadow of the wayside trees and joined him.

Thinking it over afterwards, Roger found it hard to say whether he overtook the other man or was overtaken by him. His attention had been on the house, and all he could say was that at one moment he was alone and at the next he had a companion.

The man gave him "good evening" in a low, musical voice, and Roger willingly fell in step beside him, glad of his company.

"You're out late on the hill road, mister," the man said, and Roger countered with, "Well, you're pretty late yourself, you know."

The man laughed quietly. "Suppose I am," he agreed. "Us chaps have to be about latish at times. There's a tuthree things to do."

Roger wondered whether he were a gamekeeper or poacher perhaps, and did not mind either way. In either event he was company.

They walked in silence for a while, Roger abating his quick, nervous gait to the countryman's unhurried pace, characteristic of his sort the world over. He was a well-made man with a fine pair of shoulders on him, and he looked well in his corduroys of the old country fashion and design.

"Fine night." Roger ventured at last to break the silence which was growing a little oppressive.

"Ay, good for any harvesting or plough work to be done extra-like."

"You wouldn't plough by moonlight surely?" Roger asked.

The other laughed his agreeable laugh again. "I've had to before now," he said.

"I suppose you work hereabouts?"

The man jerked his head backwards. "Up to Ladywood," he said.

"Is that the big farm I've just passed?"

"That's it. Mr. Lang's. This is all Ladywood land we're on now."

"Pretty good land, I suppose."

"It's been better," the man said cryptically, and Roger was debating this utterance, and wondering why every man is so prone to glorify the past, when the track dipped suddenly and ran by the side of a dark wood. The air was damper in the hollow, and Roger said abruptly:

"I never did like pine trees much. Why they can't plant good English oak, I don't know."

They had come to the end of the wood now, and the countryman stopped and rested his hand on a gate. "That's the Lady Wood," he said. "Gives its name to the farm, I reckon."

The upright trees, absolutely still in that windless air, looked dark and mysterious in the moonlight, almost as though there were secrets in the unexplored blackness of the wood which they were guarding and would not yield.

"There's a deal of folk don't care about coming past here o' night time," the man said suddenly, and instantly Roger's ears were pricked. He was blessed (or cursed, he could never himself be sure which) with an insatiably curious mind and was always avid to hear any new thing.

"Why's that?" he asked.

"Tales—well, one tale in particular, I reckon."

Silence. Roger broke it with an encouraging extension of his cigarette case. "Have a cigarette?"

"No, thank you, mister. I've never had no use for them things. One time o' day I used to smoke a bit o' baccy in a pipe, but that's all."

"And the story?" Roger prompted. "The tale that makes people afraid to come along here?"

"I'll tell it you if you've a mind to hear it; seeing as we've happened on each other, 'companions in the way' as the Bible says. Only it's ghosts, of course, and I reckon you're a book-learned man and maybe you don't believe in such things and aren't interested in 'em."

"I'm interested in everything," Roger said, and it was very nearly true.

The countryman hesitated a minute as though wondering how to start his tale; one hard, muscled hand rested on top of the five-barred gate; one side of him was in shadow, the other silvered by the moonlight; his eyes were fixed on the dark mystery of the wood.

"It's about old days now," he said, "though not really old in a manner of speaking. Michaelmas, eighteen-eighty-eight, it all began, the way the old chaps always tell the tale. In they days there was always a Michaelmas Mop Fair at Wenlock. Wenches used to go to be hired out for servants and chaps for work on the farms. Stood in two rows they always did, chaps in the front and wenches at the back, and each one wearing summat to show what his work was. Then the farmers 'ud come and look 'em over and pick out a likely one, and they'd strike a bargain, master and man, for a year or three years maybe, and the money was fixed and the 'ulowances and everything; and the farmer always had to pay a shilling there and then earnest money. That was a right way of striking a bargain to my mind. Master could see man and man master, and each gave his word and stuck to it. None of this writing and notices and cards and such.

"The chap this tale is about stood there Michaelmas, eighteen-eighty-eight, in the Market Square at Wenlock with a whip in his hand to show he was a horseman. Twenty-four years old he was, and knew his work.

Born the other side of the Clee at Hope Bowdler, a sleepy sort of place some reckon it; well, I daresay we are sleepy these parts, sleepy still as far as that goes. But I'll warrant he didn't feel sleepy that particular morning standing in Wenlock Square with all the noise of the fair round him, and chaps hollering and the auctioneer calling out the bids for the beasts and all the wenches about him.

"Good-looking chap they reckon he was, ought to have gone for a soldier, some say, time the 'cruiting sargent with his red sash came round and stood all beer, and then maybe he wouldn't have got into his trouble. But that's as may be. I reckon things work out to an appointed end, and if it hadn't been trouble here, it would have been trouble the other side of the world somewhere, in lands he didn't know. There was a girl or two looked at this chap in Wenlock, seemingly; I reckon he must have looked a good one to wed with, but if he me't have smiled at one or two, there was nothing more, him being married for two years and happy.

"When the farmers came out of the Arms all the argufying and bargain-making started, louder than selling the beasts. And the outcome of it was this chap, Dale his name was, engaged himself to Ladywood Farm to serve his master faithful and well for three years as horseman. Fifteen shillings a week and a cottage found, and extra money harvest time, and a bit of meal every now and again to help him keep a pig if he'd a mind to. Mr. Lang the farmer was. There was Langs at Ladywood then, of course, and always have been, pretty well.

"This Lang, Harry Lang *his* name was, he was a man about fifty, very quick-tempered and must have what he wanted; but if he did make his men work, he worked alongside them with his coat off. A great man for getting the most out of everything, fly into a temper he would if your headlands were a foot too wide when you were ploughing. But if you worked well he gave you credit for it; he was that sort. Ted Dale understood that

sort of man, and if ever they lost tempers with one another and got to widdershins he stood up to him. The horseman's cottage was in the next valley then, Well Cottage it was called. It's been pulled down since they days. A little bit of a place it was, two up and two down, and a pigsty; but a man can make his bit of heaven where's he's a mind to, so be as he's got the woman he loves and it's his home.

"Ted Dale served his three years and was happy there, and time they was up they struck another bargain, master and man, in the big stable at Ladywood Farm.

" 'You stay along o' me another three years, Dale,' Mr. Lang said, 'and I'll raise you two shillings a week.' And they shook hands on it there and then, and Mr. Lang called for a girl to bring out some homebrewed from the cellar to make a bargain of it. Mr. Lang wasn't married, then, being a widower; his wife died in childbirth and the baby died too, a little after. So Ladywood had been without a mistress for a good number of years, which didn't seem right in a farmhouse somehow, but there it was.

"Of course, they days there *was* ploughing to do; all this country was under corn then, and the old men today'll tell you the same. A man had to mind his horses then, or they'd never have stood up to the work. But this chap Dale he loved his cattle, and there was always a prize or two came Ladywood way, Wenlock or Ludlow show times.

"When Dale had been at Well Cottage four years, Mr. Lang got married again. Took everyone by surprise because no one had seen any walking-out or courting or such; and no wonder, for he didn't marry a Shropshire woman, but brought a lady straight from London, wed and all in order before he got here, and put her in at Ladywood as mistress straight away.

"Of course, there was a do after she came; they cleared the big barn and there was a supper and music and dancing and such like. And some speeches like they always make. And Mr. Lang stood up and said he'd got himself a wife as every man ought to do, and he had brought her to Ladywood to look after it for him, and he reckoned to be a farmer's wife was as good a thing as any woman, lady or no, could wish for. And when he'd done Mrs. Lang got up, a slim slip of a woman, quality-bred, as 'ad never done a day at the washtub in her life, and thanked everybody nice and proper and said she was sure she was going to be happy at Ladywood. She looked that lissom and bright-colored, like a bit of china. I'll warrant there was above a man or two there would have changed places willingly with Harry Lang.

"They days there wasn't much in the way of funning these parts; time Mayday sports was over there was nothing till Harvest Home; and then only the Mummers at Christmastime to break the winter. So a do like this wedding-feast got talked of a good deal, and everyone was saying what a proper lady Mr. Lang had brought home with him. But laborers didn't have much to do with the big house, and this chap Ted Dale didn't see his master's wife again for a tuthree months; only, times, he thought of her looking so small and dainty and so different from the heavy, yeavy things as filled his life.

"Harvest Home he saw her and she spoke to him; quick, bright words she had like the chirrup of a bird. And Christmastime, when all went to all to wish happiness, he saw her again, standing in the firelight of the big kitchen and laughing and looking like a fairy.

"There was more ploughing than ever that next spring. Corn looked to rise in price, and Mr. Lang dearly loved a bargain and was mad to grow all he could. He worked man and beast hard. They days there was no hours and agreements and Acts of Parliament about us chaps; it was up by starlight and back to bed by starlight and work all in between. And yet never enough to satisfy him. He was like that, desperate after a thing as he'd set his mind on, and everything else he'd reckon waste of time and sinful.

"April time one of Ted Dale's children went ill and one day, as was too wet to plough and he was at home mending gear, Mrs. Lang came from the farm with a basket of comforts. First he knowed about it, the bit of a hovel where he sat working was darkened, and he looked up to see her in the doorway.

"'Can I come in?' she says. And a bit of April sun came out at that second, and she looked gold and glorious all at once like she me't be a shining angel.

"That was the first time as Ted Dale ever saw her alone, and there was only two more times in his life—three in all. Strange, I always reckon that. Yet I suppose it's like these clever artists who can paint a picture with half-a-dozen quick strokes and you see the thing plain and vivid enough to make you cry out. I reckon God can do the same with us humans when He's a mind to.

"Ted Dale bid her come her ways in, and stood up a bit awkward, what with his hair tousled and sleeves rolled up and the shirt open on his chest. But I suppose the sun and the wind put a color on a man, especially one who's got a great pair of shoulder and a happy smile, as a woman likes to see above niceties of dress.

"Ten minutes and more she talked to him and never offered to go. You me't almost have thought as she was glad of someone to talk to.

"Ted talked it all over with his wife that evening. Pleasant and good, they both reckoned, it was of her to come, and charitable.

"'That's the sort of woman we want at the farmhouse,' Mary said. But, night-time, when he lay awake in the dark and Mary sleeping safe beside him, all Ted could remember was the moment when he looked up and saw her shining in the doorway, and caught his breath the instant as he had seen a vision.

"July was half done and hay harvest almost finished before he saw her again. A hot day it was, with no wind and the hum of the insects so steady on those lonely fields as would lull a man to sleep. Ted Dale was walking through the Long Meadow Coppy, which was the shortest way from the farmhouse to the far hayfield, where there was still a load or two to carry. They days the coppy was thicker than it is now, all a mass of lush and undergrowth, and so still in the midst of it a man me't be alone in all the world, only times a yaffle would startle you by its noise, or a dog-fox run across the ride. Suddenly he saw her sitting on a log in the clearing. He was on her before he could give any warning of his coming, and she looked up quickly and gave a little cry as she was frightened, and he could see that her eyes were streaming wet with tears. Very awkward and uncomfortable he felt in his corduroys although she made to smile when she saw him, but she would have him sit beside her on the log and no refusal.

"She wasn't the lady at the big house, but just a dear human heart fighting with itself and desperate unhappy.

"'Oh,' she says beating her little, white hands on the back of the log, 'I'm so lonely, Dale. Lonely, lonely, lonely. I thought Ladywood was lovely when I came to it, but I tell you it's a prison, a prison.'

"Then she told him—yet, in a way, it wasn't telling *him*, but just *telling*, just easing her heart of what it must say to someone— she told him of what it had been like in London where she lived and the menservants and parties and theaters and bright lights and all such which was like a dream to Ted Dale. Then Harry Lang had set eyes on her and, never mind her three elder sisters, he wanted her desperate bad. Would have her too, yea-word or nay-word from her parents. And her parents were dead set against him. Pride puffed up their hearts, maybe, as it has puffed up many others to their unhappiness. They wanted a London man with money for their prettiest girl, and here was a farmer from the middle of Shropshire swearing he must have her, and angry at any delay. The end of it was he was forbidden the house, and

she was told plain she must forget him and look elsewhere.

"But at twenty-one it is hard to look elsewhere when there's a man pouring out such passionate love to you as most women never hear in their lives.

"'You've got to live your own life, my dear,' Harry Lang said (and by that he meant live *his*), 'and never mind about your parents.'

"And she listened to him; with his kisses hot on hers and his arms aching to hold her closer yet, she listened; what woman wouldn't? And one night between one hour and the next she slipped out of the big London house into the gaslit streets with a lie on her lips and wonder in her heart and all life an adventure before her.

"Harry Lang had all ready, and next day they were wed at a registrar's, and he brought her to Ladywood, and she had never seen or heard of her family since.

"But Harry Lang the farmer was different from Harry Lang the lover. Beasts in the stockyard and women in the kitchen, that's what he liked to see. That was the way he reckoned life should be, and he didn't set up to understand any other. It wasn't so much the work—though that was bad enough—as the loneliness that she got to hate. All this countryside is lonely; they days it stood lonelier still, and Ladywood the loneliest of it all. Times a month will go without you see anyone outside the household; and should a stranger chance to come it sets all the parish talking. It was very different from London and the menservants and the traffic in the lighted streets.

"'Oh,' she cried, 'I hate Ladywood now. It's like a cage. I feel like a bird trapped in it all the time. It's like a cage I tell you.'

"Ted Dale understood that. He could never abear to see any caged or chained thing and had always a mind to set all free as he saw. It always seemed terrible to him to see the sunlight and not to be able to be in it. He forgot she was his master's wife; in a way, the manner of her speaking to him had made him forget it.

"'Now, dear heart,' he told her, 'don't 'ee take on so. There's up and down in life, 'tis the way of things, and 'twill all come smooth in the end.'

"Oh, but she didn't want it smooth in the end; in the end she would be old and stiff-limbed and not mind whether 'twas spring or autumn, and now she was young and warm-blooded and was lonely, lonely, lonely. And she went into a fit of weeping there and then, like a child that had broken its toy. And angry, too, against him, mad angry, for trying to fob her off with old saws that parsons use.

"And suddenly, in the midst of it, she jumped up and stood against him, and they looked at each other. 'Ah,' she said, and her voice had gone very quiet like it me't be a little stream running alongside a meadow. 'Ah, I liked you, Ted Dale, the very first time I saw you.' And quick as a flycatcher she darted down and kissed him full on his lips, and then she was up and running down the ride to the house before he could move.

"Time he did move and got to the Long Meadow, Mr. Lang was hollering from across the field at him why had he been so long and perhaps he reckoned hay harvest would wait for him and all such. And Ted Dale never answered a word; not a thing could he see in the bright sunlight, neither Harry Lang, nor the cocks of hay, nor the red and blue wagon, nor his own great horses, nor anything in the whole hayfield save only a little elfish face against him and two lips on his.

"That was the second time of his seeing her alone, and it lasted him through the end of hay harvest, right through corn harvest (and there *was* a corn harvest those times) to the beginning of the back-end. A time or two when he was at the buildings he might catch a glimpse of her in the farmhouse talking to a maid, or among the bright flowers in the garden or some such, but never to speak to. But not a day went by when he didn't think on her.

"Folks used to read the Bible a deal those

times, even rough laboring chaps would have it in their cottages. 'My soul is troubled and grievously afflicted,' Ted Dale would read, or may be, 'Beauty hath lifted up mine eyes and made me afraid.' And time he'd turn to the love song where it says, 'A cluster of grapes my beloved is to me in the vineyards of Engaddi.' And all the while he was thinking of one thing. Sinful he knew it was, because Mary was his lawful wedded wife for better or worse, through rough and smooth as long as they both lived, and he loved her.

"But this other woman had got into his blood. She haunted him like she was a ghost, so light and delicate and like a bit of china, and yet her lips so soft and warm and yes-saying on his that time in Long Meadow Coppy. Aye, and once he read, 'A man shall dream and have an image set in his heart,' and he let the Book slip and sat staring over it like he was struck.

"Well, that was a poor way for a man to be in, but he had his work of course to keep him busy. Time harvest was done and all raught in, there was winter ploughing to start, and October was always a rare month these parts for working. There was a day the end of that October as this chap Dale was sent to plough this very field here by the Lady Wood. Grass it's been long since, but they days it was plough and always had bin. Mr. Lang was away to Ludlow to buy beasts, and Ted Dale was to plough Spinner's Piece as they call it. There'd been a touch of frost in the night and there was a mist everywhere like a white curtain and the sun certain to come through by noonday. Proper October weather it was. Captain and Brownie he was plowing with, and it was music to him to hear their harness jingle as he took them down the lane to work.

"Mr. Lang was set on having the Piece ploughed as soon as me't be, and Dale stuck at it steadily all morning with the mist clearing all the time and the rooks waddling after him like aldermen in the furrows and the steam standing up off his horses in the still air.

"Noon day was gone and he was just getting to the end of a furrow when summat made him look up and there across the headland looking at him over the hedge top she was. Neither said a word for a minute, and he could only think of those words, 'A man shall dream and have an image set in his heart' because just at that moment he had been thinking of her clear and vivid and here was his image set over against him.

"Then she said, 'Busy?' And slipped off her horse and tied him to this very gate stump here. She had taken a horse from Ladywood stables and ridden out to see him. Ted Dale was struck silly at first.

"'I was just a-goöing to have my middays,' he said.

"'I reckoned you would be,' she made answer, 'and I thought I'd come and have mine with you. Mr. Lang's away to market and I'm tired of having meals alone.'

"'Well, I must finish the furrow first,' Ted said, and she laughed out loud at him, such a noise it sounded in these still fields all bright and silvery.

"'No you must *not*,' she says. 'You can finish that after.' And for the first time in his life Ted left his horses standing in the middle of a furrow; no shade or headland nibbling nor nothing. Just left them there and followed her into the Lady Wood.

"She made him sit down very close to her. 'Ah Ted,' she says, 'we ought to have seen one another before this. You've been avoiding me.' And, 'Oh Ted, I can't stand it any more, no one to talk to and nothing to do and loneliness all day long.' And she slid her arm on his, which was hot and sweaty from ploughwork, and she said, "Ted Dale, you've got wonderful powerful arms, a man's arms . . .'

"Well, that was the way of it. There'll be plenty ready to blame, but the world's made of men and women; and, times, all promises, all honor, all happiness counts nothing beside a mad hour's pleasure.

"And then, in the middle of it, when neither had been listening to aught but the other's whispers, a twig snapped, and Harry Lang stood there looking at them like a man mazed.

"Halfway to Ludlow he chanced to meet the man whose beasts he wanted to buy, and they struck a bargain there and then in a wayside inn and no need to go to market at all. And Harry Lang was so pleased at saving half-a-day he drove straight back to Ladywood to kiss his wife in high humor; but on the way he thought he'd turn aside for ten minutes to see how Dale was getting on with the Spinner's Piece. And by the roadside to his amazement he saw Bluebell, the Ladywood hacking mare, tied to a gatepost. 'What the devil's this?' he thought to himself. And when he made his way into the Wood what it turned out to be was his wife in the arms of his ploughman.

"He was that struck he couldn't do naught but stare at first; it was almost funny to see him.

"He had his shotgun with him which he always took wherever he went in case there might be a rabbit or a rook as he walked up the hedgeside. And Ted Dale thought, 'He'll shoot me certain sure.' And he made to push the woman away from him in case she got shot too.

"But Lang had his courage. He was that angry at someone daring to take what was his it wouldn't be good enough just to shoot him; he must prove himself the better man. He handled his gun, but only to put it down on the ground.

"'My God, Dale,' he says, very quiet and white all the time, 'you're going to remember this.' And he took off his market-going coat and put it down very neatly beside him.

"Then they went to it, master and man—or man and man, I should say, with the woman looking on.

"Dale had the years of the other man, but Harry Lang was like a mad person; if you hit him he didna' feel it; you could have burnt him with a bare flame and he'd not have known.

"It was naked fists, and ugly, naked anger, and blood enough soon in all conscience; and the woman forgotten you me't say, sobbing and crying in the background.

"And then in the silence of that quiet place and sending all the rooks like a handful of black stones into the sky, a noise like it was the end of the world.

"And so it was the end of the world for one of the men. The woman had picked up the gun, and from not ten yards off, no, not five either, had taken aim at one of them and fired, and the fighting stopped at once. Maybe she hit the one she aimed at, maybe the twisting and turning of their bodies defeated her—who knows? Only she; and it was too late to say. She and her husband stared at one another over the dead body of her lover, and gradually the echoes died away in the Lady Wood and the rooks settled again in the furrows, and silence came back to the place.

"Aye, that was the way of it, mister; love and anger and a dead man all in an hour as you me't say.

"And then the two of them that remained, man and woman, in the bright sunshine and the air. What to do, was what they asked themselves. Run into Ludlow town calling, 'I've shot my lover, I've shot him'? Aye, some would; but I'll not blame the woman, whoever does. Life's sweet, mister, very sweet when spring comes and Shropshire orchards are white with blossom. I'll not blame the woman. No one but those three had heard the shot; no one but them knew aught of the happening.

"There was, aye there still is, a pool in the Lady Wood, a deepish bit of water, and dark such as you get in woods. Harry Lang carried his ploughman to it and tipped him in. He made ripples like a stone would, and then the ripples ceased and all was still.

"Harry Lang put his wife on Bluebell and made her ride home beside him and never a word was said about Dale between them.

"Next day Lang asked, 'Where's Dale?' And nobody knew, and Mary all in a state at Well Cottage because he hadn't been back all night.

"'He's gone off then,' Lang said, and gave out his tale, how he had been to see Dale at work and reprimanded him and they had quarreled. ('He struck me. Look at the marks.') And he warned him he would have him up before the Bench for assault, and he must have taken fright and gone.

"It made a bit of a stir at the time, but it soon quieted down, and folks believed what the farmer said. They days one ploughman more or less didn't matter a lot; there was always a tuthree more.

"Ah, well, it's an old tale and over now. But two things Harry Lang couldn't stop: he couldn't stop Ted Dale coming back o' nights to finish his furrow; and he couldn't stop his wife going down to the Lady Wood when she'd a mind to and sitting there staring. Time after time he forbade her and was angry about it, but go she would, nay-word or no; and he daresen't speak too much about it before the maids and such-like, for someone me't ask: why shouldn't she go to the Lady Wood if so she'd a mind?

"She'd go there and sit very still, listening. Not by the pool she wouldn't sit, as a rule, but just out of sight of it, inside the wood. And as she listened times she thought she would hear horses as it me't be ploughing, and a man's voice very rich and musical (which she always had noticed about it) calling very faint and ghostly, 'Gee, *ay*, Captain,' or maybe, 'Co-oop, Brownie,' and quick as a flycatcher she would dart to the side of the wood and there was nothing but an empty, lonely field.

"But she went to the Lady Wood once too often. Christmastime she went, towards dusk one day. A proper mournful, dead sort of a place it would seem, with drippings falling *pat pat pat* from the bare branches and all the dead leaves beneath. That time she never came back, and folks would have it that the pool must be dragged.

"They found her, of course; maybe in the dark she had slipped in by mistake; maybe she thought she heard something calling her from the bottom of the black water. For there was still something else there. They found it when they were dragging, far gone, of course, but enough to see it was a man; and some said enough to tell there was a gun-shot wound all down one side—well, look, mister . . ."

The man turned so that the side of him that had been in shadow should have been silvered by the moonlight, and yet it was not silvered but dark and ugly. "Look, mister," he said in his low, musical voice, and Roger took one look and tried to scream and fainted.

A milk float passes along that lonely road soon after six in the morning. Its driver found Roger Ascham; recognized by his clothes that he was one of the mad gentlemen who walk, and brought him to the next farm down the road. Here warmth, a glass of hot milk and kindliness did their work. And Roger, who was a determined person, left again on foot by half-past seven. He walked quickly, with-out a single glance behind him. If a stranger had stepped out of the roadside to talk to him, he would have screamed with terror. By nine o'clock precisely he stood in the porch of Overley.

A typical Overley breakfast was in prog-ress, noisy, hilarious, prodigious.

"Roger!" Anne shrieked. "Darling Roger, where on earth have you come from at this hour?"

"What'll you have, Roger?" Hilary's deep voice asked from the sideboard. "There's ba-con, kidney, or the odd egg."

"I'll have," said Roger, with the greatest clarity and decision, "a double brandy-and-soda, thank you."

SUGGESTIONS FOR STUDY

1. What purpose is served by the description of Overley House in the third paragraph?
2. Why did the author not start the story with Roger trudging along the Old Track in the moonlight, thus eliminating the scene at the inn?
3. Why is emphasis laid on the age of the Shropshire countryside?
4. Of what significance is it that the plough-man says "Good evening" in a "musical" voice? Does the quality of his voice figure later in the story?
5. What elements of foreshadowing occur in the first part of the dialogue between Roger and the ploughman?
6. Examine the structure of the ploughman's story. Is the story skillfully told? Is any advan-tage gained by having the story told in dialect by a country person?
7. Is Harry Lang a thoroughly unlikable person? Is it beyond comprehension that Mrs. Lang was willing to marry him?
8. Why is it that the reader is left somewhat in doubt as to which man Mrs. Lang intended to shoot?
9. Does the story provide a possible natural explanation for Roger's experience?
10. Was the author's main aim to develop character or to build an interesting plot?
11. As the author develops the story, does it seem at all plausible?
12. This is an example of a story within a frame. Is there an advantage in this so far as this type of story is concerned?

Laura[1]

SAKI (H. H. MUNRO)

"You ARE NOT really dying, are you?" asked Amanda.

"I have the doctor's permission to live till Tuesday," said Laura.

[1] From *The Short Stories of Saki* [H. H. Munro], (New York, 1930). Reprinted by permission of the Viking Press, Inc. and John Lane, The Bodley Head, the English publisher.

"But today is Saturday; this is serious!" gasped Amanda.

"I don't know about it being serious; it is certainly Saturday," said Laura.

"Death is always serious," said Amanda.

"I never said I was going to die. I am pre-sumably going to leave off being Laura, but

I shall go on being something. An animal of some kind, I suppose. You see, when one hasn't been very good in the life one has just lived, one reincarnates in some lower organism. And I haven't been very good, when one comes to think of it. I've been petty and mean and vindictive and all that sort of thing when circumstances have seemed to warrant it."

"Circumstances never warrant that sort of thing," said Amanda hastily.

"If you don't mind my saying so," observed Laura, "Egbert is a circumstance that would warrant any amount of that sort of thing. You're married to him—that's different; you've sworn to love, honour, and endure him: I haven't."

"I don't see what's wrong with Egbert," protested Amanda.

"Oh, I dare say the wrongness has been on my part," admitted Laura dispassionately; "he has merely been the extenuating circumstance. He made a thin, peevish kind of fuss, for instance, when I took the collie puppies from the farm out for a run the other day."

"They chased his young broods of speckled Sussex and drove two sitting hens off their nests, besides running all over the flower beds. You know how devoted he is to his poultry and garden."

"Anyhow, he needn't have gone on about it for the entire evening and then have said, 'Let's say no more about it' just when I was beginning to enjoy the discussion. That's where one of my petty vindictive revenges came in," added Laura with an unrepentant chuckle; "I turned the entire family of speckled Sussex into his seedling shed the day after the puppy episode."

"How could you?" exclaimed Amanda.

"It came quite easy," said Laura; "two of the hens pretended to be laying at the time, but I was firm."

"And we thought it was an accident!"

"You see," resumed Laura, "I really *have* some grounds for supposing that my next incarnation will be in a lower organism. I shall be an animal of some kind. On the other hand, I haven't been a bad sort in my way, so I think I may count on being a nice animal, something elegant and lively, with a love of fun. An otter, perhaps."

"I can't imagine you as an otter," said Amanda.

"Well, I don't suppose you can imagine me as an angel, if it comes to that," said Laura.

Amanda was silent. She couldn't.

"Personally I think an otter life would be rather enjoyable," continued Laura; "salmon to eat all the year round, and the satisfaction of being able to fetch the trout in their own homes without having to wait for hours till they condescend to rise to the fly you've been dangling before them; and an elegant svelte figure—"

"Think of the otter hounds," interposed Amanda; "how dreadful to be hunted and harried and finally worried to death!"

"Rather fun with half the neighborhood looking on, and anyhow not worse than this Saturday-to-Tuesday business of dying by inches; and then I should go on into something else. If I had been a moderately good otter I suppose I should get back into human shape of some sort; probably something rather primitive—a little brown, unclothed Nubian boy, I should think."

"I wish you would be serious," sighed Amanda; "you really ought to be if you're only going to live till Tuesday."

As a matter of fact Laura died on Monday.

"So dreadfully upsetting," Amanda complained to her uncle-in-law, Sir Lulworth Quayne. "I've asked quite a lot of people down for golf and fishing, and the rhododendrons are just looking their best."

"Laura always was inconsiderate," said Sir Lulworth; "she was born during Goodwood week, with an Ambassador staying in the house who hated babies."

"She had the maddest kind of ideas," said Amanda; "do you know if there was any insanity in her family?"

"Insanity? No, I never heard of any. Her father lives in West Kensington, but I believe he's sane on all other subjects."

"She had an idea that she was going to be reincarnated as an otter," said Amanda.

"One meets with those ideas of reincarnation so frequently, even in the West," said Sir Lulworth, "that one can hardly set them down as being mad. And Laura was such an unaccountable person in this life that I should not like to lay down definite rules as to what she might be doing in an after state."

"You think she really might have passed into some animal form?" asked Amanda. She was one of those who shape their opinions rather readily from the standpoint of those around them.

Just then Egbert entered the breakfast-room, wearing an air of bereavement that Laura's demise would have been insufficient, in itself, to account for.

"Four of my speckled Sussex have been killed," he exclaimed; "the very four that were to go to the show on Friday. One of them was dragged away and eaten right in the middle of that new carnation bed that I've been to such trouble and expense over. My best flower bed and my best fowls singled out for destruction; it almost seems as if the brute that did the deed had special knowledge how to be as devastating as possible in a short space of time."

"Was it a fox, do you think?" asked Amanda.

"Sounds more like a polecat," said Sir Lulworth.

"No," said Egbert, "there were marks of webbed feet all over the place, and we followed the tracks down to the stream at the bottom of the garden; evidently an otter."

Amanda looked quickly and furtively across at Sir Lulworth.

Egbert was too agitated to eat any breakfast, and went out to superintend the strengthening of the poultry yard defences.

"I think she might at least have waited till the funeral was over," said Amanda in a scandalized voice.

"It's her own funeral, you know," said Sir Lulworth; "it's a nice point in etiquette how far one ought to show respect to one's own mortal remains."

Disregard for mortuary convention was carried to further lengths next day; during the absence of the family at the funeral ceremony the remaining survivors of the speckled Sussex were massacred. The marauder's line of retreat seemed to have embraced most of the flower beds on the lawn, but the strawberry beds in the lower garden had also suffered.

"I shall get the otter hounds to come here at the earliest possible moment," said Egbert savagely.

"On no account! You can't dream of such a thing!" exclaimed Amanda. "I mean, it wouldn't do, so soon after a funeral in the house."

"It's a case of necessity," said Egbert; "once an otter takes to that sort of thing it won't stop."

"Perhaps it will go elsewhere now that there are no more fowls left," suggested Amanda.

"One would think you wanted to shield the beast," said Egbert.

"There's been so little water in the stream lately," objected Amanda; "it seems hardly sporting to hunt an animal when it has so little chance of taking refuge anywhere."

"Good gracious!" fumed Egbert, "I'm not thinking about sport. I want to have the animal killed as soon as possible."

Even Amanda's opposition weakened when, during church time on the following Sunday, the otter made its way into the house, raided half a salmon from the larder and worried it into scaly fragments on the Persian rug in Egbert's studio.

"We shall have it hiding under our beds and biting pieces out of our feet before long," said Egbert, and from what Amanda knew of this particular otter she felt that the possibility was not a remote one.

On the evening preceding the day fixed for the hunt Amanda spent a solitary hour walking by the banks of the stream, making what she imagined to be hound noises. It was charitably supposed by those who overheard her performance that she was practising for farmyard imitations at the forthcoming village entertainment.

It was her friend and neighbor, Aurora Burret, who brought her news of the day's sport.

"Pity you weren't out; we had quite a good day. We found at once, in the pool just below your garden."

"Did you—kill?" asked Amanda.

"Rather. A fine she-otter. Your husband got rather badly bitten in trying to 'tail it.' Poor beast, I felt quite sorry for it, it had such a human look in its eyes when it was killed. You'll call me silly, but do you know who the look reminded me of? My dear woman, what is the matter?"

When Amanda had recovered to a certain extent from her attack of nervous prostration Egbert took her to the Nile Valley to recuperate. Change of scene speedily brought about the desired recovery of health and mental balance. The escapades of an adventurous otter in search of a variation of diet were viewed in their proper light. Amanda's normally placid temperament reasserted itself. Even a hurricane of shouted curses, coming from her husband's dressing-room, in her husband's voice, but hardly in his usual vocabulary, failed to disturb her serenity as she made a leisurely toilet one evening in a Cairo hotel.

"What is the matter? What has happened?" she asked in amused curiosity.

"The little beast has thrown all my clean shirts into the bath! Wait till I catch you, you little—"

"What little beast?" asked Amanda, suppressing a desire to laugh; Egbert's language was so hopelessly inadequate to express his outraged feelings.

"A little beast of a naked brown Nubian boy," spluttered Egbert.

And now Amanda is seriously ill.

SUGGESTIONS FOR STUDY

1. From a rational point of view this story is completely implausible. As a reader, do you resent the author's imposing on you or do you accept the situation? What gives it the air of verisimilitude?

2. What are the most humorous elements of the story to you?

3. Who are the only ones in the story who know the truth? What elements in the character of each—merely hinted at—make them willing to accept the irrational as true?

4. Could anything be omitted without damage to the story? Would the story be better if the author had quoted authorities to make the idea of reincarnation more plausible?

5. Is Laura's estimate of her own character correct, or is she really bad?

You Could Look It Up[1]

JAMES THURBER

IT ALL BEGUN when we dropped down to C'lumbus, Ohio, from Pittsburgh to play a exhibition game on our way out to St. Louis. It was gettin' on into September, and though we'd been leadin' the league by six, seven games most of the season, we was now in

[1] From the *Saturday Evening Post*, CCXIII (April 5, 1941), No. 40 (copyright by James Thurber). Reprinted by permission of the author and the *Saturday Evening Post*.

first place by a margin you could 'a' got it into the eye of a thimble, bein' only half a game ahead of St. Louis. Our slump had given the boys the leapin' jumps, and they was like a bunch a old ladies at a lawn fete with a thunderstorm comin' up, runnin' around snarlin' at each other, eatin' bad and sleepin' worse, and battin' for a team average of maybe .186. Half the time nobody'd speak to nobody else, without it was to bawl 'em out.

Squawks Magrew was managin' the boys at the time, and he was darn near crazy. They called him "Squawks" 'cause when things was goin' bad he lost his voice, or perty near lost it, and squealed at you like a little girl you stepped on her doll or somethin'. He yelled at everybody and wouldn't listen to nobody, without maybe it was me. I'd been trainin' the boys for ten year, and he'd take more lip from me than from anybody else. He knowed I was smarter'n him, anyways, like you're goin' to hear.

This was thirty, thirty-one year ago; you could look it up, 'cause it was the same year C'lumbus decided to call itself the Arch City, on account of a lot of iron arches with electric-light bulbs into 'em which stretched acrost High Street. Thomas Albert Edison sent 'em a telegram, and they was speeches and maybe even President Taft opened the celebration by pushin' a button. It was a great week for the Buckeye capital, which was why they got us out there for this exhibition game.

Well, we just lose a double-header to Pittsburgh, 11 to 5 and 7 to 3, so we snarled all the way to C'lumbus, where we put up at the Chittaden Hotel, still snarlin'. Everybody was tetchy, and when Billy Klinger took a sock at Whitey Cott at breakfast, Whitey threwed marmalade all over his face.

"Blind each other, whatta I care?" says Magrew. "You can't see nothin' anyways."

C'lumbus win the exhibition game, 3 to 2, whilst Magrew set in the dugout, mutterin' and cursin' like a fourteen-year-old Scotty. He bad-mouthed everybody on the ball club and he bad-mouthed everybody offa the ball club, includin' the Wright brothers, who, he claimed, had yet to build a airship big enough for any of our boys to hit it with a ball bat.

"I wisht I was dead," he says to me. "I wisht I was in heaven with the angels."

I told him to pull hisself together, 'cause he was drivin' the boys crazy, the way he was goin' on, sulkin' and bad-mouthin' and whinin'. I was older'n he was and smarter'n he was, and he knowed it. I was ten times smarter'n he was about this Pearl du Monville, first time I ever laid eyes on the little guy, which was one of the saddest days of my life.

Now, most people name of Pearl is girls, but this Pearl du Monville was a man, if you could call a fella a man who was only thirty-four, thirty-five inches high. Pearl du Monville was a midget. He was part French and part Hungarian, and maybe even part Bulgarian or somethin'. I can see him now, a sneer on his little pushed-in pan, swingin' a bamboo cane and smokin' a big cigar. He had a gray suit with a big black check into it, and he had a gray felt hat with one of them rainbow-colored hatbands onto it, like the young fellas wore in them days. He talked like he was talkin' into a tin can, but he didn't have no foreign accent. He might 'a' been fifteen or he might 'a' been a hundred, you couldn't tell. Pearl du Monville.

After the game with C'lumbus, Magrew headed straight for the Chittaden bar—the train for St. Louis wasn't goin' for three, four hours—and there he set, drinkin' rye and talkin' to this bartender.

"How I pity me, brother," Magrew was tellin' this bartender. "How I pity me." That was alwuz his favorite tune. So he was settin' there, tellin' this bartender how heartbreakin' it was to be manager of a bunch a blindfolded circus clowns, when up pops this Pearl du Monville outa nowheres.

It gave Magrew the leapin' jumps. He thought at first maybe the D.T.'s had come back on him; he claimed he'd had 'em once, and little guys had popped up all around him, wearin' red, white, and blue hats.

"Go on, now!" Magrew yells. "Get away from me!"

But the midget clumb up on a chair acrost the table from Magrew and says, "I seen that game today, Junior, and you ain't got no ball club. What you got there, Junior," he says, "is a side show."

"Whatta ya mean, 'Junior'?" says Magrew, touchin' the little guy to satisfy hisself he was real.

"Don't pay him no attention, mister," says the bartender. "Pearl calls everybody 'Junior,' 'cause it alwuz turns out he's a year older'n anybody else."

"Yeh?" says Magrew. "How old is he?"

"How old are you, Junior?" says the midget.

"Who, me? I'm fifty-three," says Magrew.

"Well, I'm fifty-four," says the midget.

Magrew grins and asts him what he'll have, and that was the beginnin' of their beautiful friendship, if you don't care what you say.

Pearl du Monville stood up on his chair and waved his cane around and pretended like he was ballyhooin' for a circus. "Right this way, folks!" he yells. "Come on in and see the greatest collection of freaks in the world! See the armless pitchers, see the eyeless batters, see the infielders with five thumbs!" and on and on like that, feedin' Magrew gall and handin' him a laugh at the same time, you might say.

You could hear him and Pearl du Monville hootin' and hollerin' and singin' way up to the fourth floor of the Chittaden, where the boys was packin' up. When it come time to go to the station, you can imagine how disgusted we was when we crowded into the doorway of that bar and seen them two singin' and goin' on.

"Well, well, well," says Magrew, lookin' up and spottin' us. "Look who's here. . . . Clowns, this is Pearl du Monville, a monseer of the old, old school. . . . Don't shake hands with 'em, Pearl, 'cause their fingers is made of chalk and would bust right off in your paws," he says, and he starts guffawin' and Pearl starts titterin' and we stand there givin' 'em the iron eye, it bein' the lowest ebb a ballclub manager'd got hisself down to since the national pastime was started.

Then the midget begun givin' us the bally-

hoo. "Come on in!" he says, wavin' his cane. "See the legless base runners, see the outfielders with the butter fingers, see the southpaw with the arm of a little chee-ild!"

Then him and Magrew begun to hoop and holler and nudge each other till you'd of thought this little guy was the funniest guy than even Charlie Chaplin. The fellas filed outa the bar without a word and went on up to the Union Depot, leavin' me to handle Magrew and his new-found crony.

Well, I got 'em outa there finely. I had to take the little guy along, 'cause Magrew had a holt onto him like a vise and I couldn't pry him loose.

"He's comin' along as masket," says Magrew, holdin' the midget in the crouch of his arm like a football. And come along he did, hollerin' and protestin' and beatin' at Magrew with his little fists.

"Cut it out, will ya, Junior?" the little guy kept whinin'. "Come on, leave a man loose, will ya, Junior?"

But Junior kept a holt onto him and begun yellin', "See the guys with the glass arm, see the guys with the cast-iron brains, see the fielders with the feet on their wrists!"

So it goes, right through the whole Union Depot, with people starin' and catcallin', and he don't put the midget down till he gets him through the gates.

"How'm I goin' to go along without no toothbrush?" the midget asts. "What'm I goin' to do without no other suit?" he says.

"Doc here," says Magrew, meanin' me— "doc here will look after you like you was his own son, won't you, doc?"

I give him the iron eye, and he finely got on the train and prob'ly went to sleep with his clothes on.

This left me alone with the midget. "Lookit," I says to him. "Why don't you go on home now? Come mornin', Magrew'll forget all about you. He'll prob'ly think you was somethin' he seen in a nightmare maybe. And he ain't goin' to laugh so easy in the mornin', neither," I says. "So why don't you go on home?"

"Nix," he says to me. "Skiddoo," he says, "twenty-three for you," and he tosses his cane up into the vestibule of the coach and clam'ers on up after it like a cat. So that's the way Pearl du Monville come to go to St. Louis with the ball club.

I seen 'em first at breakfast the next day, settin' opposite each other; the midget playin' "Turkey in the Straw" on a harmonium and Magrew starin' at his eggs and bacon like they was a uncooked bird with its feathers still on.

"Remember where you found this?" I says, jerkin' my thumb at the midget. "Or maybe you think they come with breakfast on these trains," I says, bein' a good hand at turnin' a sharp remark in them days.

The midget puts down the harmonium and turns on me. "Sneeze," he says; "your brains is dusty." Then he snaps a couple drops of water at me from a tumbler. "Drown," he says, tryin' to make his voice deep.

Now, both them cracks is Civil War cracks, but you'd of thought they was brand new and the funniest than any crack Magrew'd ever heard in his whole life. He started hoopin' and hollerin', and the midget started hoopin' and hollerin', so I walked on away and set down with Bugs Courtney and Hank Metters, payin' no attention to this weak-minded Damon and Phidias acrost the aisle.

Well, sir, the first game with St. Louis was rained out, and there we was facin' a double-header next day. Like maybe I told you, we lose the last three double-headers we play, makin' maybe twenty-five errors in the six games, which is all right for the intimates of a school for the blind, but is disgraceful for the world's champions. It was too wet to go to the zoo, and Magrew wouldn't let us go to the movies, 'cause they flickered so bad in them days. So we just set around, stewin' and frettin'.

One of the newspaper boys come over to take a picture of Billy Klinger and Whitey Cott shakin' hands—this reporter'd heard about the fight—and whilst they was standin' there, toe to toe, shakin' hands, Billy give a back lunge and a jerk, and throwed Whitey over his shoulder into a corner of the room, like a sack a salt. Whitey come back at him with a chair, and Bethlehem broke loose in that there room. The camera was tromped to pieces like a berry basket. When we finely got 'em pulled apart, I heard a laugh, and there was Magrew and the midget standin' in the door and givin' us the iron eye.

"Wrasslers," says Magrew, cold-like, "that's what I got for a ball club, Mr. Du Monville, wrasslers—and not very good wrasslers at that, you ast me."

"A man can't be good at everythin'," says Pearl, "but he oughta be good at somethin'."

This set Magrew guffawin' again, and away they go, the midget taggin' along by his side like a hound dog and handin' him a fast line of so-called comic cracks.

When we went out to face that battlin' St. Louis club in a double-header the next afternoon, the boys was jumpy as tin toys with keys in their back. We lose the first game, 7 to 2, and are trailin', 4 to 0, when the second game ain't but ten minutes old. Magrew set there like a stone statue, speakin' to nobody. Then, in their half a the fourth, somebody singled to center and knocked in two more runs for St. Louis.

That made Magrew squawk. "I wisht one thing," he says. "I wisht I was manager of a old ladies' sewin' circus 'stead of a ball club."

"You are, Junior, you are," says a familyer and disagreeable voice.

It was that Pearl du Monville again, poppin' up outa nowheres, swingin' his bamboo cane and smokin' a cigar that's three sizes too big for his face. By this time we'd finely got the other side out, and Hank Metters slithered a bat acrost the ground, and the midget had to jump to keep both his ankles from bein' broke.

I thought Magrew'd bust a blood vessel. "You hurt Pearl and I'll break your neck!" he yelled.

Hank muttered somethin' and went on up to the plate and struck out.

We managed to get a couple runs acrost in

our half a the sixth, but they come back with three more in their half a the seventh, and this was too much for Magrew.

"Come on, Pearl," he says. "We're gettin' outa here."

"Where you think you're goin'?" I ast him.

"To the lawyer's again," he says cryptly.

"I didn't know you'd been to the lawyer's once, yet," I says.

"Which that goes to show how much you don't know," he says.

With that, they was gone, and I didn't see 'em the rest of the day, nor know what they was up to, which was a God's blessin'. We lose the nightcap, 9 to 3, and that puts us into second place plenty, and as low in our mind as a ball club can get.

The next day was a horrible day, like anybody that lived through it can tell you. Practice was just over and the St. Louis club was takin' the field, when I hears this strange sound from the stands. It sounds like the nervous whickerin' a horse gives when he smells somethin' funny on the wind. It was the fans ketchin' sight of Pearl du Monville, like you have prob'ly guessed. The midget had popped up onto the field all dressed up in a minacher club uniform, sox, cap, little letters sewed onto his chest, and all. He was swingin' a kid's bat and the only thing kept him from lookin' like a real ballplayer seen through the wrong end of a microscope was this cigar he was smokin'.

Bugs Courtney reached over and jerked it outa his mouth and throwed it away. "You're wearin' that suit on the playin' field," he says to him, severe as a judge. "You go insultin' it and I'll take you out to the zoo and feed you to the bears."

Pearl just blowed some smoke at him which he still has in his mouth.

Whilst Whitey was foulin' off four or five prior to strikin' out, I went on over to Magrew. "If I was as comic as you," I says, "I'd laugh myself to death," I says. "Is that any way to treat the uniform, makin' a mockery out of it?"

"It might surprise you to know I ain't makin' no mockery outa the uniform," says Magrew. "Pearl du Monville here has been made a bone-of-fida member of this so-called ball club. I fixed it up with the front office by long-distance phone."

"Yeh?" I says. "I can just hear Mr. Dillworth or Bart Jenkins agreein' to hire a midget for the ball club. I can just hear 'em." Mr. Dillworth was the owner of the club and Bart Jenkins was the secretary, and they never stood for no monkey business. "May I be so bold as to inquire," I says, "just what you told 'em?"

"I told 'em," he says, "I wanted to sign up a guy they ain't no pitcher in the league can strike him out."

"Uh-huh," I says, "and did you tell 'em what size of a man he is?"

"Never mind about that," he says. "I got papers on me, made out legal and proper, constitutin' one Pearl du Monville a bone-of-fida member of this former ball club. Maybe that'll shame them big babies into gettin' in there and swingin', knowin' I can replace any one of 'em with a midget, if I have a mind to. A St. Louis lawyer I seen twice tells me it's all legal and proper."

"A St. Louis lawyer would," I says, "seein' nothin' could make him happier than havin' you makin' a mockery outa this one-time baseball outfit," I says.

Well, sir, it'll all be there in the papers of thirty, thirty-one year ago, and you could look it up. The game went along without no scorin' for seven innings, and since they ain't nothin' much to watch but guys poppin' up or strikin' out, the fans pay most of their attention to the goin's-on of Pearl du Monville. He's out there in front a the dugout, turnin' handsprings, balancin' his bat on his chin, walkin' a imaginary line, and so on. The fans clapped and laughed at him, and he ate it up.

So it went up to the last a the eighth, nothin' to nothin', not more'n seven, eight hits all told, and no errors on neither side. Our pitcher gets the first two men out easy in the eighth. Then up come a fella name of Porter or Billings, or some such name, and he lammed one up against the tobacco sign for three bases. The next guy up slapped the first ball out into left for a base hit, and in come the fella from third for the only run of the ball game so far. The crowd yelled, the look a death come onto Magrew's face again, and even the midget quit his tomfoolin'. Their next man fouled out back a third, and we come up for our last bats like a bunch a schoolgirls steppin' into a pool of cold water. I was lower in my mind than I'd been since the day in Nineteen-four when Chesbro throwed the wild pitch in the ninth inning with a man on third and lost the pennant for the Highlanders. I knowed something just as bad was goin' to happen, which shows I'm a clairvoyun, or was then.

When Gordy Mills hit out to second, I just closed my eyes. I opened 'em up again to see Dutch Muller standin' on second, dustin' off his pants, him havin' got his first hit in maybe twenty times to the plate. Next up was Harry Loesing, battin' for our pitcher, and he got a base on balls, walkin' on a fourth one you could 'a' combed your hair with.

Then up come Whitey Cott, our lead-off man. He crotches down in what was prob'ly the most fearsome stanch in organized ball, but all he can do is pop out to short. That brung up Billy Klinger, with two down and a man on first and second. Billy took a cut at one you could 'a' knocked a plug hat offa this here Carnera with it, but then he gets sense enough to wait 'em out, and finely he walks, too, fillin' the bases.

Yes, sir, there you are; the tyin' run on third and the winnin' run on second, first a the ninth, two men down, and Hank Metters comin' to the bat. Hank was built like a Pope-Hartford and he couldn't run no faster'n President Taft, but he had five home runs to his credit for the season, and that wasn't bad in them days. Hank was still hittin' better'n anybody else on the ball club, and it was mighty heartenin', seein' him stridin' up towards the plate. But he never got there.

"Wait a minute!" yells Magrew, jumpin' to his feet. "I'm sendin' in a pinch hitter!" he yells.

You could 'a' heard a bomb drop. When a ball-club manager says he's sendin' in a pinch hitter for the best batter on the club, you know and I know and everybody knows he's lost his holt.

"They're goin' to be sendin' the funny wagon for you, if you don't watch out," I says, grabbin' a holt of his arm.

But he pulled away and run out towards the plate, yellin', "Du Monville battin' for Metters!"

All the fellas begun squawlin' at once, except Hank, and he just stood there starin' at Magrew like he'd gone crazy and was claimin' to be Ty Cobb's grandma or somethin'. Their pitcher stood out there with his hands on his hips and a disagreeable look on his face, and the plate umpire told Magrew to go on and get a batter up. Magrew told him again Du Monville was battin' for Metters, and the St. Louis manager finely got the idea. It brung him outa his dugout, howlin' and bawlin' like he'd lost a female dog and her seven pups.

Magrew pushed the midget towards the plate and he says to him, he says, "Just stand up there and hold that bat on your shoulder. They ain't a man in the world can throw three strikes in there 'fore he throws four balls!" he says.

"I get it, Junior!" says the midget. "He'll walk me and force in the tyin' run!" And he starts on up to the plate as cocky as if he was Willie Keeler.

I don't need to tell you Bethlehem broke loose on that there ball field. The fans got onto their hind legs, yellin' and whistlin', and everybody on the field begun wavin' their arms and hollerin' and shovin'. The plate umpire stalked over to Magrew like a traffic cop, waggin' his jaw and pointin' his finger, and the St. Louis manager kept yellin' like his house was on fire. When Pearl got up to the plate and stood there, the pitcher slammed his glove down onto the ground and started stompin' on it, and they ain't nobody can blame him. He's just walked two normal-sized human bein's, and now here's a guy up to the plate they ain't more'n twenty inches between his knees and his shoulders.

The plate umpire called in the field umpire, and they talked a while, like a couple doctors seein' the bucolic plague or somethin' for the first time. Then the plate umpire come over to Magrew with his arms folded acrost his chest, and he told him to go on and get a batter up, or he'd forfeit the game to St. Louis. He pulled out his watch, but somebody batted it outa his hand in the scufflin', and I thought there'd be a free-for-all, with everybody yellin' and shovin' except Pearl du Monville, who stood up at the plate with his little bat on his shoulder, not movin' a muscle.

Then Magrew played his ace. I seen him pull some papers outa his pocket and show 'em to the plate umpire. The umpire begun lookin' at 'em like they was bills for somethin' he not only never bought it, he never even heard of it. The other umpire studied 'em like they was a death warren, and all this time the St. Louis manager and the fans and the players is yellin' and hollerin'.

Well, sir, they fought about him bein' a midget, and they fought about him usin' a kid's bat, and they fought about where'd he been all season. They was eight or nine rule books brung out and everybody was thumbin' through 'em, tryin' to find out what it says about midgets, but it don't say nothin' about midgets, 'cause this was somethin' never'd come up in the history of the game before, and nobody'd ever dreamed about it, even when they has nightmares. Maybe you can't send no midgets in to bat nowadays, 'cause the old game's changed a lot, mostly for the worst, but you could then, it turned out.

The plate umpire finely decided the contrack papers was all legal and proper, like Magrew said, so he waved the St. Louis players back to their places and he pointed his finger at their manager and told him to quit hollerin' and get on back in the dugout. The manager says the game is percedin' under protest, and the umpire bawls, "Play ball!" over 'n' above the yellin' and booin', him havin' a voice like a hog-caller.

The St. Louis pitcher picked up his glove and beat at it with his fist six or eight times, and then got set on the mound and studied the situation. The fans realized he was really goin' to pitch to the midget, and they went crazy, hoopin' and hollerin' louder'n ever, and throwin' pop bottles and hats and cushions down onto the field. It took five, ten minutes to get the fans quieted down again, whilst our fellas that was on base sat down on the bags and waited. And Pearl du Monville kept standin' up there with the bat on his shoulder, like he'd been told to.

So the pitcher starts studyin' the setup again, and you got to admit it was the strangest setup in a ball game since the players cut off their beards and begun wearin' gloves. I wisht I could call the pitcher's name—it wasn't old Barney Pelty nor Nig Jack Powell nor Harry Howell. He was a big right-hander, but I can't call his name. You could look it up. Even in a crotchin' position, the ketcher towers over the midget like the Washington Monument.

The plate umpire tries standin' on his tip-toes, then he tries crotchin' down, and he finely gets hisself into a stanch nobody'd ever seen on a ball field before, kinda squattin' down on his hanches.

Well, the pitcher is sore as a old buggy horse in fly time. He slams in the first pitch, hard and wild, and maybe two foot higher 'n the midget's head.

"Ball one!" hollers the umpire over 'n' above the racket, 'cause everybody is yellin' worsten ever.

The ketcher goes on out towards the mound and talks to the pitcher and hands him the ball. This time the big right-hander tries a undershoot, and it comes in a little closer, maybe no higher'n a foot, foot and a half above Pearl's head. It would 'a' been a strike with a human bein' in there, but the umpire's got to call it, and he does.

"Ball two!" he bellers.

The ketcher walks on out to the mound again, and the whole infield comes over and gives advice to the pitcher about what they'd do in a case like this, with two balls and no strikes on a batter that oughta be in a bottle of alcohol 'stead of up there at the plate in a big-league game between the teams that is fightin' for first place.

For the third pitch, the pitcher stands there flat-footed and tosses up the ball like he's playin' ketch with a little girl.

Pearl stands there motionless as a hitchin' post, and the ball comes in big and slow and high—high for Pearl, that is, it bein' about on a level with his eyes, or a little higher'n a grown man's knees.

They ain't nothin' else for the umpire to do, so he calls, "Ball three!"

Everybody is onto their feet, hoopin' and hollerin', as the pitcher sets to throw ball four. The St. Louis manager is makin' signs and faces like he was a contorturer, and the infield is givin' the pitcher some more advice about what to do this time. Our boys who was on base stick right onto the bag, runnin' no risk of bein' nipped for the last out.

Well, the pitcher decides to give him a toss again, seein' he come closer with that than with a fast ball. They ain't nobody ever seen a slower ball throwed. It come in big as a balloon and slower'n any ball ever throwed before in the major leagues. It come right in over the plate in front of Pearl's chest, lookin' prob'ly big as a full moon to Pearl. They ain't never been a minute like the minute that followed since the United States was founded by the Pilgrim grandfathers.

Pearl du Monville took a cut at that ball, and he hit it! Magrew give a groan like a poleaxed steer as the ball rolls out in front a the plate into fair territory.

"Fair ball!" yells the umpire, and the midget starts runnin' for first, still carryin' that little bat, and makin' maybe ninety foot an hour. Bethlehem breaks loose on that ball field and in them stands. They ain't never been nothin' like it since creation was begun.

The ball's rollin' slow, on down towards third, goin' maybe eight, ten foot. The infield comes in fast and our boys break from their bases like hares in a brush fire. Everybody is standin' up, yellin' and hollerin', and Magrew is tearin' his hair outa his head, and the midget is scamperin' for first with all the speed of one of them little dashhounds carryin' a satchel in his mouth.

The ketcher gets to the ball first, but he boots it on out past the pitcher's box, the pitcher fallin' on his face tryin' to stop it, the shortstop sprawlin' after it full length and zaggin' it on over towards the second baseman, whilst Muller is scorin' with the tyin' run and Loesing is roundin' third with the winnin' run. Ty Cobb could 'a' made a three-bagger outa that bunt, with everybody fallin' over theirself tryin' to pick the ball up. But Pearl is still maybe fifteen, twenty feet from the bag, toddlin' like a baby and yeepin' like a trapped rabbit, when the second baseman finely gets a holt of that ball and slams it over to first. The first baseman ketches it and stomps on the bag, the base umpire waves Pearl out, and there goes your old ball game, the craziest ball game ever played in the history of the organized world.

Their players start runnin' in, and then I see Magrew. He starts after Pearl, runnin' faster'n any man ever run before. Pearl sees him comin' and runs behind the base umpire's legs and gets a holt onto 'em. Magrew comes up, pantin' and roarin', and him and the midget plays ring-around-a-rosy with the umpire, who keeps shovin' at Magrew with one hand and tryin' to slap the midget loose from his legs with the other.

Finely Magrew ketches the midget, who is still yeepin' like a stuck sheep. He gets holt of that little guy by both his ankles and starts whirlin' him round and round his head like Magrew was a hammer thrower and Pearl was the hammer. Nobody can stop him without gettin' their head knocked off, so everybody just stands there and yells. Then Magrew lets the midget fly. He flies on out towards second, high and fast, like a human home run, headed for the soap sign in center field.

Their shortstop tries to get to him, but he can't make it, and I knowed the little fella was goin' to bust to pieces like a dollar watch on a asphalt street when he hit the ground. But it so happens their center fielder is just crossin' second, and he starts runnin' back, tryin' to get under the midget, who had took to spiralin' like a football 'stead of turnin' head over foot, which give him more speed and more distance.

I know you never seen a midget ketched, and you prob'ly never even seen one throwed. To ketch a midget that's been throwed by a heavy-muscled man and is flyin' through the air, you got to run under him and with him and pull your hands and arms back and down when you ketch him, to break the compact of his body, or you'll bust him in two like a matchstick. I seen Bill Lange and Willie Keeler and Tris Speaker make some wonderful ketches in my day, but I never seen nothin' like that center fielder. He goes back and back and still further back and he pulls that midget down outa the air like he was liftin' a sleepin' baby from a cradle. They wasn't a bruise onto him, only his face was the color of cat's meat and he ain't got no air in his chest. In his excitement, the base umpire, who was runnin' back with the center fielder when he ketched Pearl, yells, "Out!" and that give hysteries to the Bethlehem which was ragin' like Niagry on that ball field.

Everybody was hoopin' and hollerin' and yellin' and runnin', with the fans swarmin' onto the field, and the cops tryin' to keep order, and some guys laughin' and some of the women fans cryin', and six or eight of us holdin' onto Magrew to keep him from gettin' at that midget and finishin' him off. Some of the fans picks up the St. Louis pitcher and the center fielder, and starts carryin' 'em around on their shoulders, and they was the craziest goin's-on knowed to the history of organized ball on this side of the 'Lantic Ocean.

I seen Pearl du Monville strugglin' in the arms of a lady fan with a ample bosom, who was laughin' and cryin' at the same time, and him beatin' at her with his little fists and bawlin' and yellin'. He clawed his way loose finely and disappeared in the forest of legs which made that ball field look like it was Coney Island on a hot summer's day.

That was the last I ever seen of Pearl du Monville. I never seen hide nor hair of him from that day to this, and neither did nobody else. He just vanished into the thin of the air, as the fella says. He was ketched for the final out of the ball game and that was the end of him, just like it was the end of the ball game, you might say, and also the end of our losin' streak, like I'm goin' to tell you.

That night we piled onto a train for Chicago, but we wasn't snarlin' and snappin' any more. No, sir, the ice was finely broke and a new spirit come into that ball club. The old zip come back with the disappearance of Pearl du Monville out back a second base. We got to laughin' and talkin' and kiddin' together, and 'fore long Magrew was laughin' with us. He got a human look onto his pan again, and he quit whinin' and complainin' and wishtin' he was in heaven with the angels.

Well, sir, we wiped up that Chicago series, winnin' all four games, and makin' seventeen hits in one of 'em. Funny thing was, St. Louis was so shook up by that last game with us, they never did hit their stride again. Their center fielder took to misjudgin' everything that come his way, and the rest a the fellas followed suit, the way a club'll do when one guy blows up.

'Fore we left Chicago, I and some of the fellas went out and bought a pair of them little baby shoes, which we had 'em golded over and give 'em to Magrew for a souvenir, and he took it all in good spirit. Whitey Cott and Billy Klinger made up and was fast friends again, and we hit our home lot like a ton of dynamite, and they was nothin' could stop us from then on.

I don't recollect things as clear as I did thirty, forty year ago. I can't read no fine print no more, and the only person I got to check with on the golden days of the national pastime, as the fella says, is my friend, old Milt Kline, over in Springfield, and his mind ain't as strong as it once was.

He gets Rube Waddell mixed up with Rube Marquard, for one thing, and anybody does that oughta be put away where he won't bother nobody. So I can't tell you the exact margin we win the pennant by. Maybe it was two and a half games, or maybe it was three and a half. But it'll all be there in the newspapers and record books of thirty, thirty-one year ago and, like I was sayin', you could look it up.

SUGGESTIONS FOR STUDY

1. This story is of course implausible. It belongs to the same *genre* as Mark Twain's "Baker's Blue-Jay Yarn." As you read it, do you have any intense desire to question the plausibility of the incidents? On what elements does the author depend to give it the illusion of plausibility?

2. Who is the protagonist and who the antagonist? Or is the conflict between forces rather than persons? If you say the latter, name them.

3. What is the author's purpose in giving the story the title he does?

4. Give a character sketch of the narrator. Would the story gain or lose in interest if it were narrated by a sophisticated sports writer or by the author, assuming an omniscient point of view and writing in good English?

5. Are the characters well delineated, or are they simply pegs on which to hang the action?

6. Are there any elements of the story that could be omitted without in any way detracting from it?

7. What is the purpose of the last two paragraphs? Would the story be better if they were omitted?

A New England Nun

MARY WILKINS FREEMAN

IT WAS LATE in the afternoon, and the light was waning. There was a difference in the look of the tree shadows out in the yard. Somewhere in the distance cows were lowing and a little bell was tinkling; now and then a farm-wagon tilted by, and the dust flew; some blue-shirted laborers with shovels over their shoulders plodded past; little swarms of flies were dancing up and down before the people's faces in the soft air. There seemed to be a gentle stir arising over everything for the mere sake of subsidence—a very premonition of rest and hush and night.

This soft diurnal commotion was over Louisa Ellis also. She had been peacefully sewing at her sitting-room window all the afternoon. Now she quilted her needle carefully into her work, which she folded precisely, and laid in a basket with her thimble and thread and scissors. Louisa Ellis could not remember that ever in her life she had mislaid one of these little feminine appurtenances, which had become, from long use and constant association, a very part of her personality.

Louisa tied a green apron round her waist, and got out a flat straw hat with a green ribbon. Then she went into the garden with a little blue crockery bowl, to pick some currants for her tea. After the currants were picked she sat on the back door-step and stemmed them, collecting the stems carefully in her apron, and afterward throwing them into the hen-coop. She looked sharply at the grass beside the step to see if any had fallen there.

Louisa was slow and still in her movements; it took her a long time to prepare her tea; but when ready it was set forth with as much grace as if she had been a veritable guest to her own self. The little square table stood exactly in the centre of the kitchen, and was covered with a starched linen cloth whose border pattern of flowers glistened. Louisa had a damask napkin on her tea-tray, where were arranged a cut-glass tumbler full of teaspoons, a silver cream-pitcher, a china sugar-bowl, and one pink china cup and saucer. Louisa used china every day—something which none of her neighbors did. They whispered about it among themselves. Their daily tables were laid with common crockery, their sets of best china stayed in the parlor closet, and Louisa Ellis was no richer nor better bred than they. Still she would use the china. She had for her supper a glass dish full of sugared currants, a plate of little cakes, and one of light white biscuits. Also a leaf or two of lettuce, which she cut up daintily. Louisa was very fond of lettuce, which she raised to perfection in her little garden. She ate quite heartily, though in a delicate, pecking way; it seemed almost surprising that any considerable bulk of food should vanish.

After tea she filled a plate with nicely baked thin corn-cakes, and carried them out into the back-yard.

"Cæsar!" she called. "Cæsar! Cæsar!"

There was a little rush, and the clank of a chain, and a large yellow-and-white dog appeared at the door of his tiny hut, which was half hidden among the tall grasses and flowers. Louisa patted him and gave him the corn-cakes. Then she returned to the house and washed the tea-things, polishing the china carefully. The twilight had deepened; the chorus of the frogs floated in at the open window wonderfully loud and shrill, and once in a while a long sharp drone from a tree-toad pierced it. Louisa took off her green gingham apron, disclosing a shorter one of pink-and-white print. She lighted her lamp, and sat down again with her sewing.

In about half an hour Joe Dagget came. She heard his heavy step on the walk, and rose and took off her pink-and-white apron. Under that was still another—white linen with a little cambric edging on the bottom; that was Louisa's company apron. She never wore it without her calico sewing-apron over it unless she had a guest. She had barely folded the pink-and-white one with methodical haste and laid it in a table-drawer when the door opened and Joe Dagget entered.

He seemed to fill up the whole room. A little yellow canary that had been asleep in his green cage at the south window woke up and fluttered wildly, beating his little yellow wings against the wires. He always did so when Joe Dagget came into the room.

"Good-evening," said Louisa. She extended her hand with a kind of solemn cordiality.

"Good-evening, Louisa," returned the man, in a loud voice.

She placed a chair for him, and they sat facing each other, with the table between them. He sat bolt-upright, toeing out his heavy feet squarely, glancing with a good-humored uneasiness around the room. She sat gently erect, folding her slender hands in her white-linen lap.

"Been a pleasant day," remarked Dagget.

"Real pleasant," Louisa assented, softly. "Have you been haying?" she asked, after a little while.

"Yes, I've been haying all day, down in the ten-acre lot. Pretty hot work."

"It must be."

"Yes, it's pretty hot work in the sun."

"Is your mother well to-day?"

"Yes, mother's pretty well."

"I suppose Lily Dyer's with her now?"

Dagget colored. "Yes, she's with her," he answered, slowly.

He was not very young, but there was a boyish look about his large face. Louisa was not quite as old as he, her face was fairer and smoother, but she gave people the impression of being older.

"I suppose she's a good deal of help to your mother," she said, further.

"I guess she is; I don't know how mother 'd get along without her," said Dagget, with a sort of embarrassed warmth.

"She looks like a real capable girl. She's pretty-looking too," remarked Louisa.

"Yes, she is pretty fair-looking."

Presently Dagget began fingering the books on the table. There was a square red autograph album, and a Young Lady's Gift-Book which had belonged to Louisa's mother. He took them up one after the other and opened them; then laid them down again, the album on the Gift-Book.

Louisa kept eying them with mild uneasiness. Finally she rose and changed the position of the books, putting the album underneath. That was the way they had been arranged in the first place.

Dagget gave an awkward little laugh. "Now what difference did it make which book was on top?" said he.

Louisa looked at him with a deprecating smile. "I always keep them that way," murmured she.

"You do beat everything," said Dagget, trying to laugh again. His large face was flushed.

He remained about an hour longer, then rose to take leave. Going out, he stumbled over a rug, and, trying to recover himself, hit Louisa's work-basket on the table, and knocked it on the floor.

He looked at Louisa, then at the rolling spools; he ducked himself awkwardly toward them, but she stopped him. "Never mind," said she; "I'll pick them up after you're gone."

She spoke with a mild stiffness. Either she was a little disturbed, or his nervousness affected her, and made her seem constrained in her effort to reassure him.

When Joe Dagget was outside he drew in the sweet evening air with a sigh, and felt much as an innocent and perfectly well-intentioned bear might after his exit from a china shop.

Louisa, on her part, felt much as the kind-hearted, long-suffering owner of the china shop might have done after the exit of the bear.

She tied on the pink, then the green apron, picked up all the scattered treasures and replaced them in her work-basket, and straightened the rug. Then she set the lamp on the floor, and began sharply examining the carpet. She even rubbed her fingers over it, and looked at them.

"He's tracked in a good deal of dust," she murmured. "I thought he must have."

Louisa got a dust-pan and brush, and swept Joe Dagget's track carefully.

If he could have known it, it would have increased his perplexity and uneasiness, although it would not have disturbed his loyalty in the least. He came twice a week to see Louisa Ellis, and every time, sitting there in her delicately sweet room, he felt as if surrounded by a hedge of lace. He was afraid to stir lest he should put a clumsy foot or hand through the fairy web, and he had always the consciousness that Louisa was watching fearfully lest he should.

Still the lace and Louisa commanded perforce his perfect respect and patience and loyalty. They were to be married in a month, after a singular courtship which had lasted for a matter of fifteen years. For fourteen out of the fifteen years the two had not once seen each other, and they had seldom exchanged letters. Joe had been all those years in Australia, where he had gone to make his fortune, and where he had stayed until he made it. He would have stayed fifty years if it had taken so long, and come home feeble and tottering, or never come home at all, to marry Louisa.

But the fortune had been made in the fourteen years, and he had come home now to marry the woman who had been patiently and unquestioningly waiting for him all that time.

Shortly after they were engaged he had announced to Louisa his determination to strike out into new fields, and secure a competency before they should be married. She had listened and assented with the sweet serenity which never failed her, not even when her lover set forth on that long and uncertain journey. Joe, buoyed up as he was by his sturdy determination, broke down a little at the last, but Louisa kissed him with a mild blush, and said good-bye.

"It won't be for long," poor Joe had said, huskily; but it was for fourteen years.

In that length of time much had happened. Louisa's mother and brother had died, and she was all alone in the world. But greatest happening of all—a subtle happening which both were too simple to understand— Louisa's feet had turned into a path, smooth maybe under a calm, serene sky, but so straight and unswerving that it could only meet a check at her grave, and so narrow that there was no room for any one at her side.

Louisa's first emotion when Joe Dagget came home (he had not apprised her of his coming) was consternation, although she would not admit it to herself, and he never dreamed of it. Fifteen years ago she had been in love with him—at least she considered herself to be. Just at that time, gently acquiescing with and falling into the natural drift of girlhood, she had seen marriage ahead as a reasonable feature and a probable desirability of life. She had listened with calm docility to her mother's views upon the subject. Her mother was remarkable for her cool sense and sweet, even temperament. She talked wisely to her daughter when Joe Dagget presented himself, and Louisa accepted him with no hesitation. He was the first lover she had ever had.

She had been faithful to him all these years. She had never dreamed of the possibility of marrying any one else. Her life, especially for the last seven years, had been full of a pleasant peace, she had never felt discontented nor impatient over her lover's absence; still she had always looked forward to his return and their marriage as the inevitable conclusion of things. However, she had fallen into a way of placing it so far in the future that it was almost equal to placing it over the boundaries of another life.

When Joe came she had been expecting him, and expecting to be married for fourteen years, but she was as much surprised and taken aback as if she had never thought of it.

Joe's consternation came later. He eyed Louisa with an instant confirmation of his old admiration. She had changed but little. She still kept her pretty manner and soft grace, and was, he considered, every whit as attractive as ever. As for himself, his stent was done; he had turned his face away from fortune-seeking, and the old winds of romance whistled as loud and sweet as ever through his ears. All the song which he had been wont to hear in them was Louisa; he had for a long time a loyal belief that he heard it still, but finally it seemed to him that although the winds sang always that one song, it had another name. But for Louisa the wind had never more than murmured; now it had gone down, and everything was still. She listened for a little while with half-wistful attention; then she turned quietly away and went to work on her wedding-clothes.

Joe had made some extensive and quite magnificent alterations in his house. It was the old homestead; the newly married couple would live there, for Joe could not desert his mother, who refused to leave her old home. So Louisa must leave hers. Every morning, rising and going about among her neat maidenly possessions, she felt as one looking her last upon the faces of dear friends. It was true that in a measure she could take them with her, but, robbed of their old environments, they would appear in such new guises that they would almost cease to be themselves. Then there were some peculiar features of her happy solitary life which she would probably be obliged to relinquish altogether. Sterner tasks than these graceful but half-needless ones would probably devolve upon her. There would be a large house to care for; there would be company to entertain; there would be Joe's rigorous and feeble old mother to wait upon; and it would be contrary to all thrifty village traditions for her to keep more than one servant. Louisa had a little still, and she used to occupy herself pleasantly in summer weather with distilling the sweet and aromatic essences from roses and peppermint and spearmint. By-

and-by her still must be laid away. Her store of essences was already considerable, and there would be no time for her to distil for the mere pleasure of it. Then Joe's mother would think it foolishness; she had already hinted her opinion in the matter. Louisa dearly loved to sew a linen seam, not always for use, but for the simple, mild pleasure which she took in it. She would have been loath to confess how more than once she had ripped a seam for the mere delight of sewing it together again. Sitting at her window during long sweet afternoons, drawing her needle gently through the dainty fabric, she was peace itself. But there was small chance of such foolish comfort in the future. Joe's mother, domineering, shrewd old matron that she was even in her old age, and very likely even Joe himself, with his honest masculine rudeness, would laugh and frown down all these pretty but senseless old-maiden ways.

Louisa had almost the enthusiasm of an artist over the mere order and cleanliness of her solitary home. She had throbs of genuine triumph at the sight of the window-panes which she had polished until they shone like jewels. She gloated gently over her orderly bureau-drawers, with their exquisitely folded contents redolent with lavender and sweet clover and very purity. Could she be sure of the endurance of even this? She had visions, so startling that she half repudiated them as indelicate, of coarse masculine belongings strewn about in endless litter; of dust and disorder arising necessarily from a coarse masculine presence in the midst of all this delicate harmony.

Among her forebodings of disturbance, not the least was with regard to Cæsar. Cæsar was a veritable hermit of a dog. For the greater part of his life he had dwelt in his secluded hut, shut out from the society of his kind and all innocent canine joys. Never had Cæsar since his early youth watched at a woodchuck's hole; never had he known the delights of a stray bone at a neighbor's kitchen door. And it was all on account of a sin committed when hardly out of his puppy-hood. No one knew the possible depth of remorse of which this mild-visaged, altogether innocent-looking old dog might be capable; but whether or not he had encountered remorse, he had encountered a full measure of righteous retribution. Old Cæsar seldom lifted up his voice in a growl or a bark; he was fat and sleepy; there were yellow rings which looked like spectacles around his dim old eyes; but there was a neighbor who bore on his hand the imprint of several of Cæsar's sharp, white, youthful teeth, and for that he had lived at the end of a chain, all alone in a little hut, for fourteen years. The neighbor, who was choleric and smarting with the pain of his wound, had demanded either Cæsar's death or complete ostracism. So Louisa's brother, to whom the dog had belonged, had built him his little kennel and tied him up. It was now fourteen years since, in a flood of youthful spirits, he had inflicted that memorable bite, and with the exception of short excursions, always at the end of the chain, under the strict guardianship of his master or Louisa, the old dog had remained a close prisoner. It is doubtful if, with his limited ambition, he took much pride in the fact, but it is certain that he was possessed of considerable cheap fame. He was regarded by all the children in the village and by many adults as a very monster of ferocity. St. George's dragon could hardly have surpassed in evil repute Louisa Ellis's old yellow dog. Mothers charged their children with solemn emphasis not to go too near to him, and the children listened and believed greedily, with a fascinated appetite for terror, and ran by Louisa's house stealthily, with many sidelong and backward glances at the terrible dog. If perchance he sounded a hoarse bark, there was a panic. Wayfarers chancing into Louisa's yard eyed him with respect, and inquired if the chain were stout. Cæsar at large might have seemed a very ordinary dog, and excited no comment whatever; chained, his reputation overshadowed him, so that he lost his own proper outlines and looked darkly vague and enormous. Joe Dagget, however, with his good-humored sense and shrewd-ness, saw him as he was. He strode valiantly up to him and patted him on the head, in spite of Louisa's soft clamor of warning, and even attempted to set him loose. Louisa grew so alarmed that he desisted, but kept an-nouncing his opinion in the matter quite forcibly at intervals. "There ain't a better-natured dog in town," he would say, "and it's downright cruel to keep him tied up there. Some day I'm going to take him out."

Louisa had very little hope that he would not, one of these days, when their interests and possessions should be more completely fused in one. She pictured to herself Cæsar on the rampage through the quiet and un-guarded village. She saw innocent children bleeding in his path. She was herself very fond of the old dog, because he had belonged to her dead brother, and he was always very gentle with her; still she had great faith in his ferocity. She always warned people not to go too near him. She fed him on ascetic fare of corn-mush and cakes, and never fired his dangerous temper with heating and sangui-nary diet of flesh and bones. Louisa looked at the old dog munching his simple fare, and thought of her approaching marriage and trembled. Still no anticipation of disorder and confusion in lieu of sweet peace and harmony, no forebodings of Cæsar on the rampage, no wild fluttering of her little yel-low canary, were sufficient to turn her a hair's-breadth. Joe Dagget had been fond of her and working for her all these years. It was not for her, whatever came to pass, to prove untrue and break his heart. She put the exquisite little stitches into her wedding-gar-ments, and the time went on till it was only a week before her wedding-day. It was a Tuesday evening, and the wedding was to be a week from Wednesday.

There was a full moon that night. About nine o'clock Louisa strolled down the road a little way. There were harvest-fields on either hand, bordered by low stone walls. Luxuriant clumps of bushes grew beside the wall, and trees—wild cherry and old apple trees—at intervals. Presently Louisa sat down on the wall and looked about her with mildly sor-rowful reflectiveness. Tall shrubs of blue-berry and meadow-sweet, all woven together and tangled with blackberry vines and horse-briers, shut her in on either side. She had a little clear space between them. Opposite her, on the other side of the road, was a spreading tree; the moon shone between its boughs, and the leaves twinkled like silver. The road was bespread with a beautiful shift-ing dapple of silver and shadow; the air was full of a mysterious sweetness. "I wonder if it's wild grapes?" murmured Louisa. She sat there some time. She was just thinking of rising, when she heard footsteps and low voices, and remained quiet. It was a lonely place, and she felt a little timid. She thought she would keep still in the shadow and let the persons, whoever they might be, pass her.

But just before they reached her the voices ceased, and the footsteps. She understood that their owners had also found seats upon the stone wall. She was wondering if she could not steal away unobserved, when the voice broke the stillness. It was Joe Dagget's. She sat still and listened.

The voice was announced by a loud sigh, which was as familiar as itself. "Well," said Dagget, "you've made up your mind, then, I suppose?"

"Yes," returned another voice; "I'm going day after to-morrow."

"That's Lily Dyer," thought Louisa to her-self. The voice embodied itself in her mind. She saw a girl tall and full-figured, with a firm, fair face, looking fairer and firmer in the moonlight, her strong yellow hair braided in a close knot. A girl full of a calm rustic strength and bloom, with a masterful way which might have beseemed a princess. Lily Dyer was a favorite with the village folk; she had just the qualities to arouse the admira-tion. She was good and handsome and smart. Louisa had often heard her praises sounded.

"Well," said Joe Dagget, "I ain't got a word to say."

"I don't know what you could say," returned Lily Dyer.

"Not a word to say," repeated Joe, drawing out the words heavily. Then there was a silence. "I ain't sorry," he began at last, "that that happened yesterday—that we kind of let on how we felt to each other. I guess it's just as well we knew. Of course, I can't do anything any different. I'm going right on an' get married next week. I ain't going back on a woman that's waited for me fourteen years, an' break her heart."

"If you should jilt her to-morrow, I wouldn't have you," spoke up the girl, with sudden vehemence.

"Well, I ain't going to give you the chance," said he; "but I don't believe you would, either."

"You'd see I wouldn't. Honor's honor, an' right's right. An' I'd never think anything of any man that went against 'em for me or any other girl; you'd find out, Joe Dagget."

"Well, you'll find out fast enough that I ain't going against 'em for you or any other girl," returned he. Their voices sounded almost as if they were angry with each other. Louisa was listening eagerly.

"I'm sorry you feel as if you must go away," said Joe, "but I don't know but it's best."

"Of course it's best. I hope you and I have got common sense."

"Well, I suppose you're right." Suddenly Joe's voice got an undertone of tenderness. "Say, Lily," said he, "I'll get along well enough myself, but I can't bear to think— You don't suppose you're going to fret much over it?"

"I guess you'll find out I sha'n't fret much over a married man."

"Well, I hope you won't—I hope you won't, Lily. God knows I do. And—I hope—one of these days—you'll—come across somebody else—"

"I don't see any reason why I shouldn't." Suddenly her tone changed. She spoke in a sweet, clear voice, so loud that she could have been heard across the street. "No, Joe Dagget," said she, "I'll never marry any other

man as long as I live. I've got good sense, an' I ain't going to break my heart nor make a fool of myself; but I'm never going to be married, you can be sure of that. I ain't that sort of a girl to feel this way twice."

Louisa heard an exclamation and a soft commotion behind the bushes; then Lily spoke again—the voice sounded as if she had risen. "This must be put a stop to," said she. "We've stayed here long enough. I'm going home."

Louisa sat there in a daze, listening to their retreating steps. After a while she got up and slunk softly home herself. The next day she did her housework methodically; that was as much a matter of course as breathing; but she did not sew on her wedding-clothes. She sat at her window and meditated. In the evening Joe came. Louisa Ellis had never known that she had any diplomacy in her, but when she came to look for it that night she found it, although meek of its kind, among her little feminine weapons. Even now she could hardly believe that she had heard aright, and that she would not do Joe a terrible injury should she break her troth-plight. She wanted to sound him without betraying too soon her own inclinations in the matter. She did it successfully, and they finally came to an understanding; but it was a difficult thing, for he was as afraid of betraying himself as she.

She never mentioned Lily Dyer. She simply said that while she had no cause of complaint against him, she had lived so long in one way that she shrank from making a change.

"Well, I never shrank, Louisa," said Dagget. "I'm going to be honest enough to say that I think maybe it's better this way; but if you'd wanted to keep on, I'd have stuck to you till my dying day. I hope you know that."

"Yes, I do," said she.

That night she and Joe parted more tenderly than they had done for a long time. Standing in the door, holding each other's hands, a last great wave of regretful memory swept over them.

"Well, this ain't the way we've thought it was all going to end, is it, Louisa?" said Joe.

She shook her head. There was a little quiver on her placid face.

"You let me know if there's ever anything I can do for you," said he. "I ain't ever going to forget you, Louisa." Then he kissed her, and went down the path.

Louisa, all alone by herself that night, wept a little, she hardly knew why; but the next morning, on waking, she felt like a queen who, after fearing lest her domain be wrested away from her, sees it firmly insured in her possession.

Now the tall weeds and grasses might cluster around Cæsar's little hermit hut, the snow might fall on its roof year in and year out, but he never would go on a rampage through the unguarded village. Now the little canary might turn itself into a peaceful yellow ball night after night, and have no need to wake and flutter with wild terror against its bars. Louisa could sew linen seams, and distil roses, and dust and polish and fold away in lavender, as long as she listed. That afternoon she sat with her needle-work at the window, and felt fairly steeped in peace. Lily Dyer, tall and erect and blooming, went past; but she felt no qualm. If Louisa Ellis had sold her birthright she did not know it, the taste of the pottage was so delicious, and had been her sole satisfaction for so long. Serenity and placid narrowness had become to her as the birthright itself. She gazed ahead through a long reach of future days strung together like pearls in a rosary, every one like the others, and all smooth and flawless and innocent, and her heart went up in thankfulness. Outside was the fervid summer afternoon; the air was filled with the sounds of the busy harvest of men and birds and bees; there were halloos, metallic clatterings, sweet calls, and long hummings. Louisa sat, prayerfully numbering her days, like an uncloistered nun.

SUGGESTIONS FOR STUDY

1. This story stresses small details very particularly. Why is that necessary here? Study, for instance, the use of details in the opening and closing paragraphs.

2. Is this a story of plot or character? Is the change in Louisa made plausible? Is the story realistic or romantic? It was written over sixty years ago. Is it outdated? Support your answer.

3. How does the character of Lily Dyer increase the plot tension and then provide a means of resolution of that tension?

4. Study the use of mood, which is an important part of this story.

The Color of Mama Josefina's Life[1]

MARY MAIN

EVERYONE IN THE pueblo knew Mama Josefina, for she was not a woman one could easily ignore. She was so large and so very noisy. She was more grossly fat than any woman so active had a right to be; and she was noisier, Don Gumesindo said, than the bullfrogs down by the *laguna*. But, of course, Don Gumesindo owned the other *almacén* and was prejudiced.

[1] From *Tomorrow*, V (May, 1946), No. 9. Reprinted by permission of the author and *Tomorrow* magazine.

Mama Josefina was a source of amazement, envy, and righteous indignation to every other woman in the pueblo; she had been ever since the death of her husband when, instead of allowing her aunt Rosa's idle son to take charge of the *almacén,* as her aunt so charitably suggested, she herself sold the olive oil, pajama jackets, sugar, gingham, wine, and rosaries with which the shop was stocked; and bought and sold again and made a profit, too! Although, as her aunt

Rosa's idle son had said to his friend, Don Gumesindo, her *almacén* was no more than a tin shed, it had the good fortune to be so placed that everyone on entering or leaving the pueblo must pass it. Don Gumesindo's own *almacén* was an ostentatious concrete building; as it also stood on the only street in the pueblo, one might have supposed it to be equally advantageously situated.

Not only had Mama Josefina taken over her husband's business but, before the grass was green above his grave, she had cast aside her widow's weeds, crying that since she had not loved him alive she saw no reason to mourn him dead; and she blossomed once more wearing the gaudy prints she favored.

To women who were mourning half their lives, this was profoundly shocking. But there was worse to follow.

Mama Josefina had an only child, a little girl named Celia. When Celia was ten years old Mama Josefina sent her to a convent school in Buenos Aires and, when she was graduated, to college in that city. Mama Josefina had seen her daughter only half a dozen times in the past ten years. That was a wickedness impossible to condone; even her friends, and she had staunch ones, shook their heads dubiously while those who openly said they were not her friends, cried, "But what barbarity! Casting out her only child! What lack of all maternal feeling!" over this, Mama Josefina's most lamentable eccentricity.

And now Celia was twenty and she was returning to visit her mother, and the whole pueblo was agog to see what sort of daughter she had become.

Mama Josefina had been in a fever of activity ever since she had heard from Celia. She had painted the walls of her *almacén* white, and the roof red—it was made of corrugated iron and had never seen a lick of paint before. She sent for a length of silk, strawberry-colored roses sprawling on an olive green background, and made it into the shapeless sort of sack she called a dress.

Her vast, waddling figure could be seen at any hour steaming down the center of the road, her rope-soled *alpargatas* shuffling in the dust till she raised a cloud as thick as a passing troop of horse, followed by such a trail of urchins, loafers, and mongrels as might follow any circus from the city.

On the day of Celia's arrival every soul in the pueblo was at the station; this was usual, for the passing of the train from Buenos Aires—it stopped only on request—was the highlight of the week; but this day everyone was on tiptoe with expectancy.

Mama Josefina held the center of the stage, her purpling face, beaded with sweat, contorted into one beatific grin, her gold tooth flashing, her voice hoarse with emotion. Behind her the waiting crowd, the women in rusty shawls and faded gowns, the men in wide cotton *bombachas* and striped pajama jackets, the scantily clad, inquisitive-eyed children, appeared colorless and unreal, as if painted cloudily against the backdrop of a scene.

Celia had looked forward to her return with some misgiving, the cause of which she would not permit herself to acknowledge. She prepared for her reunion with her mother with as much care as she dressed to keep a date with Fernandito; indeed it was possible that she might be seeing Fernandito, for his uncle had an *estancia* not far from her home, and this link had been the first step in their friendship. But it was not of Fernandito she was thinking; it was of her mother.

Strange to be so unfamiliar with one's own mother! It was wrong, thought Celia, who had strong convictions as to right and wrong. It had been she who had insisted on this visit; her mother had not encouraged her return. Not that Mama Josefina did not love her daughter; Celia could not doubt her mother's love. Mama Josefina's love was as solid and dependable as the earth under your feet. Celia's fears were of another nature.

As the engine heralded their arrival with a piercing hoot of triumph, Celia took one last anxious look at herself in her mirror. She had that cool and unruffled air which some women seem able to maintain through fire and flood, and eighteen hours of dusty travel had in no way disturbed her.

As the train jolted to a standstill, Celia jumped down the steps with her arms held out to greet her mother.

Mama Josefina let out a bellow of joy and flung herself upon her daughter, and Celia found herself enveloped in an aura of garlic, sweat, and the tangy, vinegary smell of the *almacén*. Involuntarily she drew back, but almost before Mama Josefina could be aware of her recoil, she embraced her mother with added tenderness.

Then Mama Josefina turned, her arm still about her daughter, the tears coursing down her quivering cheeks, and cried in her hoarse, stentorian tones, "This is my daughter, people! Is she not beautiful? And brains! She has more in that pretty little headpiece than there are in all the flea-infected noddles in this hovel! Make way there, you louts! Make way for my daughter! You there, Gumesindo with the belly, carry the lady's valise instead of standing with your eyes goggling as if you had swallowed a chicken bone! Make way there!"

Celia was scarlet with mortification. She could not look her old acquaintances in the eye. Someone at the back of the crowd sniggered, for Don Gumesindo had, without thinking, obediently gathered up the valise. Don Gumesindo scowled but he did not let go of the valise, because Celia was so exceptionally pretty.

Mama Josefina had her daughter firmly by the elbow and was propelling her up the center of the road, followed by every man, woman, and child, and cur in the place. Still pink in the face and with the tears pricking her eyelids, Celia gazed at the scenes of her childhood with growing despondency. It was more dreary and sordid than ever she remembered: the mud-brick houses unrelieved by paint; the scrawny chickens scratching in the dust; the mangy, mean-eyed mongrels; the flies and the dust, the penetrating, omnipresent dust.

"I am so happy to see you, Mama, I must weep!" Celia lied bravely.

"Weep then," said her mother, "for tears relieve the heart."

That evening the *almacén* was crowded; everyone suddenly wanted to buy a kilo of maté or a liter of wine and see at closer quarters this prodigy from the city. Celia had to endure all their impertinent stares, suggestive allusions, crude jokes and laughter while she helped her mother behind the counter. It seemed as if Mama Josefina was not conscious of her suffering but egged them on by talking loudly of her daughter's charms. Yet, when Celia was not looking her mother observed her shrewdly and with sympathy, and when Don Gumesindo appeared in the doorway and stood there in a new mauve-striped pajama jacket, chewing on a toothpick while he stared at Celia in greedy silence, Mama Josefina sent him scuttling by shouting jocosely, "What, is your own wine so sour that you drink here, fat Gumesindo? Ask your wife for some from the barrel she keeps for the young Florindo. I saw him ride by and wondered why he did not stop to quench his thirst. But then, he does not have to pay cash for the wine your wife gives him!" She let out a guffaw of laughter, for Don Gumesindo was gone. Don Gumesindo's wife, Mama Josefina knew, was well able to defend herself.

When the noise was at its height, Celia went out into the back yard to breathe the cool air; the stench of stale wine nauseated her. The sun had set and left a rim of crimson on the dark horizon; above her head the stars began to twinkle; the kindly shadows hid the dust and dirt. Celia sighed, thinking lovingly of her mother and of her own fastidious shrinking with dismay.

Down the darkening road a youth came riding; he was not more than sixteen, yet he had an air of quiet serenity that blended with the wide, still world around.

"*Buenas noches,*" he said unsmilingly. "I

come in search of the señorita Celia Olivera."

"I am Celia Olivera," Celia answered, her heart beating violently.

"I have a letter for you," he said, riding right up to her but without dismounting, for it was more natural for him to remain in the saddle. "I am to await an answer."

"Oh . . ." said Celia, feeling that fierce constriction of the heart which word from Fernandito always brought her. She took the letter to the bedroom to read.

It was in the bold, flowing hand that was so characteristic of Fernandito. He was at his uncle's house, he wrote; might he come in his car tomorrow and take her and her mother to visit his uncle? His uncle was most anxious to make her acquaintance.

Celia's heart sank. She knew of Fernandito's uncle, an elegant old man with a reputation for wit. She could well imagine how such wit could be used against her mother! How they would laugh! Celia burned with the fierce defensive loyalty of youth.

She sat down and wrote the answer at great speed. She was sorry but she and her mother were too busy to receive or pay visits. Indeed, on consideration, she thought their friendship had gone far enough and had better cease.

She ran out and gave the letter, the ink scarcely dry, to the boy who had waited there motionless as a statue.

"Remain with God," he said gravely, turning his horse's head.

"Go with God," Celia whispered as he rode away. But the farewell was not for the messenger.

Celia's was a quiet and docile nature that hid a stubborn will. She was proving more stubborn than her mother; Mama Josefina said Celia must return to work in the city, and Celia said her place was at her mother's side. Celia might not have argued with such determination had she not been shamed to find how shocked she was by her mother's vulgarity and the squalor of her surroundings; if she had wanted to stay she might have been persuaded to go. It was wrong,

Celia decided, to be unhappy in your home, to be embarrassed by your mother. What was good enough for Mama should certainly be good enough for her; she must get used to this environment and prepare to devote her life to the care of her mother.

"But in the name of all the saints, child, do you think I spent that money on your education to see you spend your days measuring out wine or watching Gumesindo lest he diddle you? Your place is in the city. I can see you there," Mama Josefina clasped her hands over her stomach, "seated behind the teacher's desk. . . . Or up on the platform presenting prizes to your pupils. . . . I did not have you educated that you might choke your mind with dust and flies! And I tell you, girl, it has cost no small amount. . . . Though, bless you, I would not begrudge it if it cost my life!"

"But, Mama, it is not right that you should spend your life slaving here," Celia cried, "while I live in luxury! You are getting old and I should be here to look after you. . . ."

"Old!" Mama Josefina fairly screeched with rage. "I'll have you know, my girl, I'm as good a woman as any and better than some of these puling things the men bring home these days as brides. Old! If there were a man in this pueblo with a thought beyond his stomach or an idea above the bottom of his glass, you'd see how old I am! Old!"

"All the same, Mama, you need me here."

"And who do you think you'll find to marry in this mudhole? Tell me that!"

"I do not intend to marry," Celia said, her voice trembling for all her self-control. "I will stay here and help you in the business."

"Mother of God, have mercy on my soul!" Mama Josefina cried, flinging up her hands to heaven. "Now for sure I shall be ruined! Well, since you must help, go and tell that Hipolito he can pay his debt in kind. I want two cows with calf, fat and sleek. You can drive them home yourself."

Mama Josefina stood in the doorway watching Celia walking down the road. It was obvious that the girl was unhappy for all her determined cheerfulness. Mama Josefina's heart bled for her. The young, she thought, if they have no troubles of their own, must fabricate them! As if a girl like Celia could be happy in a hole like this! She gave one scornful glance up and down the empty road and waddled angrily back into her shop.

Celia was unhappy, but it was not only her surroundings that made her so. It was a week since she had sent Fernandito that ungracious note, and she had had no word from him. Undoubtedly he was furious, for Fernandito had a temper that flared up like dry straw. And he had every right to be! She would never hear from him again, of that she could be sure, she told herself miserably.

The thick, warm dust had seeped into her high-heeled shoes so that walking was painful, and she had to stop every so often and balance on one leg while she emptied the other shoe. Soon she would be wearing the rope-soled *alpargatas* as all the other women did; soon her clothes would take on the hue and smell of dust. If Fernandito should one day pass through the pueblo she would be indistinguishable from the rest! Only Mama Josefina had survived the dust!

Of course, Celia thought, as if she had discovered a bright new idea, Mama wears those gaudy clothes, Mama talks loudly and behaves in an eccentric fashion in revolt against the dust. Mama will not allow the dust to bury her in oblivion. Mama, thought Celia with deep feeling, is wonderful! And she sighed and mused about Fernandito, and her misery returned.

Hipolito, she found, had no intention of paying his debt at all. He told her so in no uncertain language, but Celia was not her mother's daughter for nothing, and she browbeat him into promising to have the cows driven into a corral so that next morning she might take her pick. She was frankly relieved that she did not have to drive the animals home that evening.

The shadows were long when she turned home, and a faint breeze had sprung up,

cooling to her moist brow. The countryside was beautiful at this hour, beautiful in the remote, austere fashion of the pampas.

The lamp was twinkling in the *almacén;* two hounds came rushing forth at her approach, but above their barking she could hear her mother's raucous voice. Mama Josefina was singing and, not knowing Mama Josefina, one might have supposed her drunk. The song she sang was no drawing-room ditty, and she bellowed it forth with huge Rabelaisian gusto as if she smacked her lips over each word. Suddenly a man's voice broke in with the chorus.

At this sound Celia stopped abruptly and then began to run toward the *almacén.* She burst through the curtain that hung across the door and stood on the threshold, gaping.

Mama Josefina was perched on her own counter; beside her sat Fernandito and between them lay an open tin of anchovies and a bottle of wine. Fernandito had one hand on Mama Josefina's shoulder and in the other he held a toothpick with which he speared at the anchovies. They were both singing lustily.

"Celia!" Fernandito cried when he saw her. "Why did you not tell me Mama Josefina was your mama? She is an old friend of mine. I used to come stealing her anchovies when I was a kid, didn't I, Mama Josefina, love?" He slid off the counter and came across to Celia, his brown eyes looking into hers and laughing in a way he had. "You know your letter made me so mad I swore I would never see you again! And then I had the good sense to come and tell Mama Josefina all my troubles. It was as simple as that. Mama Josefina says all girls write that sort of letter once to the man they really love!"

He said this with so disarming a grin that Celia found it impossible to be angry; besides, she was all at once so very happy. Mama Josefina got off the counter with a thud that shook the building and came waddling over and put an arm round each of them, looking from one to the other with her gold tooth flashing.

"This silly boy was always after my pickles and anchovies. Not a sweet tooth like other boys. He likes things with a nip in them!" She chuckled deeply, "But why did you tell me nothing about this handsome young fellow, girl? That to me is suspicious! The foolish things that girls are; if there are not enough troubles in the world already they must go inventing more!"

"You explain to her the way you did to me, Mama Josefina," Fernandito said, putting his arm affectionately around the old woman's waist. "Then she will see sense."

"Oh, well . . ." Mama Josefina hesitated coyly.

"Go on," Fernandito urged her gently.

"Well, it is like this, daughter," the old woman began awkwardly as if the words were drawn from the bottom of her heart. "I hate this place! I hate this pueblo and this life where nothing happens from one year to the next! Most I hate the dust! It takes all the color out of you. It takes all the juice out of you. Pah, the dust, I spit on it! But I know I am too old to escape from it, too old and too ignorant! Oh, you think I do not see myself with your young eyes? A fat, smelly old woman! No, don't interrupt! It is true. I am dirty and I stink and I know no other way of life. I cannot escape. . . ." She swung round and faced her daughter dramatically, her old body held painfully erect, and spoke with suppressed and tragic rage. "I fight the dust! I will not let it take the color from my life. I will not let it take you! Only through you can I escape! I can live, thinking of your freedom. Thinking of you I can feel myself young and lovely and full of life! Thinking of you I can

forget the dust! But if you remain here, Celia," she turned her massive head away and her voice trembled, "if you stay here, if I have to watch you lose your youth, watch the color fade from your cheek and the light from your eye, see you shuffling through the dust in *alpargatas* . . . I could not bear it! I could fight no more. The dust would bury me . . ."

There was a moment of silence and then Celia put her arm about her mother's waist. "Forgive me, Mama. Now I understand. I will go back." She felt Fernandito's hand laid over hers, and her mother gave a convulsive sob, flung her arms about her and embraced her enthusiastically.

"That's my girl!" she cried tearfully. "That's my Celia! Now come and eat some anchovy before this greedy boy guzzles the lot!" She wiped her nose with the back of her hand. "And now we will sing and enjoy ourselves, and you can hold hands all you like behind my back. . . . Eh, you think I don't know what goes on! You think I have as much fat on my brains as I have on my body!" She guffawed with laughter and nudged them both knowingly. "Come on, sing and enjoy life!"

SUGGESTIONS FOR STUDY

1. In this story there are actually two antagonists. Name them and show how each is overcome.

2. Is the method used to bring the conclusion plausible? What foreshadowing is used to make the final incident plausible?

3. Do the differences between Celia and Mama Josefina seem too incongruous?

4. Whose story is this really—Mama Josefina's or Celia's?

The Law-Abiding[1]

MARC BRANDEL

IT WAS RAINING again: the drops slapping

[1] From the *Atlantic*, CLXXXIX (May, 1952). Reprinted by permission of the author and of the *Atlantic Monthly*.

against the window of the compartment. At times it seemed to Hallam that it was always raining in Europe. Thinking of Germany, for instance, where he had spent the greater part of the last three years working in collaboration with Army Intelligence, he remembered the cold rain dripping from the eaves of the ruined buildings, the spattering pools among the rubble. And now the driving wetness of England.

The train was beginning to slow for East Croyden. He glanced warily across at the only other occupant of the narrow English compartment. But the wariness was really no more than automatic now. He wasn't afraid that Radjek would leave the train at Croyden, would try and give him the slip or even contact anyone. He knew only too well what Radjek was going to do. He was going to sit there just as he was, his large head settled back against the embroidered antimacassar provided by the Southern Railway for its first class passengers, his heavy lids closed, the infrequent restive shifting of his square reddish hands on his knees the only indication he was so much as aware of Hallam, that he was even awake. He was going to sit there until they got into Newhaven Harbor at nine tonight, and then he was going to take his bag from the rack and move slowly and ponderously ahead of Hallam down the station platform, through the customs sheds, and up the gangplank of the Channel boat to safety—carrying the figures he had been sent to England to get securely packed away inside his mind beyond any possibility of detection or recapture. And there was absolutely nothing Hallam could do to stop him.

Disgustedly he turned back to his own window, looking out over the twilit acres of identical red roofs, the row of somehow pathetically cared-for gardens running down to the base of the railroad embankment. A woman in a flowered apron stood in the shelter of a doorway holding a child in her arm. Her hand clasping the child's wrist fluttered its arm up and down, waving at the train. Hallam raised his own hand in response and then let it fall back beside him. For a moment he hated Radjek with a quite personal hatred.

"It must be such a lonely job," his sister back in Rhode Island had once said to Hallam. But he had never seen it that way. He loved his job—not for the occasional risks involved; he had as a matter of fact little stomach for that side of it: at forty-two it was a conscious effort of will for him to be even moderately courageous—but for the very reason that it gave him such a sense of belonging. In working against a man like Radjek he could feel he was working *for* so many people. People like that woman: decent, friendly, standing in the doorways of their ugly little houses waving their good will at passing strangers.

He wondered again if Radjek knew just how safe he was. And was bitterly forced once more to admit to himself that he almost certainly did. It had been a last doomed hope this: to show his own hand, to follow Radjek quite openly since last night, follow him to the station, into this empty compartment. A last hope of scaring Radjek into thinking they weren't going to let him leave the country. But Radjek hadn't seemed in the least perturbed, had scarcely even looked up when Hallam entered the compartment. And he must certainly know by now who Hallam was, that he was being followed, must surely have suspected it ever since he landed in England. To Radjek's kind it would seem unthinkable that a foreigner, any foreigner, shouldn't be kept under constant watch.

And yet, Hallam thought more hopefully, Radjek *had* taken this train, this slow halting local instead of the more obvious Channel boat express. Radjek still couldn't quite believe apparently that it could be this easy: that even a suspect foreigner might have the *right* to move freely in a "corrupt democracy," in England.

But then Radjek hadn't been at the Yard yesterday when Hallam talked to MacDonald. Good old Mac with his worn, homely face and worried eyes, his fuzzy hair and mustache. Like a little gray panda, Hallam had thought sitting across the desk from him in the small office. There was nothing disrespectful in the thought: it was a habit he had trained himself to, to settle on some simple association of this kind for each new face he encountered. It helped fix it in his memory.

"We've checked with our Passport Control people." Mac pulled a sheet of paper towards him. "Everything in order, I'm afraid. 'Naturalized Czech citizen. Visitor's visa issued by the British Consul in Prague.' Our fault, that. 'Traveling as the representative of the Continian Aluminum Company.' A bona fide firm with legitimate business connections in this country."

Hallam nodded. "You've got to hand it to them. They know exactly how to take advantage of every legality they can."

"So there it is." Mac slid the report back into the folder on his desk. "If he wants to leave the country I don't see how we can stop him. I mean we can't go around breaking our own laws, can we? We can search his luggage of course. Might even stretch a point and make a search of his . . . person. Though we don't like to do that if we can help it."

"Wouldn't do any good anyway." Stretch a point, Hallam thought. And if the positions were reversed? Radjek's kind wouldn't consider it stretching a point to commit murder in broad daylight. "He hasn't a thing on him," he continued. "Not a scrap of paper or a note of any kind. It's all in his head. That's why they sent Radjek. Because Radjek would understand what those figures meant. He wouldn't even have to memorize them exactly—only their meaning."

"I see." Mac pulled a rough-textured black pipe from his pocket and began to fill it. "Just how important are they?" he asked after a moment. "Not precisely a closed secret, would you say? Anyone doing the same experiments could get the figures for themselves."

"Sure. Sure, they could. Only it took your boys twenty-eight months and they had the best equipment in the world. Twenty-eight months that we're just handing them on a platter the moment Radjek leaves the country tomorrow." Hallam stood up, his own self-disgust suddenly overwhelming. "Right in front of me," he said. "Right there on a public bench in the bang middle of Hyde Park with me sitting within twenty feet of them. Can you imagine! All the time I'd kept thinking Radjek would have to go to Harwell himself, or they would have to smuggle copies of the figures out to him. It never even occurred to me, pinhead I am, that was how they would do it, that was how they had planned it all along. Word of mouth. I hadn't even seen that was *why* they sent Radjek. A scientist. Far too important a man for them to risk unless they were absolutely sure what they were doing. And that whole hour. That whole hour they were sitting there, Radjek and Hart, I didn't suspect a Goddam thing. Me! I didn't even know who Hart was."

"Not your fault, that." If there had been any sympathy in Mac's voice Hallam couldn't have borne it, but it was a mere statement of fact. "We didn't know about Hart ourselves until just before his death." He shook out the match he had been holding to his pipe. "Extraordinary, a fellow like that, isn't it?" he went on. "Hart, I mean. Oxford man. Senior science scholar. Brilliant record. Went all through the war. Comes of a good family too. You can imagine what this has done to them. His sister was in here this afternoon. Awfully nice girl, got a special citation for her work during the Blitz, night ferry service up and down the river. She just sat there, fidgeting with the clasp of her handbag, saying 'Isn't there anything I can do to make up for my brother?' " Mac reached gloomily for another match. "Beats me," he admitted. "Men like Hart. What makes 'em do it, do you think? Not money. Kind of a disease, I suppose."

Hallam turned back to his chair and sat down. "Why did Hart kill himself?" he asked. "Did he know you were after him?"

"No." There was a look of sadness in Mac's honest, worried eyes that might almost have been taken for pity. "No, we can be pretty sure he didn't. Do you know what I think?" he continued. "It was because of them. Radjek's lot, I mean. They didn't trust him. I don't mean to say they killed him. It was suicide all right. But they were through with him. They let him see they didn't trust him any longer. And after all he'd done for them the realization was just too much for him. He had betrayed his own country, his family, everything he had been brought up to believe in, and suddenly he had nothing left, nowhere to turn."

"Look." In his urgency Hallam leaned forward and rested his hands on Mac's desk. "Suppose I was willing to swear, go to court and swear Radjek was in touch with Hart. Wouldn't that be enough for you—at least to detain him?"

"Could you swear what they talked about?"

"No." Hallam shook his head. "No, I guess for all I can prove they talked about the weather. But we both know they didn't."

"That's not enough, though, is it?"

Hallam did not answer and after a moment Mac asked frankly: "Look here, what's your particular interest in Radjek? Is there anything you people can prove against him?"

"Not legally." Hallam felt for a cigarette and lit it. "We think . . . Hell, we know he's the coördinator of a group of agents working in the States. That's why I was sent here after him. We knew he was after those figures and we hoped we could get something on him here. Something that would stick in your courts." His own anger with himself crept into his voice again. "And now that he's got the figures on top of everything else we can't even stop him leaving the country."

"Well, after all, Old Chap." There was a strange, rather likeable embarrassment in MacDonald's gray eyes. "I mean that's rather what it's all about, isn't it? Can't go around arresting people on suspicion or we should none of us sleep safe in our beds at night. What?"

"I guess so." These English, Hallam thought. He'll be offering me a cup of tea next. But he felt a great affection for Mac at that moment. "It's too bad it doesn't work

both ways, though," he said. "Too bad a man like Radjek can come over here and take advantage of your decency, your regard for laws he despises you for having."

"Do you suppose he knows?" There was a sudden sharpness in MacDonald's voice, a look of bright speculation in his eyes. "I mean do you suppose Radjek himself knows just how safe he is, that we can't touch him without breaking our own laws? They have funny ideas about other countries sometimes, you know, these people."

Sure he knew, Hallam thought now, watching Radjek across the narrow aisle of the compartment. His taking this train, this local that stopped at Newhaven Town as well as the Harbor, was no more than an irrational reflex of caution, a way of leaving himself a last out in case he was stopped and questioned.

The train jolted to a stop, a shower of raindrops shaking loose from its roof, splashing on the platform. A wave of passengers rippled forward from the shelter of a wooden awning, disclosing a row of billboards. "Did you Maclean your teeth today?" The door of the compartment was opened from the outside: a girl entered in a flurry of parting advice. She settled her suitcase on the seat opposite Hallam and turned back to a tall woman on the platform, opening the window and leaning out.

"Have a good time."

"Oh, I shall. Don't worry. I expect I shall make an absolute pig of myself."

"Do. You deserve it, and dear . . ."

"Two eggs every morning. Just fancy . . . I wish you were coming too. It's too awful to think of your having to stay in England. I wish . . ."

"Don't, dear. Just try and forget it all. Forget *him*. Stay as long as you can and have a simply lovely time."

There was a warning whistle, a moment's silence as the brake pumps stilled, the slamming of doors up and down the train. The girl stepped back and closed the window, pulling on the heavy leather strap until the single pane slipped into place and held. The older woman's face moved slowly past. Looking out Hallam saw her turn back to the shelter of the awning. There had been two men in raincoats standing beneath it and in the instant before they were lost to sight Hallam had the impression that they had been waiting for her there. The thought caused him a slight uneasiness, like a word in a cipher that did not quite fit. Why had only the woman come to the door of the compartment?

He watched the girl as she moved briskly about, straightening her suitcase on the seat beside her, folding her coat on top of it, settling into her corner. She was rather pretty in an English way, the softness of her eyes and mouth oddly contrasting with the bones of her face, the firmness of her chin, the long capable hands. So many English people were like that, he thought; all shy apology on the surface and underneath as tough and serviceable as the shoes they made, with that curious indignant toughness that came from their assurance of being always in the right.

The girl had scarcely even glanced at either him or Radjek. Having made herself comfortable, she opened a book, a green clothbound book with no wrapper. As she raised it Hallam noticed the red sticker across the bottom of the jacket. Boots Circulating Library. He was aware again of that faint sense of disquiet, as at something that did not quite fit. "Stay as long as you can," the woman on the platform had said. Then wasn't it a little strange to be taking a library book with her?

His attention was distracted by a movement in the corridor outside. A man passed, glancing briefly in. Hallam had the impression of a white pointed face beneath an absurdly narrow-brimmed, high-crowned black hat. Like an irritable gnome, he thought. His glance shifted to Radjek. The other had not moved, but looking at his hands, Hallam felt an instant's stirring of excitement. The thumb and forefinger of Radjek's right hand were

rubbing softly, insistently together. It was a mannerism Hallam had noticed before; it reminded him of a gambler fingering his last chip; and he had come to recognize it as a sign of anxiety. What was it that had disturbed Radjek? The girl's presence in the compartment? He brought his eyes back to her.

Perhaps it was only the contrast between his hatred of Radjek and his instinctive liking for her, or perhaps something in the girl herself, her air of gentle independence, of hidden reserves; but for a moment looking at her, Hallam was aware of almost suffocating anger. It was girls like this who had stood beside the ack-ack guns in 1940, who had run the little boats up and down the Thames those too bright London nights. Who were now being edged a little closer to a still greater ordeal, an even worse Hell, because of his own stupidity and failure.

The train was beginning to slow again. Hayward's Heath. The quiet little country station, peaceful as an old print, seemed only to echo his own self-accusations. Did you Maclean your teeth today? Only one stop more now, he thought, Lewes, and then Newhaven, first the Town, and a mile further on the Harbor, and the waiting boat. A figure passed the window, glancing in, moving on down the corridor. Hallam caught a glimpse of the little white face beneath the absurd black hat. The irritable gnome again. He looked at Radjek. His hands were moving once more, the fingers whispering nervously together. He *was* afraid of something, Hallam decided. But what? What in God's name had he got to be scared of? All he had to do was walk aboard.

Opposite him the girl closed her book, laying it beside her. There was a thin white celluloid marker, the accompaniment of all Boots Library books, slipped between the pages towards the end, but she had not moved it. Had she finished the book already? He looked at her face. She was staring out of the window, thoughtfully watching the green Sussex fields, the neat hedges, the still trees slip by, but Hallam had the impression of a certain tenseness in her manner now. Like Radjek she might have been nerving herself to something.

Before he could recover from his surprise a signal box slid past the window. Lewes. The train slowed, shuddered, halted, the air brakes panting. Doors slammed shut. There was the sound of men's voices in the corridor; the train was on its way again.

The girl seemed to drag her eyes from the window and straightened a little in her seat, staring directly ahead of her.

The voices were approaching their carriage. Two men came into view and halted. At the sight of them Hallam felt a surge of hope. There was no mistaking that air of deferential firmness, of somehow apologetic authority. The two Yard men wore their profession like coats as they stepped into the compartment and stood just inside the door taking in the three passengers.

"Anyone for the Channel boat?" It was the elder of the two who had spoken.

Hallam frowned, puzzled. Then: of course, he thought, his brief hope dying. Money. They have to check your money. You're only allowed to take out so much.

"Yes, I am." The girl snapped open her bag and pulled out her passport. "I'm going to Paris."

The Yard man took it from her, opening it at the first page, reading her name. His eyes hardened unaccountably. "And just what are you going to be doing in France?" he asked.

"Taking a holiday."

"That all?"

Hallam was incredulous: he had felt a note of menace in the question.

"Plenty of nice places in England for a holiday." The Yard man gestured brusquely toward the suitcase on the seat beside the girl. "This yours?" Without waiting for an answer he bent down and unfastened the locks. "Or don't you like England?" he asked, fingering expertly through the neatly piled clothes inside.

Hallam looked at the girl's face. Within this framework of the English carriage with its old-fashioned upholstery, its fading photographs of Bognor Regis, the English Lake Country, the expression in her eyes filled him with a sense of waking nightmare. He had seen that same expression in men and women's eyes before; but then it had seemed to him a mere extension of their surroundings: the barrier, the arc lights, the booted guards, the little huddle of refugees from the Eastern Zone presenting their papers with that same look of fearful hope.

"Yes, of course I like it. Why shouldn't I?" Snap. Lock. Snap. Lock. Her voice matched the brittle staccato sound of her fingers blindly opening and closing the clasp of her handbag.

"What's this?" The Yard man picked up the book from the seat beside her. "*European Crossroads*. Ilya Ehrenburg. Russian, isn't he?"

"Yes, but . . ."

"Afraid we'll have to ask you to come along with us." He had closed the suitcase and now handed it and the book to his companion in the doorway. "Come on, Miss."

"But what for? What am I charged with?" The trembling of the girl's lips was pitiful.

"Not charged with anything . . . *yet*. Just taking you into protective custody." There was a nasty, jeering quality in the Yard man's voice. "Just on suspicion, you might say."

"Suspicion of what?" Snap. Lock. Snap. Lock. She was fighting hard to control it, but she was plainly terrified now. Hallam watched her with a kind of sickened fascination, as one might watch some scene in a Grand Guignol pantomime, some scene that bore absolutely no relation to reality. The worn, homely compartment, the quiet English countryside sliding serenely past outside had ceased to exist for him, transformed into grotesque fantasy by the incredibility of what was happening in relation to it.

"You're known to have associated with the traitor, Jonathan Hart."

"But I hardly knew him . . ."

"Come along, now. Come along." The Yard man made a quick impatient movement towards the door. "Halpert," he called, "take her outside."

Still protesting, but with an air of terrified resignation now, the girl stood up, her fingers struggling awkwardly with the buttons of her coat, and followed the younger Yard man out into the corridor. The other stood for a moment looking after her and then slipped her passport into his pocket. There was a dreadful finality in the gesture: he might have been turning a key in a lock.

"Anyone else for the boat?" He turned suddenly on Radjek. "You leaving the country?"

There was no change of expression on Radjek's heavy face, only the reddish hands moved now with increasing restive speed. He did not answer at once, but his eyes reflected no sign of hesitation, or even of thought. It was simply a moment lost, a moment Radjek might merely have been waiting to pass before replying.

"No," he said in his flat, dryly factual voice. "I'm only going as far as the town. On business. I'm returning to London tomorrow."

The words rang in Hallam's ears like a reprieve. Bewildered as he had been by what had just taken place, shocked beyond words by the Yard man's treatment of that girl, by the fact that such things could happen here, in England, he was conscious now only of a sense of quite physical relief.

Radjek had committed himself. He wouldn't dare now try and go aboard that boat—at least tonight. It was only slowly that the full implications of this fact became clear to Hallam. For the moment it was enough to realize that he had been given a second chance, a second chance to meet the harsh demands of his own New England conscience, to do his job, to stop those figures in Radjek's mind leaving the country at all, ever.

"May I see your ticket, please?"

The large hand stilled on the heavy knee, fumbled with a button, searched an inside pocket.

"This ticket is for Newhaven Harbor." The detective turned the small green pasteboard card in his fingers.

"A mistake." For all the interest in Radjek's voice he might have been correcting an error in grammar. "The ticket seller misunderstood me."

"We'll be coming into the town in a few minutes now." There was an unmistakable note of warning in the Yard man's voice. He handed the ticket back and without a glance at Hallam turned and left the compartment, sliding the door shut behind him.

Hallam was alone with Radjek once more. His mind was working desperately, trying to fit things together. MacDonald. What he had said about Hart. The Yard man's incredible treatment of that girl. "Just on suspicion, you might say. You're known to have associated with Hart." Had some confederate of Hart's come forward then, implicated a whole new group? If so, why hadn't they arrested Radjek? At least warned him directly not to try and leave the country? None of it seemed to fit.

They were beginning to slow for Newhaven Town. Feverishly Hallam searched his mind for some fact, some detail he might have overlooked that, like the key word in a cipher, would make the whole thing clear. And then all at once he had it. The library book.

Hallam did not actually smile, but his relief, his sense of impersonal victory and above all his admiration for MacDonald, to say nothing of that girl, were so great at that moment that if he had been alone he would have laughed aloud.

It was a quietly respectable hotel on a side street about a quarter of a mile from the station. Above the double glass door a flaking gilt sign announced "The Traveller's Arms" and below it in smaller letters "Licensed to sell Wines and Spirits."

Hallam waited outside until he had seen Radjek follow the aging porter in his green baize apron up the stairs and out of sight and then crossed to the desk himself and asked for a room. The gray-haired woman on duty pushed the book towards him and Hallam signed his name. On the line above in Radjek's brisk, awkward hand was the entry "Konrad Bergen, Sweden" and the room number, 119.

Radjek must be even more scared than he had imagined, Hallam thought with a flush of triumph, to have reverted, so futilely, to a false name.

"Do you have a phone?" Hallam asked. He had an idea Mac might not be very far away, might be waiting at the local police station for this very call, in fact.

"It's right down the hall, sir."

Hallam thanked her, making his way past the cheerful murmur of the public bar to the box at the end of the corridor. "Lift receiver and insert two pennies. When your party answers press Button A." Good old England, Hallam thought. Its own special way of doing everything: to the English the only, the right way. And yet what a good, just way it often was—like Mac's way of stopping Radjek. He pressed Button A.

"Hullo, Mac," he said a moment later. "Yes, it worked. You did it. That girl was wonderful. . . . Oh, is that who she is? Well, she's certainly made up for her brother now. She did a marvelous job. Sure, she fooled me. I was all ready for a moment there to denounce England as a totalitarian state. Yes, he's taken a room at The Traveller's Arms on West Street. I'm downstairs. All right, I'll wait for you. About five minutes. Fine." He hung up and whistling happily under his breath strolled back into the lobby.

"Do you want to see your room now, sir?"

"No, thank you." Hallam smiled at the woman out of sheer high spirits. "I'm waiting for a friend." He walked over to a chair from which he could watch both the door and the stairs and lit a cigarette.

He was less than halfway through it when he first noticed the shoes. They were small, very shiny, very pointed black shoes and they were standing on the top step in sight

of where he was sitting, the landing above cutting them off from the rest of the figure. For perhaps half a minute they remained quite still and then slowly and with a kind of conscious deliberation they began to descend the stairs.

The legs of a pair of narrow blue serge trousers came into view, a dark belted raincoat, a sharp little white face, and finally a narrow-brimmed, absurdly high-crowned black hat. It was the irritable gnome from the train.

Without hesitation, but with the same conscious deliberation, the little man continued down step by step until he reached the lobby. Like a hunter, Hallam thought, moving through the forest, afraid of snapping a twig. Like a gambler fingering his last chip.

In an instant Hallam was out of his chair.

The gnome turned and started back up the stairs at his approach, his livid hand moving in a curiously graceful arc towards his pocket. But Hallam was too quick for him. He felt the delicate bones of the other's wrist like something not quite living in his hands, as he wrenched the gnome's arm up behind his back. Then his other hand slid into the little man's pocket. It was a gun he had expected, but instead his fingers wounded themselves on a blade and withdrawing them Hallam found them reddened and viscid with more than his own blood.

He was aware of the gnome's feeble struggles: aware of them in a sickened, impalpable way that somehow recalled to him the doomed struggles of a dead chicken. His mind fled from them up the stairs into room 119, already knowing what he would find there. It had always been difficult for him to accept violence, even more to practice it.

He brought his hand around grasping the gnome's thin shoulder with some idea of forcing him before him up the stairs, into Radjek's room. And became conscious all at once of the lobby beneath them, the raised faces, the suddenly disturbed expressions of the guests. And then the glass door onto the street swung open, and in a moment Mac was beside him on the stairs. With his quiet matter-of-fact presence, order seemed to re-invade the scene at once.

"Come, come now. Don't want to cause a disturbance." There was something absurd and yet wholly admirable in the way the hel-meted bobby took the gnome from Hallam's hands, leading him with quiet certainty to-wards the door.

"What room?"

"119." Hallam bounded up the stairs ahead of Mac. In front of him a long corridor stretched towards a window. At its end, to the right, a door bore the number in brass.

Radjek lay face down across the bed. Ex-cept for the wide gashes in the dark cloth of his coat where the gnome's knife had ripped through to the heart, he might have been sleeping.

They didn't trust him either! Hallam thought with a kind of dazed wonder. They sent the gnome after him to make sure he got on that boat. But then Radjek made his one mistake. The words Mac had spoken the day before came to his mind: "They have funny ideas about other countries sometimes, these people." In spite of everything, Radjek had never quite been able to believe that any law could protect *him*. When Mac had had his men stage that scene in the compartment with the help of Hart's sister, Radjek had been only too ready to accept it as real. And so for a moment he had been afraid. "No, I'm only going as far as the town. I'm returning to London tomorrow." And after that he had been afraid even to try and leave, thinking those same two Yard men would surely be watching the boat. . . . While all the time he had had nothing, nothing in the whole world to fear—except from his own peo-ple. . . .

Hallam's thoughts broke off, interrupted by a sound beside him.

Mac was standing quite still, staring at the man on the bed, his lips moving in what seemed at first to be a string of indistinguish-able curses. And then gradually Hallam made out the other's words.

"Oh, damn them," the little Scotsman was muttering to himself. "Damn them. Why do they have to try it here? I don't care if they murder each other in their own country until there's not one of them left. But damn them, I won't *stand* for it here. Here amongst de-cent, law-abiding people."

SUGGESTIONS FOR STUDY

1. State the concepts about totalitarianism and democracy that form the underlying logic of this story.

2. In a sense this story is propaganda advanc-ing the virtues of the democratic way as opposed to the totalitarian way. Think over carefully the essential difference between treating such a topic through entertainment and treating it through exposition or argument. Do the feelings aroused concerning MacDonald, Hart's sister, Radjek, and the gnome bear on this difference?

3. The plot of the story unfolds by virtue of the understanding which each character has of the others. Study this imaginative conception carefully. What does Hallam understand about the British and about Radjek? What does Mac-Donald understand about Radjek? What does Radjek know about his own country but fail to understand about England? Where does the gnome fit into the plot? What does the gnome fail to understand that Hallam comprehends after a little thought?

4. What is the climax of the story? Analyze the working of Radjek's mind at this crucial time.

That Greek Dog[1]

MacKINLAY KANTOR

He received . . . praise that will never die, and with it the grandest of all sepulchers, not that in which his mortal bones are laid, but a home in the minds of men.—THUCYDIDES (more or less).

IN THOSE FIRST years after the first World War, Bill Barbilis could still get into his uniform; he was ornate and handsome when he wore it. Bill's left sleeve, reading down from the shoulder, had patches and patterns of color to catch any eye. At the top there was an arc—bent stripes of scarlet, yellow, and purple; next came a single red chevron with the apex pointing up; and at the cuff were three gold chevrons pointing the other way.

On his right cuff was another gold chevron, only slightly corroded. And we must not forget those triple chevrons on an olive-drab field which grew halfway up the sleeve.

People militarily sophisticated, there in Mahaska Falls, could recognize immediately that Mr. Basilio Barbilis had been a sergeant, that he had served with the Forty-second Division, that he had been once wounded, that he had sojourned overseas for at least eighteen months, and that he had been discharged with honor.

His khaki blouse, however, was worn only on days of patriotic importance. The coat he donned at other times was white—white, that is, until cherry sirup and caramel speckled it. Mr. Barbilis was owner, manager, and staff of the Sugar Bowl.

He had a soda fountain with the most glittering spigots in town. He had a bank of candy cases, a machine for toasting sandwiches, ten small tables complete with steel-backed chairs, and a ceiling festooned with leaves of gilt and bronze paper.

[1] From the *Saturday Evening Post*, CCXIV (August 9, 1941). No. 6. Reprinted by permission of the author.

Beginning in 1920, he had also a peculiar dog. Bill's living quarters were in the rear of the Sugar Bowl, and the dog came bleating and shivering to the Barbilis door one March night. The dog was no larger than a quart of ice cream and, Bill said, just as cold.

My medical office and apartment were directly over the Sugar Bowl. I made the foundling's acquaintance the next day, when I stopped in for a cup of chocolate. Bill had the dog bedded in a candy carton behind the fountain; he was heating milk when I came in, and wouldn't fix my chocolate until his new pet was fed.

Bill swore that it was a puppy. I wasn't so certain. It looked something like a mud turtle wearing furs.

"I think he is hunting dog," said Bill, with pride. "He was cold last night, but not so cold now. Look, I make him nice warm bed. I got my old pajamas for him to lie on."

He waited upon the sniffling little beast with more tender consideration than ever he showed to any customer. Some people say that Greeks are mercenary. I don't know. That puppy wasn't paying board.

The dog grew up, burly and quizzical. Bill named him Duboko. It sounded like that; I don't know how to spell the name correctly, nor did anyone else in Mahaska Falls.

The word, Bill said, was slang. It meant "tough" or "hard-boiled." This animal had the face of a clown and the body of a hyena. Growing up, his downy coat changing to wire and bristles, Duboko resembled a fat Hamburg steak with onions which had been left too long on the griddle.

At an early age Duboko began to manifest a violent interest in community assemblage of any kind or color. This trait may have been fostered by his master, who was proud to be a Moose, an Odd Fellow, a Woodman, and an upstanding member of the Mahaska Falls Commercial League.

When we needed the services of a bugler in our newly formed American Legion post and no bona fide bugler would volunteer, Bill Barbilis agreed to purchase the best brass instrument available and to practice in the bleak and cindery space behind his store. Since my office was upstairs, I found no great satisfaction in Bill's musical enterprise. It happened that Duboko also lent his voice in support—a Greek chorus, so to speak, complete with strophe and antistrophe.

Nevertheless, I could register no complaint, since with other members of the Legion I had voted to retain Bill as our bugler. I could not even kick Duboko downstairs with my one good leg when I discovered him in my reception room lunching off my mail.

Indeed, most people found it hard to punish Duboko. He had the ingratiating, hopeful confidence of an immigrant just off the boat and assured that he had found the Promised Land. He boasted beady eyes, lubberly crooked paws, an immense mouth formed of black rubber, and pearly and enormous fangs which he was fond of exhibiting in a kind of senseless leer. He smelled, too. This characteristic I called sharply to the attention of his master, with the result that Duboko was laundered weekly in Bill's uncertain little bathtub, the process being marked by vocal lament which might have arisen from the gloomiest passage of the *Antigone*.

Mahaska Falls soon became aware of the creature, in a general municipal sense, and learned that it had him to reckon with. Duboko attended every gathering at which six or more people were in congregation. No fire, picnic, memorial service, Rotary conclave, or public chicken-pie supper went ungraced by his presence.

If, as sometimes happened on a crowded Saturday night, a pedestrian was brushed by a car, Duboko was on the scene with a speed to put the insurance-company representatives to shame. If there was a lodge meeting which he did not visit and from which he was not noisily ejected, I never heard of it. At Commercial League dinners he lay pensive with his head beneath the chair of Bill Barbilis. But, suffering fewer inhibitions than his master, he also visited funerals, and even the marriage of Miss Glaydys Stumpf.

Old Charles P. Stumpf owned the sieve factory. He was the richest man in town; the nuptials of his daughter exuded an especial aura of social magnificence. It is a matter of historical record that Duboko sampled the creamed chicken before any of the guests did; he was banished only after the striped and rented trousers of two ushers had undergone renting in quite another sense of the word. Grieved, Duboko forswore the Stumpfs after that; he refused to attend a reception for the bride and bridegroom when they returned from the Wisconsin Dells two weeks later.

There was one other place in town where Duboko was decidedly *persona non grata*. This was a business house, a rival establishment of the Sugar Bowl, owned and operated by Earl and John Klugge. The All-American Kandy Kitchen, they called it.

The Brothers Klugge held forth at a corner location a block distant from the Sugar Bowl. Here lounged and tittered ill-favored representatives of the town's citizenry; dice rattled on a soiled mat at the cigar counter; it was whispered that refreshment other than soda could be purchased by the chosen.

The business career of Earl and John Klugge did not flourish, no matter what inducement they offered their customers. Loudly they declared that their failure to enrich themselves was due solely to the presence in our community of a Greek—a black-haired, dark-skinned Mediterranean who thought nothing of resorting to the most unfair business practices, such as serving good fudge sundaes, for instance, to anyone who would buy them.

One fine afternoon people along the main

street were troubled at observing Duboko limp rapidly westward, fairly wreathed in howls. Bill called me down to examine the dog. Duboko was only bruised, although at first I feared that his ribs were mashed on one side. Possibly someone had thrown a heavy chair at him. Bill journeyed to the Clive Street corner with fire in his eye. But no one could be found who would admit to seeing an attack on Duboko; no one would even say for a certainty that Duboko had issued from the doorway of the All-American Kandy Kitchen, although circumstantial evidence seemed to suggest it.

Friends dissuaded Bill Barbilis from invading the precinct of his enemies, and at length he was placated by pleasant fiction about a kicking horse in the market square.

We all observed, however, that Duboko did not call at the Kandy Kitchen again, not even on rare nights when the dice rattled loudly and when the whoops and catcalls of customers caused girls to pass by, like pretty Levites, on the other side.

There might have been a different tale to tell if this assault had come later, when Duboko was fully grown. His frame stretched and extended steadily for a year; it became almost as mighty as the earnest Americanism of his master. He was never vicious. He was never known to bite a child. But frequently his defensive attitude was that of a mother cat who fancies her kitten in danger; Duboko's hypothetical kitten was his right to be present when good fellows—or bad—got together.

Pool halls knew him; so did the Epworth League. At football games an extra linesman was appointed for the sole purpose of discouraging Duboko's athletic ardor. Through some occult sense, he could become aware of an approaching festivity before even the vanguard assembled. Musicians of our brass band never lugged their instruments to the old bandstand in Courthouse Park without finding Duboko there before them, lounging in an attitude of expectancy. It was Wednesday night, it was eight o'clock, it was July;

the veriest dullard might know at what hour and place the band would begin its attack on the *Light Cavalry Overture*.

Duboko's taste in music was catholic and extensive. He made a fortuitous appearance at a spring musicale, presented by the high-school orchestra and glee clubs, before an audience which sat in the righteous hush of people grimly determined to serve the arts, if only for a night.

The boys' glee club was rendering selections from *Carmen*—in English, of course—and dramatically they announced the appearance of the bull. The line goes, "Now the beast enters, wild and enraged," or something like that; Duboko chose this moment to lope grandly down the center aisle on casta-netting toenails. He sprang to the platform. . . . Mahaska Falls wiped away more tears than did Mérimée's heroine.

In his adult stage, Duboko weighed forty pounds. His color suggested peanut brittle drenched with chocolate; I have heard people swear that his ears were four feet long, but that is an exaggeration. Often those ears hung like limp brown drawers dangling from a clothesline; again they were braced rigidly atop his skull.

Mastiff he was, and also German shepherd, with a noticeable influence of English bull, bloodhound, and great Dane. Far and wide he was known as "that Greek dog," and not alone because he operated out of the Sugar Bowl and under the aegis of Bill Barbilis. Duboko looked like a Greek.

He had Greek eyes, Greek eyebrows, and a grinning Greek mouth. Old Mayor Wingate proclaimed in his cups that, in fact, he had heard Duboko bark in Greek; he was willing to demonstrate, if anyone would only catch Duboko by sprinkling a little Attic salt on his tail.

That Greek dog seldom slept at night; he preferred to accompany the town's watchman on his rounds, or to sit in the window of the Sugar Bowl along with cardboard ladies who brandished aloft their cardboard sodas. Sometimes, when I had been called out in the

middle of the night and came back from seeing a patient, I would stop and peer through
the window and exchange a few signals with
Duboko.

"Yes," he seemed to say, "I'm here. Bill forgot and locked me in. I don't mind, unless,
of course, there's a fire. See you at Legion
meeting tomorrow night, if not at the County
Medical Association luncheon tomorrow
noon."

At this time there was a new arrival in the
Sugar Bowl household—Bill's own father, re-
cruited all the way from Greece, now that
Bill's mother was dead.

Spiros Barbilis was slight, silver-headed,
round-shouldered, with drooping mustachios
which always seemed oozing with black dye.
Bill put up another cot in the back room and
bought another chiffonier from the secondhand store. He and Duboko escorted the old
man up and down Main Street throughout
the better part of one forenoon.

"I want you to meet friend of mine," Bill
said. "He is my father, but he don't speak no
English. I want him to meet all my good
friends here in Mahaska Falls, because he
will live here always."

Old Mr. Barbilis grew deft at helping Bill
with the Sugar Bowl. He carried trays and
managed tables, grinning inveterately, wearing an apron stiff with starch. But he failed to
learn much English except "hello" and
"good-by" and a few cuss words; I think that
he was lonely for the land he had left, which
certainly Bill was not.

One night—it was two o'clock in the morning—I came back to climb my stairs, step-
ping carefully from my car to the icy sidewalk in front of the Sugar Bowl. I moved
gingerly, because I had left one foot in the
Toul sector when a dressing station was
shelled; I did not like icy sidewalks.

This night I put my face close to the show
window to greet Duboko, to meet those sly
and mournful eyes which, on a bitter night,
would certainly be waiting there instead of
shining in a drifted alley where the watchman prowled.

Two pairs of solemn eyes confronted me
when I looked in. Old Mr. Barbilis sat there,
too—in his night clothes, but blanketed with
an overcoat—he and Duboko, wrapped together among the jars of colored candy and
the tinted cardboard girls. They stared out,
aloof and dignified in the darkness, musing
on a thousand lives that slept near by. I enjoy imagining that they both loved the street,
even in its midnight desertion, though doubtless Duboko loved it the more.

In 1923 we were treated to a mystifying
phenomenon. There had never been a riot in
Mahaska Falls, nor any conflict between racial and religious groups. Actually we had no
racial or religious groups; we were all Americans, or thought we were. But, suddenly and
amazingly, fiery crosses flared in the darkness
of our pasture lands.

I was invited to attend a meeting and did
so eagerly, wondering if I might explore this
outlandish nonsense in a single evening.
When my car stopped at a cornfield gate and
ghostly figures came to admit me, I heard
voice after voice whispering bashfully,
"Hello, doc," "Evening, doc. Glad you came."
I was shocked at recognizing the voices. I
had known the fathers and grandfathers of
these youths—hard-working farmers they
were, who found a long-sought freedom on
the American prairies, and never fumed
about the presence of the hard-working
Catholics, Jews, and black men who were
also members of that pioneer community.

There was one public meeting in the town
itself. They never tried to hold another; there
was too much objection; the voice of Bill
Barbilis rang beneath the stars.

A speaker with a pimply face stood illuminated by the flare of gasoline torches on
a makeshift rostrum, and dramatically he
spread a dollar bill between his hands.
"Here," he cried, "is the flag of the Jews!"

Bill Barbilis spoke sharply from the crowd:
"Be careful, mister. There is United States
seal on that bill."

In discomfiture, the speaker put away his

bank note. He ignored Bill as long as he could. He set his own private eagles to screaming, and he talked of battles won, and he wept for the mothers of American boys who lay in France. He said that patriotic 100-per-cent Americans must honor and protect those mothers.

Bill Barbilis climbed to the fender of a car. "Sure," he agreed clearly, "we got to take care of those mothers! Also, other mothers we got to take care of—Catholic mothers, Greek mothers, Jew mothers. We got the mothers of Company C, One Hundred Sixty-eighth Infantry. We got to take care of them. How about Jimmy Clancy? He was Catholic. He got killed in the Lorraine sector. Hyman Levinsky, he got killed the same day. Mr. Speaker, you don't know him because you do not come from Mahaska Falls. We had Buzz Griffin, colored boy used to shine shoes. He go to Chicago and enlist, and he is wounded in the Ninety-second Division!"

It was asking too much for any public speaker to contend against opposition of that sort; and the crowd thought so, too, and Duboko made a joyful noise. The out-of-town organizers withdrew. Fiery crosses blazed less frequently, and the flash of white robes frightened fewer cattle week by week.

Seeds had been sown, however, and now a kind of poison ivy grew within our midnight. Bill Barbilis and Duboko came up to my office one morning, the latter looking annoyed, the former holding a soiled sheet of paper in his hand. "Look what I got, doc."

The message was printed crudely in red ink:

We don't want you here any more. This town is only for 100 per cent law-abiding white Americans. Get out of town! Anti-Greek League.

It had been shoved under the front door of the Sugar Bowl sometime during the previous night.

"Bill," I told him, "don't worry about it. You know the source, probably; at least you can guess."

"Nobody is going to run me out of town,"

said Bill. "This is my town, and I am American citizen, and I am bugler in American Legion. I bring my old father here from Greece to be American, too, and now he has first papers." His voice trembled slightly.

"Here. Throw it in the wastepaper basket and forget about it."

There was sweat on his forehead. He wiped his face, and then he was able to laugh. "Doc, I guess you are right. Doc, I guess I am a fool."

He threw the paper away and squared his shoulders and went downstairs. I rescued a rubber glove from Duboko and threw Duboko into the hall, where he licked disinfectant from his jaws and leered at me through the screen.

A second threatening letter was shoved under Bill's door, but after that old Mr. Spiros Barbilis and Duboko did sentry duty, and pedestrians could see them entrenched behind the window. So the third warning came by mail; it told Bill that he was being given twenty-four hours to get out of town for good.

I was a little perturbed when I found Bill loading an Army .45 behind his soda fountain.

"They come around here," he said, "and I blow hell out of them."

He laughed when he said it, but I didn't like the brightness of his eyes, nor the steady, thrice-assured activity of his big clean fingers.

On Friday morning Bill came up to my office again; his face was distressed. But my fears, so far as the Anti-Greeks were concerned, were groundless.

"Do you die," he asked, "when you catch a crisis of pneumonia?"

It was one of his numerous cousins, in Sioux Falls. There had been a long-distance telephone call; the cousin was very ill, and the family wanted Bill to come. Bill left promptly in his battered, rakish roadster.

Late that night I was awakened by a clatter of cream cans under my window. I glanced at the illuminated dial of my watch, and lay wondering why the milkman had appeared some two hours before his habit. I was about to drop off to sleep when sounds of a scuffle in the alley and a roar from Duboko in the Barbilis quarters took me to the window in one leap.

There were four white figures down there in the alley yard; they dragged a fifth man —nightshirted, gagged, struggling—along with them. I yelled, and pawed around for my glasses, spurred to action by the reverberating hysterics of Duboko. I got the glasses on just before those men dragged old Mr. Barbilis into their car. The car's license plates were plastered thick with mud; at once I knew what had happened.

It was customary for the milkman to clank his bottles and cans on approaching the rear door of the Sugar Bowl; Bill or his father would get out of bed and fetch the milk to the refrigerator, for there were numerous cream-hungry cats along that alley. It was a clinking summons of this sort which had lured the lonely Mr. Barbilis from his bed.

He had gone out sleepily, probably wondering, as I had wondered, why the milkman had come so early. The sound of milk bottles lulled Duboko for a moment.

Then the muffled agony of that struggle, when the visitors clapped a pillow over the old man's face, had been enough to set Duboko bellowing.

But he was shut in; all that he could do was to threaten and curse and hurl himself against the screen. I grabbed for my foot— not the one that God gave me, but the one bought by Uncle Sam—and of course I kicked it under the bed far out of reach.

My car was parked at the opposite end of the building, out in front. I paused only to tear the telephone receiver from its hook and cry to a surprised Central that she must turn on the red light which summoned the night watchman; that someone was kidnaping old Mr. Barbilis.

The kidnapers' car roared eastward down the alley while I was bawling to the operator. And then another sound—the wrench of a heavy body sundering the metal screening. There was only empty silence as I stumbled down the stairway in my pajamas, bouncing on one foot and holding to the stair rails.

I fell into my car and turned on the headlights. The eastern block before me stretched deserted in the pale glow of single bulbs on each electric-light post. But as my car rushed into that deserted block, a small brown shape sped bulletlike across the next intersection. It was Duboko.

I swung right at the corner, and Duboko was not far ahead of me now. Down the dark, empty tunnel of Clive Street the red taillight of another car diminished rapidly. It hitched away to the left; that would mean that Mr. Barbilis was being carried along the road that crossed the city dump.

Slowing down, I howled at Duboko when I came abreast of him. It seemed that he was a Barbilis, an Americanized Greek, like them, and that he must be outraged at this occurrence, and eager to effect a rescue.

But he only slobbered up at me, and labored along on his four driving legs, with spume flying behind. I stepped on the gas again and almost struck the dog, for he would not turn out of the road. I skidded through heavy dust on the dump lane, with filmier dust still billowing back from the kidnapers' car.

For their purpose, the selection of the dump had a strategic excuse as well as a symbolic one. At the nearest boundary of the area there was a big steel gate and barbed-wire fence; you had to get out and open that gate to go through. But if you wished to vanish into the region of river timber and country roads beyond, you could drive across the wasteland without opening the gate again. I suppose that the kidnapers guessed who their pursuer was; they knew of my physical incapacity. They had shut the gate carefully behind them, and I could not go through it without getting out of my car.

But I could see them in the glare of my headlight—four white figures, sheeted and hooded.

Already they had tied Spiros Barbilis to the middle of a fence panel. They had straps, and a whip, and everything else they needed. One man was tying the feet of old Spiros to restrain his kicks; two stood ready to proceed with the flogging; and the fourth blank, hideous, white-hooded creature moved toward the gate to restrain me from interfering. That was the situation when Duboko arrived.

I ponder now the various wickednesses Duboko committed throughout his notorious career. Then for comfort I turn to the words of a Greek—him who preached the most famous funeral oration chanted among the ancients—the words of a man who was Greek in his blood and his pride, and yet who might have honored Duboko eagerly when the dog came seeking, as it were, a kind of sentimental Attican naturalization.

"For even when life's previous record showed faults and failures," said Pericles, with the voice of Thucydides, to the citizens of the fifth century, "it is just to weigh the last brave hour of devotion against them all."

Though it was not an hour by any means. No more than ten minutes had elapsed since old Mr. Barbilis was dragged from his back yard. The militant action of Duboko, now beginning, did not occupy more than a few minutes more, at the most. It makes me wonder how long men fought at Marathon, since Pheidippides died before he could tell.

And not even a heavy screen might long contain Duboko; it is no wonder that a barbed-wire fence was as reeds before his charge.

He struck the first white figure somewhere above the knees. There was a snarl and a shriek, and then Duboko was springing toward the next man.

I didn't see what happened then. I was getting out of the car and hopping toward the gate. My bare foot came down on broken glass, and that halted me for a moment. The noise of the encounter, too, seemed to build an actual, visible barrier before my eyes.

Our little world was one turmoil of flapping, torn white robes—a whirling insanity of sheets and flesh and outcry, with Duboko revolving at the hub. One of the men dodged out of the melee, and stumbled back, brandishing a club which he had snatched from the rubble close at hand. I threw a bottle, and I like to think that that discouraged him; I remember how he pranced and swore.

Mr. Barbilis managed to get the swathing off his head and the gag out of his mouth. His frail voice sang minor encouragement, and he struggled to unfasten his strapped hands from the fence.

The conflict was moving now—moving toward the kidnapers' car. First one man staggered away, fleeing; then another who limped badly. It was an unequal struggle at best. No four members of the Anti-Greek League, however young and brawny, could justly be matched against a four-footed warrior who used his jaws as the original Lacedaemonians must have used their daggers, and who fought with the right on his side, which Lacedaemonians did not always do.

Four of the combatants were scrambling into their car; the fifth was still afoot and reluctant to abandon the contest. By that time I had been able to get through the gate, and both Mr. Barbilis and I pleaded with Duboko to give up a war he had won. But this he would not do; he challenged still, and tried to fight the car; and so, as they drove away, they ran him down.

It was ten A.M. before Bill Barbilis returned from Sioux Falls. I had ample opportunity to impound Bill's .45 automatic before he came.

His father broke the news to him. I found Bill sobbing with his head on the fountain. I tried to soothe him, in English, and so did Spiros Barbilis, in Greek; but the trouble was that Duboko could no longer speak his own brand of language from the little bier where he rested.

Then Bill went wild, hunting for his pistol and not being able to find it; all the time, his father eagerly and shrilly informed Bill of the identifications he had made when his assailants' gowns were ripped away. Of course, too, there was the evidence of bites and abrasions.

Earl Klugge was limping as he moved about his All-American Kandy Kitchen, and John Klugge smelled of arnica and iodine. A day or two passed before the identity of the other kidnapers leaked out. They were hangers-on at the All-American; they didn't hang on there any longer.

I should have enjoyed what took place, down there at the Clive Street corner. I was only halfway down the block when Bill threw Earl and John Klugge through their own plateglass window.

A little crowd of men gathered, with our Mayor Wingate among them. There was no talk of damages or of punitive measures to be meted out to Bill Barbilis. I don't know just what train the Klugge brothers left on. But their restaurant was locked by noon, and the windows boarded up.

A military funeral and interment took place that afternoon behind the Sugar Bowl. There was no flag, though I think Bill would have liked to display one. But the crowd of mourners would have done credit to Athens in the age when her dead heroes were burned; all the time that Bill was blowing Taps on his bugle, I had a queer feeling that the ghosts of Pericles and Thucydides were somewhere around.

SUGGESTIONS FOR STUDY

1. What was the specific purpose of the author of this story—to arouse interest in dumb animals, to show the difficulties of returned soldiers in establishing themselves in business, to denounce intolerance, or to portray an interesting animal character?

2. Who are the protagonist and the antagonist in the story?

3. Does the story gain or lose in interest by being told by the doctor? Do you think it would have been better if told directly by the author, using the omniscient point of view? Does the method chosen handicap the author in any way? If so, in what way?

4. Is the plot overdrawn at any point? Be ready to defend your answer.

5. Do any of the characters come to life, or are they merely types to carry the plot? Which characters seem to you best realized as living, animate beings?

6. Is there anything symbolical in having Duboko a mongrel?

7. Is the denouement esthetically satisfactory? Would it have been a more satisfactory ending to have Duboko drive off the kidnapers and thereafter become the town hero?

8. When you have finished the story, what do you know about the narrator? Can you think of a good plot for a story in which he is the protagonist?

9. Are there any elements of this story which are still timely after the second World War?

10. What is the point of making Mahaska Falls the setting of the story? Would any small town in the United States do as well? (In this connection, if you do not know the story, go to the library and read O. Henry's "A Municipal Report.")

Suggestions for Writing

1. A good way to gain practice by one who has never written a short story is to rewrite one, using a different point of view from that of the original—for instance, "The Color of Mama Josefina's Life" by Celia, "You Could Look It Up" by the midget, and so on.

2. Write a realistic story of a high-school girl or boy who is determined to go to college, and whose antagonist is poverty and environment, or whose antagonist is ignorant relatives.

3. Write a story in which through dialogue and incident you depict the character of a certain community or section. Develop a plot, but let this be secondary to your aim of characterization.

4. Write a story in which some crisis brings out some theretofore unsuspected trait in the character of the protagonist. (For example, how some shy lad becomes a hero is one possibility, how a colorless girl becomes the belle of the J-Hop is another.)

5. Write a story in which conflict with objective forces drives the protagonist to his utmost endurance in order to win.

6. By means of dialogue alone, develop a story of conflict between persons of divergent character, and bring the story to a conclusion which is esthetically satisfactory.

7. Make an informal outline of three plots which you think might make good short stories and submit these to your instructor for comment and counsel.

The Whole Composition

꓇꓇꓇꓇꓇

III. BLENDING THE FOUR FORMS OF WRITING

A. The Research Paper

"RESEARCH PAPER," "term paper," "investigative theme," and "source paper" are various names for a composition of some length organized according to methods used by experienced scholars. These methods concern analyzing the topic, finding sources of information, gathering the material, and writing a report which shows clearly the authenticity of the information and the extent of research done. Research papers fill the journals of physicians, lawyers, teachers, engineers, and other professional folk and are indeed the standard method of communication wherever organizing accurate information is important.

The research paper may be expository or argumentative. That is, by assembling information from various sources, it may clarify what was misunderstood or unintelligible, or it may persuade the reader to change his mind concerning its subject. In any event, it presents an original idea derived from the writer's own thinking and observation and from his assembling information unearthed by other people.

CHOOSING A TOPIC

If your instructor does not assign you a research topic, you face the problem of choosing one for yourself. As a poor topic may plunge you into hopeless confusion, you should ask yourself the following questions about any topic you select.

1. *Is it interesting to me?* Choose a topic that appeals to you. It may concern a hobby of yours, a character in history who has aroused your interest, a scientific discovery, but whatever it is, let it be something you wish to investigate.

2. *Is it too big?* Here, as elsewhere in writing, you must limit the scope of your paper. You cannot, for instance, choose the Spanish Armada as your topic, for you would soon find that a whole book is needed to treat so vast a subject. You might rather select a portion of this subject, such as one reason for assembling the fleet, the effect of the disastrous storm upon the vessels, or the feeling pervasive among the crew at the time of departure to attack England. At the outset of your investigation you may not know, of course, whether your subject is too big, but as you do the necessary reading, you must be alert to the possibility of effectively limiting the topic.

3. *Is it within the range of my present ability?* Be ambitious, of course, to accomplish something bigger than you ever have before, but also be discreet. You have not time in the few weeks allotted to the research paper to master an elaborate new terminology or intricate new techniques. You cannot discuss Einstein's work if you are not well grounded in mathematical theory, or weigh the tariff problem if not well versed in economics.

4. *Is it possible to obtain the necessary material in my locality?* Not all libraries contain the same books. A technical college library may be admirably stocked with material on agriculture, engineering, or home

economics but lack works on philosophy, history, and literature. A teachers' college library is likely to be best equipped with books, magazines, and bulletins on education. Even the libraries of very large universities have their specialties.

To be sure, other sources may be available to you. The local city library may have the material you wish, or your college library may be able to borrow from other libraries the books you need. Many state and federal bureaus can furnish you with bulletins, available often too from industrial concerns. But using these sources ordinarily consumes time, and you have but little at your disposal. You would do well, therefore, to select a subject which you can investigate fully with the resources of your college library.

5. *Can I treat the topic objectively?* If you choose a controversial subject on which you are strongly prejudiced, you may find that you cannot examine the evidence impartially so that your conclusions are likely to be warped and one-sided. If you are, for instance, violently agitated about a racial problem, you should either refrain from choosing to investigate it further on this occasion or resolve to examine all sides of the problem impartially. A research paper is presumed to be scientifically objective.

NOTE. The discussion hitherto has been concerned only with acquiring information from written materials, which are indeed the basis of most research papers. But it may also aid you in choosing a topic to reflect that you yourself may have direct experience which you can utilize, or that you know someone near at hand whom you can interview for material, or that you can take a short excursion to gather information at a factory, a museum, or other place of interest. Also do not overlook the fact that the various members of the faculty may be able to assist you on topics in which they are experts.

EXERCISE IN CHOOSING A TOPIC FOR A RESEARCH PAPER

Consider each of the following topics carefully. If a topic is good, write "G" in the blank at the left. If it is bad, write the appropriate number, or numbers, corresponding to the questions in the preceding discussion.

———— Horse Racing
———— Alcohol, the Ruin of Modern Youth
———— The Functions of the Thyroid and Endocrine Glands
———— The Greatness of the Poet Shelley
———— The Causes of Earthquakes
———— Refrigeration
———— How an Electric Refrigerator Works
———— Boulder Dam
———— How Books Are Bound
———— Some Reasons for and against the Use of the Platoon System in City Schools
———— How the Medieval Church Made Use of Drama
———— How to Make a Bed
———— Platonism in the Thought of the English Humanists
———— Methods of Surfacing Country Roads
———— The Use of Light Filters in Photography
———— Some Great Books I Have Read
———— Is Bernard Shaw's Characterization of Joan of Arc Historically Accurate?
———— The Importance of Antarctica to Future Civilization
———— The Extent of the Oil Industry in Michigan
———— The Siege and Capture of Detroit during the War of 1812
———— Can the Deaf-Mute Learn to Talk?
———— How to Dig Bait
———— The Heroic Game of Football
———— The Status of Religion in Russia

THE USE OF THE LIBRARY

The Card Catalogue

In most libraries the great body of books are for practical reasons shelved in rooms to which the students do not have access. But you can find what materials these rooms contain by consulting the card catalogue, which ordinarily you will find near the main desk of the library. This catalogue is composed of a large number of cards, carefully indexed, which record extensive information about every book, bulletin, periodical, and manuscript in the library.

If the library is adequately staffed and completely up-to-date, most items in it are represented by at least three cards in the catalogue—the author card, the title card, and the subject-matter card. Thus, if you want E. K. Chambers's work on *The Medieval Stage,* you can find it by looking in the C's for the author's name, in the M's for the title, or under a subject matter caption referring to the material in the book. If your topic is "Costuming in the Medieval Morality Play" and you have no idea who the chief authorities are on that subject, by looking under such captions as "stage," "medieval stage," "costume," you will probably discover cards for the book by E. K. Chambers. The use of the subject matter indexing will be of most value in the initial stages of finding what resources the library has to offer for your topic. Use a little ingenuity in thinking of the probable catchword or phrase which the librarian has used to describe the information in which you are interested. If no caption "Spanish Armada" can be found, try "naval history," or "Spanish history."

Having discovered the general organization of the card catalogue, next acquire a clear understanding of what is on the cards themselves.

On the first line is the author's name, last name first, and the dates of his birth and (if it has occurred) death. Next comes a transcription of the title page of the book, followed by the facts of publication (place, publisher, and date). The symbols on the next line indicate that there are seven pages of prefatory material (small Roman numerals), followed by three hundred and thirty pages of text. A map is included, and the book is twenty-two and a half centimeters high. This is followed by a list of three subject-matter classifications which apply to this book. The rest of the material at the bottom of the card is chiefly for the use of librarians.

General Book Indexes

The card catalogue of your library lists only the books available in its own stacks. You will wish, however, to know if other books in other libraries may pertain to your

Anthropology; H—Social Sciences; J—Political Sciences; K—Law; L—Education; M—Music; N—Fine Arts; P—Languages and Literature; Q—Sciences; R—Medicine; S—Agriculture, and Plant

---

> JK 146 .B368 Beard, Charles Austin, 1874-1948
>
>   An economic interpretation of the Constitution of the United States, by Charles A. Beard . . . New York, The Macmillan Company, 1913.
>
>   vii, 330 p. map. 22½ cm.
>
>   1. U.S.—Constitutional History. 2. U.S.—Constitution. 3. U.S.—Economic Conditions.
>   I. Title
>
>   Library of Congress JK146.B135   13-9314
>   Copyright A 346373   [a35i²1]   342.73

At the top, in the left-hand corner, is the call number, the symbol which indicates to the librarian where the book should be shelved.[1]

[1] Most libraries adopt one of two systems, the Library of Congress system or the Dewey Decimal system. The Library of Congress uses letters to denote twenty divisions of all knowledge: A—General works and Polygraphy; B—Philosophy and Religion; C—History and Auxiliary Sciences; D—History and Topography of foreign countries; E and F—American History and Topography; G—Geography and

and Animal Husbandry; T—Technology; U—Military Science; V—Naval Science; and Z—Bibliography and Library Science.

The Dewey Decimal system divides knowledge into ten groups and designates the groups by numbers: 000—General works; 100—Philosophy; 200—Religion; 300—Sociology; 400—Philology; 500—Natural Sciences; 600—Useful Arts; 700—Fine Arts; 800—Literature; and 900—History. These groups are further subdivided to provide smaller classifications within the larger divisions. Unless the student has access to the library stacks, there is little need for him to learn these systems.

topic. In the Reference Room of your library are several volumes which will assist you to find this information. The most useful perhaps is the *Cumulative Book Index,* which lists monthly and annually the books published in English and which is bound periodically as the *United States Catalogue.* You should also examine, if pertinent to your work, the *Catalogue of United States Public Documents,* the *Children's Catalog,* the *Fiction Catalog,* and the *Standard Catalog for Public Libraries.* A special volume, not in itself an index, called the *Book Review Digest* will aid you in knowing which books are the most significant, as it prints excerpts from book reviews.

Periodical Indexes

To know what magazine articles pertain to your topic, consult the periodical indexes in the Reference Room. That index of most general use is the *Reader's Guide to Periodical Literature,* which covers from 1900 to the present a wide variety of magazines and lists articles by much the same helpful classification system used in the card catalogue—by author, title, and subject, with numerous cross references. In the front of each number is a key to the rather intricate system of abbreviation used for each entry. Useful indexes for nineteenth century periodicals are *19th Century Reader's Guide to Periodical Literature 1890-1899,* an index to subjects and authors, and *Poole's Index to Periodical Literature,* published from 1802 until 1907, an index to subjects, not authors, except when authors are treated as subjects. Of special value in science and the humanities is also the *International Index to Periodical Literature,* begun in 1907.

These three indexes do not list articles from highly specialized or technical journals. For your convenience in finding articles from these periodicals there are numerous specialized indexes. Among these are the *Agricultural Index,* the *Art Index,* the *Debate Index,* the *Dramatic Index,* the *Education Index,* the *Engineering Index,* the *Index Medicus* and *Quarterly Cumulative Index Medicus,* the *Industrial Arts Index, Psychological Index,* and the *Song Index.*

Of specialized interest also is the *New York Times Index,* a complete index to articles printed in the *New York Times.*

As these titles make no pretense at being a complete listing of reference works, they may not pertain directly to the topic you have chosen. By consulting the *Guide to Reference Books* by Constance M. Winchell (based on the *Guide to Reference Books* by I. G. Mudge) or the *Guide to the Use of Libraries* by Margaret Hutchins, Alice Johnson, and Margaret Williams, you may be able to compile a bibliography more completely and quickly.

Encyclopedias and Special Dictionaries

Encyclopedias are useful not only for their articles on a wide variety of subjects but also for their bibliographies, given at the end of important articles, which can lead you to standard sources on these subjects. In addition, the index volume may suggest other articles in the encyclopedia which bear partially on your topic. The following encyclopedias are excellent:

Chambers's Encyclopedia, revised 1950.
Encyclopædia Britannica, 14th edition, in continuous revision.
Encyclopedia Americana, in continuous revision.
New International Encyclopedia, 2nd edition, 1922.

In the section on "The Word" the standard dictionaries and thesauri have been listed, but other more specialized dictionaries often prove helpful. Among those which assist in questions of usage and meaning are:

Berrey, L. V. and Van den Bark, M. *American Thesaurus of Slang,* 1947.
Craigie, Sir William and Hulbert, J. R. *Dictionary of American English,* 1936-1944.
Fowler, H. W. *Dictionary of Modern English Usage,* 1926.
Horwill, H. W. *Dictionary of Modern American Usage,* 1944.

Mathews, M. M. *A Dictionary of American-isms on Historical Principles,* 1951.

Skeat, W. W. *Etymological Dictionary of the English Language,* 1910.

Weekley, E. *Etymological Dictionary of Modern English,* 1921.

Other dictionaries have the special purpose of explaining allusions and tracing the origins of quotations. Some of these are:

Apperson, G. L. *English Proverbs and Proverbial Phrases,* 1929.

Bartlett, John. *Familiar Quotations,* 1948.

Bartlett, John. *New and Complete Concordance . . . of Shakespeare,* 1894.

Benham, W. G. *Book of Quotations, Proverbs, and Household Words,* 1949.

Brewer, E. C. *Dictionary of Phrase and Fable,* 1948.

Mencken, H. L. *A New Dictionary of Quotations,* 1942.

Smith, W. G. *Oxford Dictionary of English Proverbs,* 1948.

Stevenson, B. E. *Home Book of Quotations,* 1949.

Modern scholarship has provided numerous biographical dictionaries; those of the type of *Who's Who* are especially plentiful. Only a very few can be enumerated here:

American Men of Science, 1906—.

Century Cyclopedia of Names, 1914.

Current Biography, 1940—.

Dictionary of American Biography, 1928-1936; supplement, 1944.

Dictionary of National Biography, 1885-1901; supplements, 1901, 1912, 1927, 1937, 1949.

National Cyclopedia of American Biography, 1892—.

Webster's Biographical Dictionary, 1943.

Who's Who; Who's Who in America; Who's Who in American Education; Who's Who in Engineering; and so on.

Reference works in special subjects. In each subject-matter area these general reference works are supplemented by more detailed reference works. In the following list are a few which may assist you in finding what writings apply to the research topic you have chosen:

AGRICULTURE

Bailey, L. H. *Cyclopedia of American Agriculture,* 1907-1909.

——— *Standard Cyclopedia of Horticulture,* 1914-1917.

Bailey, L. H. and Bailey, E. Z. *Hortus Second,* 1941.

Taylor, Norman. *Encyclopedia of Gardening, Horticulture, and Landscape Design,* 1948.

U.S. Department of Agriculture. *Year Book of Agriculture,* 1894—.

ALMANACS AND YEAR BOOKS

American Yearbook, 1910-1919, 1925—.

Kieran, John. *Information Please Almanac,* 1947—.

New International Year Book, 1907—.

Public Affairs Information Service, 1915—.

Statesman's Yearbook, 1864—.

World Almanac, 1868—.

ARCHITECTURE AND ART

A.L.A. Portrait Index, 1906.

American Annual of Photography, 1887—.

American Art Annual, 1899—.

Bryan, M. *Bryan's Dictionary of Painters and Engravers,* 1905.

Ceramic Abstracts, 1922—.

Fielding, M. *Dictionary of American Painters, Sculptors, and Engravers,* 1926.

Harper's Encyclopedia of Art, 1937.

Index of Twentieth Century Artists, 1933-1937.

Hiler, H. and Hiler, M. *Bibliography of Costume,* 1939.

Johnson, A. P. and Sironen, M. K. *Manual of the Furniture Arts and Crafts,* 1928.

Runes, D. D. and Schrickel, H. G. *Encyclopedia of the Arts,* 1946.

Searle, A. B. *Encyclopedia of the Ceramic Industries,* 1930.

Sturgis, Russell. *Dictionary of Architecture and Building,* 1901.

Wolf, M. L. *Dictionary of the Arts,* 1951.

CLASSICS

Cary, M. and others. *The Oxford Classical Dictionary,* 1949.

Harvey, Sir Paul. *Oxford Companion to Classical Literature,* 1937.

Peck, H. T. *Harper's Dictionary of Classical Literature and Antiquities,* 1897.

Sandys, Sir John. *A Companion to Latin Studies,* 1925.

Smith, Sir William. *Classical Dictionary of Greek and Roman Biography and Mythology,* 1880.

Whibley, Leonard. *A Companion to Greek Studies,* 1931.

COMMERCE, BUSINESS, ECONOMICS

American Labor Yearbook, 1916—.

Chisholm, G. C. *Handbook of Commercial Geography,* 1932.

Clark, V. S. *History of Manufactures in the United States,* 1929.

Economic Almanac, 1940—.

Encyclopedia of the Social Sciences, 1930-1935.

Horton, B. J. and others. *Dictionary of Modern Economics,* 1948.

Manley, M. C. *Business Information and Its Sources,* 1931. Supplement, 1939.

——— *Business Books,* 1920-1926, 1927.

Munn, G. G. *Encyclopedia of Banking and Finance,* 1937.

Sloan, H. S. and Zurcher, A. J. *Dictionary of Economics,* 1949.

U.S. Bureau of the Census. *Census,* 1790—.

U.S. Department of Commerce. *Commerce Year Book,* 1922—.

U.S. Bureau of Foreign and Domestic Commerce. *Statistical Abstract of the United States,* 1878—.

EDUCATION

Baird, W. R. *Baird's Manual of American College Fraternities,* 1949.

Bogue, J. P. and Eells, W. C. *American Junior Colleges,* 1948.

Brumbaugh, A. J. *American Universities and Colleges,* 1948.

Good, C. V. *Dictionary of Education,* 1945.

Monroe, Paul. *Cyclopedia of Education,* 1911-1913.

Monroe, W. S. *Encyclopedia of Educational Research,* 1950.

Rivlin, H. N. and Schuler, Herbert. *Encyclopedia of Modern Education,* 1943.

HISTORY

Adams, J. T. *Album of American History,* 1944.

——— *Atlas of American History,* 1943.

——— *Dictionary of American History,* 1942.

Beers, H. P. *Bibliographies in American History,* 1942.

Cambridge Ancient History, 1923-1939.

Cambridge Medieval History, 1911-1936.

Cambridge Modern History, 1902-1926.

Channing, E., Hart, A. B., and Turner, F. I. *Guide to the Study and Reading of American History,* 1912.

Dutcher, G. M. and others. *Guide to Historical Literature,* 1931.

Keller, H. R. *Dictionary of Dates,* 1934.

Langer, W. L. *An Encyclopedia of World History,* 1948.

Larned, J. N. *New Larned History for Ready Reference,* 1922-1924.

Pageant of America: A Pictorial History of the United States, 1925-1929.

Paullin, C. O. *Atlas of the Historical Geography of the United States,* 1932.

Shepherd, W. R. *Historical Atlas,* 1929.

Writings on American History, 1902-.

LITERATURE

Baker, E. A. and Packman, J. *Guide to the Best Fiction,* 1932.

Baker, E. A. *Guide to Historical Fiction,* 1914.

Benet, W. R. *The Reader's Encyclopedia,* 1948.

Brewton, J. E. and Brewton, S. W. *Index to Children's Poetry,* 1942.

Bruncken, H. *Subject Index to Poetry,* 1940.

Cambridge History of American Literature, 1917-1921.

Cambridge Bibliography of English Literature, 1941.

Cambridge History of English Literature, 1907-1927.

Essay and General Literature Index, 1900—.

Firkins, Ina. *Index of Plays,* 1800-1926, 1927. Supplement, 1927-1934, 1935.

——— *Index to Short Stories,* 1923. Supplements, 1929, 1936.

Hart, J. D. *Oxford Companion to American Literature,* 1948.

Hartnoll, P. *Oxford Companion to the Theatre,* 1951.

Harvey, Sir Paul. *Oxford Companion to English Literature,* 1946.

Hefling, H. and Richards, E. *Index to Contemporary Biography and Criticism,* 1934.

Logasa, H. and Ver Nooy, W. *Index to One-Act Plays,* 1924-1950.

Millett, F. B. *Contemporary American Authors,* 1940. Based on Manly, J. M. and Rickert, E. *Contemporary American Authors,* 1929.

——— *Contemporary British Literature,* 1935. Based on Manly, J. M. and Rickert, E. *Contemporary British Literature.*

Modern Humanities Research Association. *Annual Bibliography of English Language and Literature,* 1920—.

Sharp, R. F. *Short Biographical Dictionary of Foreign Literature,* 1933.

MEDICINE

Dorland, W. A. N. *American Illustrated Medical Dictionary,* 1947.

Jones, H., Hoerr, N., and Osol, A. *Blakiston's New Gould Medical Dictionary*, 1949.

Kelly, E. C. *Encyclopedia of Medical Sources*, 1948.

Merck Index, 1940.

Stedman, T. L. and Garber, S. T. *Practical Medical Dictionary*, 1946.

MUSIC

Grove, Sir George. *Grove's Dictionary of Music and Musicians*, 1928. Supplement, 1940.

Kobbé, G. *Complete Opera Book*, 1935.

Oxford History of Music, 1929-1938.

Scholes, P. A. *The Oxford Companion to Music*, 1947.

Thompson, O. *International Cyclopedia of Music and Musicians*, 1949.

MYTHOLOGY, FOLKLORE, HOLIDAYS

Chambers, R. *Book of Days*, 1899.

Douglas, G. W. *The American Book of Days*, 1948.

Eastman, M. H. *Index to Fairy Tales, Myths, and Legends*, 1926. Supplement, 1937.

Edwardes, M. and Spence, L. *Dictionary of Non-classical Mythology*, 1912.

Frazer, Sir James. *The Golden Bough*, 1907-1915.

Gayley, C. M. *The Classic Myths in English Literature and in Art*, 1911.

Gray, L. H. *Mythology of All Races*, 1916-1932.

Hazeltine, M. E. *Anniversaries and Holidays*, 1944.

Hazlitt, W. C. *Faiths and Folk Lore*, 1905. A new edition of Brand, J. *Observations on the Popular Antiquities of Great Britain*, 1888-1890.

Leach, M. *Funk and Wagnalls Standard Dictionary of Folklore, Mythology, and Legend*, 1949.

Schauffler, R. H. *Our American Holidays*, 1907-1947.

———— *The Days We Celebrate*, 1940.

PHILOSOPHY AND PSYCHOLOGY

Baldwin, J. M. *Dictionary of Philosophy and Psychology*, 1901-1905.

Harriman, P. L. *Encyclopedia of Psychology*, 1946.

Psychological Abstracts, 1927—.

Rand, B. *Bibliography of Philosophy, Psychology, and Cognate Subjects*, 1905.

Runes, D. D. *The Dictionary of Philosophy*, 1942.

Warren, H. C. *Dictionary of Psychology*, 1934.

RELIGION

Catholic Encyclopedia, 1907-1922.

Hastings, J. *Encyclopedia of Religion and Ethics*, 1908-1927.

Jewish Encyclopedia, 1901-1906.

Mathews, S. and Smith, G. B. *Dictionary of Religion and Ethics*, 1921.

Schaff, P. *New Schaff-Herzog Encyclopedia of Religious Knowledge*, 1908-1912.

SCIENCE

American Chemical Society. *Chemical Abstracts*, 1907—.

Bibliography of North American Geology, 1919—.

Biological Abstracts, 1926—.

Bolton, H. C. *Select Bibliography of Chemistry*, 1893-1904.

Botanical Abstracts, 1918-1926.

Crane, E. J. and Patterson, A. M. *Guide to the Literature of Chemistry*, 1927.

Glazebrook, Sir Richard. *Dictionary of Applied Physics*, 1922-1923.

Henderson, I. F. and Henderson, W. D. *Dictionary of Scientific Terms*, 1949.

Soule, B. A. *Library Guide for the Chemist*, 1938.

Thorpe, J. F. and Whiteley, M. A. *Dictionary of Applied Chemistry*, 1937-1949.

U.S. Geological Survey. *Publications of the Geological Survey*, 1948.

Van Nostrand's Scientific Encyclopedia, 1947.

Webster's Geographical Dictionary, 1949.

Willis, J. C. *Dictionary of Flowering Plants and Ferns*, 1931.

SOCIOLOGY

Encyclopedia of the Social Sciences, 1930-1935.

Fairchild, H. P. *Dictionary of Sociology*, 1944.

Social Science Abstracts, 1929-1933.

Social Work Year Book, 1930—.

SPORTS

Cummings, P. *The Dictionary of Sports*, 1949.

Menke, F. G. *New Encyclopedia of Sports*, 1947.

Spalding's Official Athletic Almanac, 1893—.

EXERCISE IN THE USE OF THE LIBRARY

Find the answers to the following questions. Note also the reference works in which the answers were found.

1. What are ten slang terms in America to designate political patronage?

2. What is the Irish folk belief about the cluracan?

3. Name four ways in which April 26 is celebrated in the United States.

4. For what sort of paintings was the American, J. L. Heimer, known?

5. In what sport is the term "facing circle" used?

6. On what musical instrument did the French composer Pierre Levasseur perform?

7. Name two writers who used the Americanism "deadhead" as a verb.

8. Complete the English proverb, "War is sweet to them . . . ."

9. From what poem does the line come, "The boy stood on the burning deck"?

10. What is the population of the Canadian town of Lacombe?

11. What classical author satirized Bavius and Maevius?

12. What is the mailing address of the poet Robert Frost?

13. Name four books on farm life published in 1949.

14. Name three books published by T. S. Eliot since 1948.

15. About how many species of the flower coreopsis are there?

16. Cite three lines from Shakespeare's works using the word "porridge."

17. To whom was James Bowie, inventor of the Bowie knife, married?

18. Name three magazine articles on inoculation written in 1948-1949.

19. Name three magazine articles written by Herbert Hoover in 1950.

20. Name a magazine article written in 1950 on the International Conference on Public Education.

FORMS FOR BIBLIOGRAPHY CARDS

Once you have agreed with your instructor upon a topic for your research, you must begin the actual work on your subject by going to the library and consulting some of the reference works just cited in order to compile a bibliography—that is, a list of all books, articles, and other sources of information pertaining to your subject. Make this list as complete as you can, for though some of the works you list may not be in your college library, you may be able to secure them easily at home, in a city library, or elsewhere. Should you find, however, that an extensive number of items on your bibliography are not in the college library, consult at once with your instructor; he may advise you to change your topic.

As a first device for saving you time in research, purchase a supply of cards or pads of paper measuring three by five or four by six inches, on which you can record bibliographical information and notes. Putting only *one* bibliographical entry on a card, copy each item of your bibliography on these cards and file the cards alphabetically by the authors' last names for easy reference. Each entry must be written down carefully and completely, for you do not want to waste time later by returning to the library to seek information on these books and articles when you are listing them as the bibliography at the close of the final draft of your completed manuscript. Record information according to the following forms to render it complete, recalling also the correct procedure for underlining titles or placing them in quotation marks.

A bibliography card for Carl Van Doren's *Benjamin Franklin* would look like this:

> Van Doren, Carl
> *Benjamin Franklin*
> New York: The Viking Press, 1938

For your convenience you could also note on the card such items as the library call number of the book, the total number of pages in the book, the pages in the volume which pertain to your subject, or the presence of pictures or illustrations. The following list will establish for you the correct form for almost any kind of entry you may wish to make on your bibliography cards:

Entry for a book by two editors:

> Millett, Fred B. and Bentley, Gerald E. (eds.)
> *The Play's the Thing*
> New York: Appleton-Century Company, 1936

Entry for a book by two authors:

> Beard, Charles Austin and Beard, Mary
> *The Rise of American Civilization*

New York: The Macmillan Company, 1927

Entry for a book by more than three authors:

Sizer, Theodore and others
Aspects of the Social History of America
Chapel Hill: The University of North
Carolina Press, 1931

Entry for a book which has been revised:

Hanford, James Holly
A Milton Handbook
Revised edition
New York: F. S. Crofts & Co., 1933

Entry for a work of more than one volume:

Calvin, John
The Institutes of the Christian Religion
Tr. by Henry Beveridge
Edinburgh: T. & T. Clark, 1895
2 vols.

Entry for a book which is part of a series:

Chesterton, G. K.
Robert Browning
New York: The Macmillan Company,
1926
("English Men of Letters")

Entry for a University Bulletin:

*The Articulation of High-School Studies
with Freshman Courses in the University*
A Series of Reports by the University
Committees and Representatives of the
Michigan High Schools. University of
Michigan Official Publication, Vol.
XXXVII, No. 42
Ann Arbor, Michigan, 1936

Entry for an item in a collection of readings:

Dunne, Finley Peter
"On the Victorian Era" in Walter Blair,
Native American Humor (1800-1900)
New York: American Book Company,
1937

Entry for an article in an encyclopedia:[1]

Pfeil, Stephen
"Jurisprudence"
The Encyclopedia Americana. 1940
Edition
Vol. 16

---

[1] Name of publisher and place are generally omitted for the best-known encyclopedias. Edition and date are important, however.

Entry for a magazine article:

Lane, James
"The Craze for Craziness"
Catholic World, CXLIV (December,
1936), 306-9

NOTE-TAKING AND THE USE OF SOURCES

As a true research paper is based upon wide reading in a number of different sources, it will not be possible to write the paper while you are doing your reading. You must read, take careful notes, and only then begin writing the paper with the aid of the notes. A good system of note-taking, therefore, is indispensable. The prime considerations are that the notes be clear, complete, accurate, and accessible: you must be able to find them quickly, to read them easily, and to have such complete information upon them that you never have to return to source books to recheck items or fill out information.

As a first step in taking notes, it is well to read about your subject in a general reference work, such as the encyclopedia, so that you may be able at once to make a highly tentative outline to guide you in classifying the notes you take. Suppose that you are reading about theatrical activities in the United States before 1800. After some preliminary reading and some thought on your part, you may decide that four divisions of this subject will prove useful for organizational purposes:

1. Earliest beginnings
2. Spread of theatrical activity
3. Prominent people
4. Kinds of plays

Bearing this very sketchy outline in mind, you now consult the bibliography which you have compiled on this subject. It is well even now to keep first to the more general works, so that a broad view of the topic gained in this way will help you to understand details better when you encounter them later on. Suppose, therefore, that you select P. H. Boynton's *Literature and American Life* as containing a helpful general survey of the subject. Looking up "theater" in the index, you are referred to pages 105-110. You read first that a professional theater, like a professional orchestra or an opera, is likely to come late in the growth of any society, because it is expensive and must await the existence of large communities of prosperous people who have time and interest for these kinds of entertainment. As this appears to be an interesting and valuable observation, you write in the top, left-hand corner of a note card "Earliest beginnings," that caption from your tentative four-point outline which best describes this item.

But before you write the note you must make a decision. Do you wish the exact words of the author or a summary of them? An exact quotation is useful when the point at issue is controversial, especially well phrased, or highly authoritative. But remember, *material quoted directly should always be put in quotation marks on the note card.*

The material from Boynton's book, though important, is rather obvious; no need exists for quoting it directly. The card then takes on this appearance:

Early beginnings
Professional theater, like prof. orchestra and opera, comes late in development of any society. Is expensive; therefore dependent on large communities with prosperous people who have time and interest.
Boynton, *Lit. & Amer. Life,* p. 104

For the sake of brevity abbreviations and incomplete sentences are used, but these must always be clear in meaning and easily recognized. Notice that at the bottom of the card are the author's name, the title of the work, and the page number from which the information is taken. These must always appear on a note card; you must leave nothing to your memory, which will become very treacherous after you have made a great number of cards from many different source works.

Reading further in Boynton, you soon find that, much to the indignation of some of the

citizens of Boston, someone suggested a dramatic entertainment right in the Council Chamber itself in 1714. Using another card, you make this entry:

Early beginnings   1714
Somebody suggested holding a dramatic entertainment in the Council Chamber of Boston in 1714. Some citizens indignant.
Boynton, *Lit. & Amer. Life,* p. 106

Placing the date 1714 in the upper corner of this card affords a subdivision of "Early beginnings" which may later prove useful.

In this manner you continue to read further in Professor Boynton's volume and the other works on your bibliography. To find information easily, *place only a single point from a single source on any one card.* In this way all cards bearing the caption "Early beginnings" can be filed together in a note box or folder ready for a more careful organization when the time comes to write your paper.

Further cautions about quotations seem necessary. Should the book you are reading contain a quotable item taken from another source, secure if possible that primary source to examine it yourself. Professor Boynton, for example, quotes a stern remark of the Puritan judge, Samuel Sewall, on theaters; this remark, he says, in a footnote, he has taken from an article, "Letter-Book of Samuel Sewall," in the *Massachusetts Historical Society Collections,* sixth series, II, 30. Rather than contenting yourself with accepting the statement of the quotation by Professor Boynton, consult the original article in the historical society volume in order to validate the accuracy of the quotation and to see it in context, where it may assume fresh meaning for you. If your library does not have the primary volume, write this fact on your note card and acknowledge later in a footnote that you have been unable to secure the primary volume and are depending on Boynton's transcription of it. Do not ever lead a reader to believe that you have consulted some item which has been inaccessible to you.

It is also imperative that *when you make a direct quotation, it must be absolutely true to the original.* Even typographical errors, slips in spelling, and other mistakes or peculiarities should be copied as they stand; immediately after them place in brackets the Latin word *sic* (meaning "thus it is") to indicate the error is in the original and not in your transcription.

On page 449 are listed a number of standard abbreviations for saving space. Make use of these on your note cards. Two other devices you may also find helpful. In the midst of a direct quotation, if you wish to make some comment of your own for clarification of the wording of the quotation, insert such editorial comment in brackets, as "In that year [1374] Chaucer was provided with a house in London rent-free." Then too you may wish to omit part of a quotation which is not pertinent to the point at issue. Insertion of three dots will indicate this omission: "This act of Congress . . . was made a law in 1924."

As you read carefully the items on your bibliography, a pattern should soon begin to emerge. Some works included on it will prove useless by lacking pertinence to your subject or by being too general; this information you would do well to indicate on your bibliography cards. Next, you will find that a certain body of knowledge is common to all works which bear directly or indirectly on your subject. You should transcribe this material carefully on your note cards for your own use, but under usual circumstances you need not ascribe it by footnote to any particular writer. Again, make notation to this effect on your note cards. Finally you will perceive that some writers hold opinions on the subject that no one else has advanced or have stated facts which escaped the attention of other research workers. These ideas and facts you must scrupulously ascribe to the correct author and transcribe very accurately so that you do not distort them. This pattern,

however, will usually emerge best if you begin reading the most general reference works, proceed then to what appear to be the most important and helpful works, and only finally peruse the most detailed and limited treatments of the topic.

EVALUATING SOURCES: EVIDENCE

Almost any topic involving true research will present, sooner or later, a marked difference of opinion among those scrutinizing the available facts, this usually to the complete astonishment or bewilderment of a freshman student. Dale Carnegie in an article on Shakespeare's life declares that Shakespeare had to flee from Stratford for stealing deer from the park of Sir Thomas Lucy; J. Q. Adams, in his biography of Shakespeare, believes such a conclusion entirely unwarranted. Which of these two shall you believe? Surely you must make up your mind one way or the other if your research paper bears on this subject.

Experience will demonstrate to you that all writers are human and so make errors of statement or expound questionable theories. Even the most exact scholarship can be biased or shortsighted. No one, therefore, should be read with other than a critical eye. But experience will also prove that some writers are far more accurate, better informed, and more sensible than others; nearly always you can rely upon them. One task facing you in research is to ascertain which writers are the more trustworthy.

As a first aid in evaluating evidence, notice the date of publication of the book or article. If the work is old, it may be highly inaccurate because of the discovery of new facts since its publication; we no longer believe the world is flat or that Newton's theory of light is adequate. On the other hand, an older book may be exactly what you are seeking if it contains an eyewitness account of an historical event, first-hand information on a man's appearance or character, a contemporary theory that may stimulate new ideas in you, or many other such essentials in research.

Secondly, observe the purpose of the work. Is it written to gain adherents to a cause or belief with a consequent warping of facts and ideas, or is it coolly impartial? Is it issued by an institution or industry as camouflaged advertising propaganda, or is it the effort of a detached investigator to determine facts? Beware of apparently trustworthy booklets sent by large corporations, usually free of charge. If not designed as advertising, they would not be sent free. Also examine geographical, racial, sectarian, and political affiliations carefully. A large stockholder in a private utilities corporation will ordinarily not give the most acceptable evidence on the desirability of government-owned power resources. The opinion of an editorial writer should be considered in the light of the editorial policy of his newspaper. The source of a man's bread and butter, his social prestige, or his profession almost invariably affects the objectivity of his judgment.

Thirdly, observe the documentation of the work—that is, the footnote and bibliographical apparatus which shows sources of material. Many popularized surveys of art, science, literature, history, and the like, designed for the easy reading of large audiences, do not contain such documentation, and so the authenticity of many statements in them is open to suspicion. Read also the preface or introduction of a book, for if the book represents a large amount of labor, the author will record his indebtedness to the works and the people who have helped him: libraries, owners of manuscripts, other scholars, authorities who have read and criticized his manuscript. With respect to an article, notice the kind of periodical in which it is published. Periodicals which number their readers by the hundreds of thousands or millions must cater to popular taste and present somewhat oversimplified ideas. They can seldom afford to print a widely unpopular opinion or a highly subtle, profound article.

Evaluate also the kind of evidence which is presented. Direct evidence—the testimony of an eyewitness, proved historical data, or an accurate statistical survey—may involve error, but the chances are less so than in so-called indirect evidence, which involves someone's opinion. Tramping through the woods, you may gain the direct evidence of your own eyes that a snake sheds its skin; if you have never seen this phenomenon, you must rely on indirect evidence, what is told you by others. In the library direct evidence involves *primary research* with primary sources, as for instance in a problem related to Shakespeare's *Henry V* the play itself is the primary source. Books and articles about the play constitute the indirect evidence or *secondary* sources. Just as your own research will be more accurate if you rely heavily on primary sources, so will that of others. Observe the text, footnotes, and bibliography of the work you are reading to see how frequently the author has made use of primary documents and other such sources; if he quotes frequently from them or refers often to them, you may have more confidence in his accuracy than if there is little indication of his study of them. The fact that J. Q. Adams's biography of Shakespeare is studded with quotation from primary Elizabethan sources immediately gives it an air of authority which Dale Carnegie's article on Shakespeare lacks.

Of lesser importance perhaps but well worth noting is the qualification of the author to write upon his subject. Sometimes this information may be gleaned from the title page or the dustcover of a book. For instance, you may gain confidence by reading on the title page of Carl Van Doren's *Benjamin Franklin* that the author has written among other works four biographies of literary men, six books of literary history and criticism, and edited three works including the *Cambridge History of American Literature;* and on the dustcover that he has taught at Columbia University, served as editor of the *Nation* and *Century* and as editor-in-chief of the Literary Guild, and worked on the Franklin biography for ten years. On the surface he would seem well qualified to write such a volume. Sometimes, of course, you must gather this information from biographical dictionaries, but you will profit from making such an investigation. If an author had never written biography, made a specialty of literary history or criticism, or delved especially into American colonial history, he might not be sufficiently trained to write an outstanding biography of Franklin.

THE OUTLINE

Having now read all the works on your bibliography, taken notes on them following a tentative outline, and weighed the evidence on all debatable points of opinion, you are ready to advance toward the final stages of preparation of your research project. The next step is to consider with care the sort of reader you envision for the paper, especially noting the amount of knowledge which you presume him to possess about your topic. Study well the method best suited to introduce him easily and logically to the body of information you have assembled so that he will be sure to accept your conclusions. It may be that the temporary outline which you made at the beginning of your research will still suffice, but of course an entirely new organizational pattern may be necessary. When you are satisfied that you have established the best possible method of approach, write down the thesis as a guide to unity, formulate first the main headings of the outline, and then subdivide these in detail. Though at first for the sake of time and ease of organizing you may work with the topic outline, you should translate this into a sentence outline before you actually begin writing your paper. But do not under any circumstances try to write the paper without an outline; such a procedure will only waste your time and confuse your reader.

FOOTNOTES AND FINAL BIBLIOGRAPHY

Not only does the writer of a research paper feel morally obligated to give credit to the sources which he has used, but he understands, as the foregoing paragraphs have observed, that a critical reader will look for proper documentation as one of the first signs of careful research work. Make very sure, therefore, that before you submit your term paper to the instructor, it has footnotes and bibliography accurate in substance and precise in form.

Footnotes to Acknowledge Sources

A footnote reference is necessary for every statement of fact or opinion that is not a matter of general knowledge and is not derived from the writer's own original observation. The question of what constitutes general knowledge is sometimes debatable, but if there is any doubt in the writer's mind, it is better to include the footnote than to omit it. The date of the signing of the Declaration of Independence, certainly, is common knowledge, and no source need be given for it; but a statement concerning the number of passenger cars registered in New Jersey in 1940 must be documented. The fact that Abraham Lincoln was assassinated by John Wilkes Booth is common knowledge, but a statement to the effect that Booth was a member of a ring of conspirators who had carefully planned the assassination needs footnoting.

Footnotes to Acknowledge Quotations

Be sure to state the source of all material which is quoted directly. Enclose such material in quotation marks unless it is one hundred words or more; in this event omit the quotation marks, and indent the quotation from the left margin of the page to show it is a quoted unit; sometimes these longer quotations are single-spaced, but this practice is rather widely objected to because of the difficulty of reading such spacing. When you come to copying these quotations from your note cards, you will realize the force of the injunctions given earlier in the text—to put full information on each card concerning the source of the quotation, and to make sure you put all quoted matter in quotation marks, so that you can easily distinguish between direct and indirect quotation.

Footnotes to Define Terms

Sometimes the terminology of a technical article is familiar to a person trained in that subject, but confusing to an ordinary reader. The footnote is a convenient place to present definitions of terms of this kind. Translations of foreign words and sentences can also be placed in footnotes.

Footnotes to Provide Additional Information

Sometimes material in notes is interesting and useful, but, if presented in the body of the text, would be an unnecessary digression. Illustrations, anecdotes, and biographical data, for instance, can frequently be placed in a footnote when they would only serve to clutter the paper if used along with more important information.

Form for Footnotes

A footnote need not repeat any information included in the body of the paper. Occasionally, all the data necessary to identify a source of information or a quotation occurs in the text, thus: "The essay on 'Mark Twain' written by Stuart P. Sherman for the *Cambridge History of American Literature*, Vol. III, Chapter VIII, states that . . ." When this happens, no footnote is necessary. However, the constant inclusion of documentation in the text of the paper makes the style unreadable. If the sentence reads, "The essay on 'Mark Twain' written by Stuart P. Sherman for the *Cambridge History of American Literature* states that . . . ," a footnote should provide the volume and chapter but should not repeat what has already been stated in the sentence to which it refers.

To refer a reader to a footnote, place an Arabic number just after the portion to which the footnote corresponds and in a slightly raised position (thus,[3]); number continuously throughout the whole paper. Place footnotes at the bottom of each page or at the end of the paper. The latter practice is preferred for a manuscript which is to be printed, but your instructor may prefer for his convenience that you place them at the bottom of each page. Ask him which method to follow. When typing, double space the footnotes as you do the text and leave the same margins as ordinarily. When placing footnotes at the bottom of the page, draw a line across the page to separate text from footnotes.

Manuscripts prepared for publication are generally not accompanied by a bibliography, and therefore the footnotes should include complete bibliographical data. Student papers, however, are always accompanied by a complete bibliography, and for that reason certain items which appear in the bibliography proper are omitted from the notes. The proper form for footnotes referring to books appears below:

1. Thurman W. Arnold, *The Folklore of Capitalism*, p. 123.
2. Arthur Young, *A Six Months' Tour through the North of England* (London, 1771), I, 222, as quoted in A. H. Johnson, *The Disappearance of the Small Landowner*, pp. 102-103.
3. Stuart P. Sherman, "Mark Twain," *Cambridge History of American Literature*, III, 59.
4. Rudyard Kipling, "The Courting of Dinah Shadd," *Life's Handicap: Being Stories of My Own People*, pp. 117-145.
5. "North American Indians," *Encyclopaedia Britannica*, 11th ed., XIV, 65.
6. *Chief Pre-Shakespearean Dramas*, ed. Joseph Quincy Adams, pp. 9-24.

Forms for articles in magazines appear below:

1. Lindsay Rogers, "Crisis Government: 1936 Model," *The Southern Review*, I (Spring 1936), 696.
2. Fletcher Pratt, "Crime as a Profession," *American Mercury*, XL (1937), 214.
3. "Foreign News: Canada," *Time*, August 24, 1936, p. 24.

Forms for newspaper articles and bulletins appear below:

1. "Administration Planning New Expenditures," Chicago *Daily News*, Sept. 5, 1940, p. 1.

2. Curriculum Commission for the National Council of Teachers of English, *An Experience Curriculum in English*, p. 114.

Short forms for footnotes. In a research paper of considerable length, the mechanical labor involved in composing footnotes is great. Fortunately, there is practically universal agreement concerning certain standardized short forms and abbreviations.

The first time a source is mentioned in a footnote, the citation should take the form of one of the examples given above; thereafter, future references to the same source can be shortened, if that is possible without rendering the footnote ambiguous. "W. P. Ker, *Epic and Romance: Essays on Medieval Literature*" can, after the first reference, become "Ker, *Epic and Romance.*" "Fletcher Pratt, 'Crime as a Profession,' *American Mercury*, XL (1937)" can become "Pratt, 'Crime as a Profession.'" However, no shortening of a reference is excusable if it can possibly result in confusion of one source with another.

Footnotes can be shortened even further by the use of three standardized abbreviations: *ibid.* (for *ibidem*, meaning "in the same place"), *op. cit.* (for *opere citato*, meaning "in the work cited"), and *loc. cit.* (for *loco citato*, meaning "in the place cited"). *Ibid.* (which, like the other two abbreviations, should always be underlined) is used to avoid repeating a citation when reference is made *consecutively* to the same source. It always duplicates the citation which immediately precedes it, or as much of it as is appropriate for the new citation. If *ibid.* stands alone, the entire previous citation is being repeated; if it is qualified, as in "*Ibid.*, p. 23," the previous citation is being repeated with the exception of the page number, the new page number being 23.

When one or more footnotes have intervened between a citation and a footnote which must repeat all or part of the citation, *ibid.* obviously will not do; another abbreviation, *op. cit.*, is used in these circumstances. *Op. cit.* can never stand alone, but must always appear in conjunction with the author's

name or some other part of the original reference, in order to indicate just what work is being cited. Thus, "McKerrow, *op. cit.*, p. 193" would refer the reader to a book by McKerrow cited previously, but between the citation and the present footnote something else has intervened.

Loc. cit. is used in place of *op. cit.* for references to a passage cited in a preceding footnote (see No. 10 below).

The uses of these abbreviations are easy to learn. Remember that they are not interchangeable. Each has a distinct meaning which cannot be violated. The following set of illustrations may serve to make their uses clearer:

1. *Chief Pre-Shakespearean Dramas*, ed. Joseph Quincy Adams, pp. 9-24. [This specimen is a first footnote.]
2. *Ibid.* [Repeats footnote 1.]
3. *Ibid.*, p. 26. [Repeats footnotes 1 and 2 except for page number.]
4. John Dove, *Confutation of Atheism*, pp. 25-27. [Another first note.]
5. Adams, *op. cit.*, p. 28. [Refers to work cited in 1, 2, and 3.]
6. *Ibid.* [Repeats footnote 5.]
7. Dove, *op. cit.*, p. 28. [Refers to work cited in 4.]
8. John Wilson, "Shakespeare and the Strolling Players," *PMLA*, XXXVIII (1923), 178. [Another first note.]
9. Adams, *op. cit.*, p. 89. [Refers to work cited in 1, 2, 3, 5, and 6.]
10. Wilson, *loc. cit.* [Refers to the same passage cited in 8.]

Bibliography Forms

A final bibliography, providing a complete list of all the sources actually used for reference, should be attached to the student research paper. It should be arranged alphabetically, by authors, last names first (or, if the author is not known, by the first important word in the title). If the bibliography is long, it may be well to place books and articles in two separate lists.

The arrangement of the items in each entry in the final bibliography is the same as was used for the bibliography cards, except that the entry is written in a linear fashion instead of being spread out over several lines. Some punctuation is added, also. The following examples should provide adequate models:

Adams, Joseph Quincy, ed. *Chief Pre-Shakespearean Dramas.* Boston: Houghton Mifflin Co., 1924.

Anon. *The Lottery. A Farce.* London: J. Watts, 1732.

"Chemical Costs," *Chemical and Metallurgical Engineering,* XXXIX (January, 1932), 1-8.

Evans, Michael. "Prohibition's Attempted Comeback," *Coronet,* X (September, 1941), 3-8.

Lardner, Ring. "Haircut." In Donald Davidson, *American Composition and Rhetoric.* New York: Charles Scribner's Sons, 1939.

"North American Indians," *Encyclopaedia Britannica.* Eleventh Edition. Vol. XIV.

Simms, W. Gilmore. *Charlemont; or, The Pride of the Village.* Chicago, New York, San Francisco: Belford, Clarke & Co., 1889. New and revised edition.

Trent, William Peterfield and others. *The Cambridge History of American Literature.* 4 vols. New York: G. P. Putnam's Sons, 1917-21.

University of Chicago Press. *A Manual of Style.* Chicago, 1937. Tenth edition.

Final Form for the Research Paper

Since the research paper is probably the longest and, in many ways, the most exacting written assignment required during the year, its final form should receive careful attention. If possible, it should be typed. Before it is turned in, it should be read carefully for errors, omissions, and misspelled words. When it is completed it should consist of the following parts, in order: title page, outline, text, bibliography.

LIST OF COMMON ABBREVIATIONS

bk. (pl., bks.), book
c. or ca., about
cf., compare
chap. or ch. (pl., chaps. or chs.), chapter
col. (pl., cols.), column
ed., editor (pl., eds. or edd.), edited by
fig. (pl., figs.), figure
ibid., in the same place
infra, below
l. (pl., ll.), line

loc. cit., in the passage cited
MS (pl., MSS), manuscript
op. cit., in the work cited
passim, here and there
p. (pl., pp.), page
pp. 7 f., page 7 and the following page
pp. 7 ff., page 7 and following pages

sec. (pl., secs.), section
supra, above
tr. or trans., translator; translated by

vol. (pl., vols.), volume
vs. (pl., vss.), verse

EXERCISE IN BIBLIOGRAPHY FORMS

Rewrite the following descriptions of printed material in such a way that they conform to the bibliographical usage explained in this text.

1. A book called The Handy Dictionary of Biography written by Charles Morris and published in 1905 in Philadelphia by the John Winston Company.
2. A book by H. G. Wells called The Shape of Things to Come, published by The Macmillan Company in New York in 1933.
3. A book published in New York by Albert and Charles Boni, Inc., in 1927. Title is The Bridge of San Luis Rey, and the author is Thornton Wilder.
4. A book by John Franklin Genung called A Guide to Biblical Literature, published in Boston by Ginn & Company in 1919.
5. A book called The Modern Reader's Bible edited by Richard G. Moulton, published in 1908 by The Macmillan Company in New York.
6. An article called Pardon My Harvard Accent published in the Atlantic Monthly in its September, 1941, issue, pages 318-29, volume CLXVIII.
7. An article in the magazine called Life entitled Vichy vs. France. The author is Richard de Rochemont. Volume eleven. Pages 66-73. September 1, 1941.
8. In James Whitcomb Riley's volume of poems entitled Child-Rhymes can be found a well-known poem entitled Little Orphan Annie. It appears on pages 23-8. The book was published in Indianapolis by the Bobbs-Merrill Company in 1888.
9. A newspaper story in the Chicago Daily Tribune for September 16, 1941, with the headline Manila Harbor Ravaged by $1,-000,000 Fire.
10. The article in the Encyclopaedia Britannica, volume four of the fourteenth edition, on Bascule Bridges.

Suggested Topics for Research Papers

1. The Methods of Color Photography
2. The Experiment with Army Universities in World War II
3. The Scientific Aspects of Hypnosis
4. The Importance of the Almanac in the History of American Journalism

5. The Conquering of Yellow Fever
6. Modern Tendencies in the Rules Governing College Football
7. The Conspiracy of Benedict Arnold
8. The Conspiracy of Guy Fawkes
9. Methods of Rehabilitating Drought Areas
10. The Efficiency of Federal Pure Food Laws
11. Desperados in American Folk Ballads
12. How Fur Coat Buyers Are Cheated
13. The Importance of Skeletal Traction in Surgery
14. The Sources of Income of ———— College
15. The Public Transit Problems of the City of ————
16. The Literary Sources Used by Richard Wagner in his Ring operas
17. A Brief Description of Boulder Dam (or any other engineering project)
18. The Rise of the Committee for Industrial Organization
19. The Purposes and Plans of the Civil Aeronautics Authority
20. How Phonograph Records Are Made
21. The Beginning of Methodism in America
22. The Theory of Impressionism in Nineteenth-Century Painting

23. Indemnities Imposed by the Versailles Treaty on Germany
24. The Importance of *Godey's Ladies' Book* in the Feminine Culture of the Nineteenth Century
25. A Definition of Melodrama
26. The Present Status of Prefabrication in the Construction of Houses
27. American Diplomatic Relations with Japan from the Beginning of the War with China until Pearl Harbor
28. The Organization of the National Broadcasting Company
29. The Organization of the Confederate States of America

To assist you in submitting an attractive manuscript to your instructor, the following pages present a reproduction of a research paper written by a freshman student in composition with introductory material and bibliography. Use this as a model of manuscript form. Your instructor, however, may wish you to submit a sentence outline rather than the topic outline of this research paper.

Lois Boeck
English 122
April 10, 1953
Sec. 1, file 3

THE CONSPIRACY OF AARON BURR

Subject: Aaron Burr's intentions in the Mississippi Valley

Audience: already interested in early American history, especially in the Aaron Burr conspiracy; already familiar with Burr's background as well as some of the social, political, and economic history of the country during the early 1800's

Purposes

General: to persuade

Specific: to show Aaron Burr's intentions in the Mississippi Valley in 1806

Thesis: Aaron Burr's intentions in the Mississippi Valley in 1806 were not those of a traitor but merely those of an expan-

sionist in search of new fields to conquer.

Outline

I. The argument for Burr as traitor

   A. The origins of his plan

      1. Negotiations with Merry

      2. Negotiations with Eaton

   B. Plan of conquest

      1. The attack on Mexico

      2. The empire in the Mississippi Valley

         a. The testimony of Turreau

         b. The testimony of Blennerhassett

II. The argument for Burr as expansionist and conqueror

   A. The overthrow of Spanish-dominated colonies

      1. Negotiations with foreign ministers

      2. Testimony of others

         a. Claiborne

         b. Clark

         c. Truxtun

         d. Smith

   B. The formation of a Mexican empire

      1. A benevolent aristocracy

      2. The maps for invasion

Lois Boeck
English 122
April 10, 1953
Sec. 1, file 3

THE CONSPIRACY OF AARON BURR

Ever since Aaron Burr's conspiracy in the Mississippi Valley in 1806, there have been two schools of thought as to his actual intentions. According to one belief he was trying to sever the United States and establish an empire west of the Alleghanies; according to the other he sought only a Mexican empire free of Spanish domination.

In 1806, partly as a result of the duel with Hamilton, the entire country regarded Burr as a person of low moral standards and a fugitive from justice. Because of this attitude Burr was embittered and began to calculate the possibilities of establishing a new empire somewhere in the Americas. In fact, Merry, the British minister to the United States, received a message from Burr immediately after the Hamilton duel offering his assistance to Britain in any way he might be needed, "particularly in endeavoring to effect a separation of the western part of the United States from that which lies between the Atlantic and the mountains, in its whole extent."[1] According to Henry Adams, this was the beginning of Burr's plan for severing the Union and establishing an empire west of the Alleghanies with New Orleans as capital.[2] As Burr was always an advocate of bold policies, he saw nothing to lose in his conspiracy

1 Henry Adams, History of the United States, II, 395.
2 Ibid., III, 222 ff.

except his life, which even now might be in danger, whereas on the

other hand he did see a whole new and important world to gain.[3]

Burr entered into these intrigues with an old-time friend,

General Wilkinson, now general of the United States army in the

south. To Wilkinson Adams gives credit for the plan of Mexican con-

quest and states that it was only because of Burr's influence as an

old friend that Wilkinson expanded his plan for conquering Mexico

to embrace the Burr scheme for separation of the Union.[4]

Adams also asserts that Burr at one time entertained the idea

of seizing Washington and establishing himself as dictator.[5] This

assertion is borne out by William Eaton who was approached by Burr

for aid with his plans. Eaton states that Burr not only mentioned a

plan for the invasion of Mexico, but also told of a plot to seize

the capital and establish himself there as dictator; or if he failed

in this, he planned to sail for New Orleans with stolen U. S. arms,

money, and ships. Here he would then establish an independent West-

ern empire.[6] Competent authorities, however, discount this tale

because of Eaton's financial involvement in the matter.

Burr's plan of a Western empire goes as follows, according to

Holmes Alexander:

> At a given signal the Creole population of New Orleans would
> rise and declare itself independent. Tennessee, Kentucky and
> possibly Ohio would take the moment to pronounce a secession from
> the Union, and simultaneously General Wilkinson, stationed at

---

3 Holmes Alexander, Aaron Burr, the Proud Pretender,
pp. 236-237.
4 Adams, op. cit., III, 222-223.
5 Ibid., pp. 239-240.
6 Dictionary of American Biography,
ed. Allen Johnson, III, 318.

St. Louis, would lead his dissaffected army across the Spanish
province of Texas and into the heart of Mexico. Meanwhile British men-of-war at the mouth of the Mississippi would frighten
away Mr. Jefferson's absurd navy, and Colonel Burr, having declared himself head of the new government, would impress all
ships in the harbor and sail to Vera Cruz. From there he would
lead a band of conquistadores against Mexico City, arriving in
time to co-operate with Wilkinson's overland march.[7]

Adams's whole conception of Burr's plan seems to be based upon
his analysis of Burr's character and personality: "Raising the
standard of a new empire in the Mississippi Valley seemed to an
intriguer of Burr's metal not only feasible, but certain of success."[8] While Burr denied any knowledge of a plan of this sort,
Adams interpreted this to fit his own views of Burr and his plans:
"What he [Burr] so solemnly denied was the intention to separate the
Western States 'by force' from the Eastern; what he never denied was
the plan of establishing a Western empire by consent."[9]

Burr's personality seems to have influenced most people's impressions of his plan. Turreau, the French minister to the United
States at the time of the alleged conspiracy, wrote a letter to
Talleyrand describing conditions in America. In this letter he
stated that he had met Burr and was of the opinion that while others
looked upon Burr's career as finished, Burr himself did not and
would rather sacrifice the interests of his country than renounce
celebrity and fortune.[10]

Blennerhassett, a fellow conspirator of Burr's whose home on an
island in the middle of the Ohio was the base for Burr's operations,

7 Alexander, op. cit., p. 236.
8 Adams, op. cit., III, 220.
9 Ibid., p. 276.
10 Ibid., II, 407.

seems to have been under the impression at one time that their plans were for dividing the Union, for he published a series of articles during the early stages of the conspiracy implicating Burr in a plan for separating the Western states from the Eastern.[11]

There is, however, another side to this story. Charles and Mary Beard, for instance, argue that Burr courted the Southwest to get aid for his proposed expedition to Mexico, as he knew that while the Southwest was not poor, it was full of enterprise and greedy for Mexican plunder.[12] In like way, W. F. McCaleb assumes that this brilliant man, knowing the odds against the success of his plan, could not possibly have contemplated the Washington or New Orleans plans for any reason other than to get aid from Spain, England, or France.[13]

According to McCaleb, who has uncovered much new material on this subject, Burr's own announced intention was only to overthrow the Spanish-dominated colonies in America and not to sever the United States.[14] This evidence is further substantiated by the fact that both Burr and Hamilton had previously been interested in Mexico and anxious to lead an army across the Southwest to free the Spanish colonies; Burr had always been eager to rival Hamilton in the nation's affections.[15]

After the Hamilton-Burr duel, General Wilkinson was approached by Burr with the result that they agreed upon a plan of action for

11 Dictionary of American Biography, III, 318.
12 The Rise of American Civilization, I, 412–413.
13 The Aaron Burr Conspiracy, p. 57.
14 Ibid., p. 34.
15 Dictionary of American Biography, III, 317.

the coming conquest. To effect this plan, however, they needed
money, men, and supplies. As a consequence Burr conversed with the
British, French, and Spanish ministers, but to each he described a
different plan, as if concealing his real intention:

> With all Burr's misrepresentations there is not the faintest
> hint that New Orleans was to be sacrificed; no allusion to a con-
> vention which was to be called for the purpose of declaring the
> independence of the Western States--a point which had borne great
> weight in the Spanish and English intrigues;--but we are told
> plainly that an attack was to be made on the Spanish possessions,
> possibly beginning with West Florida at Baton Rouge. If policy
> dictated . . . that Baton Rouge should remain unmolested, they
> would pass on--and to no other place than Mexico. . . . Mexicans
> were interested in the cause [their own freedom]. It was only in
> the matter of his resources that Burr attempted deception.[16]

Money was desperately needed for the proposed invasion of
Mexico, and when Yrujo, the Spanish minister from whom aid had been
solicited on the basis of a Western empire, complained of hearing
rumors of the Mexican plan, he was told that this was a falsehood
whispered for the sole purpose of drawing attention away from the
conspirators' real purpose. This, of course, was merely to blind
Yrujo to the actual plan concerning Mexico.[17]

Henry Adams takes Burr's notes to Yrujo very literally and so
credits Burr with a plan for a Western rather than a Mexican empire.
He fails, however, to take cognizance of the fact that Yrujo eventually became suspicious of the large amount of supplies which Burr
insisted upon securing and finally did realize it was to be a Mexican expedition. Wilkinson's betrayal to the Spanish was the
result.[18]

---

16 McCaleb, op. cit., pp. 69-70.
17 Ibid., p. 82.
18 Ibid., p. 86.

Burr's singleness of purpose is further borne out by the testimonies of several of those involved in the intrigues. Claiborne, governor of the territory of Orleans with whom Burr had dealings, did not believe Burr was plotting against his country but believed he sincerely loved it and was only carried away by his zeal for the liberation of Mexico.[19] Daniel Clark, an influential citizen of New Orleans and an intimate friend of both Wilkinson and Burr, steadfastly maintained that as Burr told the plot to him, it was only to be an expedition against Spanish–dominated Mexico where an empire was to be set up upon the completion of a successful invasion.[20] Commodore Thomas Truxtun, whom Burr asked to lead a naval contingent in the revolt, stated definitely that Burr had never mentioned any plans whatsoever to him concerning a severance of the United States. Burr's plans were wholly concerned with Mexico as far as he knew.[21] Senator Smith in 1806 received a letter from Burr which denied any knowledge of a plot to separate the Union and which stated that Burr "never harbored or expressed any such intention to any one," nor anyone else to him.[22]

Burr's conception of his Mexican empire was one of a benevolent government ruled by an aristocracy of accomplishment—artists, philosophers, authors. Universal education and scientific research were to be furthered by the wealth of the empire while his fellow

---

19 Ibid., p. 33.
20 Ibid., pp. 34–35.
21 Dictionary of American Biography, III, 318.
22 Adams, op. cit., III, 276.

conspirators—Blennerhassett, Wilkinson, Dayton, his daughter, his
son-in-law, and others—were to be high officials.[23]

While making plans for the invasion, Burr drew three maps which
are the best clues to his intentions. The first map was a detailed
chart of the Gulf of Mexico to serve as a guide to a fleet sailing
from New Orleans to Vera Cruz. The second was a singularly descriptive map of the land route from Vera Cruz to Mexico City. The last
map was of the empire itself—Texas, Mexico, and the Californias.[24]
These maps together with Burr's oft-reiterated statements of his
innocence furnish our best clues to his purposes. The fact that
Burr continued making plans for a Mexican conquest after being
acquitted of treason also adds further proof to his innocence of
treason.[25]

Taking these facts into consideration, we must therefore conclude that Burr was in reality only desirous of setting up a Mexican
empire free from Spanish domination. Adams's views are taken mainly
from English, Spanish, and French correspondence and are not based
on other sources of information which McCaleb has uncovered. It
seems reasonable to conclude with McCaleb that Burr's intentions in
the Mississippi Valley in 1806 were not those of a traitor but
merely those of an expansionist in search of new fields to conquer.

BIBLIOGRAPHY

Adams, Henry. History of the United States of America. 9 vols.
    New York: Charles Scribner's Sons, 1890.

23 Alexander, op. cit., pp. 223-240.
24 Ibid., p. 245.
25 Dictionary of American Biography, III, 319-320.

Alexander, Holmes. *Aaron Burr, the Proud Pretender.* New York: Harper and Brothers, 1937.

Beard, Charles A. and Mary R. Beard. *The Rise of American Civilization.* 2 vols. New York: The Macmillan Company, 1931.

Johnson, Allen, ed. *Dictionary of American Biography.* 20 vols. New York: Charles Scribner's Sons, 1929.

McCaleb, Walter F. *The Aaron Burr Conspiracy.* New York: Wilson-Erickson, Inc., 1936.

"I Have Not Yet Begun to Fight" [1]

CHARLES LEE LEWIS

THE FAMOUS WAR cry of John Paul Jones is alleged to have been uttered at the climax of one of the most renowned ship duels in history. This was the battle off Flamborough Head, England, on September 23, 1779, between the British ship *Serapis* and the American vessel *Bonhomme Richard.* The battle had been in progress for an hour or more, the ships were lying alongside lashed together, and the crisis of the bloody contest seemed to be at hand. The gunner, the carpenter, and the master-at-arms, thinking that the *Richard* was sinking and that both John Paul Jones and his first lieutenant had been killed, rushed up on deck and called loudly to the British for quarter. Captain Pearson of the *Serapis,* hearing the cry, demanded of Jones to know if he had struck. His reply, according to popular histories and biographies, was, "I have not yet begun to fight!"

Jones might have settled this question at once and for all time, if he had set down in his official report his exact reply to the British captain; but such communications are usually stripped rather bare of personal and picturesque details of that kind. In his letter of October 3, 1779, to Franklin,[1a] the only official report of the battle that he wrote, all that Jones states which bears upon the slogan is merely this: "The English Commodore asked me if I demanded quarter, and I having answered him in the most determined negative, they renewed the battle with double fury." It is necessary, therefore, to look elsewhere for the source of the exact language of the slogan.

Contemporary newspaper accounts, published in England, are of no particular value as evidence, except where they corroborate other statements; but some of them are extremely interesting as showing the widely varying versions of the war cry which have appeared in print. For example, the London *Evening Post* of September 30, 1779, gives this picturesque account: "In the engagement between the *Serapis* and Paul Jones, his vessel was so disabled, that the Captain of the *Serapis* called out to Jones to strike, else he would sink him. To which the latter replied, 'that he might if he could; for whenever the Devil was ready to take him, he would rather obey his summons, than strike

[1] From the *Mississippi Valley Historical Review* (September, 1942). Reprinted by permission of the author, who has revised the article slightly for use here.

[1a] John Henry Sherburne, *Life and Character of the Chevalier John Paul Jones: A Captain in the Navy of the United States during Their Revolutionary War* (Washington, 1825), p. 120. The original letter is in the Library of Congress.

to any one.' . . . The foregoing account is from the affidavits of seven seamen, who made their escape after the engagement, before the Mayor of Hull." [2] This account may be the source of a similar story in *Naval Heroes* by S. Putnam Waldo, 1823, which reads as follows: "The Captain of the *Serapis* said, 'I give you an opportunity to strike; if you do not, I will sink you at the next broadside.' The indignant Jones replied in a rage, 'Sink me if you can; if I must go to the Devil, I had rather strike to him than to you.'" [3] In the London *Public Advertiser* of October 20, 1779, there is another highly embroidered account, which runs thus: "One of the men escaped from Paul Jones says that in the engagement with the *Serapis*, Jones, almost exhausted with fatigue, sat down upon a hen coop. The Lieutenant of Marines went up to him and said, 'For God's sake, Captain, strike!' Jones looked at him, paused a moment, then leaped up from his seat and said, 'No, I will sink, I will never strike.'" [4] Of about the same purport are these lines from the well-known contemporary ballad:

Our gunner, affrighted, unto Paul Jones he came,
   "Our ship is a-sinking, likewise in a flame";
Paul Jones he replied, in the height of his pride,
   "If we can do no better, we'll sink alongside." [5]

It is true that some British prisoners, who had taken part in the battle, did escape at the close of the engagement. But the above accounts are not cited as reliable proof. They are referred to in passing only to show that immediately after the battle there were various and conflicting reports, and that the very

best authority should be sought before the acceptance of any version whatsoever.

The official report of Captain Richard Pearson and his evidence afterwards are interesting. He wrote his report, of course, as a prisoner of war; it was headed, "*Pallas, French frigate in Congress Service, Texel, 6 October, 1779.*" The portion which bears directly upon the question is this: "At ten o'clock they called for quarter from the ship alongside, and said they had struck; hearing this, I called upon the Captain to know if they had struck; or if he asked for quarter; but no answer being made, after repeating my words two or three times, I called for the boarders, and ordered them to board, which they did; but the moment they were on board her, they discovered a superior number laying under cover with pikes in their hands ready to receive them, on which our people retreated instantly into our own ship, and returned to their guns again till half past ten." [6] But at the court-martial proceedings in 1780 Pearson made this additional statement: "I did not myself hear the reply; but one of my midshipmen, Mr. Hood, did hear it and soon reported it to me. It was to the effect that he was just beginning to fight." [7]

We have exactly the same words reported in a French pamphlet, called *Memoir du Combat*. [8] The author was Pierre Gerard, who

[2] Quoted in Don C. Seitz, *Paul Jones: His Exploits in English Seas during 1778-1780: Contemporary Accounts Collected from English Newspapers* (New York, 1917), p. 55.

[3] S. Putnam Waldo, *Biographical Sketches of Distinguished American Naval Heroes in the War of the Revolution* (Hartford, 1823), p. 120.

[4] Quoted in Mrs. Reginald [Anna] de Koven, *The Life and Letters of John Paul Jones* (2 vols., New York, 1913), I, 461, n.

[5] Burton Egbert Stevenson, ed., *Poems of American History* (Boston, 1908), p. 224.

[6] Pearson's report is printed in *The Naval Chronicle* XXIV (London, 1810), 357; also in *The Remembrancer: or, Impartial Repository of Public Events for the Year 1780, Part I* (London), IX, 47.

[7] Augustus C. Buell, *Paul Jones, Founder of the American Navy: A History* (2 vols., New York, 1900), I, 225. Buell is notably unreliable, however. Upon inquiring of the Public Record Office in London as to the accuracy of the above statement, the author received this reply: "I am directed to inform you that the Minutes of the Court-Martial held on 10 March 1780, for the trial of Captains Pearson and Piercy and the officers and men of the *Serapis* and *Countess of Scarborough*, have been examined, but no record of the statement said to have been made by Captain Pearson during the proceedings was found."

[8] As far as the writer has been able to determine, no one but Buell has ever cited the *Memoir du Combat* as an authority. The pamphlet appears in no bibliographies relating to Jones; hence its present

is said to have been a French volunteer on the *Bonhomme Richard*. Augustus C. Buell, in a footnote in his *Life of Jones*, says that this Gerard was Jones's French orderly on the day of the battle, that he afterwards rose in the French naval service after the French Revolution, and that he was a lieutenant on the *Généreux*, one of the two French ships which escaped at the Battle of the Nile, and was second in command of the *Neptune* in the Battle of Trafalgar. Buell claims that the pamphlet is a rare one, and that it was first published at l'Orient in 1780, and a year later at Paris. According to him, Gerard wrote, "En ce moment, crie le capitaine anglais, 'Avez vous amené votre pavillon?' Auquel, férocement, et lachant un gros juron, a repondu le Commodore Jones—'Non! je vais à l'instant commencer le combat!'" [9]

Still another account, which gives practically the same language, is furnished by Dr. Benjamin Rush of Philadelphia. He was an intimate friend of John Adams, and was not only an author of medical treatises but also a careful observer of men. Among the diaries, letters, and pen portraits of his celebrated contemporaries, which have been published by his greatgrandson, Mr. Louis Biddle, is the following account of a conversation with John Paul Jones at a dinner, during which Jones declared, concerning the famous battle: "Towards the close of the battle while his deck was swimming in blood, the Captain of the *Serapis* called to him to strike. 'No, sir!' he said, 'I will not, we have had but a small fight yet.'" [10]

These three reports agree that the slogan was, in substance, "I am just beginning to fight." And they may have been the source of the slogan as it is now commonly worded, for only a slight change is needed to convert the former into the latter. But it should be remembered that scholars have shown that Buell's *Life of Jones* is thoroughly unreliable; the Gerard pamphlet is not listed in any of the John Paul Jones bibliographies, and hence it may have existed only in Buell's imagination.[11] As to the Rush account, the words therein recorded sound more like something quoted from memory than an exact transcription made at the time they were spoken. If, however, we had no further light on the slogan, we might be disposed to consider the words given above as a fairly correct approximation to what was spoken on that occasion, and there rest the case. But there is better and more definite evidence to be considered.

It is not commonly known that John Paul Jones himself has put on record the words that he used. They are to be found in the *Journal* which he prepared for Louis XVI in 1786. There is a well-authenticated French copy of the original *Journal* in the Library of Congress. It bears the following ponderous title: "Extrait du Journal de mes Campagnes, ou j'expose mes principaux Services et rapelle quelques circonstances de ce qui m'est arrivé deplus remarquable pendant le

---

[11] In the preface (p. 11, n.) to his edition of *Fanning's Narrative; Being the Memoirs of Nathaniel Fanning, An Officer of the Revolutionary Navy, 1778-1783* (New York, 1912), John S. Barnes wrote, in reference to Buell's claim that he quoted from Fanning in his biography of Jones: "The editor informed Mr. Buell of his error regarding Fanning, to which he made no reply. His book is, however, so replete with pure fabrications that it can only be classed as an interesting romance through which runs but a slender thread of truth, and its title a misleading assumption unworthy to be called history."

When Buell was questioned by George Canby, a grandnephew of Betsy Ross, as to Buell's claim in his biography of Jones that the first American flag was made in Portsmouth, Buell replied in part on October 4, 1901: "The fact is that when compiling the matter for my history I never had any idea of being made a defendant in the premises or being called upon to prove anything by proffer of original documents." See de Koven, *John Paul Jones*, II, appendix D, 453.

At the United States Naval Academy Buell is considered so unreliable that his biography is placed on reserve in order that midshipmen may not be misinformed by reading it.

---

location or place and date of publication cannot be supplied with any certainty.

[9] Buell, *Paul Jones*, I, 222, 224, 227.

[10] *A Memorial Containing Travels through Life or Sundry Incidents in the Life of Dr. Benjamin Rush . . . Published privately for the benefit of his Descendants by Louis Alexander Biddle* (1905), p. 121.

cours de la Révolution Américaine, particu-liérement en Europe." Jones's account of the slogan, when translated into English, reads as follows: "The Captain, on hearing the gun-ner express his wishes to surrender, in con-sequence of his supposing that we were sink-ing, instantly addressed himself to me, and exclaimed, 'Do you ask for quarter? Do you ask for quarter?' I was so occupied, at this period, in serving the three pieces of cannon on the forecastle that I remained totally ig-norant of what had occurred on deck; I replied, however, 'I do not dream of sur-rendering, but I am determined to make you strike!'" It is well known that Jones was a great lover of the picturesque phrase, and it seems almost inconceivable that, if he had used the more vigorous and expressive words, "I have not yet begun to fight," they would not have remained in his memory and been set down verbatim in this *Journal,* which was written only seven years after the battle in which they were used.

There is, furthermore, strange confirma-tion that he did use the substance of the language recorded in the *Journal.* A letter from Amsterdam, dated October 8, 1779, was printed in the London *Evening Post* of Octo-ber 12, 1779, and contained these words: "Captain Pearson hearing all that was said, asked Jones if he had struck? (at this time the flag was shot away). 'No, sir,' says he, 'I have not as yet thought of it, but am determined to make you strike.'" [12] It is not at all improbable that the writer of this letter heard either in Amsterdam or Texel, both of which places Jones visited after the battle, the great hero himself describe the engage-ment and use those very words. At all events, their substantial identity is most striking.

In addition to this letter there is another corroborative account. On the *Bonhomme Richard* there was a midshipman by the name of Nathaniel Fanning, who during the engagement commanded the marines and sailors in the maintop. He kept a sort of diary, which he wrote out in the form of a

continuous narrative in 1801 and published anonymously in 1806. After his death, it was published in 1808 under the title *Memoirs of the Life of Captain Nathaniel Fanning.* His version of the incident is as follows: "The enemy now demanded of us if we had struck, as they had heard the three poltroons halloo for quarter. 'If you have,' said they, 'why don't you haul down your pendant?', as they saw our ensign was gone. 'Ay, ay,' said Jones, 'we'll do that when we can fight no longer, but we shall see yours come down the first, for you must know that Yankees do not haul down their colors till they are fairly beaten.'" [13] This, as will be readily seen, is but an amplification of the words set down by Jones in his *Journal.* It is, of course, im-probable that Fanning heard Jones speak the slogan, for he was in the tops at the time. But he is reported to have acted as Jones's secretary during a part of the cruise, and, besides, all the most minute happenings of that memorable day must have been the common knowledge of all the officers of the *Bonhomme Richard.* Thomas Wilson in his *Principal American Military and Naval He-roes* (1817) must have based his account on the Fanning narrative, for he says, "Jones replied that his colors would never descend, till he was fairly beaten." [14]

What, then, was the origin of the slogan as usually written? It has already been stated that there was some slight authority for the words, "I am just beginning to fight." These, slightly edited and made more emphatic, almost certainly were the foundation of the commonly accepted wording of the war cry. They appear to have been recorded for the first time in this final form in Sherburne's *Life of Jones* (1825). When Sherburne was preparing this biography, Richard Dale, who had been the first lieutenant on the *Bon-*

[12] Quoted in Seitz, *Paul Jones,* p. 88.

[13] Barnes, *Fanning's Narrative,* p. 45. The original edition (1806) of *Fanning's Narrative* is a rare item. There is a copy privately owned in Annapolis and one in the library of the New York Historical So-ciety. The above quotation is from Barnes's edition.

[14] Thomas Wilson, *The Biography of the Principal American Military and Naval Heroes* (2 vols., New York, 1817), I, 126.

homme Richard, furnished him with an account of the battle, in which he gives the slogan in the well-known words, "I have not yet begun to fight." [15] But at the time Dale gave Sherburne this information, the former was an old man. Dale died the following year at the age of seventy. To show that he failed to remember some of the most important details of the battle correctly, the following passage is cited: "The *Serapis* soon passed ahead of the *Bonhomme Richard*, and when he thought he had gained a distance sufficient to go down athwart the fore foot to rake us, found he had not enough distance, and that the *Bonhomme Richard* would be aboard him, put his helm alee, which brought the two ships on aline, and the *Bonhomme Richard*, having headway, ran her bows into the stern of the *Serapis*. We had remained in this position but a few minutes when we were again hailed by the *Serapis*, 'Has your ship struck?' To which Captain Jones answered, 'I have not yet begun to fight.' "

That is to say, he states very clearly (and this is Dale's language and not Sherburne's) that the slogan was spoken "a few minutes" after the ships fouled each other; but both Jones and Pearson in their official reports state that the action had been going on very much longer than that when the call for quarter was heard and the answer given. Pearson says definitely that the ships were lashed together at 8:30 and that the call for quarter was heard about 10:00 o'clock. Jones plainly implies in his report that a period of about one hour intervened.

May not this confusion have been caused by Dale's feeling that the words, "I have not yet begun to fight," which had by that time become the accepted form, would have been more naturally spoken near the beginning of a close action than toward the end of a battle which had been continuing for an hour or more? That Dale's account may have been thus affected is made more credible by

an examination of James Fenimore Cooper's narrative of this incident. In his *History of the United States Navy* Cooper writes as follows: "The wind being light, much time was consumed in these different manoeuvers, and near an hour had elapsed between the firing of the first guns, and the moment when the vessels got foul of each other in the manner just described. The English now thought it was the intention of the Americans to board them, and a few minutes passed in the uncertainty which such an expectation would create; but the positions of the vessels were not favorable for either party to pass into the opposing ship. There being at this moment a perfect cessation of the firing, Captain Pearson demanded, 'Have you struck your colors?' 'I have not yet begun to fight,' was the answer." [16] He goes on to relate that the ships then broke apart and were afterwards lashed together. One will note in this account, therefore, an even greater straining of the facts in order to make this apparently exaggerated slogan fit into the context. In other words, in his endeavor to place the war cry as near as he can to the beginning of the battle, Cooper has stated that the words were spoken even before the ships were lashed together. This is a gross error, which Maclay and other naval historians have passed along.[17] It is in such errors that the slogan, as now commonly known, will be found imbedded.

---

[15] Sherburne, *Life and Character of the Chevalier John Paul Jones*, p. 127.

[16] James Fenimore Cooper, *History of the Navy of the United States of America* (3rd edition, 2 vols. in 1, Philadelphia, 1847), I, 107.

[17] Cf. Edgar S. Maclay, *A History of the United States Navy from 1775 to 1901* (3 vols., New York, 1901), I, 120. Very curiously, Alfred Thayer Mahan sidesteps the slogan. In his famous *Influence of Sea Power upon History* he makes no mention of Jones, although Jones's exploits are within the limits of the book's dates. In an article in *Scribner's Magazine* XXIV (New York, 1898), 210, he recounts the battle in detail but mentions no battle cry as having been made by Jones. The only cry he refers to is that of the frightened gunner who called for quarter. Of this Mahan writes: "This cry Pearson heard, and called to know whether his opponent had struck. Receiving no answer, for Jones had hurled his boarding pistols at the clamorer's head, breaking his skull and silencing his yells, he ordered his men to board."

It seems unreasonable, therefore, to take as an authority the account of an old man near seventy years of age, written forty-six years after the battle, rather than the record of John Paul Jones himself, the author of the slogan, who wrote it down only seven years after the occasion of its utterance. It may be that Jones did not set down in his *Journal* the exact words that he spoke; but it seems certain that we have there the substance of his famous war cry, which is so markedly different from the popular slogan. There is no question but that the latter is more forceful, more picturesque, and more inspiring; but that is not the point at issue. The simple question is, "Have we good and sufficient authority for believing that Jones said, 'I have not yet begun to fight'?" The answer is in the negative. John Paul Jones said, "I do not dream of surrendering, but I am determined to make you strike!"

SUGGESTIONS FOR STUDY

In making your analysis of this research paper, study closely Professor Lewis's method of sifting the evidence concerning Jones's war cry. Does he find it more acceptable, for example, to go directly to the primary documents, such as Jones's manuscripts, contemporary diaries kept by those in the fight, and the like, or to rely upon secondary evidence, such as later transcripts by those not present at the combat? Is his method in general the better one for research scholars?

Also consider whether it would be possible to report a scientific investigation of this sort convincingly without footnotes. Also study the different kinds of footnotes used. For example, what is the full purpose of the first footnote? Note the different devices used in the footnoting. Why did the author insert the brackets in the fourth footnote? What do the three dots mean in the tenth footnote?

Pertaining to your own selection of a topic for research, observe how excellently the author of this investigation limited his topic. But also notice how many words were demanded from him to make even so limited a topic clear and persuasive in its presentation.

B. *The Feature Article*

The term "feature article" comes from journalism, where it means a type of news story that aims to entertain as well as supply information. It well merits attention, for many people, including college students, have supplemented their incomes by writing feature articles.

The feature article is kin to the research paper but is less formal and usually more readable. It is based, however, on careful investigation, though investigation conducted by observation or interview as well as by research in the library. The livelier tone of the feature article arises primarily from the fact that, whereas the research paper is usually directed at a limited audience, the feature aims to be widely attractive. If devoted to the history of a small town, it tries to interest not only the few individuals who are already engaged in antiquarian research in the locality but also all natives and residents who are literate enough to read a newspaper. The feature writer, therefore, delights in anecdotes, personal histories, and "background" information. He interweaves narration, description, and exposition. He cherishes the dual virtues of accuracy and appeal to popular taste.

FINDING IDEAS FOR FEATURE ARTICLES

If you have written a research paper, you probably have material for at least one feature article, perhaps several. If this material is unsatisfactory, in your immediate vicinity are hundreds of possible topics, which you can read about and observe. The locality in which you live or in which you attend college affords one source of topics. Every town or community has an early history that can be made interesting. Historic landmarks, buildings, industries, organizations, and institutions are all gold mines of ideas. So are local people and their achievements; remember, however, that the local resident who lives in the finest house or has his name in the paper most frequently does not always live the most interesting life. The mail carrier, the bridge tender, the photographer, the bank messenger, the college janitor may be better subjects than the industrial magnate

or the society leader. The subject matter of courses offers another rich field to explore. The work of glaciers, the assaying of gold, the character and personality of a figure in history, the story behind a poem, the real meaning of a treaty—these are only a handful of suggestions.

Inventions and discoveries, and the people connected with them, are popular topics. Professions, businesses, and trades offer an unlimited number of opportunities for profitable investigation and observation. Games, holidays, national customs, outdoor life, health, hobbies, and travel need only mentioning to suggest their possibilities for the feature writer.

MAKING THE ARTICLE INTERESTING

Whatever the topic, make the treatment of it interesting. An article on Frederick the Great may begin, for instance, by a reference to the great admiration in which Frederick was held by the Nazi leaders of Germany. The configuration of a certain hill or moraine well known to local residents may serve to introduce a discussion of the work of glaciers.

The beginning of the article is especially important in providing the proper contact with the reader—so important that many professional writers finish the body of the article first and then return to write the beginning. It must (1) catch the reader's eye and attract him to a reading of the article, (2) give the reader an idea of the content of the article and the point of view to be maintained, and (3) provide a point of contact with interests the reader already holds. Since Americans are great readers of fiction, a beginning that makes use of a bit of narrative or dialogue is likely to be more effective than strict exposition. Description, a direct quotation, or merely a question may serve equally well, although the method last mentioned ("How many students know that . . .") is overworked by high-school writers. An opening (or *lead*, as it is called in newspaper parlance) that plunges the reader into

a concrete situation about which he can build sensory images—in other words, one based on something the reader can experience with pleasure or excitement—will serve the purpose of attracting attention and advertising the material that follows.

The lead must also be integrated with the rest of the article so that the reader will not feel he has been cheated with a showy display window that fronts a shabby store. The more striking the lead, the more difficult it is to graduate the style and content of the article down to a level that can be maintained.

THE FEATURE STORY BASED ON LIBRARY RESEARCH

If you have written an acceptable formal research paper, you should need no further instruction in using the library for purposes of the feature article. Every reference work on the shelves in the reading room can suggest topics and furnish information. Many professional feature writers make regular trips to public libraries merely to browse through the card catalogues. The suggestions for topics that an hour's time in the library can furnish are limited only by the imagination of the writer.

A never-failing source of material is anniversaries and holidays. Those best known are frequently overworked, but less familiar anniversaries can always be used for interesting articles. Here are a very few:

January 27 (1880)—Edison patents the incandescent light.

February 7 (1893)—First long distance telephone operated between Boston and New York.

February 26 (1856)—Costa Rica declares war against a single man, a soldier of fortune named Walker.

March 30 (1842)—Ether first used as an anesthetic.

March 30 (1867)—Alaska purchased from Russia for $7,200,000.

April 2 (1792)—Birthday of the United States Mint.

May 10 (1501)—Amerigo Vespucci sails on second trip to America.

July 4 (1826)—Two presidents die: John
Adams and Thomas Jefferson.

July 26 (1847)—First electrical locomotive
exhibited and operated.

September 25 (1690)—First American newspaper issued.

October 8 (1891)—Great Chicago fire.

October 27 (1904)—New York subway
opened to the public.

November 6 (1847)—First American Missionary church established in China.

December 1 (1863)—Patent granted for
making artificial limbs.

Any fair-sized library will provide sufficient
material for an article on such events. Remember that the mere retelling of the incident does not constitute a good feature article. The information must be made attractive
to ordinary people, many of whom found
history in the public school dull. Characters
must be made to emerge with real human
traits. The drama and irony of events must
be emphasized; and, if possible, a link with
some contemporary occurrence of wide interest must be contrived to make the material seem more than usually pertinent.

THE FEATURE ARTICLE BASED
ON THE INTERVIEW

The article based on the interview has the
twofold attraction of containing up-to-date
information and presenting an interesting
individual. Although the person interviewed
is usually prominent in community life, in
his profession, or in the news of the day,
any person, in some sense or other, is interesting.

Technique of interviewing. As a rule, to
get an interview, make an appointment by
letter or telephone several days in advance.
Explain briefly your purpose and the kind
of information you want. Allowing a person time to gather his thoughts before being
questioned is more courteous than plunging
into his home or office unannounced; furthermore, the person is more likely to feel that
he and the writer are collaborating on a
piece of work. Although it is sometimes better to arrange to talk somewhere other than
at the person's place of business in order to
be free from distracting influences, the interview will perhaps be more colorful and
informative if it takes place amid the operations you will try to describe in your article.

It is extremely important that you make
careful preparations before you call. First,
inform yourself as to the personality, idiosyncrasies, hobbies, and achievements of the
person you are about to question. No good
feature writer will drop into his subject's
office, sprawl on a chair, and begin, "Now,
Mr. Brown, tell me all about your business."
Prepare twenty or thirty questions, tactfully
phrased, to start the conversation and keep it
going in the desired channels. Conduct the
interview itself more like an informal conversation than the grilling of a witness on
a stand. Have your questions well in mind
and drop them in casually when the talk
lags or departs from the desired path. Invariably courtesy, intelligent enthusiasm,
and attentiveness mark the good interviewer.

Writing the interview article. The article
may consist almost entirely of direct quotation, or it may make use of direct quotation as an embellishment for material that
is partly quoted and partly derived from
sources other than the interview. The second
method of writing is usually the more effective. Most feature articles of this kind begin with a lead consisting of a description of
the subject and his surroundings, and the
opening words or most striking sentence of
the interview. Whatever the lead may be,
do not proceed far before giving a sharply
defined picture of the person under consideration. Whether the article is primarily about
him, or whether he has been chosen as one
of a class of people and his statements used
to personalize an otherwise objective treatment of the information, keep in mind the
principle that readers are usually more interested in people than in things.

Fifty Ideas for Newspaper Features[1]

To SELL these ideas to local papers, tie the idea in with local people, events, and places. For sale of the same idea to a state paper (a newspaper with a "State Edition" that is sold throughout the entire state) tie the idea in with prominent state people, places, and events. Pictures make the feature. Submit "glossy prints" about 5 x 7 inches.

1. "The Lord Is Where You Look." Any town of 250,000 or over will show, on careful investigation, many singular religious sects with their own leaders, their own curious ways, and peculiar meeting places. Normally we think of churchgoers traveling to a dignified stone building, in their Sunday best, sitting quietly through services, and nodding pleasantly to acquaintances. But there are millions of Americans whose churches have colorful names, and even more exciting services, manners, and customs.

2. Kite flying as a serious hobby; as a toy for boys; as an industry. Ben Franklin used a kite in his experiments. The weather departments use them, and there are kite flying clubs of young men who love the sport.

3. Unusual epitaphs in your community. Bob Ripley has revived interest in humorous tombstone lines. Write up not only the amusing ones in your city or state, but the dramatic ones that speak tragedy (murder, accident, fire, epidemics).

4. Origin of street and suburb names in your city. Do they reflect historical trends and fads? Were German names changed during World War I? Are there reminiscences of the Civil, Spanish-American, and World Wars? Are local heroes honored? Were the streets preplanned and prenamed before they were built (as in Salt Lake City)?

5. How successful has the police radio been in your community? Cite instances of thrilling captures of criminals by broadcasts to a squad car. Take the other side of the story, too. Have police broadcasts helped any bad men to escape?

6. How various students in college earn money performing odd chores to help pay their tuition or to help make money for their fraternities or other organizations. Part-time work in a drug store, restaurant, or typing, sweeping, grass-cutting, tutoring, garage duties.

7. Tribulations of a movie usher. Has to be a Beau Brummell, diplomat, Sherlock Holmes, night nurse, and encyclopedia, all in one. Interview some interesting ushers, learn their stories and ambitions. Be sure to mention notables who have at one time served as ushers—Tyrone Power is only one movie usher who has zoomed to the top.

8. Minerals, gems, soil strata in your community. Interview geologists, ask them about interesting items, historical facts, or new discoveries. Look into early mining in your section of the state; past gold rushes, lost gold mines, ghost towns, dignitaries of old who prospected and prospered.

9. Advent of the "gasoline buggy" in your town. What citizen owned the first car; who operated the first garage, where the mechanics were known as "car doctors"? Early motorcades. Dip into old newspaper files and look for amusing headlines—especially those stressing the danger and the daring of the "Horseless Carriage."

10. Feminine Fliers in your city or in a nearby city. What are their reasons for flying? Have they had to hurdle family opposition or financial difficulties in order to follow their aviation ambitions?

11. If there is a penitentiary nearby, interview the man who pulls the switch for the electric chair in the death house. His emotions. His recollections of "last words," "last

[1] Reprinted by permission of the *Writer's Digest*.

requests," "last suppers" of the doomed men. His observations of human courage and fears, as based upon his death house experiences. Was there an instance of a doomed man being pardoned at the last minute?

12. Early theaters in your vicinity. The first opera, play, or performance. The last. What great actors graced the stage? What great personages swelled the audiences? What romances culminated on that stage? What has become of the building?

13. Talking books for blind students. How sightless pupils get their lessons; how they amuse themselves; how they earn a living.

Are there any shut-in societies in your community? Are crippled and disabled persons encouraged to make a living through their skill and handiwork? How do they manage?

14. Adventures of a federal narcotic agent. The dangers and thrills in his work. Some characters he has met; "innocent" victims! dangerous and elusive criminals; his hairbreadth experiences in solving narcotic cases. Unsolved cases.

15. The National Guard of your state. Its duties and activities in peacetime; its activities in the defense program.

16. Interview a newsreel photographer. Make him the real "power behind the throne" or the backstage hero. Stress his risks and dangers in "getting that picture." His most humorous experience; his greatest danger; some of his hardships, black moments, his favorite stories, his favorite pictures, his favorite characters. Emphasize unsung hero angle.

17. Is there an unpublicized ventriloquist in your community? There were myriads of ventriloquists struggling to earn daily bread long before Chase and Sanborn discovered Charlie McCarthy.

18. Experiences of a local parachute jumper. Some of his narrow escapes from death. How he became interested in this thrilling profession; does he still get a thrill

with each jump or is he nonchalant and used to it all? Does he have any pet superstitions, or lucky days?

19. Experiences of a dog-catcher. His full duties. (In most cities the dog-catcher is also the Deputy Sheriff and, therefore, is an important individual. Is the hard-heartedness conception of the dog-catcher untrue in this case? Is this particular dog-catcher fond of children?)

20. Local hero feature story about neighborhood personalities who have been awarded the Carnegie medal for bravery.

21. The bicycling craze. Begin with the current Hollywood fad of bicycling for slenderness and health and the latest bike models, with handlebar brakes and other up-to-date features.

22. Evolution of the barbering trade. Old-time tonsorial shops with *Police Gazette* on hand. Changes in methods, gossip, literature. Some tonsorial oldtimers in your community.

23. Anything interesting about typewriters in your communities? Who owned the first one in your town? What is the oldest model you can find? Development of the typewriter; some of its inventors; first stenographers were men.

24. Beauty parlor operators. How they happened to go into that work. Do they find it monotonous or exhilarating?

25. Unusual collection of old firearms. Does a local citizen or police department own pistols of historical or dramatic interest? Pistols once belonging to a notorious outlaw or pirate—or perhaps to a famous soldier?

26. A veteran music teacher who has maintained a studio for 20 years or more, and has, perhaps, been a famous artist at one time. His or her experiences in guiding the hands and musical tastes of many youngsters.

27. Interview an old-time druggist in your community. Oldest drug store in town. Ancient drugs, ones most in demand in old times; newest products and fads.

28. The fingerprinting of civilians, includ-

ing schoolchildren. Individual reactions to it: objection, superstitions. How these clues have been used to trap culprits, to identify amnesia victims, find missing persons, and reconcile families. Look for dramatic stories and humorous incidents here.

29. There may be a good story in a local florist shop. How did the florist get interested in flowers? Has he or she discovered anything interesting and unusual about flowers? What types are most in demand during what seasons? Has the florist been able to trace romances through floral orders?

30. Interview a veteran veterinarian for an appealing article on the art of healing the diseases and injuries of domestic animals. How animal hospitals prolong animals' lives and cure injuries and diseases which formerly took a huge toll of pet life.

31. Experiences of a hypnotizer or a psychology professor who has hypnotized students in his experiments. Highlights of his career; interesting points and experiences concerning hypnotism; how he has told a hypnotized person to perform a certain act and how, later when the hypnotic state has been dispelled, the person will perform that act without knowing why. Conclusions the hypnotizer has drawn from his experiences. How this has effected certain benefits, caught criminals? Psychoanalysts use hypnotism.

32. Unique experience of a pawnbroker. Out-of-the-ordinary articles which people have deposited with him as security on loans.

33. Interview with a woman physician. Her preparation and the highlights of her medical career.

34. The city's most enthusiastic and successful autograph collector. Some of his (or her) most distinguished signatures; the personal favorites of the collector, and the story behind them. Interesting experiences in securing, and the story behind them.

35. History of a fraternal organization in your city or campus. The leaders, past and present. Initiation fun and terrors. Build it around one main character.

36. A genealogical expert. How he or she collects data about different families. The demand for such work, the compensation? What are this genealogist's opinions of human vanity and man's interest in himself? Does he or she connect our increasing interest in genealogy with Oriental and Biblical ancestor-worship?

37. Interview an ant or insect specialist. What started the person in this work? What has he found most interesting in the life and habits of ants and similar insects? Has the student other vocations? You might make references to Henry David Thoreau and his life at *Walden*.

38. A professional rat exterminator. How the modern "Pied Piper" conducts a campaign to rid a city of rodents. Some of the biggest triumphs.

39. Experiences of a state highway patrolman. Exciting captures of dangerous desperadoes and close calls.

40. Interview a weather prophet of note. Ask him his methods of forecasting and their accuracy. How he first became interested in weather forecasting. Ask him his theories as to the important position of his profession in modern warfare; how weather forecasts have affected war.

41. Get a story about an ancient piano in your vicinity. Who was the first citizen to own one? Did the early pioneers of your section rebel against the use of pianos in Sunday School or church services? Are there any harpsichords, clavichords, and other forerunners of the piano nearby?

42. Interview with a Judge in a Juvenile Court. How he deals with cases of young lawbreakers. His theories.

43. The growth of a local humane society. Facts about the personality and the life of the founder. Was there a personal reason for going into this charitable field? The task of finding homes for animals. Fate of animal pets in war.

44. Experiences of a theater cashier. Any holdups or humorous happenings? What

types of movies are preferred by men, by women, by children?

45. A local bridge champion. What system does he use? To what does he ascribe his success?

46. Interesting article about razors, from the oldest in your community to a stream-lined late-model electric razor. The advent of the safety razor; then the electric. Facts concerning beard. Interview someone in your town who has a full beard or a Van Dyke.

47. The history of hospitalization in your city. Pioneer hospitals and distinguished doctors of the past and present. Interesting experiences; unusual cases where patients have benefited from hospitalization.

48. Trace the history of military conscription throughout our American wars. (It really started in Biblical times.) But stress conscription in the Civil War. The age limits at various times during the War. Under the Draft Act passed by Congress in March, 1863, a drafted person could be exempted from service by hiring a substitute or by paying $300.

49. Thrills of a lifetime among local golfers. Some unique holes-in-one; how they perfected "trick" plays or characteristic shots; their superstitions, best memories.

50. Famous Indian fighters of your state. Some of Paleface's outstanding exploits, and close escapes from death.

Solo[1]

THE TALK OF THE TOWN

AT BELMONT PARK the other afternoon, we availed ourself of the opportunity to have a talk with Karl E. Rissland, official trumpeter for all New York State running-race tracks, and a man whose presence undoubtedly raises the cultural tone of those premises at least two notches. He's a cheerful, white-haired man of fifty-seven, weighing some two hundred and fifty pounds, who, as a symphonic trumpeter, has played under most of the leading conductors. It is eleven years since he abandoned the sombre evening dress of the concert stage for a neat blue uniform with a trumpet-shaped insigne on the cap. He has never regretted the change. A race track's clientele is admittedly less musical than a Carnegie Hall audience, but Rissland finds it far more responsive to his trumpet solos; it is his duty and pleasure to play two of these before each race—the Army "First Call," to summon the horses from the paddock to the track twelve minutes before post time, and "First Call" again,

[1] From the *New Yorker*, XXVIII (May 31, 1952). Reprinted by permission of the *New Yorker*.

to proclaim the arrival of the horses on the track ten minutes before post time. Rissland estimates that in his eleven years on the turf he has sounded "First Call" 32,180 times. It is his custom always to blow the first "First Call" facing the paddock and the second facing the grandstand. The point he sounds off from varies with the track. At Belmont, he blows the first "First Call" on the ramp beside the Turf & Field Club section of the grandstand and the second in the Club enclosure, whereas at Saratoga he blows the first "First Call" in the paddock, behind the clubhouse, and the second on the lawn in front of the clubhouse.

Mr. Rissland told us that in the old days the race-track trumpeter's call was usually "Boots and Saddles." He lays its disappearance to the fact that it hasn't the balance and resolution of "First Call." " 'Boots and Saddles' goes 'Ta-ta-ta-tee-tum, Ta-ta-ta ta-ta-ta tum, Ta-ta-ta tum-te-tum-te-tum,' " he said. "It leaves you in a state of suspense. 'First Call' has a ring of expectancy, but it is also musically complete." Rissland got in plenty of licks on "First Call" as a sergeant bugler in the First World War. Before the war, he studied trumpet here, at the Institute of Musical Art, and after the war he played trumpet in the New York Symphony Society Orchestra, under Walter Damrosch. His father acted as the orchestra's personnel manager and as concertmaster of the second violins under Damrosch for forty years. "Dr. Damrosch was always a perfect gentleman on the podium," Rissland said. " 'Gentlemen,' he used to ask us, as if butter wouldn't melt in his mouth, 'how can I conduct in four-four time when you insist on chewing gum in *three*-four time?' "

After glancing at the time registered on the tote board, Mr. Rissland opened his instrument case and brought out a shiny brass trumpet. "My old B-flat," he said, and patted it affectionately. "The B-flat will handle almost everything. You need a high-F trumpet for just one composition, Bach's Second 'Brandenburg' Concerto. It's got an exceptionally high trumpet solo with flute obbligato, and unless you have the high-F, you lose tonal color getting the register. What you're after is a brisk, twitty note. And, of course, you need a D trumpet for Handel's 'Messiah.' " Mr. Rissland said that he gave up orchestra work for the track purely as a result of chance. He was spending the summer of 1941 in Saratoga, and one day the track trumpeter fell ill. He was asked to fill in. "First I protested and then I consented," he told us. "And when the regular trumpeter said that he wanted to give up the job, I

decided to stay on. Fact is I *like* playing solo. There aren't enough trumpet solos in symphonic compositions to suit me. The only drawback to track trumpeting is the uncertainty of the weather." In all the thousands of "First Calls" Mr. Rissland has sounded, he figures, he has blown about a dozen false notes, and those occurred during rainstorms or under other climatic conditions unfavorable to the trumpet. "Still, I'd rather blame myself than the rain or the wind," he said. "Once or twice, I've tried playing something besides 'First Call,' just to break the monotony. One day, it was 'Don't Sit Under the Apple Tree with Anyone Else but Me,' and another day it was the trumpet call from Beethoven's 'Lenore' Overture Number Three. Nobody seemed to notice the difference. I was a little disappointed." He glanced again at the tote board, walked over to his station near the Turf & Field Club enclosure, faced the paddock, and, for the 32,181st time, blew "First Call"—clear-toned, strong on balance and resolution, and temporarily deafening.

SUGGESTIONS FOR STUDY

1. Consider this feature article from the point of view of the interviewer. What questions do you suppose he framed before talking with Mr. Rissland?

2. What is the effect of quoting the conversation directly?

3. Analyze carefully the interviewer's conception of Mr. Rissland as a man. Then observe how he makes that conception come to life by choosing pertinent parts of their conversation and pertinent details from Mr. Rissland's life.

Sidewalk Fisherman[1]

MEYER BERGER

SAM SCHULTZ has always been hydrophobic. Even as a kid, in a Central Park rowboat he

[1] From the *New Yorker*, XIV (July 23, 1938), No. 23. Reprinted by permission of the author and the *New Yorker*.

would go white with fear of the water. When he grew up and friends invited him on fishing parties he'd always refuse, saying he had a tendency to seasickness. It took a vast economic disturbance, the depression, to throw him into grate-fishing when all his natural instincts were against it, but today he is probably the world's champion grate-fisherman, the man who can haul up coins from subway gratings with more efficiency than anybody else in the business. Grate-fishing was a primitive art when Sam became identified with it after losing his job as a truckman's helper seven years ago. It was just something that bums worked at for beer money. Sam has made it an exact science, and he earns a living by it.

Sam works with a few feet of light twine and a plummet of his own design—a piece of steel five inches long, an eighth of an inch thick, and about an inch and three-quarters wide, just right to lower through a grate slot. He lets it down endways until it gets to the bottom, and then lets it fall broadside on the coin. Sam will point out that his five-inch plummet thus covers a potential working area of almost ten inches. The flat side of the plummet is greased so that the coin sticks to it; all Sam has to do then is to haul away, and he's got the money. The bums of the grate-fishing industry use tiny weights for plummets and have to maneuver their lines a long time before they hit. "My way," Sam will tell you, "is pure headwoik."

Sam's second and equally important contribution toward uplift of the industry was an all-weather stickum to take the place of the chewing gum or taxicab-wheel grease which the bums use on their casting plummets. Chewing gum was all right in summer but it hardened at the first frost. Taxi grease worked into your pores, got under your fingernails, and made your hands untidy. It took months of experiment before Sam found the right thing—white petroleum jelly, or vaseline. A thin coat of this on the plummet will pull pennies, dimes, nickels, and even big money out of any subway grate, come frost or heat wave.

Sam buys the vaseline in the Liggett's drugstore on Times Square. The clerks there know him now and they plop the jar on the counter the minute he walks in. A single jar will last a month in winter and about three weeks in summer, if you husband it and don't oversmear, which is the general fault of amateurs. Runoff, because of heat, accounts for the extra summer waste, and so far Sam hasn't found a way around that. When you're after big money (quarters and halves), it is better to thicken the vaseline coating on your plummet, but not too much. Sam figures, for example, that proper bait for a silver dollar would be around a sixteenth of an inch. That's pure theory, because cartwheels are practically extinct in New York and he has never had a chance to work on one.

Sam may not look it now, but he was a machine gunner in the World War. Hunching over grates has rounded his shoulders and has taken something from his five feet, seven inches. He keeps his hat brim far down over his face, which is red from exposure. He got into that habit when he first took up grate-fishing. He was ashamed of his work and always afraid he might be recognized by the Brooklyn crowd who used to invite him around to pinochle and poker games when he was a truckman's helper. Incidentally, he thinks that stuff about Times Square being the crossroads of the world is just a myth. He's fished the Square almost every night for seven years and hasn't seen one of his old acquaintances.

Sam's people were German-American. They died before he got through 6B in Public School 25 on First Avenue at Fifth Street. He wasn't much at school except in history and arithmetic, and most of that is gone now. He doesn't think, though, that he will ever forget the stuff about George Washington, Abraham Lincoln, and Captain John Smitz. The sturdy Captain sticks in his mind. "Captain Smitz," he will say, "was so tough a tommyhawk bounced off his neck and the Indians had to turn him loose."

Sam always liked horses, and when he got out of school in the middle of the sixth year he drove a wagon for a neighborhood fruit-and-vegetable man. That's how he came to get his first job as a truckman's helper when he lived in Harlem. He had to give that up when he was drafted into the Thirty-second Machine Gun Battalion and sent to Camp Meade. He liked machine-gunning. He recalls that it made a man feel like somebody to have a Lewis gun kicking against his shoulder. Sadness overtakes him now when he remembers how Spanish flu swept the camp in October of 1918, forty-eight hours before his outfit was scheduled to go to France. The quarantine held until the war ended.

When he got back to New York from Camp Meade, Sam looked around for another helper's job and finally landed one over in Brooklyn. He started at $12 a week and worked up to $26. That had been cut to $21 when the job was swept out from under him altogether by the depression. With that he lost all his Brooklyn interests, even his (up till then) unshaken faith in the Dodgers. He doesn't get to the ball games on Sundays as he used to, but if he could raise the price of a bleacher seat he supposes he might root for the Yanks. Sam thinks a man ought to be loyal to some team and he never liked the Giants anyway.

Grate-angling prickles with fine points that you'd never dream of if you hadn't put your mind to it as Sam has. He knows all the midtown gratings by heart and can tell you, within a few cents, what his yield has been in each one. He watches waste cans for discarded newspapers, and scans the lists of goings on in town to figure out the night's working schedule. If there is nothing happening at Madison Square Garden, for example, he will stick to Times Square, which is to the grate-angler what the Grand Banks are to a Gloucesterman. Sometimes he'll just play a hunch and go over to the East Side, now that the Kingfish has disappeared. The Kingfish was a giant Negro who would pound your ears right down to your ankles if you poached on his Lexington and Madison Avenue grates. No one seems to know what has happened to him this past month, but

he hasn't been around. Rival fishermen hope it's nothing slight; Sam, in any case, is uneasy every time he works on the East Side. He figures that the Kingfish, who used to spend all his haul for gin, may merely be doing a short bit on the Island for assault or something and may get back any day. Sam, by the way, isn't a drinking man at all, though he will take a glass of beer on hot days.

The Garden is the best spot in town on fight nights, or when there's wrestling or hockey. Patrons of those sports are A-1 droppers. If you're a fast worker, like Sam, you can fish from fifty or sixty cents all the way up to a dollar on the Garden side of Eighth Avenue, from Forty-seventh Street north, on any night when there's a good fight card. Sam keeps away, though, during the Horse Show or when there is a Communist rally. He has come to learn that the Horse Show crowd either use their own cars or, when they pay off a taxi, simply don't drop any change. Communists, he'll advise you bitterly, are the lousiest droppers in the world. You can't count much on special events, either. Sam figured from what he'd read in the newspapers, for example, that the American Legion Convention would bring a big week of fishing. He worked like hell all through the thing, and at the end, what had he? Less than if those apple-knocking wise guys with their electric shockers had stayed home on the farm. The whole thing still puzzles him. Sam hates to see his carefully worked-up theories go to pieces. Things like the flop of the American Legion Convention make him lose confidence in his judgment.

Newspaper stands set up on subway gratings are highly favored spots, for obvious reasons. When Sam first figured that out, he had wild ideas about canvassing the stand people all along Broadway and Seventh and Eighth Avenues to move their positions from building fronts to the curb. He toyed with the project for a while, but could never quite bring himself to making the proposition. Some of the papersellers looked sour, and then, too, maybe it wouldn't have been honest. Sam is a stickler for honesty. He turned down an idea advanced by a Broadway chiseler who thought Sam might induce some kid to bump into people counting out change near the gratings. Sam just walked away from the fellow.

He has a working arrangement, however, with several of the busier newsstand owners. The man who operates the big stand on the northwest corner of Forty-second Street and Seventh Avenue drops on an average of $1.80 to $2 a month. Every time Sam comes by, the stand man indicates where coins have been dropped and Sam does his stuff. If the haul is small money he keeps all of it. On quarters, though, he gets only ten cents and on half-dollars only thirty cents. He thinks that fair enough, and even if he didn't, what could he do? Let some other fisherman get the business? He had a trade argument one time with another stand owner, a woman, and before he knew it she had her own kid fishing for the drops.

Movie-house barkers will tip Sam off when people drop money, as they often do while fighting to buy tickets in a crowd. Some barkers, though, are apt to be snooty, especially the ones with fancy uniforms. Sometimes they snarl at Sam and tell him to scram. That always makes him curl up inside. Whenever it happens he tries to think of Camp Meade and the machine gun kicking away at his shoulder. One night a man dropped a twenty-dollar bill, wrapped around a half-dollar, through the grating in front of the Rialto. Sam got the flash from the barker but a subway porter beat him to the money—lifted one of the grates and got two dollars' reward for the job. Whenever Sam thinks of the incident he grows wistful. Even without the reward it was a swell chance to set a world record for grate-fishing.

Sam walks from ten to fifteen miles every night covering the grates, but never has foot trouble. The only time he ever had sore feet was a few years ago when he took a laborer's job up in Narrowsburg, New York, clearing out underbrush on the site of a Boy Scout camp. The ground was so soft and so alien to his feet that they slid all over the place and finally burst out in big blisters. He quit the sylvan quiet and was glad to get back to Times Square.

Sam usually works twelve hours a day, from five o'clock at night until daybreak. In addition to the general avenue runs he visits certain selected spots, in the manner of a trapper looking over his traps. After the early-evening rush the bus stop on the east side of the Times Building in the Square is nearly always good for twenty to thirty cents. The yield might be even better if some busybody hadn't wired boards under part of that grating. Sam doesn't know who's responsible, the *Times* people or the I.R.T. Another favored spot is the Lexington Avenue side of Grand Central Terminal in the morning and evening rush hours. Commuters use that entrance and they're very good droppers, especially on quarters; Sam can't say why. Loew's Lexington, between Fiftieth and Fifty-first, isn't bad either. At both places, of course, you've got to watch out for the Kingfish. The Waldorf is a continual disappointment—not nearly as good as Bickford's Restaurant at 582 Lexington Avenue or Foltis-Fischer's, next door to Bickford's. They're on the same side of the street as the Waldorf, one block further north.

No part of the garment center is worth working, and that goes, generally, for everything below Forty-second Street except the Hotel New Yorker. At that, the best bit of fishing Sam ever did was in front of the Hotel York, on Seventh at Thirty-Sixth, but it was just one of those freak things. He fished up a fountain pen with a lot of people watching and someone thought it might be a good idea to hold a sidewalk auction. The bid went to $1.10, the highest single sum Sam has ever earned at grate-angling. He fished another pen—a two-minute job in front of the United Cigar store at Forty-second and Seventh—but that was a flat-rate assignment from the owner and paid only fifty cents.

The pen was a gift, with initials on it, and the fellow was very grateful; couldn't get over Sam's skill.

Sam tried Brooklyn once, on a sudden inspiration, but came back disgusted. He didn't so much as make carfare and bait money there, although he surveyed every grate in the neighborhood of the Fulton Street department stores. The same goes for the Manhattan shopping district around Macy's, Saks, and Gimbels. Women drop less than men because their handbags are so big-jawed that change usually falls right back into them. He's never tried Queens, but feels instinctively it would be no better than Brooklyn.

Sam figures his fishing nets him an average of a dollar a day, or a little more. Some days, he says, you're lucky, and you may get as much as $1.65 or even $1.85. Lots of days, though, it's like going out for trout; you just don't have any luck at all. A few weeks ago, Sam hauled out only six cents in fourteen hours on the grates—a nickel in front of the Rialto and one cent from the Times island bus stop. He knew the recession was coming even before the papers began to notice it. Almost overnight Times Square was overrun with outsiders (any newcomer is an outsider to Sam) working the grates with disgustingly primitive equipment.

When the day's yield is a dollar or over, Sam feels justified in spending fifty cents for a room in the Seventh Avenue Mills Hotel. If it happens to be a little less, he puts up at the Vigilant, on Eighth Avenue near Twenty-eight, where they charge only forty cents. He prefers the Mills because the guests are more genteel—not so apt to get boisterous. You don't get soap or towels with the rooms, so Sam carries his own, neatly wrapped in newspaper. He carries two suits of underwear, too; an extra pair of socks, a Gillette, and a stick of shaving soap. He bathes once a week in the Municipal Baths on Forty-first Street, at Ninth, when it's cold, but will go two or three times in hot weather. He feels a man loses his grip altogether if he doesn't clean up at least once a week.

Sam has no fancy tastes in food, although his work in the open air sharpens his appetite. When he finishes the early-morning run of the grates he has breakfast at the Manhattan, on Seventh Avenue near Forty-first. It's pretty nearly always the same—wheat cakes and coffee, for a dime. On good days he tries to get down to Beefsteak John's, at Third Avenue and Twenty-first, where they serve a stew, coffee, and bread for fifteen cents. If the day's haul warrants it, Sam may have a cut of coconut pie, the only dessert that ever tempts him. Sometimes, but not unless he has room money reserved, there's a late snack at the Manhattan and, because Sam's imagination doesn't seem to work where food's concerned, it's very likely to be wheats and java again. He has a good stomach—always did have—and never gets sick.

It's a mistake, unless you're out to bait Sam, to bring up the subject of stinkers. You wouldn't know about them, but stinkers are the parasites of the grate-fishing industry. When they sense that Sam is having a lucky night, they run on ahead and cut in on his grates. There's nothing you can do about it, either. Gratings are more or less public domain and anybody can fish them. What stirs Sam's gall, though, is the utter lack of ethics (he says "ettics") in the business—something he's tried to correct, but without much luck. "By me," he's apt to tell you with astonishing violence, "a stinker is rat poison—in spades."

Most grate-fishermen are antisocial. They don't so much as ask one another's names. Oh, once in a while one of them may look up from a grate and say "Hya, fisherman!" but you can't count on it. On chatty occasions they may ask you about your luck, but that's more or less perfunctory, too. No oldtimer in the business will tell another fisherman how much he's made; certainly not *where* he made it. Sam does have a working arrangement with a young grate-angler who has been in and around the Square the past four years. He's a shy, shabby fellow who has an expression of constant bewilderment. Cab-drivers make him the butt of their unsubtle jokes (Shellshock is their name for him, because of that rabbity look), but he's rather handy with the plummet. Once a week he or Sam will ride down to Barclay Street on the B.-M.T. and buy a dozen flashlight batteries at a cut-rate hardware store. All grate-anglers use flashlights to show up what's at the grating bottoms. At the cut-rate stores the batteries are three cents apiece, against five cents for the same thing at Woolworth's; so Sam and Shellshock save a total of fourteen cents on the deal, even when you count in the carfare. There's always a chance, too, to fish carfare out of the downtown grates, but outside of William Street and maybe Church, financial-district fishing is lousy.

Three batteries make one fill for the flashlight and will last about three days. Sam always has three extra ones bulging his pockets, along with his portable toilet kit. Most grate-anglers are rather sloppy—carry their plummets in their pockets, grease and all. Sam is a neat fellow and packs his equipment in a Prince Albert tin. It took him quite a while to convince Shellshock that it wasn't nice to get his pockets all smeary, but he never has sold Shellshock the vaseline idea. Shellshock just wipes off his plummet after each performance and gets new grease from the wheels of the nearest cab.

People keep asking Sam if it's true that grating fishermen find valuable diamonds and things like that. He knows of but two cases. One time a traffic cop lost a diamond ring near Penn Station. This cop went home at the end of the day, rigged up a childish fishing outfit, and came back to fish. By that time, of course, the ring was gone. Sam doesn't know who got it. In the other case (Sam won't vouch for this, because it's only hearsay), the Kingfish was supposed to have done a job for a woman who lost a five-thousand-dollar bracelet on Lexington Avenue. The woman gave him a quarter, so the story goes, and the Kingfish would have busted her crumpet if she had been a man.

Right now Sam is doing some research on a pocket-battery outfit—something on the automobile-lighter principle—that will melt thin ice at the bottom of a grating. If he perfects this invention, he feels he can practically control the industry this winter. He hasn't thought the whole thing through yet, but he's the dogged type and will probably work it out all right.

SUGGESTIONS FOR STUDY

1. What do you judge to have been the author's source of information for the material in this article? Study the article to see if you can detect more than one source.

2. Cite several instances of direct and indirect quotation that give insight into Sam's character. Why does the author use such words as "lousiest," "flop," and "apple-knocking"? Enumerate several other words of this sort that are not on a standard level of diction.

3. Is Sam honest? hard-working? intelligent? thrifty? neat? a lover of the rural countryside? a gourmand? List the words used to describe him.

4. Characterize the Kingfish and "Shellshock."

5. Trace the major divisions of the sketch to show its organization.

6. List each incident and comment that you think was inserted to attract and hold the reader rather than to give information.

7. Define the following words from the selection: hydrophobic, plummet, alien, canvassing, sylvan, recession, ethics, perfunctory.

Enterprise and Old Iron[1]

JOHN PATRIC

ON A FERTILE PLATEAU above the raging Snake River, near Jackson, Wyoming, Ora Grisamer owned a ranch. Until last year, he and his neighbors were virtually marooned there. Their only way across the turbulent Snake, 300 feet wide, was riskily by skiff or along a swaying footbridge sagging from a half-inch cable.

And now Ora Grisamer's tractor had broken down. There was no way to get it to a repair shop. Once there had been a ferry across the river—a scow pulled along a cable —but a flood had washed it away. Recently Grisamer had heard that a strange fellow named McCrary—a wizard mechanic—was camping in the canyon across the river. People said that Charles McCrary could make or repair anything—out of junk; that he had gathered around him the queerest caravan of old iron ever assembled west of the Missouri.

Grisamer hunted him up. In a clearing, he found the McCrary caravan, a bizarre collection of gadgetry on wheels, a traveling Valhalla of noble junk. There was a trailer as big as a box car, hitched to a mammoth but decrepit coal truck. The truck was loaded with a donkey engine, a ton of tools belonging to all trades and professions, and a mountainous assortment of cogs, ratchets, springs, and unclassified gear that McCrary had collected in his wanderings. Near by was the family jalopy and a smaller trailer where the family ate and slept. The family included Mrs. McCrary, four children, and a white goat. Strangest of all was a home-made contraption that McCrary proudly called his "drag-line" rig—another old truck

on which was mounted a sort of power shovel whose bucket hung from pulleys at the end of a derrick.

Yes, McCrary would be glad to earn a few dollars by repairing Grisamer's tractor. The two men carried McCrary's tools over the narrow catwalk of the footbridge. "A wagon bridge would be worth $1,000 to me and my neighbors," said Grisamer, "but there's no use talking about it. Government engineers say that it would cost at least $10,000 to swing any kind of bridge across this river."

McCrary said nothing. But while he worked on the tractor, he did a little figuring in the back of his mind. Finally he said, "I'll build you a bridge for $1,250. And I'll guarantee it to hold three tons."

It sounded good to Grisamer. A bridge would make his farm more valuable. He knew his neighbors would chip in too. So that night by lamplight in a simple contract McCrary agreed for $1,250 to build—of second-hand steel and old cable—a suspension bridge eight feet wide, with railings, across the Snake. Grisamer agreed to advance $400 when actual construction began, and the remaining $850 when he could drive a three-ton load over the completed bridge.

McCrary walked home to his trailer camp, tingling with confidence. All his life he'd been making his own way, despite hard times, with supreme self-reliance, and never a penny from charity or relief. When his little repair shop in Missouri had burned in 1933, he started west with his family, in their old car, landing finally in Wyoming, where he made a living by reconditioning junked cars and selling them. Accumulating a stake, he leased an abandoned coal mine, operating it with machinery from the junk heaps, re-

[1] From the *Christian Science Monitor* (December 21, 1940). Reprinted by permission of the *Christian Science Monitor*.

conditioned by his expert hands. During a long winter he made his drag-line rig—also from junk—and with it got jobs clearing fields and building roads. Why shouldn't he likewise build a bridge from junk?

McCrary's only cash was the $6 he had charged Grisamer for repairing the tractor. But he did have his drag-line excavator. Its 900-pound bucket, made of old bridge girders cunningly welded together with a makeshift acetylene torch, would scoop up half a ton of gravel at a single bite. The rest of the machine consisted of such things as scrambled bits of gaspipe, a bicycle chain, a hay-rake seat, a locomotive coupling, and parts from automobiles and farm machines that McCrary had found on junk heaps. In cold cash, it had cost him only $3.50, mostly for bolts and screws. With this contraption he was going to dig the foundations of his bridge.

McCrary knew nothing of engineering; but he had a picture postcard of the Golden Gate Bridge: that would serve him in lieu of blueprints. He figured that his own towers, allowing for the droop in the cables, would have to be 30 feet high on Grisamer's side of the river and 40 feet on the lower Jackson side.

One morning he leveled off a shelf on the Jackson side, and set up his beloved drag-line rig. He climbed to the old hay-rake seat, started the engine, and dropped the bucket for the first load of dirt. Days later, two deep holes yawned darkly. McCrary could dig his pits no deeper; the bottom was solid rock. And now the once-rusty, bridge-steel bucket shone like a plowshare on a spring evening.

To find steel for the supporting towers of his bridge would have stymied a less ingenious fellow. But McCrary remembered a twisted heap of bridge ruins washed out in a flood of the Gros Ventre River. The mangled bridge still lay buried in the swirling river; wading out to his armpits, he cut off four girders with his acetylene torch. Then he dragged them through Jackson, one

at a time, on a rude trailer made of two auto wheels and an axle. On the bank of the Snake River he laid them in approximate position near the holes he had dug.

Now for the cables! McCrary set out in his old truck for the oil fields, a several-hundred-mile trip, made none the easier by 17 flats. He knew that the long cables used in well drilling are discarded when they develop kinks. Oil men gave McCrary all the discarded cable he could haul away. Soon, at the bridge site, he had eight flawless pieces of cable, each about 400 feet long. He was ready to begin construction of the Jackson end of the bridge.

Erecting the steel uprights was a grueling job that required patience and precision. Aided only by his 13-year-old boy, Buster, McCrary picked up a pair of bridge towers with his drag-line rig, now transformed into a derrick, and lowered them into the hole already dug. With the $400 advanced by Grisamer, he bought a small cement mixer. He swapped an old automobile engine he had found in the dump, and then repaired, for a stationary gas engine to run his mixer. With this equipment he poured tons of concrete, reinforced by scrap iron, around the bases of the towers. Behind the towers he sank a 10-foot section of steel I-beam, and buried it in concrete under 100 tons of rock and earth. This was the shoreward anchorage for eight cables which were to be festooned across the river. He did not know it, but the cost of this extra anchorage, required by the nature of the soil, had thwarted past plans for building such a bridge.

Thus far, McCrary and his boy Buster had done all the work themselves. They would have continued alone, but two jobless wayfarers turned up and McCrary hired them at 40 cents an hour. Their wages would cut into his profit, but he knew what it was to be jobless. The quartet now began the task of stringing the eight suspension cables across the river. First they pulled a light cable to Grisamer's side and with that, tugging like demons, they dragged each of the heavy bridge cables through the foaming waters of the Snake.

After the cables had been drawn across, McCrary strung two of them on a temporary scaffolding. Then he devised a sort of cablecar that ran along them on pulleys, with the drag-line rig supplying motor power. On this cablecar, tools, cement, and cement mixer went across. But now came the herculean job of transporting the 7,000-pound tower to the farthest side of the river! Would the cablecar support it? The cables sagged perilously under the burden. McCrary's face was gray with strain. But the cables held fast; the tower reached the other side. Then the four bridge builders tipped it into holes already blasted for it.

But now McCrary had ominous visitors—two U.S. Forest Rangers. "You should have gotten a permit before you started this work," they said. McCrary hurried to Grisamer. "Have we got to stop work?" he asked.

"Not unless you want to, Mac," the farmer replied, "and I don't figure you will when you hear what they're saying uptown. They're saying, 'Grisamer's hired a little boy and a couple of tramps and a dumb mechanic, who never saw a suspension bridge in his life, to build him one with stuff from the town dump.'"

"That's so," McCrary grinned. "But she'll be a bridge. I'll show 'em!"

A few days later, as the concrete tower bases were slowly hardening, the county engineer came up to McCrary: "You fellows are undertaking something pretty serious here," he said. "The United States Forest Service has been to see me. May I see your blueprints?"

"Blueprints? What blueprints?"

"Your plans and specifications."

"Ain't got any."

"But, man, you must have something!"

From his pocket, McCrary pulled his postcard of the San Francisco Bridge. "I'm making it something like that," he said. "But"—apologetically—"not so big, of course." The engineer shook his head and turned to gaze at McCrary's bridge admiringly "I don't see how you did it. But there she stands." After a careful inspection, the engineer passed judgment. "McCrary, if you'll make a few minor changes, I'll O.K. your bridge for a three-ton limit."

McCrary thanked the engineer and went back to work. Six more cables were strung and anchored in concrete. A solid plank floor was laid. Stout wooden handrails were fitted along the sides. County Commissioners, impressed by the job, agreed not only to improve the road approaches to the bridge but to pay the lumber bill also, thus saving McCrary $200. Whereupon, he promptly raised the wages of his two helpers from 40 to 50 cents an hour, with back pay from the beginning. Charlie McCrary wasn't in the bridge-building game for the purpose of getting rich!

At the opening of the bridge, just two months from the day McCrary started building it, no Government official cut any ribbons. But there was a ceremony just the same, with just a touch of sadness about it. Ora Grisamer, who had waited half his life for a bridge, passed on just before it was finished. But his tractor, driven by his daughter, headed the procession. Then came the two helpers and the McCrarys in the family jalopy, with the white goat bringing up the rear. The bridge was as steady as a cathedral under the tramping of a little cavalcade.

This story has an epilogue.

I visited Jackson last summer and found McCrary living in a real house, with his trailer rented to campers. Financially, things were a little easier with him; he owned two building lots, a bank book—and a new baby. I saw him slip a dollar into the collection plate the day he took me to church with his family. The drag-line rig was earning good money. It had moved houses, dug basements for new homes and stores. Already it was a Jackson legend, a fragment of the greater legend that is America.

The bridge, McCrary told me, had held up during the past winter even when there were —by careful reckoning—15 tons of wet snow on it. More than that, loads had gone across on the snow before the farmers found out how much it weighed.

I last saw Charlie McCrary sitting in the old hay-rake seat, digging a water-main ditch. As he swung his bucket to and fro, I saw him as a living symbol of American ingenuity and self-reliance.

SUGGESTIONS FOR STUDY

1. How much do you know about McCrary's life before he started the bridge across the Snake? Where does this information occur in the article? Why does it not occur sooner?

2. What might have been some of the sources of information used by the writer of this article?

3. Does the writer make McCrary's accomplishment plausible or not?

4. Find half a dozen places in the article where information is given which helps you to form a mental picture of McCrary.

5. Explain the meaning of the following words: epilogue, bizarre, Valhalla, decrepit, turbulent, acetylene, stymied.

C. The Book Review

The book review employs criticism, which may be defined as an impartial attempt to estimate worth. Walter Savage Landor very aptly wrote, "A perfect piece of criticism must exhibit *where* a work is good or bad; *why* it is good or bad; in what degree it is good or bad; must also demonstrate in what manner and to what extent the same ideas or reflections have come to others."

HOW TO BEGIN

First, *determine the author's general purpose*—to inform, persuade, or entertain—as you must not censure him for doing what he never intended. You would not think of condemning a chess game because it lacked wild action nor a hockey game because it was not slow and cautious. So you must not argue with a lyric poem for not telling a story as a novel would do.

Second, *determine the specific purpose.*

One work intended to entertain may attempt an exciting story, another a character study, another the creation of a mood, and so on. You must know what a writer is attempting before you can tell whether he has accomplished it. Notice, for instance, how the purposes are stated by Lilo Linke in this review of *A Handbook of Freedom*, selected by Jack Lindsay and Edgell Rickword:

> We ask of a good anthology that it should be a whole library condensed into one volume, and that it should lead us from the reading of those pages we know and cherish to others which we might never have discovered on our own. The *Handbook of Freedom* fulfills both and more. It is not just a series of excerpts in prose and verse. "Our aim was," Rickword says in his introduction, "to show history in its impact on the experience, not as it is reflected in the contemplation." To this end, a record was made of the clamoring voices of the masses offstage, and of the individuals who had the courage to face the hostile limelight on their behalf. . . . From this angle, history is seen from below, and the kings and statesmen are suddenly turned from heroes into the villains of the piece.—*Life and Letters Today* (July, 1939).

Third, *decide whether the work has accomplished what was worth doing*. Even if the general and specific purposes have been effected, the result may be trivial or useless, for some other book may have achieved the same ends equally competently or even better. You can also clarify for yourself what you think the book offers as its major contribution. This you may not be able yet to do wisely, but try your very best with the knowledge and judgment at your disposal. Here is a sample of criticism offered by T. R. Hay in reviewing F. J. Klingberg's *The Morning of America*:

> The passing of the Virginia Presidents marked the close of an era. The morning of America was ended; the middle period was begun, but the "new American shape was clearly visible." In these present days of uncertainty, when the American tradition, the American way of life, is being subjected to challenges that are tending to change its character if not its spirit, it is important to know something of the

forces and traditions which have made the United States great. Dr. Klingberg's book is a worth-while contribution to a knowledge and an understanding of this evolution.—New York *Times Book Review* (May 21, 1941).

HOW TO CRITICIZE EXPOSITION AND ARGUMENTATION

Exposition. Test the work mainly for clarity. The organization must be logical. All steps necessary for clear or thorough understanding must be explained. The language must fit the audience. If a physics book intended for a popular audience uses highly technical words and a very rapid presentation, it is a failure. The style must also suit the audience and avoid being too abstract, too complex, or too clumsy.

Argument. Though argument should meet such tests as are applied to exposition, judge it primarily by its persuasiveness. The thesis must be supported mainly by facts, not by opinions and guesses. Facts which run counter to the thesis must not be disregarded. Important statements must be documented. Prejudice must not be shown of any sort —political, national, racial, religious, professional—without your being on guard for any warping or suppression of fact as a result.

You may find it useful to look up the author in a biographical dictionary. See how he is qualified to write on this subject, what books or articles he has written, what degrees he holds or what honors have been awarded him, and the like. These facts may build your confidence in him or place you on your guard. You can scarcely expect a Republican to write impartially in an election year about a Democratic candidate.

The services you can render your reader are many. If you have read other books by the same author, you can tell whether the new work is similar in vein to the others. If you have read many books on the same subject, you can say whether the new one is routine or whether it makes a real contribution. The tone may also impress you. Sometimes an author's gaiety, irony, somberness, or other tone happily suits his topic

(as Leacock's amusing lightness perfectly fits the subject in "My Fishpond," p. 528); but once in a while an author makes a mistake and uses a quite unsuitable tone. It is your duty as a reviewer to note these facts.

HOW TO CRITICIZE NARRATION

Factual accuracy is not a major test for narration. Use more suitable standards. Narratives combine ideas with emotions to enable you to enter an experience. The main question, therefore, is whether you have been able to experience the episodes offered.

The purpose. There are many kinds of narratives: some consider very serious human problems, others are lightly amusing, still others delight with rousing adventure, and so on. So first determine the purpose. Do not insist that every novel have a happy ending; simply decide whether the ending is appropriate to the author's purpose.

Authors differ too in the way they picture life. Some may use fantasy (as in the story "Laura," p. 393), some idealize actualities, some treat the happier parts of human life, still others center on the sordid, wretched aspects of life. See what the novel attempts, and then try to determine if it does its task well.

Character. Next evaluate the main characters. Consider whether they come to life or remain wooden and inert, whether or not they undergo a change of personality, whether you may enter their minds or see them only by their actions, and especially what feeling the author tries to arouse about each.

Plot. Define clearly for yourself what conflicts produce the growth of the plot, whether any subplots assist the main plot, what the climactic moments are and whether they are effective, and whether the incidents are logically linked together so that they lead to an inevitable conclusion. Remember this test: in a good novel characters are consistent and do not suddenly change to make a plot work out cleverly.

Setting. Setting ordinarily supports plot

and character to make them better understood. So observe whether it is completely enough and well enough described to enable you to understand the circumstances surrounding the characters, to lend atmosphere, and to assist or motivate the action. Sometimes, as in Hardy's novels, the setting is so important it controls the whole work and embodies the author's philosophy; if so, you must not overlook its importance.

Style. Examine well the sentence construction, for it may greatly enhance or impair the narrative. It may consist primarily of long, loose sentences that flow gracefully; perhaps it may be involved and intricate, full of qualifying phrases and clauses, that give complexity of statement; or perhaps it may be composed of short, terse sentences that are direct and hard-hitting. But whatever the style, it should suit well the content and mood of the narrative.

For further discussion of these matters, consult the section on narration in this book.

HOW TO WRITE THE REVIEW

Having analyzed the book, then choose those considerations which seem to you to be most important; these must form your review, as you cannot in one review treat all the ideas you have had about the book. Then resolve in your review:

1. To leave no statement unsupported—always tell *why* you believe as you do.

2. To write a review that can apply to only one book. Refer to passages in the book, quote from it, speak of its characters.

The introduction. Begin vigorously. Refer at once to the book; perhaps you might even state your thesis as the opening sentence. Make clear your attitude immediately; if you are praising the volume, establish that fact and do not give the impression that you are about to cut the book to ribbons. Do not rely on such hackneyed terms as "interesting," "absorbing," "stimulating"; if you must use such words, do so later in the review where you can explain why you are applying them.

If you wish, you may also put in the introduction a word about the author, a comparison of the book with others, a statement of the author's purpose, or a short description of the type of book being reviewed.

The body. Do not make the body of the review simply a summary of the book's contents. Use it to judge the book, to explain how well or how poorly the book meets the standards you have applied to it. Of course, describe the subject matter or the main features of the plot, but devote only a brief amount of space to this feature.

Be firm but not dogmatic or sarcastic. Francis Jeffrey began a review of a poem by Wordsworth, "This will never do. . . . The case of Mr. Wordsworth, we perceive, is now manifestly hopeless; and we give him up as altogether incurable, and beyond the power of criticism." Such a tone does little good; modern critics in general avoid it.

Be fair. Make sure that you understand exactly what the author wrote and that you do not warp his ideas while discussing them.

Be open-minded. Because a writer has not done exactly as you would wish him to do, you are not always right in attacking him. Your standards may be poor or too rigid. Shakespeare's blending comedy and tragedy in one play was for many years denounced, but critics now agree that he was right.

Conclusion. Ordinarily use the end of the review to state your thesis concerning the book.

Now examine your review to see if your reader will feel satisfied that he knows the nature and scope of the book, the audience for which it is intended or by which it is best read, and whether it is in general a praiseworthy effort. Have you been concise, persuasive, and fair?

Study each of the first three reviews that follow to see how in very short compass a skillful reviewer can establish the essential points concerning a book. The remaining longer reviews illustrate various ways a book may be analyzed in detail.

SUGGESTIONS FOR STUDY

1. Go to the library, and select four or five technical magazines which pertain to your special interest. Read six or eight reviews in these magazines, and write a précis of each.

2. Read three reviews of the same book, one review at least being in a technical magazine. The *Book Review Digest* will give you assistance in finding these reviews. Then write a paragraph noting the points of agreement and disagreement. See if you can account for the disagreement.

Book Review I: Short Reviews

Sophocles, by Cedric H. Whitman.[1]

This is a poet's book about a poet, always an interesting venture, often leading to a provocative result. Mr. Whitman has read and studied the works of his subject thoroughly and sympathetically and is familiar with what others, from Aristotle down, have said about them. This has led to a dissatisfaction with the conventional portrait of Sophocles as the type of cool, classic perfection and with the attempt to force the plays into the mould sponsored by Aristotle's "Poetics." Rather Mr. Whitman views them as one of the high expressions of the Greek genius at the moment of its fullest realization in Periclean Athens, of the point of view which is denoted by the term "Humanism." Sophocles' tragic hero is the supreme embodiment of the human spirit, too large for the world about him. Hence the tragic conflict, in the resolution of which the spiritual, divine side of the hero receives its release and recognition. Whether the reader will agree with every detail of the author's interpretation is of minor importance; what really matters is the fresh insight he will derive from a sympathetic reading of these pages.

The Art of Scientific Investigation, by W. I. B. Beveridge.

Here is a book which ought to clear up a good deal of the folklore about science and what scientists do in research laboratories. Because the author is a biologist, most of the illustrations are from the history of the development of the science which he knows best, but all the physical

[1] This and the two short reviews that follow are from the *Virginia Quarterly Review*, XXVII (Autumn, 1951). Reprinted by permission of the *Virginia Quarterly Review*.

sciences are represented from time to time in the examples. Beveridge examines systematically the preparation of the scientist, and the rôles of hypothesis, imagination, intuition, chance, reason, and observation in scientific investigation. He shows the difficulties which researchers face, details the personal qualities which they need to have to get along, and appends a full bibliography to provide the reader quick access to further details in the fascinating history of scientific investigation. Only as a writer does the author fall somewhat short of grace. His style is plodding, unimaginative, unleavened by humor. It is a pity that he should have disdained the arts of literate composition, but the content is too rich to pass by on that account.

More About Words, by Margaret S. Ernst.

The entries in this little book, the third in a series on etymology, primarily for young readers, are written in a lively and discursive style, and are illustrated with apt drawings, like that of the pitchman which illustrates "beguile." Mrs. Ernst commendably avoids preaching on the use of words—she does not, for instance, take the position that "conspiracy" should be used only of people who breathe together. Nor when she says that the younger generation uses "Hi!" instead of "Hello!" does she see in such informality a threat to the integrity of the language. The stories and anecdotes of word origins here given—they are scarcely etymologies in any formal sense—are primarily designed to send the reader to dictionaries for the wealth of historical word-lore they contain. Naturally therefore, as the author properly points out, the material has been compiled from standard sources, and makes no pretense of giving matter of interest to the trained linguist. As an introduction to the use of dictionaries the book succeeds admirably, and the occasional errors and confusions in it probably matter little on the elementary level at which the book is aimed. Thus it is hard to believe that a high school student would be seriously harmed by the statement that Old English "wilde'or" meant "wild deer," rather than "wild animal," or even by the erroneous apostrophe in the middle of the Old English form. More serious, perhaps, is the presentation of such rather vague entities as "Old Aryan" and "Old Teutonic" as if they were exotic languages from which we have merely borrowed, as we have from Latin and Greek, instead of giving these forms as genuine ancestral stages in the history of our language.

Book Review II

Dictionary of American History, edited by James Truslow Adams, reviewed by Paul A. Palmer.[1]

This work contains over six thousand articles, nearly twenty-five hundred pages: "the result of the labor of four years and the collaboration of well over a thousand persons." The review must begin with praise. The editor must be complimented on the elaborate system of cross reference, involving generous and discriminating use of *qv's* and *qqv's*, and on the admirable index volume. In organization, certainly, the *Dictionary* is a model work of reference. Mr. Adams must also be congratulated on his success in enlisting the co-operation of the most eminent authorities in their respective specialties. Thus the leading articles on diplomatic history are by Samuel F. Bemis, those on technology and invention by Roger Burlingame, on Indian culture by Clark Wissler, on religious and ecclesiastical history by William W. Sweet, on the period of the Civil War and Reconstruction by J. G. Randall, and on the judiciary and constitutional law by Carl B. Swisher. Among the more distinguished of the longer essays are Carl Becker's "Declaration of Independence," Victor S. Clark's "Manufacturing," and Dexter Perkins's "Monroe Doctrine." Some of the shorter contributions, moreover, such as George Fort Milton's "Lincoln-Douglas Debates," Irving Dilliard's "Comic Strips and Funny Papers," and H. F. Gosnell's "Machine, Party," exemplify a high order of excellence. In one of these briefer articles ("Drinking Habits"), there is information which will interest social historians and may humiliate contemporary dipsomaniacs; namely, that a little more than a century ago the yearly consumption of rum in Wilbraham, Massachusetts (population 2,000), was 8,000 gallons, and the annual consumption of whiskey in Georgia (population 400,000, including slaves) was 2,000,000 gallons. Another very short article ("North Carolina, Governor of, to Governor of South Carolina"), not unrelated to the foregoing, must be quoted in full:

> "It's a damn long time between drinks," said Edward B. Dudley, Governor of North Carolina, to Pierce Mason Butler, chief executive of South Carolina, in 1838, at the home of Mrs. Nancy Anne Jones, about midway between Raleigh and Durham, N. C. About five years later, at a meeting on the state line, not

[1] Reprinted by permission of the author and the *Kenyon Review.*

far from Charlotte, Gov. J. M. Morehead said to Gov. J. H. Hammond of South Carolina, "It's a damned long time between drinks."

As well as this reviewer can judge, the accuracy which distinguishes between a gubernatorial "damn" in 1838 and a "damned" in 1843 (*circa*), is sustained throughout. It is, of course, inevitable that in a work of this scope some errors should escape the attention of the editor and his proofreaders; and of those noted two should be pointed out. George Mason, not James Madison, predicted that the electors would fail to choose a president "nineteen times in twenty" (II, 191). Herbert Croly's *Promise of American Life* was not published in 1900 as stated (IV, 302), but in 1909.

One aware of Mr. Adams's eastern background, his specialized interest and competence in New England history, and his conservative predilections might reasonably (if somewhat meanly) expect to find traces of them in the assignment, coloring, and length of the contributions; but on the whole the work is remarkably free from sectional or partisan bias. Indeed, the generous amount of space and the high level of scholarship devoted to the South, the "Valley of Democracy," and the West mark a real advance in American historiography. As regards partisan prejudice, the assertion in the article entitled "Morals" (IV, 21) that "The Federal Government itself [the cross reference is to the abrogation of the gold clause, 1933] has contributed to this feeling of irresponsibility for contracts by its own failure to fulfill its promises," sounds more like the shriek of Associate Justice McReynolds than the calm tones of an historian; and the reference (V, 207-208) to President F. D. Roosevelt's judicial reorganization plan of February 5, 1937, as a court-packing episode (without quotation marks) is likewise objectionable. But these are exceptional.

Despite its careful organization, its general accuracy and fairness, the *Dictionary* is in two important respects extremely disappointing. In the first place, it lacks a philosophy, a principle of interpretation, to bind its alphabetically-ordered parts into anything like a consistent and coherent whole. As the reflective reader refers to articles here and there or as, following the cross references, he peruses a series of related articles, he may experience considerable confusion. From one contribution he may infer that the influence of climate largely explains regional and national evolution; from another, that the influence of the frontier has been decisive; and from still others, that economic determinism is the key wherewith to unlock the secrets of past, present, and the emerging future. Admittedly, this may be less a criticism of editorial policy than a commentary on the present state of American historical scholarship.

A more serious, at all events a fairer and more pertinent, criticism relates to the failure of the *Dictionary* to fulfill the promise implicit in the Foreword. The editor writes: "A generation ago historians had done the merest spadework. Today our whole culture is their province. . . ." On close scrutiny of the work one is, therefore, amazed to discover that more than half the articles are devoted to politics, government, and war; about one fourth to economic topics; one fifth to social history; and fewer than five per cent to the arts, literature, and philosophy. For these proportions the editor must be held responsible, and also for the fact that the articles on art, music, drama, and philosophy, although written by qualified scholars, are so brief and perfunctory as to be almost worthless. To take one example, the student who resorts to the *Dictionary* for information relative to the struggles, ideas, and faiths of the so-called "Middle Period" of American history will find nearly a page on the Battle of Gettysburg but not a line on the poetry of Walt Whitman or the novels of Herman Melville. Again, one line is assigned to pragmatism; William James is given about the same amount of space as Jack Johnson; the entry under "Lindbergh Flies across the Atlantic" is about three times as long as the summary paragraph under "Transcendentalism." If, in these cases and others that might be cited, there is any criterion of selection and emphasis, it is clearly journalistic rather than historical.

Useful, even invaluable, as the *Dictionary* will be to political scientists and to those whose main concern is with political, economic, and social history, students of the history of arts and of ideas must continue to turn for reference and guidance to the Beards' *Rise of American Civilization* and *America in Midpassage,* to the incomplete Schlesinger-Fox *History of American Life,* and to the late Professor Parrington's unfinished *Main Currents in American Thought.* This, I fear, is equivalent to saying that a dictionary of American history which shall take "our whole culture as . . . [its] province" remains to be compiled.

SUGGESTIONS FOR STUDY

1. What are the excellences of the *Dictionary?*
2. Is it warped by prejudices?
3. In what two respects is it disappointing?
4. What is its main contribution?
5. Does the reviewer take into account the underlying purpose of the *Dictionary?* How well does the *Dictionary* fulfill its purpose?
6. Does the reviewer's citing of particular details of strength and weakness of the *Dictionary* give you confidence in the justice of his review? Why?
7. Why are the several direct quotations from the work effective?
8. Define the following words from the review: collaboration, discriminating, dipsomaniacs, gubernatorial, predilections, abrogation, implicit, perfunctory, pragmatism.

Book Review III

Abraham Lincoln: The War Years, by Carl Sandburg, reviewed by Charles A. Beard.[1]

Never yet has a history or biography like Carl Sandburg's *Abraham Lincoln: The War Years* appeared on land or sea. Strict disciples of Gibbon, Macaulay, Ranke, Mommsen, Hegel, or Marx will scarcely know what to do with it. It does not enclose the commonplace in a stately diction appropriate for Augustan pomp. Its pages do not stand out in the cold formalism which marks the work of those historians who imagine that they are writing history as it actually was. Nor are the personalities, events, passions, follies, blind stumblings, ridiculous performances, contradictions, and stupidities of the four years smoothed out to make them fit into "the progressive revelation of the idea of God." The struggle of classes, though more than hinted at, forms no persistent theme employed to explain everything from Lincoln's jokes to Jefferson Davis's views in the spring of 1861.

The opening chapters of Mr. Sandburg's first volume do not present, after the fashion of Macaulay, a picture of American society in 1861 —the number, posture, interests, and ideologies of the classes whose spokesmen enact the leading roles. Systematists will not discover anywhere in the four volumes "logical" and self-contained "treatments" of finance, taxation, railways, land policies, tariffs, natural resources, labor, and immigration, or the long struggle to curtail the rights of states in the interest of business enterprise. Followers of Lytton Strachey, Gamaliel Bradford, and Freud will look in vain for psychographs of personalities fashioned after their hearts' desires.

But this is not to say that Mr. Sandburg writes "without fear and without research." On the contrary, few if any historians have ever labored harder in preparation for composition. He has

[1] Reprinted by permission of the author and of the *Virginia Quarterly Review.*

traveled widely and searched widely. Great
collections of Lincolniana he has scrutinized and
used critically. He has examined mountains of
newspapers, letters, diaries, pamphlets, stray papers, documents, records, Congressional debates,
posters, proclamations, handbills, clippings, pictures, cartoons, and memorabilia, great and small.
Work with the paper sources he has supplemented by journeys all over the country, in-
terviews with survivors of the war years and
their descendants, and walks over fields and
plantations. An indefatigable thoroughness characterizes his preparations and his pages.

In arrangement our author's text is more like
a diary or saga than a "systematic presentation."
He knows that he cannot tell it all, and says
frankly, "the teller does the best he can and
picks what is to him plain, moving, and important—though sometimes what is important may
be tough reading, tangled, involved, sometimes
gradually taking on interest, even mystery, because of the gaps and discrepancies." A few
chapter titles from the first volume illustrate the
flow: "The Use of Patronage," "December '61
Message," "Opinion Makers," "Expectations of
McClellan," "Corruption," "White House Children," "Donelson—Grant—Shiloh." Even without chapters there are excursions and diversions
which could be put in or left out. Yet when the
four volumes are taken together in bulk, it would
seem that they form a realistic history of the
great conflict and that all parts and passages are
so ordered as to give a sense of verisimilitude.

An air of grave thoughtfulness hangs over the
lightest words. The searching, brooding spirit
of the laborious historian pervades the treatment of every large problem. With this, that,
and many things, specialists will doubtless quarrel more or less gently. Mr. Charles Ramsdell,
for example, will not be satisfied with the chapter entitled "War Challenge at Sumter." And
yet when I place Mr. Ramsdell's essay on the
subject down by the side of Mr. Sandburg's
chapter, with the best will in the world, I should
not like to say on oath which is the truer, that
is, which more closely corresponds to the recorded and unrecorded emotions, thoughts,
tempers, and actions in the case. But when
specialists have finished dissecting, scraping,
refining, dissenting, and adding, I suspect that
Mr. Sandburg's work will remain for long years
to come a noble monument of American literature.

The scene is viewed mainly from the Northern
standpoint. The weight of emphasis is on Northern events and personalities, despite the passages
on campaigns and battles. There is a chapter on
Jefferson Davis and his government, but ortho-
dox Southerners of the Miss Millie Rutherford
school will not like it. They will not see the
historical necessity of quoting Andy Johnson's
outburst about "an illegitimate, swaggering, bas-
tard, scrub aristocracy" in response to Mr.
Davis's reflections on "a common blacksmith or
tailor." (See Marx.) And, although Mr. Sandburg cites freely many adverse Southern judgments on Lincoln, he sees that strange figure in
the White House undamaged by the animadversions. After all, just what is *the* Southern view of
the war years or anything else? Moreover, who,
North or South, is fitted to tell the truth, the
whole truth, and nothing but the truth?

Yet Lincoln is not portrayed in these pages as
the mighty hero, the great wise man who fore-
saw things perfectly and moved with unerring
wisdom to the great end. He is shown as a poor
limited mortal, of many moods, tempers, and dis-
tempers, stumbling, blundering along, trying this
and trying that, telling jokes, bewildered, disappointed, grieved by his fractious wife, weeping
now, laughing then, ordering this, canceling
that, trying to smooth ruffled personalities, looking upon mankind, like Marcus Aurelius, as composed of little creatures playing and loving, quarreling and fighting, and making up again, all
without much rhyme or reason—Lincoln steadfast in his purpose of saving the Union, and, if
possible, reducing the area of slavery or getting
rid of it entirely.

There may have been men around Lincoln
who were greater (whatever that may mean);
many of them at least imagined themselves
greater; but I am convinced that Mr. Sandburg's
pages will dispel any illusions on this score. Even
some cold Puritans correctly educated at Harvard, with many misgivings, and reluctantly,
came to the conclusion that even they could
scarcely have managed things better in the long
run. It was hard for cultivated persons to endure
his jokes, his uncouth manners, his unexpected
sallies, and yet they at last learned that there was
something marvelous in him—an Antaeus possessing the divine powers of a Proteus. Linguistic purists who could speak of Lincoln's style as
that of a half-educated lawyer finally saw in the
rude texture of his sentences a power that none
of them could wield. Mr. Sandburg, I feel sure,
has given us a fitting sequel to *The Prairie Years*,
a truer and more majestic Lincoln than is to be
found in the pages of Nicolay and Hay, those
apologists to the bourgeois of the Gilded Age.

A week's reading, which nearly finished my
dim eyes, carried me along as in a tumultuous
flood, amused, entertained, delighted, toward a
conclusion which I had long been maturing.
Why is it that the formally educated and pol-

ished are so often futile in the presence of vast movements of history? Why is it that so many makers of history on a large scale spring from somewhere near the earth of Antaeus and manage to do things on a colossal scale, displaying profound wisdom in the operation? The answer which I had been darkly maturing, Mr. Sandburg has clinched for me. It is that the great philosophies and systems of thought which adepts pile up, teach, and parade, so far as they are valid for life, derive from a few common-sense aphorisms, fables, and maxims evolved by ordinary humanity in its varied efforts to grapple with the stuff of life. Out of the mouths of babes cometh wisdom. Lincoln was the fabulist, the aphorist of the age, strong of will yet supple, facing the storm as a farmer wrestles with the toughness of the soil and the tempests of the seasons, and speaking a language, even in crude jokes, which struck the chords of the primordial that endures at or near the bottom of every civilization and carries on when the top has rotted away.

SUGGESTIONS FOR STUDY

1. What means of development does the author use in the two opening paragraphs? Why is reference made to Gibbon, Macaulay, Strachey, and others?

2. What unspoken questions is the reviewer answering in paragraph three as a result of his remarks in the first two paragraphs?

3. Is the biography scholarly?

4. What is Sandburg's purpose in using an unusual manner of presentation? Is the reviewer conscious of and sympathetic with that purpose?

5. Is Sandburg's method of presentation in the main successful?

6. Of what significance in reference to the value of the biography is the word "gently" in paragraph five?

7. Is Sandburg's biography the last word to be said upon Lincoln?

8. Does the reviewer accuse Sandburg of prejudice? From what standpoint is the biography written?

9. What picture of Lincoln emerges from the book as a whole?

10. Why does the reviewer include the last paragraph? Does it have any relation to the rest of the review?

11. Who is Charles A. Beard, the reviewer of the biography?

12. Summarize the value of Sandburg's work as revealed in this review.

13. Define the following words from the review: systematists, curtail, scrutinize, memorabilia, indefatigable, discrepancies, diversions, verisimilitude, animadversions, fractious, Antaeus, Proteus, purists, bourgeois, adepts, aphorisms, maxims, fabulist, primordial.

Book Review IV

You Can't Go Home Again, by Thomas Wolfe, reviewed by Louis B. Salomon.[1]

My feeling about any novel by Thomas Wolfe is that even if it were not good I'd like it. I'd like it for its ebullient, electric vitality, its obvious sincerity, the glowing, almost incandescent poetry of its style, the sense which it gives, however confusedly, of a meaning, a unified current, recognized in the seemingly helter-skelter maze of human life. These qualities light up *You Can't Go Home Again* for me, just as they illuminated *Look Homeward, Angel, Of Time and the River, The Web and the Rock,* and many shorter pieces; but there is no denying that Wolfe's methods, his themes, and to a large extent his material remained the same throughout his work, with the result that his inspiration suffered a gradual diminution of intensity.

That George Webber = Eugene Gant = Tom Wolfe is an equation almost too obvious to mention, in spite of the fact that George is described in *The Web and the Rock* and *You Can't Go Home Again* as short and stocky, while Wolfe was a mountain of a man and Eugene Gant was supposed to be long and rangy. When an author bestows his own personality on a hero and surrounds him with the author's own acquaintances under the transparent disguise of altered names, it makes little difference that he knocks five or six inches off his stature. If you have read *How to Write a Novel,* Wolfe's account of the composing and publishing of *Look Homeward, Angel,* you will find the first half of this last book virtually a retelling of that bit of autobiography. The rest of the story deals with his love affair with "Esther" and its conclusion, with the stock-market crash, and with his travels in Nazi Germany, several chapters of the latter part of the book having, if my memory does not fail me, already appeared as short stories in magazines.

His two principal themes are, as always, man's essential loneliness and the mystic movement of time, like a river that seems ever the same but is constantly shifting. You can't go home again, simply because "home" isn't there; both it and you have changed, and your romanticized mem-

[1] Reprinted by permission of the author and of the *Nation.*

ory-picture of it bears no more resemblance to the sordid reality than a surrealist painting does to an unretouched photograph.

But even themes so universally applicable as these can be overworked, and the pregnant symbolism, the driving power that made *Look Homeward, Angel* stand out above the common herd of novels like a mountain dawn, has given way to a sprawling looseness of structure that becomes more and more noticeable as the book progresses. There are diversions into long essay passages bound to the narrative by only the most tenuous threads. Nor can this be attributed altogether to the fact that the work is posthumous, not subject to final revision, since the same tendency had already manifested itself all too plainly in *Of Time and the River.*

The very nature of these conventional complaints against Wolfe's art, however, makes them a sort of compliment, a grudging admission that he had something too vitally alive to be judged entirely according to the criteria of form—in short, he irritates us more, because he had the magic power and did not use it precisely as we should have liked, than does the run-of-the-mill writer who obviously was not born with the divine fire. Wolfe belongs to the tribe of Whitman, Emerson, Carlyle,—especially the last. Like Carlyle, he was emotionally disturbed by the stupidity and selfishness of the world, without having any specific formula to offer as a remedy; he had a passion for work and a transcendental scorn for the shackles of form; even his style, with its purple splendor, its heavy leaning on apostrophe and impersonation, its ironic ranting against mediocrity, echoes that "stormy sophist with his mouth of thunder" who preached Cassandra-like warnings to the Victorians. Chapter 29, "The Hollow Men," with its bitter allegory about Standard Concentrated Blots, sounds like an excerpt from *Past and Present.*

And I feel about Wolfe very much as I feel about Carlyle: though I disagree with a great many things he says, I don't know anyone who can say them more splendidly.

SUGGESTIONS FOR STUDY

1. Formulate a thesis sentence which will state concisely the reviewer's judgment on *You Can't Go Home Again.*
2. What is the theme of the novel?
3. How does this novel compare with previous novels by the same author? Does such a comparison reveal a significant weakness in this work?
4. Is the content of *You Can't Go Home Again*

entirely original, or has the author made use of similar materials before? Has the author drawn upon his own life and experiences for material?
5. Has the reviewer been careful to state at the outset of his criticism the point of view which he has toward the novel, or does he shift the tone during the course of the review? Justify your answer, and in formulating it pay particular attention to the first and last sentences of the review.
6. Why is the comparison of Wolfe to Carlyle inserted in the review? What does that tell about the audience to whom the reviewer was writing?

D. Biography

One means to success is the ability to see people as they really are, to judge their worth, and to determine how much confidence can be placed in them. Only after years of careful observation of human nature can this ability be acquired, but you can be assisted in the effort by a study of biographical sketches of different kinds.

Consideration is to be taken here of four types of character writing: the character, the character sketch, the biographical sketch, and the autobiography. The character portrays the common traits of a group of similar people; the others pertain only to individuals. The character sketch presents the individual at one specific time in his life. The biographical sketch traces his growth and the influences which molded him. The autobiography analyzes the writer's own life and achievements.

THE CHARACTER

Our modern interest in characterization owes its origin very largely to the "character," a form of writing which dates back to a Greek philosopher, Theophrastus, three hundred years before Christ, who wrote characters to amuse himself and thereby set the form which the character has followed ever since. His major aim was to satirize certain groups of foolish people: "The Flatterer," "The Boaster," "The Coward," "The Grumbler," "The Rustic." As a forceful opening sentence he usually employed his thesis, containing a concise definition of the type he was describing. The remainder of the article was devoted to details and illustrations intended to describe the group or a person typical of the group. Modern writers of the character have followed for the most part this same structure and satirical purpose, although sketches of admirable persons are not unknown. Usually, however, the stupid, the vicious, or the extravagant have been ridiculed.

Although many characters of the old type are still written today, the form is used most frequently now by historians, sociologists, and the like to portray classes of people. As their purpose is different, they ordinarily discard satire in favor of a scientific, impersonal method. The following sketch by Mark Twain illustrates the older form, and that by Macaulay a historian's use of it.

The Office Bore

MARK TWAIN

HE ARRIVES just as regularly as the clock strikes nine in the morning. And so he even beats the editor sometimes, and the porter must leave his work and climb two or three pair of stairs to unlock the "Sanctum" door and let him in. He lights one of the office pipes—not reflecting, perhaps, that the editor may be one of those "stuck-up" people who would as soon have a stranger defile his toothbrush as his pipestem. Then he begins to loll—for a person who can consent to loaf his useless life away in ignominious indolence has not the energy to sit up straight. He stretches full length on the sofa a while; then draws up to half length; then gets into a chair, hangs his head back and his arms abroad, and stretches his legs till the rims of his boot heels rest upon the floor; by and by sits up and leans forward, with one leg or both over the arm of the chair. But it is still observable that with all his changes of position, he never assumes the upright or a fraudful affectation of dignity. From time to time he yawns, and stretches, and scratches himself with a tranquil, mangy enjoyment, and now and then he grunts a kind of stuffy, overfed grunt, which is full of animal contentment. At rare and long intervals, however, he sighs a sigh that is the eloquent expression of a secret confession, to wit: "I am useless and a nuisance, a cumberer of

the earth." The bore and his comrades—for there are usually from two to four on hand, day and night—mix into the conversation when men come in to see the editors for a moment on business; they hold noisy talks among themselves about politics in particular, and all other subjects in general—even warming up, after a fashion, sometimes, and seeming to take almost a real interest in what they are discussing. They ruthlessly call an editor from his work with such a remark as: "Did you see this, Smith, in the *Gazette?*" and proceed to read the paragraph while the sufferer reins in his impatient pen and listens; they often loll and sprawl round the office hour after hour, swapping anecdotes and relating personal experiences to each other—hairbreadth escapes, social encounters with distinguished men, election reminiscences, sketches of odd characters, etc. And through all those hours they never seem to comprehend that they are robbing the editors of their time, and the public of journalistic excellence in next day's paper. At other times they drowse, or dreamily pore over exchanges, or droop limp and pensive over the chair arms for an hour. Even this solemn silence is small respite to the editor, for the next uncomfortable thing to having people look over his shoulders, perhaps, is to have them sit by in silence and listen to the scratching of his pen. If a body desires to talk private business with one of the editors, he must call him outside, for no hint milder than blasting powder or nitroglycerine would be likely to move the bores out of listening distance. To have to sit and endure the presence of a bore day after day; to feel your cheerful spirits begin to sink as his footstep sounds on the stair, and utterly vanish away as his tiresome form enters the door; to suffer through his anecdotes and die slowly to his reminiscences; to feel always the fetters of his clogging presence; to long hopelessly for a single day's privacy; to note with a shudder, by and by, that to contemplate his funeral in fancy has ceased to soothe, to imagine him undergoing in strict and fearful detail the tortures of the ancient Inquisition has lost its power to satisfy the heart, and that even to wish him millions and millions and millions of miles in Tophet is able to bring only a fitful gleam of joy; to have to endure all this, day after day, and week after week, and month after month, is an affliction that transcends any other that men suffer. Physical pain is a pastime to it, and hanging a pleasure excursion.—*Sketches New and Old.*

SUGGESTIONS FOR STUDY

1. State the tone of the sketch. List a number of the specific words which help to establish this tone.
2. List a number of examples to indicate how the author secures concreteness of writing.
3. Divide the sketch into its main parts in order to show its organization.
4. What sentence device enables the author to handle skillfully the very long sentence next to the final sentence?
5. State the purpose and thesis of the sketch.
6. Define the following words from the sketch: defile, loll, affectation, fetters, contemplate, Inquisition, fitful.

The Country Gentlemen

T. B. MACAULAY

OF THE RENT, a large proportion was divided among the country gentlemen, a class of persons whose position and character it is most important that we should clearly understand; for by their influence and by their passions the fate of the nation was, at several important conjunctures, determined.

We should be much mistaken if we pictured to ourselves the squires of the seventeenth century as men bearing a close resemblance to their descendants, the county members and chairmen of quarter sessions with whom we are familiar. The modern country gentleman generally receives a liberal education, passes from a distinguished school to a distinguished college, and has every opportunity to become an excellent scholar. He has generally seen something of foreign countries. A considerable part of his life has generally been passed in the capital; and the refinements of the capital follow him into the country. There is perhaps no class of dwellings so pleasing as the rural seats of the English gentry. In the parks and pleasure grounds, nature, dressed yet not disguised by art, wears her most alluring form. In the buildings good sense and good taste combine to produce a happy union of the comfortable and the graceful. The pictures, the musical instruments, the library, would in any other country be considered as proving the owner to be an eminently polished and accomplished man. A country gentleman who witnessed the Revolution was probably in receipt of about a fourth part of the rent which his acres now yield to his posterity. He was, therefore, as compared with his posterity, a poor man, and was generally under the necessity of residing, with little interruption, on his estate.

To travel on the Continent, to maintain an establishment in London, or even to visit London frequently, were pleasures in which only the great proprietors could indulge. It may be confidently affirmed that of the squires whose names were in King Charles's commissions of peace and lieutenancy not one in twenty went to town once in five years, or had ever in his life wandered so far as Paris. Many lords of manors had received an education differing little from that of their menial servants. The heir of an estate often passed his boyhood and youth at the seat of his family with no better tutors than grooms and gamekeepers, and scarce attained learning enough to sign his name to a mittimus. If he went to school and to college, he generally returned before he was twenty to the seclusion of the old hall, and there, unless his mind were very happily constituted by nature, soon forgot his academical pursuits in rural business and pleasures. His chief serious employment was the care of his property. He examined samples of grain, handled pigs, and on market days made bargains over a tankard with drovers and hop merchants. His chief pleasures were commonly derived from field sports and from an unrefined sensuality. His language and pronunciation were such as we should now expect to hear only from the most ignorant clowns. His oaths, coarse jests, and scurrilous terms of abuse were uttered with the broadest accent of his province. It was easy to discern, from the first words which he spoke, whether he came from Somersetshire or Yorkshire. He troubled himself little about decorating his abode, and, if he attempted decoration, seldom produced anything but deformity. The litter of a farmyard gathered under the windows of his bedchamber, and the cabbages and gooseberry bushes grew close to his hall door. His table was loaded with coarse plenty; and guests were cordially welcomed to it. But, as the habit of drinking to excess was general in the class to which he belonged, and as his fortune did not enable him to

intoxicate large assemblies daily with claret or canary, strong beer was the ordinary beverage. The quantity of beer consumed in those days was indeed enormous. For beer then was to the middle and lower classes, not only all that beer now is, but all that wine, tea, and ardent spirits now are. It was only at great houses, or on great occasions, that foreign drink was placed on the board. The ladies of the house, whose business it had commonly been to cook the repast, retired as soon as the dishes had been devoured, and left the gentlemen to their ale and tobacco. The coarse jollity of the afternoon was often prolonged till the revelers were laid under the table.

It was very seldom that the country gentleman caught glimpses of the great world; and what he saw of it tended rather to confuse than to enlighten his understanding. His opinions respecting religion, government, foreign countries, and former times having been derived, not from study, from observation, or from conversation with enlightened companions, but from such traditions as were current in his own small circle, were the opinions of a child. He adhered to them, however, with the obstinacy which is generally found in ignorant men accustomed to be fed with flattery. His animosities were numerous and bitter. He hated Frenchmen and Italians, Scotchmen and Irishmen, Papists and Presbyterians, Independents and Baptists, Quakers and Jews. Towards London and Londoners he felt an aversion which more than once produced important political effects. His wife and daughter were in tastes and acquirements below a housekeeper or a stillroom maid of the present day. They stitched and spun, brewed gooseberry wine, cured marigolds, and made the crust for the venison pasty.

From this description it might be supposed that the English esquire of the seventeenth century did not materially differ from a rustic miller or alehouse keeper of our time. There are, however, some important parts of his character still to be noted, which will greatly modify this estimate. Unlettered as he was and unpolished, he was still in some most important points a gentleman. He was a member of a proud and powerful aristocracy, and was distinguished by many both of the good and of the bad qualities which belong to aristocrats. His family pride was beyond that of a Talbot or a Howard. He knew the genealogies and coats of arms of all his neighbors, and could tell which of them had assumed supporters without any right, and which of them were so unfortunate as to be great grandsons of aldermen. He was a magistrate, and, as such, administered gratuitously to those who dwelt around him a rude patriarchal justice, which, in spite of innumerable blunders and of occasional acts of tyranny, was yet better than no justice at all. He was an officer of the trainbands; and his military dignity, though it might move the mirth of gallants who had served a campaign in Flanders, raised his character in his own eyes and in the eyes of his neighbors. Nor indeed was his soldiership justly a subject of derision. In every county there were elderly gentlemen who had seen service which was no child's play. One had been knighted by Charles the First, after the battle of Edgehill. Another still wore a patch over the scar which he had received at Naseby. A third had defended his old house till Fairfax had blown in the door with a petard. The presence of these old Cavaliers, with their old swords and holsters, and with their old stories about Goring and Lunsford, gave to the musters of militia an earnest and warlike aspect which would otherwise have been wanting. Even those country gentlemen who were too young to have themselves exchanged blows with the cuirassiers of the parliament had, from childhood, been surrounded by the traces of recent war, and fed with stories of the martial exploits of their fathers and uncles. Thus the character of the English esquire of the seventeenth century was compounded of two elements which we are not accustomed to find united. His ignorance

and uncouthness, his low tastes and gross phrases, would, in our time, be considered as indicating a nature and a breeding thoroughly plebeian. Yet he was essentially a patrician, and had, in large measure, both the virtues and the vices which flourish among men set from their birth in high place, and accustomed to authority, to observance, and to self-respect. It is not easy for a generation which is accustomed to find chivalrous sentiments only in company with liberal studies and polished manners to image to itself a man with the deportment, the vocabulary, and the accent of a carter, yet punctilious on matters of genealogy and precedence, and ready to risk his life rather than see a stain cast on the honor of his house. It is only, however, by thus joining together things seldom or never found together in our own experience, that we can form a just idea of that rustic aristocracy which constituted the main strength of the armies of Charles the First, and which long supported, with strange fidelity, the interest of his descendants.—*History of England*, ch. 3.

SUGGESTIONS FOR STUDY

1. What are the two divisions of this character?

2. What is the author's purpose? Is it satirical like that of some of the older writers of characters?

3. What is his thesis, and where is it stated?

4. Why were the country gentlemen important as a class? Is it good rhetorical practice to state the importance of a subject immediately upon beginning a paper?

5. Why does Macaulay introduce the contrast in paragraph two?

6. What was the Revolution, referred to in paragraph two?

7. Summarize the objectionable traits of the country gentlemen.

8. What attributes of the country gentlemen brighten this picture?

9. What is the major means of paragraph development that enables Macaulay to make this sketch so vivid?

10. Define the following words from the selection: posterity, mittimus, scurrilous, gratuitously, patriarchal, derision, petard.

THE CHARACTER SKETCH

The character sketch is a picture of an individual. It sets him apart from any groups to which he may belong, but it does not trace his growth, his backgrounds, or the influences shaping him—these are left to the biography. Its aim is to depict him at some specific point of his life. The writer of the character sketch formulates a strong dominant impression concerning an individual and clarifies it by the selection of pertinent details.

The character sketch may be a description of an individual, or an analysis of his personality, or preferably a combination of the two. In describing his external appearance, state the leading impression you have of him and then present such details as will illustrate this best. Although such a description is not as valuable for a character sketch as is an analysis of personality, still it can be useful. Appearances often tell much, or at least arouse suspicions. Unpressed trousers may be a sign of slovenliness; furtive eyes, of thievery; a square chin, of resolution, courage, or stubbornness; a high forehead, of a keen intellect. Sometimes, too, appearances may belie the man. A kindly, warm-hearted old gentleman may often appear to the eye a cross and unapproachable bear. A skillful writer may thus employ a description of external appearance to good advantage in his sketch.

Presenting the personality of a character is more difficult, for you are dealing with intangibles. As a first step, perhaps, classify the individual according to the type to which he belongs—identify him as a hero, villain, tough, spendthrift, idealist, ne'er-do-well, or the like. Then distinguish him from the group. Two devices will assist you: what the character does, and what he says. Any action of his may indicate his character. Ordinarily we think only of great deeds as revealing personality: bravery at the cannon's mouth, heroism in saving lives at a fire, dishonesty in absconding with the funds of a bank, or cowardice in a crucial test of nerve. These do indeed tell a great deal. Macaulay, for example, summarizes very quickly the cruelty of Captain Kidd and the moral anguish of one of his crew by means of such a striking incident: "One of his crew, whom he called a dog, was provoked into exclaiming, in an agony of remorse, 'Yes, I am a dog; but it is you that have made me so.' Kidd, in a fury, struck the man dead." But it is not alone such striking incidents that portray character. Often a small act or a quiet happening will tell quite as much. See, for example, how much you can derive from the following paragraph, taken from Dumas, about the character of the chivalric musketeer Aramis:

> This other musketeer formed a perfect contrast with his interrogator, who had just designated him by the name of Aramis: he was a stout man, of about two- or three-and-twenty, with an open, ingenuous countenance, a black, mild eye, and cheeks rosy and downy as an autumn peach; his delicate mustache marked a perfectly straight line upon his upper lip: he appeared to dread to lower his hands lest their veins should swell, and he pinched the tips of his ears from time to time to preserve their delicate pink transparency. Habitually he spoke little and slowly, bowed frequently, laughed without noise, showing his teeth, which were fine, and of which, as of the rest of his person, he appeared to take great care. He answered the appeal of his friend by an affirmative nod of his head.

For further illustration, study the following paragraph from Thackeray's *Pendennis* to understand the sort of action or incident that is valuable in expressing character:

> Arthur Pendennis's schoolfellows at the Grey Friars School state that, as a boy, he was in no ways remarkable either as a dunce or as a scholar. He never read to improve himself out of school hours, but, on the contrary, devoured all the novels, plays, and poetry on which he could lay his hands. He never was flogged, but it was a wonder how he escaped the whipping post. When he had money he spent it royally in tarts for himself and his friends; he has been known to disburse nine and sixpence out of ten shillings awarded to him in a single day. When he had no funds he went on tick. When he could get no credit

he went without, and was almost as happy. He has been known to take a thrashing for a crony without saying a word; but a blow, ever so slight from a friend would make him roar. To fighting he was averse from his earliest youth, as indeed to physic, the Greek Grammar, or any other exertion, and would engage in none of them, except at the last extremity. He seldom if ever told lies, and never bullied little boys. Those masters or seniors who were kind to him, he loved with boyish ardor. And though the Doctor, when he did not know his Horace, or could not construe his Greek play, said that that boy Pendennis was a disgrace to the school, a candidate for ruin in this world, and perdition in the next; a profligate who would most likely bring his venerable father to ruin and his mother to a dishonored grave, and the like—yet as the Doctor made use of these compliments to most of the boys in the place (which has not turned out an unusual number of felons and pickpockets), little Pen, at first uneasy and terrified by these charges, became gradually accustomed to hear them; and he has not, in fact, either murdered his parents, or committed any act worthy of transportation or hanging up to the present day.

Dialogue provides the other major means of presenting character, for it furnishes an individual an opportunity to speak for himself. In fact, it is so useful that many short story writers reserve it for crucial moments when intensity is required. The ensuing dialogue from Jane Austen's *Pride and Prejudice* will show how vivid the characters, taking part in only a small incident, make themselves by their speech:

Elizabeth Bennet had been obliged, by the scarcity of gentlemen, to sit down for two dances; and during part of that time Mr. Darcy had been standing near enough for her to overhear a conversation between him and Mr. Bingley, who came from the dance for a few minutes to press his friend to join it.

"Come, Darcy," said he, "I must have you dance. I hate to see you standing about by yourself in this stupid manner. You had much better dance."

"I certainly shall not. You know how I detest it, unless I am particularly acquainted with my partner. At such an assembly as this it would be insupportable. Your sisters are engaged, and there is not another woman in the room whom it would not be a punishment to me to stand up with."

"I would not be so fastidious as you are," cried Bingley, "for a kingdom! Upon my honor, I never met with so many pleasant girls in my life as I have this evening; and there are several of them, you see, uncommonly pretty."

"You are dancing with the only handsome girl in the room," said Mr. Darcy, looking at the eldest Miss Bennet.

"Oh, she is the most beautiful creature I ever beheld! But there is one of her sisters sitting down just behind you, who is very pretty, and I dare say very agreeable. Do let me ask my partner to introduce you."

"Which do you mean?" and turning round, he looked for a moment at Elizabeth, till, catching her eye, he withdrew his own, and coldly said: "She is tolerable, but not handsome enough to tempt me; and I am in no humor at present to give consequence to young ladies who are slighted by other men. You had better return to your partner and enjoy her smiles, for you are wasting your time with me."

Be sure to make the character a human being. Do not idealize him excessively; portray his peculiarities or faults as well as his virtues. The final emphasis of the character sketch must always be upon his individuality. Hence, if you can summon specific details and illustrations concerning him as he really is, he will appear vividly to the reader. The thesis should be clearly established, and the details should be chosen with discrimination.

Heywood[1]

CHRISTOPHER MORLEY

I THINK Heywood Broun would have been genuinely shocked by some of the tributes printed after his death; for I believe that in the later months of his life he had begun to achieve a way of thinking and feeling in which Privacy is more important than Publicity. Under the apparently naïf exhibitionism, and a sort of intellectual strip-tease which was his armor wherein he trusted, there was a deep humility and a terrified search for certainty. He always took an innocent pleasure in being what used to be known as a Man about Town; and little by little he discovered that the Town that is most interesting is the City of God. In that latter no one is pointed out; there is no consciousness of self; there is, one may believe, the blessing of anonymity and forgetfulness.

I always thought of Heywood as a kind of medieval figure; a strolling friar—how much more becoming a brown robe and knotted cord would have been—a sort of huge Santa Claus. He took his simplicity and kindliness into the most disconcerting slums there are —among night clubs and wisecrackers and Racqueteers—and was everywhere beloved for his drollery and devotion. He was overworked (as Santa Claus always will be) wrapping and delivering innumerable parcels of generosity. Anything that looked to him like cruelty or oppression enlisted his immediate and bewildered and chivalrous anger. The medieval and monkish flavor of his mind was best shown in his love of fables, parables, allegories. Even his love of his hobby, painting, was evidence of that. In a different age he would have been enormously happy coloring rubrics and fanciful

bright vignettes on old vellum chronicles. When in 1921 I reprinted his beautiful and satirical little fairy tale *The Fifty-First Dragon* in an anthology of contemporary essays, I said "Heywood Broun is likely, in the next ten or fifteen years, to do as fine work, both imaginative and critical, as any American of his era."

This, in occasional flashing swordstrokes, came to pass; but not as often as one hoped. His profession as daily columnist, his preoccupation as crusader for various causes, his diffusion among sociable and generous concerns, increased the temperamental dispersiveness of his mind. He was too humane, too genuinely interested in people, for the savage concentration required by art. His mind, I used to think, was sometimes as disorderly as his person. When he measured himself against anything precise, lucid, articulated, he was likely to fumble. The elementary French grammar that flunked him at Harvard was perhaps symbolic. But where powers of intuition and observation were concerned, whether in poker or politics, he became wise and efficient. Those of us who are relatively average in body or bearing can scarcely guess the handicap imposed upon a mind incarnated in such a conspicuous figure. That beefy and kindly bosom was the broad battleground of the most militant complexes, where opposing troops struggled in briars and thickets. It was surely this, in part, that drove our friend to so many chivalries at once.

Beneath that partly guileful naiveté there was great wisdom and shrewdness in Heywood, and humor of most endearing ricochet. His unshockable tolerance, his sympathy with all kinds of creative experiment, were of the greatest service in our Book-of-

[1] Reprinted by permission of the author and the Book-of-the-Month Club.

the-Month Club meetings—where he never once (in nearly 14 years) arrived on time. This, he said, was to avoid eating too much at the lunch table; but he always ate as much dessert as he could lay hands on, especially raspberry ice cream. In an age increasingly machined and regimented Heywood was an invaluable liaison officer, or commuter, between two worlds, the Flesh and the Spirit; the Serious and the Merry. Few of us will ever know anyone who had more of both. Two of the best things he ever wrote—in his habit of baring his bosom to the moon—were his obituary tributes to Ruth Hale and to his father. In the latter he suggested as a final inscription, *He took and*

gave much joy in life. This may well be his own.

SUGGESTIONS FOR STUDY

1. For what reason did Heywood Broun come to believe more in privacy than in publicity?
2. What were the medieval traits in his character?
3. Why did he fail to live up to the prediction made about him by Christopher Morley?
4. Summarize the central conception of Heywood Broun in a thesis sentence.
5. Study the eulogy to see by what means the character of Broun is brought out. How does the author secure concreteness of writing?
6. Define the following words from the selection: naïf, exhibitionism, humility, anonymity, allegories, rubrics, vignettes, vellum, diffusion, dispersiveness, humane, lucid, articulated, guileful, ricochet, tolerance, liaison, obituary.

Walt Whitman Old and Poor[1]

HAMLIN GARLAND

NOT UNTIL October, 1888, did I cross the river from Philadelphia in search of the poet whose presence had made Camden known throughout the world. The citizens from whom I inquired my way to Mickle Street directed me into a mean section of the town and when I came to the number designated, I could not believe that I had been rightly informed, so dim was the doorplate and so weather-worn the doorway. The street was ugly and narrow, and the house, a two-story frame structure, was such as a day laborer might have owned, and yet the poet's name was there.

In answer to my ring, a small gray man whom I guessed to be Whitman's attendant came clumping down the stairway and received my name impassively. "Wait here," he said, "I'll see if you can come up."

While he went back up the stairs, I

studied the faded paper on the walls, and the worn carpet of the hall with growing astonishment. There was nothing to indicate that a poet of world-wide fame was living here. His sordid surroundings filled me with indignation.

From the landing above the man called down, "Walt will see you for a few minutes." He emphasized the brevity of my stay and warned me not to weary the old man.

On entering the door on the left, I found myself in a fairly large, square chamber on the north front of the house, and in the center of it Whitman, standing by his armchair, with a broad white hat on his head, awaited me, a tall man clothed in gray, with a cloud of snowy hair and beard enveloping his face.

Without leaving his place he extended his hand and greeted me pleasantly in a voice rather high in key, mellow and cordial, inviting me to be seated. The grip of his hand was firm and vital.

[1] From Hamlin Garland, *Roadside Meetings* (New York, 1930). Reprinted by permission of The Macmillan Company.

He was dressed in a loosely fitting gray robe, and his linen shirt with rolling collar unbuttoned at the throat and his cuffs were all equally immaculate. I thought him one of the noblest figures I had ever seen. His head was magnificent in contour, and his profile clean-cut as a coin.

In contrast to his personal order and comeliness, the room was an incredible mess. Beside his chair rose a most amazing mound of manuscripts, old newspapers, and clippings, with many open books lying, face down, at the point where he had laid them aside.

The furnishings of the room were few and ugly. The bleak windows looked out upon a row of frame tenements whose angular roofs and rude chimneys formed a dreary landscape. It was a melancholy place of confinement for one who had roamed America's open roads and sung its sunlit vistas. No one had prepared me for this bitter revelation of the meager awards which *Leaves of Grass* had won for its author.

In spite of his surroundings Whitman looked the hero of the poems, strong, self-poised, with a certain delicacy of action and speech. His face when turned toward me discovered a pleasant, searching glance. His mouth was hidden in his great beard, but his eyes were smiling and the lines on his brow were level. Nothing querulous showed in voice or word. His speech was nobly pure with nothing of the coarseness I had been led to expect. When he dropped into homely phrase or coined a word, he did so with humorous intonation. It is because some of his interviewers failed to record his smile that so many misinterpretations of his conversation have been recorded. This use of the common phrase now and again lent additional charm to his speech.

He had no word of humor, however. He was grave without being low-spirited or grim, placidly serious in all that he said. He made no reference to his poverty or to his illness, and nothing petulant or self-pitying came into his voice.

Once he rose in order to find some book which he wished to show me, and I perceived that one side of his body was almost useless. He dragged one leg and he used but one arm. In spite of the confusion of his books and papers he seemed to know where to find what he wanted.

The attendant had said "a few minutes," but Walt was interested, I could see that, and so I stayed on with full realization of the value of every additional moment. We talked of his English friends, of his growing acceptance there, and I confidently predicted his acceptance in America. "I can sense a change in the attitude of critics in the last two years," I assured him, and he listened with an eagerness almost pathetic. "I hope you are right," he said.

He asked me about my work in Boston and seemed keenly interested in my praise of *Specimen Days.* "I find it the best introduction to your poetry," I said. "I advise all my pupils to begin by reading it."

"That is very curious," he said musingly. "Most of my readers neglect my prose."

I went on to say, "Your descriptive passages have the magic of setting me in the midst of your landscape. I feel it and see it as you saw and sensed it. I even smell it!"

As I talked he studied me with dim, gray-blue eyes, as if marveling at my youth and fervor. He had laid aside his broad Quaker hat by this time, and I thought the lines of his head the noblest I had ever known. His brow was like that of a serene and kindly philosopher, and his sentences were well chosen and concise. He had no local peculiarity of accent or pronunciation; at least he left no singularity of speech in my memory. My recorded impressions of him were all in harmony with my preconceived notions of his nobility of spirit.

He spoke slowly, choosing the best word for the place with impressive care. There was no looseness of mumbling in his enunciation. Every word came forth clear-cut and musical. He had the effect of compressing sentences into single words, but with his noble voice and subtle inflection there was no excuse for failure to apprehend his thoughts.

"I am a good deal of a Quaker," he said, as if explaining to me his peculiarities of dress. "My ancestors were Quakers, and I delight to recall and to retain certain of their distinctive customs."

One of his "whims," as he called them, was to suffer in silence the sting of the various false reports about him. He would not authorize his friends to go into print to defend him. He reminded me of Grant in this regard. "I prefer to leave all that to time," he said. "Such things clear themselves up, or at worst they deceive only the unthinking whom your explanation would not reach."

Naturally I led the talk toward things literary, and being "moved by the spirit," as he smilingly confessed, he talked freely of his contemporaries and gave me full permission to quote him.

I told him that many good people considered him unduly severe on American literature in general and "certain of our poets in particular, Stedman and Gilder for example."

He became grave. "You refer to a report by a German writer. I do not think Stedman was deceived, though many of his friends think I have the spirit to rasp him. It would have been ingratitude to have said such words even had I thought them, which I do not. I hold Stedman in high regard as a man of decided insight and culture. On personal grounds I owe him much. The traveler you mention either willfully or otherwise *twistified*," here he smiled, "what I said—if I said anything in his presence. I am beset with all kinds of visitors who go away thinking me fair game. It is one of the evils which men of any"—he hesitated —"notoriety must bear patiently.

"As for American literature in general, I have insisted, as all my readers know, on the need of distinctive flavor in our poetry. There is an old Scotch word, Burns uses it occasionally, which expresses exactly what I mean—the word 'race.' A wild strawberry, a wild grape has the racy quality—this distinctive tang. Our poetry lacks *race*. Most of it might have been written in England or on the Continent. I myself like Cooper, Bryant, Emerson, and Whittier because they have this distinctive American quality."

This led me to bring up the work of George W. Cable, Joseph Kirkland, Joel Harris, Mary E. Wilkins, and others of my friends who were getting, it seemed to me, just that flavor he was demanding. "Their books are, in my judgment, forerunners of a powerful native literature."

After a pause he said, "It may be so, but I have not read many of them. Against some of them I *have* read I might bring a grave charge. They have a deplorable tendency toward the *outré*. I call their characters *delirium-tremen characters*. These writers seem not content with the normal man; they must take the exceptional, the diseased. They are not true, not American in the deeper sense at all. To illustrate, in a hunter's camp of twenty men there will always be some who are distorted, unusual, grotesque, but they are not typical of the camp. So in an 'army mess' there are always characters more or less abnormal, men who enjoy distorting their faces and cutting up antics. And yet in all my coming and going among the camps of the Civil War, I was everywhere struck with the decorum—a word I like to use— of the common soldier, his good manners, his quiet heroism, his generosity, even his good, real grammar. These are a few of the typical qualities of the American farmer and mechanic."

All this was said quietly but with deep earnestness, as if he were working the problem out while speaking. Then turning his glance on me, he spoke with decision. "I say that the novel or drama claiming to depict American life is false if it deals mainly or largely with abnormal or grotesque characters. They should be used merely as foils."

This led me to say, "In the early stages of national literature it is natural to deal with the abnormal, the exceptional, because it startles, claims the attention; so it may be that the novelists you speak of may be just in the preparatory stage and that they will pass on to something higher."

He fell into a profound muse, and at last said with deliberate precision as if making a concession which he had not hitherto directly stated, "I don't know but you are right. I can see that the novice would find the exceptional nearest his hand and most noticeable, and it may be that these books are preparatory to a new, indigenous fiction. The public itself, moreover, seems to demand and enjoy such work. It may be as you argue, that the writers and the public will grow toward a higher perception. At any rate I want to utter my protest against such work and to demand that the really heroic character of the common American be depicted in novel and drama."

I forgot his age, his sickness, his drab surroundings as I listened to his musical voice and lofty personal convictions. He appeared a grand and ageless spirit. His sublime faith in the average American was not that of a dreamer, cloistered and bookish; it was the judgment of one who knew the farmer, mechanic, cab driver, miner, street laborer, and roustabout from personal contacts.

"I guess I am aware of our political and literary fraudulencies," he said calmly, "but as things are going on in the States—our time —I am confident of results. I have no sympathy with current pessimistic notions of life, of government, of society."

This serene and buoyant optimism in the midst of old age, poverty, and physical pain filled me with admiration. It was majestic. It was another proof of the grand and simple faith of this indomitable soul who looked into the future with the unswerving gaze of an eagle. He was still of a mind to say, "I know the future will be well, for all that is, is well."

Seeing that my interview was nearing an

end, I said, "May I carry from you a friendly message to these young novelists?"

"You may, with this advice and plea: Tell them to go among the common men, as one of them, never looking down upon them. Tell them to study their lives and find out and celebrate their splendid primitive honesty, patience, and what I like to call their heroism. When our novelists shall do that in addition to being true to their time, their art will be worthy all praise from me or any other who is insisting on native anti-class poems, novels, and plays.

"And finally I would say to the young writer, don't depict evil for its own sake. Don't let evil overshadow your books. Make it a foil as Shakespeare did. His evil is always a foil for purity. Somewhere in your play or novel let the sunlight in." Here he raised his superb head and in a grandly suggestive gesture of his arm made his point clear. "As in some vast foundry whose walls are lost in blackness, a scuttle far up in the roof lets the sun and the blue sky in."

As I rose to go I assured him that the circle of his admirers was swiftly widening, and that his influence on our literature was certain to deepen year by year.

"Burroughs tells me the same thing," he said, "and I hope you are both right."

He put on his hat, and rising painfully to his feet gave me his hand at parting. I understood the respect which this formality indicated and was proud of it.

SUGGESTIONS FOR STUDY

1. In your own words describe Whitman's appearance.

2. Also in your own words describe the house and neighborhood in which he lived.

3. What effect did poverty and ill health have upon his outlook on life?

4. What was the essence of Whitman's criticism of American literature in general?

5. What is the substance of his advice to American novelists?

6. At the time of the interview, were American critics whole-hearted in acclaiming Whitman?

7. Does Garland show admiration for Whitman as a man and a poet?

8. Does the description of Whitman's appearance prove effective in introducing the reader to the poet's character? Explain. By what means does the author portray Whitman's character?

9. Write a character sketch of Whitman, using your own words and plan of organization.

10. Define the following words from the article: impassively, sordid, mellow, immaculate, comeliness, vistas, querulous, intonation, foil, petulant.

THE BIOGRAPHICAL SKETCH

The problem of the biographer is more difficult than that of the writer of the character or the character sketch. He must acquaint himself so well with an individual that he makes him a close friend whose thoughts he shares and whose actions he understands. Further he must be aware of the antecedents and growth of the subject so that he may understand the forces of heredity and environment that produced this particular individual.

The subject of the biography may be a prominent person, but very interesting sketches can be written of those who have never made much stir in the world. The important consideration is what is done with the subject, how well he is interpreted. The first step in achieving a successful sketch is to determine the subject's real character from which all his acts radiate consistently. The great characters of fiction, for example, are based upon such central conceptions: Othello as jealous, Macbeth as ambitious, Jaques as melancholic, Uriah Heep as falsely "'umble," Becky Sharp as vain and worldly. These characters live because their humanity has been expressed through a clearly defined central characteristic.

You must be careful, however, not to jump rashly at conclusions concerning an individual. Assemble all pertinent information before you make a decision. What did he inherit from his parents and grandparents? What effects did his home life or the life of the community have upon him, intellectually or emotionally? Were his actions as a youth and a man in harmony with his feelings and beliefs, or did he have to force himself into certain acts? Did he experience material and spiritual gain or loss during his life? What were his ideals? Did they accord with his actions? What effect did the realization or frustration of his ambitions have upon him? Consider many such questions before deciding upon a thesis.

Having determined the thesis and the pertinent facts supporting it, be careful in wording the sketch not to insert unnecessary details that may be distracting or dulling to a reader. The sketch considered here is not a cataloguing of dates and accomplishments, such as are found in a *Who's Who;* it is a revelation of the character of an individual. Thus it must center on description, incidents, and dialogue to accomplish that aim. No trivial facts or dates, such as a record of the day of graduation from college, the day of marriage, the day of moving from one city to another, need be cited unless they bear directly upon the interpretation of character. Infinitely more important are the devices which were studied in connection with the character sketch.

The organization of the sketch demands careful attention. The most obvious organization would seem to be a chronological relation of the individual's life from birth to death. Although such a method is useful in skilled hands, it runs the danger of being dull in a short article. You are likely to have more success if you begin with a character sketch of your subject, an interesting incident concerning him, or some other similar device which will attract attention and arouse interest. Then proceed to what details and illustrations are required for a full comprehension of the background and growth of the character.

You may gather material concerning the subject of the sketch from several sources. If he is not a prominent person, he can be studied through his letters, the testimony of his friends, or your personal knowledge of him. If he is a man of importance, however, written material on him will be extensive.

Biographical dictionaries or other reference works will afford a start. His diaries, letters, and autobiography may produce a rich yield when taken with the oral and written statements of his friends. Very fruitful also are the biographies of him. Every biography—after the first—is to a certain extent dependent on previous researches; each biographer checks his own theories against those held by the others, and so is enabled at times to correct his own work, at times to correct that of his predecessors. You must be sure, however, to establish your own point of view and not merely copy that of other biographers.

The true biographer, let it be remembered, is also an honest man. He pursues his subject with enthusiasm, eager to find all that is important; but he never allows his enthusiasm to blind him to facts. He remains intellectually impartial as he weighs his evidence, and after deriving a conclusion, alters it freely as new testimony arises. He works by the scientific method. His conclusions embrace all the known facts, and never disregard details which he would prefer to ignore.

The biographical sketch may be defined then as a short, impartial attempt to present an individual's life and work in so vivid and accurate a fashion that his beliefs and acts and ambitions blend into a harmonious whole to distinguish him from his fellow men.

Hu Shih: Sage of Modern China[1]

MARQUIS W. CHILDS

OF ALL THE MEN who have been sent from the four corners of the earth to Washington during the past hundred and fifty years to represent their various governments, none, it is a safe surmise, is more representative of his people and his time than the present Ambassador of China. His Excellency Dr. Hu Shih has lived the transformation of his country, its agonies, its torments, its bitterly won achievements, the terror and the shock, the long, painful travail. And in his short, solid body, in his scholarly, far-ranging mind, in the clear, unwavering humanity of his outlook, is a faith he has finally won to, formed out of the old and the new, the good and the bad.

That is why for America in the present crisis Hu Shih is more than an ambassador. He is a symbol of steadfast courage, of patience, of faith and good will, of intelligence, the virtues that Americans must now draw upon. His hope in the ultimate victory of his nation and the democratic ideal it embodies has never faltered. . . . We of the West who have taken the privileges and prerogatives of democracy so lightly for granted have not a little to learn from this scholar whom China has so generously sent us.

Honors have been heaped upon him by the universities of the world. His published works in English and Chinese fill several shelves. He was instrumental in giving his people a new and simpler language, a democratic tool to replace the complex classical language. But in his life perhaps as much as in his achievements is Hu Shih's contribution.

At twelve he was already a scholar for whom the future seemed to hold great promise. For that matter, before he was three years old he knew 800 characters of the classical language, taught him by his father, who wrote them on slips of pink paper. In his twelfth year his mother, daughter of a peasant farmer, contracted for his marriage to the child of a family that had long been close in friendship. This custom of child engagement

[1] From the *Atlantic Monthly*, CLXVI (October, 1940), 424. Reprinted by permission of the author and the *Atlantic Monthly*.

went back many centuries. It occurred to no one, least of all to the boy whose future was being signed away, to question it.

Shortly afterward he left his province of Anweih to study the "new learning" in Shanghai. His mother, although she could neither read nor write, had been unsparing in her effort to perfect his education. She paid his teacher three times the usual fee of $2 silver a year so that the classics he memorized were explained to him, while ordinary pupils merely learned them by rote. Kept from play with the village children, at five he had earned the nickname "Shien-seng," the Master.

Shanghai was a vast new world. Hu Shih worked with the extraordinary concentration which has enabled him to excel in so many fields. He read incessantly in the classics of the West. And so impressed was he with the "new learning" that he took a western name. Shih means "fittest," a name taken from the Darwinian phrase "survival of the fittest."

But in his teens came a period of disillusionment, characteristic of a highly precocious adolescent, and typical, too, of the brilliant young Chinese of the time, who felt that progress was hopelessly slow. At the same time, misfortunes overwhelmed his family and he was forced to give up his studies in order to teach English and so support himself and his mother. Hu Shih and his friends wrote gloomy poetry. They drank and dissipated. One rainy night, he relates in his autobiography, when he was deadly drunk, he fought with a policeman and landed in jail.

At home the next morning, a line from the poetry of the great Li Po came into his mind: "Some use might yet be made of this material born in me." Hu Shih stopped teaching, gave up his friends, and after a month of intensive study went to Peking to take the examination for one of the university scholarships in America financed by the Boxer Indemnity fund. He passed the examination, and toward the end of his eighteenth year sailed for San Francisco.

For seven years, first at Cornell and then at Columbia, he studied philosophy, having found that he could not force himself to pursue a course in scientific agriculture. With the culture and the science of the West added to his knowledge of China's ancient wisdom, he went home to fulfill his marriage contract. His bride was a woman with bound feet, virtually illiterate. Why did he go through with this marriage, so contrary to all that he had learned from the time that he signed the contract? The answer is simple. To have failed to live up to the contract would have brought sorrow and disgrace to several people.

Two sons were born to the wife of Hu Shih. Of the loyalty and devotion that have grown up in this marriage there have been many manifestations. When the Japanese were about to take Peking, Hu Shih's wife was alone in their home. She resolved to save what she knew was most precious to her husband—his books and manuscripts. Somehow, Hu Shih says he will never understand how, she managed to have seventy big boxes containing many thousands of volumes transported to the comparative safety of a treaty port. In the confusion and uncertainty of war-torn China that was a minor miracle.

It is hard to realize, in talking with the Ambassador on the verandah of his Washington residence, how far back into the past his roots go. He speaks easily, rapidly, with only a slight accent, developing a line of thought with the careful logic that is a result, in part at least, of his study with Professor John Dewey at Columbia University. Hu Shih's quick sense of humor finds expression in an abrupt, rather startling laugh. His eyes twinkle behind horn-rimmed glasses. Ordinarily his expression is sober. And when he speaks of the sufferings of his countrymen— particularly of the trials of the government at Chungking, where 6,000 civilians were killed in a single air raid—a profound sadness is on his face. It is not despair, not hatred, not fear; only a deep sorrow.

In all his work is his humanitarianism.

When he was still a student at Cornell, he started the controversy that was to end with adoption of the pai-hua, the common speech, as the official language of China. There had been lengthy discussions of the need to publish books in the pai-hua, so that learning would be available to a larger proportion of the people. But it was taken for granted that this would be for the common people, with the literary language reserved for the literati. Declaring boldly that the pai-hua should serve for all purposes, Hu Shih began to write poetry in the common speech.

This radical break with the past soon produced a storm of criticism. But it also brought ardent followers who agreed with the young student. It was actually the beginning of a Chinese renaissance, a vast flowering of ideas and hopes expressed in the common language. Hu Shih is called the father of this renaissance. His position has been compared to that of Chaucer and Dante, who first were bold enough to write not in Latin but in the living tongue of the common people. Early in his revolt he wrote a "Pledge Poem" that was his declaration of independence. It began:—

> No more will I lament the Spring,
> No more bewail the Autumn scene—
> Here is my "Pledge song"!

Forswearing the traditional elements of the highly formalized poetry of his native land, he concluded:—

> For poetic materials, have we not at our command this modern world?

In many ways Hu Shih was an innovator. Returning to China after his American studies, he was made professor of Chinese philosophy at Peking National University. There was considerable skepticism about this young upstart who had spent so many years in the materialistic United States. The very first day he walked into the classroom and announced that the course would begin not with the mythical sages, part of the formalized classical learning for nearly 2000 years, but with the first historical events for which there is any substantiating evidence. The effect of this bombshell on the class could scarcely be exaggerated. A young student who was later to become one of Hu Shih's followers has said that it produced almost a physical revolt in the classroom, so sharp was the break with tradition.

The controversy became increasingly bitter. Classical scholars—particularly Lin Shu, who argued that the classical language was eternal—carried the dispute into the field of politics. A demand came for the dismissal of the Minister of Education, the Chancellor of the University, and all the younger professors who had brought back from the West the new science and the new critical scholarship.

It was not that Hu Shih wanted to supplant Chinese culture with the learning of the West. But he knew that China could not isolate itself from the western world. And he believed passionately that China could never become a democracy so long as the culture of the country was confined to a few scholars. It was no use, he realized, superimposing a western political system on a land made up of illiterate peasants plus a hierarchy of priestly scholars. He was quick to rebuke his young compatriots when he saw them embracing western doctrines with the same uncritical belief in which the old gods had been held.

In the period after the May Fourth Movement of 1919, Hu Shih was a restraining influence on young revolutionists who were seizing on western isms and theories. "We should study all 'isms' and 'theories,'" he wrote at this time, "but these are hypothetical solutions. You should not take them as the golden mean." In the same vein a few years later he addressed this warning to young hotheads: "You are ashamed to follow blindly Confucius and Chu Hsi, and you should be ashamed, too, when you blindly follow Marx, Lenin, and Stalin."

Hu Shih had once declared that philosophy was his profession, literature his entertainment, and politics his obligation. The troubled state of China through the twenties compelled him to more active participation. He edited the *Nu Li* weekly (the literal meaning is "Strenuous Effort") to expose corruption and inefficiency. But his friends protested that his appointed task of fusing and creating a new Chinese culture was far more important than any immediate political reform.

Gradually his intellectual interests claimed him again. One of his objectives was to bring about a recognition of the cultural significance of the popular novels written in the pai-hua that every Chinese, rich and poor alike, has read. The scholars had looked down on them, and, although they read these stirring and all too human epics of Chinese life, it was, as they had been written, clandestinely and with a sense of guilt. Now Hu Shih made his countrymen appreciate their real greatness. Furthermore, with the resources of critical scholarship, he cut through the anonymity surrounding their authorship and proved them to be the work of authors of long-established respectability.

At the same time he was working on his *History of Chinese Philosophy,* a monumental work he has never completed. With his teaching, his continuing interest in politics, his keen awareness of world events and world trends, Hu Shih's life was extremely full. He was the modern sage, in the ancient tradition of China but with all the intellectual resources of the twentieth century at his instant command.

Japan's undeclared war, beginning in 1937 with the ruthless attack on civilian Shanghai, had not been entirely unexpected. Chinese leaders were aware of the Japanese ambition to subjugate China, to stamp out all vestiges of modernism and leave nothing but a slave population dependent on Japanese masters and vitiated by the opium habit. Hu Shih knew that his academic life was over, for how long no one could say. There was no hesitation in his response. Completely independent in his political judgments, he had often been critical of General Chiang Kai-shek. Now he

offered to serve the leader who had the nation behind him.

It was recognized at once that Dr. Hu Shih's greatest usefulness would be in America, where, because of his numerous friends and his wide knowledge of the country, he could stimulate interest in the Chinese cause. Shortly after the outbreak of the war he returned to this country, and in 1938 he was named Ambassador. It is an assignment that makes heavy demands on him. Besides carrying on all the negotiations inevitably resulting from a long and costly war, he is under constant request to speak in various parts of the country. This past spring he spoke at nine college commencements. When Hu Shih talks to an American audience it is ordinarily not about the immediate problems of his country but about the democratic ideal and the need to guard that ideal in the world today.

Nothing that is happening in Europe or in Asia has shaken his belief in democracy. Realizing the seriousness of the time we are living through, he nevertheless does not subscribe to the present pessimism. Democracy has been tested, he points out, in many countries and under many circumstances. New forms have been worked out, in Australia, in Sweden, in the United States, in Great Britain. The process is a continuous and evolutionary one, and there will inevitably be interruptions, periods of profound pessimism. It is a coincidence and nothing more, in the view of Hu Shih, that democracy should seem to fail at a time when the economic system which we live under is suffering severe dislocation. But democracy, he insists, is not necessarily dependent on capitalism.

It is a striking fact that, under the pressure of war, China has extended rather than suppressed democratic controls. Faced with shortages of essential material, the Chinese have formed industrial co-operatives and by the most heroic efforts have created factories for the production of munitions, clothing, shoes. In Hu Shih's opinion this remarkable development was possible because of the underlying sense of democracy that infuses his whole people.

Primarily, he says, it has been the system of examinations for official position, open to everyone without respect to rank or degree, which has made China a classless nation, democratic in the broadest sense of the word. Education was comparatively inexpensive, and preparation for the examinations, based on the old classical learning, was possible for even very humble citizens. Then, too, as long ago as 200 B.C. the law of primogeniture, under which all property passes to the eldest son, was abolished in China, with the result that estates were not closely held for century after century. Likewise the small palace aristocracy changed with each shift in dynasty.

Even more important, perhaps, was the fact that China, of necessity because of its vast area, had always been a loose federation of semiautonomous provinces. Hu Shih puts especial stress on this. So long as certain minimum requirements were met, there was a wide degree of tolerance. "We have a saying," the Ambassador explains, "that 'Heaven is high and the Emperor is far away.' That expresses the latitude which has been allowed in Chinese life."

It is perhaps not an exaggeration to say that Hu Shih's belief in the democratic ideal, with all that it implies for human enlightenment and human decency, is his religion. He has come by his faith over a long and circuitous course that has led past the shrines of the old gods and the loud persuasion of the new dogmas.

Hu Shih's father, an educated official, held to the rationalist philosophy of Confucius. On the gate of their home, he recalls, was a sign warning away Taoist and Buddhist beggars. His father died when the boy was four years old, and a year later he worked very hard, under his mother's encouragement, to build a paper temple in honor of the great sage. He hung up the scrolls and the tablets,

copied from his books, and burned incense sticks, and his mother believed that surely the spirit of Confucius would look down and help the boy to a scholarly career of rich reward.

But the mother of Hu Shih, no longer under the stern, rationalist eye of her husband, lapsed into worship of the old deities and the ancestor rituals. Her favorite, the son remembers, was Kwan-yin, Goddess of Mercy. Once the boy and his mother went on a pilgrimage to a temple dedicated to this benevolent goddess on a mountain top. The mother walked all the way over a stony path in spite of the pain which her bound feet caused her.

As the boy grew older he rebelled against the gaudy idols that he saw around him. The folk versions of Heaven and Hell no longer had power to hold him. In his reading he had come across a brief passage describing a philosopher of the fifth century named Fan Chen, who defended before the whole Imperial Court the theory of the destructibility of the spirit or soul. These sentences summing up Fan Chen's argument made a deep impression on the boy:—

"The body is the material basis of the spirit, and the spirit is only the functioning of the body. The spirit is to the body what sharpness is to a sharp knife. We have never known the existence of sharpness after the destruction of the knife. How can we admit the survival of the spirit when the body is gone?"

The young agnostic suggested to his comrades once that they push some ancient images into the village pool, and this greatly distressed his mother. At Shanghai he absorbed Hobbes, Descartes, Rousseau, Bentham, Kant, the sages and prophets of the West. During the first World War, while he was in the United States, he became an ardent pacifist, a believer in nonresistance. (He describes himself today as an ex-pacifist.) He was an internationalist, a student of Ibsen, John Morley, and Huxley. John

Dewey's *How We Think* and *Essays in Experimental Logic* made a lasting impression on him, as did the American temper with its irrepressible optimism.

During his boyhood he had cherished the ancient doctrine of the "Three Immortalities" —Virtue, Service, and Wise Speech. For his own use he translated this into the immortality of the three W's—Worth, Work, and Words. At his mother's death he pondered this simple doctrine and came to the conclusion that it was too narrow, too restricting, ruling out too much of human activity. Finally, as expressed so perfectly in his own analysis of how he arrived at a philosophy of life, this became his faith:—

"As I reviewed the life of my dead mother, whose activities had never gone beyond the trivial details of the home but whose influence could be clearly seen on the faces of those men and women who came to mourn her death, and as I recalled the personal influence of my father on her whole life and its lasting effect on myself, I came to the conviction that *everything* is immortal. Everything that we are, everything that we do, and everything that we say is immortal in the sense that it has its effect somewhere in this world, and that effect in turn will have its results somewhere else and the thing goes on in infinite time and space. . . .

"Fourteen centuries ago a man wrote an essay on 'The Destructibility of the Soul' which was considered so sacrilegious that his Emperor ordered seventy great scholars to refute it, and it was refuted. But five hundred years later a historian recorded a summary of this sacrilegious essay in his great history. And another nine hundred years passed. Then a little boy of eleven chanced upon this brief summary of thirty-five words, and these thirty-five words after being buried for fourteen hundred years suddenly became alive and are living in him and through him in the lives of thousands of men and women."

Only forty-nine years old, Hu Shih is today looked up to as one of the sages of his time, an oracle. Some of the more radical youngsters are inclined to criticize him as a Victorian oldster with pretty antique ideas. But even among the young he is revered for the great contribution that he has made to China. They are discussing and appraising his work as though he were a philosopher of the time of Confucius. The latest study is a thesis by Miss Ya Fen Hsü, submitted for an advanced degree at Smith College. I have found her study, "An Attempt at an Evaluation of Hu Shih's Work and Influence, 1917-1927," very useful in my effort to learn more about the great man China has sent to us.

Instead of the sage's robe Hu Shih wears a common business suit. He is busy at a desk twelve hours or more each day. He goes to the State Department, to the White House, to dinners and lunches and lectures. He has put aside his researches and his philosophy, his teaching and his writing. But in his heart is an unshakable conviction that he will live to see leisure and freedom restored to his country, and, if not he, then his son or his son's son or another man's son's son. That is the faith of a scholar, an ex-pacifist turned ambassador and man of the world.

SUGGESTIONS FOR STUDY

1. What is the function of the opening two paragraphs?

2. By what principle does the author select among the factual materials of the life of Hu Shih to present the biographical account in the first third of the sketch?

3. What do the details in paragraph five tell concerning his early training? Select a number of other details throughout the article that provide insight into his character.

4. What do the circumstances of his marriage tell of his character?

5. What contribution did Hu Shih make to the Chinese renaissance?

6. Why was he chosen as the American ambassador?

7. Why does he have faith in democracy in its time of crisis?

8. Why is the sketch concluded with a discussion of his religion? What things characterize his faith?

9. Why does the author not give more of the details of Hu Shih's life?

10. Define the following words from the article: surmise, travail, ultimate, tortuous, accessible, rote, precocious, renaissance, superimposing, hierarchy, hypothetical, clandestinely, ruthless, vestiges, vitiated, autonomous, circuitous, dogma, agnostic, refute.

There Was a Young Englishman[1]

CLARENCE DAY

IN 1766 a young Englishman, a clergyman's son, sailed away to seek his fortune in India. There, in spite of his youth, he was given the command of an unruly province. By the time he was twenty-seven he had "reduced" that province to order, made a fortune by trading, and gone back to England, to live the life of a well-to-do country squire without further toil.

Six of his sons went to India, hoping to repeat his experience. None of them did. Some died in battle, some from the climate, and one died of drink.

One of these active young soldiers, who had himself conquered a province as his father had done, fell in love with and married the most beautiful English girl in Calcutta. A few years later he died, like his brothers. He left a son four years old.

This little boy had some unhappy times after that. His mother carefully dispatched him in charge of a black Indian servant to England, where he was shuttled about from one elderly aunt to another. At the great school that he was then sent away to, he got into trouble because he was nearsighted and not very strong and not at all good at games. Also, one of the boys broke his nose for him, which spoiled his appearance for life. He didn't mind that so much, because he and the fellow who did it were friends; but the masters thrashed him a lot, and, as he was a weakling, he was kicked around and beaten by all the school bullies for years.

After a while his mother, who had married an elderly major, came to England to live. She had become intensely religious; rather harshly so, it seemed to her son; but he loved her, and he loved and admired his stepfather, too.

At college he followed the hounds, drank, and gambled like other young men of fashion. He had grown strong, he was now six feet four, and his chest was broad in proportion. He traveled on the Continent, loved a princess, and attended Court Balls. He was a polished young buck in tight fitting trousers strapped under his boots, a long-tailed coat, a high collar, a big cravat tie, and a monocle.

Soon after he was twenty-one and had come into possession of the money which his father had left him, he lost it. A friend of his, a young clergyman, who had a sleek, sanctified exterior and a smooth tongue, wheedled him into making an investment that completely collapsed. Another fellow he knew, a man of good family, fleeced him on a large scale at cards. Years later he pointed out this person to one of his friends. "I have not seen that man," he said, "since he drove me down in his cabriolet to my bankers in the City, where I sold out my patrimony and paid it over to him."

Not wishing to live on his stepfather, he looked around to see what a suddenly poor youth could do. He had already had a try at the law, but he hadn't worked hard at it. He now turned to journalism in his need. He didn't work hard at that either. Although almost penniless, he was still a young man of fashion at heart. It occurred to him that, as

[1] From the *Saturday Review of Literature*, XII (June 8, 1935), 12. Reprinted by permission of the *Saturday Review of Literature*.

he had always liked drawing, art might be his best bet.

It wasn't. His amateur sketches were lifelike, they were full of freshness and fun, but they were far too unstudied to meet the demands of those conventional days. In his more ambitious moments, when he tried his hand at subjects like Hogarth's, his attempts were merely facetious, or prudish and weak. He was a splendid young man in his way, but he was very English, and Art with a capital A brought out an inferior side of him. He sniggered at the nude, for example, and he sentimentalized beauty. Nevertheless he eagerly went over to Paris to paint.

While there he met a pretty Anglo-Irish girl with whom he fell in love.

This girl's mother had been watching and waiting to get her daughter a husband. She urged the youth to find some steady job at once so he could marry. He was vague about this at first. He gave up art and tried to do illustrations, but he sold very few. A man named Charles Dickens, whom nobody had ever heard of before, was writing the adventures of a character whom he called Mr. Pickwick; and the struggling would-be artist made a number of drawings to go with these Pickwick papers. They all were rejected.

He asked his stepfather to help him find some good position, to marry on. The kindly old Major hadn't much money left, owing to the failure of a bank out in India, but he precipitately took what he had and bought a newspaper with it, merely in order to make his stepson its French correspondent.

The girl for whose sake all this was so imprudently done was going to be a wonderful wife for him, the young fellow thought. Perhaps for another husband she might have been; but although he didn't see it, she was narrow-minded, and she had had a bad training. She had been taught to be an artful young girl by her artful Mamma, who was as bad-tempered and vulgar a harridan as ever came out of Ireland. But Mamma could simper and be genteel when she tried; and neither her temper nor her matchmaking

wiles were visible to the nearsighted young man. As for the girl, she didn't venture to talk much. He was drawn to her by her singing. She sang simple songs, she made eyes at him, she had lovely white arms, and he married her.

He was only twenty-five, and he didn't find out for some months that he had been cheated again.

It was poverty that opened his eyes. The newspaper on which he was dependent had never been a success, and, under his stepfather's soldierly management, after nine months it collapsed. When his wife's mother found that he was now going downhill financially, and that his family was ruined, she reviled him so loudly and coarsely that she made his home life a hell.

He hunted feverishly for a chance to do bits of ill-paid reviewing. His indolence utterly vanished. He set to work and worked hard, and for longer hours than most men would be able to, trying to sell things to magazine editors who felt lukewarm about him.

His young wife bore him two daughters. When one of these babies died, he wrote his mother, "I think of her only as something charming that for a season we were allowed to enjoy." He added that he could not ask to have her come back to a life of degradation and pain.

At the birth of their third little girl, his wife had an attack of insanity. She never recovered.

The elegant young buck was now down at heel, a hack and a drudge. His mother-in-law screamed tirades at him. His wife became sluggish and dense, like a half-witted child. He worked late into the night trying to support her and his two little girls; and as a matter of honor he felt that he must also pay his stepfather's debts.

After long years of struggle he managed to do this, and more. All England began talking about him, and reading his books. Yet when his first great novel appeared, its tone displeased many critics. It was the work of a man who had mellowed, and who had always had a warm heart, but there was a vein of cynicism in it, and sadness. The man was Thackeray, and the book was *Vanity Fair*.

SUGGESTIONS FOR STUDY

1. State the central conception of Thackeray which is conveyed in this article.
2. Characterize Thackeray's wife and her mother.
3. What facts in Thackeray's life account for the qualities of *Vanity Fair?*
4. Study carefully the facts of Thackeray's life which are included in this article and decide how well chosen they are.
5. By what means does the author secure interest and suspense?
6. Define the following words: sleek, patrimony, harridan, tirades, mellowed.

THE AUTOBIOGRAPHY

With a little care and planning an autobiography can be made very attractive. In revealing his own conception of his character and in showing what he regards as significant in his life, the author has freedom to display the full force, charm, or humor of his personality. He has a splendid opportunity to be entertaining and refreshing, and he is under no obligation to be egotistic. Depending upon his purpose and the kind of publication for which he is writing, he can be humorous or serious, amusing or instructive.

However easy the autobiography appears to the inexperienced writer, it presents a peculiar difficulty: material is too plentiful. The incautious student beginning such a paper starts bravely with the date of his birth and plunges boldly into a medley of facts and happenings following that momentous event, soon to lose himself in masses of unimportant details. His paper emerges a mélange of dissociated bits of information concerning a trip here, a vacation there, a part-time job in this store, a full-time job in that, a pet like or dislike, and a thousand and one such odds and ends. He has found the autobiography difficult because he has had the utmost trouble in selecting the important details from the unimportant.

In meeting this difficulty, decide which one of two general kinds of autobiography you wish to write. The one is a sketch of some incident or portion of your life; the other is a more extensive survey of your life. The former kind, illustrated by the first reading selection to follow, is governed by the same principles of procedure that governed the character sketch already discussed. The second kind requires special attention here because of its more complex problems.

Once again a saving factor for you is the thesis sentence. If you can get clearly in mind the dominant principle of your life and state that concisely in one sentence, your task is nearly half done. By keeping the thesis ever in mind, you can eliminate all the details which have no bearing upon it and concentrate just on the essentials which are needed to explain it. Upon analyzing yourself, you may find that you are essentially studious, or athletic, or happy-go-lucky, or literary, or scientific, or a combination of several such traits. Your task then is to trace your growth so that this dominant trait will be clearly evident.

As an example of the method which might be used in preparing an autobiography, consider the life of a student who decides that his outstanding characteristic has been an interest in science. This interest he immediately writes down in the form of a thesis sentence. In pursuing the preliminary analysis of his life, he might reason in this way: My father was not a scientist—he was a business man—but he liked to read about scientific work. For that reason he always kept scientific magazines of a technical and popular sort around the house. My earliest memories are of leafing through the publications of the National Geographic Society, studying the maps and pictures. Later the photographs and drawings of birds in this and other publications began to absorb my interest, and I undertook the identification of the common species of birds in our neighborhood. My joining the Boy Scouts furthered these studies, for we scouts were supposed to observe the phenomena of nature very closely. I even took bird walks at surprisingly early hours in the morning. However, because my family moved to the city about the time I entered high school, I found the opportunity for nature study taken from me, and my interest in it dwindled. Yet I retained a firm desire to be a scientist of some kind. I bought the usual variety of children's chemical sets, tinkered with radio construction, built airplanes, and in general toyed with the many gadgets which high-school boys find fascinating. As yet I do not know what the outcome of all this scientific investigation will be, for I am just a freshman, but it looks at the moment as if my early browsings in the *National Geographic Magazine* are going to bear fruit; geology and geography hold a strong appeal for me, and I may desert my hobbies in chemistry and physics in favor of them.

Having reasoned in this manner, he is ready to write an interesting sketch. He now knows what details in his life will be pertinent to this paper. He will not tell of the summer vacation on Aunt Sue's farm, nor of the trip to Nova Scotia, nor of the time he broke his arm, nor of his liking for going barefoot, unless this point bears directly on the origin and growth of his interest in science. No matter how attractive in themselves, the other bits are ruthlessly discarded. He may, of course, augment the major interest in his life with selected prominent minor interests, particularly if they supplement the major interest. He might, for example, have a genuine liking for literature, perhaps closely associated with his major interest through his liking for biographies of scientists or novels and stories of outdoor life and achievement.

The following outlines are further illustrations of the method by which the student can work in planning his autobiography.

THESIS: *The controlling interest in my life has been a love of sports.*

   I. My parents
     A. My father

1. A professional baseball player
2. The owner of a sporting goods store
     B. My mother
1. The daughter of a professional golfer
2. A sports enthusiast
  II. My earliest memories
     A. In my father's store
1. Playing with the equipment
2. Listening to the stories told by customers
     B. At sporting events
1. At the baseball park
2. On the golf links
 III. The growth of my own interest in sports
     A. In grammar school
1. Competing in school athletics for physical education training
2. Playing on a junior softball team
3. Hunting balls on the golf course
     B. In high school
1. Participation in school athletics
   a. Football
   b. Baseball
2. Acquisition of golfing skill
   a. Apprenticeship as a caddy
   b. Promotion to full membership in the club
     (1) Golf lessons from my father
     (2) My first score in the 90's
     (3) Competition in club tournaments
 IV. Plans for the future
     A. Those dependent upon my acquisition of further skill in sports
1. My first choice: to become a professional golfer
2. My second choice: to become a professional baseball player
     B. Other possible plans
1. To became a sports writer
2. To become a high-school or college coach

THESIS: *My life thus far has been a constant struggle against poverty.*

   I. My background
     A. My father's occupations
1. As a farm hand
2. As a factory worker
   a. In a tractor factory
   b. In an automobile body factory
     B. Our homes
1. The first: in a poverty-stricken small town
2. The second: in the crowded worker's quarter of a large city
   a. Amid conditions conducive to crime

    b. Amid conditions affording little opportunity for physical or intellectual growth

II. My struggle as a child
  A. Collecting laundry for my mother to wash
    1. Carrying it long distances
    2. Protecting it from the assaults of neighborhood gangs
  B. Selling newspapers
    1. On the street
    2. On a route

III. School days
  A. Grammar school
    1. Selling newspapers after school
    2. Working for a grocery store on weekends
  B. High school
    1. Working as science laboratory assistant after school hours
    2. Clerking in the grocery on weekends
    3. Working on the automobile assembly line during summer vacation

IV. Results
  A. Fostering of self-reliance and independence of character
  B. Creating of a desire to get ahead
    1. My father's ambition for me: to become a white-collar worker
    2. My desire: to become a teacher of science

Having carefully built a framework of this sort, fill in the substance of your paper with all the skill at your command in order that the writing will be appealing. A straightforward chronological sequence of events might well constitute the greater part of the writing, but use all the tricks studied in the sections on the character sketch and the biography to render the sketch interesting and penetrating. Short narrative anecdotes, side glances at your personal habits and traits, concise analyses or descriptions of your environment, and many other such devices can be woven into the account to advantage. They make the sketch concrete and help remove it from the category of dull facts. The following bits from autobiographical works may give some conception of how this may be done:

Doubtless, however, either of these stern and black-browed Puritans would have thought it quite a sufficient retribution for his sins, that, after so long a lapse of years, the old trunk of the family tree, with so much venerable moss upon it, should have borne, as its topmost bough, an idler like myself. No aim that I have cherished would they recognize as laudable; no success of mine—if my life, beyond its domestic scope, had ever been brightened by success—would they deem otherwise than worthless, if not positively disgraceful. "What is he?" murmurs one gray shadow of my forefathers to the other. "A writer of storybooks! What kind of a business in life—what mode of glorifying God, or being serviceable to mankind in his day and generation—may that be? Why, the degenerate fellow might as well have been a fiddler!" Such are the compliments bandied between my great-grandsires and myself, across the gulf of time! And yet, let them scorn me as they will, strong traits of their nature have intertwined themselves with mine.—Hawthorne, *The Customhouse.*

I became convinced, that if I did not put moral courage in the place of personal, or, in other words, undergo any stubborn amount of pain and wretchedness, rather than submit to what I thought wrong, there was an end forever, as far as I was concerned, of all those fine things that had been taught me, in vindication of right and justice. . . .

I had not been long in the school, when this spirit within me broke out in a manner that procured me great esteem. There was a monitor or "big boy" in office, who had a trick of entertaining himself by pelting lesser boys' heads with a hard ball. He used to throw it at this boy and that; make the *throwee* bring it back to him; and then send a rap with it on his cerebellum, as he was going off.

I had borne this spectacle one day for some time, when the family precepts rising within me, I said to myself, "I must go up to the monitor and speak to him about this." I issued forth accordingly, and to the astonishment of all present, who had never witnessed such an act of insubordination, I said, "You have no right to do this." The monitor, more astounded than anyone, exclaimed, "What?" I repeated my remonstrance. He treated me with the greatest contempt, as if disdaining even to strike me; and finished by ordering me to "stand out." "Standing out" meant going to a particular spot in the hall where we dined. I did so; but just as the steward (the master in that place) was entering it, the monitor called to me to come away; and I neither heard any more of standing out, nor saw any more of the ball.—Leigh Hunt, *Autobiography*.

When about sixteen years of age I happened to meet with a book, written by one Tryon, recommending a vegetable diet. I determined to go into it. My brother, being yet unmarried, did not keep house, but boarded himself and his apprentices in another family. My refusing to eat flesh caused an inconveniency, and I was frequently chid for my singularity. I made myself acquainted with Tryon's manner of preparing some of his dishes, such as boiling potatoes or rice, making hasty pudding, and a few others, and then proposed to my brother, that if he would give me, weekly, half the money he paid for my board, I would board myself. He instantly agreed to it, and I presently found I could save half what he paid me. This was an additional fund for buying books. But I had another advantage in it. My brother and the rest going from the printing house to their meals, I remained there alone, and dispatching presently my light repast, which

often was no more than a biscuit or a slice of bread, a handful of raisins or a tart from the pastrycook's, and a glass of water, had the rest of the time till their return for study, in which I made the greater progress from that greater clearness of head and quicker apprehension which usually attend temperance in eating and drinking.—Franklin, *Autobiography*.

The writer of autobiography should above all write sincerely and truly about himself. He should try to make the reader conceive of him as a living human being with the frailties, sympathies, and aspirations of other humans. The calendar gives the list of dates; and to the calendar the autobiographer consigns this task. He sees his duty to make a dull listing of dates and chronological details become a living document of his life. He tries to enable the reader to experience life as he has experienced it.

Digging a Well [1]

JOHN MUIR

WE CALLED our second farm Hickory Hill, from its many fine hickory trees and the long gentle slope leading up to it. Compared with Fountain Lake farm it lay high and dry. The land was better, but it had no living water, no spring or stream or meadow or lake. A well ninety feet deep had to be dug, all except the first ten feet or so, in fine-grained sandstone. When the sandstone was struck, my father, on the advice of a man who had worked in mines, tried to blast the rock; but from lack of skill the blasting went on very slowly, and father decided to have me do all the work with mason's chisels, a long, hard job, with a good deal of danger in it. I had to sit cramped in a space about three feet in diameter, and wearily chip,

chip, with heavy hammer and chisels from early morning until dark, day after day, for weeks and months. In the morning, Father and David lowered me in a wooden bucket by a windlass, hauled up what chips were left from the night before, then went away to the farm work and left me until noon, when they hoisted me out for dinner. After dinner I was promptly lowered again, the forenoon's accumulation of chips hoisted out of the way, and I was left until night.

One morning, after the dreary bore was about eighty feet deep, my life was all but lost in deadly choke-damp,—carbonic acid gas that had settled at the bottom during the night. Instead of clearing away the chips as usual when I was lowered to the bottom, I swayed back and forth and began to sink under the poison. Father, alarmed that I did not make any noise, shouted, "What's keep-

[1] From John Muir, *The Story of My Boyhood and Youth* (Boston, 1913). Reprinted by permission of the Houghton Mifflin Company.

ing you so still?" To which he got no reply. Just as I was settling down against the side of the wall, I happened to catch a glimpse of a branch of a bur-oak tree which leaned out over the mouth of the shaft. This suddenly awakened me, and to my father's excited shouting I feebly murmured, "Take me out." But when he began to hoist he found I was not in the bucket and in wild alarm shouted, "Get in! Get in the bucket and hold on! Hold on!" Somehow I managed to get into the bucket, and that is all I remembered until I was dragged out, violently gasping for breath.

One of our near neighbors, a stone mason and miner by the name of William Duncan, came to see me, and after hearing the particulars of the accident he solemnly said: "Weel, Johnnie, it's God's mercy that you're alive. Many a companion of mine have I seen dead with choke-damp, but none that I ever saw or heard of was so near to death in it as you were and escaped without help." Mr. Duncan taught father to throw water down the shaft to absorb the gas, and also to drop a bundle of brush or hay attached to a light rope, dropping it again and again to carry down pure air and stir up the poison. When, after a day or two, I had recovered from the shock, Father lowered me again to my work, after taking the precaution to test the air with a candle and stir it up well with a brush-and-hay bundle. The weary hammer-and-chisel chipping went on as before, only more slowly, until ninety feet down, when at last I struck a fine, hearty gush of water. Constant dropping wears away stone. So does constant chipping, while at the same time wearing away the chipper. Father never spent an hour in that well. He trusted me to sink it straight and plumb, and I did, and built a fine covered top over it, and swung two iron-bound buckets in it from which we all drank for many a day.

SUGGESTIONS FOR STUDY

1. What conditions occasioned the slowness of the work in the well?
2. What is meant by "choke-damp"? How did it nearly take the life of the boy?
3. What precautions could thereafter be taken against choke-damp?
4. This sketch does not enumerate the characteristics of father or son, but it implies them. Observe especially what is to be learned of John Muir as a boy. If your instructor so desires, write a character sketch of the boy, using details from this article to make your generalizations concrete.
5. Who was John Muir?

Why I Am a Naturalist[1]

ALAN DEVOE

WHEN I WAS a boy of grammar-school age, it seemed to me that there could be nothing in the world more pleasurable to do than just to sit in a meadow in the summer sun. It seemed to me that there could be no livelier delights than going bird-nesting in the spring, going cocoon-gathering on crackling days in winter, going sugaring for moths in the long, late twilights of the summer. It seemed to me that this world, just as it was, and my own sharp senses and responses to it, just as *they* were, combined to make the life-adventure a glorious thing of splendid daily excitements and continuous rewards.

I should not at the time, of course, have thought of formulating it in this windy way. Words are for later years. Boyhood is for the living. But the view was there, unformulated, just experienced.

[1] From *Nature Magazine*, XLII (August-September, 1949). Reprinted by permission of *Nature Magazine* and of the author.

That is the way I felt and looked at things as a small boy. There was nothing extraordinary about it. It is the way most boys feel, and the reason why they are likely to dismay their elders by keeping grasssnakes in their pockets, or by attaching enormous significance to a "treasure" in the form of a queer-shaped stone, or by emitting a wild whoop and rushing out and rolling on the grass when the soft airs of the May are blowing and the sun shines bright. It is the way old Adam himself, the original boy of our tribe, may be supposed to have felt and looked at things, back in the earliest dawn-day of the adventure of human consciousness. If there is anything at all unusual about the boy-convictions and boy-enthusiasms that once made up my life-view long ago, it is only the fact that they still do.

That is probably the shortest way, I imagine, of answering the question that is asked me every now and then, and that accordingly I have been asking myself, Why are you a naturalist? Well, that is why.

In my fortieth year I still think, as I did in my tenth, that just hearing and seeing the first spring bluebird, on one of those damp, earth-smelling March mornings when the mourning-cloak butterflies are flitting in the snow-patched woods, is a much more tremendous experience than anything that can be bought. I still think that just lazing away a hot afternoon lying on a hilltop and listening to the wind is a much better way of spending it than in a furious concentration on any of the myriad projects by which "practical-minded" people are constantly endeavoring to get the world to go faster, louder, more complexly and more profitably. I still think that the smell of hemlock boughs, or pond scum, or newly laid thrush-eggs, or a plowed field, or any woods at night, are infinitely more exciting and restoring than anything that comes by the costly half-ounce in a bottle. I still think certain moss-streaked and brook-washed stones are very much treasures; and if I do not have a

grasssnake about me at the moment, it is only because I am writing in the winter.

The world, the natural world, looks very good to me, and tastes good and smells good and has a very good feel in all its textures of bark and blossom and feathers and fur and plain dark dirt. And man, the natural man, the original one, looks very good to me too, with his keenly subtle senses, his aware alertness and his joy in relaxation, his endurance and his exuberation and his glad response to living. The freshness of the morning of the world, and the freshness of the boyhood of the race . . . that is the way I want them; and I would not see the first traded for the murked skies and poison rivers of the biggest Progress procurable, nor the second traded for all the sophistication in all the libraries of philosophy.

(Words, did I say, are for later life? How they do pile up and tumble forth and get to be too many and too "wordy"!)

If the devotions of a man's heart are the sort I have been talking about, what is to become of him when he grows up? Factory directors do not get much chance for hearing the peepers in the spring marsh, or even for watching the cumulus clouds sail by. There is gold to be had in Wall Street, but no goldenrod, no goldfinches. And so . . . ?

Well, with one kind of mind, it is possible to become a clergyman. There is a great deal of Nature-closeness in Christianity, if you go digging down under all the ecclesiastical flummery; there is a lot of precious stuff about lilies of the field, and little foxes, and coneys, and threshing-time and so on. After all, the story starts, rightly enough, with man set down in a Garden; and it winds up with his being saved from his exile, and restored spiritually to that Garden, by One who was not a pompous dignitary nor a laborious philosopher but a carpentering countryman. A clergyman can find in his Gospel a plenty of good reasons for getting out under the sky, and for thinking bullfrogs are more exciting than bond-issues. Still, though, it takes a special turn of vocation to be a clergyman.

Just so, it takes a special twist of talent to be an artist. I had an uncle, when I was a boy, who was a painter. At least, when he vanished into the outdoors he had canvases and brushes and things in a knapsack; and when he came home again he would have pictures to show—sketches of a country creek, winding among sun-dappled alders, paintings of an old red barn with swallows flying around it and the cattle coming home. The pictures may or may not have had much merit; I do not know. But they served *his* purpose; they let him go scuffling through the autumn leaves, listening to the white-throats; they let him go tramping through the blue-whiteness of the snow, breathing balsam-scent and hearing the tinkle of chickadees; they let him spend his life doing things like this, and responding to them with a spiritual and sensory eagerness that is the birthright of boyhood and that he wanted never to surrender. He never did.

If not a minister, not an artist, what? Well, there is the life, and a very luring one it can be, of a plain tramp. No money, no possessions, no responsibility, none of that murderous thing called one's "dignity" to be forever guarding . . . all these freedoms should release a man almost completely for the exercise of his cherished enjoyment; just hearing and touching and smelling and exulting in the wonder of the world. But it does not work out. It cuts a man off altogether from acceptance by his fellows; and we are a social animal. More, it cuts him off from a marriage, from a home; it thwarts the deep drives of domesticity. A fox has its earth. Even a male red-winged blackbird, singing *conkerree!* in the April swamp, is staking out a territory. We are not different.

If you are not to become an Eden-dreaming minister or an artist or a hobo—and if still you think with a high passion, just as you did at the age of ten, that the blossoming of spring bloodroot is bigger news than any-

thing in the day's newspaper, and that the scream of a high hawk, wheeling in the wilderness places, is a finer thing to hear than the scream of a factory whistle—if you feel and think like this, what do you become? Why, what you become, of course, is a naturalist. In a very real sense, indeed, you already *are* a naturalist. Your deepest spirit is committed. All that remains is the question of what direction your naturalizing will take. Scientist? All-around field man? Specialist? Writer?

Myself, of course, I am a writing naturalist. That is the way my bent goes. Words come readily to me (too readily and too many, often enough), whereas, after all these years, I still have to look up Latin species-names in a textbook every time I need to recall one. My naturalizing is simply a devoted prowling around the common woods and fields and creeks, having a look into a woodchuck-burrow, seeing what the deer are up to, and writing down the things I see and the things I feel. I have been at it for a good many years now, and I expect still to be at it on the day before they print my obituary. For a naturalist is not something that a man ever stops being. A naturalist is a conviction in the bones, and in the heart a dream inalienable.

Why am I a naturalist? There come back to me across the years the words of an old naturalist long ago, talking about his love for watching birds and animals: "They are our childhood come back to us, all instinct and joy and adventure." That is just about it, I think. I suppose I am a naturalist, and always will be one, because there were some truths I knew when I was ten years old that still seem to me everlastingly the truest things in the world.

SUGGESTIONS FOR STUDY

1. Enumerate any five pleasures of boyhood which the author still enjoys.

2. Enumerate ten highly concrete nouns in the first four paragraphs. What do these contribute denotatively and connotatively to the writing?

3. What is the author's conception of "practical-minded" people?

4. Why might a nature lover be a clergyman? an artist? a tramp? Why did the author forego each of these pursuits?

5. State the thesis, answering the question, Why am I a naturalist?

6. Study the organization of this sketch. To what are the first five paragraphs devoted? If one has a real devotion to some calling, what does the author imply about the vocation to be followed? What then is the function of the paragraphs about the clergyman, artist, and tramp?

7. Observe how ably this article states the central interest of the author's life. If you write this kind of sketch, be sure to follow a similar procedure.

8. Define the following words from the selection: unformulated, myriad, coneys, inalienable, obituary.

E. The Letter

THE FRIENDLY LETTER

Since a friendly letter is meant to interest and inform your intimates and so to preserve friendships, careless letter writing is inexcusable. Haste, slovenliness, or carelessness indicates that you do not have the time nor the inclination to treat the correspondent with consideration.

Form

In a good letter both form and content receive close attention. The form, based on several conventions which may be easily learned, requires the division of the letter into five parts: the heading, the greeting, the body, the close, and the signature.

Heading. The heading is usually placed in the upper right-hand corner of the page; to be sure, writers sometimes place it on the left-hand margin at the end of the letter, but this location is not preferred. The heading can take several forms, all correct.

The block form with open punctuation:

> 160 Cross Street
> Detroit 5, Michigan
> September 23, 1958

The indented form with open punctuation:

> 160 Cross Street
> Detroit 5, Michigan
> September 23, 1958

The block form with closed punctuation:

> 160 Cross Street,
> Detroit 5, Michigan,
> September 23, 1958.

The indented form with closed punctuation:

> 160 Cross Street,
> Detroit 5, Michigan,
> September 23, 1958.

Today the block heading with open punctuation is used more often than the others. In no form of the heading are abbreviations used. It is advisable to write out *street, avenue,* and *place;* the names of states and cities, such as New York, Philadelphia, Washington; and the names of the months. This practice will obviate any confusion. If the writing is not clear, a correspondent who does not know your address may be unable to decide whether you live in Ga., Va., Pa., Ia., or La., in Cal. or Col., in Md. or Mo. Therefore, courtesy and clarity both forbid the use of abbreviations.

Greeting. The greeting is placed just below the heading and on the opposite side of the page, even with the left-hand margin. The accepted forms of greeting are:

> Dear Bill,
> Dear Mr. Jones,
> My dear Professor Smith: (a formal usage)

The greeting is usually followed by a comma, although in more formal letters—as to a mere acquaintance—a colon is better. The use of the conventional terms of greeting, "Dear ——" and "My dear ——," depends upon the intimacy of the correspondents. "My dear ——" is commonly thought more formal in the United States. Abbreviations are not used, except Mr., Mrs., and Dr. To write "My dear Prof. Smith" shows lack of good taste.

Body. The body of the letter is begun two lines below the greeting. Its structure and the rules for writing it are essentially the same as those studied in this text for other kinds of writing. The rules of rhetoric with their admonitions as to correct paragraphing, sentence structure, and grammar all apply.

Close. The close of the letter is placed two lines below the bottom of the last paragraph and is begun near the center of the page. The first word only is capitalized. A comma follows the close. The most commonly used forms are:

Sincerely yours, } these two have the great-
Yours sincerely, } est degree of formality
Faithfully yours,
Cordially yours,
Affectionately yours,

Of course, to one's parents and intimates, other and more appropriate closes are used.

A few other cautions must be made. Keep a neat letter appearance. Let the margins on all sides of the page be straight and wide, and the lines be well spaced and parallel. And above all, be legible. Your correspondent wants to know what you have said to him. Also make sure that the signature at the end of the letter is clear.

Address the envelope with the same form —block or indented—used for the heading. Place the return address in the upper left-hand corner, and the address just below center on the right-hand side of the envelope.

Content

A friendly letter is really a conversation which substitutes the written for the spoken word. Like a conversation it is rarely planned in advance and proceeds by a series of ideas which arise spontaneously in the writer's mind. Just be careful not to shift from one topic to another so swiftly as to bewilder your reader. Of course, you may jot down beforehand those ideas you wish to be sure to include in your letter, but in any event try to maintain a tone of freshness and spontaneity.

Your own personality should be revealed by the informality, leisureliness, and chattiness of your letter. William Cowper, a famous English poet and letter writer, has this to say about writing a good letter:

You like to hear from me: this is a very good reason why I should write.—But I have nothing to say: this seems equally a good reason why I should not. Yet if you had alighted from your horse at our door this morning, and at this present writing, being five o'clock in the afternoon, had found occasion to say to me—"Mr. Cowper, you have not spoke since I came in; have you resolved never to speak again?" it would be but a poor reply, if in answer to the summons I should plead inability as my best and only excuse. And this by the way suggests to me a seasonable piece of instruction, and reminds me of what I am very apt to forget, when I have only epistolary business in hand, that a letter may be written upon anything or nothing just as that anything or nothing happens to occur. A man that has a journey before him twenty miles in length which he is to perform on foot, will not hesitate and doubt whether he shall set out or not, because he does not readily conceive how he shall ever reach the end of it: for he knows that by the simple operation of moving one foot forward first, and then the other, he shall be sure to accomplish it. So it is in the present case, and so it is in every similar case. A letter is written as a conversation is maintained, or a journey performed; not by preconcerted or premeditated means, a new contrivance, or an invention never heard of before—but merely by maintaining a progress, and resolving as a postilion does, having once set out, never to stop till we reach the appointed end.

This attempt to think of grand events— inventions "never heard of before"—prevents many students from writing engaging letters. Actually your daily affairs and ideas are of greater interest to your friends than news of a stranger's going over Niagara Falls in a barrel. So write of the little things that have happened to you or notions you have had. See how the Rev. Sydney Smith, a famous humorist of the nineteenth century, follows a whim in a letter:

You are, I hear, attending more to diet than heretofore. If you wish for anything like happiness in the fifth act of life, eat and drink about half what you *could* eat and drink. Did I ever tell you my calculation about eating and drinking? Having ascertained the weight of what I could live upon, so as to preserve health and strength, and what I did live upon, I found that between ten and seventy years of age, I had eaten and drunk forty four-horse wagon-loads of meat and drink more than would have preserved me in life and health! The value of this mass of nourishment I considered to be worth seven thousand pounds sterling. It occurred to me that I must, by my voracity, have starved to death fully a hundred persons. This is a frightful calculation, but irresistibly true; and I think, dear Murray, your wagons would require an additional horse each!

One of the real masters of the friendly letter was Charles Lamb. Notice how informal, conversational, and yet engaging this letter is:

Dear Manning,—When I last wrote you, I was in lodgings. I am now in chambers, No. 4, Inner Temple Lane, where I should be happy to see you any evening. Bring any of your friends, the Mandarins, with you. I have two sitting-rooms; I call them so *par excellence,* for you may stand, or loll, or lean, or try any posture in them; but they are best for sitting; not squatting down Japanese fashion, but the more decorous use of the post—s which European usage has consecrated. I have two of these rooms on the third floor, and five sleeping, cooking, etc., rooms, on the fourth floor. In my best room is a choice collection of the works of Hogarth, an English painter of some humor. In my next best are shelves containing a small but well-chosen library. My best room commands a court in which there are trees and a pump, the water of which is excellent—cold with brandy, and not very insipid without. Here I hope to set up my rest, and not quit till Mr. Powell, the undertaker, gives me notice that I may have possession of my last lodging. He lets lodgings for single gentlemen. I sent you a parcel of books by my last, to give you some idea of the state of European literature. There comes with this two volumes, done up as letters, of minor poetry, a sequel to "Mrs. Leicester"; the best you may suppose mine; the next best are my coadjutor's; you may amuse yourself in guessing them out; but I must tell you mine are but one third in quantity of the whole. So much for a very delicate subject. It is hard to speak of one's self, etc. Holcroft had finished his life when I wrote to you, and Hazlitt has since finished his life—I do not mean his own life, but he has finished a life of Holcroft, which is going to press. Tuthill is Dr. Tuthill. I continue Mr. Lamb. I have published a little book for children on titles of honor; and to give them some idea of the difference of rank and gradual rising, I have made a little scale, supposing myself to receive the following various accessions of dignity from the King, who is the fountain of honor—As at first, 1, Mr. C. Lamb; 2, C. Lamb, Esq.; 3, Sir C. Lamb, Bart.; 4, Baron Lamb of Stamford; 5, Viscount Lamb; 6, Earl Lamb; 7, Marquis Lamb; 8, Duke Lamb. It would look like quibbling to carry it further, and especially as it is not necessary for children to go beyond the ordinary titles of subregal dignity in our own country, otherwise I have sometimes in my dreams imagined myself still advancing, as 9th, King Lamb; 10th, Emperor Lamb; 11th, Pope Innocent, higher than which is nothing but the Lamb of God. Puns I have not made many (nor punch much) since the date of my last; one I cannot help relating. A constable in Salisbury Cathedral was telling me that eight people dined at the top of the spire of the cathedral; upon which I remarked, that they must be very sharp-set. But in general I cultivate the reasoning part of my mind more than the imaginative.

A word is perhaps needed about the beginning of the letter. As most people seem to be late in answering their personal correspondence, they have the impulse to start every letter with an apology for not having written sooner. If an apology does seem to be called for, it should be offered adroitly without a host of excuses. Here are the openings of several letters from the correspondence of Thomas Moore, which will illustrate how adroitly an apology can be offered:

I am really a very good correspondent. Do you know what the chemists call "latent heat"? This I am full of. It is a property which some bodies have of keeping all their warmth to themselves; or, rather, *in* themselves; which makes them seem not half so warm as other bodies which have all their warmth on the surface. Now this is the case with me; and therefore, whenever you are long without hearing from me, set it down at once to "latent heat," and console yourself with the idea of its being all snug and warm in my heart, instead of lavishing its precious particles through the post-office.—To Miss God-FREY.

You have every reason to be very angry with me—but I really have such an unconquerable aversion to writing letters, that I have often thought Captain Brady's resolution not to answer anything but a *challenge* was the most peaceable way of getting through life. But I feel myself particularly reprehensible in not attending to *your* letter.—To JAMES CORRY.

It is a certain fact, that since I heard from you I have, in my own mind, written you five or six letters, as excellent as ever were penned, though penned they never were. How should they, when I never had a pen in my hand since I sent you off my last little flying reproach? And how could I have a pen in a hand that was never divested of a needle, thread, and thimble, except when I was nursing the sick or conversing with carpenters and upholsterers?—Miss Godfrey to Thomas Moore.

Probably a better method, however, is to open with a word of greeting to the correspondent, like that between friends on the street. Making the correspondent feel he is a valued friend is the way to his heart. Does not the following greeting from Miss Godfrey to Thomas Moore express a real cordiality?

Rogers gave me the enclosed to get franked to you. I can't resist taking the opportunity to ask after you and Bessy, and little Barbara, and the other little animal;—are you all flourishing in health and happiness? And do your absent friends ever by any accident occupy a stray thought?

A few other words of warning remain. Whenever you receive a letter that contains questions to be answered, be sure to answer those questions so that you will not make a bad impression on the correspondent. If you neglect his questions, he feels irritated and may also believe that his letter has not even been read. It is a good practice to place on the desk before you the letter which you are answering.

THE FORMAL NOTE

The formal note is a highly artificial form, written in a set manner. It is used for formal invitations, and has no heading, greeting, or signature. It is written in the third person and the present tense throughout. Contrary to the usual rule for the use of numbers, it requires that all numbers in the date should be written out. The address of the sender and the date of writing are placed below the last line and on the left, with either open or closed punctuation.

Mr. Archibald Smith requests the pleasure of Mr. and Mrs. Alfred Jones's company at dinner on Saturday evening, January the twenty-fifth, at six-thirty o'clock.

4 Park Street,
January the fifteenth.

Mr. and Mrs. Alfred Jones accept with pleasure the kind invitation of Mr. Archibald Smith to dine on Saturday, January the twenty-fifth, at six-thirty o'clock.

25 South Avenue,
January the seventeenth.

Mr. and Mrs. Alfred Jones regret that a previous engagement prevents their acceptance of Mr. Archibald Smith's kind invitation to dine on Saturday, January the twenty-fifth.

25 South Avenue,
January the seventeenth.

SUGGESTIONS FOR STUDY

1. Write one of the following letters:

   A letter of congratulation on a marriage, the birth of a child, graduation from college or high school, the selling of a story to a magazine, or an appointment to a coveted position.

   A letter of thanks for the hospitality shown you during a visit.

   A letter to a friend confined to a sickbed.

   A letter of thanks for a Christmas gift, or other present.

   A letter to a friend asking for advice on what college to attend.

   A letter of advice to a friend in high school who has asked you concerning the college he shall attend.

   A letter home during a summer vacation.

   A letter planning a summer vacation trip.

   A letter of invitation to a friend to spend some time at your home.

   A letter home for money.

   A letter to a son who has written for money.

   A letter to a man who is retiring from his position after a lifetime of service.

2. Write a formal note of invitation, a letter of acceptance, and a letter of regret.

THE BUSINESS LETTER

Being more formal than the personal letter, the business letter demands greater precision in both form and content. The recipient of the letter, not being a friend, lacks the indulgence that the writer of a personal letter can expect. So exercise care to see that your letter is proper in form, manuscript appearance, grammar, punctuation, and all the other principles of rhetoric. In the last twenty-five years, business houses and institutions have become increasingly aware of the importance of the letter in their work, and correspondingly critical of the letters written to them.

Form

The heading of the business letter is exactly the same as that of the friendly letter; again the block form without punctuation is preferred. The business letter, however, has one item of information not found in the friendly letter: an inside address. Businessmen often do not see the envelopes of letters handled by their secretaries, and so need a record of the addressee. The inside address is placed even with the left-hand margin of the letter, a space or more below the bottom line of the heading. The style of the inside address should conform to that used in the heading.

Mr. John Andrews
121 Tennessee Drive
Buffalo, New York

Dr. George Smith,
　7 Emory Avenue,
　　Cortland, New York.

Notice that both the closed and open forms of punctuation are correct, although today the open, block form is usually preferred. Simply remember to be consistent. If you have used an open block heading, use the same type of inside address. In addition to the name and address of the receiver, his business title is often given, on the same line as his name or on the line below it:

Dr. George Smith, Chairman
Athletic Committee

Dr. George Smith
Chairman, Athletic Committee

The greeting of the business letter, placed even with the left-hand margin of the page, differs slightly from that used in the personal letter. Preferred here are:

Dear Sir:　　　　Mesdames:
Dear Madam:　　Dear Mr. Hope:
Gentlemen:

In contrast to the usage in friendly letters, the colon always follows the greeting.

Sometimes you may wish to bring a letter to the personal attention of an individual in a firm. You may address this individual directly or, more formally, may write *Attention of Mr.* —— on the same line as the salutation.

Seaboard Shipping Lines
145 Front Street
New York, New York

Gentlemen:　　Attention of Mr. Robert E.
　　　　　　　　Smith

The close is usually placed in the same position as it is in the friendly letter, although a few firms now put it in block form even with the left-hand margin. The conventional business closes are:

Yours truly,　　　　Sincerely yours,
Yours very truly,　　Yours sincerely,
Very truly yours,　　Cordially yours,
Respectfully yours,　Faithfully yours,

In business letters the signature must be legible. It is well, therefore, to type your name under the signature.

Address the envelope to correspond with the inside address, placing your return address in the upper left-hand corner.

For the usual 6½″ by 3½″ business envelope, fold the letter first from bottom to top, leaving the bottom edge about a quarter of an inch short of the top edge so that when the receiver opens the letter, he will have no trouble separating the sheets. Then make a triple fold: bring the left edge two-thirds of the way toward the right edge, which you fold over on top of it. For the large-size business envelope, make a triple fold in the letter by folding up the bottom and bringing the top down over it; thus creases divide the letter evenly in thirds.

Content

To write a good business letter, use the same principles which you have employed for other forms of writing: study the reader, define your purposes, organize the material effectively, and use appropriate language.

Adapt your letter to the reader. You are ordinarily writing him to show how he can be served, and so you should pay attention to his wants. To sell him a desk, rent him an apartment, or get him to vote for a new city ordinance, stimulate him to co-operation by indicating how your proposal will benefit him.

Define your purposes carefully, so that in the letter you will make perfectly clear to the reader what action you desire him to take. Make the letter as concise as possible, but never forget to include every bit of information necessary for your reader to do as you wish. Any busy man is annoyed by a letter so incomplete that he must write back to find out what he is expected to do. Consider the following letter:

Dear Mr. Jones:
I was a student in your rhetoric class last year. This term I wish to take English by correspondence. Would you please give permission to do so? I would appreciate a prompt reply.
Sincerely yours,

This student thought he was being commendably concise. But the instructor had to write back to find out to whom the permission was to be sent, what English course was to be taken, and why the student wanted to take correspondence study. The student replied that having failed the rhetoric course and left college, he hoped while working in his home town to make up his deficiency by correspondence study. He then enclosed the name and address of the person to whom the permission was to be sent and explained what sort of permission the correspondence administrators desired. Only then could the instructor comply with the request.

In wording the letter, be natural, using simple diction and sentence structure. Those terms which the reader himself uses will please him best. Preserve a certain dignity by avoiding colloquialisms and slang. Avoid humor or cleverness, for such tricks are frequently misunderstood.

Though formerly all sorts of abbreviations and stock phrases were used, today the businessman is more careful. He no longer relies on such clichés as "Yours of the 17th ult. at hand and contents duly noted." Instead he tries to write as he would talk. Here are a few of the hackneyed expressions which he now avoids:

as per	our Mr. Jones
at an early date	permit me to state
at hand	please be advised
at your earliest convenience	please find enclosed
	recent date
contents duly noted	take pen in hand
beg to state	thanking you in advance
by return mail	
esteemed favor	your favor
has come to hand	yours of the 17th
in reply would say	

Not only are these expressions nonsensical, grammatically poor, or exhausted through use, but they commonly occur in the most important parts of the letter and so weaken the force of the entire writing. As the beginning and ending of the letter, like similar parts of the magazine article, make the strongest impression on the reader, start the letter with a direct, fresh manner of statement to stimulate attention. Likewise at the end, do not use a weak participial construction: "Hoping to hear from you" or "Thanking you in advance." A complete sentence is more forceful: "I thank you for your courtesy."

Whatever kind of letter is written, let it be courteous. The correspondent is pleased if he finds that the difficulties of his side of the transaction are appreciated. It is diplomatic to treat him as a punctilious gentleman and to reveal an interest in him and his affairs. Interest, conciseness, and courtesy will make for pleasant and efficient correspondence.

THE CLAIM LETTER

The claim letter lodges a complaint against a company or individual. Remember that even though inconvenienced in some manner, you should write a courteous letter, setting aside anger during the writing. If the recipient of the letter is treated with consideration, he is most likely to remedy the grievance promptly.

The beginning of the letter should state accurately and fully the circumstances under which the transaction or exchange of services was made. Give the nature of the business and its date of transaction in full to establish the point of contact with the reader and to put him in possession of the facts so that needless correspondence will not be occasioned. Then make the complaint. To offer some excuse explaining the difficulty which may have arisen is a courteous gesture and indicates that you are reasonable. However, such a gesture should not weaken the force of the letter.

To stimulate the reader to action, include in the letter a statement of the inconvenience to which you have been put by the error, to indicate that the complaint is not just imaginary but based on actuality. Having provided the stimulus, then point out the exact action which the firm is to take, so that it may be sure what is expected of it to give satisfaction. The tone of the letter throughout is serious, courteous, forceful, and reasonable.

Gentlemen:

On February 25, 1954, I ordered the following books from your General Catalogue of 1954:

No. 478 Fowler, H. W. *Dictionary of Modern English Usage,* 1929

No. 592 Moore, Thomas. *The Epicurean,* 1877

No. 671 Saintsbury, G. *Short History of French Literature,* 1917

The order was correctly filled for the first two items on this list, but instead of the third, you sent me *Specimens of French Literature,* by G. Saintsbury, number 672 in the Catalogue.

I have returned *Specimens of French Literature* and desire you to rush the correct volume to me, as I have immediate need of it. The delay has already caused me considerable inconvenience.

Yours truly,

THE LETTER OF APPLICATION

A letter of application tries to impress an employer and persuade him to grant an interview. He appreciates a confident manner, neither timid nor boastful. He demands that attention be lavished on manuscript appearance and form, and seldom bothers to read carefully any letter which contains errors in spelling or grammar.

The Beginning

Come to the point at once. Make a simple statement applying for the position and telling how you learned of the vacancy. Try to get the pronoun *you* in the introduction rather than *I,* as you wish to stress what service you can perform for the employer. Throughout the letter you need not avoid *I,* but do not use it blatantly.

Also do not try to be clever in seeking to be original. If you vary the theme, "I have long wished to obtain a position in this kind of work," you will make a favorable impression by showing your eagerness to work.

The Body

Tone. Do not boast by telling the employer, "Hire me and your worries are over." Be firm, serious, and if possible gracefully affable.

Statement of experience. Following the introduction, state your experience *in detail.* Do not just write, "For two years I worked in the shops of the Jefferson Tool Company"; specify exactly what you did, so that the employer may know whether you were sweeping floors or operating a machine. Also state any experience that might possibly bear on the position for which you are applying; if you apply for personnel work, for instance, say if you have taught Sunday School, been a camp counselor, handled Boy Scouts, or done any work in which you dealt with people.

Statement of education. Next state what schools you have attended, and for how long, the degree attained, the general level of your school grades, and a list of those studies which will help you to execute the duties of the job. Also list any honors which were accorded you, as membership in scholastic societies.

A list of references. List by name and address at least three people who can speak for your character, ability, and experience. Remember always to ask permission before you give a name as a reference and later to thank the individual for granting that privilege.

The Conclusion

Show your willingness to talk with an employer by asking for an interview. On that occasion he can judge for himself such matters as your personal appearance, habits of speech, and mental abilities, and can discuss salary, a consideration usually not broached in the letter of application. Close the letter firmly, avoiding hackneyed, weak phrases, such as "Hoping to hear from you."

If an employer writes you that the position has been filled, you will impress him favorably by thanking him for his courtesy in considering your letter of application, reasserting your desire to work for him, and expressing the hope that he will keep you in mind if another position becomes vacant.

Unsolicited letters of application, written on the mere chance that a position may be open, sometimes bring results. Be careful, however, to study the qualities, education, and experience demanded by the firm of its employees before you write the letter.

SUGGESTIONS FOR STUDY

1. Read the following letter, noting the cordial tone inserted in a purely business letter.

Dear Mr. Smith:

Thank you for your order dated April 30 for two volumes. The books are being shipped to you today by express, C.O.D., as requested, with our receipted invoice enclosed.

Perhaps you will find in the enclosed folder some other books to your liking.

Our facilities, of course, are not limited to the books we list. In ordering again, please feel free to order any books you may require including textbooks. On these, when ordered for classroom or similar use, we allow as liberal a discount as our own terms of purchase permit.

This is the first order we have received from you. It is a pleasure to add your name to our list of customers.

Sincerely yours,

2. Having read this example of a pleasant business letter, revise the following letters after noting carefully where the weakness lies in each. They are not all of the same level of ability.

A

Dear Mr. Thomas:

At a recent meeting of the board of the Y.M.C.A., your name was given to me for personal solicitation. I hesitate to take the time of anyone on such a mission as this, knowing that if you make a contribution you need only be reminded.

Will you therefore kindly indicate whether you are willing to help support the Y.M.C.A.? If you do, enclose your check for whatever sum you desire to contribute. If you don't, please state why.

B

Gentlemen:

In addition to sending catalog of College of Agriculture and bulletin on Correspondence study, please answer the following by letter:

1. I hold degree with major in biology but no work in Agriculture. Would you permit me to take sufficient work by correspondence between now and next Sept. so that I could complete requirements for B.S. in Agr. in one year of residence?

2. Hold scholarship to the State U. covering tuition and fees. Can you offer a similar one? I prefer a Northern institution.

3. What is size of your diploma in inches, does it have gold seal with ribbons protruding from underneath and how many signatures?

The diploma I now have is the small vest-pocket size unsuitable for framing. I desire a large one suitable for framing. Would you be willing to have large size made for me 20½ × 25 to fit frame my father used for M.D. if I pay cost?

C

Dear Sir:

Referring to yours of February 5th advising of an overcharge made you in connection with ticket purchased by you.

We have pleasure in enclosing draft to your order for $2.95 in adjustment and trust you will overlook agent's unintentional error.

3. Write a business letter on one of the following topics:

Ordering theater tickets

Placing an order with a mail-order house or department store

Writing a bank to seek information concerning your checking account

Making hotel, train, or steamship reservations

Requesting a business firm or a governmental agency to send a special bulletin which it publishes

Requesting an automobile club to send you tour maps

4. Write a claim letter on one of the following themes:

Requesting your apartment owner to make repairs in your apartment

Requesting the electric company to adjust an overcharge on the month's bill

Seeking adjustment from a firm that has put you to needless expense. You ordered a cap and gown for your graduation ceremonies, asking the firm first to send it to your home, but later to send it to your college address; they acknowledged the change of address. Two days before your graduation you had no gown; you wired to the firm to send it immediately, and received word from home that the gown was there. The cost of wiring and mailing was $2. Your letter is to secure reimbursement for the expense to which you were put by their negligence.

Seeking reimbursement from a railroad. You feel sure that the station agent overcharged you for your ticket which you bought in the Christmas rush.

Seeking quick action from a firm. You are ready to leave on a camping trip, but your equipment, which you ordered long before, has not arrived.

5. Read the following letters of application, noting the type and amount of information given:

a

The Eastern Teachers Agency informs me that you are seeking a teacher of English for the coming year. I am making application for that position.

I am a graduate of Harvard University, B.A. 1954. During my course I specialized in English, taking twelve semester hours of composition and thirty-six hours of literature. In addition, I secured twenty hours of Education, sufficient to enable me to hold a teacher's certificate in your state. The remainder of my course of study was devoted to those subjects which would assist me in being a well-rounded teacher: history, sociology, psychology, science, and language. My grade average for the four years was B, an average which placed me well within the top third of my class.

Throughout my schooling I have engaged in many activities outside the classroom. In Newton High School, from which I graduated in 1950, I was a member of the dramatics club and the debating society. I was also awarded the school letter in track and basketball. At Harvard I was a member of the dramatics club and an editor of the *Daily Crimson*. For three years I ran on the track team, winning my letter each year. Thus I feel that my interests are wide enough to enable me to be of assistance to you and to your pupils.

Although I have had no actual experience as a teacher, the grade of A which I received in practice teaching and the keen pleasure which I took in this work seem to indicate that I should be a successful classroom teacher. I have had experience in handling boys of high-school age, as I was assistant scoutmaster of Troup 8 of Newton for three years.

The Eastern Teachers Agency has already sent you my full credentials, which include recommendations by several persons and the record of my school and college work. If there is any way in which I can be of further assistance to you in providing necessary information, please feel free to call on me.

I would like very much to have the pleasure of meeting you and talking over the work in your school. I can call at any time that will be convenient for you.

b

Mr. W. P. Brown of your home office tells me that you are desirous of employing more automobile salesmen. As I am very much interested in this work and have had considerable experience, I am placing my application with you.

Age: Twenty-three years.

Experience: For three summers I have worked as salesman for the R. E. Edwards Sales Company of Wichita, Kansas, dealers in Whirlwind cars. I have also worked for one year, after school hours, as automobile mechanic for this same firm.

Education: I am a graduate (June, 1954) of the University of Kansas School of Business Administration. I am well grounded in business theory and practice, having studied both economics and accounting.

References: Mr. W. P. Brown, Thunderbolt Automobile Company, Detroit, Michigan.
Mr. R. E. Edwards, Edwards Sales Company, Wichita, Kansas.
Professor J. W. Pound, School of Business Administration, The University of Kansas, Lawrence, Kansas.

However, I desire a personal interview to talk over my qualifications with you. May I call at your convenience?

c

Your advertisement in the *Free Press* states your need for a salesman in your shoe department. I desire to be considered an applicant for this position.

For many years I have looked forward to making my way in the shoe business. My father was for ten years the owner of a shoe store, and from him I learned at an early age many important facts about the construction, quality, and selling of shoes. During each summer and after school hours, I worked in the store, first as errand boy, and then later for five years as salesman. Thus I have learned both about shoes and about meeting customers.

I am a graduate of Ardmore High School, and this June I hope to receive a B.A. degree from the University of Pennsylvania. I have tried to take those studies which would fit me best for the shoe business. Thus I have pursued a business course and studied such subjects as accounting, bookkeeping, typewriting, and economic geography. However, I have taken work in English composition, French, history, and psychology. My marks have been A and B.

The following men have kindly consented to act as references for me:

Mr. J. L. Turner, 265 Temple Street, Philadelphia, Pennsylvania.

Professor T. D. Smith, Department of Economics, The University of Pennsylvania, Philadelphia, Pennsylvania.

Dr. H. D. Thistlewaite, 4 Ontario Street, Ardmore, Pennsylvania.

May I have a personal interview to present my qualifications more fully? I am free any afternoon after two o'clock.

6. Write a letter of application for a summer position.

Assuming that you are about to graduate from college, write a letter of application for a permanent position.

F. The Informal Essay

DEFINITION

The term *essay* has been applied to so many different kinds of prose writing that it scarcely admits of definition. Its two main types are often said to be the formal and the informal essay, though these are rather loose terms. Generally speaking, the formal essay is a relatively impersonal, serious piece of writing, explaining or proving some thesis. The current magazine articles in a serious vein on politics, war, or economics are good examples of formal essays.

The informal essay, on the other hand, aims to entertain more than to instruct or persuade. In attractive fashion it suggests that some things may be true. Usually it is dominated by the personality of the writer; hence it is to prose essentially what the lyric is to poetry, a personal expression of the writer. It is a leisurely, conversational form of writing, which holds the reader as an equal to engage him in informal, intimate conversation on a variety of topics.

PROCEDURE

Your success as an informal essayist will not depend upon the size and importance of the topic you select, but upon the manner in which you treat that topic. Fine essays have been written about all sorts of unlikely subjects—going for a walk, choosing a necktie, watching television, walking a dog. Such topics become interesting and even important when you speak very naturally about them, linking your observations and experience to some sort of generalization about existence that may prove fruitful speculation for the reader. As in the personal letter you must convey what you have seen, thought, experienced, firm in the conviction that what has interested you will also interest your reader, for without this conviction no essay can be written. To be sure, the person with the fullest personality, widest thought and reading, deepest experience may write the best essay, but everyone has ample opportunity.

The informal essay does not bind you quite so rigidly as the formal essay. It gives you freedom to write much as you would talk, with spontaneity and opportunity to pursue attractive fancies. Provided that you stay within the domain of reason, you need not feel that you must prove every generalization and forge an absolutely logical chain of conviction; you may present pet ideas, cast new light on old subjects, note unfamiliar scenes, and play with the intricate psychology of mankind.

Do not, however, construe these remarks to mean that you have a free hand to do whatever you like at any moment while writing, that you may set pen to paper with the first thought that occurs to you and follow the dictates of fancy till you reach a likely conclusion, that you need not make an outline or plan the essay. Actually, nothing can be farther from the truth. An air of informality and spontaneity comes not from haphazard writing, but from the most careful preparation and skillful execution. Informality is a work of art. It can be attained only by the expenditure of the same time and effort given to the writing of a serious treatise. An artistic essay, however formless and even rambling it may appear, is based upon a carefully organized outline, judiciously concealed. In some formal prose writings the introduction enumerates the major points to follow, and the body of the paper

considers these in order. But in the informal essay such an apparent structural device is not used. Beginning with the thesis, or an observation closely related to it, you proceed toward a predetermined goal without seeming to follow an organized plan. Each point ingeniously gives rise to the next by a natural association of ideas. Careful preparation is required in order not to lose sight of the ultimate goal and to retain the interest of the reader. No awkward gaps can be left between ideas, and the shift from one idea to the next must be clearly evident.

Formulate a thesis at the outset. It serves not only as a check against excessive rambling but as a goal toward which to aim. It can be stated outright, or possibly withheld and brought out by implication. Often it is the opening sentence and so provides forcefulness to the beginning. Oliver Goldsmith, a delightful eighteenth-century essayist, made excellent use of it as a vigorous opening sentence from which he could extend his train of thought. Here are the opening paragraphs from several of his essays:

Foreigners observe that there are no ladies in the world more beautiful, or more ill dressed, than those of England. Our country women have been compared to those pictures where the face is the work of a Raphael, but the draperies thrown out by some empty pretender, destitute of taste, and entirely unacquainted with design.

Man, when secluded from society, is not a more solitary being than the woman who leaves the duties of her own sex to invade the privileges of ours. She seems, in such circumstances, like one in banishment; she appears like a neutral being between the sexes; and, though she may have the admiration of both, she finds true happiness from neither.

Animals, in general, are sagacious in proportion as they cultivate society. The elephant and the beaver show the greatest signs of this when united; but when man intrudes into their communities, they lose all their spirit of industry, and testify but a very small share of that sagacity for which, when in a social state, they are so remarkable.

You may also choose to start from that observation which gave your thoughts their initial impulse, and so proceed toward an ultimate generalization. Charles Lamb's essay "Old China" follows this plan. It begins:

> I have an almost feminine partiality for old china. When I go to see any great house, I inquire for the china closet, and next for the picture gallery. I cannot defend the order of preference, but by saying that we all have some taste or other, of too ancient a date to admit of our remembering distinctly that it was an acquired one. I can call to mind the first play, and the first exhibition, that I was taken to; but I am not conscious of a time when china jars and saucers were introduced into my imagination.

Lamb then gradually shifts to a reflection concerning the old days when he and his sister struggled to find the money to buy such china. He pictures the pleasures of poverty when each new purchase was a treasured prize. Then he turns to the thought that poverty may have been enjoyable when he and his sister were young, but now that old age has crept upon them, they need greater comfort and security. The final note is struck when he returns to the old china before him. The reader ends with the feeling that he has been through a very natural and delightful conversation which arose from a reflection concerning the beautiful old china in Lamb's possession.

There are, of course, countless other ways of starting the essay. The principle is that which governs all introductory paragraphs: the reader's attention must be aroused through interest and curiosity. An impulse must be provided him. Then he will follow the writer along the main path or through the by-paths just as long as those paths come in an orderly fashion.

One other caution must be observed. In a form which tends toward the general as does the essay, be especially careful to be concrete. Illustrations must be frequent; indeed many successful essays consist almost solely of illustrations designed to explain the different implications of the thesis.

The informal essay is therefore a brief, informal, conversational piece of writing, in which in a personal way you express yourself freely upon any subject which catches your attention. You have a definite plan and a definite thesis, but these you conceal so that you can delight and entertain the reader with the freshness, spontaneity, and informality of your writing.

SUGGESTIONS FOR WRITING

Write an informal essay on one of the following topics:

The proper time of year for swimming
The habit of smoking
The most suitable clothes to wear to class
Homesickness
Varieties of movies
Social prestige in college
Weather
Mowing the lawn
Spending the week end
Traveling
Hunting
The best kind of conversation
Where and what to eat
Passing courses in college
What a home ought to be
Setting-up exercises
Shaving
Spending the night in a day coach
Death
How to be a gentleman
The cigar-store Indian
Nature at her best
Roadhogs

Love and a uniform
The magazines in the doctor's office
In-laws
City or country?
The church choir
How to be a bore
Cutting classes
Slacks
Absurdities of college life
Candid camera fans
The ingenuity shown in gadgets
Attractive books
Antiques
Weeds
Apartment life
Building a new house
The decay of courtesy among the younger generation
Summer fashions
Where to spend the summer
Driving a truck
Movies or the stage?
Casper Milquetoasts
The practical joker
Missing the train
Ferry boats
Subways

My Fishpond[1]

STEPHEN LEACOCK

IT LIES EMBOWERED in a little cup of the hills, my fishing pond. I made a last trip to it just as the season ended, when the autumn leaves of its great trees were turning color and rustling down to rest upon the still black water. So steep are the banks, so old and high the trees, that scarcely a puff of wind ever ruffles the surface of the pond. All around, it is as if the world were stilled into silence, and time blended into eternity.

I realized again as I looked at the pond what a beautiful, secluded spot it was, how natural its appeal to the heart of the angler. You turn off a country road, go sideways across a meadow and over a hill, and there it lies—a sheet of still water, with high, high banks, grown with great trees. Long years ago someone built a sawmill, all gone now, at the foot of the valley and threw back the water to make a pond, perhaps a quarter of a mile long. At the widest it must be nearly two hundred feet—the most skillful fisherman may make a full cast both ways. At the top end, where it runs narrow among stumps and rushes, there is no room to cast except with direction and great skill.

Let me say at once, so as to keep no mystery about it, that there are no fish in my pond. So far as I know there never have been. But I have never found that to make any difference. Certainly none to the men I bring there—my chance visitors from the outside world—for an afternoon of casting.

If there are no fish in the pond, at least they never know it. They never doubt it; they never ask, and I let it go at that.

It is well known hereabouts that I do not take anybody and everybody out to my fish-

pond. I only care to invite people who can really fish, who can cast a line—experts, and especially people from a distance to whom the whole neighborhood is new and attractive, the pond seen for the first time. If I took out ordinary men, especially men near home, they would very likely notice that they got no fish. The expert doesn't. He knows trout fishing too well. He knows that even in a really fine pond, such as he sees mine is, there are days when not a trout will rise. He'll explain it to you himself; and, having explained it, he is all the better pleased if he turns out to be right and they don't rise.

Trout, as everyone knows who is an angler, never rise after a rain, nor before one; it is impossible to get them to rise in the heat; and any chill in the air keeps them down. The absolutely right day is a still, cloudy day, but even then there are certain kinds of clouds that prevent a rising of the trout. Indeed, I have only to say to one of my expert friends, "Queer, they didn't bite!" and he's off to a good start with an explanation. There is such a tremendous lot to know about trout fishing that men who are keen on it can discuss theories of fishing by the hour.

Such theories we generally talk over—my guest of the occasion and I—as we make our preparations at the pond. You see, I keep there all the apparatus that goes with fishing —a punt, with lockers in the sides of it, a neat little dock built out of cedar (cedar attracts the trout), and, best of all, a little shelter house, a quaint little place like a pagoda, close beside the water and yet under the trees. Inside is tackle, all sorts of tackle, hanging round the walls in a mixture of carelessness and order.

"Look, old man," I say, "if you like to try a running paternoster, take this one," or,

[1] From the *Atlantic Monthly*, CLVIII (December, 1936), 720. Reprinted by permission of the author and of the *Atlantic Monthly*.

"Have you ever seen these Japanese leads? No, they're not a gut; they're a sort of floss."

"I doubt if I can land one with that," he says.

"Perhaps not," I answer. In fact, I'm sure he couldn't: there isn't any to land.

On pegs in the pagoda hangs a waterproof mackintosh or two, for you never know—you may be caught in a shower just when the trout are starting to rise. Then, of course, a sort of cellarette cupboard with decanters and bottles, and gingersnaps, and perhaps an odd pot of anchovy paste—no one wants to quit good fishing for mere hunger. Nor does any real angler care to begin fishing without taking just a drop (Just a touch—be careful! Whoa! Whoa!) of something to keep out the cold, or to wish good luck for the chances of the day.

I always find, when I bring out one of my friends, that these mere preparatives or preparations, these preliminaries of angling, are the best part of it. Often they take half an hour. There is so much to discuss—the question of weights of tackle, the color of the fly to use, and broad general questions of theory, such as whether it matters what kind of hat a man wears. It seems that trout will rise for some hats, and for others not. One of my best guests, who has written a whole book on fly fishing, is particularly strong on hats and color. "I don't think I'd wear that hat, old man," he says; "much too dark for a day like this." "I wore it all last month," I said. "So you might, but that was August. I wouldn't wear a dark hat in September; and that tie is too dark a blue, old man."

So I knew that that made it all right. I kept the hat on. We had a grand afternoon; we got no fish.

I admit that the lack of fish in my pond requires sometimes a little tact in management. The guest gets a little restless. So I say to him, "You certainly have the knack of casting!"—and he gets so absorbed in casting farther and farther that he forgets the fish. Or I take him toward the upper end and he gets his line caught on bulrush—that might

be a bite. Or, if he still keeps restless, I say suddenly, "Hush! Was that a fish jumped?" That will silence any true angler instantly. "You stand in the bow," I whisper, "and I'll paddle gently in that direction." It's the *whispering* that does it. We are still a hundred yards away from any trout that could hear us even if a trout were there. But that makes no difference. Some of the men I take out begin to whisper a mile away from the pond and come home whispering.

You see, after all, what with frogs jumping, and catching the line in bulrushes, or pulling up a waterlogged chip nearly to the top, they don't really know—my guests don't —whether they have hooked something or not. Indeed, after a little lapse of time, they think they did: they talk of the "big one they lost"—a thing over which any angler gets sentimental in retrospect. "Do you remember," they say to me months later at our club in the city, "that big trout I lost up on your fishpond last summer?" "Indeed I do," I say. "Did you ever get him later on?" "No, never," I answer. (Neither him nor any other.)

Yet the illusion holds good. And besides, you never can tell: there *might* be trout in the pond. Why not? After all, why shouldn't there be a trout in the pond? You take a pond like that and there ought to be trout in it!

Whenever the sight of the pond bursts on the eyes of a new guest he stands entranced. "What a wonderful place for trout!" he exclaims. "Isn't it?" I answer. "No wonder you'd get trout in a pond like that." "No wonder at all." "You don't need to stock it at all, I suppose?" "Stock it!" I laugh at the idea. Stock a pond like that! Well, I guess not!

Perhaps one of the best and most alluring touches is fishing out of season—just a day or two after the season has closed. Any fisherman knows how keen is the regret at each expiring season—swallowed up and lost in the glory of the fading autumn. So if a guest turns up just then I say, "I know it's out of season, but I thought you might care to take a run out to the pond anyway and have a look at it." He can't resist. By the time he's in the pagoda and has a couple of small drinks (Careful, not too much! Whoa! Whoa!) he decides there can be no harm in making a cast or two. "I suppose," he says, "you never have any trouble with the inspectors?" "Oh, no," I answer; "they never think of troubling me." And with that we settle down to an afternoon of it. "I'm glad," says the guest at the end, "that they weren't rising. After all, we had just the same fun as if they were."

That's it: illusion! How much of life is like that! It's the *idea* of the thing that counts, not the reality. You don't need fish for fishing, any more than you need partridge for partridge shooting, or gold for gold mining. Just the illusion or expectation.

So I am going back now to the city and to my club, where we shall fish all winter, hooking up big ones, but losing the ones bigger still, hooking two trout at one throw —three at a throw!—and for me, behind it all, the memory of my fishing pond darkening under the falling leaves. . . . **At least it has** made my friends happy.

SUGGESTIONS FOR STUDY

1. What does the author **gain by his** opening description?

2. Why does the author **state immediately** that no fish are in his pond? **Would** he have gained anything by withholding **his** revelation until later?

3. Why are only experts invited to the pond?

4. What traits of human **nature** are depicted in the essay that make **it** of humorous significance?

5. What basic idea or thesis is the author trying to portray? What word **is** of primary importance in understanding this basic idea?

6. What means does the author use to develop his various topic ideas?

7. Although the essay is conversational and informal, do you find an underlying pattern which the author follows?

8. Define the following words from the essay: embowered, pagoda, decanters, retrospect, expiring.

On the Floor of the Library[1]

SIMEON STRUNSKY

UNFORTUNATE PEOPLE who never read detective novels; or, worse still, those who pick up a mystery story and wonder what in the world anyone can see in the book to keep him up till 1:30 in the morning with intermittent trips to the cold meat in the icebox; or, worst of all, those who read the first chapter and then turn to the end to see who did the killing—such unfortunates think they are sufficiently kind when they describe the habit as a mild vice, not so hard on the family as liquor or drugs, but pernicious for the eyesight. They think they are 100 per cent charitable when they tolerate the practice as one form of escape from the realities of a difficult world.

To such outsiders it is not given to understand that the *Mystery of the Chintz Room* or the *Smile of Gautama* is not an escape from the world but an initiation. They simply do not know that a select course in reading from Conan Doyle to Carolyn Wells is a guide to the institutions, culture, and life outlook of the nations from China to Chile. I have set down below a mere fragment of the picture of humanity which may be built up by devoting not more than one evening a fortnight to this field of research hitherto neglected by the sociologists. The list might easily be multiplied by twenty.

(1) The common belief that the British are

[1] From Simeon Strunsky, *Sinbad and His Friends* (New York, 1921). Reprinted by permission of Henry Holt & Co.

an open-air people is utterly opposed to the facts. When a member of the British nobility or upper middle classes is found dead in his bed, with a mystic Oriental symbol scrawled in blood on the sheets, the mystery is rendered all the more baffling by the fact that all the windows are hermetically sealed, the door is locked from within, the transom has not been opened for years, and the ventilators are choked up—in fact, the plumbers were scheduled to arrive on the morning after the tragedy. If it were not for that grisly Oriental symbol, the obvious conclusion would be that the victim perished for lack of a breath of fresh air. Given such a bedroom—and nearly all fatal bedrooms in our fiction are of this kind—and it is a question which is the greater puzzle: how the murderer managed to get in and escape, or how the victim managed to keep alive until the murderer got at him.

(2) Economy and resourcefulness are not among the virtues of the classes addicted to being murdered in their bedrooms or in their libraries. Twenty years after the tragedy the ghastly stain is still there on the floor. All attempts at erasing the spot in the course of twenty years have failed. What the scrubbing expense must have been, even if we reckon at a much lower rate than the prevailing scale of domestic wages today, is obvious. What the doctor's expenses have been in the way of treatment for nervous derangements inflicted by the ghastly stain on various members of the family is easily calculable. Yet no one in all these twenty years seems to have thought of replacing the bloodstained plank with a new one, at a trifling cost if done by day labor, and for a really insignificant sum if ordered from a collapsible bungalow manufacturer.

(3) Weekend guests in British baronial mansions or in wealthy residences on Long Island drink too much black coffee before going to bed. Then they lie awake all night. That is why about two in the morning they hear that queer, shuffling footfall down the hall to which at the moment they attach no particular meaning and the dread significance of which they realize only next morning when the host is found dead on the library carpet with his eyes fixed in a ghastly stare on the ceiling.

(4) The number of servants who have been in the employ of wealthy families addicted to violent deaths, for a period of forty years and up, and for whose fidelity the survivors can vouch as confidently as for their own husbands and wives, is truly astounding. Here, indeed, my friends, the psychoanalysts, may find the secret of my own passion for the mystery novel. Having in recent years never succeeded in keeping a houseworker for more than a couple of months, it is perfectly comprehensible how all my suppressed desires draw me to these faithful servants who stay forty years and then prefer to be victims of cruel suspicion by the coroner rather than bring disgrace on the family. It is not overstating the case to say that if only I could find a plain cook who will stay with us for forty years, I am perfectly willing to take a chance at being found at the end of the period upon the floor of my library with the ivory-handled paper cutter through my heart. For that matter, I should welcome an unsuccessful attempt at murder if the assassin is not apprehended until he has found the paper-cutter. As it is, I have to tear the pages open by pulling with both hands from the top.

(5) The victims of foul play in the best British and American families never, absolutely never, cut themselves when shaving, or scrape the skin, or raise a blister. That is how the investigator from Scotland Yard or from his private office in the Equitable Life Building is enabled to detect the cause of death in an almost imperceptible red spot under the chin which the local police have overlooked and which he immediately recognizes as the characteristic bite of the rare South American adder, *Megaloptera Bandanna*. That method, if applied to the average man after he has shaved a second time for the theater, would suggest that he had been

done to death by the greater part of the reptilian fauna of the South American forests.

(6) Closely allied to the preceding topic, it appears that the principal occupation of the inhabitants of South America is the manufacture or the jealous preservation of the secret of instantaneously deadly poisons unknown to modern science and leaving no visible after-effects, excepting, of course, the corpse.

(7) Insurance premiums on the lives of the British nobility must be really enormous at Lloyd's. At least one third of the members of the House of Lords are killed every year on the floor of their libraries or at the end of their yew walks close to the abandoned garden pavilion. But it is worse than that. If you have on the one hand the aged Duke of Beaucaire with an income of a million a year, and if you have on the other hand the third son of his fifth younger brother, who was wild at school and has lost himself somewhere on the Rand, and if you have no less than seven lives intervening between the scapegrace nephew and the ducal title, then these seven lives are sure to be wiped out by an earthquake or a fire or a marine disaster, and it only remains for the man who masquerades as the nephew (the real nephew having died of drink in Johannesburg) to come home and finish up the Duke.

(8) Nearly everybody in a mystery novel is a consummate athlete. They escape the vigilance of the detective who is disguised as a taxi-driver, or the pursuing avengers, by getting into a taxicab at one door and leaving by the other while the cab is in motion. This will interest people coming home from the theater who have sometimes tried to open a taxi door from the inside.

(9) The wealth of Burma and Tibet in priceless jewels would be enough to pay the German indemnity ten times over. An emerald like the Eye of Gautama, a sapphire like the Hope of Asoka, a ruby like the Doom of Dhalatpur—all of them stolen from the forehead of sacred images by European adventurers—would be enough to finance British trade with Russia for the next fifty years. The fields of Burma and Tibet are cultivated entirely by women. The male population consists solely of priests, who are off in the West for the purpose of recovering the hallowed jewels and visiting the vengeance of Brahmaputra on the sacrilegious plunderers. Usually they are disguised as elevator runners at the Savoy or the St. Regis.

People who do not know, think detective fiction is a vice, whereas, it is, like Mr. H. G. Wells, a liberal education.

SUGGESTIONS FOR STUDY

1. What is the tone of the opening paragraph? Is this tone maintained throughout the essay?
2. What criticism of detective stories is implied by the essay?
3. Is the general purpose of the writer to instruct the reader?
4. Who are Conan Doyle and Carolyn Wells?
5. Define the following words from the essay: intermittent, hermetically, imperceptible, ducal, indemnity, hallowed.

A Little Moral Advice

SYDNEY SMITH

IT IS SURPRISING to see for what foolish causes men hang themselves. The most silly repulse, the most trifling ruffle of temper, or derangement of stomach, anything seems to justify an appeal to the razor or the cord. I have a contempt for persons who destroy themselves. Live on, and look evil in the face; walk up to it, and you will find it less than you imagined, and often you will not find it at all; for it will recede as you advance.

Any fool may be a suicide. When you are in a melancholy fit, first suspect the body, appeal to rhubarb and calomel, and send for the apothecary; a little bit of gristle sticking in the wrong place, an untimely consumption of custard, excessive gooseberries, often cover the mind with clouds and bring on the most distressing views of human life.

I start up at two o'clock in the morning after my first sleep, in an agony of terror, and feel all the weight of life upon my soul. It is impossible that I can bring up such a family of children, my sons and daughters will be beggars; I shall live to see those whom I loved exposed to the scorns and contumely of the world!—But stop, thou child of sorrow, and humble imitator of Job, and tell me on what you dined. Was not there soup and salmon, and then a plate of beef, and then duck, blancmange, cream cheese, diluted with beer, claret, champagne, hock, tea, coffee, and noyeau? And after all this, you talk of the *mind* and the evils of life! These kinds of cases do not need meditation, but magnesia. Take short views of life. What am I to do in these times with such a family of children? So I argued, and lived dejected and with little hope; but the difficulty vanished as life went on. An uncle died, and left me some money; an aunt died, and left me more; my daughter married well; I had two or three appointments, and before life was half over became a prosperous man. And so will you. Everyone has uncles and aunts who are mortal; friends start up out of the earth; time brings a thousand chances in your favor; legacies fall from the clouds. Nothing so absurd as to sit down and wring your hands because all the good which may happen to you in twenty years has not taken place at this precise moment.

The greatest happiness which can happen to anyone is to cultivate a love of reading. Study is often dull because it is improperly managed. I make no apology for speaking of myself, for as I write anonymously nobody knows who I am, and if I did not, very few would be the wiser—but every man speaks more firmly when he speaks from his own experience. I read four books at a time; some classical book perhaps on Monday, Wednesday, and Friday mornings. The *History of France*, we will say, on the evenings of the same days. On Tuesday, Thursday, and Saturday, Mosheim or Lardner, and in the evenings of those days, Reynolds' Lectures, or Burns' Travels. Then I always have a standing book of poetry, and a novel to read when I am in the humor to read nothing else. Then I translate some French into English one day, and retranslate it the next; so that I have seven or eight pursuits going on at the same time, and this produces the cheerfulness of diversity, and avoids that gloom which proceeds from hanging a long while over a single book. I do not recommend this as a receipt for becoming a learned man, but for becoming a cheerful one.

Nothing contributes more certainly to the animal spirits than benevolence. Servants and common people are always about you; make moderate attempts to please everybody, and the effort will insensibly lead you to a more happy state of mind. Pleasure is very reflective, and if you give it you will feel it. The pleasure you give by kindness of manner returns to you, and often with compound interest. The receipt for cheerfulness is not to have one motive only in the day for living, but a number of little motives; a man who from the time he rises till bedtime conducts himself like a gentleman, who throws some little condescension into his manner to superiors, and who is always contriving to soften the distance between himself and the poor and ignorant, is always improving his animal spirits, and adding to his happiness.

I recommend lights as a great improver of animal spirits. How is it possible to be happy with two mold candles ill snuffed? You may be virtuous, and wise, and good, but two candles will not do for animal spirits. Every night the room in which I sit is lighted up like a town after a great naval victory, and in this cereous galaxy and with a blazing fire, it is scarcely possible to be low-spirited, a thousand pleasing images spring up in the mind, and I can see the little blue demons scampering off like parish boys pursued by the beadle.

SUGGESTIONS FOR STUDY

1. What is Smith's attitude toward suicide? State his thesis.

2. On what may one often blame a melancholy view of human life?

3. Why should one not despair when faced with misfortune?

4. What suggestions for happiness does Smith offer?

5. By what means does Smith secure concreteness of writing?

6. In what way is this an informal essay? Why can it not be called a formal treatise on morals?

7. Make a topic outline of this essay. This exercise will acquaint you with the logical organization of the writing.

INDEX

Abbreviations: 139; in research paper, 449

Abraham Lincoln: The War Years, Carl Sandburg, reviewed by C. A. Beard, 485

Abridged dictionary, 154

Absolute infinitive phrase, 75

Abstract words, 172

Active voice, 66

Adams, Henry, "Jay Gould," WORKBOOK, Exercise 48

Adams, J. T., "The Business Type," 296

Adjectives: 61, 68; distinguished from adverbs, 105; degree, 106; correct form, 106; misplaced, 109

Adjective clause: 76; diagramed, 90

"Adventure of a Turtle," John Steinbeck, 360

Adverbs: 61, 69; distinguished from adjectives, 105; in double negatives, 106; having two forms, 106; misplaced, 109

Adverbs, conjunctive, 70

Adverbial clause: 76; diagramed, 90; punctuated in introductory position, 121

Advice to Young Men, William Cobbett, 215

Agreement: subject and predicate, 98; pronoun and antecedent, 102

"Aim of a University Course, The," J. H. Newman, 215

"American Way of Life, The," Dorothy Thompson, 143

Analogy, reasoning by, 309

Analysis in exposition: 293; formal, 293; informal, 294

Antecedent of pronoun, 101

Antonyms, 157

"Apology for Idlers, An," R. L. Stevenson, 22

Apostrophe, 133

"Apparition, The," Guy de Maupassant, 372

Appearance of manuscript, 48

"Apples," John Burroughs, 335

Application, letter of, 522

Appositive: 75; punctuation of, 119; diagramed, 89

Argument against the man, 309

Argument to the people, 310

Argumentation: 304; proposition, 304; issues, 304; methods of reasoning, 305; applied to writing, 308; final precautions, 309; criticism of, 481

Arnold, Matthew, "The Last Word," WORKBOOK, Exercise 51

Art of Scientific Investigation, The, W. I. B. Beveridge, reviewed, 483

Articles, definite and indefinite, 69

Audience, 50

Austen, Jane: *Northanger Abbey,* 132; *Pride and Prejudice,* 494

Author: appraisal of, in research, 445; in criticism, 481

"Author's Account of Himself, The," Washington Irving, 209

Autobiography, 509

Autobiography, Benjamin Franklin, 512

Autobiography, Leigh Hunt, 512

Autocrat of the Breakfast Table, The, O. W. Holmes, 216

Auxiliary verb, 65

"Baker's Blue-Jay Yarn," Mark Twain, 361

Barr, Stringfellow, *Let's Join the Human Race,* 302

"Basic English for Science," T. B. Haber, 175

Basis of classification in outlining, 233, 294

"Bathtub," W. P. Gerhard, 264

Beard, C. A., review of *Abraham Lincoln: The War Years,* 485

Becker, Carl, "Where Are We?" 4

Berger, Meyer, "Sidewalk Fisherman," 471

"Be Your Own Weatherman," Carl Warden, 277

Bible, quotation from, 115, 172

Bibliography: cards, 441; form, 448

Biographical dictionaries, 438

Biographical sketch, 500

Biography: 488; the character, 488; character sketch, 493; biographical sketch, 500; autobiography, 509

Boas, Franz, *The Diffusion of Cultural Traits,* WORKBOOK, Exercise 48

Boeck, Lois, "The Conspiracy of Aaron Burr," 450

Book indexes, general, 436

Book review: 480; how to begin, 480; how to criticize exposition and argumentation, 481; how to criticize narration, 481; writing the review, 482

Book reviews, illustrative short reviews, 483

Brackets, 129

Brandel, Marc, "The Law-Abiding," 417

Brandt, J. A., "I Can't Quite Hear You, Doctor," 178

"Brandy for Breakfast," L. W. Meynell, 384

Broughton, Lord, *Recollections of a Long Life,* 246

Browning, Robert, "Prospice," WORKBOOK, Exercise 50

Buchan, John, "My America," 221

Burke, Edmund, "Speech on Conciliation with the Colonies," 204

"Burns," Thomas Carlyle, 214

Burroughs, John, "Apples," 335

Bush, Douglas, "Scholars, Poor and Simple," 203, 216

Business letter: 520; form, 520; content, 521

"Business Type, The," J. T. Adams, 296

Byron, John Nichol, 215, 218

Capitalization, 136

"Captain Ahab," Herman Melville, 341

Card catalogue, 435

Caret, 135

Carlyle, Thomas: from "The Hero as Man of Letters," 27; "Burns," 214

Case: nouns, 62; pronouns, 103; possessive for both nouns and pronouns, 133

Cause and effect, paragraph development by, 211

Character, the, 488

Character sketch, 493

Characterization: in narrative, 353; analysis of, in criticism, 481

535

Childs, M. W., "Hu Shih: Sage of Modern China," 501
"Christmas Breakfast," Herman Smith, 336
"Christmas Tree," Herman Smith, 331
Circumlocution, 170
Claim letter, 522
Classification in definition, 260
Clauses: 76; diagramed, 90; misplaced, 109
Clichés: 186; in business letters, 521
"Cliché Expert Takes the Stand, The," Frank Sullivan, 187
Climax in the sentence, 115
Cloister and the Hearth, The, Charles Reade, 204, 205
Cobbett, William: *Advice to a Young Man,* 215; "Grammar," 78
Coherence: of the paragraph, 205; of the whole composition, 231
Collective noun, agreement with, 99
"College Football 'Expendable,'" R. M. Hutchins, 219
Colloquialisms, 168
Colon, 125
"Color of Mama Josefina's Life, The," Mary Main, 412
Comma, 118
Comma splice, 122
Common adjectives, 69
Common level of usage, 166
Common noun, 62
Comparative degree: adjectives, 68; adverbs, 69
Comparison, paragraph development by, 212
Comparison, proper usage of, in sentences, 96, 104
Complements, 73
Complete predicate, 72
Complete predication, 73
Complete sentences, 95
Complete subject, 72
Complex sentence: 77; diagramed, 90
Compound-complex sentence, 77
Compound predicate: 72; diagramed, 88
Compound preposition, 71
Compound sentence: 77; diagramed, 91; punctuated, 118, 124; use of, 111, 115, 116
Compound subject, 72; diagramed, 88
Conciseness: of sentences, 116; of diction, 170; of business letters, 521
Conclusions: concluding paragraphs, 218; in narrative, 354; in letters of application, 523
Concrete words, 172, 325
"Conditions of Art, The," John Ruskin, 238
Conflict in narrative, 348
Conjugation of verbs, 66
Conjunctions: 61, 70; proper use of, 106; proper use of correlatives, 112
Conjunctive adverb, 70
Connectives: 73; proper use of, 106
Connotation: 184; in description, 326
"Conspiracy of Aaron Burr, The," Lois Boeck, 450
Conspiracy of Pontiac, The, Francis Parkman, 247
Contrast, paragraph development by, 212
"Co-operation versus Competition," John Ruskin, 174
Co-ordinating conjunctions: 70; proper use of, 107

Co-ordination, excessive, 111
Co-ordinate points in outlining, 232
Corrections in manuscript, 54
Correlative conjunctions, proper use of, 112
"Country Gentlemen, The," T. B. Macaulay, 490
Courtesy in the business letter, 522
Cowper, William, letter by, 517
Cozzens, J. G., "Foot in It," 376
Crane, Stephen, "The Merry-Go-Round," 333
"Credo," Thomas Wolfe, 145
Criticism, principles of, 480
Cross, W. L., "My Experience as a Book Agent," 56
"Customhouse, The," Nathaniel Hawthorne, 511

Dana, R. H., *Two Years before the Mast,* 204
Dangling modifiers, 109
Dash, 127
Day, Clarence, "There Was a Young Englishman," 507
Declarative sentence, 72
"Decline of Attention, The," Clifton Fadiman, 38
Deductive reasoning, 307
Definite article, 69
Definition: 260; intensive, 260; extensive, 262
De Maupassant, Guy: *Pierre et Jean,* 325; "The Apparition," 372
Demonstrative pronoun, 63
Denotation: 184; in description, 326
Dependent clause, 76
Description: 324; accurate observation, 324; choice of words, 325; point of view, 327; dominant impression, 328; choice of details, 328; sense impressions, 329
Detail, paragraph development by, 211
Details, choice of, in description, 328
Detzer, Karl, "The Metamorphosis of Hell Week," 84
Development, paragraph, 210
Devoe, Alan, "Why I Am a Naturalist," 513
Diagraming, 87
Dialogue: paragraphing, 205; punctuating, 131
Diamant, Gertrude: "Rain in Mexico," 332; "Making Tortillas," 334; "Mexico City," 337; "Finding a Room," 359
Dickens, Charles, *Sketches by Boz,* 329
Diction: levels of, 166; economy of, 170; glossary of, 197
Dictionaries: 154, 437
Dictionary of American History, ed. J. T. Adams, reviewed by Paul Palmer, 484
Differentiation in definition, 261
Diffusion of Cultural Traits, The, Franz Boas, WORKBOOK, Exercise 48
"Digging a Well," John Muir, 512
"Dinner at Cousin Lil's," Herman Smith, 336
"Dinner Party, The," Mona Gardner, 364
Direct object: 74; diagramed, 87
Direct quotation: punctuating, 131; on note cards, 443
"Do Animals Talk?" Lillian Harriman, 57
Dominant impression, 328
"Donjon," 264
Dreamthorp, Alexander Smith, 203

"Duel in the Long Shrubbery, The," R. L. Stevenson, 351

Dumas, Alexander, *The Three Musketeers*, 493

Du Pont, H. B., "Technology—Hope or Hobgoblin?" 250

"Early Morning," Siegfried Sassoon, 334

"Earthquakes," Joseph Lynch, 283

Eastman, Max, "Humor and America," 252

Economy of diction, 170

"Electrical 'Bath' in Yellowstone, An," W. B. Sanborn, 81

Elimination, paragraph development by, 213

"Elk, The," E. A. Poe, 217

Ellipsis mark, 135

Elliptical clause, dangling, 110

Emerson, R. W., "Self-Reliance," 214

"Emotional Meanings," R. H. Thouless, 188

Emphasis: sentence, 114; paragraph, 217; whole composition, 232

Emphatic form of the verb, 65

Encyclopedias, 437

"English Admirals, The," R. L. Stevenson, 217

"Enterprise and Old Iron," John Patric, 477

Erasures and corrections, 47

Errors in reasoning, 305, 307, 309, 444

Essay, informal, 525

"Essay on Johnson," T. B. Macaulay, 247

Ethics concerning sources, 55

Euphemisms, 186

"Eustacia Vye," Thomas Hardy, 341

Evaluating sources in research, 444

"Evening Service, The," R. C. Hutchinson, 366

Evidence, evaluating, 444

Excessive co-ordination, 111

Exclamation point: 127; in direct quotation, 131

Exclamatory sentence, 72

Expletive: 73; diagramed, 89

Exposition: 260; definition, 260; process, 268; mechanisms and organizations, 279; analysis, 293

Expository analysis of the sentence, 86

Extensive definition, 262

Eye movements in reading, 21

Fadiman, Clifton, "The Decline of Attention," 38

Fallacies in reasoning, 305, 307, 309, 444

"Farewell Address," George Washington, 247

"Farmhouse Cellar," Herman Smith, 339

Faulkner, William, "Nobel Prize Acceptance Speech," 249

"Featherbeds and Parnassus," Carol Hovious, 158

Feature Article: 464; finding ideas, 464; making the article interesting, 465; use of library research, 465; use of the interview, 466

Fielding, Henry, "On the Knowledge of the Character of Men," 219

"Fifty Ideas for Newspaper Features," 467

Figures of speech: 185; in description, 326

"Finding a Room," Gertrude Diamant, 359

"First Inaugural Address," Thomas Jefferson, WORKBOOK, Exercise 49

Flexner, Abraham, "The Usefulness of Useless Knowledge," 212

Foord, A. S., "Studies That Build Men of Character," 6

"Foot in It," J. G. Cozzens, 376

Footnotes, 446

Foreshadowing in narrative, 354

Foreword to students, 1

Form and appearance of manuscript, 48

Formal analysis, 293

Formal note, 519

Fors Clavigera, John Ruskin, 213

Foster, W. T., "Should Students Study?" 315

Fractions, use of hyphens with, 135

Fragmentary sentences, 95

Franklin, Benjamin: "Proposed New Version of the Bible," 172; *Autobiography*, 512

Freeman, M. W., "A New England Nun," 405

Friendly letter, 516

"Furnished Room, The," O. Henry, 340

Future perfect tense, 65

Future tense, 65

Gardiner, A. G., "On Word Magic," 195

Gardner, Mona, "The Dinner Party," 364

Garland, Hamlin, "Walt Whitman Old and Poor," 496

Gender of nouns, 62

General purpose, 51

General words, 172

"Gentleman, A," J. H. Newman, 267

Gerhard, W. P., "Bathtub," 264

Gerund: 71; diagramed, 87; dangling, 110

Gerund phrase, 75

Gilded Age, The, Mark Twain and C. D. Warner, 173

Glossary of Usage, 197

Godfrey, Mary, letters by, 519

Goldsmith, Oliver, 526

"Grammar," William Cobbett, 78

Grammar and the sentence: 61; parts of speech, 61; sentence, 72; analyzing the sentence, 86; applying grammatical principles, 95; writing effective sentences, 114; punctuation, 117; mechanics, 136

Greeting: of a friendly letter, 516; of a business letter, 520

Griswold, W. S., "A Little Learning," 9

Haber, T. B., "Basic English for Science," 175

"Happiest Man on Earth, The," Albert Maltz, 378

Hardy, Thomas, "Eustacia Vye," 341

Harriman, Lillian, "Do Animals Talk?" 57

Harte, Bret, "The Outcasts of Poker Flat," 350

Hawthorne, Nathaniel, "The Customhouse," 511

Hay, T. R., review by, 480

Hazlitt, William, "On Familiar Style," 247

Heading: of a friendly letter, 516; of a business letter, 520

Henry, O., "The Furnished Room," 340

"Hero as Man of Letters, The," Thomas Carlyle, 27

"Heywood," Christopher Morley, 495

Holbrook, Weare, "You Know Me, Allergy," 215

Holmes, O. W.: *Over the Teacups*, 216; *The Autocrat of the Breakfast Table*, 216

Hovious, Carol, "Featherbeds and Parnassus," 158

"How to Detect Propaganda," 273

"How to Learn," E. S. Robinson, 23

"How to Misunderstand the USA," Tibor Koeves, 148

"How to Write a Book," Harold Nicolson, 270

"Humor and America," Max Eastman, 252

Hunt, Leigh, *Autobiography,* 512

"Hu Shih: Sage of Modern China," M. W. Childs, 501

Hutchins, R. M., "College Football 'Expendable,'" 219

Hutchinson, R. C.: "The Wind," 335; "A Road in England," 343; "The Evening Service," 366

Hutchison, R. C., "Work Your Way through College?" 312

Hyperbole, 185

Hyphen, 134

Ibid., 448

"I Can't Quite Hear You, Doctor," J. A. Brandt, 178

"I Chose America," Percy Waxman, 141

Ignoring the issues, 310

"I Have Not Yet Begun to Fight," C. L. Lewis, 459

Illiteracies, 169

Illusion of reality in narration, 357

Illustration, paragraph development by, 212

Images in description, 325

Imaginative words, 184

Imperative mood, 65

Imperative sentence, 72

Incomplete comparison, 96

Incomplete sentences, 95

Indefinite article, 69

Indefinite pronoun, 63

Indention, 46

Independent clause, 76

Indexes: book, 436; periodical, 437

Indicative mood, 65

Indirect object: 74; diagramed, 89

Indirect quotation on note cards, 443

Inductive reasoning, 305

Inevitability in narration, 355

Infinitive: 71; absolute, 75; infinitive phrase, 76; diagramed, 87; dangling, 110; split, 112

Informal analysis, 294

Informal essay, 525

Initial situation in narration, 348

Ink, use of, 46

Intensive definition, 260

Intensive pronoun: 63; faulty use of, 105

Interjection, 61

Interrogative pronoun, 63

Interrogative sentence, 72

Interview for a feature article, 466

Intransitive verb, 63, 73

Introduction: introductory paragraphs, 217; in narration, 348; in friendly letters, 518; in claim letters, 522; in letters of application, 522

Inversion in sentence structure, 114

Irregular sentences, 78

Irregular verbs, 63

Irving, Washington, "The Author's Account of Himself," 209

Issues in argumentation, 304

Italics, 138

Its, it's, 199

Jargon, 170

"Jay Gould," Henry Adams, WORKBOOK, Exercise 48

Jefferies, Richard, "Sounds in Late Summer," 333

Jefferson, Thomas, "First Inaugural Address," WORKBOOK, Exercise 49

Jeffrey, Francis, 482

Kane, H. T., "Water Hyacinths," 331

Kantor, MacKinlay, "That Greek Dog," 426

Kazan, Elia, "Where I Stand," 147

King-Hall, Stephen, "World Government or World Destruction?" 321

Koeves, Tibor, "How to Misunderstand the USA," 148

Lamb, Charles, letters by, 518, 527

Landor, W. S.: 480; "So Then, I Feel Not Deeply!" WORKBOOK, Exercise 51

"Last Word, The," Matthew Arnold, WORKBOOK, Exercise 51

"Laura," H. H. Munro, 393

"Law-Abiding, The," Marc Brandel, 417

Leacock, Stephen, "My Fishpond," 528

Legibility, 47

Length of paragraphs, 202

Let's Join the Human Race, Stringfellow Barr, 302

Letters: 516; friendly letter, 516; formal note, 519; business letter, 520; claim letter, 522; letter of application, 522

Levels of usage: 166; common, 166; literary, 167; technical, 167; colloquial, 168; slang, 168; illiterate, 169

Lewis, C. L., "I Have Not Yet Begun to Fight," 459

Library, use of, 435

Library research for a feature story, 465

Lie, lay, 199

"Life without Principle," Henry Thoreau, 213, 216

Lincoln, Abraham: "Speech at Springfield," 213; "Speech at the Cooper Institute," WORKBOOK, Exercise 50

Linke, Lilo, review by, 480

Linking verb, 63, 69, 73

Literary indebtedness, 55, 442

Literary level of usage, 167

Litotes, 185

"Little Learning, A," W. S. Griswold, 9

"Little Moral Advice, A," Sydney Smith, 532

Loc. cit., 448

Look Homeward, Angel, Thomas Wolfe, 326

Loose sentence, 114

Lowell, J. R., "On a Certain Condescension in Foreigners," 213, 246

Lynch, Joseph, "Earthquakes," 283

Macaulay, T. B.: "Essay on Johnson," 247; "The Country Gentlemen," 490

Macbeth, William Shakespeare, 185

Main, Mary, "The Color of Mama Josefina's Life," 412

"Making Tortillas," Gertrude Diamant, 334

Maltz, Albert, "The Happiest Man on Earth," 378

"Man with Camera," R. W. Wagner, 212

Manuscript: 46; paper, 46; ink, 46; title, 46; indention, 46; margins, 46; erasures and corrections, 47; paging and endorsing, 47; legibility, 47; instructions for typing, 47

Margins, 46

"Masque of the Red Death, The," E. A. Poe, 350

Master of Ballantrae, The, R. L. Stevenson, 351

McCartney, E. S., "Some Participles I Have Met," 215

Mechanics: 136; capitals, 136; italics, 138; abbreviations, 139; numbers, 140

Mechanisms and organizations, 279

Melville, Herman, "Captain Ahab," 341

"Merry-Go-Round, The," Stephen Crane, 333

"Metamorphosis of Hell Week, The," Karl Detzer, 84

Metaphor, 185

"Mexico City," Gertrude Diamant, 337

Meyer, Rose D., "The Witch Tree," 55

Meynell, L. W., "Brandy for Breakfast," 384

Mikkelsen, Strand, "Skiing," 240

Milton, John: on the value of language, 3; "Lycidas," analyzed, 34; *Of Education,* WORKBOOK, Exercise 49

Misplaced modifiers, 108

Mixed constructions, 111

Mixed figures of speech, 185

Modifiers: 73; misplaced, 108; squinting, 109

Mood: 65; unnecessary shift of, 114

Moore, Thomas, letters by, 518

More about Words, M. S. Ernst, reviewed, 483

Morley, Christopher, "Heywood," 495

Muir, John, "Digging a Well," 512

Munro, H. H., "Laura," 393

"My America," John Buchan, 221

"My Experience as a Book Agent," W. L. Cross, 56

"My Fishpond," Stephen Leacock, 528

Narration: 347; paragraphing, 204; initial situation, 348; action, 351; conclusion, 354; essential qualities of good narration, 356; simple narrative, 358; short story, 370

"New England Nun, A," M. W. Freeman, 405

Newman, J. H.: "The Aim of a University Course," 215; "A Gentleman," 267

Nichol, John, *Byron,* 215, 218

Nicolson, Harold, "How to Write a Book," 270

"Nobel Prize Acceptance Speech," William Faulkner, 249

Nominative absolute: 75; diagramed, 89

Nominative of address: 75; diagramed, 89

Nonrestrictive phrases and clauses, 119

Note, formal, 519

Note-taking, 442

Noun: 61, 62; possessive case, 133; spelling the plural of, 162

Noun clause: 76; diagramed, 89

Number: of nouns, 62; of verbs, 66

Numbers, 140

Object of the preposition, 70

Objective complement: 74; diagramed, 89

Objective infinitive: 75; diagramed, 89

Observation in description, 324

"Of Education," John Milton, WORKBOOK, Exercise 49

"Office Bore, The," Mark Twain, 489

"Of Kings' Treasuries," John Ruskin, 29

"On a Certain Condescension in Foreigners," J. R. Lowell, 203, 246

"On Familiar Style," William Hazlitt, 247

"On Observing Colors," John Ruskin, 329

"On the Floor of the Library," Simeon Strunsky, 530

"On the Knowledge of the Characters of Men," Henry Fielding, 219

"On Word Magic," A. G. Gardiner, 195

Op. cit., 448

Orientation: a foreword to students, 1; reading and studying, 16; first considerations, 46

Ornamental phraseology, avoidance of, 117, 171

"Outcasts of Poker Flat, The," Bret Harte, 350

Outline: 232; in planning the paper, 51; for paragraph coherence, 206; form, 232; composition, 232; topic outline, 233; sentence outline, 234; use with the research paper, 446

Over the Teacups, O. W. Holmes, 214

Paging and endorsing, 47

Palmer, P. A., review of *Dictionary of American History,* 484

Paper, kind to use in writing, 46

Paragraph: 202; definition, 202; unity, coherence, emphasis, 205; paragraph development, 210; introduction and conclusion, 216

Parallelism: in sentence structure, 112; for paragraph coherence, 207; in outlining, 234

Parentheses, 128

Parkman, Francis, *The Conspiracy of Pontiac,* 247

Participle: 71; diagramed, 87; dangling, 110; participial phrase, 75

Partition in formal analysis, 465

Parts of speech: 61; noun, 62; pronoun, 62; verb, 63; adjective, 68; adverb, 69; conjunction, 70; preposition, 70; verbal, 71

Passive voice, 66

Past perfect tense, 65

Past tense, 65

Patric, John, "Enterprise and Old Iron," 477

Patterson, Mary, "Tu'imalila, Oldest Animal in the World," 79

Peel, Robert, "Woodchuck Therapy," 247

Pendennis, W. M. Thackeray, 493

Period, 126

Period fault, 95

Periodic sentence, 114

Periodical indexes, 437

Person of verbs, 66

Personal pronoun, 62

Personification, 185

Phrases: 75; misplaced, 109

Pierre et Jean, Guy de Maupassant, 325

Plagiarism, 55

Plot: in narration, 348, 351; in book reviewing, 481

Plurals of nouns, 162

Poe, E. A.: "The Elk," 217; "The Rationale of Verse," 218; "The Masque of the Red Death," 350

Point of view: in description, 327; in narration, 349

Possessive case: nouns, 62; nouns and pronouns, 133

Possessive pronoun, 105

Post hoc propter hoc reasoning, 307

Précis, 245

Predicate of sentence, 72

Prefixes, spelling of, 162

Preliminary planning: 48; subject, 49; audience, 49; purpose, 51; thesis, 51; outline, 51; tone, 52; title, 53

Preposition: 61, 70; correct use of, 108; choosing the appropriate, 165

Prepositional phrase: 70, 75; diagramed, 87; dangling, 110

Present perfect tense, 65

Present tense, 65

Pride and Prejudice, Jane Austen, 494

Principal parts of verbs, 63

Process in exposition, 268

Progressive form of the verb, 65

Pronoun: 61, 62; reference, 101; agreement, 102; case, 103; possessive case, 105, 133

Proof, paragraph development by, 211

Proofreading and revising, 54

Proper adjectives: 69; capitalization of, 136

Proper nouns: 62; capitalization of, 136

"Proposed New Version of the Bible," Benjamin Franklin, 172

Proposition in argumentation, 304

"Prospice," Robert Browning, Workbook, Exercise 50

Punctuation: 117; comma, 118; semicolon, 124; colon, 125; period, 126; question mark, 127; exclamation point, 127; dash, 127; parentheses, 128; brackets, 129; quotation marks, 129; apostrophe, 133; hyphen, 134; caret, 135

Purposes: general and specific, 51; evaluating in book reviewing, 480

Question mark: 126; in direct quotation, 131

Questions, paragraph development by, 213

Quotation, punctuation of direct, 131

Quotation marks, 129

"Radicalism and Conservatism," A. M. Schlesinger, 265

"Rain in Mexico," Gertrude Diamant, 332

Rambling sentence, 111

"Rationale of Verse, The," E. A. Poe, 218

Rationalizing, 309

Reade, Charles, *The Cloister and the Hearth,* 204, 205

Reading and studying: 16; employing different methods for different purposes, 17; hindrances to reading, 17; studying intelligently, 20; reading a sample paragraph, 22

Reasoning, methods of, 305

Reciprocal pronouns, 63

Recollections of a Long Life, Lord Broughton, 246

Red herring in argumentation, 310

Reed, V. D., "You Are One of These," 299

Reference of pronoun, 101

Reference works, 438

Reflexive pronoun, 63

Regular verbs, 63

Relative pronouns, 62

Repetition for emphasis, 115

Research paper: 434; choosing a topic, 434; use of library, 435; forms for bibliography cards, 441; note-taking and use of sources, 442; evaluating sources: evidence, 444; footnotes and final bibliography, 446; final form, 449

Restrictive elements, punctuating, 122

"Road in England, A," R. C. Hutchinson, 343

Robinson, E. S., "How to Learn," 23

Roughing It, Mark Twain, 212

Royce, Josiah, *The Spirit of Modern Philosophy,* 218

Rusby, H. H., "Struck by Lightning," 83

Ruskin, John: "Of Kings' Treasuries," 29; "Co-operation versus Competition," 174; *Fors Clavigera,* 213; "The Conditions of Art," 238; "On Observing Colors," 329; "Water," 330

Saki, "Laura," 393

Salomon, L. B., review of *You Can't Go Home Again,* 487

Sanborn, W. B., "An Electrical 'Bath' in Yellowstone," 81

Sassoon, Siegfried, "Early Morning," 334

Schlesinger, A. M., "Radicalism and Conservatism," 265

"Scholars, Poor and Simple," Douglas Bush, 203, 216

"Self-Reliance," R. W. Emerson, 214

Semicolon, 124

Sentence: parts of, 72; classes of, 76

Sentence outline, 234

Setting, analysis of, in criticism, 481

Shakespeare, William, *Macbeth,* 185

Shifts of subject, discourse, voice, mood, tense, 113

Short story, 370

"Should Students Study?" W. T. Foster, 315

"Sidewalk Fisherman," Meyer Berger, 471

Simile, 185

Simple narrative, 358

Simple predicate, 72

Simple sentence, 76

Simple subject, 72

Sit, set, 200

Skerrett, R. G., "Under Mobile River," 281

Sketches by Boz, Charles Dickens, 329

"Skiing," Strand Mikkelsen, 240

Slang, 168

Smith, Alexander, *Dreamthorp,* 203

Smith, Herman: "Christmas Tree," 331; "Christmas Breakfast," 336; "Dinner at Cousin Lil's," 336; "Farmhouse Cellar," 339; "Stina," 343

Smith, Sydney: letter by, 517; "A Little Moral Advice," 532

So, proper use of, 200

"So Then, I Feel Not Deeply!" W. S. Landor, Workbook, Exercise 51

"Solo," The Talk of the Town, 470

"Some Participles I Have Met," E. S. McCartney, 216

Sophocles, C. H. Whitman, reviewed, 483

"Sounds in Late Summer," Richard Jeffries, 333

Sources in research, evaluating, 444

Specific purpose, 51

Specific words: 172; in description, 325

"Speech at the Cooper Institute," Abraham Lincoln, WORKBOOK, Exercise 50

"Speech on Conciliation with the Colonies," Edmund Burke, 204

Spelling, 162

Spirit of Modern Philosophy, The, Josiah Royce, 218

Split constructions, 112

Squinting modifiers, 109

"Steamboat Landing at a Small Town, A," Mark Twain, 344

Steinbeck, John, "Adventure of a Turtle," 360

Stevenson, R. L.: "An Apology for Idlers," 22; "The English Admirals," 217; quoted, 218; *The Master of Ballantrae,* 351

"Stina," Herman Smith, 343

"Struck by Lightning," H. H. Rusby, 83

"Struggle for Existence, The," Henshaw Ward, 288

Strunsky, Simeon, "On the Floor of the Library," 530

"Studies That Build Men of Character," A. S. Foord, 6

Studying intelligently: 20; time allotment, 20; methods of study, 21; acquiring speed, 21; reading a simple paragraph, 22

Style, 117

Subject of a composition, choosing and narrowing of, 49

Subject of a sentence: 72; unnecessary shift of, 113

Subjective complement: 73; diagramed, 87

Subjunctive mood, 65

Subordinating conjunction: 70; proper use of, 107

Subordination, proper: 108; "upside-down," 111

Suffixes, spelling of, 162

Sullivan, Frank, "The Cliché Expert Takes the Stand," 187

Summarizing contents in the book review, 482

Superlative degree: adjectives, 68; adverbs, 69

Suspense in narrative, 351, 357

Syllogism, 307

Synonyms, 156

Synopsis of a verb, 66

Talk of the Town, "Solo," 470

Technical level of usage, 167

"Technology—Hope or Hobgoblin?" H. B. du Pont, 250

Tense: 65; proper, 100; unnecessary shift of, 114

Thackeray, W. M., *Pendennis,* 493

"That Greek Dog," MacKinlay Kantor, 426

There, as expletive: 73; diagramed, 89

There is, there are, use of, 98

"There Was a Young Englishman," Clarence Day, 507

Thesaurus, 156

Thesis, 51

Thompson, Dorothy, "The American Way of Life," 143

Thoreau, Henry, "Life without Principle," 213, 216

Thorp, W. L., "Types of Industrial Organization," 242

Thouless, R. H., "Emotional Meanings," 188

Thurber, James, "You Could Look It Up," 396

Title: placement of, on page, 46; choosing, 53

Titles: use of quotation marks with, 130; italics with, 139

Tone: 52; in narrative, 349; in letter of application, 522

Topic outline, 233

Topic sentence of paragraphs, 202

Topics for writing: 86, 153, 228, 323, 347, 370, 432, 527

Transitional expressions: 70; proper use of, 108; for paragraph coherence, 206

Transitional paragraph, 204

Transitive verb, 66, 73

Triteness: 186; in business letters, 521

"Tu'imalila, Oldest Animal in the World," Mary Patterson, 79

Twain, Mark: *The Gilded Age,* 173; *Roughing It,* 212; "A Steamboat Landing at a Small Town," 344; "Baker's Blue-Jay Yarn," 361; "The Office Bore," 489

Two Years before the Mast, R. H. Dana, 204

"Types of Industrial Organization," W. L. Thorp, 242

Typing, instructions for, 47

Unabridged dictionaries, 154

"Under Mobile River," R. G. Skerrett, 281

Unity: of the paragraph, 205; of the whole composition, 231; in narration, 356

"Upside-down" subordination, 111

Usage, glossary of, 197

"Usefulness of Useless Knowledge, The," Abraham Flexner, 212

Variety of sentence structure, 116

Verbs: 61; regular and irregular, 63; conjugation, 64; examples of conjugation, 66; correct form, 97; agreement, 98; correct tense, 100

Verb phrase: 76; split, 112

Verbals: 71; diagramed, 87; dangling, 110

Voice: active and passive, 66; shifts of, 113

Wagner, R. H., "Man with Camera," 212

"Walt Whitman Old and Poor," Hamlin Garland, 496

Ward, Henshaw, "The Struggle for Existence," 288

Warden, Carl, "Be Your Own Weatherman," 277

Warner, C. D., *The Gilded Age,* 173

Washington, George, "Farewell Address," 247

"Water," John Ruskin, 330

"Water Hyacinths," H. T. Kane, 331

Waxman, Percy, "I Chose America," 141

"Where Are We?" Carl Becker, 4

"Where I Stand," Elia Kazan, 147

"Why I Am a Naturalist," Alan Devoe, 513

"Wind, The," R. C. Hutchinson, 335

Wishful thinking, 309

"Witch Tree, The," Rose D. Meyer, 55

Wolfe, Thomas; "Credo," 145; *Look Homeward, Angel,* 326; *You Can't Go Home Again,* reviewed, 487

"Woodchuck Therapy," Robert Peel, 247

Word, the: 154; dictionaries, 154; spelling, 162; words frequently confused, 164; appropriate prepositions, 165; levels of usage, 166; right choice of words, 170; glossary of usage, 197

Wordiness, 116, 170

"Work Your Way through College?" R. C. Hutchison, 11

"World Government or World Destruction?" Stephen King-Hall, 321

"You Are One of These," V. D. Reed, 299

You Can't Go Home Again, Thomas Wolfe, reviewed, 487

"You Could Look It Up," James Thurber, 396

"You Know Me, Allergy," Weare Holbrook, 215

COMMON ABBREVIATIONS USED IN
CORRECTING STUDENT MSS.

cap	capitalize	sl	avoid slang
cf	compare	sp	correct the spelling
clar	make the meaning clear	stet	let the original construction stand
coh	improve the coherence	syl	correct the division into syllables
col	colloquialism; use formal diction	T	correct the tense
D	improve the diction	thought	make the expression more logical
dict	consult the dictionary	tr or ~	transpose
emp	make more emphatic	trans	insert proper transitions
euph	euphony; improve the sound	U	irrelevant; preserve unity of thought
FW	avoid fine writing		
G	correct the grammar	V	avoid vagueness
id	improve the idiom	W	avoid wordiness
il	illogical; correct	WW	wrong word; improve diction
inc	finish an incomplete construction	¶	begin a new paragraph
K	awkward; make more graceful	no ¶	do not begin a new paragraph
lc	remove capitalization	‖	make parallel in structure
mar	leave ample margins	on	omit
MS	make the manuscript neater	∧	insert a necessary word or words
P	correct the punctuation	⌣	no space; bring together
quot	insert quotation marks	/.	separate
ref	make the reference clear	∂	delete
rep	remove an awkward repetition	?	some question has been raised
S	improve faulty sentence structure		